Contemporary Issues in Society

EDITED BY

Hugh F. Lena
Providence College

William B. Helmreich
City College and Graduate Center CUNY

William McCord
City College and Graduate Center CUNY

McGraw-Hill, Inc.

New York   St. Louis   San Francisco   Auckland
Bogotá   Caracas   Hamburg   Lisbon   London
Madrid   Mexico   Milan   Montreal   New Delhi
Paris   San Juan   São Paulo   Singapore
Sydney   Tokyo   Toronto

Contemporary Issues in Society

2 3 4 5 6 7 8 9 0 HAL HAL 9 0 9 8 7 6 5 4 3 2

ISBN 0-07-027965-9

This book was set in Palatino by Better Graphics, Inc.
The editors were Phillip A. Butcher and Edwin Hanson;
the production supervisor was Richard A. Ausburn.
The cover was designed by Andrew Canter.
Arcata Graphics/Halliday was printer and binder.

Library of Congress Cataloging-in-Publication Data

Contemporary Issues in Society / edited by Hugh F. Lena, William B.
    Helmreich, William McCord.
        p.   cm.
    Includes bibliographical references and index.
    ISBN 0-07-027965-9
    1. Sociology.   2. Interpersonal relations.   3. Equality.
4. Social institutions.   5. Human ecology.   I. Lena, Hugh F.
II. Helmreich, William B.   III. McCord, William J.
HM51.C5996   1992
301—dc20   91-11038

Dedicated to
Jeanne and Hugh
Joseph and Deborah
and Maxwell

PART 5   # Social Environments

PART 6   # Epilogue

CONTENTS

PART 5 # Social Environments

PART 6 # Epilogue

Contemporary societies are in a state of crisis. A statement such as this may have produced anxiety or uneasiness in the past, but it is so common an expression today that as we enter the 1990s it virtually has a taken-for-granted quality. Television and print media buffet us daily with accounts of the indicators of this crisis. Law enforcement officials in the United States do not appear to be making headway in the "war on drugs." The number of homeless individuals and families who eke out their existence on the streets of our cities has grown, while programs of governmental support for the needy have been cut back. The deterioration of the environment because of toxic waste dumping, acid rain, and the destruction of natural ecosystems may mean that we will leave planet earth to our children in an uninhabitable state. The educational system in the United States is subject to heated criticism because it graduates students who are ignorant of geography, world affairs, and even basic reading and writing skills—or worse, who are functionally illiterate. The political systems of eastern Europe are experiencing critical social and economic transformation. In short, contemporary societies are confronted on all sides with a perplexing array of social troubles that seem all but intractable.

How severe are these crises? What are their causes? What is already being done to alleviate these problems? These are some of the issues that we wish to address in this reader. This book is a collection of readings for introductory sociology and social problems courses, but it may also find a place in courses on American society. The readings examine problems and issues in contemporary societies that are of interest to sociologists and students of sociology. The book was designed so that it may be used in conjunction with a text, or with several paperbacks, or it can stand alone. Great care has been taken in selecting the readings for this anthology so that they address a range of issues and problems that are considered in sociology courses from a number of levels of analysis used by sociologists. No attempt has been made to address all the relevant problems that bedevil societies and their members, but we have tried to sample the more important ones. Similarly, we make no claim to have included all the important theoretical perspectives on an issue, or even to have covered issues in a completely balanced way. While sociology is unified in a number of ways, the discipline is characterized by too much diversity, dissension, and controversy to strive for comprehensiveness in a single book with such a broad scope.

PLAN OF THE BOOK

Our objective in constructing *Contemporary Issues in Society* was to choose lucid and highly readable selections from the writings of sociologists as well as other well-known authors whose work has clear sociological import. The 51 articles are divided into seventeen chapters organized around the individual, major dimensions of social inequality, institutional settings, social environments, and emerging social issues. They have been drawn from professional sociological journals, research monographs, popular mass-market books, and articulate magazines. In the selection process, emphasis was given to the sociological relevance of the topics and to the quality and style of writing. Student and instructors will find excerpts from well-known authors who have wide popular appeal but are not often read in sociology courses, as well as less familiar pieces that bring a fresh and insightful perspective to societal analysis. The vast majority of the readings were originally published in recent years, although a few sociological "classics" that are still relevant to contemporary societal issues have been included. A special effort was made to include selections that are often cited in introductory and social problems texts but never find their way into readers. We also sought to create a blend of ethnographic and quantitative articles that are within the grasp of most undergraduate students. Our hope is that this will facilitate access to topics that are cited in textbooks, that intrigue students, and that will assist instructors in integrating course materials.

Each of the seventeen chapters presents three readings that address prominent areas of concern under that topic, and each of the three readings approaches the topic from a different level of analysis. The readings are arranged so that the three levels of analysis—cultural (**C**), individual (**I**), and cross-cultural (**C-C**)—are presented in the same order in each chapter. This permits the instructor to assign all or some of the articles on a given topic, or to assign only those readings on the same level of analysis across different topics. Naturally, some of the readings themselves address issues from multiple levels of analysis or defy easy categorization. The use of different levels of analysis is one distinctive aspect of this anthology, and the levels should not be considered definitive categories. Rather, they should be considered guides to reading the articles.

SPECIAL FEATURES

The features of this anthology are:

- High-quality, lucid readings that explore sociological perspectives on issues in societies
- Six-part organization which includes an introductory chapter on sociological perspectives on issues and a concluding epilogue on emerging issues as well as coverage of the individual, social inequalities, institutional settings, and social environments
- Readings that address problems from three levels of analysis—cultural, individual, and cross-cultural
- An explicit cross-cultural and international focus in each chapter which explores either the impact of the United States on one or more other nations or the effects of other nations on issues in America
- Inclusion of research and literature that is frequently cited in textbooks but not often included in anthologies
- Chapter introductions that profile major dimensions of inequality and societal institutions and offer a context for understanding social issues
- Discussion questions following each selection which encourage students to review the major points in the reading and to think further about the sociological import of the conclusions reached in the reading

ACKNOWLEDGMENTS

A number of colleagues have made valuable suggestions about materials appropriate for this book. The editors would like to thank William Preston and the following colleagues who reviewed various drafts of the manuscript: Bill Bailey, University of Wisconsin, Stout; William Finlay, The University of Georgia; Brad Simcock, Miami University, Ohio; and, Steven L. Vassar, Mankato State University. William Helmreich thanks his longtime friend Howard Fuchs for his incisive suggestions and for clarifying his understanding of social issues and problems. We especially thank Marcia Battle for her assistance in preparation of the manuscript. A special note of appreciation goes to Bert Lummus who was responsible for putting this project together. We are deeply grateful for his enthusiasm and encouragement in the early stages of the work. Phillip Butcher, along with Sylvia Shepard, did a wonderful job taking over the project in midstream and seeing it through to publication. Ed Hanson, our editing supervisor, was wonderfully meticulous in his efforts to improve the overall accuracy of this book. Helaine Helmreich and Susan H. Lena were, as ever, supportive of our work.

Hugh F. Lena
William B. Helmreich
William McCord

Grateful acknowledgment is made to the authors and publishers who have granted permission to reprint the following selections:

1-1 C. Wright Mills, "The Promise of Sociology," from *The Sociological Imagination* by C. Wright Mills. Copyright © 1959 by Oxford University Press, Inc.; renewed by Yaraslava Mills. Reprinted by permission of the publisher.

1-2 Erving Goffman, "The Presentation of Self," excerpt(s) from *The Presentation of Self in Everyday Life* by Erving Goffman. Copyright © 1959 by Erving Goffman. Used by permission of Doubleday, a division of Bantam Doubleday Dell Publishing Group.

1-3 Horace Miner, "The Body Ritual among the Nacirema," reproduced by permission of the American Anthropological Association from *American Anthropologist*, vol. 58, no. 3, June 1956. Not for further reproduction.

2-1 Alan M. Klein, "Pumping Iron," published by permission of Transaction Publishers, from *Society*, vol. 22, no. 6, September–October 1958. Copyright © 1985 by Transaction Publishers.

2-2 Charles Moskos, "Army Women," reprinted from *The Atlantic*, vol. 266, no. 2, August 1990. Reprinted by permission of the author.

2-3 William Ouchi, "Japanese Decision-Making," from *Theory Z*, pp. 43–55. Copyright © 1981 by Addison-Wesley Publishing Co., Inc., Reading, MA. Reprinted by permission of the publisher.

3-1 Howard Becker, "The Outsiders," from *Outsiders: Studies in the Sociology of Deviance* by Howard S. Becker. Copyright © 1963 by The Free Press. Reprinted with permission of The Free Press, a Division of Macmillan, Inc.

3-2 William McCord and Jose Sanchez, "Curing Crime," reprinted from Psychology Today, April 1982, by permission of the authors.

3-3 Rensselaer W. Lee, "Cocaine Mafia," published by permission of Transaction Publishers, from *Society*, vol. 27, no. 2, January–February 1990. Copyright © 1990 by Transaction Publishers.

4-1 Shoshana Zuboff, "New Worlds of Computer-Mediated Work." Copyright © 1982 by the President and Fellows of Harvard College; all rights reserved. Reprinted by permission of *Harvard Business Review*.

4-2 Arlie Russell Hochschild, "Airline Flight Attendants," from *The Managed Heart: Commercialization of Human Feeling*, pp. 95–101, 105–114. Copyright © 1983 by The Regents of the University of California.

4-3 Barbara Ehrenreich and Annette Fuentes, "Life on the Global Assembly Line," reprinted from *MS Magazine*, January 1981, by permission of the authors.

5-1 Richard P. Nathan, "Will the Underclass Always Be with Us?" published by permission of Transaction Publishers, from *Society*, vol. 24, no. 3. Copyright © 1987 by Transaction Publishers.

5-2 James D. Wright, "The Worthy and Unworthy Homeless," published by permission of Transaction Publishers, from *Society*, vol. 25, no. 5. Copyright © 1988 by Transaction Publishers.

5-3 S. W. Miller, "New Welfare State Models and Mixes," reprinted from *Social Policy*, Fall 1986, published by Social Policy Corporation, New York 10036. Copyright 1986 by Social Policy Corporation.

6-1 William B. Helmreich, "The Things They Say behind Your Back: Stereotypes and the Myths behind Them," reprinted by permission of the author.

6-2 Elijah Anderson, "A Place on the Corner," reprinted by permission of the author and The University of Chicago Press, 1978.

6-3 Pauline H. Baker, "South Africa on the Move," reprinted with permission from *Current History* magazine. Copyright © 1990 by Current History, Inc.

7-1 Rosabeth Moss Kanter, "Secretaries," from *Men and Women of the Corporation* by Rosabeth Moss Kanter. Copyright © 1977 by Rosabeth Moss Kanter. Reprinted by permission of Basic Books, Inc., Publishers, New York.

7-2 Arlie Hochschild with Anne Machung, "A Notion of Manhood and Giving Thanks: Peter and Nina Tanagawa," from *The Second Shift* by Arlie Hochschild with Ann Machung. Copyright © 1989 by Arlie Hochschild. Reprinted by permission of Viking Penguin, a division of Penguin Books USA Inc.

7-3 Charlotte G. O'Kelly and Larry S. Carney, "Women in Socialist Countries" from *Women & Men in Society: Cross-Cultural Perspectives on Gender Stratification*, 2d ed., by Charlotte G. O'Kelly and Larry S. Carney. Copyright © 1986 by Wadsworth, Inc. Reprinted by permission of the publisher.

8-1 Bernice L. Neugarten and Dail A. Neugarten, "Age in the Aging Society," reprinted by permission of *Daedalus*, Journal of the American Academy of Arts and Sciences, "The Aging Society," Winter 1986, vol 115, no. 1.

8-2 Matilda White Riley and John W. Riley, Jr., "The Lives of Older People and Changing Social Roles," *Annals* of the American Academy of Political and Social Science, vol. 503, May 1989, pp. 14–28. Reprinted by permission of Sage Publications Inc.

8-3 Eli Ginzberg, "The Elderly: An International Policy Perspective," reprinted by permission of the author and *The Milbank Quarterly*, The Milbank Fund, 1983.

9-1 Lillian Breslow Rubin, "Changing Expectations: New Sources of Strain," from *Worlds of Pain: Life in the Working Class Family*, by Lillian Breslow Rubin. Copyright © 1976 by Lillian Breslow Rubin. Reprinted by permission of Basic Books, Inc., Publishers, New York.

9-2 Gerald Handel, "Beyond Sibling Rivalry," from *Sociological Studies of Child Development*, vol. 1, 1986. Reprinted by permission of JAI Press, Greenwich, CT.

9-3 William Moskoff, "Divorce in the USSR," from *Journal of Marriage and the Family*, vol. 45, no. 1. Copyright © 1983 by the National Council on Family Relations, 3989 Central Ave., N.E., Suite 550, Minneapolis, MN 55421. Reprinted by permission.

10-1 Robert N. Bellah et al., "Religion," from Robert Bellah et al., *Habits of the Heart*, pp. 219, 225–227, and 237–249. Copyright © 1985 by The Regents of the University of California.

10-2 John R. Hall, "Apocalypse at Jonestown," published by permission of Transaction Publishers, from *Society*, vol. 16, no. 6. Copyright © 1979 by Transaction Publishers.

10-3 Feliks Gross, "Il Paese," reprinted from *Il Paese: Values and Social Change in an Italian Village*, New York University Press, 1973. Reprinted by permission.

11-1 Seymour Martin Lipset, "The Sociology of Politics," from *Political Man*, expanded edition, Doubleday Press, 1981. Reprinted by permission of the author.

11-2 James Miller, "A Collective Dream," from *Democracy Is in the Streets*, New York: Simon & Schuster, Inc., 1987. Reprinted by permission of the publisher.

11-3 Daniel Bell, "As We Go into the Nineties," reprinted from *Dissent* by permission of the author.

12-1 George J. Benston and George G. Kaufman, "Understanding the Savings-and-Loan Debacle," reprinted with permission of the authors from *The Public Interest*, no. 99, Spring 1990, pp. 79–95. Copyright © 1990 by National Affairs, Inc.

12-2 Michael Harrington and Mark Levinson, "The Perils of a Dual Economy," reprinted from *Dissent*, Fall 1985, pp. 417–426, by permission of the publisher.

12-3 Ezra Vogel, "Japan as Number One," from *Japan as Number One* by Ezra Vogel, Cambridge, MA: Harvard University Press. Copyright © 1979 by the President and Fellows of Harvard College. Reprinted by permission of the publisher.

General Introduction

Sociologists have long been interested in the problematic aspects of social life. Beginning with its nineteenth-century origins, sociological inquiry focused on issues and problems that affect societal institutions, as well as on the nature and extent of structured social inequality—issues that have had dramatic effects upon the chances of individual members of society to succeed in life. In this book we examine, from the perspective of sociology, some of the major contemporary issues and problems confronting societies. Sociology is the scientific study of human relationships and their consequences. You will find it one of the most interesting of all academic disciplines because its subject matter is so familiar and yet exceedingly complex and abstract. There are a number of reasons why sociological inquiry is different.

PITFALLS OF SOCIOLOGICAL INQUIRY

The study of human relationships is hampered by the fact that their most important aspect—the meaning attached to them by the people involved—is invisible and cannot be directly observed. In truth, the reality of sociological material cannot be established through use of the senses, for society, groups, and relationships cannot be seen, heard, felt, or smelled. Even so, most of us would agree that society, groups, and social relationships exist and are real. We experience them on a daily basis. Our understanding of them is further complicated by the belief that, because they are familiar to us, we are knowledgeable about them and their consequences. In this sense, we are all experts about society, groups, and human relationships. Our "expertise" influences us to hold the mistaken notion that sociology is "common sense." The results of sociological inquiry often agree with everyday experiences in social life. For example, you may accept the assertions of a newspaper editorial that suggests that divorce has adverse effects on the social and psychological development of children because these suggestions "confirm" your own experience or the experiences of others you have known. However, it is important to keep in mind that, in some instances, statements that we readily understand and accept are supported by empirical observation and scientific analysis and therefore are correct, whereas, in other cases, our commonsense ideas are not supported by data or systematic analysis and thus are wrong. Confusing *values* (what we would like to believe is true) and *facts* (what is true) is particularly dangerous in studying social problems and institutional issues that generate strong feelings and emotions.

The case of medical malpractice is illustrative. Since a malpractice suit may have devastating consequences for the offending physician, and since few people are able to acknowledge mistakes readily, it is reasonable to conclude that members of the medical profession habitually try to conceal their errors in judgment or treatment, in order to avoid blame and lawsuits. However, sociological evidence does not appear to support a "conspiracy of silence" among doctors. On the contrary, as Hilfiker reveals in Chapter 14, medical errors and uncertainty in medical practice are neither ignored nor concealed in many cases. Selections throughout this reader demonstrate that it is not possible to completely separate values from facts, but that we should strive to understand how our values and biases influence our interpretation of the facts.

Another difficulty with sociological inquiry, which is also addressed in this book, is that individuals are often held responsible for the problems they experience. The causes of unemployment, marital disruption, child abuse, and addictive disorders are often thought to be located in the individuals' personal limitations: mental illness, personality disorders, laziness, or excessive aggression. However, as C. Wright Mills has perceptively argued in *The Sociological Imagination* (1959), we must be careful not to attribute to individuals the problems and difficulties that many people share. Instead, he suggests, we should use our "sociological imagination" to distinguish "personal troubles of milieu" from "public issues of social structure."

Troubles occur within the character of the individual and within the range of his [sic] immediate relations with others; they have to do with his self and with those limited areas of social life of which he is directly and personally aware, [while] *Issues* have to do with matters that transcend these local environments of the individual and the range of his inner life (1959:8).

An "issue," then, is a public matter which many people share and is very often involved in a crisis of institutional arrangements. While personal troubles are difficulties in an individual's own life and are limited in scope, public issues are difficulties shared by many people. If many individuals experience a problem such as unemployment or divorce, Mills believed, we should look beyond the individual—beyond his or her personal biography—to the social structure and culture for an explanation of the problem. A fuller account of Mills' perspective is given in Chapter 1.

Many of the authors in this book encourage you to avoid "blaming the victim" and to look beyond individual circumstances to the larger social structural, historical, and cultural forces which affect them. In Chapter 7, for example, Rosabeth Kanter analyzes the stereotypical behavior of secretaries—their timidity and their allegiance to their bosses—not in terms of gender or personality but in the context of the dilemmas and contradictions presented by their positions in the social organization of business corporations. This approach enables her to exercise her imagination in explaining individual problems in terms of the larger social and structural forces that cause them.

Despite the pitfalls and difficulties of sociological inquiry, the value of studying individuals, inequalities, and institutional crises from a sociological perspective is apparent. Sociology permits us to obtain a clearer picture of American society as well as other societies. It allows us to escape the limitations imposed by our own origins and upbringing and to view the social world in a more objective manner, from the standpoint of an outsider. As a result of sociological study, you should be able to clarify your understanding of your own values and goals, and to assay the causes of others' values and attitudes. Learning to understand the nature of social institutions and social structure is the first step in the process of improving and reforming them.

SOCIOLOGICAL PERSPECTIVES

Rather than presenting one unitary perspective, sociology offers a variety of perspectives to help us understand social inequalities and institutional crises. Controversy is endemic to sociological interpretation. Clearly, one reason for controversy in sociology is the highly diverse nature of the field and the extensive specialization of sociologists. No single theory reigns supreme in the discipline. Moreover, another source of sociological controversy stems from the disparate levels of concern of sociologists. Some sociologists take a *macrosociological* approach, dealing with questions of the broad setup of society as a whole, while others concentrate on issues pertaining to individuals and their private interactional spheres of everyday life, using a *microsociological* perspective. Sociologists who work at these opposite ends of the spectrum are often in conflict. Macroscopic sociologists criticize the work of microscopic colleagues for its triviality and lack of generalizability; and the latter respond by critiquing the lack of scientific rigor of those who seek to explain society as a whole, or who deal with broad patterns of society.

Controversy also stems from disagreements about the uses of sociological findings. This debate takes place between sociologists who seek knowledge for its own sake, without explicit regard for the uses to which that knowledge is put, and more applied or policy-oriented sociologists who believe that knowledge must be put to use or communicated in such a fashion that others can put it to good use.

In this reader, both macroscopic and microscopic topics are addressed, and both "pure" and "applied" orientations are represented. A distinctive feature of this book that permits a more comprehensive treatment of sociological perspectives is its levels-of-analysis approach. Each chapter includes three readings, each of which considers the topic of the chapter from a different level of analysis. The levels of analysis presented here are cultural, individual, and cross-cultural, or international. Each level is described below.

1. Cultural analysis, the first level presented in each chapter, examines the sum total of the socially acquired and transmitted patterns of activity and the objects associated with them. Culture includes norms or expected patterns of behavior, attitudes, and values, as well as the material objects that are the products of patterns of social behavior. Sociological analysis of cultural phenomena sometimes calls for examination of familiar settings with a measure of detachment. For example, in Chapter 1, Horace Miner considers everyday rituals familiar to all Americans, but his detached analysis of cultural practices makes them seem strange and foreign. His approach offers a refreshing and insightful perspective on American society.

The cultural level of analysis also concerns stable features of patterned social relationships. Social life becomes organized when shared cultural meaning is attached to patterns of social order. As social interaction recurs and becomes patterned over time, it acquires shared cultural meanings and understandings. Sociologists pay attention to patterns of behavior among people according to their positions in social relationships, thus providing insights that other perspectives do not provide. Sociological examples stress the importance of individuals' positions in social structure and environments, in order to point out that social relationships exist independently of the particular individuals who participate in them. If no individuals acted in these relationships, however, they would not exist. In this book, social organization is considered in both its more stable and its more dynamic aspects.

2. The individual, or personal, level, the focus of the second reading in each chapter, is explicitly concerned with the human dimensions of issues in contemporary societies. For instance, the effects of work on personal relationships and family life are the focus of several readings. In Chapter 2, Charles Moskos describes the personal experiences of women in the military, particularly their relationship with male soldiers. In Chapter 4, Arlie Hochschild recounts the struggle of a working couple, the Tanagawas, to balance work and family responsibilities.

3. Each chapter concludes with a reading on the cross-cultural, or international, level of analysis. With a world economy and a global society fast approaching, it seems appropriate to consider problems and crises cross-nationally. In the cross-national pieces, we have tried to include work that reveals the impact of the United States on other nations and/or vice versa. You will also find that many of the articles on the other two levels of analysis have an international flavor. In Chapter 3, for example, the reading by E. D. Hirsch considers the plight of American education in light of the success of other nations, but the cross-cultural levels of analysis is most clearly revealed in Fred Strebeigh's reading on the growing numbers of China's elite who are educated in American universities.

Besides distinctive perspectives and levels of analysis, the discipline of sociology also provides new insights into contemporary issues. Sociologists' explanations of the facts and generalizations they generate are significant aspects of such insights, but since social facts are amenable to a variety of interpretations, there is often more than one theoretical explanation of a given issue. In attempting to explain contemporary societies, sociologists face a variety of choices. Fundamental to these choices are the assumptions that guide sociological thinking and form the basis for sociological theories. The three types of theoretical sociological perspectives—structural functionalism, conflict perspectives, and symbolic interactionism—are evident in this reader and are described below.

1. The theoretical framework of structural functionalism is based on the assumption that societies are composed of interrelated parts or subsystems that operate in an interdependent manner to maintain stability. Structural functional theorists emphasize the social consequences, or functions, of the elements of social structure for society. The effective performance of these functions is thought to be necessary in order for the society to persist. Structural functionalism has deep roots in sociology, having been initiated in the first half of the nineteenth century by Auguste Comte (1798–1857), the founding father of sociology. It was passed down through Emile Durkheim (1858–1917) to its contemporary proponents, Talcott Parsons and Robert Merton. Among Merton's significant contributions to sociology is the recognition that social patterns may have both positive (functional) and negative (dysfunctional) consequences.

2. Social conflict perspectives emphasize the social inequalities and conflicts between various individuals and groups in society. Conflict provides the basis for social change. While social conflict perspectives in sociology are diverse in nature, they share the belief that society is characterized by many divisions and considerable divisiveness. The structural-functional orientation acknowledges that elements of the social system may be dysfunctional, but conflict theorists stress tensions inherent in society. Elements of social structure and social relations, they argue, may be simultaneously useful to some groups of individuals while harmful to others. The research presented by Caroline Persell and Peter Cookson in Chapter 13 offers a provocative example. They indicate that children from wealthy families who can afford elite boarding school education benefit

from the special "charters" these schools enjoy and from the extensive "bartering" they engage in with the admission committees of Ivy League colleges and universities. Graduates of elite preparatory schools thus have a favored status over public high school students. The relative ease with which the children of wealthy families can gain admission to selective colleges helps to ensure the transmission of status and privilege from one generation to the next. Insofar as social conflict theorists examine who benefits from particular social arrangements and who does not, it is clear that they view society as composed of competing groups whose interests are in conflict.

3. The third major theoretical perspective in sociology is symbolic interactionism. Rather than concentrating on macrosociological issues as do functionalists and conflict analysts, symbolic interactionists are oriented to the microsociological level in their concern for patterns of social interaction. Interactionists place primacy on society as a product of the ongoing interaction of individuals in various settings. They ask how society is experienced by its members, how patterns of interaction create and change social patterns, and how patterns of interaction and symbolic communication change from one setting to another. The selection by Howard Becker on the labeling of deviance in Chapter 3 reveals some aspects of interactionists' concerns. In this excerpt from his book, *The Outsiders*, Becker describes the exchange of symbols (labels) between rule breakers and a group that judges their behavior to be outside normal boundaries. He further suggests that deviance is a social product insofar as it is created in the process of the exchange of labels.

The structural-functional, social conflict, and symbolic interactionist perspectives are the major frameworks that guide the thinking of sociologists in their understanding of society. While these simple distinctions do not do justice to the myriad sociological theories extant, they do indicate that any, or all, of these theoretical perspectives might be employed in the analysis of societal issues, but that none provides a complete explanation of the causes or consequences of societal problems.

ORGANIZATION OF THE BOOK

The topics that were chosen for inclusion in this anthology are salient in contemporary societies. The introductory chapter provides some general examples of the perspectives that sociologists bring to the analysis of society and human behavior. All three of these readings are considered "classics" in sociology. Part Two is devoted to the individual in society. The chapters on group affiliation (Chapter 2), deviance (Chapter 3), and work (Chapter 4) include readings that share a microsociological orientation but examine issues from different levels of analysis.

In Part Three we consider the nature of social inequalities. Social inequalities are often associated with distinctions between individuals and groups in terms of gender, race, age, and occupation. There is nothing inherently unequal about use of these terms to differentiate between people, for the terms themselves merely indicate physical or social differences between people without ranking the importance of these characteristics. It is generally true, however, that distinctions on the basis of gender, racial or ethnic background, age, and occupation are associated with individuals' roles in society's division of labor and thus with the allocation of scarce, and highly valued, resources such as income, power, and prestige. While many of the selections in this reader testify to the extent of structured social inequality engendered by social differentiation, the three chapters in Part Three examine issues in poverty (Chapter 5), race and ethnicity (Chapter 6), gender (Chapter 7), and aging (Chapter 8).

Part Four focuses on some of the important crises that plague societal institutions. A societal institution is a relatively permanent, organized system of social patterns that revolve around the basic needs of society. These patterns, which have the objective of satisfying specific needs, embody the ultimate values that are shared by members of society. Societal institutions are relatively permanent in that behavior patterns established within them become part of the tradition of a given culture. The social basis of a societal institution is broad enough to enable it to occupy a central place within a society. Institutional change can have dramatic consequences, since a change in one institution often produces changes in other institutions. The institution of the family, for example, functions to reproduce and care for new members, to protect the young, to socialize individuals so that they can effectively participate in social activities, and to transmit culture and status across generations. Changes in the characteristics and functions of the American family in the last century have been a consequence of, and have produced, changes in other societal institutions. You will learn about many of these changes by reading this book. Besides the chapter on the family (Chapter 9), Part Four includes separate chapters on religion (Chapter 10), power and politics (Chapter 11), the economy (Chapter 12), education (Chapter 13), and health and medical care (Chapter 14).

Part Five covers issues in the city and the community (Chapter 15) and in the environment (Chapter 16). The readings in these two chapters bear on a number of significant problems that confront human systems and ecosystems and their interdependence. The Epilogue, Part Six, addresses a number of emerging issues in the United States and the world.

References

Becker, Howard S. *The Outsiders: Studies in the Sociology of Deviance.* New York: The Free Press, 1966.

Mills, C. Wright. *The Sociological Imagination.* New York: Oxford University Press, 1959.

PART ONE

Introduction

CHAPTER 1

Sociological Perspectives on Issues

INTRODUCTION

Sociologists approach issues in contemporary society from diverse perspectives. For this chapter, we have chosen articles that reflect the three levels of analysis—cultural, individual, and cross-cultural—according to which this book is organized. Each of these three readings is a classic sociological statement about a sociological approach, the nature of sociological inquiry, or both. As in other selections throughout this reader, these three authors do not concern themselves exclusively with one level of analysis.

The first reading is C. Wright Mills' classic statement on the sociological imagination. At the heart of the sociological imagination is the ability to distinguish between personal troubles and public issues. With this ability, one can distinguish personal biography from history, and can recognize that a problem that is experienced as personal is often actually a public or social issue that is shared by many people at the same time. Mills says that we can exercise the sociological imagination by looking beyond the personal difficulties of individuals to the historical, cultural, and social structural

forces that cause them and that are beyond the scope of individuals. For Mills, the task and promise of sociology is to be aware of social structure and to use it "with sensibility" so that we will be capable of tracing linkages among a great variety of *spheres*. His is a classic statement of the value of recognizing social structure in sociological analysis.

Erving Goffman, in the second selection, sketches the outlines of his dramaturgical model of social life. In his view, social interaction may be likened to the theater, and people in everyday life to actors on a stage, each playing a variety of roles. The audience consists of other individuals who observe the role playing and react to the performances. By viewing individuals as social actors playing social roles, Goffman uncovers the invisible, and often taken-for-granted, rules that guide social behaviors as well as the various ways in which people present themselves to different publics or audiences. Goffman's analysis focuses on the individual, but his perspective is distinctly sociological. He locates individual behaviors in the context of social role performances and interaction rituals that form the basis of society. Goffman's analysis of individual behavior clearly reveals the theoretical perspective of symbolic interactionism.

The comparative or cross-cultural level of analysis is represented by Horace Miner's classic description of ritualistic practices among the Nacirema. His approach is to look at familiar features of our daily lives in an unfamiliar way. Thus, his perspective illustrates how sociological analysis involves detachment. Miner's article is apropos as a closing selection in this chapter because his analysis makes use of three themes that have been covered in the readings of this chapter—detachment, cultural relativism, and the sociological imagination. Moreover, his study turns cross-cultural or comparative analysis on its head and epitomizes the benefits of this level of analysis.

The Promise of Sociology

C. Wright Mills

Nowadays, men often feel that their private lives are a series of traps. They sense that, within their everyday worlds, they cannot overcome their troubles, and, in this feeling, they are quite correct: What ordinary men are directly aware of and what they try to do are bounded by the private orbits in which they live; their visions and their powers are limited to the close-up scenes of job, family, neighborhood; in other milieux, they move vicariously and remain spectators. And the more aware they become, however vaguely, of ambitions and of threats that transcend their immediate locales, the more trapped they seem to feel.

Underlying this sense of being trapped are seemingly impersonal changes in the very structure of continent-wide societies. The facts of contemporary history are also facts about the success and the failure of individual men and women. When a society is industrialized, a peasant becomes a worker; a feudal lord is liquidated or becomes a businessman. When classes rise or fall, a man is employed or unemployed; when the rate of investment goes up or down, a man takes new heart or goes broke. When wars happen, an insurance salesman becomes a rocket launcher; a store clerk, a radar man; a wife lives alone; a child grows up without a father. Neither the life of an individual nor the history of a society can be understood without understanding both.

Yet, men do not usually define the troubles they endure in terms of historical change and institutional contradiction. The well-being they enjoy, they do not usually impute to the big ups and downs of the societies in which they live. Seldom aware of the intricate connection between the patterns of their own lives and the course of world history, ordinary men do not usually know what this connection means for the kinds of men they are becoming and for the kinds of history-making in which they might take part. They do not possess the quality of mind essential to grasp the interplay of man and society, of biography and history, of self and world. They cannot cope with their personal troubles in such ways as to control the structural transformations that usually lie behind them.

Surely, it is no wonder. In what period have so many men been so totally exposed at so fast a pace to such earthquakes of change? That Americans have not known such catastrophic changes as have the men and women of other societies is due to historical facts that are now quickly becoming "merely history." The history that now affects every man is world history. Within this scene and this period, in the course of a single generation, one-sixth of mankind is transformed from all that is feudal and backward into all that is modern, advanced, and fearful. Political colonies are freed; new and less visible forms of imperialism, installed. Revolutions occur; men feel the intimate grip of new kinds of authority. Totalitarian societies rise, and are smashed to bits—or succeed fabulously. After two centuries of ascendancy, capitalism is shown up as only one way to make society into an industrial apparatus. After two centuries of hope, even formal democracy is restricted to a quite small portion of mankind. Everywhere in the underdeveloped world, ancient ways of life are broken up and vague expectations become urgent demands. Everywhere in the over-developed world, the means of authority and of violence become total in scope and bureaucratic in form. Humanity itself now lies before us, the supernation at either pole concentrating its most coordinated and massive efforts upon the preparation of World War III.

The very shaping of history now outpaces the ability of men to orient themselves in accordance with cherished values. And which values? Even when they do not panic, men often sense that older ways of feeling and thinking have collapsed, and that newer beginnings are ambiguous to the point of moral stasis. Is it any wonder that ordinary men feel they cannot cope with the larger worlds with which they are so suddenly confronted? That they cannot understand the meaning of their epoch for their own lives? That—in defense of selfhood—they become morally insensible, trying to remain altogether private men? Is it any wonder that they come to be possessed by a sense of the trap?

It is not only information that they need—in this Age of Fact, information often dominates their attention and overwhelms their capacities to assimilate it. It is not only the skills of reason that they need—although their struggles to acquire these often exhaust their limited moral energy.

What they need, and what they feel they need, is a quality of mind that will help them to use information and to develop reason in order to achieve lucid summations of what is going on in the world and of what may be happening within themselves. It is this quality, I am going to contend, that journalists and scholars, artists and publics, scientists and editors are coming to expect of what may be called the sociological imagination.

The sociological imagination enables its possessor to understand the larger historical scene in terms of its meaning for the inner life and the external career of a variety of individuals. It enables him to take into account how individuals, in the welter of their daily experience, often become falsely conscious of their social positions. Within that welter, the framework of modern society is sought, and within that framework the psychologies of a variety of men and women are formulated. By such means, the personal uneasiness of individuals is focused upon explicit troubles, and the indifference of publics is transformed into involvement with public issues.

The first fruit of this imagination—and the first lesson of the social science that embodies it—is the idea that the individual can understand his own experience and gauge his own fate only by locating himself within his period, that he can know his own chances in life only by becoming aware of those of all individuals in his circumstances. In many ways, it is a terrible lesson; in many ways, a magnificent one. We do not know the limits of man's capacities for supreme effort or willing degradation, for agony or glee, for pleasurable brutality or the sweetness of reason. But in our time we have come to know that the limits of "human nature" are frighteningly broad. We have come to know that every individual lives, from one generation to the next, in some society; that he lives out a biography, and that he lives it out within some historical sequence. By the fact of his living he contributes, however minutely, to the shaping of this society and to the course of its history, even as he is made by society and by its historical push and shove.

The sociological imagination enables us to grasp history and biography and the relations between the two within society. That is its task and its promise. To recognize this task and this promise is the mark of the classic social analyst. It is characteristic of Herbert Spencer—turgid, polysyllabic, comprehensive; of E. A. Ross—graceful, muckraking, upright; of Auguste Comte and Emile Durkheim; of the intricate and subtle Karl Mannheim. It is the quality of all that is intellectually excellent in Karl Marx; it is the clue to Thorstein Veblen's brilliant and ironic insight, to Joseph Schumpeter's many-sided constructions of reality; it is the basis of the psychological sweep of W. E. H. Lecky no less than of the profundity and clarity of Max Weber. And it is the signal of what is best in contemporary studies of man and society.

No social study that does not come back to the problems of biography, of history, and of their intersections within a society has completed its intellectual journey. Whatever the specific problems of the classic social analysts, however limited or however broad the features of social reality they have examined, those who have been imaginatively aware of the promise of their work have consistently asked three sorts of questions:

1. What is the structure of this particular society as a whole? What are its essential components, and how are they related to one another? How does it differ from other varieties of social order? Within it, what is the meaning of any particular feature for its continuance and for its change?

2. Where does this society stand in human history? What are the mechanics by which it is changing? What is its place within, and its meaning for, the development of humanity as a whole? How does any particular feature we are examining affect, and how is it affected by, the historical period in which it moves? And this period—what are its essential features? How does it differ from other periods? What are its characteristic ways of history-making?

3. What varieties of men and women now prevail in this society and in this period? And what varieties are coming to prevail? In what ways are they selected and formed, liberated and repressed, made sensitive and blunted? What kinds of "human nature" are revealed in the conduct and character we observe in this society in this period? And what is the meaning for "human nature" of each and every feature of the society we are examining?

Whether the point of interest is a great power state or a minor literary mood, a family, a prison, a creed—these are the kinds of questions the best social analysts have asked. They are the intellectual pivots of classic studies of man in society—and they are the questions inevitably raised by any mind possessing the sociological imagination. For that imagination is the capacity to shift from one perspective to another—from the political to the psychological; from examination of a single family to comparative assessment of the national budgets of the world; from the theological school to the military establishment; from considerations of an oil industry to studies of contemporary poetry. It is the capacity to range from the most impersonal and remote transformations to the most intimate features of the human self—and to see the relations between the two. Back of its use, there is always the urge to know the social and historical meaning of the individual in the society and in the period in which he has his quality and his being.

That, in brief, is why it is by means of the sociological imagination that men now hope to grasp what is going on in the world, and to understand what is happening in themselves as minute points of the intersections of biography and history within society. In large part, contemporary man's self-conscious view of himself as at least an outsider, if not a permanent stranger, rests upon an absorbed realization of social relativity and of the transformative power of history. The sociological imagination is the most fruitful form of this self-consciousness. By its use, men whose mentalities have swept only a series of limited orbits often come to feel as if suddenly awakened in a house with which they had only supposed themselves to be familiar. Correctly or incorrectly, they often come to feel that they can now provide themselves with adequate summations, cohesive assessments, comprehensive orientations. Older decisions that once appeared sound now seem to them products of a mind unaccountably dense. Their capacity for astonishment is made lively again. They acquire a new way of thinking, they experience a transvaluation of values: In a word, by their reflection and by their sensibility, they realize the cultural meaning of the social sciences.

Perhaps the most fruitful distinction with which the sociological imagination works is between the "personal troubles of milieu" and the "public issues of social structure." This distinction is an essential tool of the sociological imagination and a feature of all classic work in social science.

Troubles occur within the character of the individual and within the range of his immediate relations with others; they have to do with his self and with those limited areas of social life of which he is directly and personally aware. Accordingly, the statement and the resolution of troubles properly lie within the individual as a biographical entity and within the scope of his immediate milieu—the social setting that is directly open to his personal experience and, to some extent, his willful activity. A trouble is a private matter: Values cherished by an individual are felt by him to be threatened.

Issues have to do with matters that transcend these local environments of the individual and the range of his inner life. They have to do with the organization of many such milieux into the institutions of a historical society as a whole, with the ways in which various milieux overlap and interpenetrate to form the larger structure of social and historical life. An issue is a public matter: Some value cherished by publics is felt to be threatened. Often, there is a debate about what that value really is and about what it is that really threatens it. This debate is often without focus, if only because it is the very nature of an issue, unlike even widespread trouble, that it cannot very well be defined in terms of the immediate and everyday environments of ordinary men. An issue, in fact, often involves a crisis in institutional arrangements, and often, too, it involves what Marxists call "contradictions" or "antagonisms."

In these terms, consider unemployment. When, in a city of 100,000, only one man is unemployed, that is his personal trouble, and for its relief we properly look to the character of the man, his skills, and his immediate opportunities. But when, in a nation of 50 million employees, 15 million men are unemployed, that is an issue, and we may not hope to find its solution within the range of opportunities open to any one individual. The very structure of opportunities has collapsed. Both the correct statement of the problem and range of possible solutions require us to consider the economic and political institutions of the society, and not merely the personal situation and character of a scatter of individuals.

Consider war. The personal problem of war, when it occurs, may be how to survive it or how to die in it with honor; how to make money out of it; how to climb into the higher safety of the military apparatus; or how to contribute to the war's termination. In short, according to one's values, to find a set of milieux and within it to survive the war or make one's death in it meaningful. But the structural issues of war have to do with its causes; with what types of men it throws up into command; with its effects upon economic and political, family and religious institutions, with the unorganized irresponsibility of a world of nation-states.

Consider marriage. Inside a marriage, a man and a woman may experience personal troubles; but, when the divorce rate during the first four years of marriage is 250 out of every 1,000 attempts, this is an indication of a structural issue having to do with the institutions of marriage and the family and other institutions that bear upon them.

Or consider the metropolis—the horrible, beautiful, ugly, magnificent sprawl of the great city. For many upper-class people, the personal solution to the problem of the city is to have an apartment with private garage under it in the heart of the city, and forty miles out, a house by Henry Hill, garden by Garrett Eckbo, on a hundred acres of private land. In these two controlled environments—with a small staff at each end and a private helicopter connection—most people could solve many of the problems of personal milieux caused by the facts of the city. But all this, however splendid, does not solve the public issues that the structural fact of the city poses. What should be done with this wonderful monstrosity? Break it all up into scattered units, combining residence and work? Refurbish it as it stands? Or, after evacuation, dynamite it and build new cities according to new plans in new places? What should these plans be? And who is to decide and to accomplish whatever choice is made? These are structural issues; to confront them and to solve them requires us to consider political and economic issues that affect innumerable milieux.

Insofar as an economy is so arranged that slumps occur, the problem of unemployment becomes incapable of personal solution. Insofar as war is inherent in the nation-state system and in the uneven industrialization of the world, the ordinary individual in his restricted milieu will be powerless—with or without psychiatric aid—to solve the troubles this system or lack of system imposes upon him. Insofar as the family as an institution turns women into darling little slaves and men into their chief providers and unweaned dependents, the problem of a satisfactory marriage remains incapable of purely private solution. Insofar as the overdeveloped megalopolis and the overdeveloped automobile are built-in features of the over-developed society, the issues of urban living will not be solved by personal ingenuity and private wealth.

What we experience in various and specific milieux, I have noted, is often caused by structural changes. Accordingly, to understand the changes of many personal milieux, we are required to look beyond them. And the number and variety of such structural changes increase as the institutions within which we live become more embracing and more intricately

connected with one another. To be aware of the idea of social structure and to use it with sensibility is to be capable of tracing such linkages among a great variety of milieux. To be able to do that is to possess the sociological imagination.

What are the major issues for publics and the key troubles of private individuals in our time? To formulate issues and troubles, we must ask what values are cherished yet threatened, and what values are cherished and supported, by the characterizing trends of our period. In the case both of threat and of support, we must ask what salient contradictions of structure may be involved.

When people cherish some set of values and do not feel any threat to them, they experience *well-being*. When they cherish values but *do* feel them to be threatened, they experience a crisis—either as a personal trouble or as a public issue. And, if all their values seem involved, they feel the total threat of panic.

But suppose people are neither aware of any cherished values nor experience any threat? That is the experience of *indifference*, which, if it seems to involve all their values, becomes apathy. Suppose, finally, they are unaware of any cherished values, but still are very much aware of a threat? That is the experience of *uneasiness*, of anxiety, which, if it is total enough, becomes a deadly, unspecified malaise.

Ours is a time of uneasiness and indifference—not yet formulated in such ways as to permit the work of reason and the play of sensibility. Instead of troubles—defined in terms of values and threats—there is often the misery of vague uneasiness; instead of explicit issues, there is often merely the beat feeling that all is somehow not right. Neither the values threatened nor whatever threatens them has been stated; in short, they have not been carried to the point of decision. Much less have they been formulated as problems of social science.

In the 1930s, there was little doubt—except among certain deluded business circles—that there was an economic issue that was also a pack of personal troubles. In these arguments about the "crisis of capitalism," the formulations of Marx and the many unacknowledged reformulations of his work probably set the leading terms of the issue, and some men came to understand their personal troubles in these terms. The values threatened were plain to see and cherished by all; the structural contradictions that threatened them also seemed plain. Both were widely and deeply experienced. It was a political age.

But the values threatened in the era after World War II are often neither widely acknowledged as values nor widely felt to be threatened. Much private uneasiness goes unformulated; much public malaise and many decisions of enormous structural relevance never become public issues. For those who accept such inherited values as reason and freedom, it is the uneasiness itself that is the trouble; it is the indifference itself that is the issue. And it is the condition, of uneasiness and indifference, that is the signal feature of our period.

All this is so striking that it is often interpreted by observers as a shift in the very kinds of problems that need now to be formulated. We are frequently told that the problems of our decade, or even the crises of our period, have shifted from the external realm of economics and now have to do with the quality of individual life—in fact, with the question of whether there is soon going to be anything that can properly be called individual life. Not child labor but comic books, not poverty but mass leisure, are at the center of concern. Many great public issues as well as many private troubles are described in terms of "psychiatric"—often, it seems in a pathetic attempt to avoid the large issues and problems of modern society. Often, this statement seems to rest upon a provincial narrowing of interest to the Western societies, or even to the United States—thus ignoring two-thirds of mankind; often, too, it arbitrarily divorces the individual life from the larger institutions within which that life is enacted, and which on occasion bear upon it more grievously than do the intimate environments of childhood.

Problems of leisure, for example, cannot even be stated without considering problems of work. Family troubles over comic books cannot be formulated as problems without considering the plight of the contemporary family in its new relations with the newer institutions of the social structure. Neither leisure nor its debilitating uses can be understood as problems without recognition of the extent to which malaise and indifference now form the social and personal climate of contemporary American society. In this climate, no problems of the "private life" can be stated and solved without recognition of the crisis of ambition that is part of the very career of men at work in the incorporated economy.

It is true, as psychoanalysts continually point out, that people do often have the "increasing sense of being moved by obscure forces within themselves that they are unable to define." But it is *not* true, as Ernest Jones asserted, that "man's chief enemy and danger is his own unruly nature and the dark forces pent up within him." On the contrary: "Man's chief danger" today lies in the unruly forces of contemporary society itself, with its alienating methods of production, its enveloping techniques of political domination, its international anarchy—in a word, its pervasive transformations of the very "nature" of man and the conditions and aims of his life.

It is now the social scientist's foremost political and intellectual task—for here the two coincide—to make clear the elements of contemporary uneasiness and indifference. It is the central demand made upon him by other cultural workmen—by physical scientists and artists, by the intellectual community in general. It is because of this task and these demands, I believe, that the social sciences are becoming the common denominator of our cultural period, and the sociological imagination, our most needed quality of mind.

DISCUSSION QUESTIONS

1. Explain, by giving an example, what Mills means by the "sociological imagination."

2. Sociologists often caution that we should not "blame the victim" for problems such as being on welfare, getting a divorce, or dropping out of school. Briefly explain how the sociological imagination may avoid "blaming the victim."
3. What are the advantages of the sociological perspective as described by Mills? Does it have limitations?

The Presentation of Self

Erving Goffman

When an individual enters the presence of others, they commonly seek to acquire information about him or to bring into play information about him already possessed. They will be interested in his general socioeconomic status, his conception of self, his attitude toward them, his competence, his trustworthiness, etc. Although some of this information seems to be sought almost as an end in itself, there are usually quite practical reasons for acquiring it. Information about the individual helps to define the situation, enabling others to know in advance what he will expect of them and what they may expect of him. Informed in these ways, the others will know how best to act in order to call forth a desired response from him.

For those present, many sources of information become accessible and many carriers (or "sign-vehicles") become available for conveying this information. If unacquainted with the individual, observers can glean clues from his conduct and appearance which allow them to apply their previous experience with individuals roughly similar to the one before them or, more important, to apply untested stereotypes to him. They can also assume from past experience that only individuals of a particular kind are likely to be found in a given social setting. They can rely on what the individual says about himself or on documentary evidence he provides as to who and what he is. If they know, or know of, the individual by virtue of experience prior to the interaction, they can rely on assumptions as to the persistence and generality of psychological traits as a means of predicting his present and future behavior.

However, during the period in which the individual is in the immediate presence of the others, few events may occur which directly provide the others with the conclusive information they will need if they are to direct wisely their own activity. Many crucial facts lie beyond the time and place of interaction or lie concealed within it. For example, the "true" or "real" attitudes, beliefs, and emotions of the individual can be ascertained only indirectly, through his avowals or through what appears to be involuntary expressive behavior. Similarly, if the individual offers the others a product or service, they will often find that during the interaction there will be no time and place immediately available for eating the pudding that the proof can be found in. They will be forced to accept some events as conventional or natural signs of something not directly available to the senses. In Ichheiser's terms,[1] the individual will have to act so that he intentionally or unintentionally *expresses* himself, and the others will in turn have to be *impressed* in some way by him.

The expressiveness of the individual (and therefore his capacity to give impressions) appears to involve two radically different kinds of sign activity: the expression that he *gives*, and the expression that he *gives off*. The first involves verbal symbols or their substitutes which he uses admittedly and solely to convey the information that he and the others are known to attach to these symbols. This is communication in the traditional and narrow sense. The second involves a wide range of action that others can treat as symptomatic of the actor, the expectation being that the action was performed for reasons other than the information conveyed in this way. As we shall have to see, this distinction has an only initial validity. The individual does of course intentionally convey misinformation by means of both of these types of communication, the first involving deceit, the second feigning.

Taking communication in both its narrow and broad sense, one finds that when the individual is in the immediate presence of others, his activity will have a promissory character. The others are likely to find that they must accept the individual on faith, offering him a just return while he is present before them in exchange for something whose true value will not be established until after he has left their presence. (Of course, the others also live by inference in their dealings with the physical world, but it is only in the world of social interaction that the objects about which they make inferences will purposely facilitate and hinder this inferential process.) The security that they justifiably feel in making inferences about the individual will vary, of course, depending on such factors as the amount of information they already possess about him, but no amount of such past evidence can entirely obviate the necessity of acting on the basis of inferences. As William I. Thomas suggested:

> It is also highly important for us to realize that we do not as a matter of fact lead our lives, make our decisions, and reach our goals in everyday life either statistically or scientifically. We live by inference. I am, let us say, your guest. You do not know, you cannot determine scientifically, that I will not steal your money or your spoons. But inferentially I will not, and inferentially you have me as a guest.[2]

Let us now turn from the others to the point of view of the individual who presents himself before them. He may wish them to think highly of him, or to think that he thinks highly of them, or to perceive how in fact he feels toward them, or to obtain no clearcut impression; he may wish to ensure sufficient harmony so that the interaction can be sustained, or to defraud, get rid of, confuse, mislead, antagonize, or insult them. Regardless of the particular objective which the individual has in mind and of his motive for having this objective, it will be in his interests to control the conduct of the others, especially their responsive treatment of him.[3] This control is achieved largely by influencing the definition of the situation which the others come to formulate, and he can influence this definition by expressing himself in such a way as to give them the kind of impression that will lead them to act voluntarily in accordance with his own plan. Thus, when an individual appears in the presence of others, there will usually be some reason for him to mobilize his activity so that it will convey an impression to others which it is in his interests to convey. Since a girl's dormitory mates will glean evidence of her popularity from the calls she receives on the phone, we can suspect that some girls will arrange for calls to be made, and Willard Waller's finding can be anticipated.

> It has been reported by many observers that a girl who is called to the telephone in the dormito-

ries will often allow herself to be called several times, in order to give all the other girls ample opportunity to hear her paged.[4]

Of the two kinds of communication—expressions given and expressions given off—this report will be primarily concerned with the latter, with the more theatrical and contextual kind, the non-verbal, presumably unintentional kind, whether this communication be purposely engineered or not. As an example of what we must try to examine, I would like to cite at length a novelistic incident in which Preedy, a vacationing Englishman, makes his first appearance on the beach of his summer hotel in Spain:

> But in any case he took care to avoid catching anyone's eye. First of all, he had to make it clear to those potential companions of his holiday that they were of no concern to him whatsoever. He stared through them, round them, over them—eyes lost in space. The beach might have been empty. If by chance a ball was thrown his way, he looked surprised; then let a smile of amusement lighten his face (Kindly Preedy), looked round dazed to see that there *were* people on the beach, tossed it back with a smile to himself and not a smile *at* the people, and then resumed carelessly his nonchalant survey of space.
>
> But it was time to institute a little parade, the parade of the Ideal Preedy. By devious handlings he gave any one who wanted to look a chance to see the title of his book—a Spanish translation of Homer, classic thus, but not daring, cosmopolitan too—and then gathered together his beach-wrap and bag into a neat sand-resistant pile (Methodical and Sensible Preedy), rose slowly to stretch at ease his huge frame (Big-Cat Preedy), and tossed aside his sandals (Carefree Preedy, after all).
>
> The marriage of Preedy and the sea! There were alternate rituals. The first involved the stroll that turns into a run and a dive straight into the water, thereafter smoothing into a strong splashless crawl towards the horizon. But of course not really to the horizon. Quite suddenly he would turn on to his back and thrash great white splashes with his legs, somehow thus showing that he could have swum further had he wanted to, and then would stand up a quarter out of water for all to see who it was.
>
> The alternative course was simpler, it avoided the cold-water shock and it avoided the risk of appearing too high-spirited. The point was to appear to be so used to the sea, the Mediterranean, and this particular beach, that one might as well be in the sea as out of it. It involved a slow stroll down and into the edge of the water—not even noticing his toes were wet, land and water all the same to *him!*—with his eyes up at the sky gravely surveying portents, invisible to others, of the weather (Local Fisherman Preedy.)[5]

The novelist means us to see that Preedy is improperly concerned with the extensive impressions he feels his sheer bodily action is giving off to those around him. We can malign Preedy further by assuming that he has acted merely in order to give a particular impression, that this is a false impression, and that the others present receive either no impression at all, or worse still, the impression that Preedy is affectedly trying to cause them to receive this particular impression. But the important point for us here is that the kind of impression Preedy thinks he is making is in fact the kind of impression that others correctly and incorrectly glean from someone in their midst.

I have said that when an individual appears before others his actions will influence the definition of the situation which they come to have. Sometimes the individual will act in a thoroughly calculating manner, expressing himself in a given way solely in order to give the kind of impression to others that is likely to evoke from them a specific response he is concerned to obtain. Sometimes the individual will be calculating in his activity but be relatively unaware that this is the case. Sometimes he will intentionally and consciously express himself in a particular way, but chiefly because the tradition of his group or social status require this kind of expression and not because of any particular response (other than vague acceptance or approval) that is likely to be evoked from those impressed by the expression. Sometimes the traditions of an individual's role will lead him to give a well-designed impression of a particular kind and yet he may be neither consciously nor unconsciously disposed to create such an impression. The others, in their turn, may be suitably impressed by the individual's efforts to convey something, or may misunderstand the situation and comes to conclusions that are warranted neither by the individual's intent nor by the facts. In any case, in so far as the others act *as if* the individual had conveyed a particular impression, we may take a functional or pragmatic view and say that the individual has "effectively" projected a given definition of the situation and "effectively" fostered the understanding that a given state of affairs obtains.

There is one aspect of the others' response that bears special comment here. Knowing that the individual is likely to present himself in a light that is favorable to him, the others may divide what they witness into two parts: a part that is relatively easy for the individual to manipulate at will, being chiefly his verbal assertions, and a part in regard to which he seems to have little concern or control, being chiefly derived from the expressions he gives off. The others may then use what are considered to be the ungovernable aspects of his expressive behavior as a check upon the validity of what is conveyed by the governable aspects. In this a fundamental asymmetry is demonstrated in the communication process, the individual presumably being aware of only one stream of his communication, the witness of this stream and one other. For example, in Shetland Isle one crofter's wife, in serving native dishes to a visitor from the mainland of Britain, would listen with a polite smile to his polite claims of liking what he was eating; at the same time she would take note of the rapidity with which the visitor lifted his fork or spoon to his mouth, the eagerness with which he passed food into his mouth, and the gusto expressed in chewing the food, using these signs as a check on the stated feelings of the eater. The same woman, in order to discover what one acquaintance (A) "actually" thought of another acquaintance (B), would wait until B was in the presence of A but engaged in conversation with still another person (C). She would then covertly examine the facial expressions of A as he regarded B in conversation with C. Not being in conversation with B, and not being directly observed by him, A would sometimes relax usual constraints and tactful deceptions, and freely express what he was "actually" feeling about B. This Shetlander, in short, would observe the unobserved observer.

Now given the fact that others are likely to check up on the more controllable aspects of behavior by means of the less controllable, one can expect that sometimes the individual will try to exploit this very possibility, guiding the impression he makes through behavior felt to be reliably informing.[6] For example, in gaining admission to a tight social circle, the participant observer may not only wear an accepting look while listening to an informant, but may also be careful to wear the same look when observing the informant talking to others; observers of the observer will then not as easily discover where he actually stands. A specific illustration may be cited from Shetland Isle. When a neighbor dropped in to have a cup of tea, he would ordinarily wear at least a hint of an expectant warm smile as he passed through the door into the cottage. Since lack of physical obstructions outside the cottage and lack of light within it usually made it possible to observe the visitor unobserved as he approached the house, islanders sometimes took pleasure in watching the visitor drop whatever expression he was manifesting and replace it with a sociable one just before reaching the door. However, some visitors, in appreciating that this examination was occurring, would blindly adopt a social face a long distance from the house, thus ensuring the projection of a constant image.

This kind of control upon the part of the individual reinstates the symmetry of the communication process, and sets the stage for a kind of information game—a potentially infinite cycle of concealment, discovery, false revelation, and rediscovery. It should be added that since the others are likely to be relatively unsuspicious of the presumably unguided aspect of the individual's conduct, he can gain much by controlling it. The others of course may sense that the individual is manipulating the presumably spontaneous aspects of his behavior, and seek in this very act of manipulation some shading of conduct that the individual has not managed to control. This again provides a check upon the individual's behavior, this time his presumably uncalculated behavior, thus re-establishing the asymmetry of the communication process. Here I would like only to add the suggestion that the arts of piercing an individual's effort at calculated unintentionality seem better developed than our capacity to manipulate our own behavior, so that regardless of how many steps have occurred in the information game, the witness is likely to have the advantage over the actor, and the initial asymmetry of the communication process is likely to be retained.

When we allow that the individual projects a definition of the situation when he appears before others, we must also see that the others, however passive their role may seem to be, will themselves effectively project a definition of the situation by virtue of their response to the individual and by virtue of any lines of action they initiate to him. Ordinarily the definitions of the situation projected by the several different participants are sufficiently attuned to one another so that open contradiction will not occur. I do not mean that there will be the

kind of consensus that arises when each individual present candidly expresses what he really feels and honestly agrees with the expressed feelings of the others present. This kind of harmony is an optimistic ideal and in any case not necessary for the smooth working of society. Rather, each participant is expected to suppress his immediate heartfelt feelings, conveying a view of the situation which he feels the others will be able to find at least temporarily acceptable. The maintenance of this surface of agreement, this veneer of consensus, is facilitated by each participant concealing his own wants behind statements which assert values to which everyone present feels obliged to give lip service. Further, there is usually a kind of division of definitional labor. Each participant is allowed to establish the tentative official ruling regarding matters which are vital to him but not immediately important to others, e.g., the rationalizations and justifications by which he accounts for his past activity. In exchange for this courtesy he remains silent or noncommittal on matters important to others but not immediately important to him. We have then a kind of interactional *modus vivendi*. Together, the participants contribute to a single over-all definition of the situation which involves not so much a real argument as to what exists but rather a real agreement as to whose claims concerning what issues will be temporarily honored. Real agreement will also exist concerning the desirability of avoiding an open conflict of definitions of the situation.[7] I will refer to this level of agreement as a "working consensus." It is to be understood that the working consensus established in one interaction setting will be quite different in content from the working consensus established in a different type of setting. Thus, between two friends at lunch, a reciprocal show of affection, respect, and concern for the other is maintained. In service occupations, on the other hand, the specialist often maintains an image of disinterested involvement in the problem of the client, while the client responds with a show of respect for the competence and integrity of the specialist. Regardless of such differences in content, however, the general form of these working arrangements is the same.

In noting the tendency for a participant to accept the definitional claims made by the others present, we can appreciate the crucial importance of the information that the individual *initially* possesses or acquires concerning his fellow participants, for it is on the basis of this initial information that the individual starts to define the situation and starts to build up lines of responsive action. The individual's initial projection commits him to what he is proposing to be and requires him to drop all pretenses of being other things. As the interaction among the participants progresses, additions and modifications in this initial informational state will of course occur, but it is essential that these later developments be related without contradiction to, and even built up from, the initial positions taken by the several participants. It would seem that an individual can more easily make a choice as to what line of treatment to demand from and extend to the others present at the beginning of an encounter than he can alter the line of treatment that is being pursued once the interaction is under way.

In everyday life, of course, there is a clear understanding that first impressions are important. Thus, the work adjustment of those in service occupations will often hinge upon a capacity to seize and hold the initiative in the service relation, a capacity that will require subtle aggressiveness on the part of the server when he is of lower socio-economic status than his client. W. F. Whyte suggests the waitress as an example:

> The first point that stands out is that the waitress who bears up under pressure does not simply respond to her customers. She acts with some skill to control their behavior. The first question to ask when we look at the customer relationship is, "Does the waitress get the jump on the customer, or does the customer get the jump on the waitress?" The skilled waitress realizes the crucial nature of this question. . . .
>
> The skilled waitress tackles the customer with confidence and without hesitation. For example, she may find that a new customer has seated himself before she could clear off the dirty dishes and change the cloth. He is now leaning on the table studying the menu. She greets him, says, "May I change the cover, please?" and, without waiting for an answer, takes his menu away from him so that he moves back from the table, and she goes about her work. The relationship is handled politely but firmly, and there is never any question as to who is in charge.[8]

When the interaction that is initiated by "first impressions" is itself merely the initial interaction in an extended series of interactions involving the same participants, we speak of "getting off on the right foot" and feel that it is crucial that we do so. Thus, one learns that some teachers take the following view:

> You can't ever let them get the upper hand on you or you're through. So I start out tough. The first day I get a new class in, I let them know who's boss. . . . You've got to start off tough, then you can ease up as you go along. If you start out easy-going, when you try to be tough, they'll just look at you and laugh.[9]

Similarly, attendants in mental institutions may feel that if the new patient is sharply put in his place the first day on the ward and made to see who is boss, much future difficulty will be prevented.[10]

Given the fact that the individual effectively projects a definition of the situation when he enters the presence of others, we can assume that events may occur within the interaction which contradict, discredit, or otherwise throw doubt upon this projection. When these disruptive events occur, the interaction itself may come to a confused and embarrassed halt. Some of the assumptions upon which the responses of the participants had been predicted become untenable, and the participants find themselves lodged in an interaction for which the situation has been wrongly defined and is now no longer defined. At such moments the individual whose presentation has been discredited may feel ashamed while the others present may feel hostile, and all the participants may come to feel ill at ease, nonplussed, out of countenance, embarrassed, experiencing the kind of anomy that is generated when the minute social system of face-to-face interaction breaks down.

In stressing the fact that the initial definition of the situation projected by an individual tends to provide a plan for the cooperative activity that follows—in stressing this action point of view—we must not overlook the crucial fact that any projected definition of the situation also has a distinctive moral character. It is this moral character of projections that will chiefly concern us in this report. Society is organized on the principle that any individual who possesses certain social characteristics has a moral right to expect that others will value and treat him in an appropriate way. Connected with this principle is a second, namely that an individual who implicitly or explicitly signifies that he has certain social characteristics ought in fact to be what he claims he is. In consequence, when an individual projects a definition of the situation and thereby makes an implicit or explicit claim to be a person of a particular kind, he automatically exerts a moral demand upon the others, obliging them to value and treat him in the manner that persons of his kind have a right to expect. He also implicitly forgoes all claims to be things he does not appear to be[11] and hence forgoes the treatment that would be appropriate for such individuals. The others find, then, that the individual has informed them as to what is and as to what they *ought* to see as the "is."

One cannot judge the importance of definition disruptions by the frequency with which they occur, for apparently they would occur more frequently were not constant precautions taken. We find that preventive practices are constantly employed to avoid these embarrassments and that corrective practices are constantly employed to compensate for discrediting occurrences that have not been successfully avoided. When the individual employs these strategies and tactics to protect his own projections, we may refer to them as "defensive practices"; when a participant employs them to save the definition of the situation projected by another, we speak of "protective practices" or "tact." Together, defensive and protective practices comprise the techniques employed to safeguard the impression fostered by an individual during his presence before others. It should be added that while we may be ready to see that no fostered impression would survive if defensive practices were not employed, we are less ready perhaps to see that few impressions could survive if those who received the impression did not exert tact in their reception of it.

In addition to the fact that precautions are taken to prevent disruption of projected definitions, we may also note that an intense interest in these disruptions comes to play a significant role in the social life of the group. Practical jokes and social games are played in which embarrassments which are to be taken unseriously are purposely engineered.[12] Fantasies are created in which devastating exposures occur. Anecdotes from the past—real, embroidered, or fictitious—are told and retold, detailing disruptions which occurred, almost occurred, or occurred and were admirably resolved. There seems to be no grouping which does not have a ready supply of these games, reveries, and cautionary tales, to be used as a source of humor, a catharsis for anxieties, and a sanction for inducing individuals to be modest in their claims and reasonable in their projected expectations. The individual may tell himself through dreams of getting into impossible positions. Families tell of the time a guest got his dates mixed and arrived when neither the house nor anyone in it was ready for him. Journalists tell of times when an all-too-meaningful misprint occurred, and the paper's assumption of objectivity or decorum was humorously discredited. Public servants tell of times a client ridiculously misunderstood form instructions, giving answers which implied an unanticipated and bizarre definition of the situation.[13] Seamen, whose home away from home is rigorously he-man, tell stories of coming back home and inadvertently asking mother to "pass the fucking butter."[14] Diplomats tell of the time a nearsighted queen asked a republican ambassador about the health of his king.[15]

To summarize, then, I assume that when an individual appears before others he will have many motives for trying to control the impression they receive of the situation.

Notes

[1] Gustav Ichheiser, "Misunderstandings in Human Relations," Supplement to *The American Journal of Sociology*, 55 (September, 1949): 6–7.

[2] Quoted in E. H. Volkart, editor, *Social Behavior and Personality*, Contributions of W. I. Thomas to Theory and Social Research (New York: Social Science Research Council, 1951). p. 5.

[3] Here I owe much to an unpublished paper by Tom Burns of the University of Edinburgh. He presents the argument that in all interaction a basic underlying theme is the desire of each participant to guide and control the responses made by the others present. A similar argument has been advanced by Jay Haley in a recent unpublished paper, but in regard to a special kind of control, that having to do with defining the nature of the relationship of those involved in the interaction.

[4] Willard Waller, "The Rating and Dating Complex," *American Sociological Review*, 2:730.

[5] William Sansom, *A Contest of Ladies* (London: Hogarth, 1956), pp. 230–32.

[6] The widely read and rather sound writings of Stephen Potter are concerned in part with signs that can be engineered to give a shrewd observer the apparently inci-

dental cues he needs to discover concealed virtues the gamesman does not in fact possess.

[7] An interaction can be purposely set up as a time and place for voicing differences in opinion, but in such cases participants must be careful to agree not to disagree on the proper tone of voice, vocabulary, and degree of seriousness in which all arguments are to be phrased, and upon the mutual respect which disagreeing participants must carefully continue to express toward one another. This debaters' or academic definition of the situation may also be invoked suddenly and judiciously as a way of translating a serious conflict of views into one that can be handled within a framework acceptable to all present.

[8] W. F. Whyte, "When Workers and Customers Meet," Chap. VII, *Industry and Society*, ed. W. F. Whyte (New York: McGraw-Hill, 1946), pp. 132–33.

[9] Teacher interview quoted by Howard S. Becker, "Social Class Variations in the Teacher-Pupil Relationship," *Journal of Educational Sociology*, 25:459.

[10] Harold Taxel, "Authority Structure in a Mental Hospital Ward" (unpublished Master's thesis, Department of Sociology, University of Chicago, 1953).

[11] This role of the witness in limiting what it is the individual can be has been stressed by Existentialists, who see it as a basic threat to individual freedom. See Jean-Paul Sartre, *Being and Nothingness*, trans. by Hazel E. Barnes (New York: Philosophical Library, 1956), pp. 365 ff.

[12] Erving Goffman, "Communication Conduct in an Island Community" (unpublished Ph.D. dissertation, Department of Sociology, University of Chicago, 1953), pp. 319–27.

[13] Peter Blau, *Dynamics of Bureaucracy: A Study of Interpersonal Relationships in Two Government Agencies*, 2nd ed. (Chicago: University of Chicago Press, 1963).

[14] Walter M. Beattie, Jr., "The Merchant Seaman" (unpublished M. A. Report, Department of Sociology, University of Chicago, 1950), p. 35.

[15] Sir Frederick Ponsonby, *Recollections of Three Reigns* (New York: Dutton, 1952), p. 46.

DISCUSSION QUESTIONS

1. What are the differences between "expressions given" and "expressions given off," according to Goffman?

2. Give examples of sincere and cynical role performances. Are there situations in which cynical role performances are expected?

3. Describe some of your role performances in terms of Goffman's dramaturgical approach.

The Body Ritual among the Nacirema

Horace Miner

The anthropologist has become so familiar with the diversity of ways in which different peoples behave in similar situations that he is not apt to be surprised by even the most exotic customs. In fact, if all of the logically possible combinations of behavior have not been found somewhere in the world, he is apt to suspect that they must be present in some yet undescribed tribe. This point has, in fact, been expressed with respect to clan organization by Murdock. In this light, the magical beliefs and practices of the Nacirema present such unusual aspects that it seems desirable to describe them as an example of the extremes to which human behavior can go.

Professor Linton first brought the ritual of the Nacirema to the attention of anthropologists twenty years ago, but the culture of this people is still very poorly understood. They are a North American group living in the territory between the Canadian Cree, the Yaqui and Tarahumare of Mexico, and the Carib and Arawak of the Antilles. Little is known of their origin, although tradition states that they came from the east. . . .

Nacirema culture is characterized by a highly developed market economy which has evolved in a rich natural habitat. While much of the people's time is devoted to economic pursuits, a large part of the fruits of these labors and a considerable portion of the day are spent in ritual activity. The focus of this activity is the human body, the appearance and health of which loom as a dominant concern in the ethos of the people. While such a concern is certainly not unusual, its ceremonial aspects and associated philosophy are unique.

The fundamental belief underlying the whole system appears to be that the human body is ugly and that its natural tendency is to debility and disease. Incarcerated in such a body, man's only hope is to avert these characteristics through the use of the powerful influences of ritual and ceremony. Every household has one or more shrines devoted to this purpose. The more powerful individuals in the society have several shrines in their houses and, in fact, the opulence of a house is often referred to in terms of the number of such ritual centers it possesses. Most houses are of wattle and daub construction, but the shrine rooms of the more wealthy are walled with stone. Poorer families imitate the rich by applying pottery plaques to their shrine walls.

While each family has at least one such shrine, the rituals associated with it are not family ceremonies but are private and secret. The rites are normally only discussed with children, and then only during the period when they are being initiated into these mysteries. I was able, however, to establish sufficient rapport with the natives to examine these shrines and to have the rituals described to me.

The focal point of the shrine is a box or chest which is built into the wall. In this chest are kept the many charms and magical potions without which no native believes he could live. These preparations are secured from a variety of specialized practitioners. The most powerful of these are the medicine men, whose assistance must be rewarded with substantial gifts. However, the medicine men do not provide the curative potions for their clients, but decide what the ingredients should be and then write them down in an ancient and secret language. This writing is understood only by the medicine men and by the herbalists who, for another gift, provide the required charm.

The charm is not disposed of after it has served its purpose, but is placed in the charm-box of the household shrine. As these magical materials are specific for certain ills, and the real or imagined maladies of the people are many, the charm-box is usually full to overflowing. The magical packets are so numerous that people forget what their purposes were and fear to use them again. While the natives are very vague on this point, we can only assume that the idea in retaining all the old magical materials is that their presence in the charm-box, before which the body rituals are conducted, will in some way protect the worshipper.

Beneath the charm-box is a small font. Each day every member of the family, in succession, enters the shrine room, bows his head before the charm-box, mingles different sorts of holy water in the font, and proceeds with a brief rite of ablution. The holy waters are secured from the Water Temple of the community, where the priests conduct elaborate ceremonies to make the liquid ritually pure.

In the hierarchy of magical practitioners, and below the medicine men in prestige, are specialists whose designation is best translated "holy-mouth-men." The Nacirema have an almost pathological horror of and fascination with the mouth, the condition of which is believed to have a supernatural influence on all social relationships. Were it not for the rituals of the mouth, they believe that their teeth would fall out, their gums bleed, their jaws shrink, their friends desert them, and their lovers reject them. They also believe that a strong relationship exists between oral and moral characteristics. For example, there is a ritual ablution of the mouth for children which is supposed to improve their moral fiber.

The daily body ritual performed by everyone includes a mouth-rite. Despite the fact that these people are so punctilious about care of the mouth, this rite involves a practice which strikes the uninitiated stranger as revolting. It was reported to me that the ritual consists of inserting a small bundle of hog hairs into the mouth, along with certain magical powers, and then moving the bundle in a highly formalized series of gestures.

In addition to the private mouth-rite, the people seek out a holy-mouth-man once or twice a year. These practitioners have an impressive set of paraphernalia, consisting of a variety of augers, awls, probes, and prods. The use of these objects in the exorcism of the evils of the mouth involves almost unbelievable ritual torture of the client. The holy-mouth-man opens the client's mouth and, using the above mentioned tools, enlarges any holes which decay may have created in the teeth. Magical materials are put into these holes. If there are no naturally occurring holes in the teeth, large sections of one or more teeth are gouged out so that the supernatural substance can be applied. In the client's view, the purpose of these ministrations is to arrest decay and to draw friends. The extremely sacred and traditional character of the rite is evident in the fact that the natives return to the holy-mouth-men year after year, despite the fact that their teeth continue to decay.

It is to be hoped that, when a thorough study of the Nacirema is made, there will be careful inquiry into the personality structure of these people. One has but to watch the gleam in the eye of a holy-mouth-man, as he jabs an awl into an exposed nerve, to suspect that a certain amount of sadism is involved. If this can be established, a very interesting pattern emerges, for most of the population shows definite masochistic tendencies. It was to these that Professor Linton referred in discussing a distinctive part of the daily body ritual which is performed only by men. This part of the rite involves scraping and lacerating the surface of the face with a sharp instrument. Special women's rites are performed only four times during each lunar month, but what they lack in frequency is made up in barbarity. As part of this ceremony, women bake their heads in small ovens for about an hour. The theoretically interesting point is that what seems to be a preponderantly masochistic people have developed sadistic specialists.

The medicine men have an imposing temple, or *latipso*, in every community of any size. The more elaborate ceremonies required to treat very sick patients can only be performed at this temple. These ceremonies involve not only the thaumaturge but a permanent group of vestal maidens who move sedately about the temple chambers in distinctive costume and headdress.

The *latipso* ceremonies are so harsh that it is phenomenal that a fair proportion of the really sick natives who enter the temple ever recover. Small children whose indoctrination if still incomplete have been known to resist attempts to take them to the temple because "that is where you go to die." Despite this fact, sick adults are not only willing but eager to undergo the protracted ritual purification, if they can afford to do so. No matter how ill the supplicant or how grave the emergency, the guardians of many temples will not admit a client if he cannot give a rich gift to the custodian. Even after one has gained admission and survived the ceremonies, the guardians will not permit the neophyte to leave until he makes still another gift.

The supplicant entering the temple is first stripped of all his or her clothes. In everyday life the Nacirema avoids exposure of his body and its natural functions. Bathing and excretory acts are performed only in the secrecy of the household shrine, where they are ritualized as part of the body-rites. Psychological shock results from the fact that body secrecy is suddenly lost upon entry into the *latipso*. A man whose own wife has never seen him in an excretory act, suddenly finds himself naked and assisted by a vestal maiden while he performs his natural functions into a sacred vessel. This sort of ceremonial treatment is necessitated by the fact that the excreta are used by a diviner to ascertain the course and nature of the client's sickness. Female clients, on the other hand, find their naked bodies are subjected to the scrutiny, manipulation and prodding of the medicine men.

Few supplicants in the temple are well enough to do anything but lie on their hard beds. The daily ceremonies, like the rites of the holy-mouth-men, involve discomfort and torture. With ritual precision, the vestals awaken their miserable charges each dawn and roll them about on their beds of pain while performing ablutions, in the formal movements of which the maidens are highly trained. At other times they insert magic wands in the supplicant's mouth or force him to eat substances which are supposed to be healing. From time to time the medicine men come to their clients and jab magically treated needles into their flesh. The fact that these temple ceremonies may not cure, and may even kill the neophyte, in no way decreases the people's faith in the medicine men.

There remains one other kind of practitioner, known as a "listener." This witchdoctor has the power to exorcise the devils that lodge in the heads of people who have been bewitched. The Nacirema believe that parents bewitch their own children. Mothers are particularly suspected of putting a curse on children while teaching them the secret body rituals. The counter-magic of the witchdoctor is unusual in its lack of ritual. The patient simply tells the "listener" all his troubles and fears, beginning with the earliest difficulties he can remember. The memory displayed by the Nacirema in these exorcism sessions is truly remarkable. It is not uncommon for the patient to bemoan the rejection he felt upon being weaned as a babe, and a few individuals even see their troubles going back to the traumatic effects of their own birth.

In conclusion, mention must be made of certain practices which have their base in native esthetics but which depend upon the pervasive aversion to the natural body and its functions. There are ritual fasts to make fat people thin and ceremonial feasts to make thin people fat. Still other rites are used to make women's breasts larger if they are small, and smaller if they are large. General dissatisfaction with breast shape is symbolized in the fact that the ideal form is virtually outside the range of human variation. A few women afflicted with almost inhuman hyper-mammary development are so idolized that they make a handsome living by simply going from village to village and permitting the natives to stare at them for a fee.

Reference has already been made to the fact that excretory functions are ritualized, routinized, and relegated to secrecy. Natural reproductive functions are similarly distorted. Intercourse is taboo as a topic and scheduled as an act. Efforts are made to avoid pregnancy by the use of magical materials or by limiting intercourse to certain phases of the moon. Conception is actually very infrequent. When pregnant, women dress so as to hide their condition. Parturition takes place in secret, without friends or relatives to assist, and the majority of women do not nurse their infants.

Our review of the ritual life of the Nacirema

has certainly shown them to be a magic-ridden people. It is hard to understand how they have managed to exist so long under the burdens which they have imposed upon themselves. But even such exotic customs as these take on real meaning when they are viewed with the insight provided by Malinowski when he wrote:

"Looking from far and above, from our high places of safety in the developed civilization, it is easy to see all the crudity and irrelevance of magic. But without its power and guidance early man could not have mastered his practical difficulties as he has done, nor could man have advanced to the higher stages of civilization."

DISCUSSION QUESTIONS

1. Where do you think the Nacirema culture is located? How did you arrive at this conclusion?
2. Using Miner's approach, describe another situation you are familiar with in the United States.
3. How do the ideas of Goffman and Mills in this chapter assist us in stepping back from our way of life as Miner has done here?

PART TWO

The Individual in Society

CHAPTER 2

Issues in Group Affiliation

INTRODUCTION

Two basic premises of sociological inquiry are that every person is born into a social group and that the behaviors of all people may be understood in the context of the many groups of which they are members during their life cycles. A social group consists of two or more individuals who share a sense of unity and are bound together in relatively stable patterns of social interaction. Social groups include diverse social phenomena, ranging from families and close friends to voluntary associations like the Elks and religious congregations to the large organizations that we work for and are educated in. These myriad social units are central to our socialization as human beings and are critical sources of our identities and the meanings we attach to social interaction. However, the groups we belong to do not all have equal importance to us. This fact has led sociologists to distinguish between two types of groups.

Primary groups are the first and most important groups to which we belong. Examples are our family, our group of close friends, and sometimes the people with whom we work

most closely. These groups are characterized by intimate, face-to-face association and cooperation. Typically small in size, primary groups are fundamental to our social identities and are a principal source of emotion and commitment.

Secondary groups, such as colleges, labor unions, army units, and corporations, are less intimate or personal. They also tend to be more temporary and larger, and to offer fewer opportunities for face-to-face interaction than primary groups. For these reasons, secondary groups are less important to us. They also raise different issues with respect to group affiliation than do primary groups.

Primary and secondary groups share features in common. They have identifiable members and boundaries, social control mechanisms, and socially organized interaction patterns. Yet the significance of these features for our affiliations with groups depends on the type of group. For instance, primary groups are more fundamental than secondary groups because they are essential to socialization, they provide settings in which we meet most of our

31

personal needs, and they are powerful instruments for social control.

The readings in this chapter raise a number of intriguing issues about group affiliation. The first selection, by Alan M. Klein, involves group behavior in the context of subcultural beliefs and practices. As Americans have come to place increasing value on health and to recognize the benefits of regular exercise, the popularity of health clubs and fitness centers has grown. Interest in physical appearance has grown as well. Klein explores some of the consequences of a change in membership and identity of a bodybuilding gym. Klein describes the increasing popularity of bodybuilding among women and the subsequent assimilation of women into the male subculture of the weight room. His ethnography of Gold's Gym in Venice, California, focuses on the social structure of the gym, the extent of narcissism among professional and amateur bodybuilders, and changing social values regarding men's and women's participation in this sport. He traces the breakdown of traditional beliefs about women's participation in sports and changes in notions about physical attractiveness. Klein sees a continued breakdown of sexual stereotypes about women's participation in sports as media attention devoted to activities like bodybuilding subsides.

In contemporary societies, dominated by bureaucratic organization and a rationality in which work lives are suspended between deadlines and dead ends, leisure-group membership assumes extraordinary symbolic significance. However, group behavior is equally important at work.

The second reading looks at gender issues at work. Charles Moskos, a prominent military sociologist, focuses on the lives and aspirations of enlisted women and women officers in the U.S. Army. His perspective is on individual women who participated in military operations and combat in Libya and in Panama. Until recently, women had been excluded from combat roles. Besides Moskos examining women's actual combat performance in Panama in 1989, he also describes instances of sexual harassment in Army units and relates the personal experiences of female officers and soldiers. In a branch of the military in which women make up a growing but still small (11 percent) proportion of soldiers, Moskos found strained relations between the sexes, as well as women who experienced difficulties in forming friendships. He also found differences between enlisted women and officers in commitment and career aspirations, critical dimensions of group affiliation.

The final selection in Chapter 2 examines group decision-making processes from a cross-cultural perspective. Virtually all social groups engage in collective decision-making at one time or another, and sociologists are keenly interested in the strategies used by members of groups and in the stages they go through to reach collective decisions. An appreciation for cultural differences in group processes is particularly important in today's increasingly global world economy, in which businesses need to be familiar with cultural differences between trading partners. William Ouchi highlights some of the major differences between group decision-making processes in Japanese and in American organizations. Understanding these differences has been critical to the growing business and trade relations between Japan and the United States. Ouchi points out that, in contrast to the typical American pattern of decision-making, Japanese companies employ a thoroughly participative and democratic approach. A strong orientation toward collective values, holistic concern for people, and resistance to identifying individual responsibility for decisions have led, according to Ouchi, to more creative decisions and more effective implementation than does the individual decision-making style of Western businesses. An appreciation of differences in styles of decision-making between Japanese and American companies is essential to their continued economic interdependence.

Pumping Iron

Alan M. Klein

The new image of strong, independent women is exemplified in the film *Pumping Iron II: The Women* and by cover stories on women bodybuilders in *Life* and *Time* magazines. The mildly sensational and congratulatory tone of the articles panders to the world of women and fashion, yet passes it off as liberating. For donning an expensive Danskin leotard and lifting chrome-plated weights, women are presented as leading the onslaught against an exclusively male domain. An army of lithe, fashionable young women, it would appear, have literally taken over the sport. That this should be passed off as feminist is curious: it is doubtful that feminists take on an institution or behavior to enhance their attractiveness, as do the majority of women who engage in weight training.

Many serious bodybuilders have grown resentful of such reportage, feeling—correctly in most instances—that it belittles their efforts. In light of decades of neglect, bodybuilding ideologues are of the opinion that "any coverage is good coverage." In their headlong rush for cultural legitimacy, bodybuilding's officialdom has jeopardized those distinctive elements that have given rise to their subculture and brought the sport from obscurity to being the sixth largest international sports federation. The role that women play in this subculture, while recent, is substantive—filled with the clash of opposing cultural representations and the odd, sometimes cruel, drama of the "weaker sex" encountering and creating a niche within one of the more imposing bastions of manhood.

Behind the spectacle of the bodybuilding contest, behind the exotic form of self-presentation and the current mass appeal of the sport, is a distinct subculture. The men and women who daily come to contend seriously with weights do so not only to enhance their physiques, but to share a set of values and concerns with like-minded people. Their priorities in life—centering on physical development—limit their social network to people in the bodybuilding community, to the gym. Amid lively music, banging weights, and grunts of exertion, muscle politics are worked out; careers enhanced or damaged; friends and enemies encountered; and jobs and apartments procured.

The center of this subculture is found in southern California, a breeding ground of exotic lifestyles, in a place notorious even to Californians: Venice. Muscle Beach and some of the most important gyms in the world are located there, but at the core of the subculture and sport is Gold's Gym. Wielding considerable political clout in the bodybuilding community and drawing regular media coverage, as well as a steady stream of pilgrims and onlookers, Gold's, with its 700 members, has been a sometime home to every major figure in the sport. Gold's has been prominently featured in the *Pumping Iron* films as well as in various television productions. It is Gold's that brings to mind an automatic association of bodybuilding with a lifestyle.

After four years of studying the mecca of bodybuilding at Gold's Gym, I completed an ethnography of what *Life* magazine claims will be the sport of the 1980s. The dramatic rise in popularity of the sport warrants an examination of what the lifestyle represents to American culture in an era of declining expectations. Photos were critical from the beginning and are very much a part of the record. The members of this subculture have a developed appreciation for the visual media, and requested that I maintain photographic records of them throughout my study.

Few groups value the visual dimension of the human body as highly as bodybuilders.

Some say they study it. Many claim they are obsessed with it as latter-day narcissists. After reading Christopher Lasch's *The Culture of Narcissism* I became interested in the concept. Three questions guided my work: (1) Were bodybuilders really narcissistic as almost everyone imagines? (2) How useful is the concept of narcissism to the social scientist studying groups? (3) Generally speaking, what was this world like?

Until recently, as one gym member put it, Gold's was "ovary free." Gathering momentum during the 1970s, the women's movement fostered attempts to redefine conventional American sex roles. Myths surrounding women's inferiority were exploded one-by-one. Physical weakness, the cornerstone of male perceptions of women, became a special target. Women's athletic programs were fought for; the female presence in male-dominated sports such as marathon road racing was institutionalized; the Annapurna mountain climbing expedition by an all-female team succeeded—all these were part of the attempt by dedicated female athletes to integrate themselves into the highest echelons of the male sports world. Bodybuilding was one such domain.

What more formidable barrier could there be than to break into the most macho gym in the world? Even many male bodybuilders cannot bring themselves to go there. Upon discovering that I had spent three years doing research there, heavily muscled men have sheepishly asked me if I thought they were big enough to train at Gold's. What manner of woman would it take to rub shoulders with these behemoths who measure nearly one yard across?

Joe Gold, who founded the gym in 1964, did so for the hardcore bodybuilder, whether professional, amateur, or noncompetitor. The trio who bought it in 1978 had different intentions. Messrs. Grymkowski, Conners, and Kimber wanted to retain the gym's appeal to the serious bodybuilder while fostering relations beyond that. A new, more appealing public image was needed, and they seized on the idea that weight training was healthy for everyone, naturally encouraging the women who first came to the gym. Despite the welcome, there was considerable resentment on the part of many.

At 4'11" and 105 lbs. Pam Meister is no Amazon. When she came to Gold's in 1979, she had only two years of weight training experience, all of it in her home town of Canton, Ohio. Her odyssey into the weight world had begun in an effort to get back into shape following her graduation from high school. There she had been a cheerleader known for her smile and bubbly personality. As an outgoing novice powerlifter (a sport based on lifting maximum poundage), she was ill prepared for the rebuff she faced when she came to Gold's. The first day she walked around the gym, overwhelmed by the array of machines and the huge men who deftly manipulated them. No one reciprocated her attempts at friendship. The second and third days were no better. On the fourth day she stormed into the gym in a rage, loaded an olympic bar with 300 pounds (three times her body weight), and proceeded to dead lift (a required lift in powerlifting contests) the entire load three times. She let the weights crash to the floor to punctuate her anger and left. When she next walked into the gym, she was noticed and greeted with, "Hey, Pam, how's it going?" and "You gonna do squats today, Pam?" By pound-for-pound outlifting the men, she had broken the barrier.

Pam and the others were condescended to at first, perceived as toying with weights rather than actively pursuing an emerging field of bodybuilding and power training. Claudia Wilbourn, another pioneer, recalls the humiliation: "I've gone through a lot of ridicule. I've been laughed at a lot; been called grotesque; called a dyke; called a lot of names to my face as well as behind my back . . . really insulting things. At first I turned the rage inward. Then I simply had to stand up to them." She decided to directly confront these men. When someone commented on her workout, she walked over and related the facts. "Look you, I'm lifting twice my body weight on this set. Think you can do the same?" Confronted in these terms, most backed off. Figures like these are hard to refute. These days Claudia has no problems with men; they are usually her training partners.

The first women at Gold's broke down resistance within the gym by daily confronting men at their own game: strength, determination, and an unwillingness to be pushed around. Still, in 1978 and 1979 there were no women's events beyond the quasi-beauty contest. Men had the big amateur events to train for (e.g., Mr. America and Mr. Universe), not to mention the ultimate professional contest— the Mr. Olympia, or "Big O." Within the year another Gold's pioneer, Lisa Lyons, had organized and held a contest for serious female bodybuilders. Other offers from forward looking promoters followed. Women, almost overnight, managed to achieve quick success in the world of bodybuilding. The time was right: cultural movements in fitness and among women were able to draw instant responses from the media, and scores of determined women came out to take on the challenges. By virtue of taking on bodybuilding as a lifestyle, the women at Gold's had forced people to rethink conventional notions of body image.

Once in bodybuilding, women as well as men are driven by the same need for accomplishment that one finds in any athletic field. The impulse to achieve success, be it personal or sportswide, while related to the initial motive for getting into bodybuilding, is not necessarily identical with it. Psychologist Dorcas Susan Butt stresses three psychological sources that motivate athletes: competence, aggression, and neurotic conflict. These are present in any athlete in varying degrees. Cer-

tain sports by their nature tend to emphasize one over the others. For instance, boxing selects heavily for the aggressively oriented while mountain climbing attracts those who most highly value competence. Bodybuilding uses all three sources of motivation but stresses neurotic conflict. The discrepancy between the ego (actual-self) and the ideal-self as depicted in the bodies they fashion for themselves is one source of neurotic conflict in many bodybuilders. This is manifested in the persistence of the poor body image many retain even after building themselves up to extremes. Here women differ little, if at all, from men. Compare the following typical statements, the first by a man: "There are days when I feel like I look horrible . . . skinny, no chest, nothin. The contest I won just a few weeks ago might just as well never happened." This statement is by a woman: "I know I'm sensitive. Yea, I know I need to get approval from everyone. I worry about not making it, going back to the way I used to be: chronically overweight and depressed. Sometimes when I look in the mirror, I see a fat ugly body, I really do!"

For male bodybuilders, the Charles Atlas ads from childhood comic book days struck a responsive chord. While most boys dealt with the traumas of adolescence by putting it in perspective, for some it was too painful; they built their lives and egos around the struggle to overcome that pain. Compensation for male poor self-image may be transferred to a variety of accomplishments in non-physical areas. For many men there are alternative routes to achieving a sense of self, but society has historically foisted beauty upon women as a prerequisite for most achievements. Even then, beauty may turn into an obstacle, since it is often seen by men as connoting the opposite of ability—for example, the image of the dumb blond. This conflict, manifested in the struggle to overcome faulty self-perception crops up in the reasons many women, such as Claudia

Wilbourn, give for going into bodybuilding: "When I started bodybuilding, I was extremely introverted, I had severe acne, I was skinny. People used to laugh at my chest when I'd wear a bikini, call me 'chicken legs' . . . so bodybuilding has meant a lot to me. For the first time people pay me compliments. I feel proud to walk through a crowd." Pillow, an aspiring bodybuilder from Anchorage, Alaska, now training at Gold's, described herself as a chronic overeater. "I'm fat in my mind. I got into bodybuilding to control my weight."

More recently bodybuilders, such as Maria Gonzales, have come to the sport by virtue of their undeniable athletic prowess with no history of poor self-image. Maria had played a number of sports at the collegiate level and went on to pursue marathon road racing. Following an injury that permanently halted her racing, she transferred her talents and competitive temperament to bodybuilding. This is true for a number of other top female bodybuilders. The sport offers many talented female athletes a new lease on their athletic lives. For most, graduation from college represents the end of their athletic careers, but since bodybuilders can train and compete longer than other athletes, and since the sport is only now emerging, it offers an attractive alternative.

Most visitors to Gold's are struck by the uniformity of the bodybuilder's life, and the homogeneity of the subculture. The demands on their time and the goals of their lives are held in common, but real differences between men and women exist. Some of these differences result from the respective histories of each sex vis-à-vis the sport. Men developed the sport and subculture without interference. Women encountered male resistance, developing their version of the sport under a great deal of duress. Additional resentment from males comes from the greater interest shown in women's bodybuilding by the media and the press, which is in part a function of historic factors such as the women's movement and physical culture movements. Other differences between men and women have to do with class and sex role attributes, both of which are apparent in their behavior and values.

Traditionally, bodybuilding was a working-class male activity. Some of these traits are still in evidence in the gym today. Among forty men sampled, 79 percent had come from a blue-collar, working-class background. Bodybuilders continue to be primarily semiskilled laborers with 58 percent working at jobs that fall into this category, such as bricklayers, bouncers, bartenders, and bill collectors. This tendency is somewhat exaggerated because most of the men subordinate their work to their training. Educationally, this is borne out by the fact that 60 percent of the men attended some form of higher educational facility, while only 16 percent graduated.

Women, on the other hand, come from a higher socioeconomic background. In a sample of thirty-five Gold's females, 69 percent came from professional or semiprofessional homes. Their educational histories reflect this as well: 80 percent attended college, 40 percent graduated. Judy Kitchen, a Gold's member, feels that is, "because women have only recently gone into bodybuilding. Getting an education was a more likely pursuit for most women." This is evident in the jobs that women at the gym hold, which include a higher frequency of skilled occupations such as teaching, editing, business ownership, and performing arts. Women appear more capable of functioning successfully in the wider society (than Gold's men) because they are doing so. Among professional bodybuilding ranks in the gym, however, women tend to earn less than men, and fewer of them earn a living from the sport at all: 13 percent of the women gained one-third of their income from the sport as compared with 36 percent of the men.

One explanation for this discrepancy in class background might be that the higher socioeconomic background of Gold's women affords them the luxury of exploring alternative lifestyles. It might also be that these women realize that conventional pursuits open to men are not as accessible to them. In comparison with their female counterparts, middle-class men are more likely to explore conventional careers and do so successfully. Women of a lower socioeconomic background may find demands for earning a living and possibly raising children too pressing to pursue sports as a lifestyle. Their more traditional outlook on sex roles, unmediated by a college millieu or careers in athletics, also underscores their reluctance.

The noticeable difference in professional earnings by female competitors may also relate to backgrounds. The educational and professional superiority of women may make their self-image less exclusively dependent on bodybuilding than, for example, the man in unskilled labor who pursues the sport. The need to prove oneself may not be so urgent. Renie Schwartz is a serious competitor, but she is also a partner in a growing furniture business. Maria Gonzales is consumed with the sport, but she also teaches in the Los Angeles public school system. Claudia Wilbourn made it to the top of the sport, but she is now an associate editor for Weider Publications. While still competing, Claudia saw her future lying elsewhere, which is also very common among women bodybuilders: "Bodybuilding is the right thing to be doing now, but it's going to lead to other things in time . . . It's not enough for me by itself. I've worked in gyms for years, and I find them deadening." This view is held by several prominent male bodybuilders as well. Mike Mentzer retired from a sterling career, still in his prime, to take on an administrative position in the sport's leading publication. We are familiar with the film and television careers of Arnold Schwarzenegger (*Conan the Barbarian*) and Lou "The Incredible Hulk" Ferrigno. For the aver-

age male at Gold's, bodybuilding seems more an end in itself than a means to an end.

The women of Gold's differ in other ways as well. They are more social. Whereas men usually indicate that they are "loners" or make friends with difficulty, women generally claim to have friends both inside and outside of the gym. An overall lack of defensiveness on the part of women is noticeable; an observation that has received confirmation in psychological testing carried out at Gold's by Homer Sprague. The media took so readily to women partly because they were so much more approachable, as well as lacking in negative associations carried around by outsiders.

It is in the bodybuilding contest, as opposed to the subculture of the gym, that the difference in sociability is most apparent. Among men, these contests are notorious for the quality of ruthless competition. Once a bodybuilder competes, his view of those around him alters rapidly from ally to nemesis. He is apt to stop at nothing to show off his build at his rival's expense. Prior to walking on stage, men are often silent and brooding, asking for and giving nothing. Women, on the other hand, are much more likely to befriend one another.

Pillow, like many of the women at Gold's, is fairly new at the sport. Her build looks as if it were chiseled out of granite by centuries of wind and rain. Resembling a wrestler with the face of an ingenue, her incongruous career as an exotic dancer in Alaska even further jumbles stereotypes. Sensitive and insightful, she was quick to point out the differences between male and female competitors: "Women are tighter. They're real friendly. I've seen girls swap clothing, posing suits at contests. And they helped me with my hair and makeup when my hairdresser didn't show up on time. At 'The Best in the West' [a prestigious contest] these two girls were getting dressed and the one says, 'Hey, that suit doesn't look right on you.' The other one says, 'Yea, it's a little baggy.' 'Here, try one of mine.' And she gave her the most flattering one she had."

One contestant at a recent Ms. New England contest, a well-respected professional woman bodybuilder, upon waiting to hear the results of the voting by the judges said, "I really hope G. wins this one; it would be so good for her career right now." When the outcome was announced and G. won, her friend congratulated her affectionately, genuinely overjoyed. Later, a group of contestants went out to dinner. Camaraderie like this is much less likely in the world of men's competiton. Even in the gym, as contests near men will often grow sullen, turning friendships into adversary relationships. There are women who are intensely competitive just as there are men who are warm and outgoing in competitions, but they are the exception. A long-range bodybuilder, and now training partner of one of the women at Gold's, John Balik says of female competitions: "As far as I'm concerned, the women are just as tough a competitor [sic] as the men. On the amateur level everybody helps everybody else out. When money enters the picture, it's different. I don't see psyching [negative behavior], the negative remarks, an aggressive stance among women. I just see women as more passive competitors . . . . As a rule there is frustration more over judging: 'How can they judge her better than me?' rather than, 'She is better than me, and I hate her.'" If Balik is right, as money increases for women, they will succumb to pettiness and ruthlessness. This is a question for the immediate future.

Women's bodybuilding has its roots in the American beauty pageant, events that used to be tacked on to bodybuilding contests as a form of light entertainment. Serious female competitors deeply resent this ancestry. While the practice is on the wane, we can periodically still find women entered in contests who have no weight training experience. Since the late seventies women have transformed these contests by transforming their bodies using established training principles. This has led to a new controversy: What is the ideal female body? There are currently two schools of thought in bodybuilding circles. One view is that women should achieve maximum muscularity and pose more like men. The other is that women should limit muscularity and develop a posing routine that is distinctly feminine.

In 1980 Claudia Wilbourn was penalized by judges for being too muscular, placing behind women who never lifted a weight. In 1981 Pillow placed fourth in the Ms. America contest despite being more developed and striated, "cut up," than anyone on stage. In 1982 Mary Roberts faced much the same sort of discrimination at the Women's Bodybuilding Championships. The judges and purveyors of standards (male and female alike) are having difficulty dealing with women who surpass in muscularity conventional notions of the female, while men have no such restraints placed on them. Most enthusiasts and officials prefer "tastefully" developed women. "Most like the skinny model type of physique," says Stacey Bentley, who is herself in that camp; "but it's changing," she cautions.

Claudia not only helped pioneer women's bodybuilding but was its first muscular star: "I got it all the time from the people at the AAU [Amateur Athletic Union] and promoters. They don't think women should be developed. They say, 'Sure, you can come down here and compete, but I don't want any biceps, I don't want to see any muscles popping out.'" Maria Gonzales, a competitor who is midway between the two camps also advocates female muscularity: "I'd like to see more well-proportioned women and a bit more muscularity, more so than . . . or people like that. They're beauty types."

When women do help themselves to all the muscle they can carry, they are almost always indirectly accused of using steroids. In male bodybuilding, steroids—synthetic male hormones—are so widely used, they are standard. If you train without them, you don't win. Steroids help maintain size and strength during the extreme 800-calorie-per-day dieting required to rid oneself of subcutaneous body fat and achieve the critical muscle striation or "ripped look." Although steroids, especially in huge doses, are linked directly to cancer and liver damage, these men and women see themselves (and project to our society) as the vanguard of fitness. With schizophrenic self-deception male bodybuilders take these drugs, but mercilessly accuse others of using them. If it is forbidden for males to use them, it is doubly so for women.

Some women do take steroids, although it is much less common than among men. Any women who looks big is accused of using them. "I'd like to see it get to where women take on muscularity without drugs. Drugwise, you gotta stop it before it gets to be like the men's contests," warns Maria Gonzales, who estimated that 40 percent of the women may take drugs. Like other women who have achieved great muscularity, she has been accused of using steroids, a charge she flatly denies. A bigger woman like Pillow responds by claiming that since she is larger to begin with, taking steroids would destroy any symmetry she could attain, that she doesn't take them but smaller women do. Charges of steroid use abound much like witchcraft accusations.

While the women at Gold's Gym differ in their psychological profiles, class backgrounds, educational levels, and occupational histories, they do not form a distinct social presence. Only in the sport of bodybuilding do differences emerge. The most determining factors in bodybuilding subculture are its pronounced individualism, the promise of personal physical and emotional change. Within the gym, sex, race, and class become ambience rather than essence. Men are seen

training with female partners; blacks with whites and latinos. They came to Gold's as individuals, and this is evident in the emphasis that the subculture fosters among its members. The routine workout that each bodybuilder develops and daily executes, the intense respect of space and privacy within the 10,000-square-foot world of Gold's are examples of this individualism. No insider would risk using a piece of equipment until absolutely sure that the previous user was finished, nor would one break into another's concentration with conversation or questions. These people are essentially atoms in quest of their own physical perfection. In between sets, as well as before and after workouts, there is a lot of socializing. Since they share a culture, they often attend specialized events or parties for their own. Here too one sees them as social beings who modify group cohesion by their ultimate self-interest.

Like most subcultures in our society, this one exists in part because its members have been shunned by the larger society. For whatever reasons, their ostracism acts to intensify their social bonding, in time helping to establish their own socioeconomic networks, values, language, etc. To some degree Gold's exists as a subculture because of popular rejection of what it stands for. The entrance of women and other nontraditional elements into gym life has aided in some ways to break down this separation as well as in fostering new social relationships within the gym.

The assimilation of women into Gold's Gym and the world of competition presents bodybuilding with its first substantial alternative. The way women handle competition and social relationships stands in striking contrast to what has traditionally taken place in the gym. Aside from offering another possibility, it also argues against common stereotypes of women as catty and vicious. That women are generally more forthright, sociable, and down-to-earth than male counterparts in the gym may be in part related to the fact that they come to the sport with a better education and proven career skills. It may also be the result of having to prove themselves and to coexist within a hostile environment. The absence of any smugness in the light of so much media attention, and the fact that when the opportunity arises, women at Gold's share the limelight with less sought after males, not only enhances social relationships at Gold's but also may aid in altering male perceptions of women as self-serving. When the media interest eventually dies down—as it no doubt will when woman's position in the sport is less controversial—the women of Gold's will still have to their credit the creation of a sport, a contributing role in breaking down sexual stereotypes, and a corner of the gym.

DISCUSSION QUESTIONS

1. What was the initial reception of women who joined Gold's gym to lift weights?
2. Klein was interested in determining the usefulness of the concept of narcissism to the study of bodybuilding. What did he conclude?
3. How do gender stereotypes of women in bodybuilding compare with those in other women's sports?

READING 2-2

Army Women

Charles Moskos

At 0055 hours on December 20, 1989, U.S. Army helicopters lifted off from Howard Air Force Base, in Panama, to carry infantry across the Panama Canal. Their mission was to assault Fort Amador, one of the few strongholds of the Panamanian Defense Forces to offer resistance to the American forces that had invaded Panama as part of Operation Just Cause. Two of the helicopter pilots ferrying the troops were women: First Lieutenant Lisa Kutschera and Warrant Officer Debra Mann. Their Black Hawk helicopters, officially designated transport, not attack, aircraft, carried troops into what turned out to be "hot" areas, where the PDF was firing on helicopters. For their participation in the assault Kutschera and Mann (and their male counterparts) would be awarded Air Medals—a much coveted decoration.

At about the same time Kutschera and Mann were doing their jobs in the air, Captain Linda Bray, the commander of the 988th Military Police Company, was directing her unit to seize a Panamanian military dog kennel. Initial press reports stated that Captain Bray led a force of soldiers in a full-blown fire fight resulting in the deaths of three Panamanian soldiers. In fact no human casualties were suffered and what actually happened remains murky to this day. Still, the incident came to be portrayed as the first time a woman had led U.S. troops into combat.

One other incident involving women soldiers in Panama also attracted attention. Press reports of female cowardice centered on two women truck drivers who allegedly received orders to drive troops into areas where Panamanian snipers were active. A subsequent account put forth by the Army was quite different. After eight straight hours of driving during the invasion, the two drivers became concerned about whether they could continue to drive their vehicles safely. Tears were shed at some point. Fresh drivers replaced the two women. A subsequent investigation concluded that at no time was anyone derelict in her duty, and the incident was closed without disciplinary action.

All told, some 800 female soldiers participated in the invasion of Panama, out of a total of 18,400 soldiers involved in the operation. Probably about 150 of the women were in the immediate vicinity of enemy fire. Owing to the publicity that women performing hazardous duty attracted, the once-dormant issue of the ban on women in combat units suddenly came awake.

Title 10 of the U.S. Code precludes women from serving aboard combat vessels or aircraft. Although there are actually no statutory restrictions on how Army women can be deployed, the Army derived its combat-exclusion policy from Title 10 and prohibits women from joining direct combat units in the infantry, armor forces, cannon-artillery forces, and combat engineers. The Army's formal definition reads as follows: "Direct combat is engaging an enemy with individual or crew-served weapons while being exposed to direct enemy fire, a high probability of direct physical contact with the enemy's personnel, and a substantial risk of capture."

Although many obstacles to women's participation in the military have been overcome, the line that excludes women from combat units has not yet been crossed. None of the women who participated in the Panama invasion, even those who came in harm's way, were assigned to combat units. Rather, they were serving as military police, medical and administrative staff, and members of transportation, communications, maintenance, and other support units.

The issue of women in combat highlights the dramatic recent changes in the role of women in the military. Visitors at most military installations today will see women in numbers and roles unthinkable at the time the Vietnam War ended. Some 230,000 women now make up about 11 percent of all military personnel on active duty. Each branch of the military has a distinctive history with respect to women. The Air Force, which is 14 percent female, has the highest proportion of jobs open to women, mainly because none of its ground jobs involve combat. Although women are precluded from piloting bombers and fighter planes, they fly transport planes and serve on the crews of refueling planes, such as those that took part in the 1986 U.S. raid on Libya. The Navy, which is 10 percent female, did not allow women on ships other than hospital ships until 1977, but today women sailors serve aboard transport and supply ships. The Marine Corps is only five percent female, because a high proportion of its members serve in the combat arms. The Army, which is 11 percent female, has the largest total number of women (86,000), and is the vanguard service insofar as the role of women is concerned.

My research as a military sociologist has allowed me to observe at close hand the changing face of the Army since my days as a draftee, in the late 1950s. The account that follows, which briefly surveys the life, the sentiments, and the aspirations of women in the U.S. Army, draws upon my observations of Army units around the world but is based mainly on interviews with soldiers of every rank who participated in the invasion of Panama, including most of the women soldiers who were closest to the shooting.

SOME BACKGROUND

When the second World War broke out, the only women in the armed services were nurses. But manpower needs caused the precursor to the Women's Army Corps (WAC) to be established in May of 1942, followed shortly thereafter by the Navy's WAVES (Women Accepted for Voluntary Emergency Service) and the Coast Guard's SPARs (from "*Semper Paratus*: Always Ready"). Women were allowed into the Marine Corps in 1943, and, refreshingly, these volunteers were called simply Women Marines. Some 800 civilian women who served as Air Force service pilots flew military aircraft across the Atlantic. The Women in the Air Force (WAF) was created in 1948, after the Air Force had become a separate service.

The Women's Armed Service Integration Act of 1948 gave permanent status to military women, but with the proviso that there would be a two-percent ceiling on the proportion of women in the services (excluding nurses). No female generals or admirals were to be permitted. For the next two decades women averaged only a little over one percent of the armed forces, and nearly all of them did "traditional" women's work, in health-care and clerical jobs. During the Vietnam War some 7,500 women served in Vietnam, mostly in the Army. The names of eight women are engraved on the Vietnam Veterans Memorial, in Washington, D.C.

Starting in the 1970s a series of barriers fell in relatively rapid succession. On June 11, 1970, women were promoted to the rank of general for the first time in U.S. history. The new generals were Anna Mae Hayes, of the Army Nurse Corps, and Elizabeth P. Hoisington, the director of the WACs. Women first entered the Reserve Officer Training Corps on civilian college campuses in 1972. Much more traumatic was the admission in 1976 of the first female cadets into the service academies. Today one of seven entrants to West Point is female, although, if truth be told, most of the male cadets are not yet reconciled to the presence of women. Congress abolished the WACs in 1978, leading to the direct assignment of women soldiers to non-combat branches of the Army. Today 86 percent of all military occupational specialties (MOSes) for enlised personnel are open to women.

To put the combat-exclusion rule into practice and minimize the possibility that women in noncombat MOSes would be assigned to areas where they received hostile fire, the Army in 1983 implemented a system of direct-combat-probability coding (DCPC). The purpose of the probability code is to exclude female soldiers, whatever their MOS, from areas where they are likely to be, to use formal Army terminology, "collocated" with troops in direct combat. But once assigned to an area, Army policy states, female soldiers "in the event of hostilities will remain with their assigned units and continue to perform their assigned duties." This is what happened in Panama with the female helicopter pilots, military police, and truck drivers who came under fire. (In contrast, during the 1983 American invasion of Grenada four military police-women were sent to the island with their unit only to be sent right back to Fort Bragg because of the fighting on the island.) DCPC is based on a linear concept of warfare, as is clear from the guideline that women soldiers not be assigned to positions found "forward to the brigade rear boundary"—that is, not close to the front lines. The coding is hard to reconcile with checkerboard combat theaters, however. Two of the twenty-three Americans killed in the Panama operation were in noncombat MOSes—a media and a military policeman—as were thirty-six of the 324 wounded. One of the wounded was a printing and bindery specialist. None of the killed or wounded soldiers were women.

A GLIMPSE OF DAILY LIFE

I flew down to Panama shortly after the invasion and, with the Army's permission, talked to scores of soldiers and investigated their living conditions. The enlistment motivations of the men and women I spoke to differed in important respects. For the typical male, economic realities were predominant. Most admitted to having seen few job opportunities in civilian life. The decision to enlist was usually supported by family and friends. For many of the men, joining the Army seemed to be the path of least resistance. The women soldiers were much more likely to have entered the military for noneconomic reasons. They also seemed to be more independent and adventurous than the men. Often they had not received much encouragement from their parents to join the service. Many of the men, and even more of the women, were attracted by the Army's post-service educational benefits. For the women, joining the Army was the result of a decision to "do something different" and get away from a "boring" existence in some backwater community.

Sitting on her bunk in an extremely hot and stuffy room in an old PDF barracks, one female Private First Class told a not unusual story: "I worked for a while right after high school and then went to a community college. But with working so much, I couldn't be a real student. I quit school and worked as a waitress at a Denny's. I woke up one day and realized I wasn't going anywhere. There had to be more to life than this. I was afraid I would end up marrying some jerk. The Army offered me a GI Bill and a chance to do something different. My mother cried when I told her I was going to join the Army. But I did it anyway and I'm glad. I won't stay in, but I've seen and done a lot more things than my friends back home."

Many of the women had spent time on field maneuvers, living in tents. Since most of the women were assigned to combat-support functions, they were often able to live in large general-purpose tents. Work sections sleep together in one tent during field exercises whenever possible. This is true whether sections are male-only or mixed-sex. Women drape blankets over a rope between the main tent poles to gain some privacy, although someone on the other side can easily peer over the top. In mixed-sex tents the men generally display some regard for privacy, although not always as much as the women would like. Most of the women sleep in gym clothes or their BDUs (battle dress uniforms), as fatigues are now

called. Others become acrobats and manage to change clothes inside their sleeping bags. Almost all the women said they would prefer to sleep in a mixed-sex tent with workmates rather than in a female-only tent with strangers.

Personal cleanliness and hygiene are of much greater concern to women than to men in the field. Even under the tense, busy circumstances of Panama, the women tried to bathe once a day. One young female soldier insisted (wrongly) to me that Army regulations guarantee women a shower at least once every three days. How to wash became almost an obsession for women in the field. One method was to post a guard outside a tent and take a "bird bath," using a can of hot water. One unit moved garbage cans inside the tent for the women to use as stand-up bathtubs. When outside shower facilities were all that was available, women often showered in their BDUs. Female soldiers are expected to plan ahead and provide their own sanitary napkins or tampons. In Panama tampons had to be drawn from the medical-supply system rather than the regular quartermaster system. This created problems for some women in the early days of the invasion. But once life began to return to normal, tampons (and women's underwear) could be readily bought at the post exchange. All in all, menstruation did not seem to worry the female soldiers I spoke with, and it was never invoked as an excuse for absence from work.

Sexual harassment is one of the issues most frequently discussed by women in the military. Enlisted women and female officers differ on this matter in important ways. Enlisted women, like most men of any rank, define sexual harassment mainly in terms of sexual propositions and actual touching. One female sergeant put it this way: "Sexual harassment is making unwelcome advances the second time." Enlisted women also tend to see sexual harassment in almost fatalistic terms, something that "goes with the territory" and is often brought on by the behavior of the woman. But they do not consider every advance to be harassment. Fraternization between men and women among enlisted personnel in the Army (and among Army officers) is as common as it is among students at a coeducational college, and is accepted as normal if it occurs among soldiers (or officers) of the same rank. Most women soldiers who have boyfriends have boyfriends who are soldiers, and the women who are married are far more likely to be married to soldiers than married male soldiers are.

Female officers understand sexual harassment in much broader terms, to include sexist remarks, sex-based definitions of suitable work, the combat-exclusion rule, and so on. Women officers see sexism in the military as something that requires constant vigilance. One lieutenant told me that she found it a "welcome challenge to deal with male chauvinists on a daily basis."

Another form of sexual harassment was mentioned by the enlisted women: approaches from lesbians. The true incidence of lesbianism (and of male homosexuality) in the military is unknown. There are indications that lesbianism is more widespread in the armed forces than is male homosexuality. Defense Department statistics, whether they reflect selective prosecution or not, show that women are discharged for lesbianism almost ten times as often, proportionately, as men are discharged for homosexuality. Accounts of lesbianism were offered spontaneously in most of my extended interviews with female soldiers. My general impression was that lesbianism causes much less alarm among women soldiers than homosexuality does among the men. Whereas male soldiers expressed disdain for homosexuals with sardonic humor if not threats of violence, the women were more likely to espouse an attitude of live and let live.

That enlisted women must face being characterized by many men in the military as either loose or lesbian is an unfortunate reality. These attitudes decline markedly when men and women work together over the long term. Such situations also seem eventually to bring out the best in the men. But sex-related issues by no means pervade the everyday existence of female soldiers. The most common topics of concern and conversation, for both sexes, appear to have little to do with sex. They have to do with the work of the Army and with the good and bad of military life.

SERGEANTS, OFFICERS, AND ENLISTED WOMEN

The Army's noncommissioned officers inhabit the middle ground between the enlisted ranks and the officer corps. If women sometimes occupy an ambiguous position within the military, female NCOs occupy the most ambiguous position of all. One reason is that there are not many of them: only four percent of all senior sergeants are women.

One Sergeant First Class I interviewed, a personnel specialist, joined the Army in 1972. She told me, "I wanted to see the world, and I sure have—Korea, Germany, and now Panama. I was glad to see the WACs go. There were too many cliques and too much politics. The real problem now is that the female NCO is never taken as seriously as the male. Every time we are reassigned to a new unit, we have to prove ourselves all over again. Our credentials aren't portable like the men's."

Like many female NCOs, this woman admits to having few close friends in the military. "If you get too close to the men, they think you're having an affair. If you hang around with women, they think you're a lesbian. Let's face it, you can't really be one of the boys. The kind of insults men throw at each other a woman can't do, unless she wants to cross an invisible line of respect." The sergeant finally brought up the matter of marriage, which weighs heavily with female careerists in the Army: "I never married," she said, "because I just couldn't think of having children and making a go of an Army career." Only 60 percent of female senior NCOs are married, and of those only half have children. A military career works powerfully on military women to keep them single and childless.

Above the rank of noncommissioned officers in the Army is the officer corps, where today one lieutenant in six is female—but only one colonel in thirty. Only three of the Army's 407 general officers are women. Women officers feel the same pressures not to marry or raise children that female NCOs do—pressures that male soldiers do not feel. Many women officers believe that the demands of an Army career preclude having children, and they leave the service. Others make the Army a career, deciding to stay childless. A female helicopter pilot told me, "Having no children is the sacrifice I make to keep flying." In 1989 among male senior officers 94 percent were married, and 90 percent of these had children; among female senior officers only 51 percent were married, and only half of these had children.

A small but growing group of junior female officers, however, seems to have devised a form of planned parenthood that can accommodate both family and career. It works like this. First, aim to be a company commander, an important "ticket to be punched" on the way up the promotion ladder. Company commanders are usually captains with six or seven years in service, people in their late twenties. Company command is a high-pressure job, but it is often followed by a slack time, such as an assignment to an ROTC position or a staff job in a headquarters command. Women officers are coming to regard this period as the most opportune to have a child.

Almost all junior officers today are commissioned right after college. This contrasts with the biographies of today's senior women officers, who entered as WACs, often after some work experience. Brigadier General Evelyn "Pat" Foote, who was one of the Army's most

senior women officers when she retired last year, was well known in the military for being an outstanding and confident professional officer who spoke her mind. She joined the Army at age thirty after a string of white-collar jobs in which, she told me, she always seemed to be "somebody's girl Friday." In her nearly three decades in the Army, Foote served as the commander of a WAC company, as a public-affairs officer in Vietnam, as a faculty member at the Army War College, and as the commander of the Military Police Group in Mannheim, West Germany. She concluded her career as the commanding general of Fort Belvoit, Virginia. She has never married.

Foote espouses a philosophy that is embraced by most senior women officers, at least in private. They hope for a future that harks back to an era when women soldiers, in the main, were unmarried, had no children and few outside distractions, and were more committed to military service than their male counterparts. By now, of course, this is simply too much to expect of female career soldiers.

Foote recognizes that many Army women have been able to combine a military career, marriage, and children. She is adamant that there is little place in the Army for single pregnant women and single mothers. Certainly having pregnant soldiers in deployable units is "the height of folly." In 1988 eight percent of the total female enlisted force bore children; some 15 percent of all enlisted Army women are single parents. Before 1975 pregnant women were routinely discharged from the Army. Today, although pregnant women are ineligible for enlistment, they can remain in the Army. The remainder leave the service after delivery.

Foote would "feel comfortable" with a rule that expelled pregnant women but allowed waivers on a case-by-case basis. She also notes the problem of pregnant women who carry on too long with their duties to the detriment of themselves and their babies. Single parents too often present "an untenable mess," Foote says. "Anyone, male or female, who can't perform their mission has no place in the Army." She ruefully notes that female officers were never consulted on the changes that allowed pregnant women and single parents to remain in the Army. The "male hierarchy caved in to so-called liberals without thinking what this would mean for Army readiness."

WHAT ABOUT COMBAT

The various arguments for and against women in combat are complex, and the issues involved are not subject to easy empirical resolution. Whether the propensity of most males to be more aggressive than most females is due mainly to body chemistry or to cultural conditioning is a matter of controversy; so is whether male bonding is chemical or cultural. There are social realities that need to be considered, however. We should not forget, for example, that combat troops live, bathe, and sleep together for days and weeks on end. No institution in American society forces men and women into such unrelenting close contact. That women could be killed or captured in a war is a specter raised by those who oppose letting women into combat units. Is this really an issue? Female police officers have died in the line of duty without raising any particular outcry. On the touchy matter of prisoners of war, we have seen at least a symbolic change. In 1988 President Ronald Reagan signed an executive order revising the Code of Conduct for POWs. What formerly began with "I am an American fighting man" was changed to the gender-neutral and less bellicose "I am an American."

What we do know a lot about are differences between the sexes in physical strength and endurance. Statistically speaking, average female upper-body strength is 42 percent less than average male upper-body strength. Looked at another way, the statistics mean that on the average the top fifth of women in lifting capacity are the equal of the bottom fifth of men on the same measure. This means that any work requiring heavy lifting or carrying a great deal of weight—the burden of the combat soldier—puts women at a serious disadvantage. Opponents of the combat-exclusion rule poin out that much of modern warfare is technological and "push-button" and does not require the brute strength of the combat soldier of old. There is some truth to this. But women are already allowed in almost all areas of technological warfare, including holding the launching keys of nuclear missiles. The irreducible fact remains that physical strength and endurance are still the hallmarks of the effective combat soldier on the ground; indeed, such qualities may be more important in the future, when we make use of rapid-deployment forces, whose members must carry most of their equipment on their backs.

Experience from foreign countries is not very enlightening on the matter of women in combat. Contrary to popular belief, women in Israel, which is the only country with a female draft, are not assigned to duty as combat soldiers; they played only a limited, mainly defensive, role in the War of Independence, in 1948. A ruling by Canada's Human Rights Commission last year held that women could no longer be excluded from any military role except in submarines. The Canadian experience has not been heartening for those who seek to end the combat-exclusion rule in this country. Only seventy-nine women were recruited into the infantry training program and only one completed the course. She has since requested a transfer out of the infantry.

For all this, it is probably the case that most senior female officers privately second the views of General Foote on the subject of women and combat. Foote favors opening all roles to women in the Army, even in the combat arms. Being a woman per se should not, she says, be a disqualification for any military job. Of course, Foote recognizes the differences in strength between men and women. She acknowledges that few women belong in the infantry, and probably not many more belong in the armor or artillery, but says that certainly some could perform well in those roles, and there is no good reason to exclude women from combat aviation. Her basic position is this: "Never compromise standards. Be sure that anybody in any MOS can do everything required in that MOS."

The problem with the combat-exclusion rule, Foote argues, is that it "develops a whole male cadre and officer corps that doesn't know how to work with women." So long as officers in the combat branches are practicing "a different sheet of music," she says, they will not know how to use women to their full capabilities. At the very least the direct-combat-probability code—"the most counterproductive policy in the U.S. Army"—ought to be abolished, she says, because it prevents trained and qualified women from performing their assignments where they are needed.

How female officers and enlisted personnel variously gauge their future Army career opportunities makes for differing views on women in combat. Female officers see their career opportunities as diminishing as they become more senior. Without a chance for command assignments in combat units, the women officers believe, their careers are limited, especially by comparison with men's careers. Although a government study released last year showed that women are promoted at a rate similar to that for men, the fact remains that the combat-exclusion rule precludes any significant number of women from becoming generals, or even full colonels. Among the female officers I talked with in Panama, about three quarters believed that qualified women should be allowed to volunteer for combat units and about a quarter said that women should be compelled to enter combat units, just as men are. A female military-police officer expressed the sentiments of most: "If a woman

has the capability and gumption to enter a combat unit, I'd say go for it. Few of us could make it in the infantry. God forbid that the Army shoehorn women into the infantry to meet some kind of quota. But a woman is as brave as a man, and we shouldn't be kept out of jobs we could do no matter what the danger. Military women are their own worst enemy by accepting a lowering of physical standards. If we kept standards up, if we kept pregnant women out, then any woman in any MOS would be assigned wherever she was needed when the balloon goes up."

Enlisted women, on the other hand, are less subject to career disapointment, because their expectations are not high to begin with. Inasmuch as they generally did not see themselves in long-term Army roles, the women I spoke with thought of their service in Panama as a one-time-only adventure. Enlisted women foresaw their eventual life's meaning in family, in work outside the military, or, if in the military, in relatively sedentary and routine jobs. Among the enlisted women I interviewed in Panama, about three quarters said that women should not be allowed in combat units and about a quarter said that women who were physically qualified should be allowed to volunteer for combat roles. None of the enlisted women favored forcing women into combat assignments. One female driver gave a typical enlisted women's response: "I'm old-fashioned. I want to be treated like a woman. I don't want people to think I'm a man. I certainly wouldn't want to be in the infantry. A normal woman can't carry a rucksack that the guys can. Even if we could, the guys would hate us for being there. And, let's face it, we would probably make things harder on everybody all around. No way."

There is one area where the combat-exclusion rule is questioned by most women and some men: piloting helicopters. The skills required to fly a utility helicopter to transport soldiers into hot zones are not really all that different from those required on gunships such as Cobras and Apaches. In Panama the skills of the female pilots were acknowledged by all to be at least the equal of those of the male pilots. Even the British high command, that most traditional of general staffs, is studying the possibility of allowing women to train as pilots for Harriers, the jump-jet fighters that saw so much action in the Falklands War. Were women to be assigned to U.S. gunships in future hostilities, however, they would almost surely suffer casualties. Even in the small, short war in Panama four helicopters were shot down and many more were hit by enemy fire.

Two things came out loud and clear in my Panama interviews. One is that the worst thing for a woman officer is to be removed from an assignment she has trained for simply because there is danger. A helicopter pilot told me how she felt on invasion day when she was denied a flight assignment that she thought was her due: "I was insane with anger. After nine years of training they left me out. It was the ultimate slam." The second point is that not a single woman, officer or enlisted, said that she would volunteer to be an infantry rifleman. Surely, somewhere in the U.S. Army, there are women who would volunteer for the infantry. But they were not in Panama.

THE UNASKED QUESTION

Women in the military have been a troublesome issue for feminists. Feminists have also been troublesome for women in the military. Most feminists clearly want women to share equally the rights and burdens of service, but many of them abhor the combat role of the military profession and much of the basic direction of American foreign policy, which the military profession serves. That many of those who opposed the Panama invasion also advocate combat roles for women is indeed ironic. Female officers are understand-

ably distrustful of much of the civilian feminist agenda, with its not-so-veiled anti-military content. Even as they chart new ground in opportunities for women, female officers are unquestionably less liberal politically, on average, than their civilian counterparts.

Where mainstream feminists and senior women officers come together is in their wish to do away with, or at least punch holes in, the categorical exclusion of women from direct combat roles. They see the exclusion as somehow precluding women from full citizenship. Following the Panama invasion and the reports of women in combat, the push to remove the last barriers to women's full participation in the military gained new momentum. Representative Patricia Schroeder, a senior Democrat on the House Armed Services Committee, proposed legislation to set up a trial program to test the suitability of women for the combat arms. Such a program had been recommended in 1989 by the Defense Advisory Committee on Women in the Services. Last April the Army announced that it would not initiate such a trial program. But the Army's decision will not put the issue to rest. As long as there are women in the military, the pressures to end the combat-exclusion rule will remain.

On the surface, the proposal for a trial program sounds eminently reasonable. How can we know whether women will measure up to the stresses of combat without assigning them to combat training and seeing what happens? Admittedly, training is not the same as actual combat, but a pilot program would tell us more than we know now.

There is another matter to consider, however. Let us assume that the presence of women in combat units can be shown not to affect adversely the combat performance of the men in those units. Let us also assume that in the event of hostilities the death of female soldiers would not cause much more upset at home than the death of male soldiers. And let us assume that a pilot program will be established and that it will show some number of women to have the physical and psychological endurance to perform well in combat, or at least as well as some men already in combat roles. Given all this, the pressure to remove the ban on women in combat units will be difficult to resist. But will allowing qualified women to enter the combat arms finally mean the resolution of this nettlesome issue?

Unfortunately, no. The issue is not simply "opening up" combat assignments to military women. The core question—the one avoided in public debate, but the one that the women soldiers I spoke with in Panama were all too aware of—is this: Should every woman soldier be made to confront exactly the same combat liabilities as every man? All male soldiers can, if need arises, be assigned to the combat arms, whatever their normal postings. True equality would mean that women soldiers would incur the same liability. To allow women but not men the option of entering or not entering the combat arms would—rightly or wrongly—cause immense resentment among male soldiers; in a single stroke it would diminish the status and respect that female soldiers have achieved. To allow both sexes to choose whether or not to go into combat would be the end of an effective military force. Honesty requires that supporters of lifting the ban on women in combat state openly that they want to put all female soldiers at the same combat risk as all male soldiers—or that they don't.

A trial program of women in combat roles which shows that women can hold their own in battle may put one argument to rest. But it will signal the start of another.

DISCUSSION QUESTIONS

1. Compare how Army women are seen by servicemen with how they are viewed by men in general.
2. What factors in military life have made it more likely that women would be seen as equals? What factors have made that outcome less likely?
3. The 1990 conflict in Panama produced reports of the first military mission led into conflict by women. What changes do you think will result from this development? Explain your assertions in terms of gender roles in the military.

Japanese Decision Making

William Ouchi

Probably the best known feature of Japanese organizations is their participative approach to decision making. In the typical American organization the department head, division manager, and president typically each feel that "the buck stops here"—that they alone should take the responsibility for making decisions.

Recently, some organizations have adopted explicitly participative modes of decision making in which all of the members of a department reach consensus on what decision to adopt. Decision making by consensus has been the subject of a great deal of research in Europe and the United States over the past twenty years, and the evidence strongly suggests that a consensus approach yields more creative decisions and more effective implementation than does individual decision making.[1]

Western style participative decision making is by now a fairly standardized process. Typically, a small group of not more than eight or ten people will gather around a table, discuss the problem and suggest alternative solutions. During this process, the group should have one or more leaders skilled at managing relationships between people so that underlying disagreements can be dealt with constructively. The group can be said to have achieved a consensus when it finally agrees upon a single alternative and each member of the group can honestly say to each other member three things:

1. I believe that you understand my point of view.
2. I believe that I understand your point of view.
3. Whether or not I prefer this decision, I will support it, because it was arrived at in an open and fair manner.

At least a few managers instinctively follow this approach in every company, government office, and church meeting, but the vast majority do not. Some companies have officially instituted this consensual approach throughout, because of its superiority in many cases to individual decision making. However, what occurs in a Japanese organization is a great deal more far reaching and subtle than even this participative approach.

When an important decision needs to be made in a Japanese organization, everyone who will feel its impact is involved in making it. In the case of a decision where to put a new plant, whether to change a production process, or some other major event, that will often mean sixty to eighty people directly involved in making the decision. A team of three will be assigned the duty of talking to all sixty to eighty people and, each time a significant modification arises, contacting all the people involved again. The team will repeat this process until a true consensus has been achieved. Making a decision this way takes a very long time, but once a decision is reached, everyone affected by it will be likely to support it. Un-

derstanding and support may supersede the actual content of the decision, since the five or six competing alternatives may be equally good or bad. What is important is not the decision itself but rather how committed and informed people are. The "best" decisions can be bungled just as "worst" decisions can work just fine.

A friend in one of the major Japanese banks described their process. "When a major decision is to be made, a written proposal lays out one 'best' alternative for consideration. The task of writing the proposal goes to the youngest and newest member of the department involved. Of course, the president or vice-president knows the acceptable alternatives, and the young person tries like heck to figure out what those are. He talks to everyone, soliciting their opinions, paying special attention to those who know the top man best. In so doing he is seeking a common ground. Fortunately, the young person cannot completely figure out from others what the boss wants and must add his own thoughts. This is how variety enters the decision process in a Japanese company. The company relies so heavily on socializing employees with a common set of values and beliefs that all experienced employees would be likely to come up with similar ideas. Too much homogeneity would lead to a loss of vitality and change, so the youngest person gets the assignment."

Frequently, according to my informant, this young person will in the process make a number of errors. He will suggest things that are technically impossible or politically unacceptable, and will leave things out. Experienced managers never over-direct the young man, never sit him down and tell him what the proposal should say. Even though errors consume time, effort, and expense, many will turn out to be good ideas. Letting a young person make one error of his own is believed to be worth more than one hundred lectures in his education as a manager and worker.

Ultimately, a formal proposal is written and then circulated from the bottom of the organization to the top. At each stage, the manager in question signifies his agreement by affixing his seal to the document. At the end of this *ringi* process, the proposal is literally covered with the stamps of approval of sixty to eighty people.

American managers are fond of chiding the Japanese by observing that, "If you're going to Japan to make a sale or close a deal and you think it will take two days, allow two weeks and if you're lucky you'll get a 'maybe.' It takes the Japanese forever to make a decision." True enough, but Japanese businesspeople who have experience dealing in the United States will often say, "Americans are quick to sign a contract or make a decision. But try to get them to implement it—it takes them forever!"

Remember that this apparently cumbersome decision process takes place within the framework of an underlying agreement on philosophy, values, and beliefs. These form the basis for common decision premises that make it possible to include a very large number of people in each decision. If, as in some Western organizations, each of the sixty people had a fundamentally different view of goals and procedures, then the participative process would fail. Because the Japanese only debate the suitability of a particular alternative to reach the agreed-upon values, the process can be broadly participatory yet efficient. In Western-style consensual processes, by comparison, often underlying values and beliefs need to be worked out, and for that reason decision making teams are deliberately kept small.

Another key feature of decision making in Japan is the intentional ambiguity of who is responsible for what decisions. In the United States we have job descriptions and negotiations between employees for the purpose of setting crystal clear boundaries on where my decision authority ends and yours begins.

Americans expect others to behave just as we do. Many are the unhappy and frustrated American businessmen or lawyers returning from Japan with the complaint that, "If only they would tell me who is really in charge, we could make some progress." The complaint displays a lack of understanding that, in Japan, no one individual carries responsibility for a particular turf. Rather, a group or team of employees assumes joint responsibility for a set of tasks. While we wonder at their comfortableness in not knowing who is responsible for what, they know quite clearly that each of them is completely responsible for all tasks, and they share that responsibility jointly. Obviously this approach sometimes lets things "fall through the cracks" because everyone may think that someone else has a task under control. When working well, however, this approach leads to a naturally participative decision making and problem solving process. But there is another important reason for the collective assignment of decision responsibility.

Many Americans object to the idea of lifetime employment because they fear the consequences of keeping on an ineffective worker. Won't that create bottlenecks and inefficiency? Clearly the Japanese have somehow solved that problem or they couldn't have achieved their great economic success. A partial answer comes from the collective assignment of decision responsibility. In a typical American firm, Jim is assigned sole responsibility for purchasing decisions for office supplies, Mary has sole responsibility for purchasing maintenance services and Fred is solely responsible for purchasing office machines. If Fred develops serious problems of a personal nature, or if he becomes ill or has some other problem that seriously impedes his ability to function at work, a bottleneck will develop. Office machine orders will not be properly processed or perhaps will not be processed at all. The whole company will suffer, and Fred will have to be let go.

In a Japanese company, by comparison, Mitsuo, Yoshito, and Nori will comprise a team collectively responsible for purchasing office supplies, maintenance services, and office machines. Each of them participates in all significant decisions in purchasing any of those goods or services. If Nori is unable to work, it is perfectly natural and efficient for Mitsuo and Yoshito to take up his share of the load. when Nori returns to work again, he can step right back in and do his share. This does mean that Mitsuo and Yoshito probably will have to work harder than usual for perhaps six months or a year, and they may also have to draw on Masao, who used to work in purchasing but has now been transferred to the computer section. This flow of people can be accomplished only if Mitsuo and Yoshito are confident that the organization has a memory and know that their extra efforts now will be repaid later. Fairness and equity will be achieved over the long run. It also depends upon the practice of job rotation, so that short-run labor needs can be filled internally without having to hire and fire people as such needs come and go. As with all other characteristics of the Japanese management system, decision making is embedded in a complex of parts that hang together and rely upon trust and subtlety developed through intimacy.

COLLECTIVE VALUES

Perhaps the most difficult aspect of the Japanese for Westerners to comprehend is the strong orientation to collective values, particularly a collective sense of responsibility. Let me illustrate with an anecdote about a visit to a new factory in Japan owned and operated by an American electronics company. The American company, a particularly creative firm, frequently attracts attention within the business community for its novel approaches to planning, organizational design, and management systems. As a consequence of this corporate style, the parent company determined to make a thorough study of Japanese workers and to design a plant that would combine the best of East and West. In their study they discovered that Japanese firms almost never make use of individual work incentives, such as piecework or even individual performance appraisal tied to salary increases. They concluded that rewarding individual ability is always a good thing.

In the final assembly area of their new plant long lines of young Japanese women wired together electronic products on a piece-rate system: the more you wired, the more you got paid. About two months after opening, the head foreladies approached the plant manager. "Honorable plant manager," they said humbly as they bowed, "we are embarrased to be so forward, but we must speak to you because all of the girls have threatened to quit work this Friday." [To have this happen, of course, would be a great disaster for all concerned.] "Why," they wanted to know, "can't our plant have the same compensation system as other Japanese companies? When you hire a new girl, her starting wage should be fixed by her age. An eighteen-year-old should be paid more than a sixteen-year-old. Every year on her birthday, she should receive an automatic increase in pay. The idea that any one of us can be more productive than another must be wrong, because none of us in final assembly could make a thing unless all of the other people in the plant had done their jobs right first. To single one person out as being more productive is wrong and is also personally humiliating to us." The company changed its compensation system to the Japanese mold.

Another American company in Japan had installed a suggestion system much as we have in the United States. Individual workers were encouraged to place suggestions to improve productivity into special boxes. For an accepted idea the individual received a bonus amounting to some fraction of the productivity savings realized from his or her suggestion. After a period of six months, not a single suggestion had been submitted. The American managers were puzzled. They had heard many stories of the inventiveness, the commitment, and the loyalty of Japanese workers, yet not one suggestion to improve productivity had appeared.

The managers approached some of the workers and asked why the suggestion system had not been used. The answer: "No one can come up with a work improvement idea alone. We work together, and any idea that one of us may have are actually developed by watching others and talking to others. If one of us was singled out for being responsible for such an idea, it would embarrass all of us." The company changed to a group suggestion system, in which workers collectively submitted suggestions. Bonuses were paid to groups which would save bonus money until the end of the year for a party at a restaurant or, if there was enough money, for family vacations together. The suggestions and productivity improvements rained down on the plant.

One can interpret these examples in two quite different ways. Perhaps the Japanese commitment to collective values is an anachronism that does not fit with modern industrialism but brings economic success despite that collectivism. Collectivism seems to be inimical to the kind of maverick creativity exemplified in Benjamin Franklin, Thomas Edison, and John D. Rockefeller. Collectivism does not seem to provide the individual incentive to excel which has made a great success of American enterprise. Entirely apart from its economic effects, collectivism implies a loss of individuality, a loss of the freedom to be different, to hold fundamentally different values from others.

The second interpretation of the examples is that the Japanese collectivism is economically efficient. It causes people to work well together and to encourage one another to better

efforts. Industrial life requires interdependence of one person on another. But a less obvious but far-reaching implication of the Japanese collectivism for economic performance has to do with accountability.

In the Japanese mind, collectivism is neither a corporate or individual goal to strive for nor a slogan to pursue. Rather, the nature of things operates so that nothing of consequence occurs as a result of individual effort. Everything important in life happens as a result of teamwork or collective effort. Therefore, to attempt to assign individual credit or blame to results is unfounded. A Japanese professor of accounting, a brilliant scholar trained at Carnegie-Mellon University who teaches now in Tokyo, remarked that the status of accounting systems in Japanese industry is primitive compared to those in the United States. Profit centers, transfer prices, and computerized information systems are barely known even in the largest Japanese companies, whereas they are commonplace in even small United States organizations. Though not at all surprised at the difference in accounting systems, I was not at all sure that the Japanese were primitive. In fact, I thought their system a good deal more efficient than ours.

Most American companies have basically two accounting systems. One system summarizes the overall financial state to inform stockholders, bankers, and other outsiders. That system is not of interest here. The other system, called the managerial or cost accounting system, exists for an entirely different reason. It measures in detail all of the particulars of transactions between departments, divisions, and key individuals in the organization, for the purpose of untangling the interdependencies between people. When, for example, two departments share one truck for deliveries, the cost accounting system charges each department for part of the cost of maintaining the truck and driver, so that at the end of the year, the performance of each department can be individually assessed, and the better department's manager can receive a larger raise. Of course, all of this information processing costs money, and furthermore may lead to arguments between the departments over whether the costs charged to each are fair.

In a Japanese company a short-run assessment of individual performance is not wanted, so the company can save the considerable expense of collecting and processing all of that information. Companies still keep track of which department uses a truck how often and for what purposes, but like-minded people can interpret some simple numbers for themselves and adjust their behavior accordingly. Those insisting upon clear and precise measurement for the purpose of advancing individual interests must have an elaborate information system. Industrial life, however, is essentially integrated and interdependent. No one builds an automobile alone, no one carries through a banking transaction alone. In a sense the Japanese value of collectivism fits naturally into an industrial setting, whereas the Western individualism provides constant conflicts. The image that comes to mind is of Chaplin's silent film "Modern Times" in which the apparently insignificant hero played by Chaplin successfully fights against the unfeeling machinery of industry. Modern industrial life can be aggravating, even hostile, or natural: all depends on the fit between our culture and our technology.

WHOLISTIC CONCERN FOR PEOPLE

Anthropologist Thomas Rohlen has described in detail the process of inducting young trainees into a Japanese bank.[2] Training culminates in a formal ceremony held in the company auditorium. The bank president stands at the podium, the training director at his side. The young trainees sit in the front rows with their mothers, fathers, and siblings behind them. The president welcomes the new members

into the bank family, challenging them to live up to the expectations of their trainers and leaders. He speaks also to the parents, accepting from them the challenge of providing for their children not only honest work, but also accepting the obligation to see to their complete physical, intellectual, and moral development. A representative of the parents next takes the podium, thanking the bank for offering this opportunity to their offspring and reaffirming the charge to the trainees to be as loyal to their new family as they are to their blood family. Finally, a representative of the trainees rises to speak, thanking both parents and bank for their support and pledging to work hard to meet their expectations.

Most Western organizations practice an attitude of "partial inclusion," an understanding between employee and employer that the connection between them involves only those activities directly connected with the completion of a specific job. Many Western social scientists have argued that partial inclusion maintains the emotional health in individuals. Being partially included in a number of organizations makes moving from one social domain to another easy, and tensions that have built up in one setting can be released in another. The Japanese organization, by contrast, forms inclusive relationships. A set of mechanisms provide for the social support and emotional release necessary for emotional equilibrium. One such mechanism is the capacity of group members to "change hats" and alter the nature of their relationships to one another for a short time in order to provide this social release and balance. Consider one example: At one American-owned plant in Japan, a golfing day with the manager became a twice yearly tradition. A train ride of four hours each way, plus golf, consumed an entire day for this important event. The American plant manager, to prepare for the outing, made a list of critical issues of strategy and management that he felt were on the minds of his subordinates. As the group approached the first tee, he produced his list and set out the agenda for the next eighteen holes. His subordinates were discouraged and disappointed by this, and the day proceeded in a desultory fashion.

A Japanese manager interpreted the story for me. A Japanese company, he pointed out, is a quite formal and at times even an authoritarian setting. Rarely will an employee disagree openly with a superior or voice complaints. When people anticipate a lifetime of working together, they cannot afford to let deep rifts develop. Thus a stylized pattern of interaction develops. Conflict and refusal would disturb the harmony that must underlie the work relationship. On the other hand, no company can remain healthy with suppressed disagreement, conflict, and complaint. A symbolic change of roles in which different patterns of behavior are acceptable provides one outlet. In the golf outing, for example, the implication was that boss and subordinates were competing as equals. With the physical setting away from the place of work, the acceptable patterns of behavior are also meant to be far removed from the daily norm. At these times subordinates can feel free to ask questions and to raise objections suppressed in the office and expect the boss to respond sympathetically. In a similar manner, office parties with drinks and dinner permit the subordinates to adopt the guise of mild inebriation to tell the boss off and give opinions unspeakable under ordinary conditions. Thus the organization provides the group with a change of venue necessary to healthy social relations.

The wholistic orientation of Japanese organizations stems from both historical accident and underlying social and cultural forces. According to one commonly held view, the historical accident is that industrialism rushed into Japan after having been held out for decades by a feudal political system. Companies were forced to build plants near to the villages where they could recruit workers. With no long and gradual urbanization as Europe had, Japan found itself with a sparsely-distributed rural population faced with the onrush of industrialization. Each plant sent recruiters to village homes asking mothers and fathers to send their offspring to work in the plant twenty or thirty miles away. Village parents who loved their children would simply not release them to go to live and work in a strange place. The companies had to build dormitories, to provide a healthy diet, and to assure parents that their children would receive the moral, intellectual, physical and domestic training that would prepare them for life. In the case of young women, the company arranged for training in domestic skills needed by a young wife. No partial inclusion, no tentative, tenuous link between company and employee was possible in this setting. Rather, it was a complete and whole relationship which formed between employee and employer.[3]

Some Japan experts argue that the underlying social patterns developed under feudalism prepared the Japanese for dependent relationship on a paternalistic force to meet their needs and to give their loyalty in return. If such an attitude had existed, it surely would have supported the wholistic work relationship.

When economic and social life are integrated into a single whole, then relationships between individuals become intimate. Rather than a connection through a single work relationship, individuals interconnect through multiple bonds. This one closely-knit relationship makes it impossible to escape the frustrations and tensions by spending time with another, completely unrelated group. Intimacy of this sort discourages selfish or dishonest action in the group, since abused relationships cannot be left behind. People who live in a company dormitory, play on a company baseball team, work together in five different committees, and know the situation will continue for the rest of their lives will develop a unique relationship. Values and be-liefs become mutually compatible over a wide range of work and non-work related issues. Each person's true level of effort and of per-formance stands out, and the close rela-tionship brings about a high level of subtlety in understanding of each other's needs and plans. This mixture of supports and restraints promotes mutual trust, since compatible goals and complete openness remove the fears of or desires for deception. Thus intimacy, trust, and understanding grow where individuals are linked to one another through multiple bonds in a wholistic relationship.

Social scientists have long noted that wholistic relationships develop in "total in-stitutions," but have regarded these as anoma-lies limited to prisons, mental hospitals, religious orders, and military units. Amitai Etzioni of Columbia University asserts that a wholistic network comprises an effective means of social control, one in which individ-uals can be free but also capable of a peaceful co-existence.[4] But Etzioni, like others, has also contended that this form of social control is fundamentally incompatible with modern in-dustrial society, because industrialism inevit-ably leads to a high degree of specialization of labor, frequent moving between employers, and consequently only a partial inclusion in the group. The Japanese show clear evidence that wholism in industrial life is possible. The final question must address whether wholism and intimacy in industrial life are desirable. In grasping just how we Americans really differ from the Japanese lies the key to what we can learn from them.

Footnotes

[1] For a thorough and practical discussion of par-ticipative methods of decision making and their use in industry, see Edgar H. Schein, *Process Consultation* [Reading, Mass.: Addison-Wesley, 1969].

[2] See Thomas P. Rohlen, *For Harmony and Strength: Japanese White-Collar Organization in Anthropological Perspec-tive* [Berkeley: Universtiy of California Press, 1974].

[3] Sociologists and anthropologists have offered a great variety of views on the nature and extent of American influence during the post-war era on the structure of Jap-anese industry. The interpretation which I present here is not definitive, but it is representative.

[4] See Amitai Etzioni, "Organizational Control Struc-ture," *Handbook of Organizations*, ed. J. G. March [Chicago: Rand McNally, 1965].

DISCUSSION QUESTIONS

1. In which respects does decision-making in Japanese organizations differ from that in American corporations?

2. How do you think the Japanese style of decision-making might be adapted to American business? What limitations does such an approach have in the United States?

3. How has the Japanese style of business or-ganization contributed to the emergence of Japan as a world economic power? You might compare Ouchi's description with the conclusions drawn by Ezra Vogel in Chapter 12 and William McCord in Chapter 17.

CHAPTER 3

Issues in Deviance

INTRODUCTION

Who is deviant? At different times and in different ways, all of us are deviant. In one sense of the word, *deviance* merely means being different from the norm or average of a particular society. Jesus, Einstein, and Hitler were all "deviants" by this standard.

Thus, if a person has red hair or is six feet tall, she or he is deviant—simply because the majority of the population is quite different. Usually, however, we use the word "deviant" to mean a person who (1) is labeled as "strange," "sick," or "bad" by the standards of the society; (2) is condemned and sometimes punished by those who have power; and (3) suffers because of the resulting ostracism. In contemporary Western society, schizophrenics, homosexuals, and drug addicts—along with many other types of people—must endure this fate.

Deviance in American society emerges from the very nature of our social framework. A variety of thinkers—Leo Tolstoy, Friedrich Wilhelm Nietzsche, Martin Buber, Erich Fromm, Albert Camus—have contended that the central disorder of modern society is its failure to provide a common framework of meaning for the definition of what is "normal" or "good." In general, they have argued that people have lost their sense of meaning, that they are deprived of a feeling of community, that they suffer from what Emile Durkheim (1858–1917) was the first to call "anomie."

The quest for meaning is an inherent part of human nature.

- Humans are the only animals who search for meaning, the only ones who wish to know why the universe was created, why they are here, and why life must end in death.
- Humans are the only animals who create meaning. Only they invent complicated systems of religion and magic, of metaphysics and ideology, of political structures and elaborate rituals.
- Humans are the only animals who acknowledge and even celebrate the lack of meaning or significance, for they can consciously destroy themselves.

It is humans' ability to question their own significance that sets them apart and leads to deviance from society's norms. Deviance flourishes in American society for several reasons:

57

The growth of industrialism and bureaucracy often alienates people from their work and destroys their framework of meaning.

The growth of science, some people feel, has rendered many traditional religious beliefs questionable. Thus, such people feel free to create their own frameworks of meaning, and new "deviant" cults proliferate.

Urbanization brings with it both greater individual freedom and greater anonymity. Consequently, urbanites are "liberated" to participate in many forms of deviance.

The political system of the United States allows ample room for dissent and many forms of deviant behavior.

To provide a theoretical context for this chapter on deviance, no selection would better serve the purpose than the first reading, Howard Becker's "The Outsiders." Becker's classic statement of labeling theory exemplifies the view that deviant behavior is created when people "label" others' behavior as deviant. The process of social typing involves labelers, who are often members of powerful groups and who are in agreement about what constitutes appropriate and inappropriate behavior, and individuals whose behavior is judged to depart from norms acceptable to the dominant group. The labeling process involves an exchange between the labeled and the labelers in which social groups create deviance by making rules the infraction of which constitutes deviance. Becker's analysis turns on the relationships between members of cultural and subcultural groups and the individual effects of labeling.

In the contemporary United States, we imprison or place under supervision some 3 million people a year who have committed crimes, and such efforts to control deviance are fraught with problems. In the second reading, William McCord and Jose Sanchez examine a critical experiment in rehabilitating young delinquents before they enter upon an adult life of crime and deviance. They find that therapy can help dramatically in reducing crime, even among psychopaths, but that early discrimination against young men can dash their hopes in later life. McCord and Sanchez's article is presented as an account of two types of rehabilitative "therapies" for young deviants.

The 1980s saw the rise to preeminence of the so-called "war on drugs." Daily headlines in the print and television media attest to the growing problem of drugs in America. The Bush administration has described the drug problem as the "gravest threat facing our nation" and cocaine as "our most serious problem today." Some critics take umbrage at Bush's assertions, for they believe that the war on drugs is neither scientifically nor medically justified but is rather a political war waged by police officers and politicians (Lapham, 1989). Lee's cross-cultural reading, "Cocaine Mafia," attacks the war on drugs from an entirely different standpoint. South American drug barons battle the U.S. government's efforts to crush their cartel because they find it to be "anti-Latin" and a violation of their national sovereignty. Members of the "cocaine mafia," according to Lee, argue openly that they are essential to economic stability and public welfare in their countries, and thus they strive for political and social legitimacy. Lee shows how their fervent nationalism and populism have resulted in extraordinary levels of violence against political officials and citizens. This is particularly true in Colombia. An international drug cartel that produces cocaine has terrified its citizens and corrupted the political structure of this struggling Third World nation. Colombia's government is fighting back by trying to crush the drug lords, with the assistance of the United States.

References

Lapham, Louis H. "A Political Opiate." *Harper's,* December 1989, pp. 43–48.

The Outsiders

Howard Becker

All social groups make rules and attempt, at some times and under some circumstances, to enforce them. Social rules define situations and the kinds of behavior appropriate to them, specifying some actions as "right" and forbidding others as "wrong." When a rule is enforced, the person who is supposed to have broken it may be seen as a special kind of person, one who cannot be trusted to live by the rules agreed on by the group. He is regarded as an *outsider*.

But the person who is thus labeled an outsider may have a different view of the matter. He may not accept the rule by which he is being judged and may not regard those who judge him as either competent or legitimately entitled to do so. Hence, a second meaning of the term emerges: the rule-breaker may feel his judges are *outsiders*.

In what follows, I will try to clarify the situation and process pointed to by this double-barreled term: the situations of rule-breaking and rule-enforcement and the processes by which some people come to break rules and others to enforce them.

Some preliminary distinctions are in order. Rules may be a great many kinds. They may be formally enacted into law, and in this case the police power of the state may be used in enforcing them. In other cases, they represent informal agreements, newly arrived at or encrusted with the sanction of age and tradition; rules of this kind are enforced by informal sanctions of various kinds.

Similarly, whether a rule has the force of law or tradition or is simply the result of consensus, it may be the task of some specialized body, such as the police or the committee on ethics of a professional association, to enforce it; enforcement, on the other hand, may be everyone's job or, at least, the job of everyone in the group to which the rule is meant to apply.

Many rules are not enforced and are not, in any except the most formal sense, the kind of rules with which I am concerned. Blue laws, which remain on the statute books though they have not been enforced for a hundred years, are examples. (It is important to remember, however, that an unenforced law may be reactivated for various reasons and regain all its original force, as recently occurred with respect to the laws governing the opening of commercial establishments on Sunday in Missouri.) Informal rules may similarly die from lack of enforcement. I shall mainly be concerned with what we can call the actual operating rules of groups, those kept alive through attempts at enforcement.

Finally, just how far "outside" one is, in either of the senses I have mentioned, varies from case to case. We think of the person who commits a traffic violation or gets a little too drunk at a party as being, after all, not very different from the rest of us and treat his infraction tolerantly. We regard the thief as less like us and punish him severely. Crimes such as murder, rape, or treason lead us to view the violator as a true outsider.

In the same way, some rule-breakers do not think they have been unjustly judged. The traffic violator usually subscribes to the very rules he has broken. Alcoholics are often ambivalent, sometimes feeling that those who judge them do not understand them and at other times agreeing that compulsive drinking is a bad thing. At the extreme, some deviants (homosexuals and drug addicts are good examples) develop full-blown ideologies explaining why they are right and why those who disapprove of and punish them are wrong.

DEFINITIONS OF DEVIANCE

The outsider—the deviant from group rules—has been the subject of much speculation, theorizing, and scientific study. What laymen want to know about deviants is: why do they do it? How can we account for their rule-breaking? What is there about them that leads them to do forbidden things? Scientific research has tried to find answers to these questions. In doing so it has accepted the common-sense premise that there is something inherently deviant (qualitatively distinct) about acts that break (or seem to break) social rules. It has also accepted the common-sense assumption that the deviant act occurs because some characteristic of the person who commits it makes it necessary or inevitable that he should. Scientists do not ordinarily question the label "deviant" when it is applied to particular acts or people but rather take it as given. In so doing, they accept the values of the group making the judgment.

It is easily observable that different groups judge different things to be deviant. This should alert us to the possibility that the person making the judgment of deviance, the process by which that judgment is arrived at, and the situation in which it is made may all be intimately involved in the phenomenon of deviance. To the degree that the common-sense view of deviance and the scientific theories that begin with its premises assume that acts that break rules are inherently deviant and thus take for granted the situations and processes of judgment, they may leave out an important variable. If scientists ignore the variable character of the process of judgment, they may by that omission limit the kinds of theories that can be developed and the kind of understanding that can be achieved.[1]

Our first problem, then, is to construct a definition of deviance. Before doing this, let us consider some of the definitions scientists now use, seeing what is left out if we take them as a point of departure for the study of outsiders.

The simplest view of deviance is essentially statistical, defining as deviant anything that varies too widely from the average. When a statistician analyzes the results of an agricultural experiment, he describes the stalk of corn that is exceptionally tall and the stalk that is exceptionally short as deviations from the mean or average. Similarly, one can describe anything that differs from what is most common as a deviation. In this view, to be left-handed or redheaded is deviant, because most people are right-handed and brunette.

So stated, the statistical view seems simpleminded, even trivial. Yet it simplifies the problem by doing away with many questions of value that ordinarily arise in discussions of the nature of deviance. In assessing any particular case, all one need do is calculate the distance of the behavior involved from the average. But it is too simple a solution. Hunting with such a definition, we return with a mixed bag—people who are excessively fat or thin, murderers, redheads, homosexuals, and traffic violators. The mixture contains some ordinarily thought of as deviants and others who have broken no rule at all. The statistical definition of deviance, in short, is too far removed from the concern with rule-breaking which prompts scientific study of outsiders.

A less simple but much more common view of deviance identifies it as something essentially pathological, revealing the presence of a "disease." This view rests, obviously, on a medical analogy. The human organism, when it is working efficiently and experiencing no discomfort, is said to be "healthy." When it does not work efficiently, a disease is present. The organ or function that has become deranged is said to be pathological. Of course, there is little disagreement about what constitutes a healthy state of the organism. But there is much less agreement when one uses the notion of pathology analogically, to describe kinds of behavior that are regarded as deviant. For people do not agree on what constitutes healthy behavior. It is difficult to find a definition that will satisfy even such a select and limited group as psychiatrists; it is impossible to find one that people generally accept as they accept criteria of health for the organism.[2]

Sometimes people mean the analogy more strictly, because they think of deviance as the product of mental disease. The behavior of a homosexual or drug addict is regarded as the symptom of a mental disease just as the diabetic's difficulty in getting bruises to heal is regarded as a symptom of his disease. But mental disease resembles physical disease only in metaphor:

> Starting with such things as syphilis, tuberculosis, typhoid fever, and carcinomas and fractures, we have created the class "illness." At first, this class was composed of only a few items, all of which shared the common feature of reference to a state of disordered structure or function of the human body as a physiochemical machine. As time went on, additional items were added to this class. They were not added, however, because they were newly discovered bodily disorders. The physician's attention had been deflected from this criterion and had become focused instead on disability and suffering as new criteria for selection. Thus, at first slowly, such things as hysteria, hypochondriasis, obsessive-compulsive neurosis, and depression were added to the category of illness. Then, with increasing zeal, physicians and especially psychiatrists began to call "illness" (that is, of course, "mental illness") anything and everything in which they could detect any sign of malfunctioning, based on no matter what norm. Hence, agoraphobia is illness because one should not be afraid of open spaces. Homosexuality is illness because heterosexuality is the social norm. Divorce is illness because it signals failure of marriage. Crime, art, undesired political leadership, participation in social affairs, or withdrawal from such participation—all these and many more have been said to be signs of mental illness.[3]

The medical metaphor limits what we can see much as the statistical view does. It accepts the lay judgment of something as deviant and, by use of analogy, locates its source within the individual, thus preventing us from seeing the judgment itself as a crucial part of the phenomenon.

Some sociologists also use a model of deviance based essentially on the medical notions of health and disease. They look at a society, or some part of a society, and ask whether there are any processes going on in it that tend to reduce its stability, thus lessening its chance of survival. They label such processes deviant or identify them as symptoms of social disorganization. They discriminate between those features of society which promote stability (and thus are "functional") and those which disrupt stability (and thus are "dysfunctional"). Such a view has the great virtue of pointing to areas of possible trouble in a society of which people may not be aware.[4]

But it is harder in practice than it appears to be in theory to specify what is functional and what dysfunctional for a society or social group. The question of what the purpose or goal (function) of a group is and, consequently, what things will help or hinder the achievement of that purpose, is very often a political question. Factions within the group disagree and maneuver to have their own definition of the group's function accepted. The function of the group or organization, then, is decided in political conflict, not given in the nature of the organization. If this is true, then it is likewise true that the questions of what rules are to be enforced, what behavior regarded as deviant, and which people labeled as outsiders must also be regarded as political.[5] The functional view of deviance, by ignoring the political aspect of the phenomenon, limits our understanding.

Another sociological view is more relativistic. It identifies deviance as the failure to obey group rules. Once we have described the rules a group enforces on its members, we can say with some precision whether or not a person has violated them and is thus, in this view, deviant.

This view is closer to my own, but it fails to give sufficient weight to the ambiguities that arise in deciding which rules are to be taken as the yardstick against which behavior is measured and judged deviant. A society has many groups, each with its own set of rules, and people belong to many groups simultaneously. A person may break the rules of one group by the very act of abiding by the rules of another group. Is he, then, deviant? Proponents of this definition may object that while ambiguity may arise with respect to the rules peculiar to one or another group in society, there are some rules that are very generally agreed to by everyone, in which case the difficulty does not arise. This, of course, is a question of fact, to be settled by empirical research. I doubt there are many such areas of consensus and think it wiser to use a definition that allows us to deal with both ambiguous and unambiguous situations.

DEVIANCE AND THE RESPONSES OF OTHERS

The sociological view I have just discussed defines deviance as the infraction of some agreed-upon rule. It then goes on to ask who breaks rules, and to search for the factors in their personalities and life situations that might account for the infractions. This assumes that those who have broken a rule constitute a homogeneous category, because they have committed the same deviant act.

Such an assumption seems to me to ignore the central fact about deviance: it is created by society. I do not mean this in the way it is ordinarily understood, in which the causes of deviance are located in the social situation of the deviant or in "social factors" which prompt his action. I mean, rather, that *social groups create deviance by making the rules whose infraction constitutes deviance,* and by applying those rules to particular people and labeling them as outsiders. From this point of view, deviance is *not* a quality of the act the person commits, but rather a consequence of the applications by others of rules and sanctions to an "offender." The deviant is one to whom that label has successfully been applied; deviant behavior is behavior that people so label.[6]

Since deviance is, among other things, a consequence of the responses of others to a person's act, students of deviance cannot assume that they are dealing with a homogeneous category when they study people who have been labeled deviant. That is, they cannot assume that these people have actually committed a deviant act or broken some rule, because the process of labeling may not be infallible; some people may be labeled deviant who in fact have not broken a rule. Furthermore, they cannot assume that the category of those labeled deviant will contain all those who actually have broken a rule, for many offenders may escape apprehension and thus fail to be included in the population of "deviants" they study. Insofar as the category lacks homogeneity and fails to include all the cases that belong in it, one cannot reasonably expect to find common factors of personality or life situation that will account for the supposed deviance.

What, then, do people who have been labeled deviant have in common? At the least, they share the label and the experience of being labeled as outsiders. I will begin my analysis with this basic similarity and view deviance as the product of a transaction that takes place between some social group and one who is viewed by that group as a rulebreaker. I will be less concerned with the personal and social characteristics of deviants than with the process by which they come to be thought of as outsiders and their reactions to that judgment.

Malinowski discovered the usefulness of this view for understanding the nature of deviance many years ago in his study of the Trobriand Islands:

One day an outbreak of wailing and a great commotion told me that a death had occurred somewhere in the neighborhood. I was informed that Kima'i, a young lad of my acquaintance, of sixteen or so, had fallen from a coco-nut palm and killed himself. . . . I found that another youth had been severely wounded by some mysterious coincidence. And at the funeral there was obviously a general feeling of hostility between the village where the boy died and that into which his body was carried for burial.

Only much later was I able to discover the real meaning of these events. The boy had committed suicide. The truth was that he had broken the rules of exogamy, the partner in his crime being his maternal cousin, the daughter of his mother's sister. This had been known and generally disapproved of but nothing was done until the girl's discarded lover, who had wanted to marry her and who felt personally injured, took the initiative. This rival threatened first to use black magic against the guilty youth, but this had not much effect. Then one evening he insulted the culprit in public—accusing him in the hearing of the whole community of incest and hurling at him certain expressions intolerable to a native.

For this there was only one remedy; only one means of escape remained to the unfortunate youth. Next morning he put on festive attire and ornamentation, climbed a coco-nut palm and addressed the community, speaking from among the palm leaves and bidding them farewell. He explained the reasons for his desperate deed and also launched forth a veiled accusation against the man who had driven him to his death, upon which it became the duty of his clansmen to avenge him. Then he wailed aloud, as is the custom, jumped from a palm some sixty feet high and was killed on the spot. There followed a fight within the village in which the rival was wounded; and the quarrel was repeated during the funeral. . . .

If you were to inquire into the matter among the Trobrianders, you would find . . . that the natives show horror at the idea of violating the rules of exogamy and that they believe that sores, disease and even death might follow clan incest. This is the ideal of native law, and in moral matters it is easy and pleasant strictly to adhere to the ideal—when judging the conduct of others or expressing an opinion about conduct in general.

When it comes to the application of morality and ideals to real life, however, things take on a different complexion. In the case described it was obvious that the facts would not tally with the ideal of conduct. Public opinion was neither outraged by the knowledge of the crime to any extent, nor did it react directly—it had to be mobilized by a public statement of the crime and by insults being hurled at the culprit by an interested party. Even then he had to carry out the punishment himself. . . . Probing further into the matter and collecting concrete information, I found that the breach of exogamy—as regards intercourse and not marriage—is by no means a rare occurrence, and public opinion is lenient, though decidedly hypocritical. If the affair is carried on *sub rosa* with a certain amount of decorum, and if no one in particular stirs up trouble—"public opinion" will gossip, but not demand any harsh punishment. If, on the contrary, scandal breaks out—everyone turns against the guilty pair and by ostracism and insults one or the other may be driven to suicide.[7]

Whether an act is deviant, then, depends on how other people react to it. You can commit clan incest and suffer from no more than gossip as long as no one makes a public accusation; but you will be driven to your death if the accusation is made. The point is that the response of other people has to be regarded as problematic. Just because one has committed an infraction of a rule does not mean that others will respond as though this had heppened. (Conversely, just because one has not violated a rule does not mean that he may not be treated, in some circumstances, as though he had.)

The degree to which other people will respond to a given act as deviant varies greatly. Several kinds of variation seem worth noting. First of all, there is variation over time. A person believed to have committed a given "deviant" act may at one time be responded to much more leniently than he would be at some other time. The occurrence of "drives" against various kinds of deviance illustrates this clearly. At various times, enforcement officials may decide to make an all-out attack on some particular kind of deviance, such as gambling, drug addiction, or homosexuality. It is obviously much more dangerous to engage in one of these activities when a drive is on than at any other time. (In a very interesting study of crime news in Colorado newspapers, Davis found that the amount of crime reported in Colorado newspapers showed very little association with actual changes in the amount of crime taking place in Colorado. And, further, that peoples' estimate of how much increase there had been in crime in Colorado was associated with the increase in the amount of crime news but not with any increase in the amount of crime.)[8]

The degree to which an act will be treated as deviant depends also on who commits the act and who feels he has been harmed by it. Rules tend to be applied more to some persons than others. Studies of juvenile delinquency make the point clearly. Boys from middle-class areas do not get as far in the legal process when they are apprehended as do boys from slum areas. The middle-class boy is less likely, when picked up by the police, to be taken to the station; less likely when taken to the station to be booked; and it is extremely unlikely that he will be convicted and sentenced.[9] This variation occurs even though the original infraction of the rule is the same in the two cases. Similarly, the law is differentially applied to Negroes and whites. It is well known that a Negro believed to have attacked a white woman is much more likely to be punished than a white man who commits the same offense; it is only slightly less well known that a Negro who murders another Negro is much less likely to be punished than a white man who commits murder.[10] This, of course, is one of the main points of Sutherland's analysis of white-collar crime: crimes committed by corporations are almost always prosecuted as civil cases, but the same crime committed by an individual is ordinarily treated as a criminal offense.[11]

Some rules are enforced only when they result in certain consequences. The unmarried mother furnishes a clear example. Vincent[12] points out that illicit sexual relations seldom result in severe punishment or social censure for the offenders. If, however, a girl becomes pregnant as a result of such activities the reaction of others is likely to be severe. (The illicit pregnancy is also an interesting example of the differential enforcement of rules on different categories of people. Vincent notes that unmarried fathers escape the severe censure visited on the mother.)

Why repeat these commonplace observations? Because, taken together, they support the proposition that deviance is not a simple quality, present in some kinds of behavior and absent in others. Rather, it is the product of a process which involves responses of other people to the behavior. The same behavior may be an infraction of the rules at one time and not at another; may be an infraction when committed by one person, but not when commited by another; some rules are broken with impunity, others are not. In short, whether a given act is deviant or not depends in part on the nature of the act (that is, whether or not it violates some rule) and in part on what other people do about it.

Some people may object that this is merely a terminological quibble, that one can, after all, define terms any way he wants to and that if some people want to speak of rule-breaking behavior as deviant without reference to the reactions of others they are free to do so. This, of course, is true. Yet it might be worthwhile to refer to such behavior as *rule-breaking behavior* and reserve the term *deviant* for those labeled as deviant by some segment of society. I do not insist that this usage be followed. But it should be clear that insofar as a scientist uses "deviant" to refer to any rule-breaking behavior and takes as his subject of study only those who have been *labeled* deviant, he will be hampered by the disparities between the two categories.

If we take as the object of our attention behavior which comes to be labeled as deviant, we must recognize that we cannot know whether a given act will be categorized as deviant until the response of others has occurred. Deviance is not a quality that lies in behavior itself, but in the interaction between the person who commits an act and those who respond to it.

WHOSE RULES?

I have been using the term "outsiders" to refer to those people who are judged by others to be deviant and thus to stand outside the circle of "normal" members of the group. But the term contains a second meaning, whose analysis leads to another important set of sociological problems: "outsiders," from the point of view of the person who is labeled deviant, may be the people who make the rules he had been found guilty of breaking.

Social rules are the creation of specific social groups. Modern societies are not simple organizations in which everyone agrees on what the rules are and how they are to be applied in specific situations. They are, instead, highly differentiated along social class lines, ethnic lines, occupational lines, and cultural lines. These groups need not and, in fact, often do not share the same rules. The problems they face in dealing with their environment, the history and traditions they carry with them, all lead to the evolution of different sets of rules. Insofar as the rules of various groups conflict and contradict one another, there will be disagreement about the kind of behavior that is proper in any given situation.

Italian immigrants who went on making wine for themselves and their friends during Prohibition were acting properly by Italian immigrant standards, but were breaking the law of their new country (as, of course, were many of their Old American neighbors). Medical patients who shop around for a doctor may, from the perspective of their own group, be doing what is necessary to protect their health by making sure they get what seems to them the best possible doctor; but, from the perspective of the physician, what they do is wrong because it breaks down the trust the patient ought to put in his physician. The lower-class delinquent who fights for his "turf" is only doing what he considers necessary and right, but teachers, social workers, and police see it differently.

While it may be argued that many or most rules are generally agreed to by all members of a society, empirical research on a given rule generally reveals variation in people's attitudes. Formal rules, enforced by some specially constituted group, may differ from those actually thought appropriate by most people.[13] Factions in a group may disagree on what I have called actual operating rules. Most important for the study of behavior ordinarily labeled deviant, the perspectives of the people who engage in the behavior are likely to be quite different from those of the people who condemn it. In this latter situation, a person may feel that he is being judged according to rules he has had no hand in making and does not accept, rules forced on him by outsiders.

To what extent and under what circumstances do people attempt to force their rules on others who do not subscribe to them? Let us distinguish two cases. In the first, only those who are actually members of the group have any interest in making and enforcing certain rules. If an orthodox Jew disobeys the laws of kashruth only other orthodox Jews will regard this as a transgression; Christians or nonorthodox Jews will not consider this deviance and would have no interest in interfering. In the second case, members of a group consider it important to their welfare that members of certain other groups obey certain rules. Thus, people consider it extremely important that those who practice the healing arts abide by certain rules; this is the reason the state licenses physicians, nurses, and others, and forbids anyone who is not licensed to engage in healing activities.

To the extent that a group tries to impose its rules on other groups in the society, we are presented with a second question: Who can, in fact, force others to accept their rules and what are the causes of their success? This is, of course, a question of political and economic power. Later we will consider the political and economic process through which rules are created and enforced. Here it is enough to note that people are in fact always *forcing* their rules on others, applying them more or less against the will and without the consent of those others. By and large, for example, rules are made for young people by their elders. Though the youth of this country exert a powerful influence culturally—the mass media of communication are tailored to their interests, for instance—many important kinds of rules are made for our youth by adults. Rules regarding school attendance and sex behavior are not drawn up with regard to the problems of adolescence. Rather, adolescents find themselves surrounded by rules about these matters which have been made by older and more settled people. It is considered legitimate to do this, for youngsters are considered neither wise enough nor responsible enough to make proper rules for themselves.

In the same way, it is true in many respects that men make the rules for women in our society (though in America this is changing rapidly). Negroes find themselves subject to rules made for them by whites. The foreign-born and those otherwise ethnically peculiar often have their rules made for them by the Protestant Anglo-Saxon minority. The middle class makes rules the lower class must obey—in the schools, the courts, and elsewhere.

Differences in the ability to make rules and apply them to other people are essentially power differentials (either legal or extralegal).

Those groups whose social position gives them weapons and power are best able to enforce their rules. Distinctions of age, sex, ethnicity, and class are all related to differences in power, which accounts for differences in the degree to which groups so distinguished can make rules for others.

In addition to recognizing that deviance is created by the responses of people to particular kinds of behavior, by the labeling of that behavior as deviant, we must also keep in mind that the rules created and maintained by such labeling are not universally agreed to. Instead, they are the object of conflict and disagreement, part of the political process of society.

Notes

[1] Cf. Donald R. Cressey, "Criminological Research and the Definition of Crimes," *American Journal of Sociology*, LVI (May, 1951), 546–551.

[2] See the discussion in C. Wright Mills, "The Professional Ideology of Social Pathologists," *American Journal of Sociology*, XLIX (September, 1942), 165–180.

[3] Thomas Szasz, *The Myth of Mental Illness* (New York: Paul B. Hoeber, Inc., 1961), pp. 44–45; see also Erving Goffman, "The Medical Model and Mental Hospitalization," in *Asylums: Essays on the Social Situation of Mental Patients and Other Inmates* (Garden City: Anchor Books, 1961), pp. 321–386.

[4] See Robert K. Merton, "Social Problems and Sociological Theory," in Robert K. Merton and Robert A. Nisbet, editors, *Contemporary Social Problems* (New York: Harcourt, Brace and World, Inc., 1961), p. 697–737; and Talcott Parsons, *The Social System* (New York: The Free Press of Glencoe, 1951), pp. 249–325.

[5] Howard Brotz similarly identifies the question of what phenomena are "functional" or "dysfunctional" as a political one in "Functionalism and Dynamic Analysis," *European Journal of Sociology*, II (1961), 170–179.

[6] The most important earlier statements of this view can be found in Frank Tannenbaum, *Crime and the Community* (New York: McGraw-Hill Book Co., Inc., 1951), and E. M. Lemert, *Social Pathology* (New York: McGraw-Hill Book Co., Inc., 1951). A recent article stating a position very similar to mine is John Kitsuse, "Societal Reaction to Deviance: Problems of Theory and Method," *Social Problems*, 9 (Winter, 1962), 247–256.

[7] Bronislaw Malinowski, *Crime and Custom in Savage Society* (New York: Humanities Press, 1926), pp. 77–80. Reprinted by permission of Humanities Press and Routledge & Kegan Paul, Ltd.

[8] F. James Davis, "Crime News in Colorado News-

papers," *American Journal of Sociology*, LVII (January, 1952), 325–330.

⁹ See Albert K. Cohen and James F. Short, Jr., "Juvenile Delinquency," in Merton and Nisbet, *op. cit.*, p. 87.

¹⁰ See Harold Garfinkel, "Research Notes on Inter- and Intra-Racial Homicides," *Social Forces*, 27 (May, 1949), 369–381.

¹¹ Edwin H. Sutherland, "White Collar Criminality," *American Sociological Review*, V (February, 1940), 1–12.

¹² Clark Vincent, *Unmarried Mothers* (New York: The Free Press of Glencoe, 1961), pp. 3–5.

¹³ Arnold M. Rose and Arthur E. Prell, "Does the Punishment Fit the Crime?—A Study in Social Valuation," *American Journal of Sociology*, LXI (November, 1955), 247–259.

DISCUSSION QUESTIONS

1. How does Becker define deviance? How is his definition of deviance different from other sociological and nonsociological approaches to deviance?
2. According to Becker, what conditions or characteristics are relevant to the labeling of deviance?
3. Explain the "creation" of deviance using an example of your choice.

READING 3-2

Curing Crime

William McCord
Jose Sanchez

During the last decade, as juvenile crime rates have soared, several well-publicized studies have proclaimed that nothing works in rehabilitating young criminals. Indeed, some researchers have argued that early intervention in the lives of delinquents actually harms them.

We disagree. Research that we completed in 1981 shows that at least one approach—a form of rehabilitation therapy—may offer hope for altering delinquent behavior and attitudes.

The flood of pessimistic reports during the 1970s created disarray in the ranks of criminologists. In 1972, officials in Massachusetts dismantled their system of reform schools, on the assumption that incarceration only leads to more delinquency. A few scholars resurrected the 19th-century notion that criminals are born, not made—suggesting that the problem may begin in the genes, and that attempts at rehabilitation may therefore be useless.

In recent years, the general public has demanded increasingly punitive action against delinquents; laws have become harsher, and a number of well-known criminologists, like James Q. Wilson of U.C.L.A. and the late Robert Martinson of City College in New York, have advocated locking up delinquents for a minimum of three years, whatever their offense. And in Massachusetts, a new "get tough" mood among state criminal-justice officials has created a movement to re-establish prisons for teenage offenders.

We think that our study gives some basis for hope. We compared the records of former inmates of two reform schools 25 years after their release. The schools followed vastly different policies. The first was the Wiltwyck School in Yorktown Heights, New York, which offers a brand of therapy based on the philosophies of Alfred Adler, August Aichhorn, Ernst Papanek, and Bruno Bettelheim. The second was the Lyman School in Waltham, Massachusetts, essentially a jail for teenagers, which was abolished in 1972 because of brutality.

The form of rehabilitation practiced at Wiltwyck since the early 1950s, when we first studied the school, substitutes "disciplined love" for the punitive approach still most common in juvenile-detention centers. In a residential, unwalled setting, the staff combines various forms of individual and group psychotherapy. Although staff members deal with some severely disturbed, violent boys, they avoid punishment, encourage self-government, and try to build a "community of understanding" among different ethnic groups. Wiltwyck has produced such distinguished alumni as Floyd Patterson, former heavyweight champion, and Claude Brown, author of *Manchild in the Promised Land*.

The Lyman School—the first and most widely copied juvenile institution in America—stood in stark contrast to Wiltwyck. The school made no effort to offer psychological treatment. The staff emphasized punitive discipline, enforced strict rules, and added a dash of vocational training. Lyman's feared disciplinary cottage, where inmates were placed for such offenses as stubbornness or smoking, demanded absolute silence. Any boy who tried to escape received an additional sentence of three months. The boys spent their extracurricular time shoveling manure and performing other menial chores at the school farm. Lyman's most illustrious graduate was Albert DeSalvo, later known as The Boston Strangler.

Demographically, the boys incarcerated at Lyman closely resembled those at Wiltwyck: They were within the same age range, had comparable intelligence, and came from similar social classes and urban backgrounds. They had committed similar types of crimes and were diagnosed as having a comparable range of psychological problems. Ethnically, however, the two groups did differ significantly. The Lyman inmates included a large proportion of boys from Irish, Italian, and French Canadian families, while the population of Wiltwyck was largely black, and, increasingly in recent years, Hispanic.

During the early 1950s, we conducted a series of studies at the Wiltwyck School. The results showed that Wiltwyck reduced the level of anxiety, prejudice, and aggressiveness among its wards—particularly the more dangerous, severely anti-social boys. A year and a half at Lyman, on the other hand, produced no apparent change in any type of delinquent. Our studies, however, had an obvious flaw: The boys left the schools at an average age of 15. No one knows the patterns of their lives or careers.

In 1980, when the former inmates were in their late 30s or early 40s, we attempted a follow-up study to measure the long-range effects of their treatment. We drew our data from two sources: the rich case histories gathered on the boys' backgrounds and behavior in the 1950s, and information on their later criminal careers, mental health, military service, incarceration, and mortality gathered primarily from nine Northeastern states to which the men had scattered.

We studied the records of 175 men from Wiltwyck and 165 men from Lyman who had been incarcerated for at least 18 months between 1952 and 1955. In addition, we interviewed a random sample of 12 men from each of the two groups.

Measured in terms of conviction rates for felony offenses, Wiltwyck graduates had a 9 percent recidivism rate in the first five years after their release, as opposed to 67 percent for Lyman alumni. During the critical age period of 15 to 24—when, according to FBI figures, people are most likely to commit serious crimes—16 percent of Wiltwyck's graduates committed such offenses, compared with 22 percent of Lyman's men. It is worth noting, however, that 50 percent of the "de-institutionalized" boys in Massachusetts (who would have been sent to Lyman except for its abolishment in 1972) committed felonies. This shows that even brutal institutions, such as Lyman, may be more effective than none.

"Status offenders"—those who had originally been sent to the schools for nonviolent actions, such as incorrigibility or truancy—also apparently responded more to rehabilitation.

During the ages between 15 and 19, 34 percent of the Wiltwyck boys who were status offenders committed felonies; 50 percent of the Lyman status offenders were convicted for similar crimes.

Many of the status offenders at both institutions expressed bitterness over the fact that their own parents had brought them to court. One of the Lyman graduates who was interviewed recalled that period in his life: "That bitch [his mother] done thrown me out. The folks at Lyman sent me back to her. What was I to do but get out on the streets?"

Most encouragingly, Wiltwyck seemed to have a dramatic impact upon the youngsters diagnosed as psychopathic (those judged potentially dangerous or violent). During the first five years after their release, only 11 percent of the psychopathic men from Wiltwyck committed grave offenses—murder, rape, armed robbery—compared with 79 percent of Lyman's psychopathic inmates.

It should be noted, however, that Wiltwyck's approach had no apparent effect on boys diagnosed as neurotic or psychotic— those partly or largely out of touch with reality. Approximately 14 percent of the boys with such diagnoses from each school entered a mental hospital at some time after their release. The young men diagnosed as psychopathic were apparently more susceptible to the support that Wiltwyck offered.

In the higher age range, a majority of men from each school were apparently reformed by middle age—a phenomenon that many scholars would regard as a natural consequence of emotional and physical maturity and change in social roles.

The men we interviewed from the Lyman School told us that they had changed their lives merely because they were sick of repeated arrests and had found new opportunities. Men from the Wiltwyck School tended to praise the school, and claimed that it had profoundly affected their lives. And in fact it apparently had—at least for the first few years.

The evidence, then, is overwhelming that in the first years after their release, many more of the Wiltwyck boys "went straight" than did their counterparts at Lyman. For them, rehabilitation therapy worked.

Beyond those five years, however, a surprising trend became clear. The general recidivism rate of the older Wiltwyck men was consistently greater than the crime rate of older Lyman alumni. By the age of 35 to 40, for example, 32 percent of Wiltwyck alumni were still committing felonies, as opposed to only 8 percent of those from Lyman. The recidivism lines cross at age 25 for the two schools.

The key question, of course, is: Why did the pattern of felony convictions change as the men from Wiltwyck aged? Why did more of the Wiltwyck men, after such a promising start, eventually turn back to criminal behavior than men who had been at the Lyman School?

We examined a variety of possible explanations for the apparent reversal in the effects of the two schools' approaches, among them intelligence, placement after release, special treatment during the period of incarceration, and educational attainment. None of these factors convincingly explained the anomaly of the men's middle-aged recidivism. Only one factor, ethnic origin, appeared related to Wiltwyck's initial success and its loss of effect in later years compared to that of Lyman.

Most of the Lyman men reported that they had found life on the outside relatively easy upon their release. A retired policeman who had spent time at Lyman as a youth said, "I fooled around a lot when I was a kid . . . but then my uncle was on the force. When I was 20 he got me my first job as a traffic man. And look at me now—sitting on this porch enjoying life. It helps to have Irish connections."

The retired policeman is an example of what seems to be the key to eventual rehabilitation or recidivism: the opportunities open to members of various ethnic groups. Members of more deprived ethnic groups from either school were more likely to commit crimes in later life. Among Wiltwyck graduates, the recidivism rates of blacks and Hispanics went up as age increased; those of white graduates declined.

The ex-Wiltwyck men we interviewed remembered the school fondly—in one sense, perhaps, too fondly. For most of these young men Wiltwyck offered a welcome relief from the "real world." After their release, however, blacks and Hispanics encountered discrimination in education, jobs, and housing. (For example, the rate of unemployment among blacks and Hispanic youths aged 16 to 19 in New York City—currently about 50 percent—traditionally runs nearly twice as high as that for all city teenagers.) This discrimination, we suspect, engendered a feeling of frustration, dashing the hopes that their experience at Wiltwyck had raised.

This hypothesis for the former inmates of the Wiltwyck School is supported by a closer analysis of the men from Lyman. While the rate of criminal activity among most former Lyman inmates declined as they got older, this was not as true for blacks and French Canadians, whose rates or recidivism after age 25 remained relatively high. The most likely explanation is that discrimination against both groups in the 1950s made it difficult for many of the men to find employment.

Ethnicity, then, largely accounted for the differences in criminal activity after the age of 25. Wiltwyck had a higher proportion of black and Hispanic youngsters. Hence, Wiltwyck graduates faced a more difficult adjustment to the real world as they grew older. This resulted in a higher crime rate in later life.

Ten years later, more men who had been at Wiltwyck faced the tangible barriers of prejudice and discrimination, and lost the advantage given them by their treatment at the school. The pattern of our findings suggests that effective treatment in childhood must be accompanied by equitable opportunities in adulthood.

The follow-up research clearly supports the contention that rehabilitation therapy is an effective way of dealing with juvenile offenders—particularly during the age period when most offenses are committed, and especially among those prone to the most violent crimes. Sadly, the study also supports the conclusion that discriminatory treatment in later life can mitigate the best possible psychological treatment given to delinquents in childhood.

We apparently possess the knowledge to significantly reduce the toll of delinquency. Whether we can alter entrenched discriminatory patterns is something that remains to be seen. Providing the means to support rehabilitation programs that work would be a good way to start.

DISCUSSION QUESTIONS

1. How does a person's ethnic background affect his or her chances of committing a felony?
2. In what sense, if any, was Wiltwyck a "success story"?
3. What lessons can be learned from this article about the national approach to preventing crime among juveniles?

Cocaine Mafia

Rensselear W. Lee

South American drug barons over time have developed something in the nature of a political and social philosophy to give an aura of legitimacy to their drug trafficking activities. They pose as defenders of national values, as civic leaders, and as fighters for progress. Drug barons strive to convey the message that drug control is "anti-Latin," a violation of national sovereignty, and a threat to the freedom of individuals. They argue openly that drug dealers are essential to economic stability and to the public welfare. They are critical of particular administrations and even certain aspects of regime types, but not necessarily of the political status quo; some capos want to work within the system, and some want to change it.

NATIONALISM

Drug capos are first and foremost nationalists. Their nationalism may be linked to a specific aspect of U.S. drug control policy. In Colombia, the U.S.-Colombian extradition treaty has been a prime target of the cocaine establishment. Carlos Lehder wrote in the Medellín newspaper *El Colombiano* in 1982, "From any point of view, the extradition of nationals has no reason for existing, and even less reason exists for making a pact with a country which does not even have borders with the United States and where customs have not one iota of affinity with ours." A writer in *Medellín Cívico*, a newspaper controlled by Pablo Escobar, observed in a 1984 article, "The nation's face has been disfigured by the imperialist boot of the treaty." In Bolivia, Roberto Suarez said in a December 1985 letter to two national deputies that the 1983 U.S.-Bolivia accords for coca reduction violated the nation's constitution as well as the "fundamental rights of countless Bolivians."

The cocaine mafia also may target specific U.S. institutions and individuals associated with drug control. The Colombian mafia tends to pick on the U.S. DEA (Drug Enforcement Agency), accusing it of committing espionage against Colombians, controlling Colombia's borders, restricting private air travel within the country, and even committing murder. An article in the weekly magazine *Semana*—an article that U.S. officials in Bogota think was paid for by the mafia—claims that the DEA hired Cuban or Puerto Rican hitmen to kidnap and kill some traffickers in Medellín in early 1986. *El Espectador*, in a more credible account, attributed the murders to a dispute among mafia families over the payment of insurance claims for a lost cocaine shipment. In Bolivia, Roberto Suarez apparently has conceived a particular hatred for Edwin Corr, Washington's Ambassador to La Paz during the Siles administration. A 1984 letter to Siles Zuazo accused Corr of "humiliating and trampling on Bolivian national sovereignty." The same letter also accused Corr of extortion, saying, "This aspiring policeman extorted from me sums worth millions, which were carried away by special commissioners and by other servants of the North American Embassy."

A particularly virulent and extreme form of drug-based nationalism was expounded by Colombia's Carlos Lehder. Lehder used the drug enforcement issue as a springboard from which to develop an all-encompassing attack against Colombia's "monarchical oligarchy," which he sees as hopelessly dependent on "North American Imperialism." This dependence, in Lehder's view, touched every aspect of Latin American life and culture, but is epitomized by the Colombian government's willingness to extradite Colombians to the United States.

To create a new Colombia, free of U.S. influence, Lehder has advocated a broad popular alliance among groups as politically diverse as the M-19 guerrillas and the nationalist elements of the Colombian military. The struggle is to be financed by the cocaine and marijuana trade—what Lehder called "a revolutionary weapon against North American imperialism"—and spearheaded by an antiimperialist army. Lehder has talked at different times about a 500,000-man force to be created with the help of the Colombian army and about a Latin American "NATO" (North Atlantic Treaty Organization) encompassing all South American countries.

Lehder's ideology was a curious amalgam of extremism that borrowed from both the left and the right. The MLN (Latin Nationalist Movement), a political party founded by Lehder, opposed "communism, imperialism, neocolonialism, and Zionism" and also holds that "we are Catholic, Apostolic, and Roman." Lehder and his followers espoused a Latinized version of Hitler's master race theory. Admiration for Hitler, "the greatest warrior of all time," was coupled with a belief in Latin superiority. As one of Lehder's lieutenants put it, "In 50 years, the Latin race will be the dominant one; the Europeans are finished." Lehder spoke warmly of right-wing military figures such as General Landazabal Reyes, a former Minister of Defense dismissed by Betancur in early 1984, apparently for his opposition to Betancur's efforts to reconcile with the nation's major guerrilla groups. And Lehder wants the "nationalist sector" of the Colombian army to play a role in his antiimperialist revolution.

At the same time, Lehder played to the extreme left. He talked in interviews about starting a dialogue with the leaders of the M-19 movement. Confidential Colombian police reports say that M-19 guerrillas served intermittently as part of Lehder's personal guard force.

Lehder reportedly was dallying with Quintín Lamé, an Indian-based revolutionary movement in southern Colombia. In a major political turnabout, Lehder's fascist political party supported the communist candidate for president, Jaime Pardo Leal, in the May 1986 presidential election. In an interview, one of Lehder's chief political lieutenants said that the MNL backed Pardo because the communists oppose the extradition treaty. Politics, it is said, makes strange bedfellows, and Lehder's extreme anti-Americanism made him willing to welcome allies of many political stripes. The DEA official's description of Lehder as the Qaddafy of international cocaine traffickers is probably as accurate a summary as any of the man and his world view. Lehder's political antics embarrassed other more conservative members of the cocaine cartel, and this may have been part of his undoing.

To some extent, "Latin nationalism" is an elaborate projection of its architect's personal problems. Lehder has many. He has the distinction of being the first Colombian whose extradition was approved by the Colombian Superior Court and by the government (under Betancur). Also, Lehder once spent two years in a U.S. jail in Danbury, Connecticut, for possession of 200 pounds of marijuana. Probably for these reasons, he feels especially bitter toward both the Colombian government and the United States. Lehder comes from a mixed parentage: his father is a German engineer, and his mother a Colombian schoolteacher. He mounted an aggressive defense of Latin culture and values, possibly to overcompensate for his divided heritage. All of these factors contributed to, if they do not fully explain, the virulence of Lehder's political messages.

POPULISM

Drug capos try to make the case that the narcotics industry is good for progress and employment. Escobar said once that drug dollars kept Colombia from suffering "a grave crisis similar to that of other Latin American societies." He also said that drug money created new employment for the Colombian people. In a similar vein, Carlos Lehder once remarked, "If it were not for these hot dollars, Colombia would be in worse shape than Argentina."

Also, leading cocaine traffickers—such as Carlos Lehder, Roberto Suarez, Pablo Escobar, and Gonzalo Rodriguez Gacha—have won the hearts and minds of local populaces by their personal largesse; all have financed a vast array of social services in their native towns and regions, including housing projects, sports stadiums, schools, roads, and sanitation facilities. Such narco-welfare activities are the stuff of folklore and have enormously complicated the task of drug enforcement in the Andean countries. "The people love him for what he has done," said a Colombian official about Pablo Escobar's public works activities in Antioquia. The Robin Hood image of Escobar and his criminal colleagues represents an important part of their protection shield; it raises the political costs to governments of arresting these outlaws and especially of extraditing them to the United States.

Carlos Lehder's brand of populism extended far beyond philanthropy to advocacy of radical political reforms. Lehder described his Latin Nationalist Party, which he formed in 1982, as a "product of the absence of popular power." Said Lehder about the Colombian political system: "Bipartisanism has placed the people on the margin of major national decisions." Lehder called for the creation of a new Colombian political body, a congress of between 3,000 and 4,000 people in which all "popular sectors" of Colombian society— men, women, peasants, priests, and soldiers"—would be able to voice opinions. It must be stressed, however, that Lehder is not typical of the Colombian trafficking establishment, most of which prefers to work within the Colombian system.

SUPPORT FOR THE SYSTEM

Is the cocaine mafia a conservative or revolutionary force in Latin American societies? Does it represent a threat to democratic systems and values in the Hemisphere? In Colombia and Peru, these questions acquire special urgency because of the presence of Marxist revolutionary movements. Narco-ideologies do have a few anti-establishment overtones: they focus on Latin America's economic and political dependence on the United States, social inequalities, and the failure of governments to provide services to the poor. Yet, for all that, most cocaine traffickers—if not exactly pillars of society—are conservative, if not atavistic in their political thinking. In this respect, they resemble stereotypical mafia figures in Sicily and in the United States. America's king of crime, Al Capone, denounced "Bolshevism," praised the free enterprise system, and supported family values. Many South American drug lords apparently are cut from the same mold.

In Colombia, the cocaine mafia, with the apparent exception of Carlos Lehder, has never sought radical changes in the Colombian political system. A memorandum from 100 major capos to Attorney General Mimenez Gomez in 1984 stated, "We have no connection, nor do we accept any such connection, with armed guerrillas. Our activities have never been intended to replace the democratic and republican form of government." Pablo Escobar has expressed, in slightly different terms, his preference for the political status quo. Responding to efforts by U.S. Ambassador Lewis Tambs to link him to FARC (Revolutionary Armed Forces of Colombia) guerrillas, Escobar said in *Medellín Cívico*, "I share with them, [the guerrillas] a desire for a Colombia with more social equality for all, but I do not agree with their plans to obtain power by means of weapons, because to achieve power there exists a democratic system, faithfully watched over by our army, guardian of the constitution, and of the laws of the Republic."

The mafia's antidemocratic tendencies, such as they are, run more toward vigilantism than toward subversion. In 1981, more than 200 cocaine traffickers founded Death to Kidnappers (MAS). Both Pablo Escobar and Carlos Lehder reportedly were associated with the creation of MAS. Designed originally to retaliate against guerrillas who kidnapped for money, MAS evolved into an instrument for the indiscriminate persecution of leftists, including labor organizers, peasants who collaborate with guerrillas, civil rights activists, and members of the Unión Patriotic (the civilian arm of the FARC). Some Colombian army officers also have been members of MAS; in fact, the organization seemingly served as a communication channel of sorts between the mafia and the military.

Colombia's cocaine dealers have acquired huge tracts of land in the countryside, an estimated one million acres between 1983 and 1988. Some of these areas were traditionally strongholds of guerrilla groups such as the FARC and the EPL (Popular Liberation Army). The acquisition of rural property by leading drug dealers apparently has raised their political consciousness; as one Colombian government official put it, "As soon as they become landowners in guerrillas zones, they view communism as a threat and an enemy. Suddenly, they see themselves as pillars of the establishment."

The new mafia landed gentry not only have refused to pay taxes to guerrillas, but also have used their private armies to spearhead local self-defense and to destroy guerrillas' political support networks. They have received support from other groups, including traditional landholders, conservative politicians, and right-wing elements of the Colombian army. Such alliances apparently have dislodged guerrillas from large sectors of the Middle Magdalena Valley and from parts of Córdoba, Magdalena,

Santander, and Meta departments. A clandestine guerrilla radio station, Radio Patria Libre, referred to a "Narco-Military Republic of the Middle Magdalena Region" that "has control over the mayor's offices in nine municipalities and covers more than 20,000 square kilometers, equal in size to the Guajira department." Significant social changes apparently are occurring in the Colombian countryside: narco-control is replacing guerrilla control in some regions.

The narco-guerrilla thesis has become very difficult to sustain in the face of such developments. To be sure, the FARC still dominates the coca-growing region. Many of the FARC's 39 fronts maintain themselves by taxing and in some cases directly managing coca cultivation and cocaine processing facilities. Yet, most of Colombia's cocaine refining industry—the more lucrative part of the cocaine trade—is not controlled by the FARC, but is in the hands of powerful trafficking syndicates that have deployed manpower, weapons, and resources against communist guerrillas and that are hostile to the Colombian left, in general.

In Peru, the situation is somewhat different. The cocaine industry in that country is immature and fragmented; traffickers have not developed a common antileftist agenda (as they have in Colombia), nor have they been able to establish close alliances with the propertied classes and with the military. One reason is that Peru's cocaine industry is relatively underdeveloped—it still accounts for only a small percentage of South American exports of cocaine hydrochloride. Peru has no major trafficking personalities comparable to Pablo Escobar or Gonzalo Rodríguez Gacha in Colombia or Roberto Suarez in Bolivia. The minimal leadership in the existing Peruvian cocaine industry is provided mainly by Colombian traffickers. The industry's shallow roots and fragmented structure and the dominant role played by foreigners may have allowed Sendero Luminoso to penetrate some trafficking organizations. Still, there is substantial evidence of narco-guerrilla conflict in Peru; the narco-guerrilla relationship seemingly depends on the balance of forces in a given region at a given time.

In Bolivia—where there is no revolutionary movement to speak of and where the narco-bourgeoisie traditionally has had rightist leanings—the critical question is: Does the cocaine mafia favor a return to military authority? In Bolivia, the mafia and the military are related, both historically and ideologically. The military regimes of the 1970s provided state bank loans that supported the development of the cocaine industry; money borrowed ostensibly to finance cotton farming and other agricultural ventures in the Santa Cruz department apparently was diverted to building laboratories and other elements of a cocaine infrastructure. Narco-traffickers provided financial backing for Garcia Meza's coup in June 1980, and there was a virtual symbiosis between drug trafficking and the state under Garcia Meza's regime. The Bolivian writer Amado Canelas sees an ideological affinity between the mafia and the military, a common concern for "God, home, and country," and a common fear that democracy would undermine these values.

Some leaders of the democratic Siles and Paz administrations see the mafia as having a vested interest in authoritarianism. A former vice president under Siles Zuazo, Jaime Paz Zamora, argued in 1983 that the mafia—far from being politically colorless—had a definite goal: to topple democracy and to restore the military dictatorship. Some leading traffickers were clearly uncomfortable with the advent of democracy in 1982. In a 1984 letter to Siles Zuazo, Roberto Suarez referred to the "fragile foundation" of democracy, its "rotten structure of power," and the "increasing panorama of political confusion and social malaise resulting from the ineffective party system and from anarcho-syndicalism."

Suarez was no friend of democracy, although he did not openly advocate a return of the military dictatorship to Bolivia. Suarez represents the authoritarian, elitist wing of Bolivia's cocaine elite—he was a major financial backer of the 1980–1981 military regime of General Luis Garcia Meza. Yet his views may no longer be shared by most Bolivian traffickers, who by now are probably comfortable with democracy in Bolivia. By all indications, the cocaine industry has expanded enormously since the early 1980s, and there are now a significantly greater number of actors. The possibility of a cocaine-backed military coup should not be dismissed out of hand.

Cocaine trafficking is a destabilizing political force in the sense that the violence and corruption associated with the drug trade erode public commitment to democratic institutions. Yet most cocaine traffickers are not revolutionaries—they seek to penetrate and to manipulate established economic and political institutions. The rightward orientation of cocaine traffickers may itself be destabilizing—consider, for example, Garcia Meza's anti-democratic coup in 1980. Today, even Bolivia's traffickers probably prefer to corrupt people in authority rather than to overthrow them. Mafia vigilantism in Colombia arguably reduces the chance of an accommodation between the government and leftist guerrillas. Yet some observers believe that the peace process initiated by the Betancur administration in 1984 has merely provided Colombia's revolutionary groups with the opportunity to strengthen their military forces.

TACTICS

Cocaine traffickers use a combination of carrot and stick to influence drug enforcement policies in their countries. Like their counterparts elsewhere, South American mafias use coercive tactics against officials who are uncooperative or who publicly condemn their activities. Traffickers prefer to use blandishments—bribes, donations, and charitable activities—to achieve their ends. Money is by far the mafia's most important political weapon; with it, the mafia buys protection from law enforcement officials, corrupts the political establishment and builds a public following, especially among poorer classes. Violence is usually the last resort—that is, it is used against the policeman, judge, or politician who cannot be bought. Mafia-sponsored violence against government and judicial representatives has been a common feature of the Colombian political scene. The behavior of Colombian traffickers reflects a violent national culture. Colombia's murder rate is six times that of the United States, itself one of the most violent societies in the world. Murder is the leading cause of death for males between the ages of 15 and 44, and the second leading cause of death among all age groups.

COERCION

Mafia pressure tactics fall into two categories: blackmail and the threat or use of violence. In Colombia, the mafia has used money—especially campaign contributions—as a wedge for later blackmail or defamation of an official. The most famous case on record involved a Minister of Justice in the Betancur administration Rodrigo Lara Bonilla, who was accused of being on the mafia payroll. The affair almost cost the Minister his job and did cost him the support of Luis Carlos Galan, the head of the New Liberal Party to which Lara belonged.

The drug mafia's repertoire also includes threats against government officials. Many such threats apparently are linked to extradition cases. Mafia authorship is not necessarily certain—extradition aroused strong antipathy among many Colombians who have nothing to do with the drug traffic. Most of the more than 100 extradition requests by the United States to the Colombian government involve drug trafficking and related offenses, and the narcotics lobby is clearly at the forefront of national opposition to the treaty. It would be fair to say that extradition has been the number-one bone of contention between the mafia and the Colombian government, and will in all likelihood continue to be so in the future.

The cocaine mafia tries to dictate the national rules of the game on narcotics control. The traffickers' primary political objective is to force the Colombian government to scuttle the U.S.-Colombian extradition treaty and to adopt a policy of not extraditing Colombians to the United States. The mafia seeks to paralyze the top echelons of the nation's criminal justice system and to discourage potential crusaders against the cocaine industry. There has been a veritable parade of mafia-sponsored hits against prominent Colombians in recent years. Where national drug policy is concerned, violence, rather than bribery, has been the traffickers' main political weapon.

The result of all this bloodshed has been the destruction of the confidence of Colombians in their political institutions. A national Colombian survey taken in March 1987 reported that nearly one-half of the population believed that the drug traffickers were too powerful to combat. In a 1988 interview, former president Belisario Betancur said, referring to the drug mafia, "We are up against an organization stronger than the state."

Aside from exercising a "veto by assassination" over national drug policy, the Colombian mafia is also progressively destroying the nation's judicial system. Judges trying drug trafficking cases in Colombia are offered the proverbial choice of *plomo o plata* (lead or silver)—death if they convict, a bribe if they set aside the charges. Not surprisingly, few judges opt to convict. In the past two years, criminal court judges released from jail or dropped charges against four major cocaine dealers: Gilberto Rodríguez Orejuela, Jose Santa Cruz Londono, Evaristo Porras, and Jorge Luis Ochoa.

COCAINE TRAFFICKING AND THE STATE

The Colombian mafia has accomplices and informants in law enforcement institutions, in key government ministries (such as Justice, Defense, and Foreign Relations), in the diplomatic community in Bogota, and in the national and local news media. The network extends well beyond Colombia and also includes political or military leaders in several Central American and Caribbean countries. The network probably encompasses corrupt police, customs officials, and air traffic controllers in the United States, as well as some members of Latin American diplomatic missions overseas.

Cocaine traffickers buy protection from police, prosecutors, judges, and, where necessary, the military. *Time* magazine reported in February 1985 that at least 100 Colombian air force personnel and 200 national policemen had been discharged because of drug connections. Four hundred judges were also under investigation by the Colombian Attorney General's office for alleged complicity in the trade. Documents captured during a Colombian army raid on traffickers' hideouts in Medellín in early 1987 provided solid evidence that traffickers had infiltrated the Ministries of Justice and Foreign Affairs. In April 1988, the intelligence chief of the Colombian army's Fourth Brigade, based in Medellín, was dismissed, because investigations verified that he had "contacts with drug traffickers." Such extensive penetration of the state apparatus protects trafficking operations up to a point; at the very least, the mafia has acquired an excellent early-warning system a capacity to anticipate raids on laboratories, police dragnets, and other official forays against the cocaine industry.

Cocaine traffickers sometimes try to sway official policy by capitalizing on governments' financial problems. Roberto Suarez, in a meeting with President Siles' narcotics advisor in June 1983, offered to give the Bolivian government $2 billion in four $500-million installments to help pay off Bolivia's foreign debt. Suarez, according to accounts of the meeting, wanted the Siles government to acknowledge the independence of his cocaine trafficking enclave in Beni. (If genuine, the offer was possibly underwritten by Colombian trafficking syndicates—it is hard to believe that Suarez could have raised such a large sum in Bolivia). In another instance, according to a Bolivian police official interviewed in May 1986, Bolivian traffickers at the end of 1985 helped the financially strapped government of Victor Paz Estenssoro to pay a traditional end-of-the-year bonus to government employees.

South American mafias seem to intrude more directly into their nations' politics than do criminal syndicates in the United States. They spend large sums on financing electoral campaigns (both national and local), building a favorable public image, and—in Colombia—mounting direct bids for political office. Such initiatives do not always increase the mafia's influence. In Colombia, for example, the mafia may have made a mistake by going too far public. Yet they represent an interesting commentary on mafia political strategies and on South American politics in general.

Campaign contributions are one of the ways that drug mafias seek to extend their influence in the political realm. Such contributions do not in themselves ensure influence, but nevertheless constitute a hold of sorts over office holders. The more open the mafia's funding—or, at least, the more visible it is to the candidate—the greater the likelihood of compliance. An incumbent may feel gratitude toward his mafia backers. He may perceive mafia financing as essential to his future political plans, such as getting reelected. He may fear exposure and blackmail if he knowingly received contributions from traffickers. On the other hand, he may act completely contrary to his backers' expectations and, in fact, may take a principled stand against the drug industry. So the mafia takes what amounts to a calculated risk. The odds are, however, that its financial leverage will corrupt some politicians and—in numerous subtle ways—weaken a country's political will to fight against drug trafficking.

Drug dollars are important to aspiring politicians in Colombia. Colombian law makes no provisions for public financing of campaigns, and in some regions of the country—in cocaine and marijuana strongholds—drug income may be the leading source of private political funds. Money is a tool of influence, but in ways that are complex and—to the eye of the outsider—somewhat opaque. Mafia contributions do not necessarily bear a signature, but candidates may be generally aware that part of their funding comes from dubious sources.

NEGOTIATING WITH GOVERNMENTS

The South American cocaine mafia has been called variously an "empire without frontiers" and "a state within a state." In Bolivia and Colombia, governments on two recorded occasions have acknowledged the mafia's independent political clout by conducting quasi-official discussions with drug traffickers. In June 1983, Rafael Otazo Vargas, the head of President Siles Zuazo's Advisory Commission on Narcotics, held a meeting with Roberto Suarez at one of the latter's hideouts in the Beni. In May 1984, a former President of Colombia, Alfredo López Michelsen, and President Betancur's Attorney General, Carlos Jiménez Gómez, held

separate meetings with Pablo Escobar, Jorge Ochoa, and other major Colombian capos in Panama. It seems likely that the presidents of both countries authorized the discussions. According to two Colombian writers who closely follow the drug industry, President Betancur "not only had prior knowledge" of the Panama meetings, but actually hoped that the participation of López and Jiménez would produce a national accord with the mafia. Jiménez had conducted a previous (and unreported) meeting with mafia leaders in Colombia in late 1983. Otazo says that "he interviewed Suarez with the complete knowledge and support of the chief executive"—that is, Siles Zuazo—and his version is accepted by most U.S. and Bolivian observers.

Neither episode seems to have resulted in a government-mafia deal; yet the discussions conferred an aura of legitimacy on the cocaine mafia and as a result, caused major national scandals in Bolivia and Colombia. The Suarez-Otazo meeting was condemned in a resolution by the Bolivian Congress, and may have hastened the departure from office of the Siles government. In Colombia, Minister of Justice Enrique Parejo and many members of congress denounced the talks. Two Colombian senators called for Jiménez Gómez to resign because of his participation in the Panama meetings. Possibly the idea of giving official recognition to the drug mafia bothered opponents most. As one *El Tiempo* columnist cynically observed, congressmen said it was a "moral impossibility to have a dialogue with narcos," but saw nothing wrong when "the same narcos gave generously to their political campaigns."

Escobar, Ochoa, and other major capos who met with López and Jiménez in Panama claimed to represent "100 persons who constitute the dome of the cocaine organization" in Colombia—the cocaine establishment. The traffickers made clear to the Colombian leaders that they did not speak for Carlos Lehder. Yet the proposal can be considered as representing the mainstream Colombian mafia thinking at the same time.

When the meetings in Panama took place, Colombia's cocaine traffickers were more or less on the run, attempting to avoid the consequences of the wave of national antidrug hysteria that followed the assassination of Colombia's Justice Minister Rodrigo Lara Bonilla. The government declared a state of siege and initiated a series of reprisals against the drug industry. Police, sometimes accompanied by soldiers, broke into the houses and offices of suspected traffickers. Airplanes, boats, and automobiles were seized on the presumption that their owners were engaged in drug dealing. The government decreed that narcotics cases would be judged by military tribunals rather than by (more lenient) civilian courts. Government officials were forbidden under pain of dismissal to maintain friendships with traffickers. The Betancur administration indicated that it would begin honoring the 1979 extradition treaty with the United States. López Michelsen, who met with Ochoa and Escobar in Panama, said that the traffickers were "very frightened" hence receptive to the idea of coming to terms with the Colombian government.

The proposal that the capos presented to López and Jiménez reflected their status as fugitives. According to the version published in *El Tiempo* in July 1984, the traffickers requested what amounted to official amnesty— "reinstatement in Colombian society in the near future." They also wanted the extradition treaty revised so that they would have the right to be judged under Colombian law. The traffickers drew a parallel between their proposal and the peace agreement that the government had worked out with the guerrillas. The government, they said, offered the guerrillas the "opportunity to return to civil life with dignity," and they wanted the same deal.

To support the case for amnesty, Colombia's capos tried to cast themselves in the most

favorable possible light. They did not assassinate the Justice Minister, they claimed. They supported the "democratic and republican form of government in Colombia" and had no connection with the guerrillas who were trying to overthrow that government by force. They made a point of criticizing the "inaccurate image of the drug trafficking guerrilla," which, they claimed, was "suspiciously and maliciously coined in the days after the assassination of Lara Bonilla." They also asserted that they were in the business of exporting cocaine, that their cocaine business did not rely on home-grown coca, and that they were not involved in selling bazuco to the Colombian masses. In other words, the capos were saying, they did not constitute a threat to the Colombian state or to Colombian society.

What the traffickers offered in return for amnesty was radical indeed. The main feature was the dismantling of their cocaine infrastructure: the surrender to the government of laboratories, clandestine runways, and aircraft "used in the shipment of raw materials and of the finished product." The traffickers announced that they would get out of business of producing, shipping, and distributing cocaine. They claimed that their organizations accounted for 70 to 80 percent of Colombian exports, that their organizations had taken years to develop, and that it would be " difficult to replace or duplicate" them in less than ten years. Acceptance of the traffickers' proposal would seemingly result in a significant, if temporary, decline in the availability of cocaine in world markets.

To make the deal more attractive, the mafia included some additional inducements. They offered to repatriate their capital to Colombia. The proposal as recorded in *El Tiempo* did not indicate an amount; however, most Colombian observers estimated that traffickers' bank deposits abroad amounted to several billion dollars. In addition, traffickers proposed to help the Colombian government combat the remainder of that country's drug trade. They said they would cooperate in "campaigns to abolish consumption of bazuco and to rehabilitate addicts." They also indicated that they would help the government replace the coca and marijuana grown in Colombia with other crops. The cocaine mafia would now be in the front lines of the war against drugs. Finally, in a gesture to Colombia's traditional political elites, the mafia promised to refrain from overt political activity. Past participation of "some members of our organization in politics," they explained, had been prompted by a "desire to work against the extradition treaty signed with the United States."

Public reaction to the news of the talks was largely unfavorable, at least on the surface. As *El Tiempo* commented, "The announcement of the contacts was received with stupor and later with indignation. The political parties, the economic interest groups, almost the entire country completely rejected the idea, which would legalize one of the most scabrous criminal activities." Some political leaders took the line that negotiating with criminals would undermine Colombia's legal and institutional order. Others were skeptical that the traffickers would keep their part of the bargain. Said Ernesto Samper Pizano, a Liberal senator from Bogota, "To ask the drug traffickers to teach us how to end the drug traffic is like inviting bank robbers to a symposium on bank security."

The U.S. response also was essentially negative. A few U.S. officials saw the traffickers' offer as a real opportunity to reduce world supplies of cocaine, at least temporarily. This view did not prevail. Officially, the United States, which had indictments against many of the proposals' sponsors, adopted the position that it could only deal with cocaine traffickers individually and not with the mafia as a group. The United States refused to recognize the mafia as a "political" entity. The U.S. government rejected the entire thrust of the Panama meetings. The purported idea behind the meetings was negotiating a collective withdrawal by most of the mafia's chief executive officers from the drug trade.

Not everyone condemned the meetings. Some (unnamed) businessmen supported the mafia's proposal on the grounds that massive repatriation of drug money could help solve Colombia's major economic problem—at the time, the country's growing fiscal deficit and its declining international reserves. A law professor at Bogota's National University, Emilio Robledo Uribe, believed that traffickers could help fight the drug traffic. He argued, "The primary responsibility of Colombia's leaders is to deracinate the drug dealing business, and if the drug dealers offer to cooperate in such an effort, is it not the duty of the government to listen to them?" Furthermore, said Uribe, "using drug traffickers' power in the service of the nation" is better than "forcing them into permanent opposition" by rejecting their overtures for a dialogue.

López and Jiménez defended the talks and urged that the government accept the mafia's proposal as a starting point for serious negotiations. Both saw negotiations as a logical extension of the peace process that was underway between the government and various guerrilla groups. López even believed that the government could strike a better deal with the mafia than with the guerrillas: "The difference between the [proposed] surrender of narco-traffickers and the surrender of guerrillas is that the former gave up everything while the latter hold on to their shotguns." There were also some congressmen—albeit a small minorty—who argued in favor of government-mafia negotiations. One conservative parliamentarian felt that, if anything, traffickers were more deserving of amnesty than guerrillas. Drug money, he said, was "invested in important enterprises" and created jobs for "thousands of Colombians." Guerrillas, in contrast, had contributed to "thousands of Colombian deaths and incalculable losses in production" over a 30-year period.

Colombia's political establishment seemed to overwhelmingly oppose striking a bargain with cocaine dealers, and, eventually, Betancur himself killed this initiative. The president issued a communiqué on July 19, 1984, that said in part, "There has not been, there is not now, nor will there ever be any kind of understanding between the government and the signers of the memorandum." So ended an extraordinary chapter in the history of mafia-government relations, although individual Colombian officials may have continued to engage in low-key, sporadic, and highly informal discussions with drug traffickers.

The discussions aroused strong political resistance. Congressional leaders, and to some extent the public, view cocaine dealers as political pariahs and blanch at the thought of any official dealings with them. The same congressmen may welcome financial support for traffickers for their political campaigns. There seemingly is a world of difference in Latin American societies between accepting the drug traffickers as a kind of necessary social evil and granting them political legitimacy. The United States, for its part, has more or less rejected out of hand the idea of a bargain with the mafia. "We do not negotiate with criminals" apparently is the predominant reaction of U.S. officials to the idea.

Yet the idea of negotiating with the mafia was not totally without redeeming features. The Colombian capos' offer, on the face of it, had merit if one accepts its two most important assumptions: that the traffickers who authorized the proposal controlled 70 to 80 percent of the cocaine market in Colombia and that their cocaine infrastructure had taken ten years to build. Amnesty for Colombia's cocaine establishment seems a small price to pay for reducing world supplies of cocaine and U.S.

consumption of the drug. The Colombian economy clearly would have benefited (especially at the time the proposal was made) from the repatriation of narco-dollars held abroad. The fundamental issue is whether the traffickers would or could keep their word. International commissions would have to be established to supervise the dismantling of laboratories and other elements of the traffickers' infrastructure. The government would have to be in a position to impose severe sanctions on traffickers should they decide to reinvolve themselves in the cocaine business.

The Colombian and U.S. governments would also have to be willing to accept the political costs involved in negotiation. Such costs would be considerable—one can imagine the screams of outrage from the Colombian political establishment, the U.S. Congress, and world leaders in general. One notes in this connection that the Reagan Administration paid a high political price for negotiating with General Manuel Noriega in Panama. The Administration tried to persuade Noriega indited by a federal court in Miami on drug smuggling and money laundering charges—to step down as head of the Panamanian defense forces. The negative political fallout from the Noriega affair prompted both candidates for U.S. President in 1988 to assure the American public that they will never under any circumstances negotiate with drug dealers.

With the extradition treaty crippled since 1987, and with the climate for negotiations becoming more hostile, progress in tackling the cocaine industry remained at a standstill. Extradition of Colombian nationals to the United states did not resume until the assassination of Luis Carlos Galan, a leading Liberal Party candidate for President, on August 18, 1989. The assassination gave the government an excuse to issue several emergency decrees, one of which revived the extradition process. There was some initial public support for the new policy: a public opinion poll taken in Colombia's four major cities in late August or early September, 1989, showed that 63.4 percent of the respondents were in favor of extradition. Virtually all previous polls in Colombia had shown a majority of Colombians to be against extradition.

Yet there are signs that the popular consensus underlying the crackdown on cocaine trafficking is beginning to unravel. Colombians are growing weary of the violence and the economic costs (such as the abrupt decline in tourism and retail sales and the disruption of real estate markets) associated with the crackdown. A poll in mid-October 1989 found considerable support for the idea of a dialogue with cocaine traffickers; Colombians by a margin of 2:1 preferred a dialogue to repression. Cocaine traffickers and their allies will no doubt pressure the Supreme Court to overturn the emergency decree that reopened the doors for extradition. The Medellín mafia will probably continue its campaign of assassinations and terrorist bombings until the government agrees to stop delivering Colombian nationals to U.S. justice.

Rather than insisting on extradition, which many South Americans regard as a violation of national sovereignty, the United States should do more to strengthen criminal justice institutions in Colombia and the other Andean countries. These institutions are presently no match for the cocaine industry—probably the most powerful criminal enterprise that the world has ever known. Countries must be persuaded to introduce more effective anti-drug legislation; this should include stronger conspiracy statutes, stiffer penalties for drug trafficking, and laws (as opposed to government decrees) permitting seizures of criminally obtained assets. The judiciary needs to be professionalized; this means creating special cadres of judges that would handle only drug investigations, compensating these judges adequately, and providing them with adequate clerical support. Court systems will require modern word processing and data processing equipment and improved statistical procedures to manage their huge backlogs of cases effectively. In Colombia, shielding judges from syndicate hit squads is a first order priority; and this will cost several times the $5 million that the Bush administration has allocated for the purpose.

Overhauling criminal justice systems in the main cocaine-source countries will require considerable finesse (a major problem is how to reconcile Anglo-Saxon and Napoleonic legal codes); no doubt it will also require a substantial commitment of U.S. resources. U.S. anti-drug programs in Andean countries have up to now been largely a waste of money because they have not addressed the need for structural changes in these societies. What Colombia, Bolivia, and Peru need is not more weapons and helicopters (the Bush administration's $65 million military aid package for Colombia will hardly make a dent in the cocaine industry), but rather stronger and more effective civilian institutions. Investments in building these institutions will make more of a difference in the drug war than any other steps that governments involved in the battle against the cocaine mafia could take.

DISCUSSION QUESTIONS

1. On what grounds do drug barons of South America defend their activities?
2. Why haven't political officials been more effective in stopping the production and distribution of drugs in South America?
3. What are the similarities and differences between the current "war on drugs" and other "wars" Americans have waged (such as the "war on poverty" or the "war on crime")?

CHAPTER 4

Issues in Work

INTRODUCTION

While the majority of people in the world must till the land in order to eke out a bare subsistence living, the United States, western Europe, and Japan have passed into a new economic stage: the "postindustrial society." Daniel Bell, the preeminent analyst of post industrial societies, argues that such economies have freed human beings from both tilling the soil and laboring in industrial assembly lines. The changes effected by this transition in advanced economies have many implications:

1. "White-collar" and "service" workers now outnumber people who engage in farming or industrial production. (Bell draws a dividing line in 1956 when, for the first time in history, the number of workers engaged in white-collar work in the United States surpassed the number involved in direct industrial activity.)
2. The coming of postindustrial societies has entailed a great leap in the numbers of technical and professional workers. These new technocrats have often displaced land-owners and business titans as major political powers.
3. Theoretical knowledge has become a primary source of technological innovation, policy formation, and powerful decisions that affect all citizens.
4. As jobs in farming and "rusting" industries have become redundant, many Americans work in service jobs—as secretaries, salespeople, fast-food servers—which typically offer low pay and require little technical knowledge.
5. As Max Weber originally predicted, postindustrial societies have spawned a growth in bureaucrats—government officials, clerical staffs, and managers—whose sole job is to keep the lower workers in a service economy functioning.
6. In such an economy, face-to-face, interpersonal relations become increasingly important. Consequently, managers and theorists place increasing importance upon development of techniques to enhance "human relations."

Significant work-related issues in contemporary societies are addressed in a number of selections in this book. In Chapter 2, Charles Moskos explores relations between men and women on military duty and William Ouchi describes the nature of group decision-making in Japanese corporations. Gender issues at work are the subject of the articles by Rosabeth Kanter and Arlie Hochschild in Chapter 7. Michael Harrington and Mark Levinson, in Chapter 12, outline shifts in the occupational structure which promote the decline of middle-wage jobs.

In this chapter, the impact of the new economy on workers and the workplace is described from three levels of analysis. The first selection shows the effect of a dramatic cultural change—the rise of information technology—on contemporary workers. The second demonstrates some effects of organizational recruitment and socialization on workers.

The third takes a critical cross-cultural look at the reliance of industrialized nations on the cheap labor that is available in Third World countries. These three readings describe the impact of work on various people ranging from women working on assembly lines in poor countries to the new breed of corporate entrepreneurs in America's most successful corporations.

In the first reading, Shoshana Zuboff examines the unprecedented rates at which computers are being introduced to the workplace in America's service-dominated economy. In 1981 alone there was a 25 percent expansion in the number of data terminals applied to business use. Though increasing reliance on computer technology permits greater business efficiency and higher worker productivity, it does not come without costs. Amid concerns about the health hazards of exposure to cathode-ray tube (CRT) terminals, restricted social interaction between workers and supervisors, and lower morale among workers associated with computer-mediated work, Zuboff sees potentially more damaging consequences. Increasing reliance on computers may contribute to "de-skilling" of labor, as employees are robbed of decision-making opportunities. Computer technology also requires that knowledge and managerial assumptions be "packaged" in computer-accessible language. Such packaging may be inconsistent with workers' skills, and thus their satisfaction will be lowered. Zuboff does not, however, view the effects of the computer revolution in entirely negative terms but points out that it may offer workers a more complete and abstract understanding of their tasks and roles in the organization. However paradoxical the effects of computer-mediated work, Zuboff maintains that understanding the responses of workers at all levels to the pervasive use of computers will become increasingly important.

The second reading is taken from Arlie Hochschild's *The Managed Heart*. In this excerpt Hochschild reports on Delta Airlines' efforts to screen and train candidates for jobs as flight attendants so that they will project the "right kind" of personality and emotion. The personal consequences of the obvious "worked-up warmth" are also described. This reading highlights the profound effects that organizations have on the style and behavior of their employees.

The third article in this chapter, by Barbara Ehrenreich and Annette Fuentes, describes the shift to an international division of labor in which low-paid, unskilled jobs are being exported to industrializing countries with an energetic, primarily female, workforce. The theoretical perspective of this article is critical and falls within a world-systems approach that views the economic prosperity of industrialized nations as dependent upon the exploitation of poorer nations. While many multinational corporations that rely on a poorly paid labor pool maintain that their presence in Third World countries contributes to national development, improves the standard of living, and creates jobs, Ehrenreich and Fuentes portray the lives of the more than 2 million women employees of these companies as extremely harsh. Many such workers live in squalid conditions, perform dangerous work for inadequate wages, and are continuously exposed to a variety of work-related health hazards. Moreover, they have little job security, and their skills are not easily transferable to other jobs. The lesson in this reading, much like that of the other readings in this chapter, is that we must closely examine the personal and social consequences of work in contemporary societies.

References

Bell, Daniel. *The Coming of the Post-Industrial Society.* New York: Basic Books, 1973.

Hochschild, Arlie Russell. *The Managed Heart: Commercialization of Human Feeling.* Berkeley, CA: University of California Press, 1983.

New Worlds of Computer-Mediated Work

Shoshana Zuboff

One day, in the 1860s, the owner of a textile mill in Lowell, Massachusetts posted a new set of work rules. In the morning, all weavers were to enter the plant at the same time, after which the factory gates would be locked until the close of the work day. By today's standards this demand that they arrive at the same time seems benign. Today's workers take for granted both the division of the day into hours of work and nonwork and the notion that everyone should abide by a similar schedule. But, in the 1860s, the weavers were outraged by the idea that an employer had the right to dictate the hours of labor. They said it was a "system of slavery," and went on strike.

Eventually, the owner left the factory gates open and withdrew his demands. Several years later, the mill owner again insisted on collective work hours. As the older form of work organization was disappearing from other plants as well, the weavers could no longer protest.

In general, industrialization presented people with a fundamental challenge to the way they had thought about behavior at work. The employer's desire to exploit the steam engine as a centralized source of power, coupled with the drive to closely supervise workers and increase the pace of production, resulted in a greater degree of collectivization and synchronization in the workplace. Employers imposed an exact discipline on workers that required them to use their bodies in specified ways in relation to increasingly complex forms of equipment. By the early 1900s, "scientific management" had given supervisors a systematic way to measure and control the worker's body.

Although most workers have accepted the work behavior that industrialization fashioned, the issues behind the New England weavers' resistance lie at the heart of modern labor-management relations. Using collective bargaining, later generations of workers have developed elaborate grievance procedures and work rules that carefully limit an employer's right to control a worker's body.

New forms of technology inevitably change the ways people are mobilized to work as well as the kinds of skills and behavior that are critical for productivity. These changes are rarely born without pain and conflict—nor do they emerge exactly as planners envision them. Instead, new conceptions of work organization and behavior emerge from an interaction between the demands of a new technology, its social organization, and the responses of the men and women who must work with the new technological systems.

In this regard, the weavers' example is doubly instructive. First, it illustrates that during a period of technological transition people are most likely to be aware of and articulate about the quality of the change they are facing. When people feel that the demands a new technology makes on them conflict with their expectations about the workplace, they are likely, during the initial stage of adaptation, to resist. Many managers maintain that employees are simply denying change when they cling to familiar patterns and complain as these forms of sustenance are threatened. But resistance can also reveal an eloquent appraisal of the *quality* of change—a subtle commentary that goes beyond a stubborn attachment to custom.

Second, the weavers' example shows that as a major technological transition recedes into the past, and with it the sense of psychological crisis, older sensibilities tend to become sub-sumed or repressed. However, original sources of resistance, if they are not properly resolved, can continue to influence the man-agement-labor agenda for many years, even though employees may accommodate the de-mands of a new technology.

Business is now witnessing a period of tech-nological change that shares some important features with the first industrial revolution. Information technology is rapidly reorganizing the kind of work people do across industries and organizational strata. It is affecting clerical workers through the automation of high-vol-ume back-office operations as well as with word processing and electronic mail. Manag-ers are more frequently making use of com-puter conferencing, decision-support systems, sophisticated modeling procedures, and new on-line management information systems. Blue-collar workers are increasingly required to interact with computer technology in order to monitor and control a variety of manufactur-ing and continuous-process operations. Dur-ing the past year, business people bought one million data terminals, worth $2.6 billion, to supplement the four million terminals already in use. The market for intelligent terminals is expected to grow 25% annually during the coming decade.

This increased use of information tech-nology is altering the technological infrastruc-ture of the workplace. More and more, production in office and factory depends on the computer and large-scale information sys-tems that can control increasingly complex sets of data. And just as with industrial tech-nology, people who are required to use infor-mation systems often resist their introduction. When managers allow employee discontent with new computer-based technology a voice, they can learn a great deal about the more subtle effect of this technology and the issues that are likely to challenge their practices in the coming decade.

During the last few years I interviewed ap-proximately 200 employees, supervisors, pro-fessionals, and managers from several different organizations in three countries to discover how people at distinct organizational levels respond to their work when it has been fundamentally reorganized by information technology. . . . In this article, I outline the principal themes that emerged repeatedly from my interviews and observations, both as they pertain to employees' experiences of in-formation systems and as observable, often unintended consequences for the organiza-tion. Finally, I identify some of the implica-tions of these findings for human resource management policies.

The data reported in this article are principally based on research in three kinds of organiza-tions—banking, retail, and consumer goods. Each of these applications had been in place from six months to one year before I began the inter-views.

The information systems in the bank in-cluded: 1 a decision-support system in the credit analysis department that was about to perform "routine" calculations for analysts; 2 information systems for account officers that provided over-views and analyses of account activity in relation to the key business criteria of a company; 3 infor-mation systems that converted front-end pro-cesses such as foreign exchange, letter of credit, and current accounts to an on-line real-time basis, thus altering the work of both back-office employees and a range of managers.

The retail application was the automation of collections activities in the back office of a large discount store chain. Before automation, collec-tors functioned as entrepreneurs, each with an individual tray of accounts to be collected. The automated system pooled all accounts that were then automatically queued in order of priority and randomly distributed among collectors each day.

In the consumer goods organizations, profes-sionals and managers coordinated and commu-nicated their activities through the use of computer conferencing and electronic mail.

MANAGEMENT POLICIES TOWARD AUTOMATION

In many ways, management policies can determine the effectiveness of automation and the quality of the workplace culture that emerges. In this regard, my discussions with employees and managers reveal two primary concerns.

Substitution and Deskilling of Labor

The purpose of the intelligent technology at the core of a computer system is to substitute algorithms of decision rules for individual judgments. This substitution makes it possible to formalize the skills and know-how intrinsic to a job and integrate them into a computer program. As decision rules become more explicit, the more they are subject to planning, and the less they require a person to make a decision at each stage of execution. For some jobs the word "decision" no longer implies an act of human judgment, but an information processing activity that occurs according to rules embedded in a computer program.

At present, most programmed decision making has been limited to the most routine jobs in an organization such as high-volume operations where tasks can be simplified and rationalized to maximize outputs and minimize skill requirements. For example, partly by limiting a collector's discretion regarding how or in what order he or she should work on an account, an automated collection system makes it possible to increase production goals and reduce the time spent on each account.

Thus for that activity the key to revenue generation becomes volume instead of collection skills. Collection managers I interviewed believe that the system enables them to recoup more funds while reducing their dependence on skilled collectors. One collection manager described the value of the system:

"It gives us a tighter lock on the collector, and we can hire less skilled people. But there's a real loss to the job of skills and know-how. You are being told what to do by the machine."

But job deskilling is not exclusive to the most routine jobs in the organization. A decision-support system installed for a bank's 20 credit analysts was supposed to free them from the most mechanical and boring aspects of the job. Six months after the system was in place, not a single analyst had used it. As one analyst explained it, "I think, then I write down my calculations directly. I know the company and the problem. With this system, I am supposed to type into the machine and let it think. Why should I let it do my thinking for me?"

Automation of Managerial Assumptions

Information systems can embody management's assumptions and values about its employees, especially about their commitment and motivation. The automated collection system provides an example of how this happens.

Bill Smith had managed collection activities for 30 years, and management considered his perspective invaluable. In creating the system, designers spent long hours debriefing Smith, and he helped them make many important design decisions. Senior managers explain key design decisions by saying: "We tried to build Bill Smith's brain into the computer. If we did not build it into the system, we might lose to the competition."

When I talked to Bill Smith, some of the reasons the system eliminated most discretion from the job became clear. As Smith put it: "I like to see people work. I'm a good worker. I don't like to see people take time off. I don't do it."

The depth of memory and extent of communications that computer systems are capable of mean that managerial biases can surround the employee as never before. The cost of Smith's managerial assumptions in the collections operations system was high. A year after the system was in place, turnover had reached almost 100%, and the corporate personnel and employee counseling offices were swamped with complaints from replacements. The new and less-educated collectors presented a different set of problems for management and training. Even with the new staff, turnover remained about three times higher than in the rest of the back-office organization.

COMPUTER MEDIATION OF WORK

As the Bill Smith example illustrates, managerial assumptions can easily get embedded in information systems. But what impact do the new systems have on the organization of work and what actually happens to the people who interact with them?

Work Becomes Abstract

When information technology reorganizes a job, it fundamentally alters the individual's relation to the task. I call the new relationship "computer mediated." Usually, this means that a person accomplishes a task through the medium of the information system, rather than through direct physical contact with the object of the task.

Computer mediation can be contrasted to other forms of task relationships in terms of the way in which one *knows* about the object of the task. The potter who turns a pot with his or her own hands has a direct experience of the task's object through a continual series of sight and tactile sensations. These sensations form the basis for moment-by-moment judgments regarding the success of the process and any alterations that the potter should make. Machines, such as a press or a welding torch, usually remove the worker as the direct source

of energy for the labor process, but leave the task's object within sensuous range. Those who work with paper and pencil usually feel "in touch" with the objects of their tasks through the activity of writing and because they are the sources of what they write.

With computer-mediated work, employees get feedback about the task object only as symbols through the medium of the information system. Very often, from the point of view of the worker, the object of the task seems to have disappeared "behind the screen" and into the information system.

The distinction in feedback is what separates the linotype machine operator from the clerical worker who inputs cold type, the engineer who works with computer-aided design from one who directly handles materials, the continuous process operator who reads information from a visual display unit from one who actually checks vat levels, and even the bill collector who works with an on-line, real-time system from a predecessor who handled account cards. The distinctiveness of computer-mediated work becomes more clear when one contrasts it against the classic image of work from the nineteenth century in which labor was considered to be the transformation of nature by human muscle. Computer-mediated work is the electronic manipulation of symbols. Instead of a sensual activity, it is an abstract one.

Many employees I spoke to reported feeling frustrated because in losing a direct experience of their task it becomes more difficult to exercise judgment over it. In routine jobs, judgment often becomes lodged in the system itself. As one bill collector said:

"In our old system, come the end of the month, you knew what you were faced with. With the automated system, you don't know how to get in there to get certain accounts out. You have to work the way the system wants you to."

People in even more complex jobs can also lose direct experience of their tasks. The comptroller of a bank that was introducing information systems to a variety of functions commented:

"People become more technical and sophisticated, but they have an inferior understanding of the banking business. New people become like systems people and can program instructions that don't necessarily reflect the spirit of the operation."

The auditor at one bank is working with a new information system that frees him from traveling to regional branches. The branches feed financial data directly into the information system that he can access in real time. He described his job this way:

"The job of auditing is very different now. More imagination is required. I am receiving data on-line. I don't go to the branches if I don't want to. I don't see any books. What do I audit in this situation? I always have to be thinking about what is in the system. I may be auditing, but it doesn't feel like it."

The auditor now has access to a new level of complexity in his data. He has the possibility of comparing branches according to criteria of his choice and searching out new relationships in the data. But in order to do this, he must now develop a theory of the auditing process. He needs to have a conceptual framework that can guide him through the mass of available information. Theoretical insight and imagination will be the keys to his effectiveness on the job.

By creating a medium of work where imagination instead of experience-based judgments is important, information technology challenges old procedures. Judging a given task in the light of experience thus becomes less important than imagining how the task can be reorganized based on new technical capabilities. In the banking industry, for example, planners are not automating the old, but inventing the new.

While working through information systems seems to require a more challenging form of mental effort, it can also induce feelings of frustration and loss of control.

A collections supervisor described the difference between the manual and computer systems:

"If you work with a manual system and you want to see an account on a given day, you have a paper file and you simply go to that particular section and pull out the file. When you're on the computer system, in a sense all your accounts are kind of floating around in space. You can't get your hands on them."

Some people cope with this frustration by creating physical analogues for their tasks. In one bank branch, an on-line system had been installed to update information on current accounts. Instead of making out tickets that would be sent to a data center for overnight keypunching, operators enter data directly into terminals; the system continuously maintains account information. Despite senior management's efforts to persuade them to change, the branch manager and his staff continued to fill out the tickets. When asked why, they first mentioned the need for a backup system. The real reason came out when the branch manager made the following comment: "You need something you can put your hands on. How else can we be sure of what we are doing?"

People are accustomed to thinking of jobs that require employees to use their brains as the most challenging and rewarding. But instead, the computer mediation of simple jobs can create tasks that are routine and unchallenging, while demanding focused attention and abstract comprehension. Nevertheless, the human brain is organized for action. Abstract work on a mass scale seems likely to create conditions that are peculiar if not stressful to many people. While it does seem that those who shift from conventional procedures to computer-mediated work feel this stress most acutely, it's impossible to forecast what adaptation to the abstraction of work will do to people over the long term.

Social Interaction is Affected

Doubtless, once information technology reorganizes a set of jobs, new patterns of communication and interaction become possible. In time, these patterns are likely to alter the social structure of an organization.

When resources are centered in the information system, the terminal itself can become employees' primary focus of interaction. This focus can lead people to feel isolated in an impersonal situation. For example, because functional operations in the back office of one bank have been reorganized, a clerical worker can complete an entire operation at his or her "professional" work station, rather than repeat a single procedure of it before passing the item on to someone else. Although employees I talked to were split in their attitudes toward the new back-office system, most of them agreed that it created an uncomfortable isolation. Because they had few remaining reasons to interact with co-workers, the local social network was fragmented.

Decades of research have established the importance of social communities in the workplace and the lengths to which people will go to establish and maintain them. Since people will not easily give up the pleasures of the workplace community, they tend to see themselves at odds with the new technology that transforms the quality of work life. The comments of one employee illustrate this point.

> I never thought I would feel this way, but I really do not like the computer. If a person makes a mistake, dealing with the computer to try and get that mistake corrected is so much red tape. And it's just taken a lot of feeling out of it. You should have people working with people because they are going to give you what you want, and you're going to get a better job all around.

In a very different kind of application, professionals and managers in the R&D organization of a large consumer goods company find the range of their interaction greatly extended with computer conferencing. While there is some evidence of reduced face-to-face interaction, the technology makes it relatively easy to initiate dialogues and form coalitions with people in other parts of the corporation. Clearly, information technology can offset social life in a variety of ways. It is important to realize, however, that the technology has powerful consequences for the structure and function of communication and social behavior in an organization.

New Possibilities for Supervision and Control

The dream of the industrial engineer to create a perfectly timed and rationalized set of activities has never been perfectly realized. Because face-to-face supervision can be carried on only on a partial basis, employees usually find ways to pace their own activities to meet standards at a reasonable rate. Thus, traditionally, supervision depended on the quality of the relationship between supervisor and worker. If the relationship is a positive one, employees are likely to produce quality work without constant monitoring. If the relationship is adversarial, the monitoring will be continual.

But because work accomplished through the medium of video terminals or other intelligent equipment can be recorded on a second-by-second basis, the industrial engineer's presence can be built into all real-time activities. With immediate access to how much employees are producing through printouts or other visual displays, supervisors and managers can increase surveillance without depending on face-to-face supervision. Thus the interpersonal relationship can become less important to supervision than access to information on the quality and quantity of employee output. One bank supervisor described this new capability: "Instead of going to someone's desk and physically pulling out files, you have the ability to review people's work without their knowledge. So I think it keeps them on their toes."

Another variant of remote supervision involves controls that are automatically built into systems operations, as in the collections system described earlier. These rules are substitutes for a certain amount of supervisory effort. Because the system determines what accounts the collector should work on and in what order, a supervisor does not have to monitor collectors' judgments on these issues. Managers also see automatic control as the organization's defense against the potentially massive pollution of data that can occur through access by many people to an on-line real-time system.

Remote supervision, automatic control, and greater access to subordinates' information all become possible with computer-mediated work. In some cases, these capabilities are an explicit objective, but too often management employs them without sufficiently considering the potential human and organizational consequences.

With remote supervision, many employees limit their own risk-taking behavior, such as spotting an error in the data and correcting it, developing a more effective approach to the work than the procedures established by the information system, or trying to achieve quality at the expense of keeping up with new production standards.

One reason the initiative to design a custom-made approach to a particular task has become too risky is that many people have difficulty articulating why their approach might be superior to other alternatives. Usually, management has developed a clearly articulated model of the particular task in order

to automate it, and if employees cannot identify their own models with equal clarity, they have little hope of having their views legitimated.

Another reason for decreased employee initiative is that the more an information system can control the details of the job, the less even relatively trivial risk-taking opportunities are available. Finally, the monitoring capabilities increase the likelihood that a supervisor will notice a deviation from standard practice. As one bank employee noted:

"Sometimes I have a gut feeling I would rather do something another way. But, because it is all going to be in the computer, it changes your mind. If somebody wouldn't listen to the reason why you did it that way, well, it could cause you quite a problem."

Another frequent response to the new relationships of supervision and control involves perceptions of authority in the workplace. Employees can tend to see technology less as an instrument of authority than as a source of it. For instance, one group of bank employees with an especially easygoing manager described the work pace on their computer-mediated jobs as hard-driving, intense, and at times unfair, but thought the manager was friendly, relaxed, and fair-minded.

One collector told about the difference in her attitudes toward her work under the manual system and under the automated system:

"When I worked with the account cards, I knew how to handle my responsibilities. I felt, 'Hey! I can handle this!' Now I come in every day with a defeatist attitude, because I'm dealing with the tube every day. I can't beat it. People like to feel not that they are necessarily ahead of the game, but they have a chance. With the tube I don't have a chance."

While this employee knows that her manager is the actual authority in the office, and that he is in turn accountable to other managers, she has an undeniable feeling that the system, too, is a kind of authority. It is the system she must fight, and, if she wins, it is the system she vanquishes.

In the Volvo plant in Kalmar, Sweden, a computer system was installed to monitor assembly operations.[1] A feedback device was programmed to flash a red light signalling a quality control problem. The workers protested against the device, insisting that the supervisory function be returned to a foreman. They preferred to answer to a human being with whom they could negotiate, argue, and explain rather than to a computer whose only means of "communication" was unilateral. In effect, they refused to allow the computer to become, at least in this limited situation, an authority. Yet clearly, the issue would never have arisen in the first place were the technology not capable of absorbing the characteristics of authority.

Finally, these capacities of information systems can do much to alter the relationships among managers themselves. A division or plant manager can often leverage a certain amount of independence by maintaining control of key information. Though a manager might have to present the data in monthly or quarterly reports, he or she has some control over the amount and format. With information technology, however, senior managers in corporate headquarters increasingly have access to real-time systems that display the day-to-day figures of distinct parts of the company's business. For instance, a division vice president can be linked to the information system that transmits raw production data from a processing plant in another state. Such data can provide the vice president with a view of the plant that only the plant manager or midlevel managers in the operation previously had.

This new access raises several questions for a corporation. First, some policy decisions must be confronted that address the kind of information appropriate to each level of management. Top managers can quickly find themselves inundated with raw data that they do not have the time to understand. It also creates a tendency for top managers to focus on the past and present when they should be planning the future.

It would seem that this new access capability would expand top management's opportunities to monitor and direct and, therefore, improve the performance of subordinate managers. But as the on-line availability of such information reaches across management hierarchies (in some companies all the way to board chairpersons), reduced risk taking and its effects begin to take hold. Managers are reluctant to make decisions on the basis of information that their superiors receive simultaneously. As one plant manager said to his boss in division headquarters: "I'm telling you, Bob, if you're going to be hooked up to the data from the pumps, I'm not going to manage them anymore. You'll have to do it."

Birth of the Information Environment

Another consequence of information technology is more difficult to label, but its effects are undeniable. I call it the "information environment." It refers to a quality of organizational life that emerges when the computer mediates jobs and begins to influence both horizontal and vertical relationships. In the information environment, people generally have greater access to data and, in particular, data relevant to their own decision making. The capacity for followup and reorganizing increases as information retrieval and communication can occur with greater ease and convenience than ever before.

One effect of this immediate access to information is a rise in the volume of transactions or operations. This increase, in turn, compresses time and alters the rhythm of work. While people were once satisfied if a computer system responded in 24 hours, those who work with computers now are impatient if information takes more than five seconds to appear. Timely and reliable functioning of the system determines workers' output, and these effects extend up the managerial ladder. Once managers become accustomed to receiving in two hours a report that once took two weeks to compile, they will consider any delay a burden. This speed of access, retrieval, and information processing is allegedly the key to improving the productivity of the organization, but few organizations have seriously considered the appropriate definition of productivity in their own operations. In the meantime, more transactions, reports, and information are generated in an ever-shorter amount of time.

Responses to the information environment usually are accompanied by feelings about power and orderliness. To some people, the increased access to information enhances their power over the contingencies of their work. An account officer for one bank states:

"I never had such a complete picture of a particular customer before. I can switch around the format of the base for my reporting purposes and get a full picture of where the bank is making money. This gives me a new power and effectiveness in my work."

While most people agree that the information environment makes the workplace more orderly, responses to this orderliness tend to be bipolar. Some see the order as "neat and nice," while others perceive it as increasing the regimentation of the workplace. Responses of two collections managers illustrate these differences. The first described the system this way:

"The computer simply alleviates a lot of paperwork. Everything is lined up for you instead of you having to do it yourself. If you are sloppy, the system organizes you."

Another manager in the same organization regards the collections system in a different way:

"Things were a lot more relaxed before the tubes. Before, you scheduled your day yourself; now the machines line it up for you. This means a more rigid environment because we can track things better."

Greater regimentation can also affect the environment of the professional. A vice president in one organization where professionals have come to rely heavily on electronic mail and computer conferencing puts it this way:

"I used to make notes to myself on things I had to follow up. Now those notes go into my electronic mail system. The system automatically tracks these things and they are there in front of me on the screen if I haven't followed up yet. Nothing slips through the cracks, but certainly for the way professionals usually operate, it's more regimented."

Many of the managers and professionals I talked to are wary of systems that seem to encroach on their judgment, their freedom, or the "artistry" of their professional assessments. Instead of feeling that increased information augments their power, these people resist information systems that they see limiting their freedom or increasing the measurability of their work.

At present, most professionals and managers function in fairly ambiguous environments. Information is imperfectly exchanged (often in corridors, washrooms, or over lunch), and considerable lag time usually occurs before the quality of decisions can be assessed. A continual flow of complete information, however, reduces ambiguity. For example, in the marketing area of one bank, an information system provides complete profits of all accounts while it assesses their profitability according to corporate criteria. Top management and systems developers believed the system could serve as a constant source of feedback to account officers and senior managers, allowing them to better manage their account activities and maximize fee-based revenues. But some bankers saw the flow of "perfect" information as not only reducing ambiguity but also limiting their opportunities for creative decisions and resisted using it.

Limited information may create uncertainty in which people make errors of judgment, but it also provides a "free space" for inspiration. This free space is fundamental to the psychology of professional work. The account officers in the bank had traditionally been motivated by the opportunity to display their artistry as bankers, but as increased information organizes the context of their work, the art in their jobs is reduced.

Employees in back-office clerical jobs also tend to perceive the increased time and volume demands and the measurability of operations as limits on their opportunities to experience a sense of mastery over the work. To overcome these effects, many of the collectors keyed fictitious data into the system of account files. Their managers were confronted with high productivity figures that did not match the size of monthly revenues.

Many managers first respond to such a situation by searching out ways to exert more control over the work process. I am convinced that the more managers attempt to control the process, the more employees will find ways to subvert that control. This response is particularly likely when outsmarting the system becomes the new ground on which to develop and test one's mastery. Managers may dismiss these subversive activities as "resistance to change," but in many cases this resistance is the only way employees can respond to the changes they face. Such resistance can also be understood as a positive phenomenon—it is evidence of an employee's identification with the job.

LISTENING TO THE RESISTANCE

Critics of technology tend to fall into one of three camps. Some bemoan new developments and see them as a particular form of human debasement and depersonalization. Others are ready to applaud any form of technology as progress toward some eventual conquest of dumb nature. Finally, others argue that technology is neutral and its meaning depends on the uses to which human beings press its application. I have found none of these views sufficient.

It is true that information technology provides a particularly flexible set of technical possibilities, and thus can powerfully embody the assumptions and goals of those whom it is designed to serve. Yet, while the value and meaning of a given application must be read, in part, from management's intentions, beliefs, and commitments, this does not imply the ultimate neutrality of the technology itself. To say that information technolgoy is neutral is like saying an airplane is neutral because it can fly to either Washington or Moscow. We know that airplanes are not neutral because we all live in a world that has been radically altered by the facts of air travel—the globe has been shrunk, time and space have collapsed.

If one accepts that technology is *not* neutral, it follows that information technology must have attributes that are unique in the world view they impose and the experience of work to which they give shape. The flexibility, memory, and remote access capabilities of information systems create new management possibilities and, therefore, choices in the design of an application.

This argument suggests three general areas for management deliberation and action in the deployment of new information systems. The first concerns policies that shape the quality of the employment relationship. The second involves attitudes toward managerial control, and the third concerns basic beliefs about the nature of an organization and the role of management.

The Quality of the Employment Relationship

Because the computer mediation of work can have direct consequences for virtually every area of human resources management including skills training, career paths, the social environment, peer relationships, supervision, control, decision making authority, and organization design, managers need to think through the kind of workplace they want to foster. They need to make design choices that reflect explicit human resource management policies.

For example, consider the automated collections system I described earlier. Although the system minimizes individual decision making, most managers I interviewed in that organization believe that collector skill and judgment are critical variables in the organization's ability to generate payments and have compelling financial data to support that view.

A management policy commitment to maintaining skill levels, providing challenging jobs, and promoting collector loyalty and motivation could have resulted in an information system that preserves the entrepreneurial aspects of the collector's job while rationalizing its administration with on-line record-keeping. But to assess the likely consequences of an approach to automation that strictly rationalizes procedures, managers need to understand the human logic of a job. In many cases, this human logic holds the clue to the motivational aspects of the job that should be preserved in the conversion to new technology.

What do managers do when faced with some of the more intrinsic features of information technology? First, they need to understand the kinds of skill demands that the computer mediation of work generates, and to construct educational programs that allow employees to develop the competencies that are most relevant to the new environment.

If a more theoretical comprehension of the task is required for effective utilization of the information system, then employees should be given the opportunity to develop this conceptual understanding. If an information system is likely to reduce the sense (if not the fact) of the individual control over a task, is it possible to redesign the job to reinvest it with a greater self-managing capacity? As elements of supervision and coordination are loaded into jobs that have been partially drained of challenge, new learning and career development opportunities can open up. The astonishing quantity of information that is available can be used to increase employees' feedback, learning, and self-management rather than to deskill and routinize their jobs or remotely supervise them.

New systems are often presented with the intention of providing "information resources" for more creative problem solving. Unless employees are actually given the knowledge and authority to utilize such resources in the service of more complex tasks, these systems will be undermined, either through poor utilization or more direct forms of resistance.

The Focus of Managerial Control

Because of the many self-management opportunities the information resource makes possible, managers may have to rethink some classic notions of managerial control. When industrial work exerted stringent demands on the placement and timing of physical activity, managers focused on controlling bodies and stipulating the precise ways in which they should perform.

With the burgeoning of office work, physical discipline was less important than reading or writing and, above all, interpersonal behavior. Because people needed to learn how to behave with superiors, subordinates, and the public, managers began to control less what people did with their bodies and more what they did with one another—their communication, teamwork, meeting behavior, and so forth.

With computer-mediated work, neither physical activity nor interpersonal behavior appear to be the most appropriate targets of managerial control. Instead, patterns of attention, learning, and mental engagement become the keys to effectiveness and high-quality performance. Obviously, people have always had to "pay attention" to their work in order to accomplish it properly. But the quality of attention computer-mediated work requires is essentially different.

For instance, in almost all accounts of routine work, researchers report that employees are daydreaming and bantering with one another while they accomplish their tasks. Of course, they must pay attention with their eyes, but not so much with their brains. In contrast, people concentrating on a visual display unit must pay a very different sort of attention. If employees are to understand and properly respond to information, they must be mentally involved.

Managers can experiment to find how to make the most of people's attending and learning qualities as well as their overall engagement in the information environment. One observation that emerges from my current field research is that imposing traditional supervisory approaches on the computer-mediated environment can create considerable dysfunction. Supervisors and managers who concentrate on the physical and interpersonal behavior of employees working with information systems simply exacerbate tensions instead of creating an environment that nurtures the kind of learning and attention computer-mediated work makes necessary and compensating for some of its less obvious but potentially negative attributes.

The Nature of Organizations and Management

With information technology, managers will do a variety of tasks that others once did for them. Because of this, we are likely to see a gradual shift in the overall shape of the organization from a pyramid to something closer to a diamond-shape with a diminishing clerical support staff, swelling numbers of professionals and middle managers, and a continually more remote, elite, policy-making group of senior managers.

While these considerations should be of central importance to management policy in the coming years, as a society we are sure to see a continuing challenge to the salience of work and the workplace in our daily lives. The traditional importance of occupational distinctiveness may be further eroded as what it means to "accomplish a task" undergoes a fundamental change. When a person's primary work consists of monitoring or interacting with a video screen, it may become more difficult to answer the questions, "Who am I?" and "What do I do?" Identification with an occupational role may diminish, while the transferability of on-the-job skills increases. Will this have implications for individual commitment to an organization and for the relative importance of work and nonwork activities?

Information technology is also likely to introduce new forms of collective behavior. When the means of production becomes dependent on electronic technology and information flows, it is no longer inevitable that, as in the case of the weavers, work be either collective or synchronous. As long as a terminal and communications links are available, people will be able to perform work in neighborhood centers, at home, or on the road. At the same time, electronic technology is altering the traditional structure and function of communication within the organization. Who interacts with whom in the organization? Can the neat chain of command hierarchy be maintained? Should it be? What does it take to lead or influence others when communication itself becomes computer mediated? Finally, who is likely to gain or lose as we make the transition to this environment?

These developments make it necessary to rethink basic conceptions of the nature of organization and management. What is an organization if people do not have to come face to face in order to accomplish their work? Does the organization itself become an abstraction? What happens to the shared purpose and commitment of members if their face-to-face interaction is reduced? Similarly, how should an "abstract" organization be managed?

If information technology is to live up to its promise for greater productivity, managers need to consider its consequences for human beings and the qualities of their work environments. The demands for a thoughtful and energetic management response go deeper than the need for "friendly interface" or "user involvement." The underlying nature of this technology requires understanding; the habitual assumptions used in its design must surface. Managers' ability to meet these demands will be an important determinant of the quality of work in future organizations.

Note

1 "Social Effects of Automation," *Internationaal Federation of Automated Control Newsletter*, No. 6, September 1978.

DISCUSSION QUESTIONS

1. How has the increasing use of computers to process information in businesses changed the kind of work people do?
2. Explain, by citing an example, how computer-mediated work can both (1) lower workers' morale by incorporating managerial assumptions into computer-accessible language and (2) provide workers with a more abstract and complete understanding of their roles in the organization?
3. How will the changing nature of work due to the increased use of computers affect workers' involvement in, and commitment to, their organizations?

READING 4-2

Airline Flight Attendants

Arlie Russell Hochschild

Even before an applicant for a flight attendant's job is interviewed, she is introduced to the rules of the game. Success will depend in part on whether she has a knack for perceiving the rules and taking them seriously. Applicants are urged to read a preinterview pamphlet before coming in. In the 1979–1980 *Airline Guide to Stewardess and Steward Careers*, there is a section called "The Interview." Under the subheading "Appearance," the manual suggests that facial expressions should be "sincere" and "unaffected." One should have a "modest but friendly smile" and be "gener-

ally alert, attentive, not overly aggressive, but not reticent either." Under "Mannerisms," subheading "Friendliness," it is suggested that a successful candidate must be "outgoing but not effusive," "enthusiastic with calm and poise," and "vivacious but not effervescent." As the manual continues: "Maintaining eye contact with the interviewer demonstrates sincerity and confidence, but don't overdo it. Avoid cold or continuous staring." Training, it seems, begins even before recruitment.

The recruits are screened for a certain type of outgoing middle-class sociability. Sometimes the recruitment literature explicitly addresses friendliness as an *act*. Allegheny Airlines, for example, says that applicants are expected to *"project a warm personality* during their interview in order to be eligible for employment." Continental Airlines, in its own words, is "seeking people who convey a spirit of enthusiasm." Delta Airlines calls simply for applicants who "have a friendly personality and high moral character."

Different companies favor different variations of the ideal type of sociability. Veteran employees talk about differences in company personality as matter-of-factly as they talk about differences in uniform or shoe style. United Airlines, the consensus has it, is "the girl-next-door," the neighborhood babysitter grown up. Pan Am is upper class, sophisticated, and slightly reserved in its graciousness. PSA is brassy, fun-loving, and sexy. Some flight attendants could see a connection between the personality they were supposed to project and the market segment the company wants to attract. One United worker explained: "United wants to appeal to Ma and Pa Kettle. So it wants Caucasian girls—not so beautiful that Ma feels fat, and not so plain that Pa feels unsatisfied. It's the Ma and Pa Kettle market that's growing, so that's why they use the girl-next-door image to appeal to that market. You know, the Friendly Skies. They offer reduced rates for wives and kids. They weed out busy women because they don't fit the image, as they see it." . . .

The trainees, it seemed to me, were also chosen for their ability to take stage directions about how to "project" an image. They were selected for being able to act well—that is, without showing the effort involved. They had to be able to appear at home on stage.

The training at Delta was arduous, to a degree that surprised the trainees and inspired their respect. Most days they sat at desks from 8:30 to 4:30 listening to lectures. They studied for daily exams in the evenings and went on practice flights on weekends. There were also morning speakers to be heard before classes began. One morning at 7:45 I was with 123 trainees in the Delta Stewardess Training Center to hear a talk from the Employee Representative, a flight attendant whose regular job was to communicate rank-and-file grievances to management and report back. Her role in the

training process was different, however, and her talk concerned responsibilities to the company:

> Delta does not believe in meddling in the flight attendant's personal life. But it does want the flight attendant to uphold certain Delta standards of conduct. It asks of you first that you keep your finances in order. Don't let your checks bounce. Don't spend more than you have. Second, don't drink while in uniform or enter a bar. No drinking twenty-four hours before flight time. [If you break this rule] appropriate disciplinary action, up to and including dismissal, will be taken. While on line we don't want you to engage in personal pastimes such as knitting, reading, or sleeping. Do not accept gifts. Smoking is allowed if it is done while you are seated.

The speaker paused and an expectant hush fell across the room. Then, as if in reply to it, she concluded, looking around, "That's all." There was a general ripple of relieved laughter from the trainees: so that was *all* the company was going to say about their private lives.

Of course, it was by no means all the company was going to say. The training would soon stake out a series of company claims on private territories of self. First, however, the training prepared the trainees to accept these claims. It established their vulnerability to being fired and their dependence on the company. Recruits were reminded day after day that eager competitors could easily replace them. I heard trainers refer to their "someone-else-can-fill-your-seat" talk. As one trainee put it, "They stress that there are 5,000 girls out there wanting *your* job. If you don't measure up, you're out."

Adding to the sense of dispensability was a sense of fragile placement vis-à-vis the outside world. Recruits were housed at the airport, and during the four-week training period they were not allowed to go home or to sleep anywhere but in the dormitory. At the same time they were asked to adjust to the fact that for them, home was an idea without an immediate referent. Where would the recruit be living during the next months and years? Houston? Dallas? New Orleans? Chicago? New York? As one pilot advised: "Don't put down roots. You may be moved and then moved again until your seniority is established. Make sure you get along with your roommates in your apartment." . . .

Training seemed to foster the sense that it was safe to feel dependent on the company. Temporarily rootless, the worker was encouraged to believe that this company of 36,000 employees operated as a "family." The head of the training center, a gentle, wise, authoritative figure in her fifties, appeared each morning in the auditorium; she was "mommy," the real authority on day-to-day problems. Her company superior, a slightly younger man, seemed to be "daddy." Other supervisors were introduced as concerned extensions of these initial training parents. (The vast majority of trainees were between nineteen and twenty-two years old.) As one speaker told the recruits: "Your supervisor is your friend. You can go to her and talk about anything, and I mean *anything*." The trainees were divided up into small groups; one class of 123 students (which included three males and nine blacks) was divided into four subgroups, each yielding the more intimate ties of solidarity that were to be the prototype of later bonds at work.

The imagery of family, with mommies and daddies and sisters and brothers, did not obscure for most trainees the reminders that Delta was a business. It suggested, rather, that despite its size Delta aspired to maintain itself in the spirit of an old-fashioned family business, in which hierarchy was never oppressive and one could always air a gripe. And so the recruit, feeling dispensable and rootless, was taken in by this kindly new family. Gratitude lays the foundation for loyalty.

The purpose of training is to instill acceptance of the company's claims, and recruits naturally wonder what parts of their feeling and behavior will be subject to company control. The head of in-flight training answered their implicit question in this way:

> Well, we have some very firm rules. Excessive use of alcohol, use of drugs of any kind, and you're asked to leave. We have a dormitory rule, and that is that you'll spend the night in the dormitory. There's no curfew, but you will spend the night in the dormitory. If you're out all night, you're asked to leave. We have weight standards for our flight attendants. Break those weight standards, and the individual is asked to resign. We have a required test average of 90 percent; if you don't attain that average, you're asked to resign. And then we get into the intangibles. That's where the judgment comes in. . . .

The claim to control over a worker's physical appearance was backed by continuous reference to the need to be "professional." In its original sense, a profession is an occupational grouping that has sole authority to recruit, train, and supervise its own members. Historically, only medicine, law, and the academic disciplines have fit this description. Certainly flight attendants do not yet fit it. Like workers in many other occupations, they call themselves "professional" because they have mastered a body of knowledge and want respect for that. Companies also use "professional" to refer to this knowledge, but they refer to something else as well. For them a "professional" flight attendant is one who has completely accepted the rules of standardization. The flight attendant who most nearly meets the appearance code ideal is therefore "the most professional" in this regard. By linking standardization to honor and the suggestion of autonomy, the company can seem to say to the public, we control *this* much of the appearance and personality of *that* many people—which is a selling point that most companies strive for. . . .

Beyond this, there were actual appeals to modify feeling states. The deepest appeal in the Delta training program was to the trainee's capacity to act as if the airplane cabin (where she works) were her home (where she doesn't work). Trainees were asked to think of a passenger *as if* he were a "personal guest in your living room." The workers' emotional memories of offering personal hospitality were called up and put to use, as Stanislavski would recommend. As one recent graduate put it:

You think how the new person resembles someone you know. *You see your sister's eyes in someone sitting at that seat.* That makes you want to put out for them. I like to think of the cabin as the living room of my own home. When someone drops in [at home], you may not know them, but you get something for them. You put that on a grand scale—thirty-six passengers per flight attendant—but *it's the same feeling.*

On the face of it, the analogy between home and airplane cabin unites different kinds of experiences and obscures what is different about them. It can unite the empathy of friend for friend with the empathy of workers for customer, because it assumes that empathy is the *same sort of feeling* in either case. Trainees wrote in their notebooks, "Adopt the passenger's point of view," and the understanding was that this could be done in the same way one adopts a friend's point of view. The analogy between home and cabin also joins the worker to her company; just as she naturally protects members of her own family, she will naturally defend the company. Impersonal relations are to be seen *as if* they were personal. Relations based on getting and giving money are to be seen *as if* they were relations free of money. The company brilliantly extends and uses its workers' basic human empathy, all the while maintaining that it is not interfering in their "personal" lives.

As at home, the guest is protected from ridicule. A flight attendant must suppress laughter, for example, at seeing a passenger try to climb into the overhead storage rack, imagining it to be a bunk bed. Nor will she exhibit any idiosyncratic habits of her own,

which might make the guest feel uncomfortable. Also, trainees were asked to express sincere endorsement of the company's advertising. In one classroom session, an instructor said: "We have Flying Colonel and Flying Orchid passengers, who over the years have always flown Delta. This is an association they're invited to join. It has no special privileges, but it does hold meetings from time to time." The students laughed, and one said, "That's absurd." The trainer answered, "Don't say that. You're supposed to make them think it's a real big thing." Thus, the sense of absurdity was expanded: the trainees were let in on the secret and asked to help the company create the illusion it wanted the passengers to accept.

By the same token, the injunction to act "as if it were my home" obscured crucial differences between home and airplane cabin. Home is safe. Home does not crash. It is the flight attendant's task to convey a sense of relaxed, homey coziness while at the same time, at take-off and landing, mentally rehearsing the emergency announcement, "Cigarettes out! Grab ankles! Heads down!" in the appropriate languages. Before takeoff, safety equipment is checked. At boarding, each attendant secretly picks out a passenger she can call on for help in an emergency evacuation. Yet in order to sustain the *if*, the flight attendant must shield guests from this unhomelike feature of the party. As one flight attendant mused:

Even though I'm a very honest person, I have learned not to allow my face to mirror my alarm or my fright. I feel very protective of my passengers. Above all, I don't want them to be frightened. If we were going down, if we were going to make a ditching in water, the chances of our surviving are slim, even though we [the flight attendants] know exactly what to do. *But I think I would probably*—and I think I can say this for most of my fellow flight attendants—*be able to keep them from being too worried about it.* I mean my voice might quiver a little during the announcements, but somehow I feel we could get them to believe . . . the best.

Her brave defense of the "safe homey atmosphere" of the plane might keep order, but at the price of concealing the facts from passengers who might feel it their right to know what was coming.

Despite the generous efforts of trainers and workers themselves to protect it, the living room analogy remains vulnerable on several sides. For one thing, trainees were urged to "*think* sales," not simply to act in such a way as to induce sales. Promoting sales was offered to the keepers of the living room analogy as a rationale for dozens of acts, down to apologizing for mistakes caused by passengers: "Even if it's their fault, it's very important that you don't blame the passengers. That can have a lot of impact. Imagine a businessman who rides Delta many times a year. Hundreds, maybe thousands of dollars ride on your courtesy. Don't get into a verbal war. It's not worth it. They are our lifeblood. As we say, the passenger isn't always right, but he's never wrong." . . .

"Think sales" had another aspect to it. One trainer, who affected the style of a good-humored drill sergeant, barked out: "What are we always doing?" When a student finally answered, "Selling Delta," she replied: "No! You're selling yourself. Aren't you selling yourself, too? You're on your own commission. We're in the business of selling ourselves, right? Isn't that what it's all about?"

In this way, Delta sells Southern womanhood, not "over their heads," but by encouraging trainees to think of themselves as *self*-sellers. This required them to imagine themselves as self-employed. But Delta flight attendants are not making an independent profit from their emotional labor, they are working for a fixed wage. They are not selling themselves, they are selling the company. The *idea* of selling themselves helps them only in selling the company they work for.

The cabin-to-home analogy is vulnerable from another side too. The flight attendant is asked to see the passenger as a potential friend, or as like one, and to be as understanding as one would be with a good friend. The *if* personalizes an impersonal relation. On the other hand, the student is warned, the reciprocity of real friendship is not part of the *if* friendship. The passenger has no obligation to return empathy or even courtesy. As one trainer commented: "If a passenger snaps at you and you didn't do anything wrong, just remember it's not you he is snapping at. It's your uniform, it's your role as a Delta flight attendant. Don't take it personally." The passenger, unlike a real friend or guest in a home, assumes a right to unsuppressed anger at irritations, having purchased that tacit right with the ticket.

Flight attendants are reminded of this one-way personalization whenever passengers confuse one flight attendant with another ("You look so much alike") or ask questions that reveal that they never thought of the attendants as real people. "Passengers are surprised when they discover that we eat, too. They think we can go for twenty hours without being allowed to eat. Or they will get off the plane in Hong Kong after a fifteen-hour flight—which is a sixteen- or seventeen-hour duty day for us—and say, 'Are you going on to Bangkok?' 'Are you going on to Delhi?' Yes, right, sure—we go round the world and get sent back with the airplane for repairs." Just as the flight attendant's empathy is stretched thin into a commercial offering, the passenger's try at empathy is usually pinched into the narrow grooves of public manners.

It is when the going gets rough—when flights are crowded and planes are late, when babies bawl and smokers bicker noisily with nonsmokers, when the meals run out and the air conditioning fails—that maintaining the analogy to home, amid the Muzak and the drinks, becomes truly a monument to our human capacity to suppress feeling.

Under such conditions some passengers exercise the privilege of not suppressing their irritation; they become "irates." When that happens, back-up analogies are brought into service. In training, the recruit was told: "Basically, the passengers are just like children. They need attention. Sometimes first-time riders are real nervous. And some of the troublemakers really just want your attention." The passenger-as-child analogy was extended to cover sibling rivalry: "You can't play cards with just one passenger because the other passengers will get jealous." To think of unruly passengers as "just like children" is to widen tolerance of them. If their needs are like those of a child, those needs are supposed to come first. The worker's right to anger is correspondingly reduced; as an adult he must work to inhibit and suppress anger at children.

Should the analogy to children fail to induce the necessary deep acting, surface-acting strategies for handling the "irate" can be brought into play. Attendants were urged to "work" the passenger's name, as in "Yes, Mr. Jones, it's true the flight is delayed." This reminds the passenger that he is not anonymous, that there is at least some pretension to a personal relation and that some emotion management is owed. Again, workers were told to use terms of empathy. As one flight attendant, a veteran of fifteen years with United, recalled from her training: "Whatever happens, you're supposed to say, I know just how you feel. Late for a connection? I know just how you feel. Didn't get that steak you were counting on? I know just how you feel." Flight attendants report that such expressions of empathy are useful in convincing passengers that they have misplaced the blame and misaimed their anger. . . .

Company language is aimed not only at diffusing anger but at minimizing fear. As one Pan Am veteran recalled:

We almost turned upside down leaving Hong Kong. They call it an "incident." Not an accident, just an incident. We went nose up and almost flipped over. The pilot caught the plane just before it went over on its back and made a big loop and dropped about 3,000 feet straight down and then corrected what happened. They pulled out at 1,500 feet over the harbor. We knew we were going to die because we were going nose down and you could see that water coming. I was never really afraid of flying before, but turbulence does shake me up now. I'm not as bad as some people, though.

The very term *incident* calms the nerves. How could we be terrified at an "incident"? Thus the words that workers use and don't use help them avoid emotions inappropriate to a living room full of guests.

Finally, the living room analogy is upheld by admitting that it sometimes falls down. In the Recurrent Training classes held each year for experienced flight attendants, most of the talk was about times when it feels like the party is over, or never began. In Initial Training, the focus was on the passenger's feeling; in Recurrent Training, it was on the flight attendant's feeling. In Initial Training, the focus was on the smile and the living room analogy; in Recurrent Training, it was on avoiding anger. As a Recurrent Training instructor explained: "Dealing with difficult passengers is part of the job. It makes us angry sometimes. And anger is part of stress. So that's why I'd like to talk to you about being angry. I'm not saying you should do this [work on your anger] for Delta Airlines. I'm not saying you should do it for the passengers. I'm saying do it for *yourselves*."

From the beginning of training, managing feeling was taken as the problem. The causes of anger were not acknowledged as part of the problem. Nor were the overall conditions of work—the crew size, the virtual exclusion of blacks and men, and required accommodation to sexism, the lack of investigation into the considerable medical problems of flight attendants, and the company's rigid antiunion position. These were treated as unalterable facts of life. The only question to be seriously discussed was "How do you rid yourself of anger?"

The first recommended strategy is to focus on what the *other* person might be thinking and feeling: imagine a reason that excuses his or her behavior. If this fails, fall back on the thought "I can escape." One instructor suggested, "You can say to yourself, it's half an hour to go, now it's twenty-nine minutes, now it's twenty-eight." And when anger could not be completely dispelled by any means, workers and instructors traded tips on the least offensive ways of expressing it: "I chew on ice, just crunch my anger away." "I flush the toilet repeatedly." "I think about doing something mean, like pouring Ex-Lax into his coffee." In this way a semiprivate "we-girls" right to anger and frustration was shared, in the understanding that the official axe would fall on anyone who expressed her anger in a more consequential way.

DISCUSSION QUESTIONS

1. Hochschild contends that service jobs require *emotional labor*, or work that influences other's emotional states. Explain and give examples of how flight attendants engage in emotional labor.
2. Provide other examples, perhaps from your own work experience, of service workers who engage in emotional labor. Are the responsibilities of emotional labor written in the job description?
3. What are the effects of the management of emotion by employers on employees' working and nonworking lives?

READING 4-3

Life on the Global Assembly Line

Barbara Ehrenreich
Annette Fuentes

In Ciudad Juárez, Mexico, Anna M. rises at 5 a.m. to feed her son before starting on the two-hour bus trip to the *maquiladora* (factory). He will spend the day along with four other children in a neighbor's one-room home. Anna's husband, frustrated by being unable to find work for himself, left for the United States six months ago. She wonders as she carefully applies her new lip gloss, whether she ought to consider herself still married. It might be good to take a night course to become a secretary. But she seldom gets home before eight at night and the factory where she stitches brassieres that will be sold in the United States through J. C. Penney pays only $48 a week.

In Penang, Malaysia, Julie K. is up before the three other young women with whom she shares a room and starts heating the leftover rice from last night's supper. She looks good in the company's green-trimmed uniform and she's proud to work in a modern, American-owned factory. Only not quite so proud as when she started working three years ago—she thinks as she squints out the door at a passing group of women. Her job involves peering all day through a microscope, bonding hair-thin gold wires to a silicon chip destined to end up inside a pocket calculator, and at 21, she is afraid she can no longer see very clearly.

Every morning between four and seven, thousands of women like Anna and Julie head out for the day shift. In Ciudad Juárez, they crowd into *ruteras* (run-down vans) for the trip from the slum neighborhoods to the industrial parks on the outskirts of the city. In Penang they squeeze, 60 or more at a time, into buses for the trip from the village to the low, modern factory buildings of the Bayan Lepas free trade zone. In Taiwan they walk from the dormitories—where the night shift is already asleep in the still-warm beds—through the checkpoints in the high fence surrounding the factory zone.

This is the world's new industrial proleteriat: young, female, Third World. Viewed from the "first world," they are still faceless, genderless "cheap labor," signaling their existence only through a label or tiny imprint "made in Hong Kong" or Taiwan, Korea, the Dominican Republic, Mexico, the Phillippines. But they may be one of the most strategic blocs of womanpower in the world of the 1980s. Conservatively, there are 2 million Third World female industrial workers employed now; millions more looking for work, and their numbers are rising every year. Anyone whose image of Third World women features picturesque peasants with babies slung on their backs should be prepared to update it. Just in the last decade, Third World women have become a critical element in the global economy and a key "resource" for expanding multinational corporations.

It doesn't take more than second-grade arithmetic to understand what's happening. In the United States, an assembly-line worker is likely to earn, depending on her length of employment, between $3.10 and $5 an hour. In many Third World countries, a woman doing the same work will earn $3 to $5 a *day*. According to the magazine *Business Asia*, in 1976 the average hourly wage for unskilled work (male or female) was 55 cents in Hong Kong, 52 cents in South Korea, 32 cents in the Philippines, and 17 cents in Indonesia. The logic of the situation is compelling: why pay someone in Massachusetts $5 an hour to do what someone in Manila will do for $2.50 a day? Or, as a corollary, why pay a male worker anywhere to do what a female worker will do for 40 to 60 percent less?

And so almost everything that can be packed up is being moved out to the Third World; not heavy industry, but just about anything light enough to travel—garment

manufacture, textiles, toys, footwear, pharmaceuticals, wigs, appliance parts, tape decks, computer components, plastic goods. In some industries, like garment and textile, American jobs are lost in the process and the biggest losers are women, often black and Hispanic. But what's going on is much more than a matter of runaway shops. Economists are talking about a "new international division of labor," in which the process of production is broken down and the fragments are dispersed to different parts of the world. In general the low-skilled jobs are farmed out to the Third World, where labor costs are minuscule, while control over the overall process and technology remains safely at company headquarters in first world countries like the United States and Japan.

The American electronics industry provides a classic example: circuits are printed on silicon wafers and tested in California; then the wafers are shipped to Asia for the labor-intensive process by which they are cut into tiny chips and bonded to circuit boards: final assembly into products such as calculators or military equipment usually takes place in the United States. Garment manufacture, too, is often broken into geographically separated steps with the most repetitive labor-intensive jobs going to the poor countries of the southern hemisphere. Most Third World countries welcome whatever jobs come their way in the new division of labor and the major international development agencies—like the World Bank and the United States Agency for International Development (AID)—encourage them to take what they can get.

So much any economist could tell you. What is less often noted is the *gender* breakdown of the emerging international division of labor. Eighty to 90 percent of the low-skilled assembly jobs that go to the Third World are performed by women—in a remarkable switch from earlier patterns of foreign-dominated industrialization. Until now, "development" under the aegis of foreign corporations has usually meant more jobs for men and—compared to traditional agricultural society—a diminished economic status for women. But multinational corporations and Third World governments alike consider assembly-line work—whether the product is Barbie dolls or missile parts—to be "women's work."

One reason is that women can, in many countries, still be legally paid less than men. But the sheer tedium of the jobs adds to the multinationals preference for women workers—a preference made clear, for example, by this ad from a Mexican newspaper: *We need female workers; older than 17, younger than 30; single and without children; minimum education primary school; maximum education one year of preparatory school (high school): available for all shifts.*

It's an article of faith with management that only women can do, or will do, the monotonous, painstaking work that American business is exporting to the Third World. Bill Mitchell, whose job is to attract United States businesses to the Bermudez Industrial Park in Ciudat Juárez told us with a certain macho pride: "A man just won't stay in this tedious kind of work. He'd walk out in a couple of hours." The personnel manager of a light assembly plant in Taiwan told anthropologist Linda Gail Arrigo, "Young male workers are too restless and impatient to do monotonous work with no career value. If displeased, they sabotage the machines and even threaten the foreman. But girls? At most, they cry a little."

In fact, the American businessmen we talked to claimed that Third World women genuinely enjoy doing the very things that would drive a man to assault and sabotage. "You should watch these kids going to work," Bill Mitchell told us. "You don't have any sullenness here. They smile." A top-level management consultant who specialized in advising American companies on where to relocate their factories gave us this global generalization: "The [factory] girls genuinely enjoy themselves. They're away from their families.

They have spending money. They can buy motorbikes, whatever. Of course it's a regulated experience, too—with dormitories to live in—so it's a healthful experience."

What is the real experience of the women in the emerging Third World industrial work force? The conventional Western stereotypes leap to mind: You can't really compare, the standards are so different. . . . Everything's easier in warm countries. . . . They really don't have any alternatives. . . . Commenting on the low wages his company pays its women workers in Singapore, a Hewlett-Packard vice-president said, "They live much differently here than we do. . . ." But the differences are ultimately very simple. To start with, they have less money.

The great majority of the women in the new Third World work force live at or near the subsistence level for one person, whether they work for a multinational corporation or a locally owned factory. In the Philippines, for example, starting wages in U.S.-owned electronics plants are between $34 to $46 a month, compared to a cost of living of $37 a month; in Indonesia, the starting wages are actually about $7 a month less than the cost of living. "Living" in these cases should be interpreted minimally: a diet of rice, dried fish, and water—a Coke might cost a half-day's wages—lodging in a room occupied by four or more other people. Rachael Grossman, a researcher with the Southeast Asia Resource Center found women employees of U.S. multinational firms in Malaysia and the Philippines living four to eight in a room in boardinghouses, or squeezing into tiny extensions built on to squatter huts near the factory. Where companies do provide dormitories for their employees, they are not of the "healthful" collegiate variety implied by our corporate informant. Staff from the American Friends Service Committee report dormitory space is "likely to be crowded, with bed rotation paralleling shift rotation—while one shift works another sleeps, as many as twenty to a room." In one case in Thailand, they found the dormitory "filthy" with workers forced to find their own place to sleep among "splintered floorboards, rusting sheets of metal, and scraps of dirty cloth."

Wages do increase with seniority, but the money does not go to pay for studio apartments or, very likely, motorbikes. A 1970 study of young women factory workers in Hong Kong found that 88 percent of them were turning more than half their earnings over to their parents. In areas that are still largely agricultural (such as parts of the Philippines and Malaysia), or places where male unemployment runs high (such as northern Mexico), a woman factory worker may be the sole source of cash income for an entire extended family.

But wages on a par with what an 11-year-old American could earn on a paper route, and living conditions resembling what Engels found in 19th-century Manchester are only part of the story. The rest begins at the factory gate. The work that multinational corporations export to the Third World is not only the most tedious, but often the most hazardous part of the production process. The countries they go to are, for the most part, those that will guarantee no interference from health and safety inspectors, trade unions, or even free-lance reformers. As a result, most Third World factory women work under conditions that already have broken or will break their health— or their nerves—within a few years, and often before they've worked long enough to earn any more than a subsistence wage.

Consider first the electronics industry, which is generally thought to be the safest and cleanest of the exported industries. The factory buildings are low and modern, like those one might find in a suburban American industrial park. Inside, rows of young women, neatly dressed in the company uniform or T-shirt, work quietly at their stations.

For many Third World women, electronics is a prestige occupation, at least compared to other kinds of factory work. They are unlikely to know that in the United States the National Institute on Occupational Safety and Health (NIOSH) has placed electronics on its select list of "high health-risk industries using the greatest number of toxic substances." If electronics assembly work is risky here, it is doubly so in countries where there is no equivalent of NIOSH to even issue warnings. In many plants toxic chemicals and solvents sit in open containers, filling the work area with fumes that can literally knock you out. "We have been told of cases where ten to twelve women passed out at once," an AFSC field worker in northern Mexico told us, "and the newspapers report this as mass hysteria."

In one stage of the electronics assembly process the workers have to dip the circuits into open vats of acid. According to Irene Johnson and Carol Bragg, who toured the National Semiconductor plant in Penang, Malaysia, the women who do the dipping "wear rubber gloves and boots, but these sometimes leak and burns are common." More commonly, what electronics workers lose is the 20/20 vision they are required to have when they are hired. Most electronics workers spend seven to nine hours a day peering through microscopes, straining to meet their quotas.

One study in South Korea found that most electronic assembly workers developed severe eye problems after only one year of employment: 88 percent had chronic conjunctivitis; 44 percent became nearsighted; and 19 percent developed astigmatism. A manager for Hewlett-Packard's Malaysia plant, in an interview with Rachael Grossman, denied that there were any eye problems: "These girls are used to working with 'scopes.' We've found no eye problems. But it sure makes me dizzy to look through those things."

Electronics, recall, is the "cleanest" of the exported industries. Conditions in the garment and textile industry rival those of any 19th-century sweatshop. The firms, generally local subcontractors to large American chains such as J. C. Penney and Sears, as well as smaller manufacturers, are usually even more indifferent to the health of their employees than the multinationals. Some of the worst conditions have been documented in South Korea, where the garment and textile industries have helped spark that country's "economic miracle." Workers are packed into poorly lit rooms, where summer temperatures rise above 100 degrees. Textile dust, which can cause permanent lung damage, fills the air. When there are rush orders, management may require forced overtime of as much as 48 hours at a stretch and if that seems to go beyond the limits of human endurance, pep pills and amphetamine injections are thoughtfully provided. In her diary (originally published in a magazine now banned by the South Korean government), Min Chong Suk, 30, a sewing-machine operator wrote of working from 7 a.m. to 11:30 p.m. in a garment factory. "When [the apprentices] shake the waste threads from the clothes, the whole room fills with dust, and it is hard to breathe. Since we've been working in such dusty air, there have been increasing numbers of people getting tuberculosis, bronchitis, and eye diseases. Since we are women, it makes us so mad when we have pale, unhealthy, wrinkled faces like dried-up spinach. . . . It seems to me that no one knows our blood dissolves into the threads and seams with sighs and sorrow."

In all the exported industries, the most invidious, inescapable health hazard is stress. Lunch breaks may be barely long enough for a woman to stand in line at the canteen or hawkers' stalls. Visits to the bathroom are treated as a privilege: in some cases, workers must raise their hands for permission to use the toilet, and waits up to a half hour are common. Rotating shifts—the day shift one week, the night shift the next—wreak havoc with sleep patterns. Because inaccuracies or failure to meet production quotas can mean substantial pay losses, the pressures are quickly internalized: stomach ailments and nervous problems are not unusual in the multinationals' Third World female work force. In some situations, good work is as likely to be punished as slow or shoddy work.

As if poor health and the stress of factory life weren't enough to drive women into early retirement, management actually encourages a high turnover in many industries. "As you know, when seniority rises, wages rise," the management consultant to U.S. multinationals told us. He explained that it's cheaper to train a fresh supply of teenagers than to pay experienced women high wages. "Older" women, aged 23 or 24, are likely to be laid off and not rehired.

We estimate, based on fragmentary data from several sources, that the multinational corporations may already have used up (cast off) as many as 6 million Third World workers—women who are too ill, too old (30 is over the hill in most industries), or too exhausted to be useful any more. Few "retire" with any transferable skills or savings. The lucky ones find husbands.

One of the most serious occupational hazards that Julie and millions of women like her may face is the lifelong stigma of having been a "factory girl." Most of the cultures favored by multinational corporations in their search for cheap labor are patriarchal in the grand old style: any young woman who is not under the wing of a father, husband, or older brother must be "loose." High levels of unemployment among men, as in Mexico, contribute to male resentment of working women. (Ironically, in some places the multinationals have increased male unemployment—for example by paving over fishing and farming villages to make way for industrial parks.) Add to all this the fact that certain companies—American electronics firms are in the lead—actively promote Western-style sexual objectification as a means of insuring employee loyalty: there are company-sponsored cosmetics classes, "guess whose legs these are" contests, and swimsuit-style beauty contests where the prize might be a free night *for two* in a fancy hotel. Corporate-promoted Westernization only heightens the hostility many men feel toward any independent working women—having a job is bad enough, wearing jeans and mascara to work is going too far.

Anthropologist Patricia Fernandez, who has worked in a *maquiladora* herself, believes that the stigmatization of working-women serves indirectly to keep them in line. "You have to think of the kind of socialization that girls experience in a very Catholic—or for that matter, Muslim—society. The fear of having a reputation is enough to make a lot of women bend over backward to be 'respectable' and ladylike, which is just what management wants." She points out that in northern Mexico, the tabloids delight in playing up stories of alleged vice in the *maquiladoras*—indiscriminate sex on the job, epidemics of veneral disease, fetuses found in factory rest rooms. "I worry about this because there are those who treat you differently as soon as they know you have a job at a *maquiladora*," one woman told Fernandez. "Maybe they think that if you have to work, there is a chance you're a whore."

There has been no international protest about the exploitation of Third World women by multinational corporations—no thundering denunciations from the floor of the United Nations' general assembly, no angry resolutions from the Conference of the Non-Aligned Countries. Sociologist Robert Snow, who has been tracing the multinationals on their way south and east-ward for a number of years, explained why: "The Third World governments *want* the multinationals to move in. There's cutthroat competition to attract the corporations."

The governments themselves gain little revenue from this kind of investment, though—especially since most offer tax holidays and freedom from export duties in order to attract the multinationals in the first place. Nor do the people as a whole benefit, according to a highly placed Third World woman within the UN. "The multinationals like to say they're contributing to development," she told us, "but they come into our countries for one thing—cheap labor. If the labor stops being so cheap, they can move on. So how can you call that development? It depends on the people being poor and staying poor." But there are important groups that do stand to gain when the multinationals set up shop in their countries; local entrepreneurs who subcontracted to the multinationals; Harvard- or Berkeley-educated "technocrats" who become local management; and government officials who specialize in cutting red tape for an "agent's fee" or an outright bribe.

In the competition for multinational investment, local governments advertise their women shamelessly, and an investment brochure issued by the Malaysian government informs multinational executive that, "The manual dexterity of the Oriental female is famous the world over. Her hands are small and she works fast with extreme care. . . . Who, therefore, could be better qualified, by nature and inheritance, to contribute to the efficiency of a bench-assembly production line than the Oriental girl?"

The Royal Thai Embassy sends American businesses a brochure guaranteeing that in Thailand, "the relationship between the employer and employee is like that of a guardian and ward. It is easy to win and maintain the loyalty of workers as long as they are treated with kindness and courtesy." The facing page offers a highly selective photo-study of Thai Womanhood: giggling shyly, bowing submissively, and working cheerfully on an assembly line.

Many "host" governments are willing to back up their advertising with whatever amount of brutality it takes to keep "their girls" just as docile as they look in the brochures. Even the most polite and orderly attempts to organize are likely to bring down overkill doses of police repression.

The governments advertise their women, sell them, and keep them in line for the multinationals. But there are other parties to the growing international traffic in women—such as the United Nations' Industrial Development Organization (UNIDO), the World Bank, and the United States government itself.

UNIDO, for example, has been a major promoter of "free trade zones." These are enclaves within nations that offer multinational corporations a range of creature comforts including freedom from paying taxes and export duties; low-cost water, power, and buildings; exemption from whatever labor laws may apply in the country as a whole; and, in some cases, such security features as barbed-wire, guarded checkpoints, and government-paid police.

Then there is the World Bank, which over the past decade has lent several billion dollars to finance the roads, airports, power plants, and even the first-class hotels that multinational corporations need in order to set up business in Third World countries. The Sri Lankan garment industry, which, like other Third World garment industries, survives by subcontracting to major Western firms, was set up on the advice of the World Bank and with a $20 million World Bank loan. This particular experiment in "development" offers young women jobs at a global low of $5 for a six-day week. Gloria Scott, the head of the World Bank's Women and Development Program, sounded distinctly uncomfortable when we asked her about the bank's role in promoting the exploitation of Third World women. "Our job is to help eliminate poverty. It is not our responsibility if the multinationals come in and offer such low wages. It is the responsibility of the governments." However, the Bank's 1979 World Development Report speaks strongly of the need for "wage restraint" in poor countries.

But the most powerful promoter of exploitative conditions for Third World women workers is the United States government itself. For example, the notoriously repressive Korean textile industry was developed with the help of $400 million in aid from the U.S. State Department. Malaysia became a low-wage haven for the electronics industry, thanks to technical assistance financed by AID and to U.S. money (funneled through the Asian Development Bank) to set up free trade zones. Taiwan's status as a "showcase for the free world" and a comfortable berth for multinationals is the result of three decades of financial transfusions from the United States.

But the most obvious form of United States involvement, according to Lenny Siegel, the director of the Pacific Studies Center, is through our consistent record of military aid to Third World governments that are capitalist, politically repressive, and are not striving for economic independence." Ironically, says Siegel, there are "cases where the United States made a big investment to make sure that any unions that formed would be pretty tame. Then we put in even more money to support some dictator who doesn't allow unions at all." And, if that doesn't seem like a sufficient case of duplicate spending, the U.S. government also insures (through the Overseas Private Investment Corporation) outward-bound multinationals against any lingering possibility of insurrection or expropriation.

What does our government have to say for itself? It's hard to get a straight answer—the few parts of the bureaucracy that deal with women and development seem to have little connection with those that are concerned with larger foreign policy issues. A spokesman for the Department of State told us that if multinationals offer poor working conditions (which he questioned), this was not their fault: "There are just different standards in different countries." Offering further evidence of a sheltered life, he told us that "corporations today are generally more socially responsible than even ten years ago. . . . We can expect them to treat their employees in the best way they can." But he conceded in response to a barrage of unpleasant examples. "Of course, you're going to have problems wherever you have human beings doing things." Our next stop was the Women's Division within AID. Staffer Emmy Simmons was aware of the criticisms of the quality of employment multinationals offer but cautioned that "we can get hung up on the idea that it's exploitation without really looking at the alternatives for women." AID's concern, she said, was with the fact that population is outgrowing the agricultural capacity of many Third World countries, dislocating millions of people. From her point of view, multinationals, at least, provide some sort of alternative. "These people have to go somewhere."

DISCUSSION QUESTIONS

1. How have the growth of multinational corporations and the internationalization of the economy influenced the division of labor in Third World countries?
2. What *is* life like on the "global assembly line"?
3. What would be the effects on American companies and the U.S. economy if corporations shifted assembly-line work to American soil?
4. Why do people seek employment in multinational factories if conditions are so miserable?

PART THREE

Social Inequalities

CHAPTER 5

Issues in Poverty

INTRODUCTION

The U.S. government's role in assisting its citizens with obdurate human problems has a long history, but only in the last half-century has the United States become a welfare state in the modern sense. In different nations, the role of government in public assistance has developed at different rates and in different ways. Some European countries have a much longer history of welfare than the United States has. Health insurance and pension programs for workers, for example, arose in Germany and Austria before they did in Britain, and long before they emerged in the United States. Some European nations have generally also been leaders in the provision of public housing and health care. Clearly, the United States lags behind many other nations in the provision of public assistance in various areas; the exception is education. Today, issues of welfare policy and programs are debated around the world, and in the United States criticism of social welfare has become more and more clamorous.

In 1988 32 million residents of the United States were poor. This chapter contains evidence about the sources and extent of poverty in this country, and also provides an opportunity to examine some of the policies that have been directed toward alleviating welfare problems. While the articles selected for this chapter neither exhaust the scope of U.S. welfare policy nor deal with selected issues in great depth, they do provide some insights into contemporary issues and debates about poverty. A cross-cultural approach is important to an understanding of social welfare policy since it avoids the limited frame of reference inherent in an examination of the welfare state of only one country. A wider, comparative approach to welfare policy enables one to study general patterns of social life and to identify causal linkages between economic and social forces and the problems faced by individual citizens.

At the most general level, social welfare encompasses programs for *social security*, such as health insurance, public assistance, and family allowances, and *personal social services* in the form of day care, child welfare, health care, and community- and institution-based services

115

for targeted groups. In the United States, the two largest categories of welfare recipients are single-parent families with children and the aged, two targeted groups for whom assistance was greatly increased as a result of the "war on poverty" of the mid-1960s.

The war on poverty, which began in 1964, was conceived in great haste and rapidly pushed through Congress, with the goal of eradicating poverty in the midst of affluence. Though the war on poverty has been judged a failure, it did significantly increase government involvement in the problems of individuals. Recently, the programs germinated during that period have increasingly come under attack from many sides. An underlying theme in antiwelfare rhetoric is that the welfare system contributes to the very problems it seeks to eradicate. Many critics maintain that the U.S. welfare system provides disincentives for recipients to resolve their family problems and to find employment. Though the stereotype of the lazy, shiftless, and morally decrepit welfare recipient is inaccurate, the cultural premises of the American welfare system continue to be based on unwarranted stereotypes and a singular vision of morality. One sociological theory that underlies this explanation of poverty is that of the "culture of poverty" (Lewis, 1961). According to this theory, certain people have become trapped in a subculture, a group life, that emphasizes fatalism, instant gratification, and little control over impulsive behavior. The problems experienced by the poor are attributed to flawed individual characteristics that are perpetuated by the vicious cycle of poverty endemic to this culture. A considerable amount of social science literature has been written in opposition to this thesis and in an effort to dispel stereotyping of the poor.

The published work of social scientists has also fashioned, sometimes in dramatic ways, responses to poverty in the United States. The publication, for example, of Michael Har-

rington's *The Other America* (1963) helped spark the war on poverty. Ken Auletta's *The Underclass* (1982) introduced a new concept in reference to the chronically poor people living in America's central cities. William Julius Wilson's *The Truly Disadvantaged* (1987) went even further, describing the plight of poor urban blacks whose dismal conditions were, by his account, caused less by overt racial discrimination than by more complex economic and social forces. The readings in this chapter examine controversies stemming from these works and issues in welfare systems in light of current events and evidence.

In the first reading, Richard Nathan persuasively argues that "underclass" is an accurate term for designating a distinctive class of urban dwellers, particularly racial minorities, whose conditions of poverty are seemingly immutable. This reading has been chosen to represent certain features of a cultural perspective on poverty. While there is still disagreement among social scientists and policymakers about the exact causes and characteristics of the underclass, individuals so designated are thought to have no marketable skills and no opportunity to enjoy the benefits of participation in the economic system. The underclass is beset with rising problems of teenage pregnancy, female-headed households, welfare dependency, and criminal behavior. Nathan provides some evidence on the size and racial composition of the "truly disadvantaged" in central cities and offers policy recommendations to alleviate their dismal conditions. While Nathan is optimistic about the effects that changes in social policy might have, he nonetheless believes that the underclass will be with us for a long time to come.

C. Wright Mills (1959) describes the sociological imagination as the ability to stand back from human events and distinguish the "personal troubles" that afflict an individual from "public issues," or difficulties that many people share in common. In making such a distinction, Mills calls on us to look to the larger social structure and institutional forces for the causes of social problems. Use of the sociological imagination helps one to avoid the mistake of "blaming the victims" for the difficulties they experience. In the second article in this chapter James D. Wright takes the most destitute citizens of the United States—the homeless—and explores issues connected with blaming the homeless for their problem. He maintains that Americans continue to distinguish between the "worthy" and the "unworthy" homeless—those whose difficulties are beyond the scope of their control and "merit" assistance and those who are unworthy of assistance because of personal limitations. He describes the scope of the problem of homelessness on a continuum from the more deserving homeless families on one end to the least deserving "shiftless bums" on the other. In the course of his admittedly superficial account, Wright delineates some of the many different kinds of homeless people and shows that very few of them are homeless by choice—very few deserve to be blamed for being homeless.

In the third reading, S. M. Miller brings a perspective that is both macrosociological and cross-cultural to the study of poverty and related welfare issues. His report on changes in European welfare states identifies four models of welfare systems: (1) defend and change; (2) participation and economic transformation; (3) social integration; and (4) privatization. He believes that European experimentation with mixes of diverse welfare models and goals offers insights into, and implications for, the American welfare system.

References

Auletta, Ken. *The Underclass.* New York: Random House, 1982.

Harrington, Michael. *The Other America in the United States.* New York: Macmillan, 1963.

Lewis, Oscar. *The Children of Sanchez.* New York: Random House, 1961.

Mills, C. Wright. *The Sociological Imagination.* New York: Oxford, 1959.

Wilson, William Julius. *The Truly Disadvantaged: The Inner City, The Underclass, and Public Policy.* Chicago: The University of Chicago Press, 1987.

Will the Underclass Always Be with Us?

Richard P. Nathan

Ken Auletta added a word to the popular vocabulary with his series of *New Yorker* articles and book on the underclass. At first, people interested in social policy balked at the term, concerned that it would have an adverse labeling effect, stigmatizing the people in what the *Economist* in a March 15, 1986, article termed America's "huge and intractable, largely black underclass." I have written this article as an essay on the word *underclass* (what does it mean?); the condition (is it new; why has it developed?); and the response (how should we deal with this condition?). This is not a research paper; it is more of a personal statement with emphasis on the policy response to underclass conditions.

USING THE WORD

It is not a happy conclusion, and in my case it did not come easily, but I conclude that the word *underclass* is an accurate and functional term and that we should use it in diagnosing and prescribing for American social problems in the current period. One reason for this conclusion is purely practical. The word has caught on. Nothing social scientists could do would change matters very much. There is also a second and more important reason for this conclusion—that the word is functional.

Regrettably, I conclude that the word *underclass* reflects a real and new condition in the society with which we must come to terms. It is a condition properly described by the term *class*. Sociologist Ralf Dahrendorf, in *Class and Class Conflict in Industrial Society*, defines class as a group emerging from societal conditions that affect structural changes.

My essential argument is that there has been a distinctive structural change in social conditions in the United States over the past two decades that is expressed by the term *underclass*, and that there is now a broad consensus among politicians and experts that this has occurred. The word is increasingly used in the media as a shorthand expression for the concentration of economic and behavioral problems among racial minorities (mainly black and Hispanic) in large, older cities. For those of us interested in urban and social policy, the time has come to shift our focus from diagnosis to prescription. There are still important research issues on our agenda relating to the causes and characteristics of the underclass, but there is no longer as much to be achieved by debate on underclass conditions compared to attention devoted to how we deal with these conditions. In particular, research by William Julius Wilson provides a convincing analysis of the "problems that disproportionately plague the urban underclass." Says Wilson, in an article in P.G. Peterson's *The New Urban Reality*:

> Included in this population are persons who lack training and skills and either experience long-term unemployment or have dropped out of the labor force altogether; who are long-term public assistance recipients; and who are engaged in street criminal activity and other forms of aberrant behavior.

Researchers, government officials, and organizations and foundations interested in social and urban policy should place more emphasis on the strategies that can be adopted, and can be expected to work, in dealing with this problem. While I present a description, which I think reflects a widely shared view on the nature of the underclass, my emphasis remains on the response to this critical new reality in American society.

EMERGING CONSENSUS

The existence of a distinctive underclass, in an ironic way, is a result of the success, not the failure, of American social policy. The successes of the civil rights revolution (surely not complete, but extraordinary nonetheless) have caused a bifurcation of the racial minority groups that were the focus of the civil rights laws of the fifties and sixties and the big-spending social programs from the mid-sixties into the seventies.

I remember my first visit to a southern state in the mid-fifties. Driving through a rural area, I saw signs that said "Colored" on run-down cabins and motels. My reaction was to think how remarkable it was that such accommodations could already have what were then brand-new colored television sets. It did not take long for me to realize that these were segregated facilities.

Such outward manifestations of discrimination are gone now from our official language and the behavior of our leading and large institutions. This is not to deny that discrimination exists in more subtle forms; it is meant to call attention to the fact that the opportunity structure of our society has changed. Members of racial minority groups who are educated, talented, and motivated can assimilate in ways that a generation ago would have been thought inconceivable.

There are unanticipated results of social change. As avenues of opportunity have opened for upwardly mobile and educated members of racial minority groups to move to suburbs and better-off urban neighborhoods,

| | | | TABLE 1 | | | |

Central city	1980 population	Population below poverty in 1979	Population below poverty and living in poverty areas
Newark, N.J.	326,105	106,895	94,988
Atlanta, Ga.	409,424	112,622	93,192
Birmingham, Ala.	280,004	61,658	45,222
St. Louis, Mo.	444,308	96,849	76,456
Montgomery, Ala.	173,334	33,556	27,780
Detroit, Mich.	1,182,733	258,575	189,002
Chicago, Ill.	2,965,648	601,410	429,940
Cleveland, Ohio	564,407	124,860	93,784
Philadelphia, Pa.	1,653,164	340,517	248,735
New York, N.Y.	6,963,692	1,391,981	985,770
Oakland, Calif.	333,263	61,609	37,409
Los Angeles, Calif.	2,907,573	477,976	290,786
Kansas City, Mo.	440,001	57,965	34,441
Houston, Tex.	1,578,359	199,763	90,181
100 largest central cities	47,507,225	8,125,233	5,191,114

Source for tables 1–3: U.S. Census of Population, 1980: Subject Reports: Poverty Areas in Large Cities (PC 80-2-8D). Washington, D.C.: Government Printing Office, February 1985.

the people left behind in the ghetto—the hidden city—are more isolated. The role models of an earlier day—a teacher, postman, civil servant—have left. There is no reason they should not have left; however, the result is that the dangerous inner-city areas festering in our land have become an increasingly more serious social and economic problem.

It is useful to put this point as a hypothesis: underclass conditions are multifaceted. They are economic, behavioral and geographically focused. This is not to say that we can easily put our social science calipers to the task of measuring the underclass. The underclass involves more than things we can measure with conventional economic and demographic indicators—such as low income, long-term unemployment, limited education, and the incidence of welfare dependency. The underclass condition is also attitudinal and behavioral. It involves alienation, and for the long-term welfare subgroup what Thomas Pettigrew, in V.T. Corello's *Poverty and Public Poverty*, calls a feeling of "learned helplessness." It is often manifest in crime and vandalism, which serve to further isolate underclass groups.

Although a great deal of research has been done on poverty and underclass conditions, there are bound to be differences in interpretation. The main point that needs to be made here is like the cautionary label on cigarette packs: "Be careful when you read the work of social policy experts." We need social policy experts, and there are important areas yet to be studied under the heading of the underclass. Nevertheless, it is possible to draw different conclusions from the same data. At the very least, thoughtful observers of this subject should look at the work of a range of experts rather than unquestioningly accepting a single interpretation of the nature and reasons for underclass conditions—mine included.

Having given this warning, I feel more comfortable in summarizing my own conclusions.

My view of the situation, based on what we know at present, is that the underclass is a distinctively urban condition involving a hardened residual group that is difficult to reach and relate to. This condition represents a change in kind, not degree, although it must always be added that we are talking about a relatively small subgroup among the poor. Census Bureau data are available for 1980 on the population by race in urban poverty areas in the nation's 100 largest cities. They show disturbingly high concentrations of black and Hispanic urban poverty. These data indicate that the black and Hispanic population of urban poverty areas accounts for between 6 to 15 percent of all persons in poverty in the United States, depending on the definition used for poverty areas. If we define urban poverty areas as census tracts with 20 percent or more poverty population, there were 4.1 million black and Hispanic poor persons in poverty areas of the 100 largest cities in 1980. This is 15.1 percent of all persons classified as being in poverty. If we use a more highly concentrated definition of poverty areas—40 percent or more of the population in poverty—6 percent of all persons in poverty reside in these areas. The concentration of poor black and Hispanic persons in poverty areas in selected cities is shown in the tables. Over the past decade, census data indicate that the concentration of poor blacks and Hispanics in poverty areas rose by some 40 percent in the most severe urban poverty areas, although the 1970 and 1980 data are not precisely comparable.

The politics involved in dealing with urban underclass conditions are difficult because, overall, the numbers of people affected are small, the people involved tend not to vote, they do not have powerful interest groups that support them, and the places in which these problem conditions are concentrated can be dangerous and threatening to outsiders.

This situation has important implications for government policy. That underclass condi-

	TABLE 2			
Central city	Black & Hispanic population below poverty in 1979	Black & Hispanic population below poverty and living in poverty areas	Percent black & Hispanic poor living in poverty areas	Percent city population that is poor, black or Hispanic, and lives in poverty areas
Newark, N.J.	94,925	87,952	92.7%	27.0%
Atlanta, Ga.	95,628	85,043	88.9%	20.8%
Birmingham, Ala.	49,461	40,310	81.5%	14.4%
St. Louis, Mo.	69,018	63,731	92.3%	14.3%
Montgomery, Ala.	26,231	24,630	93.9%	14.2%
Detroit, Mich.	205,114	160,736	78.4%	13.6%
Chicago, Ill.	472,653	390,220	82.6%	13.2%
Cleveland, Ohio	83,334	73,563	88.3%	13.0%
Philadelphia, Pa.	229,140	204,940	89.4%	12.4%
New York, N.Y.	988,933	848,671	85.8%	12.2%
Oakland, Calif.	45,206	31,605	69.9%	9.5%
Los Angeles, Calif.	322,288	240,199	74.5%	8.3%
Kansas City, Mo.	31,655	25,646	81.0%	5.8%
Houston, Tex.	146,299	84,272	57.6%	5.3%
100 largest central cities	5,169,529	4,139,976	80.1%	8.7%

tions are so intractable and that they involve alienation and criminal behavior is one of the reasons underlying the current conservative-retrenchment mood of the nation on social policy. There has been a shift over the past decade not just on social spending and not limited to our belief about what we can achieve under social programs. This shift involes a perceptible and disturbing change in public opinion on race and civil rights issues. The way we came to believe we are supposed to behave toward the members of minority groups in the sixties and seventies has changed in the eighties. This often unspoken—although sometimes privately conceded—shift in opinion was partially caused by the increased severity of urban underclass conditions, and this situation in turn is manifest in heightened racial intolerance. In the long-run, these developments, unless we respond to them wisely, could threaten the social and civil rights policy gains of the earlier and more hopeful period beginning in the mid-sixties that lasted throughout most of the seventies.

A MATTER OF VALUES

My third topic is a response to underclass conditions. My purpose is not to discuss specific programs, but rather to present ideas on the strategy for dealing with underclass conditions. Here, I have better news to report. New thinking is emerging in the current period about government social policies that represent a fortuitous development. It reflects a synthesis of conservative and liberal ideas on a basis that includes the best features of both. It is useful to view this development in historical perspective.

To a considerable degree, the motivating spirit of social policy in the United States in the Great Society period was a feeling of guilt about the conditions of a society that blocked, rather than facilitated, the movement of racial minorities into the social and economic mainstream. Associated with this spirit was a sense of discovery that the culture and ideas distinctive to racial minorities should be recognized and more widely appreciated. Soul food, Gospel music and the dress, language, and humor of blacks, in Tom Wolfe's wonderful satire, all came to be part of a new, socially-motivated form of radical chic. White liberals especially reached out in well meaning ways to understand and identify with the black community.

This attitude carried over to government programs. Among the central ideas of Lyndon Johnson's war on poverty were compassion and power to the people. Again, Tom Wolfe captured the feeling of this concept in the popular literature. In his "Mau-Mauing the Flak Catchers," published in *Radical Chic and Mau-Mauing the Flak Catchers,* he wrote about going downtown to mau-mau the bureaucrats. "The poverty program encouraged you to go in for mau-mauing." Otherwise, the bureaucrats at City Hall and in the Office of Economic Opportunity, said Wolfe, wouldn't know what to do. "They didn't know who to ask." The answer in San Francisco, the locale of Wolfe's story, depended on "the confrontation ritual."

Well . . . they used the Ethnic Catering Service . . . right. . . . They sat back and waited for you to come rolling in with your certified angry militants, your guaranteed frustrated ghetto youth, looking like a bunch of wild men. Then you had your test confrontation. If you were outrageous enough, if you could shake up the bureaucrats so bad that their eyes froze into iceballs and their mouth twisted up into smiles of

		TABLE 3		
Central city	**1980 population**	**Whites below poverty level in 1979**	**Poor whites in poverty areas**	**Percent white poor living in poverty areas**
Newark, N.J.	326,105	10,959	6,337	57.8%
Atlanta, Ga.	409,424	16,058	7,600	47.3%
Birmingham, Ala.	280,004	11,858	4,676	39.4%
St. Louis, Mo.	444,308	27,085	12,191	45.0%
Montgomery, Ala.	173,334	7,240	3,122	43.1%
Detroit, Mich.	1,182,733	50,646	26,472	52.3%
Chicago, Ill.	2,965,648	117,218	33,851	28.9%
Cleveland, Ohio	564,407	40,401	19,416	48.1%
Philadelphia, Pa.	1,653,164	104,992	39,001	37.1%
New York, N.Y.	6,963,692	360,469	114,502	31.8%
Oakland, Calif.	333,263	11,439	2,971	26.0%
Los Angeles, Calif.	2,907,573	119,998	29,140	24.3%
Kansas City, Mo.	440,001	25,154	8,088	32.2%
Houston, Tex.	1,578,359	46,867	3,996	8.5%
100 largest central cities	47,507,225	2,658,750	902,278	33.9%

sheer physical panic, into shit-eating grins, so to speak—then you knew you were the real goods. They knew you were the right studs to give the poverty grants and community organizing jobs to. Otherwise they wouldn't know.

As I read the tea leaves of social policy, this deferential attitude carried over into the Nixon-Ford period in the mid-seventies. It determined what was permissible in both the rhetoric and substance of social policy. The now widespread frustration with Great Society programs did not become a part of the popular mindset on social issues until the latter part of the seventies.

George Will makes an observation, in *Statecraft as Soulcraft*, that is helpful in understanding the new philosophy of social action that began to emerge in the late nineteen seventies. He notes that politicians, although they may not concede that this is so, are often involved in shaping and changing moral values.

> . . . statecraft is soulcraft. Just as all education is moral education because learning conditions conduct, much legislation is moral legislation because it conditions the actions and the thought of the nation in broad and important spheres in life.

This idea is the key to the hopeful point that we appear to be moving toward a new formula for dealing with underclass conditions that corrects for the miscalculations and excesses, however well-intended, of the Great Society. Social policy is now evolving in a way that reflects an increased belief on the part of both liberals and conservatives that there should be a behavioral *quid pro quo*. There was reluctance on the part of people in the field of social policy from the mid-sixties through the mid-seventies to intrude on the culture and value system of the groups that in Lyndon Johnson's presidency were discovered as a new focus for social policy. Allowing people to do their own thing was felt to be (and there is a good argument for this) the right approach to helping the poor. The guaranteed income or negative income tax idea reflects this view. The problem of the poor is that they do not have enough money; providing resources—preferably in the most flexible form, hard currency—was seen as enabling them to make their own choices.

Imperceptibly at first, a movement developed in the late seventies on the part of social policy intellectuals questioning these assumptions. There is a concept in economics that is helpful for this analysis: signaling. We may not be doing people a favor if we transmit signals about welfare rights and entitlements in a society that has a deep and strong Calvinist tradition that practically deifies the work ethic. The change that has occurred in our ideas about signaling under social programs is best seen by looking at the welfare field, and particularly at the most controversial welfare program for ablebodied working-age poor people with children—the Aid to Families with Dependent Children (AFDC) program.

There have been three main theories of welfare reform for AFDC over the past twenty years, all of which have been publicly prominent. One theory is the guaranteed-income approach. Another is the employment approach (jobs are the answer). The third, for which Ronald Reagan was the principal spokesman in the seventies, is the devolutionary or block-grant approach to welfare reform. Its aim is to turn back responsibility for the welfare population to the states on the premise that states (and also local governments) are in the best position to provide services and make the fine-grained determinations necessary to enable (or better yet, push and require) working age, ablebodied poor persons to move into the labor force.

The synthesis I see emerging in the current period contains elements of all three approaches, although the dominant themes are work (the employment approach) and devolution (relying more heavily on the states). A single word captures the shift that is occurring: workfare.

In the seventies the word *workfare* was used in a narrow way to refer to the idea that people should work off their welfare grants, that is, that welfare recipients should be required to work, even in make-work jobs, in exchange for receiving their benefits. Liberals on social policy issues—and this included most welfare administrators—heaped abuse on this idea, calling it "slavefare" and rejecting it out of hand. Efforts to tie welfare to work in a binding way were often undermined by the welfare establishment. This occurred, for example, in Massachusetts, where such an effort was made by Governor Edward King, and in California under Governor Ronald Reagan. Reagan's 1971 California welfare reform plan, which included an AFDC work requirement and a work-experience component, never got off the ground. At its peak, only 3 percent of the eligible population participated in work-experience programs.

Something happened on the way to the forum—in this case the U.S. Congress. Ronald Reagan as president won grudging acceptance from the Congress to include authority under the AFDC program in the 1981 budget act to allow states to test new employment approaches to welfare reform, including the workfare approach. What emerged out of the efforts to implement this legislation is what I call "new-style workfare." The history of the nomenclature is interesting.

The 1981 budget act included a provision permitting the states to experiment with what was termed in Washington CWEP, standing for "community work experience programs." The same acronym had been used in California in the seventies, only the "C" was for "California," and not "community" under this California program.

The big difference in the 1980s—and this is a critical point—is that liberals and the welfare establishment began to shift their ground politically and, at the same time, to shift their terms of reference. The term *workfare* is increasingly being used in a new way. It takes the form of obligational state programs that involve an array of employment and training services and activities: job search, job training, education programs, and also community work experience. Over two-thirds of the states are now developing new-style workfare programs along these lines. Research by the Manpower Demonstration Research Corporation in eight states, with 35,000 people assigned to program and control groups, shows promising—although not large and dramatic—results from these programs in terms of increased earnings and reduced welfare dependency. Whether this shift to new-style workfare is intellectual or tactical is hard to say. My reading of new-style workfare is that the initial response of the welfare establishment and liberals among social policy experts was expedient and tactical, but that as events transpired conviction followed suit.

One reason for the increasingly positive response, particularly on the part of state government officials, to the new authority in the 1981 budget act reflects the opinion held by many observers of urban conditions: the critical need in distressed urban areas is jobs. In effect, new-style workfare creates jobs (short-term, entry-level positions very much like the CETA—Comprehensive Employment and Training Act—public service jobs we thought we had abolished in 1981). At the same time, new-style workfare provides a political rationale and support for increased funding for education and training programs; it also discriminates under these employment and job preparation programs in favor of the most disadvantaged people. The latter effect (discrimination in favor of the most disadvantaged) corrects for the problem of "creaming" under employment and training programs, a practice which has been the subject of strong and justifiable criticism on the part of experts in the field of employment and training.

The California story for new-style workfare is particularly interesting. Under a conservative governor, George Deukmejian, a deal was struck between the governor and liberals in the legislature, notably Arthur Agnos, on legislation that involves a fundamental restructuring of the welfare system to shift its orientation from a payment and social service system to a new system strongly oriented toward training, education, job placement, and work—including in some cases the assignment of welfare family heads to obligatory work experience positions.

At first, the language was oblique. Work experience was called PREP in California, the letters standing for preemployment preparation. Increasingly the press and participants in the debate on this legislation came to call the whole program and process by one word, workfare. This newspeak of welfare reform in California—and also in many other states—now uses the term *workfare* to refer to the array of job-focused programs and child care and other services to reduce welfare dependency. New-style workfare is a blend of conservative and liberal themes. In finding this nice balance, there is reason to hope that politicians have detoxified the welfare issue. This shift is healthy and encouraging for social policy in the United States. The basic strategy involves state initiatives, institutional change at the state level, and the idea of obligation.

This is not to say that the obligational concept in social policy can be expected to take hold everywhere and expand rapidly. Successful policy change must have a foundation in values. It is in these terms—in terms of building a new foundation of values as a basis for policy change—that I see some grounds for a modest sense of hopefulness in the current period.

We make our greatest progress on social reform in the United States when liberals and conservatives find common ground. New-style workfare embodies both the caring commitment of liberals and the themes identified with conservative writers such as Charles Murray, George Gilder, and Lawrence Mead. It involves a strong commitment to reducing welfare dependency on the premise that dependency is bad for people, that it undermines their motivation to support themselves, and isolates and stigmatizes welfare recipients in a way that over a long period feeds into and accentuates the underclass mindset and condition.

The new message is a familiar one: "You have to go along to get along." You have to go along, that is, with a set of values about work, job skills, behavior in the workplace, and attitudes toward success in the economy. Society is behaving like a supportive parent. Rather than telling people, "there is something wrong with you, you need help" we do better by telling them, "you are as good as the next person, you should make it on your own." Confidence rather than deference is the essence of this new approach to social policy.

In the long run, the test of the society's will to move in this direction requires two things: money and a willingness on the part of governments at all levels to focus training, educational, and employment services on those who need them the most. This includes both female welfare family heads and unemployed young males in distressed urban areas. Fortunately, research shows that such a targeting policy—discriminating in favor of the most disadvantaged people—has positive results. Yet even if we respond to this challenge, underclass conditions will not be alleviated quickly or easily. The task requires time, patience, and a willingness to experiment and adapt in social policy. To this question about the underclass: will it always be with us?, the answer is that, even with the best of efforts, it will be with us for a long time. Nevertheless, I believe there is reason now for a more hopeful mood about our ability to make a dent in America's most challenging social problem which tests the very mettle of our democracy.

DISCUSSION QUESTIONS

1. What evidence does Nathan offer that there is an underclass in America?

2. Have welfare policies mitigated conditions of America's urban poor?

3. Develop a theoretical explanation for the persistence of an underclass in America.

READING 5-2

The Worthy and Unworthy Homeless

James D. Wright

Americans have always found it necessary to distinguish between the "deserving" and "undeserving" poor—the former, victims of circumstances beyond their control who merit compassion; the latter, lazy, shiftless bums who could do better for themselves "if they wanted to" and who therefore merit contempt. The ensuing tension in our collective attitude toward the poor is reflected both in public policy and in public opinion surveys. A 1984 survey asked people to agree or disagree, that "most people who do not get ahead in life probably work just as hard has people who do." Forty-seven percent agreed with this sentiment, 44 percent disagreed, and the remainder were neutral or had no opinion. In the same survey, 84 percent agreed that "any person who is willing to work hard has a good chance of succeeding" but 80 percent also agreed that "even if people try hard they often cannot reach their goals."

Poverty in America has become visible again, both as a phenomenon and as a public policy issue. I refer specifically to the apparently dramatic increase in homelessness that has occurred in the past several years and to the media and political attention that the problem of homelessness has received. These days, homeless and destitute people can be found wandering the streets of any large urban area; no one can possibly remain oblivious to their existence. What to do about or for the homeless has likewise become an important political issue, with some thirty-two separate bills introduced in the Hundredth Congress that deal with one or another aspect of the homelessness problem.

So far, the homeless seem to be included among the "deserving poor," at least by the general public. A recent national survey by the Roper Organization reported by *Newsweek* on September 21, 1987, asked what problems we should be spending more money on. "Caring for the homeless" was the top priority item, favored by 68 percent. (In contrast, foreign aid was mentioned by only 5 percent, and "military, armaments, and defense" by only 17 percent.) Thus, most people seem to feel that the homeless deserve our help, if not our compassion. But an opposite, more mean-spirited view has also begun to surface. On December 1, 1986, Stuart Bykofsky wrote a "My Turn" column for *Newsweek* magazine entitled "No Heart for the Homeless." The analysis turned on the division of the homeless into three groups: "(1) the economically distressed, who would work if they could find work; (2) the mentally ill, who can't work; (3) the alcoholic, the drug-addicted, and others who won't work." His solution to the problem was workfare for the first group, mental institutions for the second, and indifference to (or outright hostility toward) the third.

Bykofsky's simplistic categorization was unburdened by numbers or percentages, and so we are not told how many of the homeless fit his various types. Concurrent with the increased media and political attention being given to the problem, there has also been an outpouring of research studies that provide reliable guides to the relative proportions of "worthy" and "unworthy" homeless. My aim here is to review the findings of some of these studies, to see if we cannot be more precise about how many homeless deserve our sympathies and how many do not.

The many recent studies available for our use are uneven in coverage and quality. The largest and most geographically dispersed sample of homeless people available is that contained in *Homelessness and Health,* my study of clients seen in the National Health Care for the Homeless Program (HCH). Data for the first year of the HCH program describe nearly 30,000 homeless people seen in health clinics in sixteen large cities all over the country. Because of its size, geographical dispersion, and my familiarity with the results, I use the findings from this study extensively in the following discussion.

A second study upon which I have drawn is the Peter H. Rossi et al. survey of homeless people in Chicago, *The Condition of the Homeless in Chicago.* One problem faced by many studies is that they are based exclusively on shelter users; it has long been recognized that the shelter users are only one of two important components of the homeless population, the other being "street homeless" who, for whatever reason, rarely or never use the shelter system. One among many virtues of the Rossi et al. survey is its extremely thorough and systematic sampling of the street homeless. This fact, coupled with the breadth of topics

covered and the general degree of sophistication in the conduct of the research, make the Chicago survey especially useful.

Neither of the above sources provides answers to all the important questions, and so in some cases I have relied on other research. In all cases, I have sacrificed technical niceties for completeness of coverage, knowing full well that new and better research will no doubt change the picture, at least in small details.

For convenience, it is useful to begin by imagining a sample of 1,000 homeless people, drawn at random, let us say, from the half million or so homeless people to be found in America on any given evening. Based on the research I have sketched, we can then begin to cut up this sample in various ways, so as to portray as graphically as possible the mosaic of homelessness in this country. Our strategy is to work from "more deserving" to "less deserving" subgroups, ending with the absolutely least deserving—the lazy, shiftless bums. Along the way, I call attention to various characteristics of and problems encountered by each of the subgroups we consider.

HOMELESS FAMILIES

Among the many tragedies of homelessness, there is none sadder than the homeless family—often an intact family unit consisting of a wife, her husband, and one or more dependent children, victims of unemployment and other economic misfortune, struggling in the face of long odds to maintain themselves as a unit and get back on their feet again. How many members of homeless families can we expect to find among our sample of 1,000 homeless people?

Although the rising number of homeless families has become a matter of considerable policy concern, evidence on their proportion in the larger homeless population is hard to come by. Most of the pertinent research has been done in homeless family shelters, or in facilities for homeless women and children; and while this material is useful for descriptive purposes, it does not tell us anything about relative proportions.

Some useful information appears in my HCH study. Across the sixteen cities covered in the study, 16 percent of all clients seen were described as members of homeless family groups. In six of the sixteen cities, family status was not systematically reported; among the 18,842 clients seen in the remaining ten cities, 28 percent were members of homeless family groups. Thus, somewhere between 160 and 280 of our 1,000 homeless people will be members of homeless families—whether male or female, adult or child. Let us take the midpoint of the range, 220 members of homeless families, as our best and final estimate, consistent with most other studies of the topic. The remainder are lone individuals.

The HCH study further suggests that among the 220 members of homeless families, 99 will be children (under age sixteen) and 121 will be adults; among the adults will be 83 adult women and 38 adult men. One important conclusion, then, is that nearly a tenth of the homeless on the streets of American cities today are homeless children in the care of their adult parent or parents.

A second important conclusion, one that follows from the relative preponderance of women to men among the adult family members, is that most homeless families consist of single mothers with their children rather than intact nuclear families. (There would also be a few single fathers with children, but their numbers are minuscule in all studies.) If each of the 38 adult men is coupled with one of the 83 adult women, then we get 38 male-female pairs and 45 single females among the total of 121 adult family members in our hypothetical sample of 1,000. Somewhat more than half of the homeless families are single-parent (typically, single mother) units, somewhat less than half are intact nuclear families.

Most of the intact nuclear families have children of dependent age, but only about half of them actually have their children with them. The most common arrangement among the remainder is that the children are living with other relatives; in some cases, the children are in foster care. Thus, only 17 or 18 of the intact male-female pairs would also include children as part of the family unit. The 99 children would thus be distributed among, say, 18 mother-father pairs and 45 single parents (mostly mothers). Thus, most homeless children live in broken families, one among the many problems homeless children face.

Studies of the effects of homelessness on children paint a uniformly shocking and depressing picture. According to Ellen Bassuk, in the *American Journal of Public Health* in 1986, developmental delays of varying severity are observed in more than half. My research has confirmed that homeless children suffer various physical disorders at rates two to ten times those seen among children in general. Some of the problems encountered by homeless children are depression, anger, anxiety, low self-esteem, and uncertainty about life (at a psychological level); and inadequate nutrition, dangerous living conditions, violence and abuse, a lack of parental authority, no quiet place to do homework, and so on (at a more concrete, palpable level). One homeless child that I have met—she lives with her mother and siblings in a welfare hotel in New York City—described her "dream" as "a clean apartment and a safe place to play out of doors." This does not seem like too much to ask. We might wonder what kind of world it is where this can only be a dream to some children.

As for the adult members of homeless family units, the picture is somewhat brighter; among both men and women, rates of alcohol and drug abuse, and mental illness, are lower than they are among lone homeless individuals. The adult family members also suffer fewer chronic physical disorders, are more likely to be short-term (or situationally) homeless, and are rated as having better housing and employment prospects than the lone homeless are. In general, their prospects for the future are much brighter; compared to the lone homeless, the adult family members are simply more intact. Many of these families need little more than a "helping hand" to get them through a rough stretch. Many of the single mothers with dependent children need little more than an expedited Aid to Families with Dependent Children (AFDC) process. Helping hands and more efficient AFDC processing would certainly not solve all the problems these families face, but it would make a considerable dent.

Members of homeless families constitute a significantly large fraction of the homeless population; my guess is that we would find 220 of them in a sample of a thousand homeless people, nearly half of them homeless children. Not only would most people look on homeless families as most deserving of help, there is also reason to believe that they need the least help (in that they appear to have the fewest disabling problems and tend generally to be the most intact), and that even relatively modest assistance would make a substantial difference in their life chances and circumstances. If the available resources are such as to require triage, then homeless families should be the top priority.

LONE WOMEN AND CHILDREN

By these calculations, there remain in our hypothetical sample of 1,000 some 780 lone homeless persons—single individuals on the streets by themselves. Based on the HCH study, some 6 percent of these 780 are children or adolescents age nineteen or less (which amounts to 47 additional children in the sample of 1,000), 20 percent are adult women (156 additional women), and 74 percent are adult

men (which leaves, from the original sample of 1,000, only 580 adult males not members of homeless family groups). Adding these to the earlier results, we get two significant conclusions: First, among the total of a thousand homeless persons, 99 + 47 = 146 will be children or youth aged nineteen or less, approximately one in every seven. Second, among the remaining 854 adults, 156 + 83 = 229 will be women, which amounts to 229/854 or 27 percent of all adults. Combining all figures, homeless children and homeless adult women themselves comprise 146 + 299 = 375 of the original 1,000—three of every eight. Adult men comprise the majority of the homeless, but not the overwhelmingly majority; a very sizable minority—nearly 40 percent of the total—are women and children.

Most of the lone children found in these calculations are teenagers, which is also to say that nearly all homeless preteen children are still living with one or both of their parents. Still, children as young as twelve or thirteen will be found in sizable numbers in these data. Although men predominate among homeless adults, boys and girls are found in equal numbers among homeless children and teenagers; in the HCH data that form the basis for the preceding calculations, 51 percent of the lone homeless aged nineteen or less are boys, and 49 percent are girls; among all children (under age sixteen) in these data (whether lone individuals or members of homeless family groups), the split is also nearly 50:50. The heavy preponderance of males to females is observed only among the adults.

Although precise numbers are hard to come by, there is little doubt that many of these homeless teenagers are runaway or throwaway children fleeing abusive family situations. Among the girls, the rate of pregnancy is astonishing: 9 percent of the girls age thirteen to fifteen, and 24 percent of the girls ages sixteen to nineteen, were pregnant at or since their first contact with the HCH clinic system;

the rate for sixteen-to-nineteen-year-olds is the highest observed in any age-group. There is impressionistic evidence, but no hard evidence, to suggest that many of these young girls are reduced to prostitution in order to survive; many will thus come to possess lengthy jail records as well. Drug and alcohol abuse are also common problems. Indeed, the rate of known drug abuse among the sixteen-to-nineteen-year-old boys—some 16 percent—is the highest rate recorded for any age-group in our data.

I am discussing a time in life when the average adolescent's biggest worries are acne, or whom to invite to the high school prom, or where to go to college—a time of uncertainty, but also a time of hope and anticipation for the future. In contrast, homeless adolescents must worry about where to sleep tonight, or where the next meal is coming from, or who is going to assault them next. What hope for the future can be nourished under these conditions? Many of these kids—tough kids on mean streets, but kids nonetheless—face an unending downward spiral of booze, drugs, crime, and troubles with the law. They too must surely be counted among the "deserving" homeless; indeed, anything that can be done should be done to break the spiral and set them back on the path to an independent and productive adult existence.

Among the 854 adults remaining in our initial sample of 1,000 homeless will be 229 adult women, or 27 percent of all adults. Again, this is very close to the figure reported in most studies. In the Chicago survey, 24 percent were women, and no recent study has reported a figure of less than 20 percent. Homeless women are not a new phenomenon; studies by D. L. Jones in Massachusetts, published in the 1974 *Journal of Social History*, and by P. F. Clements in Philadelphia confirm sizable fractions of women among the homeless, at least since colonial times. (Clements's work is published in E. H. Monkkonen's *Walking to Work: Tramps in America*.) Compared to homeless adult men, homeless women are younger by about two years on the average: 42 percent of the adult HCH women, but only 30 percent of the adult men, are under thirty. Compared to the men, the women are much more likely to have psychiatric impairments, but much less likely to abuse alcohol and drugs.

There are many different kinds of homeless women, and it is a mistake to think of "the" problems of homeless women as though all homeless women faced the same problems. One large and important subgroup is comprised of the lone mentally impaired women from whom the "bag lady" stereotype has been derived. This is the subset of homeless women that in some sense has been created by deinstitutionalization and related changes in our mental health treatment system. A reasonable guess is that they constitute about a third of all homeless women. Compared to other homeless women, they are much older (the median age of the group is forty) and predominantly white (58 percent); their principal need is for vastly improved community mental health services.

A second group, accounting for more than a quarter of the total, are mothers with dependent children in their care. These women tend to be young (the median age is twenty-seven), and their rates of mental disorder and substance abuse are relatively low. Only about half receive AFDC; many would presumably be employable if day care were available. Yet a third group are the homeless teenage girls, some of whose problems I have already discussed. The remainder of the women fall into a residual "other" category; the distinctive feature of this group is that alcohol and drug abuse is much more widespread than among the other women, rivaling the rates found generally among homeless men.

Most people would feel comfortable counting the adult women among the "deserving" homeless as well. Just as women and children are the first to be evacuated from a sinking ship, so too should women and children be the first to be rescued from the degradations of street life or a shelter existence. If we add to the group of "deserving" homeless the relatively small number of adult men in homeless family groups, then our initial cut leaves but 580 persons from the original 1,000 yet to account for.

LONE ADULT MEN

What is to be said about those who remain— the 580 lone adult males, not members of homeless families? A small percentage of them, much smaller than most people would anticipate, are elderly men, over age sixty-five; in the HCH data, the over-sixty-fives comprise about 3 percent of the group in question, which gives us 17 elderly men among the remaining 580. In fact, among all HCH adults, just about 3 percent are over age sixty-five; the lone adult men are not exceptional in this respect.

Since, in the national population as a whole, about twelve percent are over sixty-five, our 3 percent figure means that there are many fewer elderly homeless than would otherwise be expected—a "shortage" or "deficit" of elderly homeless that has been remarked upon in several studies. What explains the apparent shortage of homeless persons over sixty-five? First, a number of entitlements become available to persons once they turn sixty-five, chief among them Medicare and Social Security payments. It is possible that these benefits are adequate to get most older homeless persons off the streets or out of the shelters and into some sort of reasonably stable housing situation. A second possibility is premature mortality; homeless persons, that is, may only rarely survive to age sixty-five in the first place.

Little research has been done on mortality among the homeless, but the few studies that are available suggest that the mortality hypothesis is not to be taken lightly. Alstrom and his colleagues, in a study reported in the *British Journal of Addictions* in 1975, followed 6,032 homeless Swedish men for a three-year period. Observed mortality during the study period (n = 327 deaths) exceeded the age-adjusted expected mortality (n = 87 expected deaths) by a factor of approximately four; the average age at death among the 327 men was about fifty-three years. My own study of the topic has produced a similar result; among 88 deaths occurring among clients seen in the HCH program, the average age at death was fifty-one. Based on these findings, we can conclude that homeless men die some twenty or so years earlier than they "should." Thus, premature death must certainly account for at least some portion of the elderly "deficit."

The shortage of over-sixty-fives is not the only striking aspect of the age distribution of the homeless; the fact is, homeless people are surprisingly young. The median age of HCH adults is thirty-four years; all recent demographic studies of homeless populations have remarked on the low average age, perhaps because the stereotype is that the homeless tend to be old. Today, the average homeless adult male is somewhere in his early to middle thirties.

The low average age of the homeless sustains an important and often overlooked conclusion, namely, that the rise of the "new homeless" is in some sense a result of the so-called baby boom, the immensely large generations born in the United States between 1947 and 1964. As a cohort, the average age of the baby boom is now in the early thirties, almost identical to the average age of homeless people.

The baby boom has posed serious problems for virtually every institution it has touched in the course of its life span, beginning with the crisis in elementary education that commenced in the early 1950s, continuing through to a serious national housing shortage today, and ending ultimately with what will be a serious shortage of burial space around the year 2020 and thereafter. The more affluent members of the baby boom generation have come to be known as "Yuppies" (young urban professionals), whose housing preferences and purchasing power are in many respects responsible for the current housing crisis. What is often overlooked in discussions of the Yuppies is that they sit at the upper end of an income distribution, the other end of which reaches down into the poverty population. In the lowest reaches of this income distribution one finds the "new homeless," whose numbers have clearly begun to strain the capacity of the existing social welfare system.

As for the elderly, those over sixty-five, surely they are to be included within the "deserving" group. As it happens, only about half of them receive Social Security benefits. Many of those who do receive Social Security payments find that no housing can be purchased or rented within their means. Well over half have chronic physical health problems that further contribute to their hardships. Certainly, no one will object if we include the elderly homeless among those deserving our sympathies.

LONE VETERANS

We are now left with, let us say, 563 nonelderly lone adult men. If we inquire further among this group, we will discover another surprising fact: at least a third of them are veterans of the United States Armed Forces. Indeed, over a number of recent studies, reviewed by M. Robertson in Bingham, Green, and White's *The Homeless in Contemporary Society*, the percentage of veterans among the men varies from a low of 32 percent to a high of 47 percent. The one-third figure is clearly conservative; the true figure might be as high as one-half. As a point of comparison, 41 percent of all adult men in the United States are also veterans; in this respect, the homeless are not much different.

The studies reviewed by Robertson show the homeless veterans to be slightly older and proportionally more white than homeless nonveteran men; compared to the national veteran population, Vietnam-era veterans are overrepresented. About one in five have service-related disabilities sufficiently serious to prevent them from working; service-related psychiatric difficulties, while not always disabling, are also widespread. Among the Vietnam-era veterans, posttraumatic stress syndrome may be the most common psychiatric problem. Most of the veterans, especially the younger ones, report chronic unemployment problems as well. No more than about a third receive any form of assistance from the Veteran's Administration.

Most homeless veterans are drawn from the lower socioeconomic strata, having enlisted to obtain, as Robertson has put it, "long term economic advantages through job training as well as postmilitary college benefits and preferential treatment in civil service employment," only to find that their economic and employment opportunities remain limited after they have mustered out. The lure of military service proves to have been a false promise for many of these men: "Despite recruitment campaigns that promote military service as an opportunity for maturation and occupational mobility, veterans continue to struggle with postmilitary unemployment and mental and physical disability without adequate assistance from the federal government." One of the Vietnam veterans in Robertson's study summed up the stakes involved: "If they expect the youth of America to fight another war, they have to take care of the vets."

Many of the homeless veterans are alcoholic or drug abusive, and many are also mentally ill; the same could be said for other subgroups that we have considered. Whatever their current problems and disabilities, these men were there when the nation needed them. Do they not also deserve a return of the favor?

LONE DISABLED MEN

Sticking with the admittedly conservative one-third estimate, among the 563 adult men with whom we are left, 188 will be veterans; 375 nonelderly, nonveteran adult men are all that remain of the initial 1,000. Sorting out this subgroup in the HCH data, we find that a third are assessed by their care providers as having moderate to severe psychiatric impairments—not including alcohol or drug abuse. Many among this group have fallen through the cracks of the community mental health system. In the vast majority of cases, they pose no immediate danger to themselves or to others, and thus they are generally immune to involuntary commitment for psychiatric treatment; at the same time, their ability to care for themselves, especially in a street or shelter environment, is at best marginal. Compassion dictates that they too be included among the "deserving" group.

Just what they "deserve" is hotly contested; I cannot do justice here to the many complex issues involved. Some, for example New York's Mayor Ed Koch, think that they deserve involuntary commitment if their lives or well-being are imperiled by the material conditions of their existence; civil libertarians think they deserve the right to die on the streets if they want to. Many mental health professionals seem to feel that reopening the large state mental institutions is the only viable solution; others think that coming through on the promise of community-based mental health care—the explicit promise upon which deinstitutionalization was justified—is the only morally defensible approach. All agree that for many of the mentally ill homeless, the least restrictive treatment has meant a life of scavenging food from street sources and sleeping in alleys and gutters—and this, no one intended.

Subtracting the 125 or so mentally disabled men from the remaining group of 375 leaves 250 of the original 1,000. Among these 250 will be some 28 or so men who are physically disabled and incapable of working. This includes the blind and the deaf, those confined to wheelchairs, the paraplegic, those with amputated limbs, and those with disabling chronic physical illnesses such as heart disease, AIDS, obstructive pulmonary disease, and others. Like the mentally disabled, these too can only be counted among the "deserving" group. Subtracting them leaves a mere 222 remaining—nonelderly, nonveteran adult males with no mental or physical disability.

Of these 222, a bit more than half—112 men—will be found to have some sort of job: my data suggest that 7 will have full-time jobs, 27 will have part-time jobs, and 78 will be employed on a sporadic basis (seasonal work, day labor, odd jobs, and the like). Rossi's Chicago data show largely the same pattern. The remainder—110 men—are unemployed, and among these some 61 will be looking for work. All told, then, among the 222 will be 173 who are at least making the effort: looking for work, but so far with no success, or having a job but not one paying well enough to allow them to afford stable housing. This then leaves us with 49 people from the initial 1,000 who are not members of homeless families, not women, not children, not elderly, not veterans, not mentally disabled, not physically disabled, not currently working, and not looking for work. Call these the "undeserving homeless," or, if you wish, lazy shiftless bums. They account for about 5 percent of the total—a mere one in every twenty.

NO EASY SOLUTION

There are many different kinds of homeless people, and it is pointless even to think of "the" homeless as though they were a homogeneous, undifferentiated group. Many of them—some 40 percent by my estimates—are alcohol abusive; a tenth abuse other drugs; a third are mentally ill; many have long-term chronic employment problems; most are estranged from their families and disaffiliated from the larger society. But very few of them are "homeless by choice" (to adopt a most unfortunate, although characteristic, phrase of Ronald Reagan), and all but a residual fraction merit our compassion on one or more counts.

There are no cheap or easy solutions to the problems of homelessness. At varying levels of analysis, homelessness is a housing problem, an employment problem, a demographic problem, a problem of social disaffiliation, a mental health problem, a substance abuse problem, a family violence problem, a problem created by cutbacks in social welfare spending, a problem resulting from the decay of the traditional nuclear family, and a problem intimately connected to the recent increase in persons living below the poverty level, as well as others.

In puzzling through the complex array of factors that cause homelessness, in the hopes of finding some solutions, coldheartedness is not the proper sentiment. Should we, as Bykofsky suggests, have "no heart" for a disabled thirty-three-year-old Vietnam veteran suffering from posttraumatic stress syndrome, or for a pregnant fifteen-year-old runaway girl whose father has raped and beaten her once too often, or for a feverish infant in the arms of her homeless mother, or for an entire family that has been turned out because the factory where the father worked was shut down, or for an arthritic old gentleman who has lost his room in the "welfare hotel" because he was beaten savagely and relieved of his Social Security check? These are very much a part—a large part—of today's homeless population, no less than the occasional "shiftless bum." Indifference to the plight of "shiftless bums" comes all too easily in an illiberal era; but indifference to the plight of homeless families, women, children, old people, veterans, and the disabled comes easily only to the cruel.

DISCUSSION QUESTIONS

1. Who are the unworthy homeless and why are they considered unworthy?
2. Distinguish different types of homeless people and offer policy recommendations which might alleviate their plight.
3. Why is it that America has so many homeless people while so many other countries have far fewer homeless?

READING 5-3

New Welfare State Models and Mixes

S. M. Miller

Changes, expectations about changes, and belated recognition of new conditions are reshaping welfare states in Europe as well as in the United States. While Europe is experiencing more profound changes and issues than have yet been faced in the United States, Americans can learn from the positives and negatives of the European shifts and debates. There have been a number of important changes in welfare state contexts in Europe from which four models have emerged.

CHANGES IN CONTEXTS

First is the widespread feeling that a growing and glowing economic future is unlikely. The enormous economic growth of post-World

War II Europe and the near-full employment that accompanied it are not deemed possible in many countries. Indeed, European unemployment rates have been at levels once regarded as intolerable, and Europe seems to have learned to live with the high rates.

In the '60s British social scientists told their American counterparts that if the U.K. had U.S. unemployment rates of 5 or 6 percent, a revolution would occur. Today, of course, all of Western Europe outside of Scandinavia and Austria have scandalously high unemployment rates. Their political tenability suggests that expectations about the future have collapsed rapidly and deeply and/or unemployment can coexist with "good times" for many others. Or, that unemployment benefits and informal economy participation make unemployment less burdensome today, which is the conclusion of neoclassical economists.

Whatever the reason, continuing high unemployment is a shock. Fear of competition from Japan, the United States, and the newly-industrializing countries of the Third World is lowering economic hopes. One set of consequences is high unemployment, which increases welfare state outlays, and financial stringency that reduces governmental funds for welfare. Another consequence is a drive to lower taxes, wages, and fringe benefits in order to increase a nation's international competitiveness. A continually expanding welfare state—the condition of postwar European capitalism—is no longer anticipated. The political talk is much more of contraction of social programs than of their expansion.

Second, unemployment has led to a reevaluation of the sources of employment. For some time the unexamined belief has been that large and modern industries and firms furnished the bulk of jobs. Increasingly, it is clear that medium-sized and small firms provided the majority of employment opportunities. In some nations these smaller enterprises have been the growth centers, constituting a major

absorber of the increased labor supply. Indeed, in Britain, this recognition has led to the enshrinement of the small businessperson, "the entrepreneur," as a major hope for economic recovery and employment expansion.

Great importance has been assigned to the "discovery" that an informal economy resides alongside the mainstream economy of easily identified large and medium-sized firms. "Informal economy" is an exceedingly elastic term with many synonyms and connotations: irregular economy, black economy, gray economy, off-the-books economy, penny capitalism, dual economy, illegal economy. Sometimes it refers to illegal evasion of taxes by large and small enterprisers engaged in legitimate business activities; sometimes, it refers to the income and evaded taxes of illegal enterprises. Often, it refers to under-reported wage income and "home work," the domestic putting-out system of yore. Legal operations also have this label as in the case of smaller enterprises, the household economy—particularly the unpaid household labor of women—self-help cooperatives, voluntary activities, or exchanges of labor (reciprocity) and goods (barter) without the exchange of money.

It is not clear whether informal activities have grown or are newly discovered. That part of the informal economy that refers to tax evasion has certainly grown as have purely illegal activities. But the other parts of what are sometimes lumped under the informal-economy rubric may not have grown; they are only receiving attention after neglect.

As presently used, "informal economy" carries too much freight to do much analytical good except to point out that official measures of national and individual production, income, and wealth are grossly inadequate, at times misleading. If one could legislate usage, the term might be restricted to legal activities like small businesses, household labor, home work, volunteerism, and the like, even if some tax evasion occurs. Basically illegal activities would have another term, like "illegal economy."

One result of the renewed interest in the informal economy is to stress the level and possibilities of legal employment and the desirability of some of the flexible arrangements (reciprocity, cooperative behavior) and processes (self-help, mutual aid) involved in it. In some nations the informal economy is complacently regarded as improving the well-being of many who are officially designated as unemployed or poor; therefore, these economic and social problems are deemed to be less severe than they appear.

For many who think in terms of a new welfare state with greater choices, autonomy, and cooperativeness, the informal economy is an important avenue of experimentation and modeling for flexibility, self-help, and solidarity. For some with this viewpoint, it is the arena in which a new type of economy and society can be constructed on a smaller scale with less bureaucracy and more self-determination.

In a period of intense internationalization of trade and spread of new and expensive technologies, the amount and kind of employment that can be provided by smaller enterprises may be limited. On the other hand, at least half of the great expansion of U.S. employment in the '70s and '80s is attributed to small enterprises largely in service fields; the negative side of this expansion is that much of it is low-paid with low fringe benefits and non-career-ladder jobs. While frequently providing the flexibility of part-time employment, they do not offer much income support.

Third, irregular employment patterns are becoming more frequent, especially for households. Instead of the expansion of full-time jobs with security of employment and rising real wages and fringe benefits, which would be accompanied by a labor force attached to a particular firm, unemployment, reduced hours of work, or part-time jobs are a frequent expe-

rience of many workers. Good jobs have become less good as labor market regulations are curtailed or softened by government. Low-wage jobs have grown, real wages are frequently threatened, and protection against layoff—a great gain of the European postwar era—is eroding as the Western European labor force is being made more "flexible" and "adaptable." This process is occurring rapidly and will have important negative effects on unions, wages, and the welfare state. Slow or no real wage improvement impinges on the welfare state because revenues fail to keep up with growing needs.

The great hopes for European employment, according to their respective enthusiasts, seem to rest in high-technology or informal-sector activities. While certainly high-tech jobs (which have many definitions, yielding very different estimates of employment effects) have grown, they have made only a minor contribution to the great job spurt in the United States. How much high-tech growth can offer in terms of European employment is uncertain as competition grows. Similarly, estimates of employment in the informal-economy sectors are very uncertain. Even if prospects for expansion are great, these jobs do not offer high security or income.

The European employment discussions are dominated by hard-nosed neoclassical economists espousing high unemployment, lower wages and fringe benefits, and welfare state programs. Opposing viewpoints are scarce and fail to present an attractive, realistic-appearing alternative.

Fourth, this jagged pattern of unemployment, low wages, and job shifts is particularly common among particular groups who have become an increasingly significant part of the European (and American) labor force: women, youth, and immigrants. Much of new social policy is oriented to dealing in some way with the fears arising from widespread and prolonged youth unemployment. To a lesser extent, the problems of female-headed families and immigrants have also received attention.

Fifth, the welfare state is becoming economized in two senses: one is to reduce welfare state expenditures, seeking economies by not maintaining cash benefits in real terms and contracting the level of services or demanding some payment for services (medical care is the main area for such efforts). The other effort is to enforce economic criteria and conceptualizations in decisions about the organization and benefit level of benefits and services. Of special concern are the level and duration of unemployment benefits as providing a disincentive to accept employment at lower than previously attained wages. (In the United States, Aid to Families with Dependent Children (AFDC) is sometimes seen as offering higher income than minimum-pay jobs, thereby discouraging female heads of households from moving off welfare rolls to these jobs. "It pays not to work" is the assertion.)

Sixth, social programs are increasingly used to deal with unemployment or, at least, to reduce official unemployment rates. One way is to reduce competition for employment by drawing older workers out of the labor market by providing early retirement and disability benefits through the Social Security system. (The Netherlands is spending great sums on such programs.)

Also widespread are efforts to promote youth employment by setting up temporary work programs administered, usually, by nongovernmental organizations. In Italy, transfer payments ("cassaintegrazione") are used to supplement the income of workers whose weekly hours of employment have been reduced. In France, the estimate is that 40 percent of unemployed youth are in such programs; the British counterpart, though smaller, is still substantial. Also, in Britain, unemployed workers who start an enterprise

may continue to receive their unemployment benefits for a year.

The notion of "autonomous social policy," which is independent of and offsetting to some extent market outcomes, is overturned, and the possibilities of using social programs as part of a transformational agenda are much reduced. Instead, social policy is becoming a micro-employment policy as transfers are used to promote employment, not to maintain income for those who have suffered in the labor market.

This tendency to use social policy as a micro-employment policy has some positive effects, but it is part of the increasing push to make all things subservient to economic pressures. That tendency would not seem to aid efforts to deepen and expand welfare state benefits and challenge the supremacy of the narrow economic calculus.

One issue is how effective these micro-employment policies will be; their possibilities seem oversold. Another question is whether they will become a substitute for economic policies that deal with more basic, structural realignments; a third is what will happen to the transfer benefits of those who are not in the labor market or who fail to attain employment through the micro-employment programs.

Seventh, feminist critiques of the welfare state have made clear the extent to which the welfare state provides services to women and through them to their children and the continuing importance of women's (unpaid) activities in the overall welfare functions of society. The welfare state performs, then, only an important slice of societal welfare activities that still mainly occur within the family. Welfare state programs in many nations also provide many of the better (professional and semiprofessional) jobs that women hold.

The welfare state is thus largely about women. But that understanding has not shaped the discourse about the welfare state.

One important implication is that shifts in welfare state activities have to be viewed particularly in terms of their impact upon women. For example, decreasing the role of formal governmental welfare agencies is likely to mean increasing the burdens on women, while diminishing the number of good jobs available to them.

Reshaping welfare state services and benefits so that they are more useful to women, especially those with children and without a spouse, is a major need. A major difficulty here is that welfare state benefits are tied in many countries to labor-market status. Fewer women are in the labor market than men (although their numbers are rapidly increasing), and they receive lower wages, which affect benefit levels. The result is that women tend to get inferior benefits, especially when there is not a male breadwinner in the household. The growth of female-headed families and the pressures toward increasing means-testing of programs are likely to result in more women using welfare state programs but receiving meager benefits from them.

The rethinking of the welfare state in terms of women has not proceeded effectively in Europe or the United States. Trade unions as well as governments and political parties have been slow to adjust to the changing labor force and welfare state. Changing labor markets and demography disturb and challenge welfare states.

Eighth, the post-World War II political consensus around the achievability of full employment and the continuing expansion of the welfare state no longer exists in many nations. In some, the size, scope, performance, and financing of the welfare state are important political questions. Welfare state policies have shifted from relatively easy acceptance of expansion to criticism, reform or change, retrenchment, and privatization.

The welfare state is not simply "evolving" as the population ages. It is assigned new roles, undermined by economic difficulties, and made into a political issue. Partisan political considerations will affect it to a greater extent than in the '60s. In short, the welfare state is politicized in new and deeper ways, particularly in the rise of political groups opposing its size, cost, and performance. This situation pushes the discourse about the welfare state from an analytical-policy framework to a political-economic one.

Surprisingly, the welfare state appeared more politically durable and attractive in the middle '80s than seemed to be the case at the beginning of the decade, when many pundits described or foresaw "the crisis of the welfare state": economic constriction and escalating costs (especially in medical programs) would threaten the economics and politics of welfare state funding. The economic crisis in Western Europe and the criticism of the welfare state in many countries, e.g., Italy, seemed to make reductions politically inexpensive. That expectation was wrong.

The welfare state has many critics, but that has not meant that people do not recognize its value. Apparently, the near-universality of programs and the variety of household needs met by the welfare state have maintained or garnered support of social programs. Also, continuing high levels of unemployment have not prevented national economies from experiencing some positive growth. The post-'73 "economic crisis" may not be over, but it is not as severe as feared (at least for households with employed members). Many national economies are in a "recovery" stage. But a deep recession could reduce welfare state support.*

The durability of the welfare state has been an agreeable surprise. If the crisis worsens, there may be stronger pressure to reduce social welfare expenditures and wages. But the support for the welfare state may resurge in those circumstances.

Obviously, it is misleading to speak of the

European welfare state; there are many European welfare states. Particularly striking has been the range of responses to current pressures for change. Across-the-board cutting has not prevailed; new programs have been added with characteristics that differentiate nations even where they have a common purpose like alleviating youth unemployment.

COMPETING GOALS AND MODELS

Questions about goals, as well as effects, are also reshaping the way that the welfare state is thought about. Those who espouse some form of privatization usually advocate greater choice for citizen-consumers of social programs as a prime need; others decry the bureaucratic and alienating character of public programs and call for the promotion of social integration as the major objective. Still others want to promote independent, autonomous initiative and see self-help and self-direction playing the central role. Democratic control of services by its users compels the devotion of others. These competing goals and models can be categorized as: defend and change, participation and economic transformation, social integration, and privatization.

Defend and Change

Because of attacks on the welfare state, many once-critical supporters have become uncritical defenders of it. But few want to maintain or restore the welfare state exactly as it was. Unfortunately, a careful elucidation of what is to be defended or changed has not emerged.

This uncertainty is not surprising since critical supporters fear that negative comments will be misused to attack the fundamentals of the welfare state. But that worry is not the only reason for slow movement along the defend-and-change channel.

A major reason for this hesitation is that the sources of resistance to change are diverse and deep. The staff of the welfare state agencies are frequently reluctant to change, fearing reductions in employment, shifts in routines, and diminution of professional control. Recipients or clients worry about reductions in benefit eligibility and levels and in provision of services. Finance ministries are sometimes fearful of changes that do not directly reduce costs; often, a change in a program has the opposite effect. Indeed, to win better coordination and acceptance of changes frequently requires increasing expenditures.

The basic issue, of course, is what is to be changed and what is to be defended? The questions are about cost and effectiveness, organization and performance, allocation and finance. Cost and effectiveness are troublesome issues. Should some programs be reduced or eliminated because they have limited effectiveness or yield little benefit in relation to their costs? Or can they be changed to improve their effectiveness and benefit-cost ratio? Underlying these issues is the difficulty in defining, estimating, and measuring effectiveness. Furthermore, should the impact of changes and the possibilities of measuring or reducing long-run political support be factored into the economics of cost-effectiveness calculations?

The operations of the welfare state are criticized as bureaucratic, alienating, disempowering, inflexible, and providing low-quality services. The frequent call is for more participation by clients and less unnecessary professionalism, red tape, and control, more local control by service recipients, providing incentives for higher quality services or to induce recipients to find employment.

Allocational decisions involve such issues as providing cash payments that can be spent as the recipient desires or non-cash, in-kind services that limit choices; or relative expenditures on medical care or education, or on programs for the young or for the elderly. (The generational issue is likely to swell into an important political issue in the United States.

In Europe, the belief is that both young and old should be helped and that they should not be put into competition for governmental benefits.) Finance concerns the source of revenues for the welfare state—through pinpointed taxes or general revenues, through national or local taxation, through user charges or free services. The type of financing affects political support for programs.

A political base has to be built to make the important changes involved in these sets of questions and challenges. Can welfare state staff and beneficiaries be brought together early to forge joint programs of change? Can the broader public be better informed about the need to both defend and change? So far the answer seems to be no to both questions.

Obviously, it has been easier to defend than to advocate defend and change. But changes, e.g., tightening of eligibility criteria, unwelcome to the defenders of the welfare state are taking place even where the defenders seem to have been successful. Can the defenders take the initiative for pursuing positive directions of changes rather than responding to the pressures of the critics? This is likely only if they believe that the best defense of the welfare state requires changing it to meet old problems and new desires, especially for empowerment.

Participation and Economic Transformation

Stimulated by the left movements of the sixties, some critics of the welfare state call for much greater participation of clients-recipients-beneficiaries in the welfare state. They call for local-neighborhood control and empowerment themes, more emphasis on self-help in usually professionalized medical, social work, and economic development activities. Supported in part by some conservative critics

of the welfare state, this is a value-oriented, perhaps populist, agenda.

Another starting point has been the analysis that argues from the assumption that full employment will not occur again in late capitalist nations (a perspective notably found in West Germany). Even reductions in the normal work week or early retirements, it is asserted, will not overcome grave unemployment problems. Since national (macro) economic policies will be only limitedly effective, the scope for local (micro) activities should be enlarged.

The participatory adherents have to accept that not all welfare state functions, e.g., pension programs, can be turned over to localities. And that funding for programs, especially in lower-income areas, requires taxation on a broader basis. Who pays the piper will always influence the conduct of programs.

Despite its democratic focus, localism has problems. It can create inequalities as some communities do much better than others. Those with high resources of physical and human capital are likely to gain more than those with low levels of these resources. Nonlocal government will have to play an equalizing role as well as assuring that localities do not discriminate against particular groups such as minorities.

Nor is localism an effective answer to all ills, as some localists imply. Localism can mean xenophobia, parochialism, autocracy, manipulation, segregation, and narrowness. How localism is done is important—which again means that some controls need to be lodged outside the locality and that ways of building democracy and tolerance be enforced.

Localism is likely to be used by retrenchers as a way of reducing welfare state expenditures. Rather than providing funding to promote participation and empowerment, conservative populism aims to reduce public spending on general welfare. "Individuals can do it" becomes a substitute for "government funds are needed for an effective welfare program."

The desirability of self-help and allied activities is high but not unalloyed. The fear is that increasing reliance on self-help, family, volunteerism, and community rather than national or city governmental agencies means more work for women. In practice, decreasing the governmental role in welfare functions is likely to increase the already heavy burdens borne by women. Studies point to little increase in male involvement in the basic welfare functions of the family, even in the two-earner family.

These doubts about the participation and empowerment approach are not arguments against them as goals. The issue is how they are carried through. Indeed, those who want to defend the welfare state need to adopt many of the objectives of the empowerment adherents.

The transformationalists go further than those advocating participation and empowerment. They are determinist in approach and regard the capitalist economic system as requiring a drastic change if decent jobs are to evolve and all are to have an adequate standard of living.

Many new jobs are low-wage and boring, nor are old jobs desirable in terms of wage satisfaction. People should not be forced by income pressures to take such jobs. The need is for a broad political coalition that will seek a transformational agenda to reduce the nexus between employment and income. This rupture can be accomplished by a vast expansion of the cash-transfer system of the welfare state and more self-help and voluntary activities. Paid work will absorb less of the hours of people's lives and be less important in attaining the household's standard of living, which in any case will be redefined in more qualitative terms. Current difficulties are not regarded as a phase of the economic cycle but as a dramatic

change in late capitalism to a condition thought of as "post-industrial."

Unemployment, poor jobs, and low wages will be rife unless the transfer system is greatly expanded. This transfer expansion would push up the wage levels of jobs for individuals who would now have the option to receive public transfers rather than take low-wage jobs. The number of poor jobs will decline as they are unable to meet the rising expectations about wage levels; workers will have an alternative—public transfers—to low wages. This is desirable because workers should not be subsidizing employers by working for substandard wages. The link between employment and income will be broken. A transformation in the nature of society is envisaged: work will be less significant for people in terms of time, standard of living, and self-image; the creativity of leisure or non-paid time would become more significant for self-actualization.

These are indeed bold objectives, involving more transformational aims than other approaches to reforming and reorienting the welfare state and welfare functions. What questions does the transformational agenda face?

In 1945 if someone had prognosticated that the next 25 years in Western Europe would see full employment and rapidly expanding and deeply significant welfare states, great restrictions on employers' rights to fire or lay off workers, enormous gains in the real income of working classes, an opening of higher education to those of lower-income families, reductions in the normal work week—that economist or social analyst would have been characterized as delusional. Or, to move to the Far East, if that economist had predicted that Japan would become a high-quality, high-value-added producer and the new nations like Taiwan, South Korea, or Singapore would become "newly-industrializing countries" and effectively compete with the high-capitalist nations in the production and sale of mass production and high-technology goods, he would have seemed a prophet not deserving of honor anywhere.

True, this is a glossy picture of what occurred in the post-war period but it should lead to hesitation about predictions in general and in particular to those insisting on late capitalism's inability to adapt to changing conditions. Certainly, the United States has experienced great job growth and not all in low-wage jobs.

Without political pressure, capitalist nations will try to have high levels of unemployment as a way of making wage rates and work conditions more flexible. It is dangerous, in my opinion, to accept high unemployment levels as inevitable and not fight to reduce them. The result will be higher unemployment rates than would have occurred in the absence of struggle against them.

Even if the transformationalists are right about the low possibility of "real full employment," the economic-political-social psychological differences between a 9 percent and 5 percent unemployment rate are exceedingly important. At 9 percent, unions are weaker, wage rates, working hours and incomes are down, conservative economic policies are likely to be ascendant in today's intense international competitiveness, low tax revenues lead to pressures to contract the welfare state, and the already bad situation of many youths would worsen.

If real full employment is unlikely, we do not want to make high-level unemployment economically and politically feasible. If Barbara Wooton is right in her conclusion that full employment did more for working classes than did the welfare state, the future looks bleak unless full employment or something akin to it can be reachieved.

A strong and more expensive welfare state in the absence of an expanding economy is hard to picture, both economically and politically. If unemployment rates were high, as transformationalists expect, then funding for livable welfare state benefits would be threatened. If national income is not increasing rapidly, then tax rates would have to increase in order to cover increased cash transfers of the welfare state.

Perhaps the great productivity and value-added production believed to be associated with the post-industrial state would advance national income, but then the political obstacle would be garnering part of the rising incomes of some so that the state could support adequately others who are not working. It is difficult to imagine today the source of the solidaristic feelings that would promote such a political development.

New forms of stratification would likely emerge between those whose employment yields much of their command over resources and those whose resource command comes primarily from governmental transfer programs. The former are likely to do better as lines of cleavage between the two grow, especially if general economic conditions are bad, as the transformationalists expect.

The transformational agenda envisions a profound change in the way individuals are viewed and valued, a change that is difficult to see coming about through the device of expanding transfer benefits. I value decommodification, taking many goods and services out of the market, autonomy, reduction of work hours, solidarity, making command over resources less tied to work, and increasing equality. But can cash nexus be enduringly cut by expanded transfers? While embracing the transformational goals, I do not see the political, economic, or socio-psychological basis for those goals.

Can the goals be achieved partially through reforms of the welfare state that do not veer towards the dramatic change envisaged by the transformationalists? The localists/autonomy/ self-help groups seem to believe so as do some of the defend-and-changers.

The transformationalists may be right in their doubts about what can be achieved by these reformers; on the other hand, transformationalists' apparent acceptance of high unemployment rates as givens would make these rates more likely, an outcome that would undercut the welfare state, as spending exceeded what is politically feasible as revenues.

Three observations about the transformationalists' approach intrigue me. One is the assumption that under conditions of high unemployment and international competition great redistributive gains can be won, that the economic difficulties facing nations produce a propitious time for profound transformations. This might be feasible if part of the economy is doing so well that it can lose substantial income to lagging parts and maintain its effectiveness. Is it likely that prosperous sectors of the economy would generate sufficient income to make a substantial difference? Is the assumption that international trade need not be very important and that the domestic economy could be self-generating and expanding? The present moment of "crisis" appears a very unfavorable time for making positive and sweeping social changes. Activities are becoming increasingly economized, rather than less as is emphasized in the transformationalist outlook.

Another question is why the transformationalists have emerged and are strongest in West Germany, for that country has by far the largest percentage of its labor force in traditional industrial production of any advanced industrial nation. Whatever "post-industrial" means, it certainly is not pointing to traditional industrial activity.

The contrast between West Germany's industrial present and putative post-industrial future leads to my final observation that there is a danger of self-deception if we are not careful in delineating between our desires for the future and our analyses and predictions of what is likely to occur. Self-deception is a parent of political failure.

The Social Integration Approach

This approach has important similarities with the localistic model but differs in its emphasis on social integration as the important principle for restructuring the welfare state. The present welfare state is seen as contributing to the sense of social isolation, excessive individualism, atomism and anomie, which is said to prevail in many societies. The objective is to change the system of social welfare so that it becomes part of the solution to the overall problem of social fragmentation rather than an important contributor to it.

Changes in the welfare state are deemed necessary at the policy level as well as at the organizational level. In policy, the need is to strengthen family activities and encourage the stability of families, thereby avoiding female-headed households, by providing policy incentives to stay together. Some adherents might advocate policies that reduce the pressure for women to work by improving family and children's allowances. Community-help and mutual aid activities are to be encouraged.

At the organization level, the intention is to move from government-centered social programs to non-governmental, non-profit agencies that would carry out social policies that are framed and financed by legislation. These non-profit agencies would be locally based and would be free of what are regarded as the bureaucratic and alienating effects of governmental organizations. They would strive to promote a sense of closeness and sharing. Fewer professionals and civil servants would be employed as volunteers and neighbors became more important in providing services and assistance.

Religious organizations might be the agencies providing services. In Ireland, they do provide many social and educational services; in Italy, some important intellectuals pursue the objective of widening the role of religious agencies by providing them with government funds to provide services that governmental agencies had provided. The government would discontinue certain services and give the funds involved to religious organizations who would then establish these services.

In many countries, welfare state programs are not exclusively, or even mainly, provided by governmental agencies. What Martin Rein calls "the public-private mix" is very extensive and significant. The social integrationists, then, are calling for a much more dramatic shift to an already prominent non-governmental sector. On the other hand, the social integrationists, while calling for strong support for voluntarism, do not advocate the grassroots, informal, uncentralized form that is advocated by those seeking participation and localism. The social integrationists seek an institutionalized voluntary sector based on a national organization or organizations, while the participation-minded desire a non-institutionalized, locality-controlled development.

The social integration approach faces some important issues. Some see it as having a traditional orientation that would be coercive and burdensome to women. They fear that women will be pushed back toward more traditional, less liberating roles and will be forced to spend more time in welfare activities. Voluntarism, in this view, usually means more work and responsibilities for women.

The organizations that would administer the social integrationalist programs are unlikely to be democratically run: neither beneficiaries, staff, or volunteers would have an important part in decisions. As private non-profit agencies, the voluntary organizations would not accord rights to those they serve as governmentally-administered programs do. Creaming and inequality would likely grow. Some of the difficulties might be checked by strong monitoring and accountability administered by governmental agencies. How effective this policing activity could be—especially where the private agency is politically strong—is uncertain.

The personalism that is an appealing quality of the social integrationist approach has problems. In some circumstances anonymity, impersonality, and bureaucracy have advantages in preserving privacy and dignity. People needing aid may not want friends and neighbors to know their plight. Where one cannot reciprocate and mutual aid is one-sided, a sense of becoming a beneficiary of "charity" may emerge and be harmful.

Whatever difficulties the social integrationist approach faces, it is raising a crucial question about the objectives of the welfare state. Its ambition is that the welfare function to encourage a feeling of national cohesion, integration, community and mutuality, a concern for "the other," "the stranger." The social integrationists see the only possibility for this moral vision to occur if the welfare state becomes less governmentally-centered.

Privatization

Privatization is heralded as an alternative to governmental programs. Like "informal sector," privatization is a broad, ambiguous term.

The general theme is to move to market relationships. Rather than governmentally-provided services, individuals would purchase current government social services in "the market" where private firms would compete in attracting customers. Poorer individuals and households would be enabled to choose among private services by governmental cash grants or vouchers that would be earmarked for purchase of specific services, as in the case of educational vouchers or food stamps. Better-off individuals would be able to choose and pay for these services because their Social Security and like taxes would be reduced.

In another form of privatization, government would purchase services from private firms rather than providing them itself as it once did. The competition of private market firms in the social welfare field, it is asserted, would reduce costs and promote efficiency; it would also assure better treatment of the users of the service because they would be customers, not clients, who could move their business elsewhere. The social control element in governmental-controlled and provided services would be eliminated.

The proponents of privatization seek efficiency, less governmental expenditures, and increased choice through market competition. They differ among themselves in the weights attached to these different goals. They are united in regarding the governmentally-based welfare state as inefficient because of its monopoly state and what they see as inevitable bureaucratic structuring. Current difficult economic times, in this view, call for reduced public expenditures to lower taxes and for lower social benefits so that they do not support wage levels and disincentives to hard work, conditions that are harmful to a nation's competitive position in the world economy.

On the negative side, would consumer-clients have adequate knowledge to make choices? Would they be well-enough organized to exert political pressure to improve or change services? The sorry condition in the United States of private nursing homes, paid for out of public funds under Medicare and Medicaid programs, does not offer high hopes for the cash nexus leading to a high degree of care and concern.

The elimination or reduction of state provisioning is likely to lead to greater inequalities as those with more private funds can purchase services not available to those with meager governmental vouchers or cash benefits. The business organizations providing social services are likely to cream. The aim of reducing governmental social welfare expenditures is likely to harm the scope and quality of services available to lower-income individuals. Greater "choice" does not necessarily result in more equality, adequacy, and concern.

WHAT MIX?

The myth of the government welfare state dies hard. Despite Richard Titmuss's emphasis on the importance of fiscal and occupational benefits, despite the variety of household, self-help, and mutual aid activities, despite the importance of non-governmental organizations in providing social welfare aid with or without governmental funding, and despite the sale of medical care, the belief still seems to persist that governmental activity encompasses the welfare functions. True, new ideas about organization and structure are loose on both sides of the Atlantic, but the basic theorizing still seems to focus on the state in welfare activities.

What we see in the four models are adaptations or recommended adaptations to changing economic circumstances and life-styles. Not only does the welfare state have many critics; they want to move it in very different ways. Some of these objectives might be reconciled with each other but others (e.g., private markets and social integration) are not easily brought together.

One result is that "experimentation" and "innovation" are becoming fashionable terms in social welfare in Europe as they have long been in the United States. A number of countries permit, perhaps encourage, small-scale experimenting with different ways of conducting social programs. Even in the large, well-established Swedish welfare state, flexibility and adaptability are evident. A group can take over the operation of social programs in small geographic areas or take responsibility for local economic development. In Social Democratic Bremen and Christian Democratic West Berlin, the city-state governments provide funds for local groups to initiate new activities. In many nations small-scale projects are permitted that deviate markedly from the national model.

As is frequent with social innovation, the issue is whether the experiment is a forerunner of broad policy changes or becomes encapsulated, restricted to a narrow slice of the policy arena and gradually declines in significance as it placates critics of mainstream policies.

Judging from the American experience, experiments run the danger of encapsulation and fragmentation: they are not planting a flag and exercising sovereignty over a sector of social policy; they need to spread and root if they are to occupy a policy territory. If not, the main sectors of social policy may continue with little change, while those who seek transformational change will busy themselves with approach roads while the highways of social programs continue largely as before. The U.S. policy landscape is littered with experiments that became approach roads to nowhere.

Looked at more positively, experimentation can indicate the recognition of the need to change. In that sense, experimentation can lead to new mixes that are significant. Whether the desire for change can outmatch the pressures for contracting welfare state expenditures is the main issue. The experiments may be flowers that singly break through the concrete of fiscal conservatism, but they may not produce a garden.

Organizational structure is not seen as a given in the four approaches. The general orientation is to reduce the organizational role of the formal governmental structures or, at least, decentralize to smaller governmental units as repositories of authority and service provision. Despite the differences in the four approaches,

some common threads seem to emerge: more participation, local control, flexibility, mutual aid, and voluntarism. Significant differences appear in the locus of authority and organization sought by the four approaches.

The main issue lies, however, not in differences about organizational loci but in the values that are regarded as central. In the defend and change model, equality and lessened stratification accompany adequacy as dominant goals with decentralization and participation becoming more important than before. The transformationists prize autonomy and self-development. The social integrationists focus on the links among individuals, while those seeking privatization are most concerned about reducing costs and increasing choices through greater reliance on private markets.

These are quite different sets of agendas. They seem difficult to reconcile despite some overlap. Obviously, political strength will determine which road will be followed.

Surprisingly, none of the goals or models is primarily oriented to the specific interests of the new groups that require special attention today: immigrants, youth, female-headed households. Since these groups are now the most likely to receive any new, flexible funds, they would seem to be the sectors in which change might be easiest to structure. In practice, however, a major way that the differences in outlook is being played out is in the definition of what is the central group to help today: the traditional family, the female-headed family, unemployed youth, the unemployed, immigrants, the marginalized, traditional proletarians, the elderly, or cultural and countercultural opt-outs. The choice is made in the context of strong pressures to reduce welfare state spending.

For an American it is heartening to learn about the variety of new ideas and approaches that are debated in Europe, because in the United States the policy arena lacks imagination. The discussion veers largely between disturbing contraction and uncritical defense of the welfare state as it was.

The Western European nations that pioneered the diverse welfare states may again point the ways in which it should be changed. Clearly, welfare states are being changed; the issue is how? Today's welfare states are vastly different from what existed in 1945, and the next 20 years will see significant changes. That is what is debated in Western Europe and largely ignored or mystified in the United States.

Note

* The inroads into welfare state aid for female headed families in the United Kingdom have been drastic and disheartening even though Prime Minister Thatcher has been unable to reduce the percentage of GNP devoted to social programs. While some important programs have been reduced or terminated, the costs of unemployment benefits have risen because of the continuing high level of unemployment. Apparent stability in terms of spending masks harshness in policy.

DISCUSSION QUESTIONS

1. Describe the welfare models derived from European experience.
2. Do you believe that welfare policies based on localism and grass-roots participation will work in the United States?
3. What are the advantages and disadvantages of "privatizing" governmental programs?

CHAPTER 6

Issues in Race and Ethnicity

INTRODUCTION

What are some of the causes of prejudice? What can be done about discrimination? Why are certain groups stereotyped unfavorably? These and other questions trouble social scientists as well as members of societies throughout the world. Favorable resolution of the problems that cause such questions to arise could improve the quality of life for millions of people. Failure to find answers to such questions could cause current social problems to become even more severe.

In the United States, blacks and Hispanics in particular have experienced oppression and the denial of equal opportunities. Though their lives have improved markedly in the past two decades, there is still much room for improvement, as even a quick trip through America's slums indicates. Nor is the problem of prejudice confined to the United States. In Great Britain, for example, conflict exists between Protestants and Catholics and between Asians, people from the West Indies, and white Britons. Throughout Africa, in countries such as Nigeria, Rwanda, and Uganda, tribal conflicts have often led to serious problems. In the Middle East, Arabs and Jews face a similar dilemma.

Sometimes the problem can be traced to different outlooks and lifestyles. In other instances, economic inequalities are among the most prominent issues. Whatever the case, developing a deeper understanding of other groups' cultures can lead to an easing of tensions. While it may not be possible to compel people to literally "switch places" with others whose backgrounds differ sharply from their own, we can at least provide them with opportunities to learn about each other.

That is the purpose of the essays in this chapter. The reading on the cultural level of analysis, by William B. Helmreich, focuses on a concept that is basic to the literature on prejudice and discrimination—stereotypes. While stereotypes, which are basically exaggerations of existing traits, may not cause prejudice, they often justify and reinforce it. Thus, if a group of people have an unfavorable opinion of blacks, the notion that blacks are stupid or lazy can become widely accepted and increase prejudice against them. Such a notion can also be used as a rationalization to explain existing prejudiced attitudes toward blacks.

In his study of over ninety stereotypes, Helmreich found about one-third of them to be more or less accurate and traced them back to the particular culture of the group. Given the relationship between prejudice and stereotypes, the stereotypes that were borne out by the study tended to be positive, while the ones that were found to be inaccurate tended to be negative. What is important is to evaluate each stereotype on its own merit in terms of its orgins and validity, whether it be that Jews are shrewd in business, Hispanics are emotional, or blacks are gifted in music.

That blacks are seen negatively by many whites is, more than anything else, a reflection of the depths of racism in this country. The negative stereotypes are often directed toward group members who are poor and uneducated. It is, therefore, crucial that the world in which poor blacks live be presented in an unbiased and informative manner.

Elijah Anderson, in his book *A Place on the Corner*, has done just that. The selection presented here from the individual level of analysis focuses on status and how black ghetto dwellers achieve it. Most Americans who pass through ghetto areas, either on foot or in a car or bus, tend to see them as threatening places. They do their best to ignore the inhabitants, and they view the men lounging on the streets as failures and criminals and, sometimes less than human. Through Anderson's writings we enter a bar in a ghetto community and meet some of its individual members. His descriptions broaden and enrich our understanding of what is important to the men who frequent the bar and why it is important to them. We learn how they look at outsiders and how they create the social living space necessary for survival. Participant observation is one of the classic approaches in sociological research. Anderson, a gifted field worker, shows us how he established contact and developed rapport with the men. We come to see them as individuals who have aspirations, who want to be respected, and who have feelings just as the rest of us do. Most of all, the excerpt clearly demonstrates the complexity and diversity of this community.

It is sometimes useful to examine race relations in other societies in order to better understand our own problems and prospects. South Africa has become synonymous with racism and oppression in the minds of most Americans. President Frederik W. de Klerk's decision to relax some restrictions on blacks and the release of Nelson Mandela from twenty-seven years of confinement has given rise to optimism about social changes in that country. Sociologists have written a great deal about the causes of social movements and how they come into being, as well as their likelihood of success given a certain set of circumstances. Many of the conditions cited by these sociologists already exist in South Africa, including a liberal movement for change among some whites, precipitating incidents, growth of a generalized belief system, genuine conditions of oppression, and leaders and masses whose level of consciousness has been raised. The question is, how will these factors coalesce and interact with each other?

In the cross-cultural reading on race, Pauline Baker examines some recent events in South Africa and concludes that movement to a future multiparty, nonracial democracy is possible. However, she finds that "the legacy of apartheid, the scars of violence and the polarization of society have left their mark."

The Things They Say Behind Your Back: Stereotypes and the Myths Behind Them

William B. Helmreich

Everyone knows that most Italians either belong to the Mafia or have a relative who does. And of course they're great shoemakers and tailors, though they tend to gamble too much.

"Do you know that the first present the new Pope got was a pair of slippers with gold initials inside them that said T.G.I.F. Now you know what that stands for. Right?"

"Sure. It stands for Thank God It's Friday. We say it every week at the office."

"Wrong. It means Toes Go In First. You know how those Polacks are."

The problem with this country is that the Jews control everything. They run the TV stations, movies, newspapers, and whatever else they can get their grubby hands on. Worst of all, they're cheap and sneaky.

The Blacks think they got everything coming to them. They can't think ahead more than one day. They never come on time when you make an appointment with them. All they wanna do is drink, shoot up, and play the numbers.

Now you take the Japanese. There's a people that are hardworking, smart, and ambitious. But remember—you can never turn your backs on them, for a minute. They're really sly and treacherous. And don't ever talk politics with them. They're so chauvinistic it's ridiculous, even though, you know, they just imitate everything we do.

The well-known journalist and writer Walter Lippmann called "these pictures in our heads" stereotypes. Basically, a stereotype is an exaggerated belief, oversimplification, or uncritical judgement about a category. The category may be a neighborhood, a city, a newspaper, members of a profession, believers in a religion, or even a highway (e.g., "The Long Island Expressway is always packed."). Although stereotypes are most often exaggerations or distortions of reality, they are often accepted by people as fact. When they concern a highway, they do little damage, but when they are used to indict an entire group of people, great harm can be done.

Naturally, not all stereotypes about different nationalities are negative. Some, in fact, are quite complimentary. "The Italians are very family oriented," "the French are great lovers," and "the Chinese are so courteous," are examples of stereotypes that reflect well on various peoples. Nevertheless, they are equally exaggerated generalizations and a person who accepts such statements as factual can easily believe less positive views.

Groups are sometimes responsible for creating, or at least abetting, their own stereotypes. This is especially true when the stereotype is a positive one. Thus, an after-dinner speaker at an Irish affair may begin his speech by saying something like, "As we know, the Irish have always been regarded as good politicians." The Jewish American Princess (JAP) is another case in point. While not a very positive statement about the Jewish people, it has been given a tremendous boost in popularity by Jews themselves, particularly Jewish comedians, who have found it makes great copy.

When people employ stereotypes they are usually making judgments about a given individual's potential to fit into a certain category based upon that person's racial or ethnic origins. In other words, they say that a Pole is more likely to be stupid because he is Polish, an Italian is more apt to talk with his hands because he is Italian, and so forth. Some people even believe such traits to be true of all members of a given group. What needs to be determined is when a statement about a member of a certain group has little basis in fact and when it has a good deal of basis in fact. In short, to what extent is a stereotype based on reality?

Why do we often stereotype people, even when deep down we "know better than that?"

A great deal has been written about this question, with almost as many answers given as there are types of people. Among the most common explanations is that it is simply a very efficient way of coping with our environment, an environment so complex that we have to break it down into categories before we can understand it. It would clearly be impossible for us to function if everything that happened were dealt with on an individual basis. Without stereotypes everything would be treated as if it were taking place for the first time. Thus, stereotypes are convenient though often inaccurate. Frequently they eliminate the need to learn about people for those who simply do not, either because of fear or sheer laziness, wish to make the effort.

Another cause of stereotypes may be the cultural background of the individual. Most cultures encourage prejudiced attitudes toward other groups. These attitudes are ingrained in people beginning with early childhood, and are therefore very difficult to overcome. In general, the longer one has such attitudes, the harder it is to change them. In one study done on this question, a group of whites were shown a photograph of a white person holding a razor blade while arguing with a Black person in a New York City subway. They were shown the photo for a split second and then asked to write down what they saw on a slip of paper. More than half of the respondents said they saw a Black man holding a razor blade against the throat of a white man. Culture is such a strong factor that persons who do not agree with the particular stereotypes will remain silent simply because they "want to be like everyone else."

Quite often people are unable to accept the blame for their own shortcomings, and when this happens they search for convenient targets upon whom they can vent their frustrations. Some of the more typical victims are friends, parents, and others who are "safe" because they won't reject you for such outbursts, providing that it doesn't happen too often. In many cases, however, people select minority group members as scapegoats because they are powerless, relatively speaking, and/or easily identifiable. Thus General Brown talked about "the Jewish lobby," as did Billy Carter, and former Governor George Wallace talked about "Nigras and pointyheads."

Professors Bruno Bettelheim and Morris Janowitz have argued that stereotypes are often caused by a complex process known as projection. When people accuse others of motives or characteristics they sense in themselves but can't admit to openly, it is called projection. Noted psychologist Gordon Allport, in his famous work *The Nature of Prejudice*, notes that in Europe, where there is no large Black population, the Jew is the one accused of unbridled sexual lust, violence, and filth. Americans, having peoples such as Blacks, Puerto Ricans, and Chicanos to personify these traits, find it unnecessary to use Jews for this purpose. As a result, Americans can attribute other, more specialized, traits to Jews, such as defensiveness, aggressiveness, and shrewdness.

Stereotypes also allow us to justify our behavior toward a group that we already dislike or are mistreating. In other words, they enable us to rationalize our actions. An example would be General Westmoreland's comment during the Vietnam War. When asked to justify the napalming of innocent villagers, he replied, "These Asians don't value life the way we do." Further evidence for the use of stereotypes to rationalize behavior comes from the fact that people often assign contradictory stereotypes to members of a group. The writer Harry Golden once said, "The Jew is probably the only person who can be called a communist and a capitalist—by the same person—at the same time."

The media also play a role in stereotypes, though it is more a case of reinforcing rather than creating stereotypes. Certain TV shows portray the Irish, Jews, Blacks, and other groups in a stereotyped manner. The same is true of films, plays, and magazines. Still, the media mainly reflect our pre-existing attitudes as opposed to inventing them.

Do stereotypes actually cause prejudice? Not necessarily. More often they justify prejudice, but in doing so they reinforce prejudice. It is difficult to separate one from the other. If one has a stereotyped view of nationality, it can result in prejudice toward that group, and if one is prejudiced one can either create or find stereotypes justifying one's attitudes. Whatever the case, since stereotypes often guide our behavior, an understanding of them is extremely important.

Knowing the causes of stereotypes is indeed helpful—and there are many books on the subject—but it does not tell us how particular stereotypes developed. Growing up in a certain culture may result in a person having negative views toward, say, Italians, but it does not tell us how that culture acquired these views in the first place. Understanding that people pick on certain groups when they need a scapegoat does not tell us why particular groups are chosen as scapegoats and not others. Why the Jews and not the Danes? Why the Poles and not the Bulgarians? To answer this question, we need to know much more.

Many stereotypes change over time because they are often a function of political, economic, and social developments. For example, American views of the Chinese and Japanese have been linked by researchers to U.S. relations with China and Japan at different times in history. When such relations were good, the stereotypes in this country tended to be positive; when they deteriorated, the stereotypes focused on the negative characteristics.

How have particular groups come to be identified with particular characteristics? Puerto Ricans are not thought of as grasping in a business sense, but Jews are. Blacks are sometimes categorized as lazy and shiftless, but the Chinese are not. We have the fighting Irish, the stupid Poles, the clannish Italians,

the cold and insensitive WASP's. Where did these ideas originate?

Contrary to what many people may think, a large number of stereotypes possess more than a kernel of truth. There is some basis for saying that Jews are adept at business, Blacks musically gifted, and Hispanics emotional. True, the *majority* of stereotypes do not fall into this category, but it is important to know which do, which do not, and why. Regardless of the accuracy of stereotypes, it can be said that all of them stem, in some measure, either from the historical experiences and culture of the group or from the historical experiences and culture of the group of the nations that had contact with the group. To clarify these points let's look at some of the previously mentioned stereotypes in greater depth.

Are Jews better businessmen than others? This is impossible to prove. Yet there is enough evidence present to suggest that they indeed might have an edge in this area. For one thing Jews have been in business for centuries. Forbidden to own land by the Roman Catholic Church and denied entry into the craft guilds during medieval times, Jews were forced to turn to moneylending to survive.

The Jewish religion and, in particular, the Talmud, with its emphasis on abstract thinking, also has played a role. From childhood on, the stress was on sharpening the mind, and when economic opportunities arose the Jew was able to apply his intellectual acumen to that sphere as well. After all, interests, futures, options, stocks, and, most importantly, money itself, were also abstractions. Yet another factor was that lacking a homeland for centuries, never certain when persecution might strike, Jews came to see money as the only means of survival, something with which to buy protection or acquire certain rights.

Are Blacks more musically gifted than others? Certainly music was a central feature of their African heritage, which had hunting songs, drinking songs, work songs, funeral songs, etc. Music was integral to the Black churches founded in this country. It was in them that African exiles were able to fully express themselves as they prayed, rocked, shouted, sang, and danced.

When white society's fascination with Blacks reached unprecedented heights during the Harlem renaissance in the 1920's, music became a way in which Blacks could move up the socio-economic ladder. This meant, of course, that Black parents were more likely to encourage their children as soon as they demonstrated any abilities in this area. Whatever the reasons, probably no other group in the United States has contributed as much to music, song, and dance.

Are Hispanics apt to be warmer and more emotional than members of other groups? There seems to be an almost universal agreement on the validity of this stereotype among professionals and lay people who work with Hispanics. Latin American politics, for example, are known for warmth of personal relationships and are based more on mutual trust than on written agreements. The pattern is similar in business relationships but its clearest expression can be found in the family.

The anthropologist Oscar Lewis often observed that Hispanic families he studied had warm, emotional ties, especially between mother and child. Psychiatrists have pointed out that Hispanic mothers kiss and cuddle infants more than Anglo mothers and remain intensely involved with their children throughout their lives.

Researchers have attributed such behavior to the extended family structure common among Hispanics. As a result, the child learns to regard a greater number of people with warmth and affection. Others note that historically Hispanics have come from societies where the individual was born into a social and economic system that remained fixed throughout his life. They therefore tended to place more importance on personal qualities to make distinctions among those with whom they lived.

At the same time, there are other stereotypes which are, more or less, inaccurate. One example is the stereotype that large numbers of Italians belong to the Mafia, or Cosa Nostra. According to Richard Gambino, a noted authority on the Italian-American community, the Mafia has about 5,000–6,000 members in the United States, a small figure when one considers that there are over twenty million Italian-Americans in the United States. Why then, has the stereotype survived? For one thing, the Mafia makes excellent copy. With its Black Hand symbol, its code of silence, and its unique customs and rituals, it has provided material for countless books, movies, and television programs. As a result, the Mafia has become synonymous with crime of every sort, thus perpetuating the stereotype. Also the fact that virtually all members of the Mafia are of Italian extraction makes it easy for others to exaggerate the entire group's involvement in the organization and this is therefore another contributing factor to the stereotype.

Another type of dubious validity is that of the "sneaky Jap." Most people assume it originated with the surprise attack by the Japanese on Pearl Harbor. In truth Japanese-Americans were already described as sneaky at the turn of the century when a rumor spread that Japan was planning to attack the U.S. from a base in Mexico. Americans in general feared that the Japanese, having defeated the Russians in the Russo-Japanese War, might try to extend their power to the Western Hemisphere.

Americans pointed to the fact that many Japanese-Americans lived in strategically important areas. Therefore, they must be spying for Japan. In truth, they lived there for reasons related to economic conditions and their history. They settled near the railroad because, having laid the tracks for them, they were often paid in the form of land grants along the way. Similarly, Signal Hill had been farmed by the Japanese long before oil was discovered there.

Another explanation for the popularity of this stereotype may be the success of the Japanese-Americans. They have done well in the U.S. as a group and the problem for prejudiced whites was how to account for the success of relatively new immigrants. By accusing them of having used guile and deceit to outwit their competitors, bigots were able to rationalize their own shortcomings. In many cases, the media played up to such charges and were often encouraged to do so by unscrupulous politicians.

Differences in culture have also contributed to the stereotype. This is no one's fault, yet it must be taken into account. For example, the Japanese smile not only when pleased or amused but also when they wish to indicate that a line of inquiry should not be pursued any further. The same smile can also be used to hide shame or anger. Among Americans such misunderstandings are quite common in business dealings between the two groups. "In principle I am all for it," translated from polite Japanese, almost unfailingly means "We have a lot of problems." This is part of a general community pattern of deference and hesitancy in embarrassing others, known by insiders as *enryo*.

To sum up, there is no evidence that the Japanese are more sly and treacherous than the rest of us, although the reasons previously given, plus certain cultural differences, might lead people to think so.

Probably no other stereotype in America has been as common as the one about the "dumb Polack." Do the jokes have basis in fact? The answer is, from a scientific perspective, definitely not. According to Thomas Sowell, who has analyzed data on this questions for The Urban Institute that compared the IQs of Poles to other groups who immigrated to America, their IQs approximate the national average in this country.

Another IQ test of Polish children living in Warsaw, found the average IQ to be about 109—considerably higher than the average score of 100. A study of London's population showed that the average IQ was 102, seven points below that of the much maligned Poles.

Why then do so many people in the U.S. think otherwise? The answer can be partially found in recent history. Polish jokes became popular in the late 1950s and early 1970s precisely the period when the civil rights movement began to emerge. The show "Amos 'n Andy" which had lampooned Blacks came to be seen as highly objectionable as whites were confronted by angry Blacks demonstrating for their rights. Many felt guilt about their own prejudices and hostile about having to face up to them. White America searched for and found new scapegoats in the seemingly innocuous Poles. They had no NAACP to protect them and they had already been described somewhat unflatteringly in Tennessee Williams' classic play, *A Streetcar Named Desire* (Stanley Kowalski.) The fact that Poles were the largest single group of Eastern Europeans also helped solidify them as a stereotype (In this sense the Czechs, Hungarians, Yugoslavians, Rumanians, Slavs, and Ukrainians were just lucky.)

Two recent developments are likely to make this stereotype less popular in the years to come. First, the ascension of John Paul II and his emergence as a strong, forceful, and *intellectual* pope has contributed much to changing the image. Then there is the Solidarity Movement which has enhanced the self-respect of Polish-Americans. In any event, the stereotype itself has no factual basis and is likely to eventually die out.

Bigots will not find much support for their prejudices from the relatively high number of valid stereotypes. This is so because most of the stereotypes for which support can be found are positive and flattering to the group involved, whereas those that seem highly inaccurate tend, by and large, to be negative. It is here that we see the linkage between stereotypes and prejudice most clearly. Stereotypes are used by prejudiced people to rationalize their biases, and it is important to refute them.

Part of the joy, or at least the excitement, of living in this world is learning how and why people think and act the way they do. Creating myths and distortions about a people's history and their culture prevents us from doing so. Moreover, the uniqueness and variety represented by the different nationalities that comprise the American people ought not to be something we are ashamed to speak about. It should be a source of pride. Those aspects of a culture that are negatively perceived by others

cannot, however, be ignored since most people are aware of them anyway, at least on a subjective level. Perhaps by examining their origins we can make people more tolerant and understanding of each other.

DISCUSSION QUESTIONS

1. According to the author's discussion, are stereotypes true or false? Explain your answer.
2. Why do people stereotype? Give two examples from your own community that explain the creation of stereotypes.
3. Is there a connection between stereotypes and prejudice? If so, what types of stereotypes help explain that linkage? If not, what types of stereotypes account for the lack of a linkage?

A Place on the Corner

Elijah Anderson

THE SETTING

Urban taverns and bars, like barbershops, carryouts, and other such establishments, with their adjacent street corners and alleys, serve as important gathering places for people of the "urban villages" and ghetto areas of the city.[1] Often they are special hangouts for the urban poor and working-class people, serving somewhat as more formal social clubs or domestic circles do for the middle and upper classes. The urban poor and working-class people are likely to experience their local taverns as much more than commercial businesses.[2] They provide settings for sociability and places where

neighborhood residents can gain a sense of self-worth. Here people can gather freely, bargaining with their limited resources, their symbols of status, and their personal sense of who and what they are against the resources of their peers and against what their peers see them *really* to be. Here they can sense themselves to be among equals, with an equal chance to be somebody, even to be occasional winners in the competition for social esteem.[3] This is their place. They set the social standards. And when they feel those standards are threatened, they can defend them. Other settings, especially those identified with the wider society, with its strange, impersonal standards and evaluations, are not nearly as important for gaining a sense of personal self-worth as are the settings attended by friends and other neighborhood people.

"Jelly's," the subject of this study, is a bar and liquor store located in a run-down building on the South Side of Chicago. Situated at a corner of a main thoroughfare, Jelly's is a hangout for working and nonworking, neighborhood and nonneighborhood black people, mostly men. They gather at Jelly's at all times of the day and night, and some even sleep on the streets or in the nearby park.

A few doors away from Jelly's is a laundromat; down the street are a dry cleaner, a grocery store, and, farther on, a poolroom. As cars and buses pass, their passengers sometimes gawk at the people of Jelly's. From the safety of their cars, often with rolled-up windows and locked doors, passersby can see wineheads staggering along, a man in tattered clothing "nodding out," leaning on Jelly's front window, and a motley, tough-looking group of men gathered on the corner, sometimes with a rare white man among them. Those on foot hurry past, not wanting to be accosted by the people of Jelly's.

Periodically, the humdrum routine is punctuated with some excitement. An elderly black woman bursts out of Jelly's, clutching her jug of wine and her pocketbook as she hurries along, minding her own business. The group on the sidewalk comes to life as one of the men grabs her purse and yells, "Gimme some o' what you got there, woman!" "I'll geh ya' this fist upside yo' head!" she responds, shaking her fist and confidently moving on about her business. Children play nearby and among the men. They rip and run up and down the street and occasionally stop a man, apparently unmindful of how he looks, to say, "Got a quarter, mister?" The man bends over, puts his hands on his knees, negating any "tough" look he might have had, and begins to kid with the children, teaching them about being "good li'l kids" and giving up a quarter or whatever he can spare. Later that same evening the same man may show his tough side by drawing a switchblade and placing the edge against another man's throat, desperately "threatening" his victim. Blue-and-white police cars cruise by, each with two policemen, one black

and one white. The police glance over and slow down, but they seldom stop and do anything. Ordinarily they casually move on, leaving the street-corner men to settle their own differences.

After being around Jelly's neighborhood for a while and getting to know its people, the outside observer can begin to see that there is order to this social world. For example, the wineheads turn out to be harmless, for they generally do the things people expect them to do: they drink on the street, beg passersby for change, and sometimes stumble up and down the street cursing at others. One also begins to understand that what looks like a fight to the death usually doesn't come near a fatal end. Often such a "fight" turns out to be a full-dress game in which only "best friends" or "cousins" can participate—but at times even they can't play this game without it ending in a real fight. After a while one gets to know that old black woman leaving Jelly's with the "taste" as Mis' Lu, "a nice ol' lady who been 'round here fo' years," and "studs 'round dese here streets'll cut yo' throat 'bout messin' with her. She hope raise half the cats 'round here." Secure in her knowledge of how she is regarded, she walks the streets unafraid, "back-talking" to anyone "messin'" with her.

On these streets near Jelly's, one can't help noticing the sidewalks and gutters littered with tin cans, old newspapers, paper sacks, and whatever. The city does not pay as much attention to this area as many residents would like, but somehow it doesn't really seem to matter to anyone. People go about their business. One storefront has been boarded up for months and wineheads sometimes sleep there. The inset doorway is a perfect place to lie in wait for an unsuspecting holdup or rape victim. Most people who use this general area have come to accept their deteriorated physical world as it is. They simply make the best of it. Many have become so resigned that they would find it extraordinary if someone took an active interest in trying to do something about it—even something as minor as fixing up and painting. This is Jelly's neighborhood.

But once inside Jelly's, people don't have to be concerned with the conditions outside. They become involved as soon as they meet others on the corner, or as soon as they walk through Jelly's door. Somebody is waiting at least to acknowledge their presence, if not to greet them warmly. They come here "to see what's happenin'"—to keep up on the *important* news. They meet their "runnin' buddies" here, and sometimes they commune with others. Inside, or outside on the corner, they joke, argue, fight, and laugh, as issues quickly rise and fall. In this milieu it is time-out and time away from things outside. It's time-in for sharing one's joys, hopes, dreams, troubles, fears, and past triumphs, which are all here and now to be taken up repeatedly with peers whose thoughts about them really matter.

As this short description indicates, there is more to social life in and around Jelly's than might be suggested by a cursory inspection, informed by the stereotypes and prejudices of those not involved. Life here cannot be understood as simple "social disorganization."[4] Nor can one reach a full understanding by viewing social relations here simply as "effortless sociability."[5] When one gets close to the life of Jelly's and develops the necessary meaningful relations with its people, he can begin to understand the social order of this world. People make him aware of the general prescriptions and proscriptions of behavior by somehow fitting him in, including him as they attempt to sort out and come to terms with their minute-to-minute, ordinary everyday social events. Individuals are thus seen acting collectively, interpreting and defining one another; they make distinctions between and among those with whom they share this social space. They are seen fitting themselves in with one another's expectations and collective lines of action, each one informed by a sense of what

actions are allowed and not allowed to different kinds of people in varying sets of circumstances.

THE BARROOM

Jelly's bar and liquor store has two front entrances, one leading to the barroom and the other to the liquor store. Each room has its own distinctive social character. The barroom is a public place; outfitted with bar stools, a marble-topped counter, and mirrors on the wall, it invites almost anyone to come in and promises he will not be bothered as long as he minds his own business. In this sense it is a neutral social area. Yet people who gather on this side of Jelly's tend to be cautiously reserved when approaching others, mainly because on this side they just don't know one another. In contrast, the liquor store is more of a place for peers to hang out and outwardly appears to have a more easygoing, spontaneous ambience.

An open doorway separates the two rooms, and some people gravitate from side to side, the regular clientele usually settling in the liquor store. The social space of the barroom is shared by regular customers and visitors. Sometimes these visitors are people who have been seen around Jelly's but who have yet to commit themselves to the setting. Sometimes they are total strangers. At times there will be as many as twenty visitors present, compared with eight or nine regular customers. Regular customers are interspersed among the visitors, but though the space is shared, they seldom come to know one another well. The visitors tend to arrive, get their drinks, sit at the bar for a while, then leave. The regular clientele, on the other hand, do their best to ignore the visitors; they treat them as interlopers. And there exists a certain amount of distrust and suspicion between the two groups.

Owing to this suspicion and distrust, the barroom is characterized by a somewhat cautious and reserved atmosphere. When strangers accidentally touch or bump one another, the person in the wrong quickly says "'scuse me." On occasions when the "'scuse me" is not forthcoming and further agression seems likely, other precautionary measures may be taken. One night during the early stages of my fieldwork, when I was talking with John, a visitor I had just met, a stranger to both of us seemed drunk and unruly. He tried to enter our conversation. Putting his hand on John's shoulder, he asked "What ya'll drinking'? Lemme' drink wit you!" John tried to ignore the man, but he persisted. Abruptly and firmly John said, "Al'right, now. Man, I don't know you, now! I don't know you." Taking this comment as the warning it was, the stranger cut short his advances. Immediately he sobered and walked away without saying another word. John then looked away from him, rolling his eyes toward the ceiling, and we continued our conversation.

On this side strangers can demand some degree of deference, for people here are usually uncertain of just what the next person has in mind, of what he is capable of doing, and of what actions might provoke him to do it. On the barroom side, people often don't know *who* they're sitting or standing next to. In the right circumstances the next person might show himself to be "the police" or "the baddest cat in Chi." Or he could be waiting to follow somebody home and rip him off. In the words of the regular clientele, unknown people on this side generally "bear watching."

One consequence of the suspicion and distrust on this side is that social relationships between visitors and the regular customers tend to be guarded. Often people engaged in a conversation at the bar will screen what they say so as not to reveal their telephone numbers or addresses to anyone unless he has been proved trustworthy. Before talking to a stranger, a person often will try to "read" him carefully to get some sense of what kind of person he is, to know how far he is to be trusted. For this people pay close attention to a variety of symbols the person displays, using them to interpret and define him so they will know better how to treat him. They listen to the person's language or, as the men say, his "total conversation" and examine it for clues to his residence, associates, and line of work. They check out the way he is dressed. They watch him interact with others, with an eye and ear to "who they are" and how they treat him. They may even ask someone else, either secretly or publicly, about his trustworthiness. When talking, many tend to check themselves if the wrong people are listening too closely. When people give their names they sometimes use "handles" like Wooly or Bird or Homey, names that permit interaction without allowing others to trace them to their homes or to other settings they feel protective about. Before giving personal trust, they feel a great need to place the next person.

Another consequence of this distrust is the emergence on the barroom side of a civility based not so much on the moral dictates of the wider society as on the immediate potentially violent consequences of uncivil acts. People have been known to pull guns and knives on this side of Jelly's—and to use them. One man was shot to death, ostensibly for stepping on another's carefully spit-shined "fifty-dollar Stacy-Adams" shoes and not saying excuse me. Once a short, slight man was pushed around by a bigger man. The little man is said to have gone home to get his "roscoe" (pistol), returned, and made the larger man crawl on his knees and swear never to do him wrong again. Cases like these, kept in the lore of Jelly's, remind people of what can result from unmindful interaction, and help keep people discreet and civil with one another. People often just don't know the capabilities of others on this side—what they will do and why.

The strange visitors of the barroom side are usually in the process of making their rounds to various drinking places on the South Side. They pass through Jelly's on their way to someplace else and have a relatively small social stake there. Most of them know few of the regular customers, and they usually do not know Jelly at all; those who do know him often know only that he is the owner of the place. Generally speaking, the regular customers see the visitors as outsiders in search of "action"— "on the hustle," as "trying to get over," or as "trying to get into something." Thus they tend to keep them at some distance and try to seek and maintain advantage during encounters. To the regular customers, the visitors, by and large, remain unknown. This makes for a certain amount of apprehension on the part of both groups and works to maintain distrust between them.

Although most of the visitors respect this definition of affairs, a visitor sometimes ventures into the liquor-store area and begins to hang. He is usually not encouraged to linger. When such a person enters, others usually stop talking or at least quiet down until he leaves. Their eyes follow him, reminding him that he is an intruder. Among the regular clientele he is regarded as an outsider, as one of "Jelly's customers," or even as "just a customer." Sensing that the liquor-store area is either beneath him or apart from him, or that it is too dangerous, the visitor usually finishes his business and returns to the barroom or goes on to another joint. Normally the visitors come to the bar, spend some time, then leave, remaining somewhat unknown to Jelly's regular clientele.

GETTING IN

My first few weeks at Jelly's were spent on the barroom side among the visitors and others. This side, for the reasons shown above, was the place most accessible to new people, where strangers could congregate. It was also a place where I could be relatively unobtrusive, yet somewhat sociable. It was here that the process of getting to know Jelly's began, where increasingly I gained some license to exist and talk openly with people. Initially this meant getting to know the people and becoming somewhat involved in their relationships with one another, becoming familiar with the common, everyday understandings people shared and took for granted, the social rules and expectations they held for one another.

After I had been in the field at Jelly's for about four weeks I met Herman, a forty-five-year-old janitor. He wore a baggy army fatigue jacket, blue gabardine slacks, and black "keen-toed" shoes. On his head was a beige "high-boy" hat with a black band. Herman was a small brown-skinned man, about five feet eight inches tall and weighing about 145 pounds. At our first meeting I had been sitting at the bar for about twenty minutes, carrying on a conversation with Rose. Herman took the seat next to me and joined in the conversation. In this first encounter, Herman and I talked in much the same way as I had talked with other visitors to the barroom. At this point in the study, of course, I had not yet begun to make careful distinctions among the different types of people at Jelly's; the very notion of visitor, for instance, came to me only later. Herman was witty and seemed very easygoing, yet at times he spoke in a slow drawl. He impressed me as a person experienced on the ghetto streets, for his conversation was spiced with well-placed references to such experiences. Because of my previous encounters in the barroom, which on the whole had not been outstandingly productive, I at first took Herman as just another person I probably would not see again. But, as I was to find out, Herman was not just another visitor, but a member of the regular clientele of Jelly's.

In the course of our initial encounter Herman and I talked briefly but became very involved. Among other things, he mentioned that he had seen me around before, though I had not noticed him. During this conversation, his questions centered on the issue of what I was doing there. Although he never stated this directly, he did ask some leading questions. Not broaching it at first, he led up to it in a subtle conversation of gestures and words. Interested in "who I was," Herman asked me, "What do you do, Eli?" He wanted to know how I spent my time and whether I was gainfully employed. As I was to discover, around Jelly's whether someone works for a living is an important clue to his definition. For most people this helps to determine whether he is to be trusted within the setting, and to what degree.

In response to Herman's inquiries about my occupation, I said, "I'm a graduate student over at the University of Chicago."

"That's nice," said Herman, seeming a little surprised. "How long you been over there?" As I answered his questions, he seemed to take this as a kind of license to ask more and more about me. And I took his inquiries as cues that I could do the same. Taking this license, I asked him more about himself. During this exchange of information I noticed a marked change in Herman's demeanor toward me. He became more relaxed and sure of me. He gestured more as he spoke, punctuating his words with hits and jabs to my shoulder. He was a very friendly and affable man. At times I reciprocated by punctuating my own words with smiles and friendly exclamations. On the ghetto streets and in ghetto bars friendly students are not to be feared and suspected but are generally expected to be "square" and bookish. With all the information he had about me, including my willingness to give it, he could place me as "safe" within his own scheme of standards and values.

My openness encouraged Herman to be open with me. As a result, there was now some basis for trust in our relationship. In telling me more about himself, Herman said he was a janitor but quickly added, "I'm a man among men," implying that, contrary to what some might expect of a janitor, he held himself in high esteem. Then he told me about his work and about how early he had to get up in the morning. After more of this familiarizing talk, we parted company on good terms. We had spent more than two hours laughing and talking together. I had held this kind of information exchange with others before, and I didn't expect anything unusual to come from this particular meeting. But it was encounters like this that made me conscious that who I was and how I fit into the cognitive picture of Jelly's did preoccupy some of its more persistent members. When I went to Jelly's the next day, I met Herman again. As I entered the barroom I greeted Rose and others as I usually did. I took a seat at the bar and from my stool watched the activities of the men in the liquor-store room.

In that room people were engaged in spontaneous fun—laughing, yelling, playing with one another, and being generally at ease. To me that room seemed very exciting, but it was clear that I would have been out of place there for it seemed to be only for peer-group members. I sensed that there I would have been reminded of my outsider status again and again. While in the barroom, among the visitors and a few of the peer-group members who gravitated over now and then, I felt *in place*. Looking into the liquor-store room, I saw Herman. Catching his attention, I beckoned to him, and he came over to me in the barroom. We shook hands and greeted each other, then held a friendly conversation over a couple of beers. But soon he returned to the liquor-store area, where more of his buddies seemed to be. That Herman had buddies, and so many of them, was one of the important distinctions between him and many of the visitors I had previously met at Jelly's.

In contrast to the visitors on the barroom side of Jelly's, the regular customers on the liquor-store side tend to be spontaneous, loud, and relatively sure of themselves during interactions. Herman and the others acted very much at home there—and they were. Herman was a very sociable person and seemed to be in and out of everyone's affairs. I could see that very little went on at Jelly's without his knowledge. Recognizing this turned out to have important consequences for my entrée to the social world of Jelly's, for it was clear that not many new people stayed around without his soon getting to know them. It became apparent that Jelly's was very much Herman's place; it was his turf, a place where he felt protected from the wrong kind of outsiders.

Apparently he saw me as the right kind of outsider, because when I saw him again in a few days, Herman invited me to share his turf. Again, I was sitting in the barroom, while Herman was laughing and talking with a group of men in the liquor-store room. When I saw them through the open doorway that divided the two areas, I was about to leave. I decided to go through the liquor store to greet Herman, but also to get a closer view of the activity of that room.

As I approached the men I heard Herman say, "Hey, here come my friend, Eli!" Then he said to Sleepy, one of the other men, "He al'right. Hey, this the stud I been tellin' you about. This cat gettin' his doctor's degree." At this point Herman shook my hand and greeted me. I returned the greeting. The others of the group seemed cautious and somewhat incredulous about accepting the "me" presented by Herman. Yet they were polite and approving and remained silent while he and I went through the greeting action. The men just watched, checking us out and talking among themselves. Shortly, Herman began introducing me to the others.

"Hey, Eli. Meet Jake, T. J., and this here's Sleepy." The men then acknowledged me, nodding and saying their hellos. I exchanged greetings with them.

Herman, beer in hand, boasted to the men about a Christmas party he was going to attend where he worked. While he bragged, the others looked on and listened. Much of the conversation and interaction within small groups like this one involves people's attempts to present themselves as important—as "somebody" according to some standard the group values. This situation was dominated by one of these presentations, and it was Herman's show. Herman bragged on about the party. To make it especially meaningful he accentuated the occasion, describing it as something extravagant and special. Herman talked of the "foxy chicks" he would be kissing under the mistletoe and of the "intelligent folks" he would be "conversin'." . . .

The men of the group continued to check us out. Herman was treating me as a friend, as an insider, as though my status in the group were somehow already assured. Certainly Herman would not invite just anyone to a party at work. Other group members wouldn't have expected this and in fact would have been surprised if he had asked one of them. After this demonstration by Herman, I could feel the others in the group warm up to me; they looked at me more directly and seemed to laugh more easily.

I began to feel comfortable enough to stand around in the group and listen to the banter, but not to participate in it, my reticence reflecting my sense of my visitor status. But I did laugh and talk with the fellows, trying to get to know people I had often wondered about during the past four or five weeks. These were people I had seen around but had never before attempted to "be with."

For the next fifteen or twenty minutes Herman busied himself boasting about his various exploits, while other members of the group tried to show inconsistencies between Herman's accounts and the facts they knew. In the language of Jelly's, they tried to "shoot him down." Some of the men even took sides, attempting to counter each other's disputes over the validity of Herman's accounts of his role-to-be at the Christmas party. This style of banter is rather normal among peers on the liquor-store side of Jelly's. It moves from topic to topic as issues rise and fall, become important or trivial. After a while, I told Herman and my new friends I had to be getting home.

When Herman introduced me to his friends I was in effect being sponsored, and in many ways this made my status passage into the peer group relatively easy.[6] For those present, his introduction expressed who I was to be at Jelly's—mainly Herman's "decent" friend. I say decent because Herman used this word when he introduced me around. Through this association, others were encouraged to invest a certain degree of trust in me and to become friendly toward me. To be sure, this was a slow process, but from then on those present, and many who had not been there, acted as though I had some license to be around. . . .

> Herman and I laughed and talked with two other group members in the barroom. We sipped our beers, talked, and watched other people. Soon another of Herman's friends approached and spoke to us.
> "What's happenin'?" he asked.
> "You got it," responded Herman.
> This man was wearing a sporty overcoat and was neatly dressed. He and Herman talked for a while before Herman said,
> "Eli, this my main man, Jimbo. Jimbo, this my cousin Eli. He go to the University of Chicago."
> "Aw, how you doing, Eli?" said Jimbo.
> "Hey, how you doing?" I said.
> "He intelligent! You know I don't be hangin' 'round with no unintelligent people, Jimbo. That's why I been hanging 'round with you so long," joked Herman.
> Everyone laughed. Herman then proceeded to tell the man how we have partied together on his job. The man showed interest, as I nodded in verification of the story. Then we finished our beers, "hatted up," and started for the door.

Thereafter Herman referred to me as his cousin and introduced me to others that way.

In a sense this was the place I had lobbied for, however unwittingly. We hung together and treated each other as close friends, and the men followed suit. The more I hung with Herman and verified his stories, the closer we seemed to become. We began to "go for cousins," as the men say. Many of the men knew, of course, that we were not real cousins, and, perhaps even more important, Herman knew they knew. This was not a case of deception. Rather, the fictive kinship term of cousin was used by Herman, as it is by so many men on the streets around Jelly's, to signify that we were close friends. We were "going for cousins."[7]

One of the important implicit aspects of this developing relationship concerned its protective nature. Herman and I would often hang together and leave Jelly's together to go home or to a movie or somewhere else. Among peer group members, an unspoken rule requires those who hang together to help or "take up for" one another in times of need—particularly during physical fights, but also on general social matters. My relationship with Herman gave me a certain implicit status in the group, a place interconnected with the "rep" and rank Herman was sensed to have. A set of mutual obligations and expectations began to form, so that group members expected us to take up for each other.

My growing awareness of these developments contributed to my own self-confidence around Jelly's liquor-store room, as I slowly secured a right to be there. During the course of this entrée, I increasingly came under Herman's tutelage and guardianship. But why did Herman engage me in friendship at all? What was in it for him? After getting to know Herman better, I became aware that he regards himself as very knowledgeable about the ghetto streets. There is a certain amount of esteem to be gained by demonstrating that one knows his way around the streets, and Herman sees and presents himself as someone who has been "through it all."

Born and raised in Chicago, Herman has spent a good part of his life coming to terms with "the streets." He has been "through World War II," has been "a pimp, a hustler, a junkie" among other things—and has survived to talk about it all, something he does whenever "the streets" becomes an issue around Jelly's.

Because he carries this extensive and widely known personal biography, Herman is able to command a certain measure of esteem from the men who constitute Jelly's regular clientele. Other regulars usually agree with this definition of him and will work collectively to maintain it. At the same time, Herman wants to see himself as "decent." However, he knows that such an identity—about which I will have much to say later—is difficult to maintain for anyone hanging out at Jelly's.

As I said, in our relationship I provided Herman with a kind of verification of his identity and status on the streets and in "decent" society. Specifically, as I provided him with a "decent" pupil, one who had "all that education," I reflected well upon him and could thus verify his own claims to "decency." Of course I could also verify Herman's claims to street prowess by allowing him to teach me about the streets. And this really was important to me, since I needed to know the streets if I were to survive and carry out my fieldwork. By taking me under his wing, Herman could thus show that he knew the streets very well and at the same time could "be somebody" when "decent" friends became the issue.

All this fit nicely with the low-key, non-assertive role I assumed at the beginning of my study. I behaved in this way to prevent unwieldy challenges from those who might have felt threatened by a more aggressive demeanor, especially from a stranger. It is the kind of role any outsider must play—is forced

into—if he is not to disrupt the consensual definition of social order in this type of setting.

WORKING AT SOCIABILITY

At first glance the atmosphere of the liquor store is reminiscent of the ambience attributed to the old general store, with its pot-bellied stove and stereotyped, easygoing social relations. Relations among people of the liquor-store room seem effortless; the room buzzes with happy conversation, loud laughter, and play. The people here joke, shout, and argue from time to time. Unlike the barroom, this appears to be a place of spontaneity where friends and others who know each other well can really be sociable. Compared with the barroom, or what people of the peer group call "that side" or the "other side," relations here seem utterly unstructured.

But this view is deceptive. On examination, the initial association with the old general store fades. One begins to find that the sociability is not so effortless after all. People must work at it. Sociability here involves an elaborate set of subtle rules that emerge more clearly during interaction and that peer group members come to know and act in accordance with—or soon find themselves reprimanded.

On this side it appeared at first that there were no clear and stable seating arrangements—that people sat wherever they could find room. They sat on any old Coke or liquor case or leaned on Jelly's wobbly old counter. These places seemed to go to the lucky person. But as one spends time on this side of Jelly's he learns that the scarce seat goes to a person not so much because he is lucky as because the others feel somehow that he deserves it. On numerous occasions I saw people actively defer to others over seating. They did not need to be asked but would surrender a seat even at a look from a person who apparently had more right to it. To be sure, at times such assertions of right were made verbally or even resulted in arguments. . . .

Herman continued to sponsor my participation in the peer group. He still told people I was his cousin, a label that suggested that in times of trouble we would "take up" for each other. Yet the principle of reciprocity was at work in our relationship; Herman and I needed help from each other, but in different ways. Given our situations and positions in the group, Herman did not need my protection, and since I was the one defined as in need of such help, he probably would have been reluctant to accept it from me had the need arisen. On one occasion Herman demonstrated my need for his help by intervening in what could have developed into a troublesome situation.

> It was a balmy Saturday evening in April. Herman, Leroy, Charlie, Tony, and I were standing in front of Jelly's liquor-store window. An ice-cold can of Budweiser, wrapped in a brown paper sack, changed hands. Each man took a swig and passed the can on. Cars and buses passed by and their passengers glanced over, but the men were oblivious to this. Pedestrians quickly moved on. An old flea-bitten brown mutt limped by. Tony was in a playful mood and began poking me in the side. The poking soon turned into shoulder-bumping. Herman, who had been watching this play, said to Tony, in a half-kidding yet firm way. "Why don't you cut all that weak shit, Tony." Tony stopped at what was taken as a warning from Herman.

This is one example of the way Herman gave help in situations that might have become problematic. In this instance I felt no tension between Tony and myself. But Herman, being very familiar with the social order of the group, understood that such "playful" games can quickly develop into trouble.

Equally important, Herman helped me learn what situations could lead to trouble by giving me information about the various men in the peer group. After introducing me to someone around Jelly's, for example, he would often pull me aside and give me a small biography, to inform me how I should treat the person and how I should allow him to treat me. In effect, Herman not only was introducing me to the peer-group members but was also informing me of his conception of their consensual agreements on rank and social order. Such information is regularly exchanged at Jelly's, often through actions and subtle gestures as well as words, and provides a way of knowing people without always having to "try" identities. For example, one night Herman introduced me to Charlie, still spry at seventy-two. We talked to Charlie for about a half-hour, then at the opportune moment Herman pulled me aside and filled me in on his record. At times, such an exchange of information would wait until the next day and at other times, it did not occur at all. In "Ol' Charlie's case," Herman told me that

> He's still gettin' pussy, stays sharp [dresses well], keeps a pocket full of money, keeps his shit [pistol] on him all the time, and he talks mo' shit than any one o' them jitterbugs out there. Charlie's got three grown kids, and he's a gangster from way back. That ol' stud still will blow a mug away [shoot] quick. So you can't play him cheap, and any mug up in here [member of the peer group] will cut yo' throat 'bout messin' with him. They all love him.

In effect, Herman was giving me Charlie's script and preparing me to accept and defer to it in the interest of social order.

Another of my early lessons from Herman concerned the importance of being able to "read the signs" people display during sociability. Most people value this ability on the streets around Jelly's and like to claim proficiency at it. As I mentioned earlier, "reading" involves paying close attention to a person's self-presentation to gain clues about how he deserves to be treated, especially if he is new.

One notices the person's dress, his language, how he moves at Jelly's, the things he takes for granted, the kinds of questions he asks, even the way he formulates his questions. How much "room" he gets from others at Jelly's—that is, what certain others will allow him to get away with when he interacts with them—is also important. Such interactions can become behavioral cues signaling how he can be treated by still others in the setting. From all of this, others can gain some sense of how the person sees himself and what this might mean for their relations with him and others in the group. In effect, they learn how he deserves to be treated and thus are able to assess quickly the behavioral limits appropriate in their own dealings with him.

If the ability to read such signs is valuable, it is just as valuable to be able to display them to create the desired effect. This was demonstrated to me one evening when Herman and I encountered Oscar, a fast, street-wise former street-gang member of thirty-three who is now a hustler of the streets. Herman went through an elaborate display for my benefit. As Oscar entered the liquor-store room and approached us, Herman said, "Hey, Oscar!"

"Hey, dude," said Oscar, in a slow, cautious drawl. This statement and its tone were enough to alert Herman to Oscar's mood. The tone indicated that Oscar felt a certain distance, Herman believed. It was as though Oscar had his "pistols on," perhaps only because I was a stranger.

Herman and Oscar exchanged a few words, as Herman moved astutely and almost effortlessly to Oscar's "level" by his speech and demeanor. Herman spoke "hip street shit," spiced with a few "motherfuckers," "son' bitches," or whatever it took. I just sat at the bar with my beer in hand and watched Herman in action. Though he does not act this way in all circumstances, he seemed to sense the necessity for such behavior now to main-

tain Oscar's respect or, more to the point, to keep him in his place. To do this Herman knew he must in some measure meet the standards Oscar deemed important. Such standards are here expressed and met through adroit use of "tough" and "manly" gestures and street language, a posture Oscar could readily appreciate.[8]

After a few moments of this exhibition, which amounted to a kind of reestablishment of who was who, Oscar said,

"Who that you got with you?"

"Oh, Oscar, this is my cousin Eli."

"Hey, brother-man. What's to it?" said Oscar, as he extended his hand to me for a soul handshake.

"You," I responded, as I shook his hand.

In this situation Herman did not emphasize the side of me that Oscar might take as "square" by saying, as he so often did when introducing me, "Hey, this stud's gettin' his Ph.D." Herman just let that part of my status and identity lie dormant in this situation.

After a few minutes Oscar began to "hit on me" to buy some of the "hot" record albums he had tucked under his arm, with which he usually makes his rounds "hustlin'" from joint to joint.

Before long Herman interrupted, "Dig it, Oscar, Eli don't need none of what you sellin'!" He then tugged me away, as Oscar moved on. Herman and I retired to a corner of the liquor-store room where he began to fill me in on Oscar. Considering Oscar a "bad egg," he said,

> I've known the boy all his life. I even raised him [meaning that he taught Oscar a good deal]. The boy ain't no good, no 'count. He ain't nothing but a jive-time gangster. Just a li'l hustler who'd sell his own momma to get over. So you know what he'll do for me or you. The boy think he slick, always tryin' to get over, trying to test somebody, and if you give him any leeway, he'll try to beat you. That's what he was tryin' to do

with you, tryin' you, seein' what you'd stand. You got to stand up to dudes like him, or they'll play you cheap. Then they'll always be tryin' to get over on you, you know? Dig me, you'll learn.

The ability to interpret a person's actions accurately and then to define the boundaries proper to place takes on special significance on the streets around Jelly's, compared with the relatively serene middle-class setting. One of the main differences is in what the participants in such interaction may have at stake—especially their sense of what is at stake. In the middle-class setting, when such boundaries are not taken seriously, or are ignored, ridiculed, or slighted, one stands to lose face.[9] Around Jelly's, a person not only stands to lose face, he may even lose his life—or at least come to sense a clear danger to his life. Awareness of the high stakes encourages people to pay close attention to their relations with others during interaction and sociability around Jelly's.

For Herman and others at Jelly's, there exists a variety of circumstances and situations during sociability that require different postures and strategies of personal demeanor. In the social setting of Jelly's both working and nonworking black people can gather among others enough like themselves to matter socially. Here they seek out certain others to spend their leisure time with—friends and companions with whom they can act sociably, talking, laughing, arguing, and joking. It is in this setting that they can feel themselves among equals, especially in relation to the wider society. In a fundamental sense, this setting represents their league, where they stand a chance to win in the competition for social esteem and rank. In this respect Jelly's serves as a kind of arena of social life. Here people present themselves in the roles that peers allow them. Here they engage in ritual exhibitions of deference and demeanor that,

when properly reacted to by significant others, allow them a certain affirmation of self.[10] The people here create and work to sustain the principles and standards by which they can measure themselves and others. At Jelly's people can be somebody—and this is one of its main attractions.

Notes

[1] For comparisons in the sociological literature, see Gerald D. Suttles, *The Social Order of the Slum* (Chicago: University of Chicago Press, 1968); Herbert Gans, *The Urban Villagers* (New York: Free Press, 1962); William F. Whyte, *Street Corner Society*, 2d ed. (Chicago: University of Chicago Press, 1955); Horace Cayton and St. Clair Drake, *Black Metropolis* (New York: Harper and Row, 1962); Elliot Liebow, *Tally's Corner* (Boston: Little, Brown, 1967); Ulf Hannerz, *Soulside* (New York: Columbia University Press, 1969); William Kornblum, *Blue Collar Community* (Chicago: University of Chicago Press, 1954); and James F. Short, Jr., and Fred L. Strodtbeck, *Group Process and Gang Delinquency* (Chicago: University of Chicago Press, 1965).

[2] For comparative observations on informal drinking settings, see Sherri Cavan, *Liquor License* (Chicago: Aldine, 1966); E. E. LeMasters, *Blue Collar Aristocrats* (Madison: University of Wisconsin Press, 1975); James P. Spradley, *You Owe Yourself a Drunk: An Ethnography of Urban Nomads* (Boston: Little, Brown, 1970); James P. Spradley and Brenda J. Mann, *The Cocktail Waitress* (New York: Wiley, 1975); Samuel Wallace, *Skid Row as a Way of Life* (New York: Harper and Row, 1968).

[3] For a classic account of this kind of social process, see Georg Simmel, "The Sociology of Sociability," trans. Everett C. Hughes, *American Journal of Sociology*, vol. 55, no. 3 (1949).

[4] Critiques of this perspective may be found in Maurice Stein, *The Eclipse of Community* (Princeton: Princeton University Press, 1960), esp. pp. 13–46; John Madge, *The Origins of Scientific Sociology* (New York: Free Press, 1962); and David Matza, *Becoming Deviant* (Englewood Cliffs, N.J.: Prentice-Hall, 1969), esp. pp. 25–100.

[5] Elliot Liebow used this term to suggest why the men he studied came together at Tally's Corner.

[6] For an imaginative and provocative theoretical discussion of microsocial aspects of status mobility, see Barney Glaser and Anselm Strauss, *Status Passage* (Chicago: Aldine, 1972).

[7] See Carol Stack, *All Our Kin* (New York: Harper and Row, 1974); and Liebow, *Tally's Corner*. Notably, Liebow uses the phrase "going for brothers" to describe a close relationship between men not related by blood. In my research experience, the men used the fictive kinship term "going for cousins." Although logically it might seem that

"going for brothers" indicates a closer and more involved relationship than "going for cousins," this was not borne out by my data. The terms seem very similar in import. Such relationships as I observed moved from "low" to "high" involvement and intensity, yet the kinship term never changed.

[8] For sociological interpretations, see Dell Hymes, "Ways of Speaking," *Exploration in the Ethnography of Speaking*, ed. Richard Bauman and Joel Sherzer (New York: Cambridge University Press, 1975).

[9] See Erving Goffman, "On Face-Work," in his *Interaction Ritual: Essays on Face-to-Face Behavior* (Chicago: Aldine, 1967).

[10] See Erving Goffman, "On the Nature of Deference and Demeanor," ibid.

DISCUSSION QUESTIONS

1. Based on the author's experiences, what are some of the key factors that make a person a good participant observer?
2. How is status attained in the black ghetto? Explain your answer.
3. Explain why Herman was treated with considerable respect by the others in his community.

READING 6-3

South Africa on the Move

Pauline H. Baker

Just as 1989 was a watershed year for East Europe, 1990 is a historic turning point for South Africa. The year marked a new international environment, a new regional situation and, most dramatically, a new initiative by South Africa's President Frederik W. de Klerk to break the country's racial impasse. From revolutionary upheaval and economic decline in the 1980's, South Africa seems poised—albeit delicately—on a threshold of change that will result in a totally different political dynamic in the 1990s.

"The old South Africa is burdened by inheritances from many sources of the past which are really blocks around our neck," said de Klerk. "We're getting rid of those blocks. . . . That is why things are so dynamic in South Africa."[1] De Klerk's remarks were made in a televised interview with ABC correspondent Ted Koppel, after the February 11 release of Nelson Mandela, the country's most respected black nationalist, who spent 27 years in prison.

The interview itself was an extraordinary event. Having been all but excluded because of tight censorship imposed during the four-year state of emergency, the international media flooded the country with a press corps of 2,000 to cover the Mandela story. All the major American television networks broadcast Mandela's historic walk to freedom, live from South Africa. Virtually overnight, the world's major pariah state was catapulted into the international spotlight, this time inspiring hope rather than despair.

By releasing Mandela from prison, de Klerk began to release whites from this self-inflicted international isolation. He first took some small steps to test the political waters. Within the first 100 days of taking office, he released eight political prisoners of Mandela's generation, seven of whom were leaders of the African National Congress (ANC) and one who belonged to the breakaway Pan-Africanist Congress (PAC), an organization that is more suspicious of the role of whites and negotiations. He also permitted mass demonstrations to celebrate the freedom of these leaders; he desegregated beaches; and he designated four undeveloped areas as mixed residential zones.

However, the most important action taken by the South African President to pave the way for Mandela's release was the dismantling of the state security management system. In effect, this was a secret parallel government built up by then-President P. W. Botha as part of the counterrevolutionary strategy the government adopted to confront black unrest. Hundreds of committees blanketed the country, from the State Security Council at the top to provincial and municipal councils at the bottom.

Dominated by the security and intelligence forces, this apparatus of control had multiple functions, including citizen surveillance, welfare distribution and the counter-organization of the black population to create an alternative leadership willing to cooperate with the state. With this machinery, the government grew more repressive than it had been in any other period in the country's history. Within the last five years, 5,000 people died because of political unrest and more than 30,000 were jailed without charge.

In addition, de Klerk shifted decision-making control back into civilian hands by cutting in half the two-year compulsory military service for whites, reducing the military budget, ending cross-border raids against neighboring states, and suspending military assistance to rebel groups in Mozambique and Angola. These measures reduced the power of the "securocrats," the political class of military, police and intelligence chiefs who, together with an inner circle of ministers and functionaries, were in charge of crushing the revolutionary uprising of 1984–1987.

These actions went a long way toward demilitarizing society, but the threat of right-wing violence and conservative opposition remains. Many white security officers, especially in the police, are supporters of the Conservative party (CP), the official parliamentary opposition that captured 30 percent of the white electorate, or approximately 680,000 votes, in the September, 1989, election. The CP accuses de Klerk of treason and vows to rally 1 million whites in a campaign to stop him.

In addition, neo-Nazi groups, like the Afrikaner Weerstandsbeweging (AWB), the Afrikaner Resistance Movement, represent dangerous pockets of opposition. The AWB has a parliamentary wing, a youth brigade modeled on the German SS (Nazi elite police), and a fiery leader, Eugene Terre Blanche, a former police officer and an admirer of Adolf Hitler. Formed in 1973, the AWB has been shaken by recent scandals and infighting, spawning a splintering of the far right into a cluster of organizations that insist on a hard-line apartheid ideology. Another, possibly more serious, concern is the existence of extremists within the security forces. The army and the police have been implicated in charges of "death squads" that engage in political assassinations, prompting de Klerk to establish a special judicial commission to investigate the allegations.

Notwithstanding the intransigence of the right, de Klerk probably won more white support than he lost when he crossed the proverbial Rubicon. Clearly, he picked up supporters of the Democratic party, a newly formed alliance of liberal whites that captured over 20 percent of the electorate in the last election by campaigning on a one-person, one-vote platform. In fact, although most whites are anxious about the future, they were relieved at de Klerk's actions. Students and the business community welcomed the breakthrough, openly demonstrating their support and placing advertisements in newspapers to greet Mandela. (Only a few years ago, the chief executive of Barclays National Bank was publicly castigated by President Botha and subjected to a judicial inquiry for financing a newspaper advertisement that called for the very steps de Klerk is taking.)

On the day he was freed, thousands of ordinary whites lined the streets to cheer Mandela as he made his way to Cape Town, displaying an outpouring of emotion and support that amazed the black hero. Actually, many whites—perhaps even the majority—have been ahead of the government in wanting genuine reforms. De Klerk's actions thus represent a shrewd political calculation. He has shed the far right and has consolidated his political power among the rest of the white population, reducing the decade-long erosion of support in the ruling National party's electoral base.

The most dramatic political move de Klerk made before Mandela's historic walk to freedom, however, was taken on February 2, exactly one year to the day after the resignation of President Botha as head of the National party. In a speech at the opening of Parliament in Cape Town, de Klerk announced the legalization of the ANC and the PAC, both of which had been banned for 30 years, and the South African Communist party (SACP), which had been banned for 40 years. Restrictions were also ended on 33 other antiapartheid organizations operating within South Africa. In addition, de Klerk announced the release of many political prisoners, a selective relaxation of media censorship, the intended repeal of the Separate Amenities Act (which segregates public facilities) and the suspension of executions until new regulations make the death penalty more difficult to impose. Eight days later, the state President revealed at a news conference that Mandela would be released from prison unconditionally.

Although it was anticipated for months, Mandela's release rejuvenated the country's black population more than the legalization of the ANC and other proscribed organizations a week earlier. Mandela had achieved a stature of Olympian proportions. His calm self-confidence, regal bearing and principled defiance symbolized the irrepressible resistance of black people. His remarks during his first days of freedom were directed not to the world community, but to his people, his party and his country. Mandela restated his loyalty to the ANC, reiterated his belief in the philosophy of nonracialism, and reassured whites that he was sensitive to their concerns. He called de Klerk "a man of integrity." But he affirmed his intention to use all means possible, including the "armed struggle," to pursue full political rights for blacks.

THE REACTION

Despite the euphoria of the moment, the hard reality was that apartheid remained in force, negotiations seemed a long way off and contentious issues were left unresolved. De Klerk reserved powers that ensured he would remain in control, triggering objections from the ANC. The ANC insisted on freedom for all political prisoners, including hundreds whom de Klerk refused to release because they had been convicted of violent crimes. The ANC also called for an end to the state of emergency, which permitted troops to remain in the black townships and gave the police extraordinary powers to contain dissent. And the ANC wanted to obtain guarantees of immunity from arrest for returning exiles, including members of the ANC's military wing. Despite these stumbling blocks, the ANC national executive committee decided at a meeting on February 16 at its exile headquarters in Lusaka, Zambia, to resume activities openly inside South Africa and to prepare for direct contacts with the government.

The international community applauded de Klerk for his bold decisions and praised the ANC for its willingness to respond to the challenge. United States President George Bush invited de Klerk and Mandela separately to the White House. British Prime Minister Margaret Thatcher, an ardent opponent of sanctions, defied her European Community partners and unilaterally lifted the British voluntary ban on new investments. And foreign investors rushed to purchase South African stocks with renewed optimism about the future.[2]

In the week following the legalization of antiapartheid organizations, $400 million in new funds poured into the country. In the first two months of the year, in fact, foreign reserves increased by $1 billion, a tantalizing foretaste of the payoffs that could come from a comprehensive political settlement. The market dipped after Mandela endorsed the nationalization of key sectors of the economy, but the rapid response of the private sector to fast-breaking developments and the generally positive reaction of foreign leaders buoyed hopes in spite of this volatility. "It is likely that every hiccup in talks between the ANC and Pretoria could move the market quickly in one direction or another," noted *The New York Times*.[3] But a director of one of South Africa's brokerage houses calmly observed that "everyone here thinks [Mandela] is doing no more than staking out his position from where he will negotiate."[4]

As difficult as it was for Pretoria and the ANC to have come this far, the hard part had only just begun. The government's initiative and the ANC's response were decisions made by caucuses within each political grouping. Apart from Mandela's contacts with the government during his internment, no negotiations had taken place, no elections had been held and no legislation had been enacted to institutionalize the process. The curtain is therefore going up on a new type of engagement that will pit two old antagonists in a wholly untested political arena. The ruling Nationalist party will be moving out of power while the ANC and other extraparliamentary groups, power brokers and anti-apartheid allies will be moving in.

The negotiations, if and when they take place, will be burdened by a deep legacy of distrust, divided constituencies, and a complex political tapestry that includes dedicated ideologues and militant rivals standing in the wings who claim to be the true torchbearers of African and Afrikaner nationalisms. For that reason, the process must be as inclusive and democratic as possible from the outset. As Thabo Mbeki, ANC secretary for international affairs, warned, "it must be stated plainly that no South African can now be certain that negotiations, once they start, will succeed."[5]

THE INTERNATIONAL ENVIRONMENT

The changes that took place in South Africa occurred against a backdrop of a radically changing world order. Mandela walked out of prison at the moment when the Communist party of the Soviet Union was deciding to permit a multiparty system and ownership of private property, steps that repudiated not only former Soviet leader Joseph Stalin, but Karl Marx and V. I. Lenin as well. Mandela went into jail at the height of the cold war; he came out as it was drawing to a close.

The ANC had been witness to decades of sweeping global changes, none of which had previously had much impact on the struggle inside South Africa. Formed in 1912, before other nationalist movements emerged in sub-Saharan Africa, the ANC saw the rise and fall of communism, the consolidation and collapse of colonialism, the success of the American civil rights movement, and the march to majority rule and independence of the rest of the African continent, including—in 1990—neighboring Namibia, Africa's last colony.

At the same time, South Africa is no longer the white citadel it used to be. Its military forces, though still strong, discovered in the 1980's that there were limits to its ability to achieve its objectives in the region and to suppress internal black dissent. The South African economy is dependent on international trade and foreign capital as never before. Sophisticated communications have undermined the work of censors, exposing whites and blacks to ideas that can no longer be kept out. And internal demographic and political trends are breaking down white enclaves of privilege. The walls of apartheid have been crumbling under the cumulative weight of these trends just as the walls of communism have been crumbling under similar pressures in East Europe.

Among the most interesting examples of the effect of world developments on South Africa are developments in the Eastern bloc. The rapid pace of change there has set new international standards for democratization, heightening pressures on Pretoria for black enfranchisement. The spectacle of popular masses overthrowing tyrannies once thought impregnable has encouraged Pretoria's leaders to get ahead of the trend.

But developments in East Europe and the Soviet Union have also eased the transition because of the diminished threat of communism. Moscow's policy change in southern Africa, which began to be evident some years ago, dismayed Pretoria at first, but was eventually taken seriously. The Soviet Union downplayed the "armed struggle," put aside the goal of socialism, cautioned its allies not to meddle with the productive sectors of the community and advised blacks to take account of white fears. These shifts suggested to Pretoria that the military capabilities of the ANC were being weakened as the Soviet Union fostered a political settlement. It "created a scenario," said de Klerk, "where the Communist threat . . . lost its sting."[6]

Joe Slovo, the leader of the South African Communist party, revealed how the ripples of Soviet "new thinking" had reached the distant shores of Africa, affecting anti-apartheid forces as well. Slovo questioned the wisdom of nationalization, pointing out that state domination of the economy is a feature of apartheid. And he rejected the one-party state as incompatible with democracy. "We have to face up to our failure in East Europe," he said. "We have to recognize that those were popular re-

volts against unpopular regimes. It's no good complaining that this was some kind of capitalist conspiracy. We did it all on our own."[7]

There have been more subtle, but no less significant, shifts in the West, particularly in the United States. Washington not only distanced itself from Pretoria as a result of a bitter national debate over President Ronald Reagan's policy toward South Africa, but Congress took tangible steps to encourage the end of apartheid. In 1986, sanctions became the law of the land in the country recognized as the leader of the free world.

Wanting to avoid confrontation with Congress over this issue, the administration of President George Bush has been sensitive to public sentiment. The administration appears to be more willing than the Reagan administration to cultivate sustained and high-level contacts with anti-apartheid leaders, both through its embassies in the region and in Washington, D.C. One of President Bush's first moves was to invite Albertina Sisulu (the wife of Mandela's colleague Walter Sisulu), a widely respected anti-apartheid voice who was banned at the time, to the White House.

The administration is also more balanced in its assessment of the impact of sanctions, despite the President's personal lack of enthusiasm for these measures. Assistant Secretary of State for African Affairs Herman J. Cohen noted that sanctions have had an effect on white South African thinking. He and other members of the administration have consulted on Capital Hill with leading sanctions supporters, including members of the Black Caucus. By nurturing a bipartisan consensus, the administration has thus far been able to maintain some influence on the situation, including credibility with blacks and a working relationship with whites in South Africa.

The most concrete result of its efforts was an agreement between the Executive Branch and Congress in 1989 to delay pressing for more sanctions for a period of six to nine months to "give de Klerk a chance." If that consensus is sustained, the United States could facilitate negotiations. A tilt in the other direction that would lift sanctions prematurely, however, could divide American opinion, squander American leverage and paralyze Washington in a pointless debate.

The conciliatory approach adopted by the Bush administration is based on a recognition that South Africa has become a domestic political issue. No other major Western ally has a grass-roots constituency of comparable weight, one that sees South Africa not in strategic or economic terms, but overwhelmingly as a human rights problem.

As a consequence, George Bush's approach to South Africa has been linked closely to contemporary partisan politics. A decision by the Republican National Committee to try to win more African-American votes in the 1990 election is a key element in this calculation, especially in light of recent gains made by this constituency in local and state politics, notably, the election of Douglas Wilder as governor of Virginia and David N. Dinkins as mayor of New York.

Many southern white congressmen are also in office thanks to African-American votes. The visit of civil rights leader Jesse Jackson to South Africa, which coincided with Mandela's release, was the most recent reminder of this political reality. Among other advantages, the trip provided an opportunity for one of the most celebrated African-American leaders to help shape the American response.

The debate over South Africa has also reached a new audience in the wider American public. Increasingly, analysts have acknowledged that sanctions have helped put the South African economy in a straightjacket of debt, capital outflow and loss of credit that affected white attitudes.

Stephen Lewis, author of *The Economics of Apartheid*, estimated the loss of capital to the South African economy at roughly $2 billion a year. "Economic pressures have played a major role in forcing the South African government to change its policies on a wide range of issues from labor reform to the release of political prisoners," he wrote.[8] William Claiborne, a correspondent for the *Washington Post*, admitted that

> I . . . remained [skeptical] . . . for a good part of my [three-and-a-half-year] tour in South Africa. It seemed to me that punitive economic sanctions might be effective as a threat, but once they were imposed the stiff-necked, self-reliant nature of the Afrikaners who rule this country would come to the surface . . . and [they would] perhaps become even more intractable . . . I was wrong. For all of their faults . . . sanctions were beginning to work, finally.[9]

A new regional calculus also emerged in 1989. The Angolan-Namibian agreement signed in December, 1988, set in motion a process that had multiple repercussions. First, it gave South Africa an internationally recognized role as a peacemaker in the region, despite earlier policies that had contributed to conflict in the area. Second, it helped reduce cold war tensions in Africa. The Soviet Union supported the agreement, which called for the removal of Cuban troops from Angola over a 27-month period. Third, it launched Namibia, a territory that South Africa had controlled since World War I, on the road to democracy, providing a model of peaceful racial reconciliation on South Africa's doorstep.

Lastly, the agreement enabled South Africa to conclude a military retreat from the region without losing face. Although the civil war in Angola raged on with a new intensity and the insurgency in Mozambique was no closer to resolution, South Africa had officially withdrawn from these wars and pledged not to interfere, whatever happened to the Union for the Total Independence of Angola (UNITA) and the Mozambican National Resistance (Renamo), anti-government guerrilla groups that were Pretoria's clients.

Furthermore, while the agreement was being negotiated and implemented, the Angolan and Mozambican governments embarked on economic and political reforms, with the latter—formerly one of Africa's most committed socialist states—rejecting Marxism-Leninism. Even the ANC guerrilla threat was reduced. As part of the accord, military camps that had been located in Angola before the Angolan-Namibian agreement were moved to Tanzania and Uganda. There were now "no immediate prospects of inflicting an all-around military defeat on the enemy," noted the South African Communist party in a document assessing the new strategic situation in the region.[10] However, in August, 1989, the ANC launched a fresh diplomatic offensive with its adoption of the Harare Declaration, which set forth a plan for negotiations. The document was endorsed by the Front-Line States, the Non-Aligned Movement, the Organization of African States and, with some modification, the United Nations General Assembly.

Internal pressures within South Africa also mounted. Having been battered severely by the state of emergency, anti-apartheid forces began a defiance campaign of nonviolent resistance. Detainees arrested under emergency regulations went on a hunger strike, forcing the government to negotiate their release with leaders of the Mass Democratic Movement, as the anti-apartheid forces restyled themselves after their organizations were banned. Some prisoners escaped from custody and took refuge in foreign embassies. Those who were placed under restriction ignored government orders, defying Pretoria to rearrest them in peaceful protests. Sit-ins were organized, political rallies convened, and negotiations with local authorities started to resolve some of the burning issues in the black townships, like housing and education. Blacks were moving—literally—into cities, universities, hospitals, recreational areas and public facilities that had been historically reserved for whites.

Politically, the white community had also reached a moment of truth as the full implications of the results of the 1989 election set in. From that September poll, the Conservative party showed that, while it did not do as well as expected, it was there to stay. The rift in Afrikanerdom could not be healed. The Democratic party, doing better than expected, showed that a new challenge had emerged on the left. Marginal victories by the National party in several close constituencies raised the possibility of a hung Parliament in the next election, due in 1994.

The handwriting was on the wall: either the National party had to make a political breakthrough or it would be caught in a political vise. A party man all his life, de Klerk saw the tides of world opinion, white fragmentation and the resurgence of black resistance playing against the white establishment.

At this juncture, South Africa's future depends on how the two primary actors—the ANC and the National party government—play their cards. The situation has never looked more promising, but it is also highly dangerous. Expectations are running ahead of negotiations; rhetoric is glossing over real political differences; and time is not on anyone's side. The National party must reach a settlement before the next election, when it could be voted out of office. The ANC must move quickly or it may lose ground, not only to the government, but to other political rivals.

South Africa may well enter a period of political realignment that will cut across racial barriers even before a transition to a new government takes place. That would be a hopeful sign, leading to the creation of a new body politic. But before that occurs, Pretoria must shift from unilateral reforms to multilateral negotiations, and the ANC must make the transition from liberation struggle to participatory politics.

If an elected body, a constitutional convention or a constituent assembly, is convened, a national debate could take place that would permit all groups and alliances to test their political strength and their political ideas. Whatever mechanism is used it must be democratic or it could invite outside interference, provoke renewed conflict and lost international credibility.

Whether South Africa's transition will lead, with a minimum of violence, to a multiparty, nonracial democracy is unclear. At least that future appears possible. But the legacy of apartheid, the scars of violence and the polarization of society have left their mark. Without a commitment by all major parties to a common future, South Africa could still plunge into the abyss of race war or the violent throes of partition. The range of alternative outcomes is as broad in South Africa as it is in East Europe, and democracy hangs in the balance.

Notes

1 "ABC Nightline," interview with F. W. de Klerk, President of South Africa, February 13, 1990.

2 *Washington Post*, February 9, 1990; and *The New York Times*, February 6, 1990.

3 *The New York Times*, February 18, 1990.

4 Ibid.

5 *The New York Times*, February 4, 1990.

6 "ABC Nightline," op cit.

7 *Washington Post*, January 21, 1990.

8 Stephen R. Lewis Jr., *The Economics of Apartheid* (New York and London: Council on Foreign Relations Press, 1989), p. 167. See also *Washington Post*, February 18, 1990.

9 *Washington Post*, January 14, 1990.

10 "The Path to Power," as quoted in *The Weekly Mail* (Johannesburg), January 18, 1990, p. 11.

DISCUSSION QUESTIONS

1. What changes have taken place in South Africa that lead Baker to be optimistic about the future of race relations in that country?

2. How are the changes in South Africa related to political change in the international environment?

3. How does the history of race relations in South Africa differ from that in the United States?

CHAPTER 7

Issues in Gender

INTRODUCTION

"Is it a boy or a girl?" This is the first question asked when a baby is born, and the answer is likely to have a profound effect on that child's future. Each society differentiates among its members on the basis of gender, and the distinctions made between males and females are embedded in the cultural fabric and social structure of all societies. To some extent, all societies treat males and females differently. The expectations that are applied to the two genders fashion the social roles they play. Sociologists distinguish the biological bases of sexual identity from the culturally patterned modes of behavior associated with the sexes.

Gender is composed of the social distinctions between males and females that are used to organize social arrangements and influence social behavior. *Gender roles* are expectations about the activities of men and women that are socially learned through the process of socialization. Traditionally, most people have thought that practically all differences between

men and women are innate and thus biological in origin, but today, many of the sex-linked differences in male and female behavior have come under serious question. Most social scientists hold the view that differences in the behavior of men and women are a result of complex interactions between biological and cultural factors, but that the cultural factors offer the more powerful explanations.

Critical to an understanding of this concept is a recognition of the important role played by family members and significant others in the socialization of young people. Sociologists are deeply involved in studying the issues surrounding general socialization. They are also concerned with the pervasive influence of gender roles on many aspects of society and culture. Sociologists study the effects of gender differences in the microprocesses of daily life, such as patterns of verbal and nonverbal communication. They investigate the influence of gender socialization and interactional experiences on the concept of self and on self-esteem. They explore the ways in which individuals' work lives are affected by sexual differentiation: division of labor along gender lines results in differential access to the valued resources of society, such as income, power, and prestige—in other words, it results in structured sexual inequality. On a macrosociological level, sociologists have developed theories about the use of sexism to justify sexual discrimination. These are just some of the broad categories of issues which social scientists in general, and sociologists in particular, have explored.

Gender differences and inequalities are not only a consequence of cultural beliefs and socialization practices; they are also embedded in social structure and organizational relationships. Rosabeth Moss Kanter offers an insightful analysis of the ways in which gender, among other differentiating characteristics, is related to power, opportunities for personal advancement, and the perceptual consequences of tokenism in bureaucratic organizations. Classical approaches to bureaucratic organization emphasized its elaborate division of labor, formal patterns of authority, and extensive reliance on explicit rules and written communication. Contemporary theories of bureaucracy, however, recognize that organizations are also composed of informal patterns of relationships and personal considerations.

In her book *Men and Women of the Corporation* (1977), Kanter analyzes the roles people play in Indsco, a large multinational corporation. Instead of explaining the infusion of personal considerations in bureaucratic relationships between men and women in terms of their individual characteristics, Kanter locates a large measure of responsibility of gender behavior at work in the structure of work systems themselves. That is, the behavior of men and women at work, and their organizational fates, are explained by Kanter as consequences of typical coping responses to the dilemmas

and contradictions posed by their organizational roles. Their behaviors are not merely stereotypically male and female, nor can they be simply explained in terms of individual, personal characteristics. In our selection from Kanter's work, we see that the critical problems for secretaries at Indsco stem from the patrimonial relationship they have with their bosses. The role pressures they experience encourage secretaries to become timid, emotional, parochial, praise-addicted, and "wedded" to a single boss. Kanter attributes these qualities to three important aspects of the social organization of the boss-secretary relationship: status contingency, principled arbitrariness, and fealty. Thus, Kanter argues that the "masculine" and "feminine" images embedded in organizational roles are inherent neither in the nature of the tasks related to those roles nor in the characteristics of men and women; rather, they are developed in response to the typical problems faced by men and women in modern bureaucratic organizations.

Men and women not only face dilemmas and contradictions in their work role but also experience strains in fulfilling their familial roles. Arlie Hochschild describes the "second shift"—child care and housework—in dual-career families in which both parents work outside the home and struggle to share responsibilities at home. Women's increased participation in the labor force and families' growing dependence on two incomes have exacerbated problems of deciding the division of responsibilities in housework. Hochschild studied patterns in the division of labor of second-shift work and gender ideology among fifty-five working couples. In this excerpt from her work, we get a glimpse of the personal struggle between Peter and Nina Tanagawa as they attempt to balance their respective careers and their joint family obligations. We gain some insight into the Tanagawas' feelings for each other, their strategies for coping with second-shift responsibilities, and the effects of their coping styles upon each other, upon their jobs outside the home, and upon their daughter Alexandra.

We have already said that each society distinguishes its members by gender and that gender roles are culturally learned. It is also apparent that while men are different from women in all societies, the extent of these differences and the content of role differences varies considerably from one society to the next. Some social scientists attribute gender differences in the United States to forces inherent in capitalist economic systems. The last selection in this chapter, by Charlotte O'Kelly and Larry Carney, questions this assertion by presenting evidence drawn from socialist societies. These authors find noticeable differences between men and women in the Soviet Union, Israeli kibbutzim, the People's Re-

public of China, and Cuba. They acknowledge that these socialist societies have made advances in breaking down certain aspects of gender stratification and in improving the position of women in ways comparable to those in capitalist societies, and that they have done these things in a far shorter time. They point out, however, that these societies have failed to achieve a degree of gender equality that would be consistent with their socialist ideologies. Cross-cultural analysis such as this is essential to understanding the sources and effects of gender role differences.

References

Kanter, Rosabeth Moss. *Men and Women of the Corporation*. New York: Basic Books, Inc., 1977.

Secretaries

Rosabeth Moss Kanter

Secretaries added a personal touch to Industrial Supply Corporation [Indsco] workplaces. Professional and managerial offices tended to be austere: generally uniform in size and coloring, and unadorned except for a few family snapshots or discreet artworks. ("Welcome to my beige box," a rising young executive was fond of saying to visitors.) But secretaries' desks were surrounded by splashes of color, displays of special events, signs of the individuality and taste of the residents: postcards from friends' or bosses' travels pasted on walls, newspaper cartoons, large posters with funny captions, huge computer printouts that formed the names of the secretaries in gothic letters. It was secretaries who remembered birthdays and whose birthdays were celebrated, lending a legitimate air of occasional festivity to otherwise task-oriented days. Secretaries could engage in conversations about the latest movies, and managers often stopped by their desks to join momentarily in a discussion that was a break from the more serious business at hand. It was secretaries who were expected to look out for the personal things, to see to the comfort and welfare of guests, to show them around and make sure that they had what they needed. And it was around secretaries that people at higher levels in the corporation could stop to remember the personal things about themselves and each other (appearance, dress, daily mood), could trade the small compliments and acknowledgements that differentiated them from the mass of others and from their formal role. In many ways—visually, socially, and organizationally—the presence of secretaries represented a reserve of the human inside the bureaucratic.

Nowhere were the contradictions and unresolved dilemmas of modern bureaucratic life more apparent than in the secretarial function. The job, made necessary by the growth of modern organizations, lay at the very core of bureaucratic administration; yet, it often was the least bureaucratized segment of corporate life. The product of the rationalization of work and the vast amount of paperwork that entailed, it still remained resistant to its own rationalization. At Indsco, secretarial positions were unique in a number of ways; for one thing, they were the only jobs in the company ranked merely by the status of the manager, and attempts to change this arrangement were resisted. The secretarial job involved the most routine of tasks in the white-collar world, yet the most personal of relationships. The greatest time was spent on the routine, but the greatest reward was garnered for the personal.

Understanding the nature of this bureaucratic anomaly sheds light on several features of life in the corporation: the functions served by pockets of the personal inside the bureaucratic, but the tradeoffs for people who become trapped as an underclass in those pockets; the sources of both the intensity and the awkwardness that can emerge in relationships between bosses and secretaries; and the origin, in job conditions, of those work orientations that tend to be adopted by secretaries. Secretaries' characteristic ways of managing their organizational situation—their strategies for attaining recognition and control—as well as the behaviors and attitudes they develop, can all be seen as a response to the role relations surrounding the secretarial function. . . .

THE SECRETARIAL LADDER AT INDSCO

The first fact about the several thousand secretaries at Indsco was that they were all women, except for two men at headquarters who were classified as typists. If they entered at the bottom, Indsco secretaries were generally hired out of high school or a secretarial finishing school like Katharine Gibbs. There was a tendency in corporate headquarters to recruit from parochial schools, which meant that a very high proportion of secretaries were white and accustomed to hierarchical discipline. The bulk of hiring took place in June after high school graduation. New hires, who had to have typing and shorthand skills, were put in the entry-level position of "stenographer." After a several-day orientation, covering the cafeteria, library, medical department, policies and benefits, and classes in Industrial Supply style for letters and telephone calls, new stenographers entered a "pool."

Pool arrangements at Indsco were dispersed throughout its offices rather than centrally located, but secretaries were considered part of a pool as long as they had no permanent assignment (filling in as vacation relief, for example) and were supervised by secretarial assignment coordinators rather than by those whose work they were doing. For about six months, all correspondence they handled was sent to a training staff member, who evaluated it for proficiency. After six months, they were promoted to Secretary I and given a permanent assignment, typically working for more than one boss. From this point, there was little training or retraining, although secretaries were sometimes encouraged to go back to school on their own, and the management of secretaries was decentralized, either in the hands of their bosses, most frequently, or under secretarial coordinators, in one department that retained the pool longer. . . .

The secretarial ladder was short, and rank was determined by bosses' statuses. A secretary with three to four years' experience was eligible for promotion to Secretary II, working for a PRO (person-reporting-to-officer). Secretary IIIs had seven to twelve years' experience and worked for divisional vice presidents. Secretary IVs worked for division presidents and executive vice presidents. At the top were executive secretaries of corporate officers. . . .

The ceiling for secretaries was set by how high a boss they could snare. . . .

There was little chance of leaving the secretarial ranks for another job at Indsco. And there were decided benefits to escaping from the pool, where one was an interchangeable machine, to an assignment to a particular boss or two, where one was at least a noticeable person. So secretaries learned to count on a relationship with a boss for their rewards. The secretary–boss relationship, in turn, was a relic of patrimony within the bureaucracy. . . .

PATRIMONY IN BUREAUCRACY

Max Weber, in his classic rendering of the character of modern organizational life, considered the universalism, legalistic standards, specialization, and routinization of tasks in the bureaucracy the antithesis of traditional feudal systems ruled by patrimonial lords. As Weber saw it, bureaucracy vested authority in offices rather than in persons and rendered power impersonal, thereby undercutting personal privilege that stood in the way of efficient decisions. But despite Weber's claims, not all relationships in modern organizations have been rationalized, depersonalized, and subjected to universal standards to the same degree. The secretary–boss relationship is the most striking instance of the retention of patrimony within the bureaucracy. Fewer bureaucratic "safeguards" apply here than in any other part of the system. When bosses make demands at their own discretion and arbitrarily; choose secretaries on grounds that enhance their own personal status rather than meeting organizational efficiency tests; expect personal service with limits negotiated privately; exact loyalty; and make the secretary a part of their private retinue, moving when they move—then the relationship has elements of patrimony. . . .

There were three important aspects of the social organization of the relationship: *status contingency* (the fact that secretaries, primarily, and bosses, secondarily, derived status in relation to the other); *principles arbitrariness* (the absence of limits on managerial discretion); and *fealty* (the demand of personal loyalty, generating a nonutilitarian aura around communication and rewards).

STATUS CONTINGENCY

Reflected status was part of the primary definition of the secretarial position. *Secretaries derived their formal rank* and level of reward not from the skills they utilized and the tasks they performed but *from the formal rank of their bosses.* A promotion for secretaries meant that they had acquired a higher-status boss, not that their own work was more skilled or valuable. Most often, above the early grades, secretaries were not actually promoted at all on their own; they just remained with a boss who himself received a promotion. It was common practice at Indsco for secretaries to move with their bosses within the same geographic area, as though they were part of the private retinue of a patrimonial dignitary.

. . . Some people thought that secretarial promotions meant secretaries had *less* work to do and made less use of their skills. Secretaries felt that the hardest work, with the most demands and variety in technical requirements, was performed on the lowest levels. Women at the higher levels consequently talked about their work with a degree of discomfort, indicating the trouble they had justifying their greater pay and lighter work, except by insisting, as many did, "I worked hard to get here." . . .

Even more important was the fact that the *boss's status determined the power of the secretary.* . . . Higher up, secretaries' power derived from control of bosses' calendars. They could make it easy or difficult to see a top executive. They could affect what managers read first, setting priorities for them without their knowing it. They could help or hurt someone's career by the ease with which they allowed that person access.

If the secretary reflected the status of the boss, she also contributed in minor ways to his status. Some people have argued that *secretaries function as "status symbols"* for executives, holding that the traditional secretarial role is developed and preserved because of its impact on managerial egos, not its contribution to organizational efficiency. . . . One writer was quite explicit about the meaning of a secretary:

> In many companies a secretary outside your door is the most visible sign that you have become an executive; a secretary is automatically assigned to each executive, whether or not his work load requires one. . . . When you reach the vice-presidential level, your secretary may have an office of her own, with her name on the door. At the top, the president may have two secretaries. . . .

At Indsco, the secretary's function as a status symbol increased up the ranks as she became more and more bound to a specific boss. "It's his image, his status, sitting out in front," a personnel administrator said. "She's the first thing people see about him." For this reason, personal appearance—attractiveness and social skills—was a factor in the career prospects of secretaries, with task-related skills again playing a smaller role as secretaries moved up the ranks. "We have two good secretaries with first-rate skills who can't move up because they dress like grandmothers or housewives," another official complained. "Even those executive secretaries who are hitting sixty don't look like mothers. Maybe one or two dowdy types slipped in at that level, but if the guy they work for moves, they couldn't be sold elsewhere at the same grade." Appearance was so important that secretaries would be sent to Katherine Gibbs as much for the personal side as for the skills training. Gibbs taught posture, hand care, the use of deodorants, and the importance of clean underwear in addition to filing methods and telephone responses. . . . This was all designed to make the secretary into a "pretty package." . . .

Derived status between secretaries and bosses spilled over in informal as well as formal ways. *The parties became fused in the awareness of other organization members.* Secretaries became identified with bosses in a number of personal and informal ways. Secretaries could get respect from their peers because of feelings about their bosses, but they could also be disliked and avoided if their bosses were disliked. "There are problems for secretaries if they become trapped in their managers' fights," a secretary said. "They are usually the ones who are caught, and they have few resources with which to defend themselves." There were also "shadow hierarchies" at Indsco, in which secretaries to higher-level executives received deference at informal social events from the secretaries of lower-level staff and were more likely to assume leadership of employee events. . . .

Despite the fact that bosses could derive some informal status from characteristics of their secretaries, *status contingency operated in largely nonreciprocal ways.* It was the boss's *formal* position that gave the secretary formal rank; he, in turn, wanted to choose someone whose *personal* attributes made her suitable for the status he would be conferring. As in the patrimonial official's private ownership of his servants, the secretary was seen by the boss as "my girl." This attitude was made clear to a personnel administrator who was finding secretaries for two vice presidents under the new, centralized system. She located two candidates and sent them both to see both men, who called her in anger when they discovered this: "You mean *the women* are making the choice?" One of the executives made an offer to a candidate, only to find that she still wanted to see the other manager. He told the administrator, "If she looks at the other job, I don't want her." (The secretary made her own angry retort, and took the second job.)

The secretaries' position in the organization, then—their reward level, privileges, prospects for advancement, and even treatment by others—was contingent upon relationships to particular bosses, much more than on the formal tasks associated with the job itself.

PRINCIPLED ARBITRARINESS

The second patrimonial feature of secretarial role relations was the *absence of limits on managerial discretion*, except those limits dictated by custom or by abstract principles of fair treatment. Within the general constraints of Indsco tradition and the practice of other managers, bosses had enormous personal latitude around secretaries. . . . Thus, it was left to bosses to determine what secretaries did, how they spent their time, and whether they were to be given opportunities for movement. . . .

Managerial discretion in job demands combined with another feature of secretarial work to contribute to the sense of personal dependence on arbitrary authority. It was a job with low routinization in terms of time planning, characterized instead by a *constant flow of orders*. Unlike other parts of the bureaucracy, where the direct exercise of authority and the making of demands could be minimized through understood routines and schedules of expectations, secretarial work might involve only the general skeleton of a routine, onto which was grafted a continual set of specific requests and specific instructions. The boss did not merely set things in motion; he might make demands on the half hour. Even if boss and secretary developed a set of routines that reduced the number of direct face-to-face demands (e.g., he put work to be typed in an inbox; she knew to bring coffee in at 10:15), continual demands and new orders could not be eliminated entirely. Indeed, the secretarial position was often there in the first place to provide a person capable of responding to momentary demands and immediate requests generated on the spot. . . . Power could not be rendered impersonal by the use of routinized schedules.

Arbitrariness was embedded in the *personal services* of secretaries. . . . Some secretaries included personal services in the core definition of their job, giving them equal importance with the communication functions (like typing and telephones) for which Indsco had hired them. One secretary included among her major responsibilities: "office household duties: watering plants, cleaning cups, sharpening pencils, straightening desks, etc." . . . And despite media publicity for the controversy over whether or not secretaries should make and serve coffee, Indsco secretaries still performed this service, especially for visitors to their bosses' offices.

. . . One secretary told a writer: "His wife does everything for him at home; I do everything for him here. The only thing he does for himself is well, you know." Many Indsco secretaries seemed to feel the same way. Resentment over personal work was the biggest single issue raised by secretaries when Industrial Supply brought an experimental group of them together with their bosses for "expectation exchanges." The secretaries felt that the official definition of their jobs was fuzzy enough that they were concerned about refusing to do personal things for their bosses even when they would have preferred not to. Demands were limited only by customary practice, the boss's conscience, or the secretary's negotiating skills or ability to embarrass her boss enough that he would stop asking for personal favors. But there was disagreement among secretarial administrators and supervisors themselves about how much the managers' right to expect personal service was built into the job. At a meeting in which the secretarial function was discussed, a woman supervisor of several dozen secretaries, who herself had been promoted to this exempt job from an executive secretary's slot, insisted that, in her words, "The 'girl' is there to serve the man." A reform-minded personnel administrator countered, "No. The secretary is there to *assist* a manager."

There was another kind of personal service that was even more difficult for secretaries to talk about, since it trod the fine line between official and unofficial, legitimate and illegitimate. This was the secretaries' involvement as critical ingredients in their bosses' presentation of a "front." They participated in the behind-the-scenes transformations of chaos into order, or rough ideas into polished, businesslike letters and documents. They had access to confidential files that told the real story behind the front. They knew how bosses really spent their time. They set the stage for an atmosphere that was designed to awe or impress visitors. They served as a buffer between the boss and the rest of the world, controlling access and protecting him from callers. . . .

The secretarial job thus rested on a *personal set of procedures and understandings* carved out by secretary and boss. As we have seen, the corporation provided only the merest skeleton for the relationship; its substance depended on the unique qualities and agreements of the two people involved. Unlike other bureaucratic relations, which certainly included *some* component of special understandings generated by the unique personalities of those who interact, the secretary–boss relation was defined *largely* by the special relationship developed by two particular individuals. Secretaries and bosses created unique relationships that did not remain, that were not necessarily institutionalized as part of the built-in structure of that secretarial job. When either of the parties left, the job reverted to its skeletal outline, again to be remade. . . .

FEALTY

Fealty became the third feature of the ideal boss-secretary relationship, from the boss's perspective, making the relation a highly personal rather than a purely instrumental one. *Secretaries were rewarded for loyalty and devotion to their bosses.* They were expected to value nonutilitarian, symbolic rewards—which did not include individual career advancement—and to take on the emotional tasks of the relationship. Secretaries were rewarded for their attitudes rather than for their skills, for their loyalty rather than their talent. Given the low skill required by the actual tasks they were given to do, and the replaceability of personnel with basic secretarial skills, secretaries found it to their advantage to accept fealty as their route to recognition and reward.

Expectations of loyalty were bound up with the sense on the part of bosses that they were making secretaries part of their personal estate. This was behind the outrage experienced by some executives at the thought that secretaries might shop around for a job rather than wait to be chosen by a particular manager. . . . Members of an Indsco task force on upward mobility for clerical workers considered a major barrier to change the fact that "some men felt the secretaries worked for them personally, not for the corporation." They found managers reluctant to suggest competent secretaries for other positions; instead, bosses wanted to claim ownership and, in turn, demand loyalty. . . .

After collecting data on a hundred [performance appraisal] forms, I found that there were two "central traits" that recurred and tended to determine a secretary's overall rating . . . : "initiative and enthusiasm" and "personal service orientation" (as one manager put it, "ability to anticipate and take care of personal needs"). Content analysis showed that where variants of these traits were found, the secretary was generally rated high on most other abilities, including basic skills like typing. Where they were not present, or where managers commented on their absence, secretaries tended to be rated low on basic skills, too. In other words, secretaries were rewarded for the quality of their relationship with bosses; appearing to like their jobs and being willing to take care of bosses' personal needs. They were also rewarded for minimizing the bosses' need to give orders. Such attitudes created a halo for the secretary who had them. But they were not necessarily rewarded for professional skills. . . .

If secretaries were evaluated on non-utilitarian grounds, they were also *expected to accept nonutilitarian rewards*. In many cases, secretaries willingly did so. . . . "Love" was one nonmaterial reward secretaries were supposed to appreciate. Some Indsco secretaries reported that their bosses managed to turn their complaints about salary or working conditions into expressions of concern about whether or not they were "loved," assuming that women at work were motivated by such noneconomic, emotional factors. . . .

The idea that women wanted "love" above all was translated into constant praises for secretaries. Women were supposed to be managed through flattery. Especially at the upper levels, it was common for the constant flow of orders for particular tasks to be accompanied by a constant flow of "thank you's" and compliments for jobs well done. The rapid cycle of beginnings and completion meant that there were many tasks for which secretaries could be thanked, and bosses assumed that being a good boss was to generate these courtesies. . . . When secretaries' rights organizations began to agitate for "raises, not roses," they were challenging this notion of what motivated women.

Yet many Indsco secretaries *were* content to settle for symbolic rewards, for prestige and daily flattery rather than higher pay, job control, and independent recognition. There was a shared feeling on the part of some secretaries that women did better in the higher-level executive secretarial positions than they did in the lower exempt jobs, even taking into account the pay differential. "I'd have to give up my drapes and my outside office and settle for a tiny inside cubicle," one executive secretary said. Despite the large numbers of routine and boring tasks secretaries carried out, the little corners of reflected power in the job gave some of them a sense of reward. The upper-grade secretary had access to inside information. She knew who the "fast track" people were; whom the boss would see no matter how busy he was; who goes to lunch, who goes to meetings, who got invited to personal dinners at home. The gifts of knowledge, the invitations to special events, the bits of power secretaries picked up from their bosses' status—all this made it hard for some secretaries to see any other options for themselves. . . .

The symbolic rewards of identification were related to another aspect of the secretary–boss relationship. A *tone of emotional intensity* may come to pervade it. A "division of emotional labor" may be developed, in which the secretary comes to "feel for" the boss in both senses: to care deeply about what happens to him and to do his feeling for him. Secretaries represented a reserve of permissible emotional expression in the office. Executives unwound to their secretaries, according to an Indsco informant. "They say things they would not say anywhere else. If something goes wrong at a meeting, they will tell their secretary more than their wife." . . .

In return for the secretary's devotion and emotional support, the boss may take on the traditional patrimonial ruler's attitude of caretaking toward his underlings. An Indsco manager told a group of managers, who were discussing the position of women in the company, how his feelings of responsibility changed when he acquired a secretary of his own, after years of sharing secretarial services with other bosses:

> In the old job I shared a secretary with up to six people, and I didn't feel very personally responsible. Now I have this personal feeling that I am responsible for the care and feeding of that person—my secretary—the nurturing of her emotions, giving her a shoulder to cry on. I'm the one who remembers her anniversary. I'm the one constantly checking on her sensitivities, treating her emotions, stopping to notice that, hey, she's not having a good day. I have to make sure she's feeling all right.

Note the certainty of this man that what his secretary wanted existed primarily in the emotional realm.

In a relationship of fealty, then, secretaries were expected to be bound by ties of personal loyalty, to value nonutilitarian rewards, and to be available as an emotional partner. The image of what secretaries wanted—and, by extension, working women—was shaped by these expectations.

THE MARRIAGE METAPHOR: SECRETARY AS "OFFICE WIFE"

The three patrimonial elements in secretarial role relations (status contingency, principled arbitrariness, and fealty) have led to the frequent use of the marriage metaphor to describe the relationship between secretaries and bosses. The metaphor aptly fits many elements of the position: reflected and derived status; greater privileges and lesser work for women attached to higher-status men; choice of a secretary on the basis of personal qualities like appearance; fusion of "the couple" in the eyes of others; a nonrationalized relationship with terms set by personal negotiation; expectations of personal service, including office "housework"; special understandings that do not survive the particular relationship; expectations of personal loyalty and symbolic or emotional rewards; and an emotional division of labor in which the woman plays the emotional role and the man the providing role. Indeed, the progression from the secretarial pool and multiple bosses to a position working for just one manager resembles the progression from dating to marriage, echoed in managers' own comments about special feelings of responsibility toward a private secretary. . . .

But the marriage metaphor is not just a catchy description used by critics. It was also implicit in the way many people at Indsco talked about the relationships between secretaries and bosses. Over time, a serious emotional bond could develop. One executive secretary promoted into management described leaving her old boss as a "divorce."

> I worked with a really fine man before this slot opened, which is one of the hazards of a secretarial job. You work for truly fine people, and you get so identified with them that you really don't have a career that's your own. I'm sure I really felt a marriage was ending when we both talked about my moving. It was almost as sad as getting a divorce. I was as emotionally involved in it. While in my explanations to myself I said it was fear of going to a new job, I think it was also fear of ending a relationship with a man I really enjoyed.

For the first few months after her promotion, she stopped in to see him every morning, hanging her coat in her old office instead of the new one, and finding herself concerned if he had a cold or looked unhappy.

Some secretaries made the inevitable comparison between how *they* treated a boss and how the wives did. As a secretary said:

> I think if I've been at all successful with men, it's because I'm a good listener and interested in their world. . . . Most of the ones I'm referring to are divorced. In looking through the years they were married, I can see . . . what probably happened. I know if I were the wife, I would be interested in their work. I feel the wife of an executive would be a better wife had she been a secretary first. As a secretary, you learn to adjust to the boss's moods. Many marriages would be happier if the wife would do that.

On the other hand, there were also executive wives to whom I spoke who compared what *they* did for their husbands to the tasks of a good secretary. And, one manager suggested a *ménage à trois* in his remark to the real husband of a woman assisting him, "You have her body; I have her head."

If the marriage image had applicability, it also needed to be differentiated. There were *types* of office marriages at Indsco. Some were very traditional, perhaps among the remaining bastions of female submissiveness and deference. The traditional secretary, usually an older woman, knew her place, served with a smile, was willing to be scapegoated and take the blame for the boss's mistakes, and did not presume. . . .

At the other end of the continuum were the new "liberated" office marriages, generally involving younger women. Some secretaries refused to do "housework" and insisted on participating in a process of contracting that defined the relationship as they wanted it defined, indicating their needs and limits. The secretary to the manager of a field office, who proved herself intelligent and capable, made her job an administrative one. She demanded (and won) the title of assistant to the manager and the right not to type unless absolutely necessary. (A special typist was hired part time.) The manager, a casual, easygoing, and very liberal man, gave her highly desirable office space, taking less for himself, and tried to accommodate all of her wishes. But he wistfully mentioned that he longed sometimes that she would take more responsibility for seeing that the office stayed clean. And even this liberated secretary was still merely "the wife," without a clear career territory of her own, but in a new kind of "marriage" in which she could demand privileges.

DISCUSSION QUESTIONS

1. According to Kanter, what are the critical elements of the social organizations of the boss-secretary relationship?
2. Women in corporations suffer from relative powerlessness, limited opportunities for advancement, and tokenism. What recommendations would you make to increase women's power, increase their opportunities, and balance their numbers in corporations?
3. How do the absence of limits on managerial discretion and fealty to bosses contribute to sexism and sexual harrassment in the workplace?

A Notion of Manhood and Giving Thanks: Peter and Nina Tanagawa

**Arlie Hochschild
with Anne Machung**

Peter Tanagawa, a dark-haired man of thirty-three with twinkly brown eyes that express exuberance, leans forward in the leather chair of the small office attached to a technical books store. Speaking in a low voice, he sums up something small but key. "Nina wants me to do more with the kids, to be more concerned with their education and development, be more of a family person. And I am! But not as much as *she* is."

The issue of how much of a "family person" he should be was not new for Peter. Early on in their vibrant courtship, riding their bicycles, talking for hours on end, Peter and Nina had explored their ideas about "men" and "women," as couples do. Nina had wanted to anchor her basic identity at home, to ground only what was psychologically left over at work. In this she stood between Carmen Delacorte (who wanted to stay home and put Frank out in the world) and Nancy Holt (who wanted to balance herself and Evan equally between home and world). When Nina and Peter first met, each was attracted to the way the other felt about the roles of men and women. Peter's career in book sales, they agreed, would take priority over any job Nina would pick up later, but she'd want to pick up something. They were right for each other, both transitionals.

Just as in the Holts' marriage, tension developed between their two notions of gender. Like Nancy Holt, Nina Tanagawa pressed Peter to do more at home, and like Evan Holt, Peter resisted. But because Nina started on more traditional footing, she was to turn to an irresistible job offer as "the reason" she was venturing further into the world, and as the reason he should move further into the home. More than the Holts and Delacortes, the story of the Tanagawas is a story of how their traditionalism made Nina feel lucky and how Nina's feeling lucky affected the second shift, and about what happened to their daughter Alexandra along the way.

As a child growing up in a close-knit Japanese community in Hawaii, Peter had been his mother's favorite, and he had been distant from his father, who worked long hours and came home tired and distracted. Now, as a father himself (his two children, Alexandra and Diane, were five and three), he felt more engrossed in their lives—like a mother—and more discontent with his book business than his gender ideology would allow. He seemed to need Nina *between* himself and the children for things to feel right.

Nina, a stunning, slender blue-eyed blonde of thirty-three, is slightly shy in manner. When I interviewed her in the evening at home, she seemed still ready for the office, dressed in a white skirt and jacket that was decorated with a tasteful small red pin—a fairy princess in a business suit. Like her father, Nina is resourceful and practical. Her mother, a lifelong housewife and busy volunteer, had been intermittently restless with her husband's refusal to "allow" her to work. Nina had been determined to have "a job that gave me some sort of satisfaction" but she also expected to be the center at home. Yet, now inadvertently, she had been drawn by her own success toward a desire to be the linchpin of Telfac's personnel department. Gradually she was shedding the feminine identity she'd had when she was twenty—or was she?

PETER'S STRATEGY: EMOTIONAL SUPPORT INSTEAD OF INVOLVEMENT

Peter believes that Nina should tend the home not because her anatomy is her destiny, not because God intended men to dominate women, nor because Peter earns more money. Peter believes she should tend the home because she is more *interested* and *competent* in it and has freely chosen to put her time and energy into it. Nina agrees with that. Accordingly, she does 70 percent of the childcare and about 80 percent of the housework. (They agree on this estimate.) Nina stays home if the children are sick; she retrieves a child's forgotten jacket from a friend's house; she waits for the new sofa to be delivered. Although Peter describes his daughters as "daddy's girls" and he seems to me to do quite a bit around the house, they both agree that he has little responsibility for the daily work of caring for them.

One evening when I was visiting their home, Nina took the children upstairs to bed to say their prayers; Peter whispered to me, pleased and proud, *"Now* they're getting *quality* time." Then, since I had asked both parents to go through the evening as they normally would, he settled down with the newspaper. I wasn't sure whether he really meant to imply that *he* couldn't give his children "quality time." But it was clear that he saw his parental role as supporting *Nina's*: he mothered Nina; Nina mothered the children.

This did not mean that Peter was not an able, interested father. Both agree that Peter is more intuitive about the children's feelings. For example, he is quick to sense just what favor to Diane had made Alexandra feel slighted. He knows when Alexandra is really hurt and when she is faking it. Often he tells Nina, and Nina does something about it. Nina tends the children's physical needs, organizes their social lives, and in a kindly way "administers" them. An absence of warm communication with her own mother had left Nina slightly anxious about being a good mother herself, so she welcomes every little bit of Peter's appreciation. And Peter appreciates Nina's mothering.

Peter is at one remove from the children,

but he is enormously interested in them. When he talks to me about himself, he weaves in extraneous reminders of his wife and children. Unlike many men, he describes his typical workday morning with a consensual "we"—as in "We get up at six." When he describes a typical day, his work seems like an interlude between more emotionally charged periods of time with his family. As he recounted:

> Nina will get up first and take a shower. When the door closes, that's my cue to get up. I go downstairs and make coffee for both of us, and while the water is heating, the paper arrives. I glance at the front page, the sports page, then read the business section, make the coffee, bring the paper and two cups of coffee upstairs, as she's coming out of the bathroom. She and I both drink coffee. Then Nina brings out Diane, our youngest child. I start to change her clothes, and put her on her little potty seat. Then I towel her off so she's fresh and put on her day clothes. Alexandra is getting up and I dress her in her school uniform—she needs the *attention* when she sees me doing it for Diane, it's not that she needs the assistance. So I do it with *that* understanding.

In contrast, Peter's description of his workday is brief and perfunctory: "I arrive at work at eight-thirty or nine. Then once I get here, it's just another daily routine. I leave around five or five-thirty." Once home, Peter disappears upstairs to change into his jeans (after work, Nina remains in her white business suit). He describes mealtime, bath time, and "quality time" all in spontaneous, appreciative, and loving detail, recalling just what Nina had packed in Alexandra's lunchbox, exactly which clothes she had laid out for Diane.

In Nina's account of her typical day, the morning is short, a matter of warmly, efficiently dispatched routine. The detail begins when she gets to the first morning meeting, the morning calls and appointments over an impending crisis at the company. She slows down to talk at length about the challenging issues that would come before an important committee next week, and about a bristling rivalry between two members of her staff. Just as Peter lives less intensely at his office than he had intended, Nina lives more intensely than she had intended at hers. But far more than most men who did not share, Peter could visualize clearly just what sharing *would* be like. Recalling the preparations for Alexandra's fifth birthday, he describes a vast array of tasks *he* has *not* done:

> I've done nothing for Alexandra's birthday party this weekend except wrap a few gifts. Nina's the one who has had to write out the invitations, order the cake, buy Alexandra all her presents, figure out where we're going, figure out the lunch menu for the kids. That has all been *her* responsibility, and I think she would like me to participate more in this. I did the decorations, blew up the balloons, threw the confetti all over the place. And I made all twenty-two sandwiches and set up the Betamax. But Nina still does seventy percent to my thirty percent.

Like Frank Delacorte, Peter probably *did* more to make the children have a good time than his self-image allowed him to accept real credit for. One evening when I was having dinner with them, Diane began to whimper and suddenly threw up some purple chewing gum. The two parents spontaneously leapt to their feet; Peter rushed to Diane, and Nina rushed for the mop. Peter comforted Diane: "It's okay, Diane. You tummy's okaaaay." After cleaning up the floor, Nina took Diane's clothes off to be washed. Nina, it seemed, was the "maid" of the house—putting in a load of laundry, changing a light bulb, packing the lunches, calling the sitter. Peter was the "nanny," the understander and comforter. To reconcile the conflict between their gender ideology and the inner reality of their personalities, they developed a family myth: Nina was "naturally better with children," and "naturally more interested" than Peter.

NINA'S COLLISION COURSE

In 1973, Nina Tanagawa was one of five women in her entire college class to go on to earn a master's degree in business administration. In the early 1970s, when just a few companies were beginning to see the profit in female talent from top business schools, Nina was hired to work in the personnel department of Telfac, a large and expanding computer company. The job was enjoyable, challenging, and it paid enough to put Peter through business school.

Nina leapt with astonishing speed through the managerial ranks from one promotion to another, until in 1982, her salary put her in the top half of 1 percent of women nationally. She was five years younger than the youngest employee at her level in the company, and one of the top three women in the entire company; the other two had no children. By either female or male standards, she was a fabulous success.

After Nina had worked for five years in the company, the Tanagawas began their family. First came Alexandra. Nina took a year off to stay home with her. Looking back, she felt it had been the right thing to do. She sang songs to Alexandra, wallpapered her room in candy stripes, and sewed her tiny jumpers. But Nina also admitted to feeling bored taking care of the baby alone at home; she shouldn't have felt bored, she thought, but she did. She also thought she was becoming boring to Peter. So her reason for going back to work, as she told me, was to "be a better wife." Then, when her boss called to ask if she wanted to come back to work part time, she hired a housekeeper/babysitter and jumped at the chance.

When there was a fall in the computer market, Nina was put in charge of the company's "unhiring" program in several offices, and her hours increased. In the evenings, after Alexandra was in bed, she would read reports and write office memoranda about her "unhired clients." To maintain her managerial image, she arrived half an hour earlier than her staff in the morning and stayed half an hour later at night. When staff members stayed late, she bit her tongue and left first. Under the watchful eye of conscientious coworkers and subordinates, her work hours steadily increased. As Nina recalled: "I came back to work three days a week, then four days a week. But the job grew too rapidly. I was running—Go, go, go! I'd drop into bed at night and realize I'd been working for seventeen or eighteen hours a day."

After about two years of this, Nina's second child, Diane, was born. This time she stayed home for six months before she once again received a call from her boss and once again went back. But this time there was more to do at home and less of her to go around. As Nina put it: "The house got messier. There was that much more laundry with two kids. The dinner action and noise between the kids got worse."

She had hired a housekeeper who insisted on "no windows, no floors" and leaving at five-thirty. So after long sieges of work during the week, Nina became the consummate housewife and mother on Saturdays. On Sunday mornings, when Peter played tennis, Nina washed the children's hair, cut their fingernails, and cleaned the house. As she put it wryly, "Peter lets me take over a lot." In one sense, though, Nina felt it was a *relief* to "take over."

All the top brass of Nina's computer company were workaholics, actually or virtually single. At first she tried to pretend to be as involved as they were. But one day, just as Nina was beginning to feel she couldn't pretend anymore, her boss burst into her office, smiling broadly. "Congratulations! You've just been promoted!" Well-wishers crowded into her office to celebrate, and Nina felt pleased and flattered. But as she drove home that night, what would prove a lengthy depression was already taking hold. She recalled hearing a

speaker at an office seminar on work and family life declare, "I don't know of a working mother who can balance a career, children, and marriage; one of these has to give." Nina remembered secretly thinking, I'm proving you wrong. Now she wasn't sure.

Peter supported Nina's career, in the way "transitional" men often do. He talked with her about her problems at work, he soothed her brow at night. He worried about her health. He did a bit more here, a bit more there at home. But even these bits seemed to take reminders. As Nina put it:

> I say to him, "Do you want to bathe the kids tonight or do you want to clean up the kitchen?" That's the way I usually put it to him, because if I don't, he'll go watch TV or read the paper. Usually he does the kitchen but he doesn't want to do the bathing, so I end up bathing them and reading to the kids.

Nina hinted to Peter that she needed more help. But she put it in such a way that her "circumstances," not she herself, demanded help. Unlike Nancy, she didn't say a word about "fairness." She stuck to this new job offer: she didn't want to say yes but how could she possibly say no?

Peter heard the hints, but took them as signs of "Nina's problem." So in time, Nina let her fatigued condition speak to him. Great rings appeared around her eyes; she had grown almost alarmingly thin. As she told the story later, she even began to move and talk listlessly. Finally, Nina confided to Peter that she was getting close to a certain emotional edge. Instead of having a nervous breakdown, however, she got pneumonia and took the first ten days of pure rest she had taken since Diane's birth. It was as if her illness had said what she could not say directly herself: "Please help. Be a 'mother' too." However, although Peter was concerned about Nina, he considered the problem to be a conflict between *her* career and *her* motherhood.

Nina was changing. But Peter was not convinced that the foundations of Nina's opinion of *him* as a man had been altered. In truth, Peter didn't want to change, but because of his uncertainty about Nina's perception of his role, he also didn't quite dare.

In addition, another source of tension arose: the awkward fact that Nina was now earning much more than Peter. Nina felt fortunate to be able to add so much money to the family coffers. As she noted: "My salary would make it possible for Peter to get out of technical books, if he wanted, and go into psychology. Sometimes he talks about wanting to become a therapist. He'd be wonderful at it. I've reminded him he can if he wants. We can afford it." By offering to be the main provider for a while so he could get into work he loved, Nina was offering Peter a gift.

Peter appreciated the spirit of Nina's gift, and the opportunity. Her salary also allowed them a new home, a new car, and a private school for Alexandra—even when he was not quite settled in his career. But Peter felt uneasy about Nina's salary. He certainly didn't feel as grateful to Nina as she would have felt to him, had their salaries been reversed. This was not because Peter thought Nina was "competing" with him. He put it this way: "Nina is successful, but she isn't ambitious. I'm more ambitious than she is. Nina also isn't competitive, maybe just a little, and I am, just a little." Peter did not feel the problem was competition. It was that Nina's higher earnings *shamed him as a man*. He felt that friends and relatives—especially older males—would think less of him if they knew his wife earned more. Given that Peter wanted their good opinion, he could not gracefully accept Nina's gift. Indeed, he and Nina treated her salary as a miserable secret. They did not tell his parents; if Peter's father found out, Peter said, "he would die." They didn't tell Nina's father, because "Nina even outearns him." And they didn't tell Peter's high school buddies back home because, Peter said, "I'd never hear the end of it." Over lunch one day, Nina told me in a near whisper: "I was interviewed for an article in *Business Week*, and I had to call the fellow back and ask him please not to publish my salary. When he interviewed me I was proud to tell him my salary, but then I thought, I don't want that there—because of Peter."

Nina was giving Peter the kind of gift that, under the old rules, a man should give a woman: relief from the pressure to provide. Peter wanted to give Nina "the choice of whether to work or not." He wanted her to want to work—sure, why not?—but not to need to work. But Nina did not need *that* particular gift: given her combination of skill and opportunity, she would always choose to work.

With his notion of manhood under new pressure, Peter made one of these unarticulated "moves" that serve the goal of preserving a man's relation to a "man's sphere," and his notion of the "right" amount of marital power. He summoned the feeling that it was not Nina who gave him the gift of her high salary. It was he, Peter, who was giving the important gift because he was suffering in his sense of manhood on her behalf. People "out there" in the world Peter came from and cared about ridiculed men whose wives outearned them. They shook their heads. They rolled their eyes. In order to live with Nina's salary, he had to absorb a cultural assault on his manhood. As Peter said, looking me in the eye, "Only one in a hundred men could take this." Nina was lucky to be married to such an unusual man. And Nina gave him credit: she though Peter was "unusual" too. Her salary *was* hard to take. She was lucky.

Curiously, because Peter and Nina allowed them to, it was their parents, the guys in Peter's office, his buddies at home, society "out there"—not the two of them privately—who defined the value of the gifts they exchanged. What was it that had ultimately lowered

Nina's credit with Peter and reduced her side in their balance of gratitude? One thing was their joint appreciation of the injury he had suffered to his male pride—an appreciation based on their feeling that a man *should* be able to base his pride on traditional grounds. And this pride hinged on the attitude of others "out there." Through both their ideas about gender, the outside came inside and lowered Nina's "private account": given what people out there thought, she owed him one.

On the surface, Peter adapted to her salary; it was "fine"; he wished her well. But, as he had to make this hard concession to his older view of himself "as a man," he wanted her gratitude. After all, it was *she* who had passed on the pressure from her irresistable opportunities at Telfac to him, forcing him to adjust his role as husband.

Through this invisible "move"—to expect Nina to be grateful to *him*—Peter unwittingly passed on the strain of a larger social change (of which the call for female executives at Telfac in the early 1970s was one sign) back to Nina—through their marital economy of gratitude. Now *she* owed *him* something—gratitude for "being willing to take it." Like a great storage closet crowded with objects that would otherwise clutter the house, her indebtedness made the rest of their relationship more "tidy." Peter Tanagawa seemed to adapt to his wife's higher salary—he supported and took pride in her work—but only by storing in this hidden emotional closet the tension between his unchanged idea of himself and Nina's new salary. It was like a bite taken but not swallowed. Had he actually altered his views about men and money in response to Nina's new salary and changing self-image, *he* would have been saying the thanks; or at the least, they would have been even. Instead, their economy of gratitude absorbed and encapsulated the fact that Peter had not adapted to these recent changes in his wife.

Nina's sense that Peter was doing her a favor in being that "one in a hundred" kind of guy also had a bearing on his participation in the second shift. She told me:

> I've wondered if my salary bothers him. Because if we're having a disagreement over something, he sometimes says he thinks I'm acting high and mighty—like "Who do you think you *are*?" I said to him once, "You never used to say that." And he told me, "I do think you've gotten much more assertive than you used to be." Peter might equate my assertiveness with my income. I don't know if the money has anything to do with it, or if I'm just tired of doing all the housework.

Normally open and articulate, Peter made it clear in conversations with me that Nina's salary was painful. He felt he couldn't be the man Nina would still love thirty years from now if he *both* earned less than she did *and also* shared the second shift. That would amount to two assaults on his manhood and present him with a line he felt he couldn't cross. If he did, he would feel like a failure compared to other men, and subliminally a failure in her eyes, too. In his heart of hearts, Peter didn't really care about his career success. What he did care about was his marriage to Nina, and for things to feel right between them, she could not be that far ahead at work, that disengaged from home. Peter wanted to be involved in family life, but only if Nina were also *more* involved. He was doing more at home now than when they first married. He wanted credit for all the changing he had already done on her behalf. He felt perilously close to the "line" that marked the limits of his ability to change, and which he guarded by his "move" to win credit for sacrificing his honor, credit for being the one to adapt when, as Nancy Holt had said, usually women do that.

One sign of this "line" emerged spontaneously in an interview. I had asked Peter to look at a long list of household chores—laundry, sewing, car repairs, and so on—and tell me who did each one. Expecting a series of perfunctory replies, I was taken aback—as I think he was himself—when we came to the item on lawn mowing. "Lawn mowing!" he burst out suddenly, "*I* do the mowing!" He jabbed the page with his finger and exclaimed:

We share the weeding, but I do the mowing! I do not like the idea of a *woman* doing the mowing. I think a father, if he's got the time to mow the lawn and edge it, should not let his daughter do that, or his wife. I think it's lazy! I don't like it. I don't like parents that ask their children to do things when they either could or should do it themselves. I wouldn't want to see my wife mowing the lawn. The logical extension of that is that I don't want people seeing my daughter do that either! And another thing—I don't think girls should drive cars in high school. I wouldn't let Alexandra or Diane drive a car in high school. *No way!*

In the woman he deeply loved, in the home that mattered most, and in the world of work, a whole gender revolution was under way. But the old-fashioned ways still held for Peter Tanagawa's lawn and car. . . .

ALEXANDRA'S FRIENDS

Difficulties arose with their dark-haired Alexandra, an observant, somber child who seemed somehow older than her five years. From the first, these difficulties were defined as a "Nina-Alexandra" problem. Peter had routed his own feelings for Alexandra through Nina. Alexandra glumly explained to me one day, "I'm driven to school by Annie's mom, Sarah's mom, Jill's mom. My mom doesn't drive." Alexandra distinguished between school friends (friends she played with at school) and home friends (friends invited home). She had school friends but no home friends. She explained that in order to invite friends home, you needed *a mother* at home. By all three—Nina, Peter, and Alexandra—it was considered a truth that a girl can't make home friends without a mother at home.

If Peter had an urge to plunge more fully into the children's routines, he controlled that desire. If he had a different urge, to leave it to Nina, he acted on it. He helped Alexandra unreverse her printed *B*'s and *D*'s. He read Dr. Seuss books to her, and buttoned her dress in the mornings. But the rest of "quality time," he said with anxious reverence, was up to Nina. In this way he again shaped his inclinations so as to separate himself from the ultimate responsibility for the second shift but to identify lovingly with each family episode through the medium of his wife.

Sensing her father's gender strategy, which placed domestic responsibilities on her mother, Alexandra turned to Nina. When Alexandra began to compare her lot to that of school friends with mothers who stayed home, it was to her mother that she addressed a silent protest, and it was Nina who felt guilty.

If Mommy wasn't going to be home, it seemed, Alexandra wasn't going to "be home" either—not in conversation, not in weekend play. One day, Alexandra came home with a note in her lunchbox addressed to Nina from Alexandra's teacher. As Nina recalled: "The teacher said that even though this was Alexandra's second year at school, she still had no friends."

This was disturbing news. On the following Saturday, a week before Valentine's Day, something worse happened. Nina had taken Alexandra to a stationery store to buy valentine cards for her classmates. Alexandra picked the prettiest card for herself because, as she explained to her mother in a low voice, "I don't think anyone at school is going to give me one."

Sometimes a way of life collapses because of a very tiny but stunning episode. So it was with the valentine card. That night, Nina told Peter, "We have a crisis." Peter empathized with Nina's anguish. The incident had been tiny, but they agreed it wasn't minor. "Handle it the best way you can, honey," he said, "I'm a hundred percent behind you."

THE COMPANY LOYALTY TEST AND DROPPING OUT OF SUCCESS

A week later, Nina asked her boss if she could take a cut in pay and work only three days a week, and he said she could. She broke the good news to Alexandra at dinnertime, hoping for a delighted response. For three days, Alexandra said nothing about it. Then, one evening, she asked nonchalantly if she might invite a girl friend over the following Friday. As Peter drove Nina to work the next day, he said to her in a warm, excited tone, "Doesn't that make it worth it, honey?"

During this time, Peter made no modifications in his own work schedule. By telling Nina that she could do "whatever she needed to do" but refusing to become more involved with Alexandra himself, Peter had effectively robbed Nina of the choice he had so lovingly offered her, to work full time or not, as she saw fit. Ironically, he worked even harder at extending the market for technical books, work that bored him, while Nina curtailed the work she loved. Neither one saw anything strange about this.

Until this point in her career, Nina had been the showcase woman in top management at a company that prided itself on personnel policies that enabled mothers to work—flex time, part-time work, job sharing. Now Nina had a chance to show the world that workers can be good mothers and part-time workers can have real careers. Her immediate boss assured her, "Don't worry, we support you."

But trouble began almost immediately. Nina had handled four departments; she gave up three. Word had it that management was saying, "What Nina does can't be *that* important if she just works three days a week." Her immediate boss became more "realistic." "I fought for you with the higher-ups, I've been holding them off," he told her. "Now there's only one thing I want from you—to work full time." They had trained and groomed her; now they wanted their money's worth.

Fellow employees gossiped about how "serious" Nina was. The longer your hours, they reasoned, the more serious and committed you were. Men whose lives ran on traditional tracks had a far better crack at passing this seriousness test than a woman like Nina, who already felt lucky to live with a man who had "taken a lot." Despite its formal progressive policies, the company latently rewarded traditional marriages and punished other kinds. Nina summed up her predicament now this way:

> Working three days a week is barely holding them off. I thought to myself that maybe with the four-day weekend, I could at least meet my carpool obligations. And I'd have more time with Alexandra. If I go back to full time pretty soon, I'll be okay. But if I keep this up much longer, I won't be. I may already be out. My boss says, "You're walking alone right now. You're not committed here." Which isn't true. I *am* committed to the company—*on a part-time basis.*

More and more, Nina was punished for being an uncommitted worker. First she was moved from her large office, facing the San Francisco bay, to a tiny, windowless office. Then she was told to report to a peer instead of a higher-ranking officer "until she came back full time." Her participation in a company bonus program, all along assured her, was terminated. One older man—whose own marriage to a career woman had come to a stormy end and who had quietly resented Nina's success for years—finally confessed to her, "When you went part time, I realized you weren't really serious."

Some of her colleagues in upper management were happily remarried to women who, in second marriages themselves, were more cautiously dedicating themselves to the family. Others were married to wives who worked on timeless graduate degrees, or did volunteer work that offered them a private fantasy of some future public life but never interfered with their husbands' long hours at work. Some of these wives simply stayed home and seemed to have an easier life. A few men in upper management had career wives, but even they didn't seem to face a dilemma like this one with Alexandra.

Nina was becoming keenly aware of how her male coworkers were, like Peter, protected from the crisis she faced. Were they sacrificing anything to make sure their children got all they needed? She noticed that male coworkers were happy to pin a "mother identity" on her; passing her in the halls, they often said, "Hi, Nina, how are the kids?" She used to give a happy reply. Now she sensed certain asymmetry in such greetings; seldom did she or anyone in the company greet *men* in this way.

One day when I went to visit Nina at work, I found her gazing at family photos on her desk. She told me that for the first time she felt like a stranger in her own company. She was taking a hard look at her job: "In my job I lay people off. I have to. We've been going through layoffs. I counsel people and help them solve problems. It hasn't hit me until this year that they're *good* people. They're not poor performers. They're people I can really relate to, people who've worked hard. It wasn't their fault. Their division went under."

As I looked at Nina now, I could see how her delicate, almost Cinderella-like look of innocence, combined with her sharp intelligence and high emotional control, could have convinced her boss that she was just the person to give employees bad news kindly. Her helpful manner and mindfulness of corporate purpose had probably saved the company millions in lawsuits. How could a laid-off worker sue after dealing with someone so kind and helpful in suggesting relocation with other companies? I could imagine Nina as the velvet glove on the hard hand of the corporate profit motive. Now, in her spirit of detachment, she saw this too.

She held the company off while she looked for part-time jobs at other companies. Before long, another computer company offered her a vice-presidency, full time. Hearing of this offer, Nina's company itself suddenly offered her a vice-presidency, with a higher salary and unbelievably high bonuses, again full time. She agonized about Alexandra. She talked and talked with Peter. And then she accepted the job with her company. She told her boss she would not be able to work late on weekdays or on weekends, but she would work five days a week. As with her last success, she had a sinking feeling. But she told herself that this was a decision "for now"; she could quit if Alexandra's problem got worse.

And it did. Not long after she accepted the new job, she opened Alexandra's lunchbox and found another note from her teacher: "Dear Mrs. Tanagawa, I wanted you to know that Alexandra has made more friends at school. But I have to say that other things still concern me. Recently I assigned the children a story to write and Alexandra wrote a strange story about killing her sister and hating her mother." Nina talked to Alexandra's teacher, and within two weeks, engaged a family therapist. When I last saw them, Peter was still being supportive of Nina in "her" crisis.

Nina's circle of relatives and friends offered no solution. Her "progressive" workplace offered no relief. She had started out a transitional, had pushed softly toward Nancy Holt's position, and like Nancy, met resistance. The Holts' family myth was that they shared the second shift "as much as we can, given the difference in interest." Peter didn't, like Evan Holt, believe he shared more than he actually did. But the Tanagawas' myth, like that of the Holts, disguised the fact that Peter *had* a gender strategy, based on the ideology and feeling rules of the transitional. Although he'd been forced to accept his wife's higher salary and the extension of her identity outside the home, Peter's feeling rules were still fairly traditional, as were his feelings. Given his view of how a man should earn appreciation, he had thought he "should feel" anguished if his wife earned more than he. And he did feel anguish. On the other hand, Nina's growing involvement with her career led her to begin to outgrow the rules with which she'd begun her marriage, though she couldn't quite bring herself to re-align their marital roles.

Peter's move was to resist Nina's passive attempts to renegotiate their roles, and to push her into playing the supermom. He partly did this to preserve the marriage by shoring up the traditional male role on which he felt it emotionally depended. His "solution" was thus the problem. Currently, in about 20 percent of the nation's two-job couples (though slightly fewer in my study), women earn more than their husbands. Though the tune may differ a little each time, the beat is usually the same.

As is probably true for many such women, Nina's conflict is hardly resolved. For Nina and Peter's marriage is the stalled revolution in microcosm, and like that revolution, their story is unfinished.

DISCUSSION QUESTIONS

1. Describe the differences between "second-shift" work and the larger world of work.
2. What were Nina's reasons for choosing to cut back on her work hours and responsibilities? What do you think will be the effects of this decision upon her career?
3. To what extent do you think the Tanawagas have an egalitarian marriage?

READING 7-3

Women in Socialist Societies

Charlotte G. O'Kelly
Larry S. Carney

. . . The early socialists often argued that problems associated with gender stratification would simply disappear under socialism. The leadership in socialist countries today still gives ideological lip service to the ideal of gender equality and includes it among its long-term goals.

Ideological support and official rhetoric are certainly not sufficient to achieve gender equality or women's liberation. To overcome the legacy gender stratification inherited from the social structures of the past requires a high degree of commitment, a willingness to allocate important and often scarce resources to this end, and programs designed to change men's attitudes and behavior. Contemporary social societies have not been willing to undertake such commitment. The following exam-

ination of the history of the "woman question" in the Soviet Union, the Israeli kibbutz, the People's Republic of China, and Cuba under Castro indicates the problems and pitfalls that befell these societies' limited attempts to institute gender equality. . . .

THE U.S.S.R.

The Economic Sphere. Women's representation in the economic sphere is far higher than in the non-Communist world. Women constitute 51 percent of the civilian labor force and women are found in large numbers in occupational categories such as professional employment (for example, medical doctors and technicians), which are dominated by males in the West.[1] Women's work is facilitated by a widespread, though still inadequate, network of nurseries, day-care centers, boarding schools, and after-school programs for older children. Women receive generous maternity leaves, maternity benefits, and pension plans. There is also a large body of protective legislation limiting the type of work women can do and barring women from many of the more strenuous jobs. Legislation forbids discrimination against women workers and requires equal pay for equal work.

But the work world in the Soviet Union is as gender segregated as it is in the West, and the gender segregation produces similar consequences. There are women's jobs and women's industries and men's jobs and men's industries. The distribution of men and women in the labor force has not changed significantly since 1939. Also, just as in the West, the women's sector of this dual labor market is paid substantially less than the men's sector. The average female worker earns 65 percent of the average male worker's salary.[2] The Soviet emphasis on heavy industry includes the policy of better pay for workers in this area to attract more personnel to these occupations. These are the occupations in which men predominate and from which women are often barred by protective legislation.

Even in occupations in which men and women both participate, fewer and fewer women are found as one moves up the scale of power, pay, and prestige. For example, it is a much publicized fact that women constitute 69 percent of the physicians in the Soviet Union. Yet the more prestigious positions and the administrative positions are disproportionately male. Over 90 percent of the pediatricians are female, yet the more prestigious field of surgery has only 6 percent females. The gender stratification within medicine is further evidenced by the fact that almost all nurses are female. Moreover, current policies are aimed at reducing the overrepresentation of females among medical doctors and the percentage of females in the field is dropping. Male applicants to medical schools are being given preferential treatment over female applicants. Thus this avenue of professional advancement for women may be closing somewhat while other avenues are not opening at a comparable rate.[3] . . .

Women have been integrated into middle and lower levels of the economic sphere and into the lower levels of the political spheres, but at no time in Soviet history have men been integrated into the domestic sphere of housework and child care. This has been particularly burdensome because of the inadequate service sector. Shopping, for example, is a much more frustrating and time-consuming process in the Soviet Union than in the West. Shortages, long lines, discourteous clerks, and the necessity of going to several specialty shops instead of supermarkets have characterized Soviet shopping for decades.

Housing is also crowded and often substandard by Western standards. This makes upkeep more difficult. Few labor-saving devices have been available until recently and now that appliances are available the better off and better educated are the people who purchase them. Among poorer, less-educated couples, the husband usually judges it more important to spend the family's savings on a television than on a refrigerator or washing machine. . . .

Gender Role Stereotypes. Child rearing and children's education still embody traditional conceptions of gender roles. Girls are socialized toward "feminine" interests and occupations and boys toward "masculine" activities. In Soviet schools, girls but not boys are given home economics training. Traditional gender roles predominate in Soviet children's literature.[4] The effects of this gender role socialization show up very early in the occupational aspirations of boys and girls, and there is little reason to expect change in the near future. Soviet authorities and the public continue to believe that anatomy is destiny and that gender roles are embedded in the different biological natures of women and men. They see no reason to attempt to socialize girls and boys away from gender roles and traditional femininity and masculinity. . . .

In fact, with increased affluence has come renewed emphasis on femininity for females. This is expressed through concern for feminine and stylish clothing available only through the black market, for cosmetics, and for work assignments and domestic appliances that preserve a woman's hands and complexion.

There is little or no support for feminism among most Soviet women today. One young divorced mother in love with a married man told a researcher that there was no women's movement. "We don't need a women's movement. Here we're all convinced that everything is the way it ought to be. But I think when women were emancipated, it actually amounted to man's liberation from the family."[5]

THE ISRAELI KIBBUTZ

An alternative to the patterns of social organization and development in most modern industrial societies can be found in the planned communities of the Israeli kibbutzim. The founders of the kibbutzim consciously rejected the class and gender stratification systems as they knew them in their home countries. Although Israel as a whole has never been a socialist society, the local kibbutz communities represent one of the most important and enduring attempts to put the collective ownership and communitarian institutions idealized in socialist theory into practice. . . .

The Woman Problem

The kibbutz movement has been successful in fulfilling its ideals of abolishing class inequality and competition; it successfully established communal housekeeping and a child-care system that produced healthy, well-adjusted children and adults; it has been successful in its rural life-style. It has not, however, been successful in establishing gender equality or in abolishing gender differentiation in social roles and social participation. The kibbutzim have instead been plagued for years by what they call the "woman problem." Men are more satisfied as kibbutz members than women are, and women are more likely than men to want to leave the kibbutz. When couples do leave, it is usually at the insistence of the wife. Women are also more likely than men to oppose kibbutz principles regarding the family structure. In recent years women have agitated for more "feminine prerogatives," in particular for the right to keep their children in their apartments overnight. In all but the most radical federation of kibbutzim, women have been successful in their demand to reinstate the nuclear family. Children live with their parents and go to the children's houses only during the day. Apartments are larger and more housework is done in the nuclear family setting.

. . . The lack of prestige combined with poor working conditions further decreased women's satisfaction with and commitment to the kibbutz. The men reaped most of the benefits of kibbutz life.

The prestige differential between the male-dominated agricultural sector and the female-dominated service sector also served to undermine political equality. The kibbutz still accords equal rights to all members, and each member has an equal right to take part in political discussion and debate. But the general feeling is that those who actively participate in and have expertise in a particular area are the appropriate discussants. Thus matters concerning new investments in agriculture are debated almost exclusively among the male agricultural workers. Policy regarding the children's houses or kitchens is debated by women. Yet the most serious decisions, especially about economic allocations, are likely to involve agriculture rather than services. Thus these norms effectively exclude women from political participation in the most important decisions. Furthermore, a great deal of decision-making authority is vested in the economic committees that organize and run each sector. Again, the most important committee is the one for the agricultural sector and women rarely hold office in it. The prestige of this committee and of agriculture in general gives its workers an edge in running for other kibbutz offices. The general management of the kibbutz is predominantly male.

A further factor contributing to the failure of gender egalitarianism in the kibbutz is the wider social, political, and cultural environment in Israel and the international setting. . . .

The Threat of War. A . . . factor in the wider environment of the kibbutz that has negatively affected the position of women has been the impact of war and the constant threat of war. In the years of struggle preceding the founding of the Israeli state, females often participated in combat duties. Several female soldiers are national heroines. Today females continue to serve in the Israeli army and are subject to the draft just as males are but they are not given combat training; they do not serve as long as men do; and there are many more exceptions for females such as marriage, pregnancy, or orthodox religious beliefs.[6] Females are given clerical jobs and other noncombatant tasks which free men for combat. Female soldiers also also given lessons in beauty "to improve the morale of the men," emphasizing their role as sex objects.[7] . . .

The constant threat of war has also led to an increased emphasis on the maternal role for women. Throughout Israel, including on the kibbutz, mothers of sons in combat are expected to play important supportive roles for their sons. They are to keep in close touch with their soldier sons and provide emotional support in their letters and telephone calls. They should send food packages and other homemade luxuries to comfort the soldiers. They should also follow the war-related news closely as a demonstration of their concern for their sons' welfare. Again, this serves to emphasize male importance in society and females as supporters of the more important males.

Fear of being "outreproduced" by the Arabs increases the pressures on Israeli women to marry early and to have many children. A pregnant women may be congratulated for producing another "little soldier" for the nation.[8] . . .

The Experiment That Never Took Place. From the beginning women were assumed to be "naturals" in the laundries and kitchens, and after the children arrived, in the nurseries and schools as well. With the increased birthrate, this work eventually required half the labor of the kibbutz, and as men would not enter such work, women were drawn from what few agricultural and productive work assignments they had. A rigid gender division of labor was the result of men never relinquishing the traditional male role. . . .

The extent of the socialization of children into traditional roles is also clear in the practice of giving high school boys work assignments only in the productive spheres and girls assignments only in the children's houses. Educators who have attempted to reverse this pattern and mix up the assignments were prevented from doing so by the work foremen who refused to accept girls.[9] These early work assignments are very important for adult occupations. The training received during the work assignments is a primary consideration for career patterns after the young men and women return from their compulsory military service. Women's prior compulsory experience in the children's houses keeps them assigned to domestic and service tasks while males' previous experience in the productive sphere is the ostensible reason for giving them full-time adult assignments in the same area.[10] Occupational choice and training opportunities are actually lower for kibbutz women than for other Israeli women or for Western women. The degree of gender segregation in the labor force is one of the highest in the world. One woman complained, "I didn't want to be a child-care worker, but I am one . . . the people here are very narrow minded. When you are younger, you are working with children, and then in the kitchen, and when you are older—in the clothes' care, laundry, and sewing. . . ."[11]

Shepher and Tiger's assertion that women forced traditional gender roles on reluctant males who eagerly supported gender role equality and the dedifferentiation of the genders is incorrect. The men had never been committed to abolishing traditional gender roles; they only resisted the women's turning away from the system of female-run cooperative child-care arrangements which had become an accepted principle of kibbutz life, which as Blasi points out, is hardly a sufficient basis for female liberation.

Dead-End Jobs. As Rosabeth Moss Kanter has found, women and men in low-mobility, routine, dead-end jobs, "the stuck," react in typical ways.[12] They cease to be ambitious and striving. They turn their interests to family, friends, hobbies, or relationships with coworkers. The social aspects of the job come to be preeminent. Although Kanter was describing reactions to being "stuck" in a large, competitive, profit-oriented corporation, her analysis may apply equally to kibbutz women.

These women are blocked by the structural barriers of gender-based training and work assignments from advancement to the prestigious leadership and productive sectors of the kibbutz. Young kibbutz women are described as reacting to their lack of opportunity with resignation and withdrawal and with more symptoms of emotional and personal problems than nonkibbutz girls.[13] It is not surprising that they seek to make as comfortable an environment as possible in the service and domestic sector. This includes an emphasis on the emotional benefits of closer attachments to children and the social relationships of private family life.

Since the men are not as likely to be stuck, they are less likely to resist the kibbutz communal child-care and minimalized family practices. But little research has been conducted on kibbutz men. Men who are stuck may be making similar accommodations to their situation. In the corporation men and women responded similarly to dead-end career lines.

THE PEOPLE'S REPUBLIC OF CHINA

The development of socialism in China has followed a very different path from that in the Soviet Union or the kibbutz. Both the USSR and the kibbutzim faced difficult if not desperate settings for putting their ideals into practice. But when the Chinese Communist Party (CCP) came to power in 1949 it faced what was perhaps an even bleaker situation. Centuries of agrarian despotism, followed by colonial domination by Western powers and the Japanese, the destruction of World War II, and the ravages of the civil war left a massive population; backward, crippled agriculture and industry; and mammoth social problems, not the least of which was widespread famine. Despite the limitations of the authoritarian society the CCP has constructed, the gains in economic well-being and personal security are vivid to the majority of the population, particularly to those who lived under preliberation conditions.

Economic and Domestic Spheres. Almost all working-age women in the cities are employed outside the home, but as with the rural women, the work is highly gender segregated and women earn considerably less than men. Despite a strong ideological emphasis on socializing the domestic sphere, housework and child care remain quite private. Communal dining arrangements proved to be unpopular and they are rather limited today. Subsidized child care is available to many but it is insufficient to meet the needs. Couples rely heavily on the services of the elderly. Since adult children are required by law to support their aging parents, many multigeneration households continue even in crowded urban households. The grandparents will also help with the housework, but the main responsibility lies with the wife. There have been some educational campaigns to encourage men to share the domestic burdens, but they have been largely ineffective. Women therefore suffer the same limitations in terms of competing for promotions and better jobs and for advancing through party work as the women of the Soviet Union. Chinese women have entered many previously male-dominated occupational categories, but they are still concentrated in the lowest-paying, low-prestige jobs, primarily in the service sector or marginal industries and often in jobs seen as extensions of the domestic role.

Economic production in China is still uneven and of variable quality. Shortages and shoddy goods hurt men and women both but they make the housewife's burden even heavier. China cannot, of course, afford the household appliances and labor-saving devices common in the West. But inadequate housing, lack of running water, and time-consuming shopping bedevil the urban housewife as well as her rural cousins. Women's concerns are focused on practical improvements within the immediate situations in which they live. Interest in feminism is limited. . . .

Marriage. Chinese adults are ideally more committed to their work unit than to their marriage. They should be willing to accept work assignments that will keep them separated for months if not years, willing to work late night after night to meet production goals, and willing to devote leisure time to study or political work. Whether individuals agree with this ideology or not, they will be strongly controlled by their work unit. It is through this unit that they receive not only their salary, but also their ration coupons and their housing assignment and perhaps the clearest expression of public patriarchy is that it is in the work unit that they receive permission to marry and permission to have a child.

Marriage choices are often made on the basis of the desirability of the prospective spouse's work assignment and the housing assignment or other privileges that come with it. A man with one of the coveted state industry positions (who receives much better benefits than nonstate workers) will have a wider selection of potential brides than a man with a less desirable work unit. Marriage is the primary means people have of changing their residence from the country to the city or to a more desirable city.

Even in the city marriages are still arranged, but it is not a matter of the patriarchal father looking for the best match from his point of view as it is young people having little opportunity to find a mate and friends and relatives helping out with introductions. Courtships still tend to be formal and short. There does seem to be some loosening of the public condemnation of courtship, and visitors to China now report young couples openly showing affection in the public parks.

CUBA

Castro and his revolutionaries fought a long and difficult guerrilla war to restructure Cuba along more equalitarian lines. Many women as well as men fought in the revolution, and Castro began his leadership announcing his support for dismantling gender stratification as well as class and racial stratification and rural/urban differentials.

Structural Hindrances to Gender Equality. Material conditions in Cuba have prevented the Castro regime from achieving its ideal of equal rights for women. Castro has given strong ideological support to women's equal participation in the political and economic spheres and men's equal participation in the domestic sphere. In 1975 Cuba enacted a new Family Code that explicitly requires that husbands must share the responsibilities for housework and child care equally with their wives. Passage of the Code was preceded by months of public debate and discussion of the Code and of women's position in the family and society. The government wanted feedback from the people and changed some aspects of the law as a result of this input. More important, however, the debate was a powerful tool for consciousness raising in the population. But despite all this attention to the problem a decade after its enactment it is clear that the law has not decisively affected the behavior of Cuban husbands.

The government recognized at a very early stage that to undermine gender stratification along with class stratification, it would be necessary to socialize many aspects of housework and child care. Muriel Nazzari points out that the crucial factor in gender stratification in Cuba and elsewhere as well is probably the burdens of child care and not housework.[14] Housework can almost always be postponed, but child care cannot. The more children a person has to care for, the less time the person will have for other activities.

Castro began with a strong commitment to providing free child care to all who needed it. But the problems of economic development facing a nation trying to pull itself up from the poverty typical of peripheral societies proved to be more difficult to solve than the new government had anticipated. The economic growth required to absorb the costs of taking women's domestic services out of the private sphere to the public sphere has not been achieved. Free child care is no longer available. Women are not paid for their housework in

any way, but their duties in the home are recognized by law in the requirement that all men must work outside the home, while for women this is a choice. . . .

Divorced women who have children and heavy domestic responsibilities do work, however. It is the availability of the husband's wage combined with a heavy domestic load that explains why married women constituted only 18 percent of the female labor force in 1972, while divorced women represented 43 percent, single women 30 percent, and widows 9 percent.[15] Because married women stay out of the labor force, women compose only 30 percent of the Cuban labor force. This is true even though women have access to the higher-ranking jobs and even though the pay gap between male and female workers is probably narrower than in many other societies where women participate in much larger ratios. Women workers also receive generous maternity leave benefits, and some absenteeism for family responsibilities is a legal right. Gender segregation does exist, however, with females dominating in the lower-paid service-sector jobs and males filling the better-paid industrial jobs.

Nazzari argues that it is the material conditions in Cuban society that hinder female participation in the public sphere, although the persistence of *machismo* and male-dominated cultural traditions and attitudes may play some role. The Cuban government has as an ideal the communist maxim "From each according to his ability, but to each according to his needs," and it has made impressive progress in providing food, housing, education, medical care, and other important services for free or at very low cost. The government found, however, that if it wanted to increase productivity substantially, moral exhortations to work hard were insufficient to motivate workers who had their basic needs taken care of for little money and for whom extra money was meaningless because of the lack of a significant market in consumer goods. The state responded by raising prices, charging for many previously free services such as telephones, and increasing the importance of one's wage-earning ability. Increasing the importance of wages in a society where husbands are still likely to earn substantially more than wives is a strong structural hindrance to shared roles within the family and a strong support for the maintenance of gender stratification. It emphasizes the husband's importance as the chief breadwinner for the family; and it makes it much more likely that his wife will defer to his needs and take up the slack for a better job, or pursue political work to enhance his position. . . .

Another economic policy enacted to enhance growth and productivity is the new requirement that industries should show a profit; that is, they should produce more than it costs to run the industry. This gives managers a powerful disincentive for hiring women, especially married women with children. Maternity leave, absenteeism for domestic problems, and other special benefits for female workers add to the cost of the plant and may decrease productivity as well. . . .

The Political Sphere. As an example of the federation's work in support of gender equality, when the first experiments with local elections produced very few female officeholders or delegates, the federation was empowered to study the problem. It ascertained, not unlike the situation in other socialist and capitalist societies, that women's domestic burdens deprived them of the free time necessary for politics. It had reached similar conclusions in its studies of married women's failure to participate in the labor force outside the home. The federation has repeatedly recommended that the government undertake policies to ease what Cubans call women's "second shift." But

this interferes with policies designed to increase economic growth, which is seen as vital to Cuba's long-term development. In the short term, gender stratification is allowed to remain largely unchallenged.

Lack of progress in eliminating gender segregation is not solely a matter of economic scarcity. The government has shown little enthusiasm for integrating women into the political structure or for appointing women to high-ranking administrative or policy-making positions. The few women who do hold important government positions are concentrated in the Federation of Cuban Woman and in general confined to the "social housekeeping sphere." Even the war heroines receive less mention and fewer banners at public rallies than the war heroes. Women politicians and women in general would have little basis for protecting women's interests if the next leader should reject Castro's position favoring gender equality. . . .

CONCLUSION

When compared with their presocialist past, most socialist societies have made remarkable advances in breaking down certain aspects of gender stratification and in improving the general position of women. Most socialist societies also compare very favorably with the major capitalist countries in both these areas. Moreover, the socialist societies have achieved these advances within a very brief historical time span.[16] Nevertheless, the real achievements in the area of gender equality have, as yet, noticeably fallen short of the ideals of socialist ideology. How is this to be explained?

Evaluating relative progress toward gender equality in socialist societies is difficult not only because of the various biases that both ideological defenders and opponents of socialism bring to this task, but also because of the complex historical, cultural, and political *international* realities which have informed the development of socialism in each society where it has been established. The Soviet, Chinese, Cuban, and other socialist regimes have existed in extremely hostile international environments since their inception. However much weight one is to give to the actions of these regimes themselves in stimulating such hostility, the antisocialist ideologies and activities of the capitalist powers have had decisive effects in shaping the social, economic, and political institutions of these societies. They have been societies on the defensive, distorting whatever genuine goals of socialist egalitarianism they may have pursued (or may have wished to pursue) into conformity with what their political leaders have perceived as necessary programs for political, economic, and military survival in the face of threats from both internal and external enemies. After all the morally compelling condemnations and criticisms of the cruelties, repressions, and despotisms perpetuated by certain of these regimes have been made, the siege-environment in which twentieth-century socialism had developed still stands as one of the principal factors that must be taken into account in evaluating both its successes and failures.

Even without the international threats and constraints faced by developing socialist societies, the challenges of internal economic and social transformation would have been formidable. . . .

The alternative goals of achieving human liberties, democratic participation, and egalitarianism have not only typically been given secondary consideration in these efforts, but have often been perceived as contradictory to the prospects of advancing economic development itself. Clearly, the movement toward full gender equality has been hindered by this order of priorities in socialist societies.

Notes

1 Alistar McAuley, *Women's Work and Wages in the Soviet Union* (London: George Allen & Unwin, 1981); William Mandel, *Soviet Women* (Garden City, NY: Anchor Books, 1975) argues it is 75 percent.

2 Gail Lapidus, *Women in Soviet Society: Equality, Development, and Social Change* (Berkeley: University of California Press, 1978) p. 188.

3 Lapidus, 1978, 188.

4 Mollie Schwartz Rosenhan, "Images of Male and Female in Children's Readers," in Dorothy Atkinson, Alexander Dallin, and Gail Lapidus, Eds., *Women in Russia* (Stanford, CA: Stanford University Press, 1977), pp. 293–305.

5 Carola Hansson and Karin Liden, *Moscow Women: Thirteen Interviews* (New York: Pantheon Books, 1983).

6 Nira Yuval Davis, *Israeli Women and Men: Divisions Behind the Unity* (London: Change International Reports, n.d.), pp. 10–13; also Lesley Hazelton, *Israeli Women: The Reality Behind the Myths* (New York: Simon & Schuster, 1977); pp. 38–62; Nancy Datan, Aaron Antonovsky, and Benjamin Maoz, *A Time to Reap: The Middle Age of Women in Five Israeli Subcultures* (Baltimore: Johns Hopkins University Press, 1981).

7 Davis, pp. 13–18.

8 Davis, pp. 17.

9 Dorit Padan-Eisenstark, "Girl's Education in the Kibbutz," pp. 210–215 in Michal Palgi and Menachem Rosner, eds., *Sexual Equality: The Israeli Kibbutz Tests the Theories* (Newark, PA: Norwood Editions, 1982); Rosanna Hertz and Wayne Baker, "Women and Men's Work in an Israeli Kibbutz: Gender and the Allocation of Labor," in Palgi et. al., 154–173.

10 Quoted in Amia Lieblich, *Kibbutz Makom: Report from an Israeli Kibbutz* (New York: Pantheon Books, 1981), p. 260.

11 Quoted in Hertz and Baker, 165.

12 Rosabeth Moss Kanter, *Men and Women of the Corporation* (New York: Basic Books, 1977): 136–139, 155–159. See also Hertz and Baker, 166; Seymour Parker and Hilda Parker, "Women and the Emerging Family on the Israeli Kibbutz," *American Ethnologist* 8 (1981): 758–773; Dorit Padan-Eisenstark, "Are Israeli Women Really Equal? Trends and Patterns of Israeli Women's Labor Force Participation: A Comparative Analysis," *Journal of Marriage and the Family* 35, no. 3 (August 1973); 538–545.

13 Padan-Eisenstark, 214.

14 Muriel Nazzari, "The 'Woman Question' in Cuba: An Analysis of Material Constraints or its Solution," *Signs* 9, No. 2 (Winter 1982): 246–263.

15 Nazzari, 257.

16 On all these points, see Nuss, 1980, 1981, 1984; Joan Ecklein, "Obstacles to Understanding the Changing Role of Women in Socialist Countries," *Insurgent Sociologist* 12, nos. 1–2 (Winter/Spring 1984): 7–12; Joan Ecklein, "Women in the German Democratic Republic: Impact of Culture

and Social Policy'' in Janet Zollinger Giele, ed., *Women in the Middle Years: Current Knowledge and Directions for Research and Policy* (New York: John Wiley, 1982): 151–198.

DISCUSSION QUESTIONS

1. Compare and contrast the position of women in the United States with that in one of the socialist societies described by O'Kelly and Carney.

2. According to O'Kelly and Carney, have socialist societies been able to achieve their ideal of gender equality? Why or why not?

3. What lessons about gender stratification can be learned from cross-cultural study?

CHAPTER 8

Issues in Aging

INTRODUCTION

Like gender, race, and ethnicity, age is an important dimension of social structure and a basis for social inequalities. The reduced mortality rates, increased life expectancy, and lowered birth rates which accompanied industrialization have placed the United States in the midst of a demographic revolution which will impact each individual and every societal institution. This revolution is the inexorable aging of our population and the "graying of America" (Macionis, 1989). While the aging of America is not a new phenomenon, what is most startling about the aging trend is the rapid pace at which it is proceeding and the resulting "squaring" of the population pyramid (Pifer and Bronte, 1986). Though the aging of a population is very different from the aging of an individual, we will be concerned with both processes in this chapter.

Aging processes are important from a cultural perspective because of the changing social meanings attached to stages in the life cycle, both across societies and within a society as its population profile shifts. Social definitions have implications for the assumption of social roles, age inequalities, and social policy. The importance of these issues has given rise to a relatively new field of social science: gerontology, the study of aging and the elderly. Gerontologists are concerned with the physical process of aging as well as with how age is culturally defined. Their research has contributed to an understanding of the biological and psychological changes attendant upon the aging process and has explored the causes and consequences of age stratification. It has given rise to a variety of theories of aging and has produced new conceptions of age group distinctions. One such distinction, precipitated by the rapid growth of persons aged sixty-five and over and their social diversity, is the division of older people into the "young old" and the "oldest old." For convenience, the young old are defined as relatively healthy, active, and reasonably well-off financially, while the oldest old—individuals aged 85 and over—represent a growing segment of our population and have a distinctive set of human problems.

The readings in this chapter, which deal

with issues in aging from three levels of analysis, critically examine the limitations of age distinctions and age-based public policies. Bernice Neugarten and Dail Neugarten have taken an approach that is both macrosociological and cultural in dealing with the social meanings of age. The writing of Matilda Riley and John Riley examines aging from an individual level of analysis, and Eli Ginzberg's focus is on a cross-cultural understanding of aging. Let's look more closely at their respective arguments.

Neugarten and Neugarten explore age as a major dimension of social organization and a base from which individuals organize and interpret their experiences throughout their lives. In this selection from their work, the Neugartens examine the changing social meanings of stages in the life cycle, the potential for divisiveness between age groups based on these meanings, and the limitations of age-based social policy. They see a blurring of the distinctions between childhood, adulthood, and old age, and they argue that the significance of age is decreasing in some ways and increasing in other respects. Agreeing with earlier research on the so-called "generation gap," the Neugartens find little evidence for age polarization or age divisiveness in the United States. Research on support for social causes, political attitudes and beliefs about economic issues, particularly Social Security, does not reveal clear age-group demarcations. From a policy perspective, then, the Neugartens see no need for age-based decisions since age has become an unreliable indicator of individuals' needs and competencies. Existing public and private policy decisions targeted by age group do not meet the needs of all the aged but do encourage inappropriate stereotypes. Consequently, these authors believe that policies based on age should be replaced with policies predicated on actual needs and competencies.

One interesting dimension of our aging society is that the elderly population is itself aging. The most rapidly growing segment of our population is individuals aged 85 and over (Rosenwaike, 1985). The oldest old are a demographically distinct subpopulation. The major reason for their spectacular increase in numbers has been declining mortality, but since male mortality exceeds female mortality at every age, the sex ratio (number of males for every 100 females) for the oldest old has seen a rapid decline over the last sixty years. The sex ratio for individuals aged eighty-five and over was 43.7 in 1980, down from 75.4 in 1930 (Rosenwaike, p. 193). The imbalance in the sex ratio results in an imbalance in the marital status of the oldest old. Females in this age group are much less likely than males to be married and to live in family situations. However, convenient distinctions between age groups generate inaccurate stereotypes that reinforce anxieties about conflicts between different age groups over the allocation of scarce resources for health and social welfare. Just as Neugarten and Neugarten question journalistic and policy-based compassionate stereotypes of the aged based on disease (morbidity), poverty, and social dependency, the authors of the second reading question the limited opportunities available to the elderly because of unwarranted stereotypes.

Matilda White Riley has long been a strong advocate of a sociological understanding of aging and the life course. In this article, she and John Riley address the central dilemma of the mismatch between the strengths and capacities of the increasing numbers of older people in the United States, on the one hand, and the inadequate social-role opportunities to utilize, reward, and sustain these strengths, on the other. From the perspective of the aging individual, Riley and Riley believe, the quality of aging can be enhanced by interventions in the ways individuals grow older and in the various dimensions of social structure in which their lives are embedded. They offer a host of small-scale interventions as well as an analytic framework of the relationship between aging and broad social changes in an effort to redesign our conceptions of the life course.

Eli Ginzberg examines the problems of aging from evidence on sixteen nations. According to forecasts by advanced industrial countries, slow economic growth, high inflation, and high unemployment pose threats to economic, health care, and social service supports for the elderly. Many of these problems are also mentioned by developing nations, whose difficulties are exacerbated by additional resource-population imbalances. While recognizing the validity of some of these problems, Ginzberg questions the pessimistic scenarios they have generated in light of the history of economic changes. His is a more optimistic economic outlook. In the areas of income, work, medical care, and social services, Ginzberg believes that a shift in policy emphasis from social supports to social involvement would yield positive results.

References

Macionis, John J. *Sociology*, 2d ed. Englewood Cliffs, N.J.: Prentice-Hall, 1989.

Pifer, Alan, and D. Lydia Bronte. "Introduction: Squaring the Pyramid," *Daedalus*, vol 115, no. 1 (winter), 1986, pp. 1–11.

Rosenwaike, Ira. "A Demographic Portrait of the Oldest Old," *Milbank Memorial Fund Quarterly/ Health and Society*, vol. 63, no. 2, pp. 187–205.

Age in the Aging Society

Bernice L. Neugarten
Dail A. Neugarten

The focus of this essay is not on older persons as an age group, nor on the processes of aging. Instead, the essay deals with age as a major dimension of social organization, and a major touchstone by which individuals organize and interpret their experiences throughout their lives. From both perspectives, the changing society has brought with it new questions regarding the social meanings of age. The first part of the essay is addressed to these questions and suggests that, while in many ways the significance of age is decreasing, in other ways it is increasing.

The aging of the population has brought with it a new concern about the relations between age groups and the possible age divisiveness that may arise in the political arena. The second part of this essay is addressed to that issue and argues that age divisiveness is not necessarily inevitable or even likely to occur.

The third section of this essay moves to issues of public policy. The contention is that if policy-making is to match the social realities, programs based on age might better be played down rather than played up.

Finally, we suggest that the aging society provides not only a new context, but a new opportunity to rethink our traditional views of age in ways that might prove constructive both to individuals and to the society at large.

THE CHANGING SOCIAL MEANINGS OF AGE

Our society is changing in many ways that relate to age. Perceptions of the periods of life

are being altered, as well as role transitions, social competencies, and the ages that mark their boundaries. New inconsistencies with regard to age-appropriate behavior are appearing in informal age norms as well as in the norms codified in law. Some of these changes are occurring because of increasing longevity; others are taking place because of the rising educational demands of a technological society, alterations in family structure, changes in the economy and in the composition of the labor force, and changes in formal systems of health and social services.

Periods of the Life Cycle

In all societies, lifetime is divided into socially relevant units, and biological time is translated into social time. The social systems that emerge are based in a general way on functional age; that is, as the individual's competencies change over lifetime, those competencies are nurtured and utilized in the interests of society. Social age distinctions are created and systematized, and responsibilities and rights are differentially distributed according to social age.

Even the simplest societies define at least three periods of life: childhood, adulthood, and old age. In more complex societies, the periods of life become more numerous as they reflect other forms of social change. Different patterns of age distinctions are created in different areas of life, such as in education, the family, and the work force. Chronological age becomes an expedient index of social age.

Historians have described the ways in which life periods became increasingly demarcated in Western societies over the past few hundred years. In the sixteenth and seventeenth centuries, with the appearance of industrialization, a middle class, and formally organized schools, childhood became a clearly discernible period of life, identified by special needs and particular characteristics. Adolescence took on its present meaning in the late nineteenth century and became a widespread concept in the twentieth, as the period of formal education lengthened and the transition to adulthood was increasingly delayed. A stage called youth was delineated only a few decades ago, as growing numbers of young people, after leaving high school and before marrying or making their occupational choices, opted for a period of exploring life roles.

It was only a few decades ago, too, that middle age became identified, largely as a reflection of the historically changing rhythm of events in the family cycle. With fewer children per family, and with births spaced closer together, the time when children grow up and leave the parental home was described as the major marker of middle age. In turn, old age came to be regarded as the time following retirement, and it was usually perceived as a distinct and separable period marked by declining physical and intellectual vigor, chronic illness, social disengagement, and often by isolation and desolation. Life periods became closely associated with chronological age, even though age lines were seldom sharply drawn.[1]

The Blurring of Life Periods

The old distinctions between life periods are blurring in today's society. The clearest evidence for this is the appearance of the young-old.[2] It is a new historical phenomenon that a very large group of retirees and their spouses are healthy and vigorous, relatively well-off financially, well integrated into the lives of their families and communities, and politically active. The term "young-old" has become part of everyday parlance, and it needs little elaboration here other than to point out that the concept was originally based, not on chronological age, but on health and social characteristics. Thus, a young-old person might be fifty-five or eighty-five. The term represents the social reality that the line between middle age and old age is no longer clear. What was

once considered old age is now recognized to be pertinent only to that minority of persons who are the old-old, that particularly vulnerable group in need of special care.

When, then, does old age now begin?[3] The societal view has been that it starts at sixty-five, when most people retire from the labor force. But in the United States today, most people retire before that age. The majority begin to take their Social Security benefits at age sixty-two or sixty-three, and at ages fifty-five to sixty-four fewer than three of every four men are presently in the labor force. At the same time, with continued good health some persons are staying at work full-time or part-time until their eighties. So, age sixty-five and the event of retirement are no longer clear markers between middle age and old age.

Alternatively, old age is often said to begin when a person requires special health care because of frailty or chronic disease, or when health creates a major limitation on the activities of everyday life. Yet half of all persons who are now seventy-five to eighty-four report no such health limitations. Even in the very oldest group, those above eighty-five, more than one-third report no limitations due to health, about one-third report some limitations, and one-third are unable to carry out everyday activities.[4] Thus, health status is also becoming a poor age marker.

It is not only in the second half of life that the blurring of life periods is occurring. Adults of all ages are experiencing changes in the traditional rhythm and timing of events of the life cycle. More men and women marry, divorce, remarry, and redivorce up through their seventies. More stay single; more women have their first child when they are fourteen or fifteen, and more have their first child at thirty-five or forty. This produces first-time grandparenthood for persons who range in age from thirty-five to seventy-five. There are more women, but also increasing numbers of men, who raise children consecutively in two-parent, then one-parent, and then two-parent households. More women, but increasing numbers of men as well, exit and reenter our educational institutions, enter and reenter the labor force, change jobs, and undertake second and third careers up through their seventies. It therefore becomes more difficult to distinguish the young, the middle-aged, and the young-old either in terms of major life events or of the ages at which those events occur.

The line between adolescence and adulthood is also becoming obscured. The role transitions that traditionally marked entry into adulthood and the social competencies they implied—full-time jobs, marriage, and parenthood—are disappearing as markers of social age. For some men and women, the entry into an occupation or profession is being delayed to age thirty as education is being extended. For others, entry into the labor force occurs at ages sixteen and seventeen. And not only are there more teenage pregnancies; there are more teenage women who are mothering their children. All this adds up to what has been aptly called "the fluid life cycle."[5]

This is not to deny that our society still recognizes differences between adolescents, young people, and old people, and that persons still relate to each other accordingly. Yet we are less sure where to put the punctuation marks in the life line, what should be the nature of those punctuation marks, and therefore how we should draw boundaries between the periods of life. All across adulthood, age has become a poor predictor of the time of life events, as well as a poor predictor of a person's health, work status, family status, and therefore, also, of a person's interests, preoccupations, and needs. We have multiple images of persons of the same age: there is the seventy-year-old in a wheelchair and the seventy-year-old on the tennis court; there is the eighteen-year-old who is married and supporting a family and the eighteen-year-old college student who brings his laundry home to his mother each week.

Differences among individuals, multiple images of age groups, and inconsistencies in age norms were surely present in earlier periods of our history, but as our society has become more complex, the differences are becoming more evident. It is the irregularities that are becoming the social reality.

These trends are mirrored also in public perceptions. Although systematic research is sparse, there are a few studies that show a diminishing public consensus about the periods of life and their markers. In the early 1960s, for instance, a group of middle-class, middle-aged persons were asked their opinions about the "best" ages for major life transitions to occur (such as completing school, marrying, retiring), or the ages they associated with such phrases as "a young man," "an old woman," and "when a man (or woman) has the most responsibilities." When the same questions were asked of a similar group of people two decades later, consensus had dropped regarding every time of the questionnaire. In the earlier study, nearly 90 percent of the respondents replied that the best age of a women to marry was between nineteen and twenty-four; in the repeat study, only 40 percent chose this brief period of years. In the first study, "a young man" was said to be a man between eighteen and twenty-two; in the repeat study, "a young man" was anywhere from eighteen to forty. These findings are based on very small study populations, but they serve to illustrate how public views are changing in line with the social realities.[6]

Childhood and Adulthood

In some respects, the line between childhood and adulthood is also fading. It is a common thesis now that childhood is disappearing. Styles of dress, forms of language, games, and preferred television programs—all are becoming the same for both children and adults. Children have more knowledge of once-taboo topics such as sex, drugs, alcoholism, suicide, and nuclear war. They also engage in more adult-like sexual behavior, and in more adult-like crime. At the same time, with the pressures for achievement we have witnessed the advent of "the hurried child" and "the harried child."[7]

We also have become familiar with the many descriptions of today's adults as the "me" generation: narcissistic, self-interested, and self-indulgent. There are fewer lasting marriages, fewer lasting commitments to work roles, more uncontrolled expressions of emotion, more frequent expressions of a sense of powerlessness—in short, more childlike behavior among adults.

This description may be overdrawn. In a wide range of formal and informal settings, both children and adults are continually exhorted to "act your age," and they seldom misunderstand what is meant. Yet there is something real in the argument that the expectations of appropriate behavior for children and adults are becoming less differentiated. We are less sure of what intellectual and social competencies to expect of children—not only because some children are teaching their teachers how to use computers, but also because so many children are streetwise by age eight, and so many others are the confidants of their parents by age twelve.

Some observers attribute the blurring of childhood and adulthood primarily to the effects of television, which exposes the total culture and which reveals the secrets that adults have traditionally withheld from children. But it is not only television that accounts for the differences in socialization. One example may serve to underline the fact that children are being socialized in different ways today by parents, schools, churches, and peer groups as well:

> The Girl Scouts of America recently announced that it had spent much effort in the last ten years studying its role in the society. Among many other changes, the decision was made to admit five-year-olds. The national executive director said, "Girl Scouts are not just campfire and cookies sales anymore . . . career education is part of the program for Brownies as young as six . . . The decision to admit five-year-olds reflects the changes in the American labor market. Women are working for part or all of their adult lives now. . . . The possibilities are limitless, but you need to prepare. So we think six is not too early to learn about career opportunities, and we also think that girls need to learn about making decisions. When you're five, you're not too young. . . ."[8]

All this is not to say that age norms are disappearing altogether. The person who moves to the Sun Belt to lead a life of leisure is approved of if he is seventy, but not if he is thirty. An unmarried mother meets with greater disapproval if she is fifteen than if she is thirty-five. At some levels, our society still distributes rights and responsibilities in traditional ways. But age distinctions and age norms operate inconsistently in a complex society.

Age Distinctions and the Law

The inconsistencies are nowhere better illustrated than in the norms that are formally codified into law. Laws establishing age distinctions pervade most areas of life: education, family, housing, entry and exits from various occupations, the allocation of public resources, the extension and denial of benefits, the imposition and the relaxation of legal responsibilities. At both state and federal levels, scores of statutes refer to age.

Age is used in the law just as it is used in other social institutions, as a proxy for a wide range of characteristics: intellectual and emotional maturity (for example, minimum ages for entering school), readiness to assume adult responsibilities (minimum ages for voting, drinking, driving, and marrying), physical strength or speed of response (maximum ages for policemen, bus drivers, or airline pilots), economic productivity (age of eligibility for various occupational licensing or age of retirement), and various types of debility (ages of eligibility for federally subsidized medical and social services).

Perhaps the use of age as a proxy is indispensable in a society like ours. It renders decision-making easier, not only for employers, but for lawmakers. It is less costly than using individualized assessments of competency. The major disadvantage is that the validity of using age as a proxy depends on how well age corresponds with the characteristic for which it stands. And the presumed correspondence is often based, not on good evidence, but on age stereotypes.

Laws change over time, and as might well be anticipated, they reflect some of the present incongruencies in the wider society regarding the significance of age. One pair of examples demonstrates recent changes in legal definitions of maturity. A California law passed a few years ago, known as the Emancipation of Minors Act, was designed to help teenages who have fled intolerable family situations. The law specifies that if they are at least fourteen and are living away from home and supporting themselves, they can be declared independent of their parents and, for most legal purposes, can be treated as adults. In this instance, the individual's social competency is assessed by the court, and age (after fourteen) is not used as its proxy. Some dozen states have now passed similar laws.

In contrast, many states, faced with the problem of drunk driving and with the fact that more highway accidents involve drunk teenagers than drunk adults, are raising the age at which it is legal to purchase alcohol. In this instance, age is being used as the proxy for social responsibility. Despite the fact that only a small minority of eighteen-year-olds are drunk drivers, the laws apply to all eighteen-year-olds as an age class. In the first example, then, the law is saying that all fourteen-year-olds are not alike; but in the second example, it is saying that all eighteen-year-olds are alike.

At the same time that we are generating age-based laws, age discrimination is becoming a matter of social concern. With reference to both the young and the old, age rights constitute a new focus in the arena of civil rights. One example is the recent legislation passed by Congress that abolishes age as the basis for retirement until age seventy in the private sector, and that removes the mandatory retirement age altogether for most federal employees. In this case, age is not treated as entirely irrelevant, but the law is nevertheless a step in that direction. Another example is the recent Age Discrimination Act, which applies across the age spectrum to both young and old, and prohibits discrimination on the basis of age in any program that receives federal support (for example, community mental health centers) unless that program was specifically aimed at a particular age group (e.g., Medicare). While the regulations allow for major exceptions that have the effect of watering down its strength, the Age Discrimination Act is nevertheless a formal step toward making age equality a civil right, and toward treating age as an irrelevant characteristic in the distribution of public goods and services.[9]

The problems of deciding what constitutes age discrimination are enormous, and perhaps will become even more so. Is it discriminatory towards younger people when special benefit programs like Medicare are created only for older people? At the state level, is it just to require a sixty-five-year-old—but not a sixty-four-year-old—to pass a vision test before obtaining a driver's license? At the local level, is it discriminatory to bar children from age-segregated housing—especially when that housing is subsidized by public funds? Such distinctions are presently legal, but they may come to be regarded as unjust if public consciousness rises regarding age distinctions and age rights.[10]

The Significance of Age to the Individual

The changing meanings of age are both causes and effects of the ways people lead their lives, and it is therefore artificial to think about individuals as separate from the society in which they live. Yet there is another dimension of social reality that applies directly to individuals. As they reach adolescence, most persons develop concepts of normal, expectable life sequences, and anticipations that major transitions in education, work, and family will occur at relatively predictable times. They internalize social clocks that tell them whether they are on time. Being on time or off time is a compelling basis for self-assessment as people compare themselves with others in deciding whether they are doing well or poorly for their age.

In many ways, social timetables in today's society do not lead to the regularities so often anticipated by adolescents or young adults. We have noticed the ways in which timetables are losing their cogency, yet in other contexts some of those timetables may be more compelling than before. A young man feels he will be a failure if he does not "make it" in his corporation by the time he is thirty-five. Or an older business executive is invited to retire just when he thinks of himself as at the peak of his competencies. A young women delays marriage because of her career, and then hurries to catch up with parenthood because of her biological imperative. The same young woman might feel pressed to marry, bear a child, and establish herself in a career, all within a five-year period. And this, even though she recognizes that she is likely to live to be eighty-five.

Sometimes new perspectives sit uneasily with traditional views, even in the mind of the same individual. A young woman who deliberately delays marriage may be the same woman who worries that she has lost status because she is not married by twenty-five. A middle-aged man who starts a second family

feels compelled to explain that he has not behaved inappropriately, for he expects to live to see his new children reach adulthood. Or an old person reports that because he did not expect to live so long, he is now unprepared to take on the "new ways" of his age peers. Some people live in new ways, but continue to think in old ways.

Given such complications, shall we say that individuals are paying less or more attention to age as a prod or a brake upon their behavior? That age consciousness is decreasing or increasing? Whether or not historical change is occurring, it is fair to say that one's own age remains highly salient to the individual all the way from early childhood through advanced old age. A person uses age as a guide in accommodating to the behavior of others, in forming and re-forming the self-image, in giving meaning to the life course, and in contemplating the time that is past and the time that is left ahead.

All of this gives us an outline of the multiple levels of social and psychological reality that are based on social age, and, in modern societies, on calendar age as the marker of social age. The complexities are no fewer for the individual than they are for the society at large.

RELATIONS AMONG AGE GROUPS

At the societal level, the relations among age groups are influenced by changing perceptions of the periods of life and changing age norms, as well as by the relative numbers of young, middle-aged, and old. Policy-makers and journalists frequently comment that an aging society may bring with it age polariziation or age-divisiveness. The issue is often posed in terms of intergenerational conflict, reminiscent of the ways in which the so-called generation gap was described during the 1960s. Now, as then, the phenomenon may be more image than reality.

Many social scientists discovered during the late 1960s that it was difficult to find evidence of a generation gap. While some college students were demonstrating against the United States participation in the war in Vietnam, others of similar age, both in and out of college, were strongly supporting it. Further, a number of studies showed that college students shared the political views of their parents more often than not; and that although the forms of their behavior might be different from those of their parents, most left-wing students had left-wing parents, and most right-wing students, right-wing parents.

Today, many observers are expressing concern about the possibility of so-called intergenerational conflict between the working-age and the retired; they fear the conflict will center on economic issues, specifically on the Social Security program, and on whether workers will rebel against paying increases in Social Security taxes to support the growing proportion of retirees. The aging society does face real problems of resource distribution that are complicated by demographic changes in the population. But is it true that different age groups perceive the solutions to those problems so differently?

First, it would be well to frame the issues in terms of age groups, not generations, for the two terms are by no means synonymous. If the issues were truly intergenerational, they might drop from public attention entirely, for there are adhesives between generations in the family that appear to be as strong today as they were in earlier periods of our history. A wide range of research shows that, as long as they live, parents remain invested in the welfare of their offspring, and that ties of obligation, whether or not they are also ties of affection, remain strong in offspring. The fragility of horizontal family ties is not paralleled in vertical family ties, particularly those between grandmothers, mothers, and children. Despite the shifts of financial responsibility to the government, the evidence is clear that the family remains the major social support of older people, just as it is for children.[11]

It appears that people's views of their own intergenerational relations become intertwined with, or projected onto, their views of age groups. So far as the evidence goes, workers in the United States are not protesting the rise in Social Security taxes. Repeated surveys show this to be the case.[12] One reason is that most people prefer a strong Social Security system to the alternative of placing the financial responsibility for older people back on the family.

The evidence also shows that it was not older people who were responsible for the passage of the Social Security Act in the 1930s, but younger and middle-aged workers. And throughout the postwar period, it has been labor unions, by and large, not the organized advocacy groups for older people, that have been the major advocates of expanded Social Security benefits.[13] The reason is, that public policy for older people is usually also a public policy that benefits younger people, today as well as tomorrow.

Some young people now believe they will not enjoy as high a material standard of living as their parents, and some point to the federal budget deficits and to demographic changes to support their assertions that they will not receive as much in Social Security benefits when they grow old. But there is no evidence that young people are blaming old people for what they perceive as this deplorable state of affairs. One reason might be that "the older generation" often refers to their own parents, whose wealth they have the valid expectation of inheriting.[14] The few studies presently available indicate that during the lifetimes of parental generations, a larger amount of financial assistance flows down the family ladder than flows up that ladder, even though we would benefit from more data on what that trickle-down effect amounts to.[15] How many parents or grandparents are providing the down payments on homes for young-adult children? How many are providing funds to help divorced daughters who have young children to support?

Neither have we yet seen any movement on the part of older people that might be regarded as the expression of age-group conflict. Although it is true that there are more elderly voters than before and that a higher proportion of older people than younger people are exercising the franchise, older voters will remain a minority of voters for the foreseeable future. Further, the continuing agreement among political scientists is that no politics of age is developing in the United States, nor is there evidence of an old-age "bloc," largely because older persons are very heterogeneous in social, political, and economic terms.[16] It appears to be the case that, in old age, people continue to vote more in accord with their economic status than with the number of their birthdays. Nor is there evidence that when, in a given locality, older people vote against school bonds, they are voting against children rather than voting against increased taxes.

There are still other reasons to be cautious about using the phrase "intergenerational conflict." Some observers, concerned over conflict or equity among age groups, pose the issue in terms of a zero-sum game in which, if federal expenditures for the old were reduced, more funds for children would automatically be available.[17] It is undeniable that the increasing number of poor children is a disgrace to the affluent society, and that the implications are calamitous.[18] But the problem is part of a larger and more complex one: what proportion of federal resources should go to social programs, and how should those resources be allocated to the various subgroups who need assistance? This question, too, is more complex than it appears from examining federal expenditures. For one thing, although the data are not easily summarized, state government

expenditures for children are probably equal or higher than federal allocations. But even all government expenditures together constitute only one of two major components in the total system of economic transfers, for the family remains by far the major economic support for children.

To refer to the issue as age-group equity rather than age-group conflict may serve only to make it more murky. How is equity to be assessed in the context of the life cycle? Most public programs are future-oriented in the sense that an expenditure today is intended to affect, not only the present, but the future of those who are the beneficiaries. To help today's old is to help today's young, and presumably therefore to help those young when they are old tomorrow. But few policy-makers are intrepid enough to predict tomorrow's value of today's outlays, whether that value be reckoned in economic or social terms. And how is equity to be assessed along another time line, that of successive birth cohorts? If outlays for old people are today nearly 30 percent of the federal budget, but a decade ago were only 20 percent, is the society therefore more generous to old people today, even when reckoned on a per-capita basis? And when we talk about saddling future generations with today's large federal deficits, is it really young persons we will be saddling, or all persons, young or old, who will constitute tomorrow's society?

Until philosophers as well as economists can shed more light on such questions, it is doubtful that we are much aided in facing the problems before us by framing the issues in terms of equity among age groups.[19]

AGE AND SOCIAL POLICY

From the policy perspective, there is another and more radical framework within which to consider the relations among age groups and the goal—implied whenever the issue is raised at all—of maintaining an age-integrated society. Is it more constructive for society to create policies designed for age groups, or instead, policies for persons who, irrespective of age, share a problem or a life condition that calls for intervention by a public or private agency?[20]

Despite the fact that age is becoming a less relevant basis for assessing adult competencies and needs, and even as traditional age norms and conceptions of age groups are becoming blurred, we are witnessing a proliferation of public and private policy decisions in which the basis for defining target groups is age. The trend is most evident when we look at older people. At federal, state, and local levels of government, programs are created that provide elderly persons with income, health services, social services, transportation, housing, and special tax benefits.[21] Private, civic, educational, and religious bodies create special programs in health care, education, recreation, and other community services. For the past few decades, we have been engaged in what might be said to be a wide range of affirmative-action programs for older people. There is little doubt that the economic and social situation of older people as a group has been dramatically improved.

Despite these large outlays, there remain sizable sub-groups of very poor elderly people. And when all federal programs are considered together—the direct payments, the in-kind transfers, the tax benefits—it is evident that most of the benefits are going to those older people who are in the top third of the income distribution. Further, if these programs continue in their present direction, they will not only maintain the present inequalities, they will create even further disadvantage for those older persons who are poor.[22]

Age-based decisions present still other problems. Some observers believe that to create programs directed at older people is to encourage the stereotype that older people are themselves a problem group, and is to add inadver-

tently to age separation and age segregation. Given that the proportion of poor among persons over sixty-five is now lower than in other age groups, others believe that older persons are becoming an advantaged rather than a disadvantaged group. Some commentators are concerned by what they regard as the possibly divisive political power of older voters; others fear a possible political backlash in which older people will become the scapegoats in an attempt to contain federal expenditures.[23] Such positions often reflect the kind of distortions that arise whenever "the old" are described as a homogeneous group. The opinions diverge even more sharply when the debate focuses directly on age-targeted vs. age-neutral programs. Some point out that until age-targeted federal programs were established, older people failed to receive adequate attention because of ageist attitudes in the society at large, and that to abandon or even to alter age-targeted programs would jeopardize the great progress older people have realized over the past few decades.

Although the "age or need" issue may become more salient in the next few years and the political debate more heated, the policy issues are, in truth, more complex. In practice, they do not usually take the form of simple either/or decisions, but involve complicated combinations of age and need. It is not always an easy matter to disentangle the issue of age-irrelevancy. One example relates again to Social Security.

While their programs differ one from the next, all industrialized countries have some system of public pensions based on age-eligibility. Whether or not the present Social Security system in the United States is changed in major or minor ways, we are not likely to abandon public programs of income maintenance for older people. In the latest amendments to the Social Security Act, age has been manipulated as a major variable, with the age of eligibility for full benefits to be slowly raised from age sixty-five to age sixty-seven. For the first time, however, the income levels of the beneficiaries are also to be considered. For those older persons whose incomes surpass a given dollar level, half their Social Security benefits will be taxable. Thus, both age and need have become relevant. From the broader perspective, however, should we concentrate first on providing a guaranteed minimum income for persons of all ages, and only then shape the Social Security programs to fit that wider framework? And how shall we think about children, whose needs have not yet attracted the same degree of public attention?

Unlike the situation for older people, we have not shifted much of the responsibility for children away from the family and the voluntary organization to the federal government.[24] The inescapable fact that government can assist children only indirectly, and mainly through the family, complicates the issues enormously, for there is no public consensus today regarding the principle, let alone the method, of government support for families. But if government does begin to take a greater role, how shall we deal with the problem of poverty among children? Shall we create programs targeted towards children as a group? Or towards poor children? Or towards poor people, whatever their age? And will we continue to act on the conviction that programs for the poor must necessarily be poor programs, and that income-tested programs must necessarily be demeaning to the beneficiaries? Or will we be willing to reexamine that conviction, and to find ways of offering support that are not stigmatizing?

As we look ahead, it seems clear that some of the policy issues regarding age will be less troublesome than others. It is probably not controversial to suggest that the aging society will need a broader definition of productivity than the one that is current today. Such a definition should go beyond participation in the labor force and extend to non-paid roles. These would include not only those that are

attached to formally organized voluntary associations, but also to services that individuals provide to family members both inside and outside the household, services to neighbors and friends, and self-care activities.[25] The need is to seek out and nurture the potential for social productivity, in this broad sense, wherever it is to be found—not only among the young-old, but among younger people as well.

Along the same lines, it is probably not controversial to observe that in an aging society it will be increasingly important to remove the irrelevant age constraints that now exist for the young as well as for the young-old in various areas of employment, housing, education, and community participation.

But many of the problems that an aging society will pose will be much more difficult, for they will involve fundamental ethical as well as political questions. Some will raise issues that have not yet been clearly articulated. If, for instance, there is growing recognition that rising health costs are due less to the rising numbers of old people than to the rising costs of high-technology medicine and rising levels of reimbursement to health-care professionals, shall we be able to deal directly with these problems? Difficult though it may be, it will probably be easier to reach consensus that the quality of life should take precedence over the length of life. But as questions of health-care rationing take new forms, will society be willing to ration this care on an age-neutral basis?[26] To push that question a step further: it has been suggested that high-technology medicine might be reserved for those persons who can be expected to have five to ten more years of a decent quality of life.[27] Shall we be willing to apply that standard, not only to old persons, but to the young as well—to withhold high-technology treatment from those infants and children whose futures show no such promise? Shall we weigh the value of a lifetime, not on the basis of years since birth, but on the basis of years of decent life that lie ahead? Will we ever agree that an extra five years of good life have as much value to society when they are produced for a seventy-year-old as for a seven-year-old? Or shall we, instead, give young people a chance to live at least to the age of average life expectancy? Is it likely that a society of such diverse social, ethical, and religious values as our own can reach consensus on such difficult questions?

Baffling as they are, questions like these, are likely to become more compelling as the aging of the population becomes even more dramatic in the decades ahead. Can we use today's aging society as an appropriate context for re-thinking our traditional views of age and age distinctions? Perhaps the most constructive ways of adapting to an aging society will emerge by focusing, not on age at all, but on more relevant dimensions of human needs, human competencies, and human diversity.

Endnotes

1 For a fuller treatment of the historical appearance of childhood, adolescence, and youth, see Philippe Aries, *Centuries of Childhood* (New York: Random House, 1962); John Demos and Virginia Demos, "Adolescence in Historical Perspective," *Journal of Marriage and Family*, Nov. 1969, pp. 632–38; John R. Gillis, *Youth and History* (New York: Academic Press, 1974); Kenneth Keniston, "Youth as a Stage of Life," *American Scholar*, Autumn 1970, pp. 631–54; Panel on Youth, President's Science Advisory Committee, *Youth: Transition to Adulthood* (Washington, DC: U.S. Government Printing Office, 1973). The book edited by Erik Erikson, *Adulthood* (New York: W. W. Norton & Co., 1978) asks whether the historical obsession with childhood and adolescence may now be giving way to "the century of the adult."

2 Bernice L. Neugarten, "Age Groups in American Society and the Rise of the Young-old," *Annals of the American Academy of Political and Social Science*, Sept. 1974, pp. 187–98.

3 For a differently focused discussion of this issue, see *How Old is "Old?" The Effects of Aging on Learning and Working*. Hearing before the Senate Special Committee on Aging, 96th Congress, 2nd Session (Washington, DC: U.S. Government Printing Office, 1980).

4 Lewis H. Butler and Paul W. Newacheck, "Health and Social Factors Relevant to Long Term Care Policy," in Judith Meltzer, Harold Richman, and Frank Farrow, eds., *Policy Options in Long Term Care* (Chicago: University of Chicago Press, 1981).

5 Larry Hirschhorn, "Social Policy and the Life Cycle: A Developmental Perspective," *Social Service Review*, Sept. 1977, pp. 434–50.

6 B. L. Neugarten, Joan Moore, and John Lowe, "Age Norms, Age Constraints, and Adult Socialization," *American Journal of Sociology*, May 1965, pp. 710–17; and Patricia Passuth, David Maines, and B. L. Neugarten, "Age Norms and Age Constraints Twenty Years Later," paper presented at the Midwest Sociological Society meetings, Chicago, April 1984.

7 Among the growing number of publications on the changing nature of childhood, see David Elkind, *The Hurried Child: Growing Up Too Fast Too Soon*. (Reading, MA: Addison-Wesley, 1981); John Holt, *Escape from Childhood* (New York: Dutton, 1974); Joshua Meyrowitz, "The Blurring of Childhood and Adulthood," chap. 13 in *No Sense of Place* (New York: Oxford University Press, 1985). (An essay drawn from that chapter was published in *Daedalus*, Summer 1984, under the title, "The Adultlike Child and the Childlike Adult: Socialization in an Electronic Age.") See also Neil Postman, *The Disappearance of Childhood* (New York: Delacorte Press, 1982); and Marie Winn, *Children Without Childhood* (New York: Pantheon, 1983).

8 Reported in the *New York Times*, Oct. 28, 1984.

9 The two federal laws being referred to are the Age Discrimination in Employment Act of 1967, as amended (29 U.S. Code Sections 621–634); and the Age Discrimination Act of 1975, as amended (42 U.S. Code Sections 6101–6107).

10 For an analysis of the legal issues related to age distinctions and age discrimination, see Howard Eglit, "Age and the Law," chap. 18 in the *Handbook of Aging and the Social Sciences*, Robert H. Binstock and Ethel Shanas, eds. (New York: Van Nostrand Reinhold, 1985).

11 See, for instance, Elaine Brody, "Parent Care as a Normative Family Stress," *The Gerontologist*, Feb. 1985, pp. 19–29; and Ethel Shanas, "Social Myth as Hypothesis: The Case of the Family Relations of Old People," *The Gerontologist*, Feb. 1979, pp. 1–9.

12 This fact has often emerged from newspaper polls and other public opinion polls. For a fuller context, see the two surveys published by the National Council on the Aging, *The Myth and Reality of Aging in America* and *Aging in the Eighties: America in Transition* (Washington, DC: National Council on the Aging, 1975 and 1981).

13 For an analysis of the role of old-age advocacy groups, see Henry J. Pratt, *The Gray Lobby* (Chicago: University of Chicago Press, 1976) and "The 'Gray Lobby' Revisited," *National Forum*, Fall 1982, pp. 31–33.

14 For an analysis of family inheritance patterns, see Marvin Sussman, Judith Cates, and David Smith, *The Family and Inheritance* (New York: Russell Sage Foundation, 1970).

15 In summarizing one major set of studies on this topic, James M. Morgan, an economist, reports that in the general picture of who helps whom, relatively little regular financial assistance goes to family members who live outside the household, but that the amount expended in offering emergency help—in the form of time or money— is considerable. The middle-aged do most of the giving, but the receiving appears to be mostly by the young (18 to

35) rather than by the old (65 and over). James M. Morgan, "The Redistribution of Income by Families and Institutions and Emergency Help Patterns," in *Five Thousand Families—Patterns of Economic Progress*, vol. X, ed. by Greg J. Duncan and James M. Morgan (Ann Arbor, MI: Institute for Social Research, 1983), and by the same author, "Time in the Measurement of Transfers and Well-being," in Marilyn Moon, ed., *Economic Transfers in the United States* (Chicago: The University of Chicago Press, 1984).

[16] In the most recent review of research on political orientations, values and ideologies, party attachments, voting, and other forms of political behavior, the authors conclude—as have other reviewers—that older persons are more notable for their similarities to other age groups than for their differences. This results from the heterogeneity that exists within all age groups. The authors point also to the general absence of policy-relevant age-consciousness. Robert B. Hudson and John Strate, "Aging and Political Systems," chap. 19 in Binstock and Shanas, eds., op. cit.

[17] See, for example, Samuel H. Preston, "Children and the Elderly in the United States," *Scientific American*, Dec. 1984.

[18] A recent report of the Congressional Research Office and the Congressional Budget Office shows that in 1983, the latest year for which the data are complete, over 22 percent of children under age 18 were living below the poverty level. This is the highest figure since the mid-1960s. (*New York Times*, May 23, 1985, p. 1.)

[19] For a philosopher's approach to these issues, see Norman Daniels, "Justice Between Age Groups: Am I My Parents' Keeper?" *Milbank Memorial Fund Quarterly/Health and Society*, Summer 1983, pp. 489–522. The economist Marilyn Moon comments that a recurrent and controversial issue is how to define meaningful time periods in studying economic transfers; she further observes that estimating intergenerational equity remains a relatively unexplored area. See Moon, ed., op. cit., p. 6.

[20] B. L. Neugarten, ed., *Age or Need? Public Policies for Older People* (Beverly Hills, CA: Sage Publications, 1982).

[21] See, for example, Elizabeth A. Kutza, *The Benefits of Old Age* (Chicago: University of Chicago Press, 1981) for an analysis of federal programs; and for a critique of how many of those programs are failing older people, see Carol L. Estes, *The Aging Enterprise* (San Francisco: Jossey-Bass Publishers, 1979).

[22] See, for instance, Gary M. Nelson, "Social Class and Public Policy for the Elderly," *Social Service Review*, March 1982, pp. 85–107 (reprinted in B. L. Neugarten, *Age or Need?* op. cit.).

[23] Binstock, "The Aged as Scapegoat," in *The Gerontologist*, April 1983, pp. 136–43; and by the same author, "The Oldest Old: A Fresh Perspective or Compassionate Ageism Revisited?" *Milbank Memorial Fund Quarterly/Health and Society*, Spring 1985.

[24] See the essay by Richman and Stagner in this volume.

[25] See the report, *Productive Roles in an Aging Society*, prepared by the Committee on an Aging Society of the National Academy of Sciences, Feb. 1986.

[26] See, for example, Henry J. Aaron and William B. Schwartz, *The Painful Prescription: Rationing Hospital Care* (Washington, DC: The Brookings Institution, 1984).

[27] See the essay by Daniel Callahan in this volume.

DISCUSSION QUESTIONS

1. According to the Neugartens, what are some changes in the social meanings of age?
2. Is there any evidence for age polarization or age divisiveness, according to the authors? Why or why not?
3. The Neugartens argue against age-based policies and in favor of policies directed at people who share a problem or life condition regardless of age. What are some of these need-based problems?

The Lives of Older People and Changing Social Roles

Matilda White Riley
John W. Riley, Jr.

Over just this one century in the United States, some 28 years have been added to the average length of a person's life. This is more than was previously added in all of human history. The effects of this change continue to swirl around us.[1] Their implications are so staggering as to be barely discernible. As people begin to glimpse these implications, they ask how good these added years are.[2] Our answer is, We do not know, but recent research findings tell us that the quality of these years can be improved for most older people—through interventions designed on the basis of scientific evidence and considered thought. Research in the social and behavioral sciences is demonstrating that such interventions are possible. This is the message of this special issue of *The Annals*.

Yet, to bring such possibilities into reality is an all-encompassing challenge. It entails literally redesigning the life course. It involves massive societal and global changes—many of them beyond our immediate control—changes that are continually shaping and reshaping both individual lives and the environing social structures. Interventions are but one contribution to these alterations, and they must be guided by a full awareness of the complexity of social change. We are not social engineers, but the challenge is to design interventions that can have positive, not negative, influences on human lives.

In this introductory article, we address this challenge. We explore one of the central and most perplexing problems in our period of history: the problem of the imbalance—or the mismatch—between the strengths and capacities of the mounting numbers of long-lived people and the lack of role opportunities in society to utilize and reward these strengths. This is the problem we call structural lag,[3] because the age structure of social-role opportunities has not kept pace with the rapid changes in the ways people grow old. To enhance the quality of aging, interventions are needed not only in the life course of individuals but, even more critically, in the social matrix in which these lives are embedded. Redesigning the life course, then, involves adaptation of role opportunities and role constraints in the family, at work, in education, in shopping centers, in public affairs, in recreation and leisure, in health care institutions and hospice facilities, and in all the social structures where people relate to other people and interact with them.

At the outset, we want to call attention to two very different meanings of being old.

First, regardless of age, we like to think of the healthy old, because some people of any age—even 90 or older—can still be healthy and still be able to function effectively. The generic category of old people is essentially heterogeneous.[4] Thus, when we think of the aging process, chronological age in itself has little meaning.

Second, we like to speak of recent cohorts of older people, because those people now entering old age—say, just turning age 65—are very different from those earlier cohorts who entered old age in the past—the ones to which most current studies refer—and they are very different from those very new cohorts who will enter old age in the future. So when we speak of a cohort—people born at the same time—chronological age does have meaning, but this meaning—the meaning of age 65, for example—varies widely from one period of history to another. Our grandparents at age 75 were very different from what either of us was at 75.

We shall come back later to this distinction

between aging and cohorts, because it is highly relevant to the discussions throughout this special issue of *The Annals*.

In this introductory article, by making use of familiar research findings as evidence, we first report on older people's strengths and capacities. We then suggest the potential for interventions that can help to optimize these strengths. In similar fashion, we report on the inadequacies of role opportunities for older people and try to identify some of the interventions that could reduce these inadequacies. Along the way, we shall note some of the hazards of ad hoc interventions and shall offer an analytical framework as a guide for thinking about interventions in individual aging, in role opportunities, and in the sources of the mismatch between them. A few glimpses into the future will illustrate the use of this framework for anticipating the kinds of interventions needed to enhance the quality of aging. We conclude by considering possible interventions in the process of dying, as the years added to the life course call for deeper concern with the implications of the postponement of death for the redesign of the life course.

STRENGTHS AND CAPACITIES OF OLDER PEOPLE

First, then, with respect to the strengths and potential strengths of older people, a variety of interventions in the aging process are feasible.

The Fallacy of Inevitable Aging Decline

We know that such interventions are feasible because social science research has clearly demonstrated that the doctrine of inevitable aging decline is a fallacy. This fallacy was initiated by faulty interpretation of biological data, and, despite all the evidence to the contrary, it is still widely accepted, not only by professional practitioners and the public at large, but

even inadvertently by some outstanding scholars.[5] In the inner sanctum of the National Institutes of Health, the stereotype of inevitable decline remains stubborn. For example, in the current attack on acquired immune deficiency syndrome (AIDS), it is taken for granted that older people cannot provide sexual channels for transmitting the virus since they are believed to be no longer interested in sex!

Yet, for those who listen to the accumulating evidence on the aging process, it is simply not true that, because of aging, older people are destined to be ill, impoverished, cut off from society, sexually incapacitated, despondent, or unable to reason or to remember. Of course, everyone dies, and some older people—a minority—are seriously disadvantaged and in need of both personal and societal support. But the vast majority are reasonably well and are able to function independently and effectively.

Massive research evidence demonstrates that the aging process is neither fixed nor immutable. Biologists are now showing that many symptoms that were formerly attributed to aging—for example, certain disturbances in cardiac function or in glucose metabolism in the brain—are instead produced by disease. Sociologists and psychologists are showing how the aging process varies with social conditions, how individuals grow old in widely diverse ways depending on their family life, their socioeconomic status, or their work conditions. Sociologists are also showing how the aging process changes over time as society changes.[6] As we noted earlier, cohorts of people already old differ markedly from cohorts not yet old in: education, work history, and standard of living; diet and exercise; and physical stature, age at menarche, or experience with chronic rather than acute diseases. Perhaps the most notable of the historical alterations in the aging process spring from the unprecedented increases in longevity. These increases allow recent cohorts of young people to stay in school many years longer than their predecessors did; prolong retirement; postpone many diseases of old age; and extend family relationships, as husbands and wives in intact marriages now typically survive together for four, even five, decades or more.

Potentials of Interventions

To this point, our argument has demonstrated that the aging process is flexible. Most older people—ranging from the young old to the oldest old—have far greater and more diverse strengths and competences in intellect, health, and interest in affairs than is generally recognized. In addition, we have argued that there are potentials for optimizing these strengths still further. Although death is inevitable, the course of the aging process is not, and it is the quality of the later years that is at issue here.

What kinds of interventions, then, might sustain or even enhance this quality? Numerous studies[7] have been producing some surprising findings:

1. Among older workers, intellectual functioning improves with age if the work situation is challenging and calls for self-direction.[8]
2. Very old people, if their performance on intelligence tests has deteriorated, can be brought back to their performance levels of 17 years earlier, if the social environment affords incentives and opportunities for practicing and learning new strategies.[9]
3. Memory can be enhanced, if the impoverished context often characterizing retirement is altered to include the challenges of a stimulating and complex environment.[10]
4. Even slowed reaction time, long attributed to irreversible aging losses in central nervous system functioning, can be speeded up if the social situation provides training and consistent feedback.[11]
5. In nursing homes, changing the social environment to increase the sense of personal control and independence in aging patients can result in greater social activity, changed immune functioning, and perhaps even lowered mortality.[12]

Moreover, even when alterations in behavior, life-styles, and social contacts are made late in life, such alterations can still reduce morbidity and mortality.[13] To stop cigarette smoking in old age can make a difference.

INADEQUATE ROLE OPPORTUNITIES

A moment's reflection on the foregoing instances of interventions, and on many other similar instances, shows that all are characterized by one common theme: the older person's functioning is contingent upon social conditions. Bereft of social opportunities, resources, or incentives, older people cannot utilize or sustain their mental or physical strengths and capacities. So bereft, the doctrine of inevitable aging decline becomes a self-fulfilling prophecy. The root of the mismatch does not lie entirely in people's capacities or in the aging process itself; it also lies in the lack of suitable roles through which individuals move as they grow older. There are too few roles for older people, and the roles that do exist are too often ill designed to utilize, optimize, or reward older people's strengths.

Evidences of Structural Inadequacies

This brings us to the role structure of the aging society and to the problem of structural lag. Various accounts depict today's social structures and norms as vestigial remains of an earlier era when most people had died before their work was finished or their last child left home. For over a century, opportunities for older workers have been declining. As one example, by 1982, only 45 percent of men aged 55 and over remained in the labor force; predictions are that by 2000, the percentage could drop below 40 percent. For women, the comparable figures are 23 and 21 percent.[14] In the family, many older people are widows who live entirely alone. In society, older people's place aptly has been called—in Ernest Burgess's term—a "roleless role." Modifications in the role structure of society have indeed lagged behind the rapid changes in the strengths and potential strengths—as well as increases in the numbers—of older people themselves.

There are, however, few pertinent facts about changes in structures. Systematic research on roles is sparse and far more primitive than research on the aging process. Conceptions of the individual life course, and methodologies for longitudinal analysis, are by now highly developed. By contrast, there are few conceptual or methodological tools for examining the age structures of economic, political, or family systems; or for focusing on the operation of laws and age norms; or for investigating how age-graded roles shape the relationships and interactions among individuals over their respective lives.[15] We shall have to fight many battles before we win the war for real comprehension of the aging society—not only as a population in which the proportions of older people are increasing, but also as a system of structures, roles, and relationships for which age is a fundamental basis.

Potentials for Interventions

Despite all the conceptual and methodological obstacles, research on the inadequacy of roles for older people is beginning to show that here, too, interventions to correct the structural lag are possible. Like the individual aging process, social structures are also flexible. Capable people and empty role structures cannot long coexist, and old people are beginning to press for more favorable role opportunities. A nationwide survey of the labor force[16] showed that three-quarters of older workers wanted to continue some kind of paid part-time work after retirement that was characterized by, for example, working a day or two a week at home, freedom to set their own hours, or sharing a job with someone else. Yet the numbers of older persons working part-time do not begin to equal the numbers who report that this would be desirable. Whether or not particular individuals want to work in their late years—either for pay or on a volunteer basis—no one wishes to be disregarded, disesteemed, denigrated, or dependent.

Moreover, scattered attempts at optimizing role structures are already under way. In education, there are varied opportunities to engage in teaching: for instance, teaching adults who cannot read or who cannot manage the English language, or performing new roles as paid assistants in child-care centers.[17] There are also opportunities for older people to go back to school. Many corporations offer training programs, and nearly 1000 colleges now make places for students over age 65.[18]

In leisure, there are opportunities for recreation. For example, special tours are made available, as to historic places. There are also opportunities for a variety of serious cultural pursuits.

Throughout the health care system, there is pressing demand for assistance from older people in a range of positions from nursing home aides to management consultants—a demand currently being enlarged by the imminent spread of the AIDS epidemic. For the frail elderly who themselves need long-term care—in their own homes, in community care facilities, and in institutions—there is gradual improvement in opportunities to function independently and with dignity.[19]

In the workplace, as the supply of youthful workers diminishes, opportunities for older people, though inadequate, are beginning to open up.[20] There are provisions for part-time work, job sharing, and flexible hours. Some companies have model programs for rehiring retired employees, and legislation has now abolished age as a basis for mandatory retirement.

Indeed, we are beginning to see in practice what we once regarded as a visionary hope: education, work, and leisure, which have been organized in three separate stages of life, are now beginning to be spread more evenly over the life course. There are provisions for educational leaves from work, for retraining older adults or preparing them for new careers. There are now innovative programs in which companies allow their workers several years of leave, to be spent—according to choice—in family care, in continuing education, in preparation for a second career, or, as in the International Business Machines' program,[21] to take advantage of a once-in-a-lifetime personal opportunity.

Many such role changes are literally being forced upon us by the paradox created by two contemporary trends: longevity is increasing, but the half-life of most technologically driven occupations is decreasing. For example, medical doctors or nurses, after many years of training, find themselves out-of-date after only a few years of practice. Most skilled workers today—not just the old—are finding it necessary to intersperse periods of work with periods of training.

Yet the task of designing interventions to enhance the places for older people in the aging society is only beginning. It will inevitably require far larger effort. Many individuals today are contributing to this effort, as they invent new ways to deal with the daily-life problems of older people; and many small interventions, as they accumulate, can become institutionalized into more appropriate role structures.

Moreover, added to these changes in the social environment are interventions in other aspects of the environment. Czaja and Barr, in their article on human factors research in this issue of *The Annals*, describe ways of designing the physical environment to meet the needs of older people. As producers of consumer goods become increasingly aware of the so-called older market, easy-to-prepare foods are packaged for single servings, easy-to-use household utensils and various safety devices are made readily available, and cosmetics for care of the aging skin are widely advertised.

Meantime, we are surrounded by great debates on an ever widening range of social issues in which the place of older people is centrally involved: Social Security, Medicare, educational reform, housing, organization of health care, use of age as a cutoff point for allocation—even rationing—of medical resources, and issues of the meaning of life and death. All of us will participate in these debates—in family councils, doctors' offices, nursing homes, the workplace, the ballot box, neighborhood and community forums, hospice programs, and our everyday lives and most intimate relationships.

AN ANALYTICAL FRAMEWORK

Just as these debates pose far-reaching issues, they are also fraught with enormous complexities—which brings us to another topic: the hazards of ad hoc intervention and the consequent need for an analytical view of the processes involved. Of course, all social interventions involve dangers of unintended or undesired consequences; but these dangers are exacerbated in the case of the elderly because older people's strengths and their roles in society are interdependent. Without role opportunities, their strengths will not be sustained; in turn, without competence and power, older people cannot press for changes in the social structure. They will, instead, predictably tend to deteriorate, to become burdens to themselves and to others. A central principle of the sociology of age[22] has been forged here: there is a continuing interplay between the process of aging and changes in society. Each influences the other in a complex system of interrelationships. This means that an intervention in one is bound to have repercussions in the other.

This interdependent system of social structures and cohorts of aging people is so complex that we have long been concerned with how to simplify it enough to be able to analyze it. A number of us have been developing a paradigm that can be useful here, we believe, in understanding the potentials for interventions. This paradigm is schematized in Figure 1.

The Process of Aging

Figure 1 outlines a social space bounded on its vertical axis by years of age—from 0 to 100—and on its horizontal axis by dates—from 1890 to 2040—that index the course of history, the changes—economic, political, demographic, and cultural—that occur in society with the passage of time. Within this space, each diagonal bar represents a cohort of people who were born roughly at the same time and who are aging. As they age, they move diagonally across time and upward through the social structure—through the successive roles in family life, school grades and work careers, retirement, and, ultimately, death.

While they are growing older, the society is changing around them. A recent headline—"The 60s meet the 80s"—points to this linkage between the age of cohort members and their location in historical time. Members of that cohort who flouted traditional norms when they were young in the 1960s must now, when they are twenty years older, confront the seemingly more conservative standards of the 1980s. People who are old today grew up in a

FIGURE 1
Aging and social change: a schematic view.

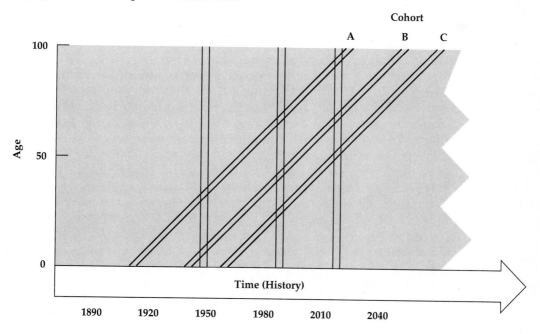

far different society, just as people who are young today will not be old in the same society in which they began their lives.

In addition, the space in this paradigm contains not one single diagonal line but a succession of diagonal lines following each other across the space. These diagonals represent a succession of cohorts. Because successive cohorts are born at different dates and live through different segments of historical time, people in different cohorts age in different ways. Thus a 20-year-old man in 1900 could scarcely have looked ahead to retirement at all; today such a man can expect to spend one-quarter of his adult lifetime in retirement. The process of aging has obviously been transformed.

The Changing Society

Now consider what is happening in the meantime to the society and to old people's place within it. At a particular moment in time—say, the year 1980—a cross-sectional slice cuts through all the cohorts that coexist in the society at that time. This vertical line represents the age structure of society at a given time in history. It indicates how both the people and their social roles are organized roughly in age groupings, from the youngest to the oldest. Over time, as society moves through historical events and changes, one can imagine this vertical line moving across the space from one time period to the next. Over time, the age-related norms and role opportunities are shifting. Moreover, the people in particular age strata are no longer the same people: they have been replaced by younger entrants from more recent cohorts with more recent life experiences.

Thus the paradigm makes provision for analysis of both processes of concern: the aging of individuals in successive cohorts and the changing structure of society. It also indicates the interplay between the two, as each

influences the other. Thus it serves as a broad conceptual framework for comprehending the possible outcomes of interventions in the aging process—along a particular diagonal line—or in the social structure, along a particular vertical line.

Moreover, a few moments' thought suggests how the two processes of aging and social change can never be perfectly synchronized. Aging people are moving along the axis of the life course, the diagonal lines. But social change—the moving vertical line—travels along its own axis of historical time. These two sets of lines are continually criss-crossing each other, producing an asynchrony. It is this asynchrony that accounts for the current mismatch between the strengths and capacities of older people and the lack of adequate roles for them in society.

An Example

Even when simplified, however, this paradigm in the abstract is complicated. Perhaps one concrete example will help to clarify its utility. The twentieth-century aging of the U.S. population has been accompanied by budgetary interventions that allocate and reallocate economic resources between old people and children. Some scholars regard these allocations as creating "intergenerational inequity," as favoring the old to the detriment of the young.[23] Use of the paradigm clarifies what has actually been happening. When the age strata in society are viewed in cross section—when young and old are compared—there has indeed been remarkable improvement from the 1960s to 1980s in the comparable economic position of the old relative to the very young.[24] Yet, to explain this change in social structure requires examination of the two underlying processes of aging and cohort succession.

Looking first at aging, when the structural change is traced back through the individual lives of people, a very different picture emerges, just as one might expect. Within a cohort, as children have grown older and entered their adult careers, they have tended to gain in economic well-being. By contrast, the economic status of elderly persons has tended to deteriorate as they have grown older, since income typically drops in retirement.

When we go on to compare the successive cohorts involved, however, it appears that the more recent cohorts, who have benefited from more advantageous employment histories, are now entering old age in a better financial position than previous cohorts. Thus it is the cohort differences that explain much of the improved relative position of the older strata in society as a whole. It is not that individuals become richer as they age—even with Social Security, Medicare, and other large-scale societal interventions. Many individuals continue to become economically deprived in old age, and further, small-scale supportive interventions from family or community are often needed.

In this example, the paradigm allows us to disentangle the interplay between aging processes and structural changes. It was not so much the societal budgetary interventions[25] that improved the relative income position of older people; rather, the improvement was due in large part to the cohort differences in the ways people grew older. In such ways, use of the paradigm can provide insights into the often hidden processes underlying changes in aging and society. The paradigm provides only a perspective, not a proof.

WINDOWS ON THE FUTURE

This analytical approach is useful not merely in explaining past consequences of interventions; it also has implications for possible future trends and the need for future interventions as the shape of the life course will, predictably, continue to change. The paradigm enables us to trace into the future the lives of people already born, since we can use actual knowledge about their earlier lives as a basis for estimating how they may eventually grow old. In the case of income, if we look at the newest cohorts, whose members are young today, we know that they are no longer starting at successively higher levels than their predecessors; instead, they have recently been starting, on the average, at comparatively lower levels. Thus, by the year 2020, when the members of these cohorts enter old age, many will predictably have lower economic status than do those entering old age today.[26]

Positive and Negative Outcomes

This particular instance is just one of several recent reversals of earlier trends that emphasize the importance of looking ahead toward the possible needs for interventions at various points in the future. In some ways, as in income, the future cohorts of old people may be less advantaged than their predecessors. For example, they will include larger proportions of the less privileged blacks and Hispanics. They will include the increasing proportions of those young people today who are failing to meet accepted standards of academic achievement.

In other ways, cohorts entering old age in the future may be better off than their predecessors. With improved nutrition, exercise, and reduced cigarette smoking in early life, they may be less subject to heart disease when they reach later life. Two trends among women are especially provocative: increasing proportions of young women in each successive cohort participate in the labor force, and increasing proportions experience a divorce before old age. We sometimes think of these trends as having entirely negative consequences, but do they perhaps mean that, as these young women become the older women of the future, they will have acquired greater independence, skills, and competence than their predecessors for living out their own lives? Will the fact of their early work-life experience have mitigated the economic insecurity of those older women who spend their later years living alone?[27] These, it seems to us, illustrate some of the issues confronting society today as we contemplate timely interventions that might optimize the design of the life course and the quality of aging in the future.

Yet, in one sense, the future is now. All of the trends and interventions we have been discussing will emerge during the twenty-first century as major transformations of both the human life course and the surrounding social structure. Nothing less than major transformations, it seems to us, are implicit in the revolutionary twentieth-century trends in longevity, the postponement of death, the aging of society, the advantages in technology and communication, the breakdown of national boundaries, and the struggles for survival of capitalist and democratic societies as we have known them. In a world where, barring nuclear cataclysm, older people will be increasingly predominant, we dare not disregard the need for interventions.

Some Caveats

At the same time, it is noteworthy that the discussions of interventions in this introductory article and throughout this special issue of *The Annals* are limited. The discussions are largely time bound. Moreover, for the sake of brevity, many of the formulations are greatly oversimplified. Average tendencies obscure the infinite diversity of human lives.[28] Differences by gender, race, ethnicity, and socioeconomic class are overlooked. Cohorts are too often treated as if they were composed of aggregates of discrete individuals, rather than of human beings embedded in social structures and closely engaged in interactions with other human beings whose lives are intricately intertwined. No estimates of the future can

properly guide interventions without taking such limitations into account.

Most neglected throughout these discussions are the issues of values: the norms and expectations built into the social structure about what is good and right and beautiful.[29] As we look toward a brighter future, seeking to intervene—to optimize the quality of aging—the fundamental question is, after all, What do we mean by "optimal."[30]—either for the aging individual or for society as a whole? What is the *summum bonum* to be used as a standard?

The answer to this central question of values is that there is still no answer. In our time, the pendulum has swung wildly from the liberal optimism of the 1930s, to the good life of the 1960s, to the reactionary leanings of the 1980s. In the short run, the success of interventions must be gauged by the shifting standards of the times. In the longer run, there may be tendencies toward more universal values that will gradually become institutionalized in social structures and internalized by the many people who, as they grow older, can also become wiser. The fundamental question of values seems worthy of an entire future issues of *The Annals*.

FINAL INTERVENTIONS

In our time, perhaps the most critically needed, and certainly the most poignant and neglected, of all interventions are the final ones—interventions designed to improve the quality of dying. These interventions can affect both the life course and the surrounding social structures.

The Role of the Dying Person

Two related current trends require us to take note of the role of the dying person in the ultimate phase of the aging process. First, during the twentieth century, the dramatic increase in longevity means that most deaths are recorded for older people. In contrast to earlier times, when most deaths occurred in infancy or young adulthood, today in the United States people over age 65 account for three-fourths of all deaths. Second, in place of the earlier rapid deaths from pneumonia and other acute diseases, today the process of dying—typically from chronic diseases—is often distressingly prolonged.

Much has been written about the experience of dying, and many wrenching questions have been debated: When does death occur? Do people die biologically before they die sociologically? When, if at all, should life-sustaining procedures be withdrawn? Does the living will have any force at law? Is there such a thing as a good death? We have contributed to these debates[31] and cannot rehearse them in detail here. Instead, we shall simply mention one of the interventions, hospice care, that can influence the quality of dying as the last phase of the aging process.

Hospice Care

Research has shown that there is often a time in the lives of those terminally ill older people who are sentient that is known as the living-dying interval. It is during this interval that the dying person often feels the need to negotiate with close kin and friends, to express previously unspoken affirmations of love and affection, to resolve old grievances and misunderstandings, to write—as it were—the final chapter. Yet this potential inherent in the living-dying interval is typically curtailed by the modern hospital setting in which most people die. The hospital is geared for treatment and cure, it functions according to standards of efficiency and bureaucratic rules, its environment is sterile and unwelcoming to those who would visit patients *in extremis*. With its overriding purpose to maintain life, the hospital is not organized to deal with the

subjective complexities of dying. Physiological processes are monitored, not states of loneliness or threats to selfhood.

It is not surprising, then, that the hospice movement has been rapidly spreading throughout the United States. Begun in Great Britain, the hospice was originally conceived as a freestanding facility dedicated solely to the care of terminal patients. Operating as the antithesis of hospital bureaucracy, the hospice put care at the top of the priority list and cure at the bottom. Its avowed purpose was to make the patient as comfortable as possible, using both analgesic medications and social supports. Today, in the United States, we speak of hospice care as a regimen rather than as a place where care is delivered. As the movement has developed, it has tended to locate such care in the home. The unit of care is both the patient and the family, but they are under the supervision of a physician, and there is a supporting team typically consisting of a nurse, a social worker, and, if needed, a specialized paramedical aide.

Under hospice conditions, the process of dying ideally involves joint decision making by the dying person and those who are about to become survivors.[32] More important, it enables the dying person to maintain a sense of identity, providing opportunities for open expressions of loneliness and fear of loss—all within a network of significant others and social-emotional supports. It also allows for active participation by those significant others, the about-to-be-bereaved, for whom death is often more painful than for the dying persons themselves.

We are not naive about the benefits of this particular intervention. We do not suggest that hospice care can transform the miseries of dying into a sentimental and soothing experience. Nor is this regimen suitable for many circumstances in which older people die, as in the instance of patients with Alzheimer's disease. Nevertheless, the record is clear: this form of care, or some modification of it, can avoid the bizarre calculus of medical settings that all too often strip both self-esteem and dignity from those who are dying. Today, hospice care is available in most parts of the United States. It is an evolving and increasingly significant model for interventions that can help to mitigate the pain of the final role in the life course.

In summary, we have called attention in this article to a contemporary mismatch between the strengths and capacities of older people and their roles in society. We have taken care to point out that research is beginning to show how carefully planned interventions in both human lives and social structures can help to reduce, if not to eliminate, this mismatch. We repeat our essential thesis: increasing numbers of competent older people and diminishing role opportunities cannot long coexist. Something has to give. It seems evident that carefully guided interventions—especially small-scale, cumulative interventions—can help to enhance the quality of aging now and in the future.

Notes

[1] One forecast suggests that average life expectancy at birth—currently estimated to be 75 years—could be increased well beyond age 85 if the known risk factors for heart disease, including smoking, high blood pressure, and obesity, were eliminated. Kenneth Manton, unpublished data. Such a forecast, which is based on simulation and makes many assumptions that may or may not be appropriate, merely indicates that maximum longevity is still unknown and may be extendable. See Kenneth G. Manton "Life-Style Risk Factors," this issue of *The Annals* of the American Academy of Political and Social Science.

[2] For a fuller discussion, see Matilda White Riley and John W. Riley, Jr., "Longevity and Social Structure: The Added Years," in *Our Aging Society: Paradox and Promise*, ed. Alan Pifer and Lydia Bronte (New York: Norton, 1986), pp. 53–77.

[3] Matilda White Riley, "On the Significance of Age in Sociology," in *Social Change and the Life Course*, vol. 1, *Social Structures and Human Lives*, ed. Matilda White Riley, Bettina J. Huber, and Beth B. Hess (Newbury Park, CA: Sage, 1988), pp. 24–45.

[4] There are today over 25,000 centenarians in the United States leading lives that, from all accounts, are in total disregard of chronology as a marker of age-related dependency. U.S. Department of Commerce, Bureau of the Census, *Current Population Reports*, series P-23, no. 153, *America's Centenarians* (Washington, DC: Government Printing Office, 1987).

[5] See, for example, John W. Rowe and Robert L. Kahn, "Human Aging: Usual and Successful," *Science*, 237:143–49 (July 1987). For a discussion of the persistent fallacy of ageism, see Robert N. Butler, "Dispelling Ageism: The Cross-Cutting Intervention," this issue of *The Annals* of the American Academy of Political and Social Science.

[6] Matilda White Riley, Anne Foner, and Joan Waring, "Sociology of Age," in *Handbook of Sociology*, ed. Neil J. Smelser (Newbury Park, CA: Sage, 1988), pp. 243–90.

[7] Many of these reports are from studies supported by the National Institute on Aging.

[8] Joanne Miller, Kazimietz M. Slomczynski, and Melvin L. Kohn, "Continuity of Learning Generalization: The Effect of Men's Jobs on Intellective Process in the United States and Poland," *American Journal of Sociology*, 91:593–615 (1985).

[9] For an overview, see K. Warner Schaie, "The Hazards of Cognitive Aging" (Kleemeier Award Lecture delivered at the Annual Meeting of the Gerontological Society of America, San Francisco, CA, Nov. 1988). See also Ursula M. Staudinger, Steven W. Cornelius, and Paul B. Baltes, "The Aging of Intelligence: Potential and Limits," this issue of *The Annals* of the American Academy of Political and Social Science.

[10] The evidence here comes from comparing tests in a laboratory context with the more complex environment of everyday life. Matthew J. Sharps and Eugene S. Gollin, "Memory for Object Locations in Young and Elderly Adults," *Journal of Gerontology*, 42(3):336–41 (1987).

[11] Laura L. Faltudo and Alan Baron, "Age-Related Effects of Practice and Task Complexity on Card Sorting," *Journal of Gerontology*, 41(5):659–61 (1986).

[12] See Judith Rodin, "Sense of Control: Potentials for Intervention," this issue of *The Annals* of the American Academy of Political and Social Science.

[13] George A. Kaplan and Mary N. Haan, "Is There a Role for Prevention among the Elderly? Epidemiological Evidence from the Alameda County Study," in *Aging and Health Care: Social Science and Policy Perspectives*, ed. Marcia Ory and Kathleen Bond (London: Routledge, 1989), pp. 27–51.

[14] U.S. Department of Labor, Bureau of Labor Statistics; data supplied by Malcolm H. Morrison. See also Harris T. Schrank and Joan M. Waring, "Older Workers: Ambivalence and Interventions," this issue of *The Annals* of the American Academy of Political and Social Science.

[15] As one exemption, see Riley, Huber, and Hess, eds., *Social Structures and Human Lives*.

[16] Louis Harris and Associates, *Aging in the Eighties: America in Transition* (Washington, DC: National Council

on the Aging, 1981). For fuller discussion, see Schrank and Waring, "Older Workers."

[17] As part of an intergenerational movement throughout the country, a Maryland pilot program called "Grandcare" reports considerable success in training older people to work in day-care centers for children aged 3 to 12. *Washington Post*, 15 Nov. 1988.

[18] *New York Times*, 12 Nov. 1987.

[19] See Marjorie H. Cantor, "Social Care Family and Community Support Systems," this issue of *The Annals* of the American Academy of Political and Social Science; David Mechanic "Health Care and the Elderly: Balancing Medical and Social Interventions," ibid.; Marcia G. Ory and T. Franklin Williams, "Rehabilitation: Small Goals, Sustained Interventions," ibid.

[20] See Schrank and Waring, "Older Workers."

[21] *Washington Post*, 19 Oct. 1988.

[22] Riley, Foner, and Waring, "Sociology of Age."

[23] The debate over "intergenerational equity" was sparked by Samuel H. Preston, "Children and the Elderly: Divergent Paths for American Dependents," *Demography*, 21:435–57 (1984). The analysis presented in this article was developed by Gregg I. Duncan, Martha Hill, and Willard Rodgers, "The Changing Fortunes of Young and Old," *American Demographics*, 8:26–34 (1986).

[24] U.S. Department of Health and Human Services, *Aging America: Trends and Projections, 1987–88 ed.,* LR 3377 (188).D 12198, pp. 57–59.

[25] To be sure, there were also benefit increases enacted in Social Security from 1968 to 1972. Department of Health and Human Services, *Aging America: Trends and Projections,* pp. 56–59.

[26] A combination of factors portend lower levels of future retiree income than are currently expected. These include today's all-time low in personal savings, added to reductions in benefits from private pensions because of the long-term trend toward increasing job changes over a person's work life. Moreover, rising numbers of older jobholders, many of them part-time, are not eligible for pension benefits in the first place. Indeed, it has been suggested that "we may now be witnessing the golden age of the golden years." Mark H. Weinstein, "The Changing Picture in Retiree Economics," *Statistical Bulletin* (Metropolitan Life Insurance Company), July-Sept. 1988, pp. 2–6.

[27] Peter Uhlenberg, "Differentiated Cohort Influences on Age Structures" (Manuscript, University of North Carolina, 1988).

[28] Cf. Dale Dannefer, "Aging as Intracohort Differentiation: Accentuation, the Matthew Effect, and the Life Course," *Sociological Forum*, 2(2): 211–36 (1987).

[29] For example, at the Paralympics following the 1988 Olympic Games in Seoul, handicapped athletes from many countries gave dramatic proof that expectations and norms are subject to change.

[30] This question of the underlying values that set criteria for "good" aging is largely overlooked in the literature. "Normal aging" is a common expression among clinicians, who wish to distinguish between health and disease; but this term effectively reduces to "average" patterns of aging at the same time that it neglects the sociological meaning of "norm" as a value-based standard of social expectations. Another expression is "successful aging," which again begs the question of the meaning of success.

[31] Note illustrative articles written by John W. Riley, Jr., over a twenty-year period: "Death and Bereavement," in *International Encyclopedia of the Social Sciences*, ed. D. L. Sills (New York: Macmillan and Free Press, 1968), 4:19–26, "What People Think about Death," in *The Dying Patient*, ed. O. G. Brim, Jr., et al. (New York: Russell Sage Foundation, 1970), pp. 30–42; "Dying and the Meanings of Death: Sociological Inquiries," *Annual Review of Sociology*, 3:191–216 (1983); with Matilda White Riley, "Longevity and Social Structure."

[32] The medical ambivalence here is severe. While formal hospital care proceeds on one set of norms, one recent study reports that 60 percent of the attending physicians proceed on another, believing that terminal patients should have a voice as to when they want to die. Anonymous, "A Time to Die," *Psychology Today* (Sept. 1988).

DISCUSSION QUESTIONS

1. In which respects do Riley and Riley find an *imbalance* between the strengths and capabilities of older people and their social-role opportunities to use these strengths?

2. Describe the essential elements of Riley and Riley's analytical framework for aging.

3. Do you think more economic resources should be devoted to programs to assist the aged even if it means reducing support for children's programs? Defend your response.

The Elderly: An International Policy Perspective

Eli Ginzberg

As a contribution to the world assembly on aging (Vienna, 26 July to 6 August 1982) the Sandoz Institute for Health and Socio-Economic Studies undertook a 16 nation survey on the problems of the elderly (defined as persons aged 60 and over) in consultation with the United Nations Center for Social Development and Humanitarian Affairs. The participating advanced industrial countries were Australia, the Federal Republic of Germany, France, Italy, Japan, Sweden, the United Kingdom, and the United States and the less industrialized countries included Brazil, Egypt, India, Israel, Kenya, Nigeria, the Philippines, and Poland (Selby and Schecter 1982).

Questionnaire responses were provided for each country by a small working group of three experts representing the broad areas of health, sociology, and social policy. There were two rounds of questions, the first focused on a ranking of the following problem areas— health, housing, health services and social services, family, community activities, income, work and employment, and retirement. The second round focused on the diversity of the elderly, employment, research, and political factors in policy making.

I was invited by the Sandoz Institute to prepare an economic commentary. Since it was not published, presumptively because it was judged not congruent with the aims of the assembly, I have taken the opportunity of making some changes and clarifications in preparing it for the present issue of the *Milbank Quarterly*.

Many of the returns from the sixteen nations were downbeat because of the anticipated rapid rise in the number of the elderly during the next twenty years, the anticipated high levels of unemployment, and the presumption of slow economic growth in the future.

Although economics in its formative years had earned the sobriquet of "the dismal science" because one of its founding fathers, the Reverend Thomas Malthus, saw famine, disease, and war as the great equilibrators when population expands faster than the food supply, the gerontologists and the sociologists who answered the questionnaire appeared to be unduly pessimistic. In my view, they were extrapolating from the unsatisfactory present for too many years into the future. A moderation of inflation together with renewed economic growth and an improved employment outlook, at least in the economies of the advanced industrial nations, is surely possible, even likely, before the end of this century.

In developing my commentary, my approach was to review critically the assumptions and conclusions of the experts who contributed to the survey, to delineate realistic parameters within which future policies for older persons should be designed, and, finally, to make a limited number of concrete suggestions for constructive action in the public and private domains that hold promise of contributing to the well-being of older persons. Each of the respondent nations is unique, but this analysis will proceed with a simplified typology in which the developed nations are distinguished from the faster and slower growing less-developed countries (LDCs).

THE PRESENT UNFAVORABLE ECONOMIC ENVIRONMENT

The respondents from the developed countries noted the following trends that threaten the viability of existing economic supports for the elderly and that will impede efforts to improve their circumstances in the future. The combination of slow economic growth, high inflation, and high unemployment represents a triple threat. Slow economic growth means that there will be only a small surplus available for improving the well-being of the total population, including the elderly, and in some years there will be no surplus. Under such strained circumstances, one cannot expect a society to use its small surplus solely to improve the well-being of the elderly to the exclusion of competing groups such as children, minorities, families with low incomes, and, especially, the working population who are producing the surplus and require incentives to increase it.

Continuing inflation is the second serious threat. On the one hand, inflation increases the difficulties that national pension schemes face in their efforts to remain solvent, by distorting the rates of savings, interest, and investments. On the other hand, inflation erodes the value of private pensions. If employers act to index these private plans, the costs to them through raising wage and benefit payments can result in the loss of future markets and jobs. If the costs of indexing private plans are absorbed in the national budget, taxes will increase, the nation's competitive position will be weakened, and income and employment are likely to decline. High inflation also leads to the erosion of personal savings that individuals accumulate during their working years to help them through their later years when they are no longer employed.

The respondents were also pessimistic about the future trends in employment. The combination of slow growth and high inflation are almost certain precursors of a low level of new job creation. Slow growth of new jobs at a time when more young people and women are entering the labor force points to continuing high unemployment. Moreover, automation is likely to result in displacing considerable num-

bers who currently hold jobs and further job losses will follow as additional manufacturing jobs are lost as a result of plant relocations from developed to less-developed nations. Since an inadequate number of jobs will be available for persons of prime working age, older workers will face increasing pressures to retire early.

A second set of adverse economic developments identified by the respondents included: the increasing costs of health care; the growing determination of governments to bring and to keep their budgets under control; and the difficulties of finding sources of funding in the private sector to provide improved services for the elderly as well as for other priority groups who need assistance.

The respondents from the developing nations cited many of these same factors: the difficulties of assuring the financial viability of embryonic pension schemes in periods of high level inflation; the growing imbalance between a rapidly increasing work force and a slower growth of employment opportunities; the intensified pressures to keep governmental expenditures under control. The developing nations called attention to additional problems to which they were particularly vulnerable, such as: the large-scale inflow of the rural population into crowded urban centers; the erosion of the extended family which had formerly provided for its elderly members; the acute competition for limited resources between economic development goals and the maintenance needs of many groups, including the elderly.

A MORE OPTIMISTIC ECONOMIC SCENARIO

No economist will minimize the dangers of a prolonged period of high inflation such as has characterized most of the developed and developing nations since the early 1970s. Governments are now increasing efforts to contain and reduce such inflationary pressures. With a reasonable admixture of continuing fiscal restraint and the absence of renewed oil or other raw material shortages, inflation could by 1990 represent a considerably reduced threat.

The assumption of continued slow economic growth can also be challenged. Included in the sixteen nations surveyed are several that have been able to sustain high or satisfactory levels of growth in recent years even though most nations have experienced a slowing of their previous rates of growth. For the developed nations, the 1950s and 1960s represented an epoch of above-average growth because of the rapid rebuilding of capital plant and equipment after many years of war and economic stagnation. For many LDCs these decades saw rapid growth aided and abetted by much enlarged international lending, following their achievement of national independence. After two decades of rapid expansion some slowdown was to be anticipated. However, the attraction of low-cost labor that has proved its ability to cope with modern technology points to an eventual quickening of investment in LDCs once the world's economy again begins to expand.

Attention must also be called to a subtle factor imbedded in the ways in which growth is measured. Some economists believe that the actual growth in both developed and developing economies may be considerably higher than the official statistics suggest. In developed economies we have seen a rapid growth in tax evading, illicit and illegal activities, as well as an expansion in noncash transfers as when dentists and accountants exchange professional services. In developing countries the shifting boundaries between the money and the nonmoney economies also create doubts about how well the statistical reporting systems provide a true reflection of real growth in employment and income.

There are also good reasons to question the forecasts of respondents from the developed nations about continuing weaknesses in the job market resulting from the continued rapid growth of the labor force. The odds favor increasing pressure from the side of adult women who are currently not working. More and more of them are likely to seek paid employment and to increase their years in active employment. But the situation is different with respect to young persons. In some developed nations the surge in the numbers of youth has already crested and in other countries the crest will occur shortly. Manpower planners in Germany are presently designing policies that will help compensate for the substantial decline in the absolute number of young people who will be entering the labor force some years hence. In the United States the number of young people reaching the working age of 16 to 24 will decline by 15 percent in the 1980s.

Technological advances usually cut both ways. Along with the benefits come dislocations; some workers lose their jobs and others find their skills obsolescent. But over the long pull, technological advances—a substitute term for automation—are likely to expand the total number of jobs and raise the skill levels of the labor force. That is the only reasonable deduction to be extracted from the record of the last two centuries.

The developed regions of the world do face a challenge from the loss of jobs incident to the relocation of manufacturing plants to the less-developed nations. But these job losses in manufacturing are the beginning, not the end of this important transition. The evidence favors Adam Smith's insight that a broadening of the market results in expansion, not contraction, of both income and employment for all who trade.

Two developments—the expansion of the service sector and increased bilateral and multilateral trade—have, in the past, helped to cushion the relative decline in manufacturing employment that has been occurring in most developed nations, and there is every reason to assume that these trends will continue.

In the more rapidly growing developing

countries—such as Brazil, Israel, and Nigeria—continuing inflation, some slowing in economic growth, and a surplus of job seekers represent threats to large-scale improvements in the standard of living, including better prospects for the elderly. But these potential threats are not to be equated with certain evils of stagnation and high unemployment and reduced funding for the elderly. If developed nations experience an easing of inflationary pressures, the same forces will contribute to moderating inflation in the developing world. Many of the developing countries should be able to continue to make good progress because of, among other reasons, the expansion of manufacturing incident to the transfer of plants from the developed nations. However, even if several LDCs are able to achieve a continuing satisfactory rate of growth, they will not be able to provide regular jobs for all of the new entrants into their labor forces, because of the larger numbers of young people who will reach working age; the many rural migrants who are relocating to the cities to find jobs; and the increased numbers of urban women who want to work outside their homes. But if past is prelude, these countries will also face selective shortages of skilled workers even while they are encountering difficulty in absorbing the large numbers of unskilled workers.

The prospect is definitely bleaker for the LDCs at the lower levels of income because even a much reduced inflation rate, a satisfactory economic growth rate, and reasonable gains in total employment will fall far short of providing adequate jobs and income for their rapidly increasing populations.

It may be that the survey respondents will be proved right by events and their bleak forecasts confirmed. But I, for one, see little basis in history or in theory to accept their pessimistic forecasts. The human and material bases for continuing gains in productivity, particularly if assisted by reductions in the rates of population growth, remain strong.

At the beginning of the 1970s, a group of futurologists, who came to be known as the Club of Rome, put forward a number of highly pessimistic forecasts about the interaction of population, raw material, and economic trends which suggested that the world would soon start becoming poorer, not richer (Meadows et al. 1972). They and their forecasts have been discredited. Only a major collapse of the international financial system and a long-term shrinkage in world trade would restore their credibility.

KEY ELEMENTS IN IMPROVING THE POSITION OF THE ELDERLY

The survey focused on obtaining critical information on a selected number of key elements including income, work, medical services, and social services, which I will address seriatim, primarily with respect to the advanced industrial countries with occasional specification for the developing countries as well.

Income

If older persons want to enjoy a standard of living in retirement approaching the level they enjoyed in the years preceding retirement, they must continue to work past the age of 60 and the economies of which they are a part must be restructured to make room for them. No national pension plan will be able to transfer from the working population the income required to keep retirees at a desirable standard of living for 20 or more years. Once the different age groups within a population are no longer growing or declining, active workers would have to pay over a third of their annual income solely to cover this one societal obligation. The financial pressures that currently afflict most national pension plans are a warning of worse trouble ahead, when the ratio of contributors to beneficiaries will decline as the longevity of the beneficiaries continues to increase and the proportion of active workers diminishes.

The pension enthusiasts will question this alarmist conclusion and point to the prospects of encouraging more personal savings (easier to do in a noninflationary period) and more private pensions (costly to fund and even more costly to index for inflation) to relieve some of the pressures on the public treasury. I see relatively limited scope for either or both of these alternatives to provide significant amounts of income to retirees without squeezing the working population. The simple fact is that income for retirees can only come out of current production. Only the cost of housing can be covered from earlier production and this disregards the costs of maintenance, heating, and taxes. While a higher rate of savings on the part of employed workers can broaden and deepen the nation's capital stock above what it would otherwise have been, and thereby increase its future GNP, the claims of workers when they retire can be covered only from current output.

Work

The only prospect for large numbers of older persons to enjoy a satisfactory level of income is to remain at work as long as possible and thereby reduce the years when they are dependent on pensions. But the survey respondents are pessimistic about jobs, full-time or part-time, that will be available to older workers if by choice or necessity they want to work until their late sixties or even into their seventies. True, if the current high levels of unemployment were to continue over many years, the prospects of older persons to continue to work would not be bright. But if the unemployment rate were to decline, the prospect for older workers could improve quickly and dramatically. Their employability would be assisted by their improved health, the lowered demand for physical labor as the economy shifts from

manufacturing to service industries, and the gains that will accrue to employers from retaining experienced workers knowledgeable about the ways in which their organizations operate.

Since lack of skill, experience, and know-how are among the constraints which impede the rate at which the modern sectors of developing countries are able to grow, one can stipulate that they too should encourage the productive members among their older workers to remain at their jobs as long as possible. Since larger employers using modern machines in developing nations are less constrained by government regulations and trade union agreements, they should face fewer difficulties in retaining such older workers.

Medical Care

The steadily growing sophistication of modern medicine expands the possibility for new useful interventions, many of which, such as open-heart surgery, carry a steep price and often an uncertain outcome. When it comes to the provision of medical care for the elderly, developed countries confront difficult decisions. For example, because of economic stringency the United Kingdom has found it necessary to deny access to the elderly to various costly procedures and other, more affluent countries are under increasing financial pressure to place limits on medical interventions on behalf of persons whose prospects of regaining functionality are problematic.

Broad access to improved medical care is clearly one of the ways in which developed nations can continue to contribute to the well-being of the elderly in the decades ahead. But an open-ended commitment to use all possible curative interventions on all older patients, without reference to their prospects of regaining functionality for self-care and work, should be reassessed in the best interests of both society and the elderly.

Developing nations should profit from the

experience of the more affluent countries and proceed cautiously in developing sophisticated hospitals and staff and in committing themselves prematurely to broad entitlement programs for costly inpatient care not only for the elderly but for all their citizens. Improved health care has a significant role to play in economic growth and development but the investment should be focused primarily on classic preventive health measures, targeted in the first instance on children and young adults, including improved water supplies, the suppression of malaria and other scourges, immunization, family planning, and improved nutrition. To the extent that these interventions succeed, future cohorts of elderly persons will be better off.

Social Services

The fourth parameter is shorthand for a wide range of supports that older persons require or can utilize. These involve assistance in the maintenance of family ties, living in one's own home, participating in social and community affairs, admission when necessary to a nursing home, and much more. The guiding principle should be caution on the part of governments in designing programs that speed the shifting of responsibility from the family to the state, both because of the burdens that such shifts place on the public treasury and the further difficulty of the bureaucracy to deliver human services of high quality. The introduction of social service programs for the elderly has been limited to the more affluent of the developed nations. The developing nations, with small resources, cannot afford to follow in the footsteps of the affluent. Their governments must move circumspectly in taking on responsibilities that have long been carried by family and community. When conventional family ties are cut, as when migrants move from the countryside to the city, some modest new public services for the elderly may well be needed.

IN SEARCH OF POLICY

What policy directions for enhancing the well-being of older persons in both developed and developing nations can be extracted from the foregoing analysis? The earlier analysis suggested that the present difficulties facing the world economy—reflected in slowed growth, continuing inflation, and excessive unemployment—are likely to be reversed, and that many current economic difficulties will be eased. Even if this optimistic forecast proves to be more accurate than the pessimistic extrapolations that now dominate the thinking of most academicians and politicians, it does not mean that it will be easy to improve the status of the elderly. The most that can be claimed is that the environment in which future solutions are developed will be more propitious.

Before considering the specific recommendations that the leaders of developed and developing countries should weigh in designing new and improved policies to improve the welfare of older persons, I will review briefly a series of propositions that have wide currency.

- *Additional income at the command of retired persons will help to stimulate the economy and create jobs.* It is true that additional disposable income at the command of the elderly has created new demands and, therefore, new jobs, ranging from the development of retirement communities to the manufacture of prepared foods. The critical question is whether the additional income of the elderly comes from transfers from younger workers in a stagnant economy, in which case the latter will have less to spend, or from an expanding economy in which both workers and the retired are better off. The best case of all would be that in which the economy expands to a point where the heretofore unused labor of the elderly would be in demand and their increased income would stem from additional wages and salaries, not from income transfers.

- *Additional jobs for the elderly can be specified and governments can create them.* It is clear that as the elderly have more income they spend it on high priority goods and services, from nursing home care to recreation. It does not follow, however, that if governments decide to increase their outlays for improved housing, health, and other services for the elderly, this would be beneficial to the economy. Money spent on the elderly must be raised by taxes that reduce the disposable income of other groups, so that jobs created to serve the elderly will, in large measure, be at the expense of jobs that would have been created to provide goods and services for children or young adults.

- *It is necessary and desirable to look to international arrangements and agreements among nations to "balance out" benefit levels for the elderly.* International trade has been expanding for the last two centuries to the advantage of both high- and low-wage countries. Because "fringe benefits" amount to between 35 and 50 percent of the basic wage, some developed nations are finding it increasingly difficult to compete with low-wage countries. But we must remember that consumers in high-wage countries are able to buy imported goods at lower prices. Large differentials in the labor supplies and cost structures of nation states will increase the mobility of both firms and workers, but it is doubtful that recourse to governmental interventions will lead to gains in efficiency or equity. With regard to benefits for the elderly, it is unlikely that they will reach a level where, on their own, they will have a seriously distorting influence on the international competitiveness of high-income, high-wage nations.

- *Lessons can be drawn from the experience of developed countries with the highest proportions of elderly persons.* In several west European countries—such as the United Kingdom, France, Italy, the Federal Republic of Germany, and Sweden—about 1 in 5 of the population is 60 or older. Moreover, estimates by the United Nations point to substantial gains in the over-60 population by the year 2000. The optimists point to the success that the above-mentioned countries have had in supporting so many elderly persons, but the pessimists point to the vulnerable financial condition of their social security and health care systems. Policy makers should refrain from attempting to improve benefits for the elderly on the ground that enlarged expenditures will stimulate their economies, that international agreements will protect their countries from loss of competitiveness, or that their experience up to the present in supporting the elderly provides assurance of the long-term future solvency of their social security systems.

A more cautious approach would aim to increase the employment opportunities for the elderly, to constrain high-cost medical interventions that offer little promise of adding to the individual's functionality, and to provide more and better social services via family and community.

For more developed nations, the following agenda requires early assessment and action:

- Hard-nosed appraisals of the financial positions of the national pension plans well into the 21st century under at least two sets of assumptions—optimistic and pessimistic—which take into account such matters as future rates of inflation, unemployment, demographic trends, and labor force participation. If these prospective assessments reveal a growing gap between current commitments and potential resources of the pension system, politicians must explore alternative ways of closing the gap and initiate early corrective action (Ginzberg 1982).

- In several developed countries the marginal tax rate is already so high as to be dysfunctional. In others, there may be some room for selective new taxes from which part of the revenues might be used to raise benefits for the elderly, if analysis demonstrated that they were seriously in need. But the preferred approach, as indicated below, would be to reduce the pressures on the pension systems by encouraging or requiring older persons, if they are capable, of continuing to work longer.

- In many countries, the national pension plans have accumulated additional obligations, some of which violate the principles of social insurance. As part of the process of shoring up the financial viability of national pension plans, such additions should not be grafted onto insurance plans.
- Many west European countries that are faced with rising unemployment have resorted to special measures aimed at reducing the retirement age to 60 or even earlier in the hope and expectation that this action will open additional opportunities for young persons to find jobs. These policies should be reappraised in light of the following: young workers frequently cannot substitute for older skilled workers, surely not on a one-for-one basis; since more and more jobs are in the service sector, most men and women entering their sixties will not find continuing to work a strain on their health or capabilities; since longer periods are spent in skill acquistion both prior to initial employment and during an active career, the payout period should be lengthened; when expectations of early retirement become entrenched, they are difficult to change; the costs of maintaining people twenty or more years in retirement status are prohibitive.
- The United States recently revised its Social Security System to raise the future age of retirement from 65 to 67, and to increase the monetary incentives for people to remain at work beyond 65.
- Reductions in the age of retirement will not bring the labor markets of countries with 8 to 13 percent unemployment into balance. Such approaches are doomed to failure and involve high, long-term costs. In an expanding economy, which alone can provide new jobs for the excessive number of unemployed persons and new entrants into the labor force, further gradual reductions in hours per week and per year hold some promise of contributing to long-term equilibrium. So too does paid time-off for continuing education and training which should result in higher productivity over an increased number of years. Another adjustment device that can contribute to a more balanced labor market is an increase in the number of less than full-time jobs. When both spouses work, many couples prefer to have one or both work less than full time.

- Employers should reassess policies and programs that currently contribute to forcing older workers out of jobs rather than encouraging them to remain.
- The Swedish approach, whereby workers have an opportunity to continue working part-time while drawing a part of their pensions, is one of a number of innovations that commend themselves to study and replication. Employers in the United States are calling back retired employees to help out at peak seasons but the heavy "penalties" (recently reduced) for earning more than the maximum allowed under the Social Security System currently limits this approach.
- There are many private and public policies that require modification if older persons are to be encouraged to remain at work. These policies involve such matters as group insurance rates, taxes, and future benefits from public and private pension plans for workers who stay on their jobs.
- Persons approach retirement in different health status, with different occupational skills, energy levels, income, prospects for employment. The fact that some may no longer be capable of working in their long-

term occupations—coal miner, steel worker, lumberjack, and other physically demanding assignments—should not be used as an excuse to retain the current, early retirement systems. Rather, national pension plans should be modified so that "spent" workers can retire without encouraging all others to stop working prematurely.

- We need an early dialogue among political leaders, the medical profession and other providers of health care, and the public about the range and depth of medical interventions for the elderly which the public treasury is expected to underwrite. A developed nation can surely afford to pay for basic ambulatory, inpatient, and home care for its older citizens, even though it may decide to draw the line at costly therapeutic interventions of questionable efficacy. A major frontier, where sizable economies and little loss of welfare (possibly even some gains) may be found, is in restricting major medical interventions among terminal patients.
- In most developed countries the feeble aged are institutionalized largely at public expense or continue to be cared for by relatives and friends at home or in the community where they have long lived. The United Kingdom probably has the most to teach other countries about caring for the feeble aged in their own homes and using public funds to supplement family resources by paying for a housekeeper when the family needs relief.
- More effort should be directed to developing programs whereby the functioning elderly can be employed part-time or full-time in assisting the home-bound. The costs of this kind of assistance are likely to be far below the costs of institutionalization. In the United States, large and small for-profit organizations are rapidly expanding personal services to the aged, most of whom prefer to remain in their own homes. The fact that more and more women are working and that increasing numbers of older persons live

alone makes it necessary to look more to paid workers to provide essential services for the feeble elderly. There is also a continuing role for volunteers to help care for friends and neighbors.

Suprisingly, the principles underlying these suggestions require only slight modification to fit the agendas of developing nations. In brief:

- Developing nations should delay establishing national pension systems until they are well along on the path of economic development. Otherwise, deflection of limited tax revenues to improve the condition of the elderly can result in making everybody poorer.
- If and when they establish national pension schemes, LDCs should attempt to keep them actuarially sound and avoid encumbering them with desirable but costly benefits that should be dealt with outside the insurance framework, by government programs that are means-tested.
- LDCs should encourage public and private policies that aim at keeping older workers in their jobs as long as they are capable of performing effectively.
- LDCs should avoid sweeping commitments to provide sophisticated therapeutic care for all the population, including the elderly. Rather, they should use their limited health care budgets primarily to improve the health of the present and future working populations.
- LDCs should encourage the family, religious orders, and the local community to continue to provide services that they have traditionally made available to the elderly. When they are able to direct some public funds to the support of the elderly they should provide them through these established instrumentalities.

One concluding observation: The developed countries have commitments to the elderly which, even under our optimistic forecasts, are not likely to be fulfilled, surely not in their entirety. But the proposed shift in policy and tactics from income maintenance to work may be less disturbing than most experts suspect. The well-being of the elderly does not rest on a prolonged period of check-collecting and check-cashing, but on active engagement in a world where work remains the principal arena of social involvement. Those who can work should be encouraged to do so. They will be better off and society will be better off. If those who can work do so, the developed nations will be able to support those who cannot. The governments of the developing nations have little option but to leave most of the responsibility for the elderly with their families until such time that their annual economic surplus permits some transfer of responsibility to the state. As more and more of the developing nations increase their national and per capita income, they will surely want to devote some of their "surplus" to making life better for their elderly citizens who will have only a relatively short time to enjoy the economic and social gains that these nations are achieving.

References

Ginzberg, E. 1982. The Social Security System. *Scientific American* 246 (1):51–57.

Meadows, D. H., D. L. Meadows, and J. Randers, 1972. *The Limits to Growth*. A Report for the Club of Rome's Project on the Predicament of Mankind. New York: Universe.

Selby, P., and M. Schechter, eds. 1982. *Aging Two Thousand: A Challenge for Society*. Hingham, Mass.: MTP Press.

DISCUSSION QUESTIONS

1. How does Ginzberg repond to the assertion that the economic climate is poor for improved policies for the elderly?
2. What recommendations does Ginzberg offer to improve policy for the elderly in less developed countries (LDCs)?
3. What are the difficulties associated with adopting another country's programs for alleviating social problems of aging?

PART FOUR

Major Institutional Settings

CHAPTER 9

Issues in the Family

INTRODUCTION

When you think of the family, what probably comes to mind is an independent unit made up of parents and siblings. The reality, however, is far more complex, for families exist within a social and cultural environment that affects how they are formed, whether or not they break up, and what goes on inside them. These influences are of interest to sociologists, for they are the key to understanding the structure and role of family life in America and elsewhere in the world.

Regardless of where they are found, families share certain characteristics, including reproduction, nurturing, production and consumption of goods, provision of status, socialization, and regulation of sexual behavior. While the family is universally viewed as a social institution, it varies not only from one society to the next but even within a given society. Thus, one can generalize that in the United States fathers are more dominant in the family than mothers, but there are many exceptions to this rule. Similarly, one can say that couples usually have two children and that grandparents do not live with their grand-

children, but everyone knows of cases in which these generalizations are not true.

Family structure and the roles of family members are based on cultural values, norms, and attitudes. Thus, the value that Americans place on the notion of romantic love affects their patterns of social interaction; but in traditional Hasidic, Hindu, and Arab cultures, romantic love plays almost no role in mate selection. Values about virginity and adultery also differ from one culture to the next. Norms in the United States generally require selection of mates from groups that are similar in social characteristics (a practice referred to as *endogamy*). Thus, Americans are most likely to marry individuals who are similar in age, educational attainment, social class, and race. Norms also determine how family members will relate to one another. Thus, in our society, sexual relations between close relatives such as uncle and niece are generally frowned upon, and marriage within one's gender or nuclear family is prohibited (embodied in rules of *exogamy*). Attitudinally, we view the family as extremely important; we pity people who have

245

no family. We sometimes contradict our own values by lampooning mothers-in-law while viewing Mother's Day as an important family event.

Families are strongly influenced by the environment and by technology in particular. To take a historic overview, as U.S. society industrialized, children lost their economic value; this resulted, among other things, in smaller families. In addition, many of the functions once attributed to the family became the responsibilities of other institutions and individuals. Thus, schools tremendously expanded their role in educating children, and individual performance and merit replaced family ties as predictors of success and social status. It was because of the shift to a more formal societal structure that romantic love replaced economic and social reasons as factors influencing the choice of a marriage partner. The role of women changed also as the family lost control over the destinies of its female members.

In terms of family stability, the changing family created certain dysfunctions. As the nuclear family gained in importance, members of the extended family lost their roles in emotional support systems. Conversely, the increased interdependency of nuclear family members created social strains that did not exist when conflict was diffused among numerous members of the family. The separation of older generations from the nuclear family further exacerbated tensions by causing parents and grandparents to feel unwanted and useless. Clearly, although the nuclear family is an inevitable outgrowth of industrial society, it brings with it many problems that need to be addressed.

One of the major dilemmas facing modern society is the divorce rate. Divorce itself is not new; it has been a feature of organized human life for centuries. What makes divorce problematic today is its *rate*, which, in the United States, has stabilized at almost one out of every two marriages. The increase in divorce has been accompanied by profound changes in attitudes. Many people no longer consider divorce sinful or wrong, in striking contrast to the attitude that prevailed as recently as thirty years ago. Divorce has become simply a fact of life. The declining importance of extended family members, the increasing independence of women, changing gender roles, and even the increase in the number of divorced people have contributed to the rise in divorce. One way of looking at the issue in perspective is to contemplate the fact that, in the old days when people married "till death do us part," many marriages lasted twenty years because that is how long people lived after getting married. Had life expectancy been longer, there might have been many more divorces. Nevertheless, it cannot be denied that most of the causes of divorce are a function of modern life itself.

Whatever happens, the family is likely to remain with us for the foreseeable future. People in the United States divorce often, but they remarry almost as often. True, the family has changed radically, as other institutions in society have taken over some of its functions. However, commitment to the institution of marriage remains high, and people show no enthusiasm for doing away with it.

The first selection in this chapter, by the well-known author, Lillian Breslow Rubin, looks at life within the working-class family. Rubin writes about the feeling of emptiness experienced by many married men and women within this culture, and about their lack of communication and their tendency to look down on displays of feeling and warmth. Rubin explains why these views emerge and what perpetuates them. She examines the role of early socialization, the media, and the occupations of parents in terms of what the parents expect life to offer their children. These attitudes are brought home by the extensive use of quotes from in-depth interviews that allow working-class people to express themselves in their own language. What emerges is a portrait of a community that knows something is amiss and has begun to make an effort to do something about it.

The second reading, by Gerald Handel, a well-known expert on the family, looks at some of the issues surrounding sibling relationships. He begins by asking why some siblings remain friends in later life and others do not. Handel identifies four problems that exist in families as they relate to sibling relationships: shared parentage, differing ages, the individuality of each child, and differing genders. What is unique about Handel's approach is its nonconfrontational aspect. Much has been written about sibling rivalry, but very little about the conditions under which it does not develop and why it might not occur. Handel's article examines the family and sibling relationships on the individual level of analysis.

William Moskoff, in the last piece in this chapter, offers another look at divorce, this time in an international context. Given the rapid advance of Glasnost, U.S. ties with the Soviet Union have become even more crucial. The marriage of a Russian space scientist to a granddaughter of former President Eisenhower made headlines not too long ago. Such marriages may become far more common in the future as contact between the two nations increases. William Moskoff, an economist, analyzes divorce in the U.S.S.R. We see that—besides alcoholism, adultery, and incompatibility—the shifting role of women and problems in obtaining housing also tear away at the fabric of family stability. Moskoff presents information on the adverse effects of divorce on children, especially in regard to their school performance. Russian couples who divorce are far less likely to remarry someone else than are American ones, and Moskoff explains why. His discussion shows that, while certain patterns of family life may be more or less universal, their causes and the solutions proposed are not.

References

Cherlin, Andrew J. *Marriage, Divorce, Remarriage*. Cambridge, Mass.: Harvard University Press, 1981.

Lasch, Christopher. *Haven in a Heartless World: The Family Besieged*. New York: Basic Books, 1977.

Straus, Murray, Richard J. Gelles, and Suzanne K. Steinmetz. *Violence in the American Family*. New York: Doubleday, 1978.

Willie, Charles V. *A New Look at Black Families*, 2d ed., Bayside, N.Y.: General Hall, 1981.

Changing Expectations: New Sources of Strain

Lillian Breslow Rubin

I give her a nice home, a nice car, all those fancy appliances. I don't cheat on her. We got three nice kids—nobody could ask for better kids. And with all that, she's not happy. I worry about it, but I can't figure out what's the matter, so how can I know what to do? I just don't know what she wants.

[Twenty-nine-year-old truck driver, married nine years]

"I just don't know what she wants"—that's the plaintive and uncomprehending cry of most working-class men, the cry that bedevils most marriages. Sadly, she often also doesn't know what she wants. She knows only that the dream is not being fulfilled—that she's married but feels lonely:

It sounds silly, I know, but here I am in a house with three kids and my husband, and lots of times I feel like I might just as well be living alone.

. . . that life feels curiously empty:

you wake up one day and you say to yourself, "My God, is this all there is? Is it really possible that this is what life is all about?"

. . . that she's often filled with an incomprehensible anger:

I feel like I go crazy-angry sometimes. It makes me say and do things to Randy or the kids that I hate myself for. I keep wondering what makes me do those things when one part of me knows I don't really mean it.

. . . and that guilt and anxiety are her steady companions:

I don't know what's the matter with me that I don't appreciate what I've got. I feel guilty all the time, and I worry about it a lot. Other women, they seem to be happy with being married and having a house and kids. What's the matter with me?

"What's the matter" with her is that, even apart from the financial burdens incurred in buying all those goods, they add little to the emotional satisfactions of life. The advertisers' promises of instant happiness prove to be a lie—good for the gross national product but not for the human soul.

Sure, it's great to show those goodies off to friends and neighbors. After all those years of poverty, it makes you feel good finally to have something and to let people see it. Besides, they make life easier, more comfortable. Now there's time for things other than household drudgery. But what things? Companionship? Intimacy? Sharing? What are those things? And how does one find them?

She has a vague idea. Television shows, the women's magazines—they all talk about something called communication. Marriage partners have to communicate, they say; they have to talk, to tell each other how they feel. So she talks. And he tries to listen. But somehow, it doesn't work. He listens, but he cannot hear. Sometimes sooner, sometimes later, he withdraws in silence, feeling attacked:

When she comes after me like that, yapping like that, she might as well be hitting me with a bat.

. . . vulnerable:

It makes me feel like I'm doing something wrong, like I'm not a very good husband or something.

. . . and helpless:

No matter what I say, it's no good. If I try to tell her she's excited over nothing, that only makes it worse. I try to keep my cool and be logical, but nothing works.

This is the dilemma of modern marriage—experienced at all class levels, but with particular acuteness among the working-class families I met. For once marriage is conceived of as more than an economic arrangement—that is, as one in which the emotional needs of the individual are attended to and met—the role segregation and the consequent widely divergent socialization patterns for women and men become clearly dysfunctional. And it is among the working class that such segregation has been most profound, whether there has been least incentive to change.

Thus, they talk *at* each other, *past* each other, or *through* each other—rarely *with* or *to* each other. He blames her: "She's too emotional." She blames him: "He's always so rational." In truth, neither is blameworthy. The problem lies in the fact that they do not have a language with which to communicate, with which to understand each other. They are products of a process that trains them to relate to only one side of themselves—she, to the passive, tender, intuitive, verbal, emotional side; he, to the active, tough, logical, nonverbal, unemotional one. From infancy, each has been programmed to be split off from the other side; by adulthood, it is distant from consciousness, indeed. . . .

When they try to talk, she relies on the only tools she has, the mode with which she is most familiar; she becomes progressively more emotional and expressive. He falls back on the only tools he has; he gets progressively more rational—determinedly reasonable. She cries for him to attend to her feelings, her pain. He tells her it's silly to feel that way; she's just being emotional. That clenched-teeth reasonableness invalidates her feelings, leaving her sometimes frightened:

> I get scared that maybe I'm crazy. He's always so logical and reasonable that I begin to feel, "What's the matter with me that I'm so emotional?"

. . . sometimes angry:

> When he just sits there telling me I'm too emotional, I get so mad, I go up the wall. Sometimes I get so mad I wish I could hit him. I did once, but he hit me back, and he can hurt me more than I can hurt him.

. . . almost always tearful and despairing:

> I wind up crying and feeling terrible. I get so sad because we can't really talk to each other a lot of times. He looks at me like I'm crazy, like he just doesn't understand a word I'm saying.

Repeatedly, the experience is the same, the outcome of the interaction, predictable. Yet, each has such a limited repertoire that they are consigned to playing out the same theme over and over again—he, the rational man; she, the hysterical woman.

But these almost wholly sociological notions—notions which speak to socialization patterns—tell only one part of the story of human development. The other part is told in the language of psychology—a language that is given its fullest and most complex expression in psychoanalytic theory. From that theory, Nancy Chodorow has presented us with a brilliant and provocative reformulation of Oedipal theory which successfully crosses the sociological with the psychological as it accounts for the dynamics of both the inner and outer world as they affect sex-role development.

Her argument starts from the premise that the differences in male and female personality are rooted in the structure of the family—in particular, in the fact that women are the primary childrearers. As a result, the mother becomes the first object with which an infant—male or female—identifies, the first attachment formed. Coincident with the forming of these identifications and attachments, other developmental tasks emerge in the period between infancy and childhood—a primary one being the development of an appropriate gender identity. For a girl, that task is a relatively straightforward one—a continuous and gradual process of internalization of a feminine identity with mother as model. For a boy, however, role learning is discontinuous involving, as it must, the rejection of his early identification with his mother as he seeks an appropriate masculine identity.

Since a girl need not reject that early identification in order to negotiate the Oedipal phase successfully, feminine personality is based on less repression of inner objects, less fixed and firm ego-splitting, and greater continuity of external relationships. With no need to repress or deny their earliest attachment, girls can define and experience themselves as part of and continuous with others. Consequently, women tend to have more complex inner lives, more ability to engage in a variety of interpersonal relationships, and more concern with ongoing relational issues.

On the other hand, boys must repress these same attachments as they shift their identification from mother to father. That means that they must distinguish and differentiate themselves in a way that girls need not. In doing so, they come to define and experience themselves as more separate from others and with more rigid ego boundaries; and adult masculine personality comes to be defined more in terms of denial of connection and relations.

Such ideas present profound implications for the marriage relationship. For if it is true that their earliest experiences in the family mean that men must deny relations and connection while women must be preoccupied with them, we are faced anew with the realization—this time from the psychoanalytic perspective—that the existing structure of family relations, especially in its delegation of the parenting function solely or dominantly to the mother, makes the attainment of compatible relations between women and men extraordinarily difficult.

It hardly need be said that such relationships between men and women are not given to the working-class alone. Without doubt, the description I have been rendering represents the most common interactional pattern in American marriage. These are the behavioral consequences of the dominant sex-role socialization patterns in the culture and of the existing structure of family relations within which boys and girls internalize an appropriate identity—patterns which generate the role stereotypes that women and men bring to marriage and which effectively circumscribe their emotional negotiations.

Still, it is also true that the norms of middle-class marriage for much longer have called for more companionate relationships—for more sharing, for more exploration of feelings, and for more exchange of them. Thus, middle-class women and men have more practice and experience in trying to overcome the stereotypes. And, perhaps more important, they have more models around them for how to do so. This is not to suggest that they have done it so well, as a casual glance at the divorce rate will show; only that the demands on the marriage partners for different behaviors have been around for much longer, that there is a language that gives those demands legitimacy, and that there has been more experimentation in modifying the stereotypes.

Among working-class couples, the demand for communication, for sharing, is newer. Earlier descriptions of working-class family life present a portrait of wives and husbands whose lives were distinctly separate, both inside and outside the home—the wife attending to her household role, the husband to his provider role. He came home at night tired and taciturn; she kept herself and the children out of his way. For generations, it was enough that each did their job adequately—he, to bring home the bacon; she, to cook it. Intimacy, companionship, sharing—these were not part of the dream.

But dreams change—sometimes before the people who must live them are ready. Suddenly, new dreams are stirring. *Intimacy, com-*

panionship, sharing—these are now the words working-class women speak to their men, words that turn *both* their worlds upside down. For while it is the women who are the discontented, who are pushing for change, they, no less than their men, are confused about what they are asking:

I'm not sure what I want. I keep talking to him about communication, and he says, "Okay, so we're talking; now what do you want?" And I don't know what to say then, but I know it's not what I mean.

. . . and frightened and unsure about the consequences:

I sometimes get worried because I think maybe I want too much. He's a good husband; he works hard; he takes care of me and the kids. He could go out and find another woman who would be very happy to have a man like that, and who wouldn't be all the time complaining at him because he doesn't feel things and get close.

The men are even worse off. Since it's not *their* dream, they are less likely still to have any notion of what is being asked of them. They only know that, without notice, the rules of the game have been changed; what worked for their fathers, no longer works for them. They only know that there are a whole new set of expectations—in the kitchen, in the parlor, in the bedroom—that leave them feeling bewildered and threatened. She says:

I keep telling him that the reason people get divorced isn't *only* financial but because they can't communicate. But I can't make him understand.

He says:

I swear, I don't know what she wants. She keeps saying we have to talk, and then when we do, it always turns out I'm saying the wrong thing. I get scared sometimes. I always thought I had to think things to myself; you know, not tell her about it. Now she says that's not good. But it's

hard. You know, I think it comes down to that I like things the way they are, and I'm afraid I'll say or do something that'll really shake things up. So I get worried about it, and I don't say anything.

For both men and women, the fears and uncertainties are compounded by the fact that there are no models in their lives for the newly required and desired behaviors. Television shows them people whose lives seem unreal—outside the realm of personal experience or knowledge. The daytime soap operas, watched almost exclusively by women, *do* picture men who may be more open and more available for intimacy. But the men on the soaps don't work at ordinary jobs, doing ordinary things, for eight, ten, twelve hours a day. They're engaged either in some heroic, life-saving, glamour job to which working-class viewers can't relate or, worse yet, work seems to be one long coffee break during which they talk about their problems. Nighttime fare, when the men are home, is different, but no less unreal, featuring the stoic private eye, the brave cop, the tight-lipped cowboy.

The argument about the impact of the mass media on blue-collar workers is complex, contradictory, and largely unsatisfactory. Some observers insist that the mass media represent the most powerful current by which blue-collar workers are swept into conformity with middle-class values and aspirations, others that blue-collar men especially resist exposure to middle-class manners and mores as they are presented on television—minimizing that exposure by exercising great discrimination in program choices; still others that the idealized and romanticized figures on television are so unreal to the average blue-collar viewer that they have little impact on their lives and little effect on their behavior.

Perhaps all three of these seemingly irreconcilable perspectives are true. The issue may not be *whether* television or other mass media affect people's lives and perceptions. Of course they do. The question we must ask more precisely is: In what ways are Americans of any class touched and affected by their exposure to television? For the professional middle class, it may well be an affirming experience; for the working class, a disconfirming one since there are no programs that deal with their problems, their prospects, and their values in sympathetic and respectful ways.

If their own lives in the present provide no models and the media offer little that seems relevant, what about the past? Unfortunately for young working-class couples, family backgrounds provide few examples of openness, companionship, or communication between husbands and wives.

> I don't think we ever had a good concept of what marriage was about. His family was the opposite of mine. They didn't drink like mine did, and they were more stable. Yet he feels they didn't give him a good concept either. There wasn't any drinking and fighting and carrying on, but there wasn't any caring either.

Even those few who recall their parents' marriages as good ones don't remember them talking much to one another and have no sense at all that they might have shared their inner lives:

> *Would you describe a typical evening in the family when you were growing up?*

A twenty-five-year-old manicurist, mother of two, married seven years, replies:

> Let me think. I don't really know what happened; nothing much, I guess. My father came home at four-thirty, and we ate right away. Nobody talked much at the table; it was kind of a quiet affair.

> *What about your parents' relationship? Do you remember how they behaved with each other; whether they talked to each other?*

> Gee, I don't know. It's hard to think about them as being *with* each other. I don't think they talked a lot; at least, I never saw them talking. I can't imagine them sitting down to talk over problems or something like that, if that's what you mean.

Yet, that *is* what I mean. But that was the last generation; what about this one?

> *Would you describe a typical evening in your own family now?*

For some, less than half, it's better—a level of companionship, caring, and sharing that, while not all they dream of, is surely better than they knew in their past. Fathers attend more to children; husbands at least try to "hear" their wives; couples struggle around some of the emotional issues I have identified in these pages. For most, however, nothing much has changed since the last generation. Despite the yearning for more, relations between husband and wife are benumbed, filled with silence; life seems empty and meaningless; laughter, humor, fun is not a part of the daily ration. Listen to this couple married seven years. The wife:

> Frank comes home from work; now it's about five because he's been working overtime every night. We eat right away, right after he comes home. Then, I don't know. The kids play a while before bed, watch TV, you know, stuff like that. Then, I don't know; we don't do anything except maybe watch more TV or something like that. I don't know what else—nothing, I guess. We just sit, that's all.

> *That's it? Nothing else?*

> Yeah, that's right, that's all. [*A short silence, then angrily.*] Oh yeah, I forgot. Sometimes he's got one of his projects he works on. Like now, he's putting that new door in the kitchen. It's still nothing. When he finishes doing it, we just sit.

Her husband describes the same scene:

> I come home at five and we eat supper right away. Then, I sit down with coffee and a beer and watch TV. After that, if I'm working on a project, I do that for a little while. If not, I just watch.
> Life is very predictable. Nothing much happens; we don't do much. Everyone sits in the same place all the time and does the same thing every night. It's satisfying to me, but maybe it's not for

her, I don't know. Maybe she wants to go to a show or something once in a while, I don't know. She doesn't tell me.

Don't you ask her?

No. I suppose I should, but it's really hard to think about getting out. We'd need someone to stay with the kids and all that. Besides, I'm tired. I've been out all day, seeing different people and stuff. I don't feel like going out after supper again. . . .

Not once in a professional middle-class home did I see a young boy shake his father's hand in a well-taught "manly" gesture as he bid him good night. Not once did I hear a middle-class parent scornfully—or even sympathetically—call a crying boy a sissy or in any way reprimand him for his tears. Yet, these were not uncommon observations in the working-class homes I visited. Indeed, I was impressed with the fact that, even as young as six or seven, the working-class boys seemed more emotionally controlled—more like miniature men—than those in the middle-class families.

These differences in childrearing practices are expressed as well in the different demands the parents of each class make upon the schools—differences that reflect the fact that working-class boys are expected to be even less emotional, more controlled than their middle-class counterparts. For the working-class parent, school is a place where teachers are expected to be tough disciplinarians; where children are expected to behave respectfully and to be punished if they do not; and where one mark of that respect is that they are sent to school neatly dressed in their "good" clothes and expected to stay that way through the day. None of these values is highly prized in the professional middle class. For them, schools are expected to be relatively loose, free, and fun; to encourage initiative, innovativeness, creativity, and spontaneity; and to provide a place where children—boys as well as girls—will learn social and interpersonal skills. The children of these middle-class families are sent

to nursery school early—often as young as two and a half—not just because their mothers want the free time, but because the social-skill training provided there is considered a crucial part of their education.

These differences come as no surprise if we understand both the past experience and the future expectations of both sets of parents. Most highly educated parents have little fear that their children won't learn to read, write, and do their sums. Why should they? They learned them, and learned them well. Their children have every advantage that they had and plenty more: books, games, toys—all designed to excite curiosity and to stimulate imagination—and parents who are skillful in aiding in their use.

Working-class parents, however, have no such easy assurances about their children's educational prospects. Few can look back on their own school years without discomfort— discomfort born of painful reminders of all they didn't learn, of the many times they felt deficient and inadequate. Further, when they look at the schools their children attend now, they see the same pattern repeating itself. For, in truth, the socio-economic status of the children in a school is the best indicator of school-wide achievement test scores—that is, the lower the socio-economic status, the lower the scores.

Observing this phenomenon, many analysts and educators argue that these low achievement records in poor and working-class schools are a consequence of the family background—the lack of culture and educational motivation in the home—an explanation that tends to blame the victim for the failure of our social institutions. Elsewhere, I have entered the debate about *who* is to blame for these failures on the side of the victims. Here, the major point is simply that, regardless of where we think responsibility lies, working-class parents quite rightly fear that their children may not learn to read very well; that they may not be able to do even the simple arithmetic required to be an intelligent consumer. Feeling inadequate and lacking confidence that they can pass on their slim skills to their children, such parents demand that the schools enforce discipline in the belief that only then will their children learn all that they themselves did not.

This, however, is only one part of the explanation of why the sons of the professional middle class are brought up in a less rigidly stereotypic mode than are the sons of the working class—the part that is rooted in past experience. But past experience combines with present reality to create future expectations, because parents, after all, do not raise their children in a vacuum—without some idea of what the future holds for them, some sense of what they will need to survive the adult world for which they are destined. In fact, it is out of just such understandings that parental attitudes and values about childraising are born. Thus, professional middle-class parents, assuming that their children are destined to do work like theirs—work that calls for innovation, initiative, flexibility, creativity, sensitivity to others, and a well-developed set of interpersonal skills—call for an educational system that fosters those qualities. Working-class parents also assume that their children will work at jobs roughly similar to their own. But in contrast to the requirements of professional or executive work, in most working-class jobs, creativity, innovation, initiative, flexibility are considered by superiors a hindrance. ("You're not getting paid to think!" is an oft-heard remonstrance.) Those who must work at such jobs may need nothing so much as a kind of iron-willed discipline to get them to work every day and to keep them going back year after year. No surprise, then, that such parents look suspiciously at spontaneity whether at home or at school. No surprise, either, that early childhood training tends to focus on respect, orderliness, cleanliness—in a word, discipline—especially for the boys who will hold these jobs, and that schools are called upon to reinforce these qualities.

Finally, men in the professional middle class presently live in an environment that gives some legitimacy to their stirrings and strivings toward connection with their emotional and expressive side. The extraordinary proliferation of the "growth-movement" therapies, which thrive on their appeal to both men and women of the upper middle class, is an important manifestation of that development. Another is the nascent men's movement—a response to the women's movement—with its men's groups, its male authors who write to a male audience encouraging their search for expressiveness. While it may be true that numerically all these developments account for only a small fraction of American men, it is also true that whatever the number, they are almost wholly drawn from the professional middle class.

For working-class men, these movements might as well not exist. Most don't know of them. The few who do, look at their adherents as if they were "kooks," "queers," or otherwise deficient, claiming to see no relevance in them to their own lives. Yet if one listens carefully to what lies beneath the surface of their words, the same stirrings for more connection with other parts of themselves, for more intimate relations with their wives are heard from working-class men as well. Often inchoate and inarticulately expressed, sometimes barely acknowledged, these yearnings, nevertheless, exist. But the struggle for their realization is a much more lonely and isolated one—removed not only from the public movements of our time but from the lives of those immediatley around them—a private struggle in which there is no one to talk to, no examples to learn from. They look around them and see neighbors, friends, brothers, and sisters who are no better—sometimes far worse off—than they:

> We're the only ones in the two families who have any kind of a marriage. One of my brothers ran out on his wife, the other one got divorced. Her sister and her husband are separated because he kept beating her up; her brother is still married,

but he's a drunk. It makes it hard. If you never saw it in your family when you were growing up, then all the kids in both families mess up like that, it's hard to know what a good marriage is like. I guess you could say there hasn't been much of a model of one around us. . . .

Do you talk to your friends about some of the things we've been discussing—I mean about your conflicts about your life and your marriage, and about some of the things you dream about and wish for?

No, we don't talk about those kinds of things. It's kind of embarrassing, too personal, you know. Besides, the people I know don't feel like I do, so it's no point in talking to them about those things.

How do you know how they feel if you don't talk about it?

You just know, that's all. I know. It's why I worry sometimes that maybe there's something the matter with me that I'm not satisfied with what I've got. I get depressed, and then I wonder if I'm normal. I *know* none of my friends feels like that, like maybe they need a psychiatrist or something.

It's all right to complain about money, about a husband who drinks or stays out late, even about one who doesn't help around the house. But to tell someone you're unhappy because your husband doesn't talk to you—who would understand that?

You don't talk about things like that to friends like I've got. They'd think I was another one of those crazy women's libbers.

Yes, there is concern among these working-class women and men about the quality of life, about its meaning. Yet, there is a deep wish for life to be more than a constant struggle with necessity. The drinking, the violence, the withdrawn silences—these are responses of despair, giving evidence that hope is hard to hold on to. How can it be otherwise when so often life seems like such an ungiving, uncharitable affair—a struggle without end? In the early years, it's unemployment, poverty, crying babies, violent fights. That phase passes, but a whole new set of problems emerge—problems that often seem harder to handle because they have less shape, less definition; harder, too, because they are less understandable, farther outside the realm of anything before experienced. But if there is one remarkable characteristic about life among the working class, it is the ability to engage the struggle and to survive it—a quality highly valued in a world where life has been and often remains so difficult and problematic. With a certain grim satisfaction, a twenty-six-year-old housewife, mother of two, summed it up:

> I guess in order to live, you have to have a very great ability to endure. And I have that—an ability to endure and survive.

DISCUSSION QUESTIONS

1. What are some of the problems faced by working-class families when husband and wife try to relate to one another? Which of these are caused by economic problems, and which have to do with their value system?
2. What are the differences between working-class and middle-class families in terms of sources of strain?
3. Do you see the same sorts of things happening in your family? If so, what are they and how are they resolved?

Beyond Sibling Rivalry

Gerald Handel

SIBLING RELATIONS IN THE FAMILY CONTEXT: CENTRAL ISSUES

The purpose of this [reading] is to present a conceptualization of the central issues that siblings deal with in constructing their relationships. The effort is guided by an organizing question: Why do siblings in some families grow up to be friends and in other families not? This question implies that some kinds of events early in the lifespan of siblings influence their relationship later in the lifespan. What I attempt here is to identify and define a set of issues that arise in the interaction between/among siblings, and in their relation to parents, whose resolution likely affects later outcomes. Modes of resolution are not studied here, nor are outcomes; the data for those tasks are not at hand, and they must await subsequent research. The fruit of the present study is the delineation of significant issues in sibling relationships in childhood.

The theoretical antecedents of the study lie in sociological social psychology, particularly in the work of those thinkers recognized as the founders of "the Chicago School," especially W. I. Thomas and George Herbert Mead. What is essential from their work for our present purpose may be distilled into two axiomatic propositions: (1) human adaptation to the environment rests upon the interpretation of it; (2) social relationships are constructed through interaction. To these may be added a third, formulated by a contemporary scholar: (3) "human action . . . is directed to whatever is identified as problematic, as requiring that action be taken in one kind of situation or another" (Lofland, 1976:40). The task of scientific inquiry is thus to examine how persons are interpreting their situation, constructing their relationships, and taking action to deal with their problematic situation. The third proposition will be briefly developed below to formulate its applicability to the task of this chapter.

Sibling Rivalry and Sibling Solidarity

Sibling rivalry has long been recognized as one of the primary features of sibling relationships. Its significance is highlighted in a recent study of 40 first-born children whose mothers gave birth to a younger sibling when the firstborns were between 18 and 43 months old. The investigators report that "By the time the first-born children were 6 years old, their discussion of their feelings about the sibling and their views on what kind of person the sibling was were dominated by descriptions of fighting and aggression" (Dunn and Kendrick, 1982:181). Sociologists who study family violence report that sibling violence is the most frequent type and that fifty-three of every hundred children attack a brother or sister in a year by kicking, biting, punching, hitting with objects, or "beating up" (Straus, Gelles, and Steinmetz, 1980:82). These recent studies reiterate a point established in a large and diverse literature: rivalry, hostility, and aggressive action are basic features of sibling relations.

A contrasting literature that illuminates sibling solidarity is much smaller, though also diverse. Cumming and Schneider (1961) argue that sibling solidarity is a norm of American kinship and, in their study of aging adults, they found that those who have siblings living nearby tend to have better morale than those who do not. Sussman's (1959) study of help patterns found that 47% of adults had given some form of help to a sibling in the preceding month. Several recent studies add to our knowledge of positive sibling relations. In a study of 75 adults covering a very wide age range, Ross and Milgram (1982) found that shared experiences in childhood often led to reported closeness among siblings. Cicirelli (1982:273) states that: "Considerable evidence exists that most siblings feel close affectionally and provide psychological support to each other throughout the course of their adult lives." Bank and Kahn (1982a, 1982b) studied intense loyalty among siblings, a concept they explicitly distinguish from Cumming and Schneider's concept of solidarity. They regard intense loyalty as a response to defective parenting or loss of a parent. Leaving aside the special case of intense loyalty, and focusing only on ordinary solidarity and affectional closeness, the literature cited opens up a large question: How do children who at age six define their siblings largely in terms of fighting and rivalry and who, throughout their childhood are prone to some violence with one another, evolve into reciprocally helpful, affectionate adults who boost morale in old age? Is Cicirelli right that most sibling relationships so evolve? If, as seems more likely, some do so evolve and some do not, can we address, in a single framework, these two main classes of outcome (and, perhaps, their many variants)? . . .

This chapter is based on interviews with children and parents in 33 intact working-class and middle-class families of northwest European ancestry in a large metropolitan area. Each family had either two or three children between 6 and 18 years old. Interviews were obtained from each parent and each child. The aim of the interview was to obtain as wide a range of information about the family as was feasible. For the present study, the interviews were read with a specific focus on sibling relationships. Every mention of a sibling by a child and of the children's relationship by the parents—whether a general characterization or a recounting of a specific incident—was noted. All of these interview excerpts were studied and examined by asking, what is this about? From this study a set of categories emerged. These categories gained coherence when placed within a framework of the three ax-

iomatic propositions. The concept of the family situation as problematic now must be further specified.

THE FAMILY AS A PROBLEMATIC CONTEXT

Children growing up as members of the same family, sharing a common household with their parents, participate in constructing a world that is both unique to the family and dependent upon the society beyond the family (Handel, 1967). This situation encompasses four conditions which make for problematic relations between or among brothers and sisters. The first and most fundamental is the fact of shared parentage. There is a general social expectation that parents have an obligation to give care to the children they have begotten and that each of their children has a rightful claim upon this care. The children who have the same mother and father come to know through family interaction that they have a relationship with each other, that they do not share with children who have other mothers and fathers. They learn the importance of this from their parents who usually teach it, and they learn it from outsiders who define them as brothers and sisters.

Shared parentage is problematic for two reasons: (1) because each child sees the same persons as vital for providing the resources the child wants and requires from others; (2) because the parents define the children's shared parentage as a basis for solidarity between or among the children. Thus, children of the same parents come to find themselves under pressure to feel affection and/or to act with consideration or moderation in relation to someone who is also competitive for parental affection, time, and other benefits.

A second condition which makes the relations of siblings problematic is that they are different ages. Thus a second basis of strain is found in the contrast between pressures towards solidarity which derive from shared parentage and the differences in social expectation directed toward children of different chronological age. The pressures toward solidarity also are not readily congruent and harmonious with age-related differences in social and cognitive competence.

A third condition which makes the relations of siblings problematic is that each has a psycho-socio-biological individuality along with their shared parentage. Each newborn presents himself or herself as a uniquely developing configuration of characteristics. Each evokes a somewhat individualized response from each parent. The extent of one sibling's perceived differences from an earlier-born may be great or small, but some consequential difference is likely to be perceived by parents. Perceived differences will enter into the interactive histories of the family members and become part of the ground for establishing relationships. The differences will need to be negotiated in family interaction.

Finally, if siblings are of different sex, this fact becomes a fourth condition which makes the relationships among them problematic. The difference in sex is met with different expectations concerning roles. Adult justifications for the different expectations are not routinely understandable or acceptable to the children.

These four conditions make the relationships between or among siblings problematic. In the course of dealing with these problematic conditions, issues arise in sibling interaction and in parental actions bearing on sibling interaction. The delineation of these issues is the task of this study. We turn now to present its results.

ISSUES IN SIBLING RELATIONS

Equity

Perhaps the most pervasive, most fundamental issue in sibling relationships is the issue of equity. Commonly, children are sensitive to the way parents treat them and their siblings. They are attentive and make comparisons between rewards and punishments distributed to self and sib. Parents ordinarily feel some obligation within themselves to be fair to their children, to reward and punish in ways that satisfy both themselves and their children that they are neither excessively harsh nor excessively indulgent toward one as compared to the other(s). When parents do show favoritism, they may be under some pressure to modify it, from the adversely affected child if from no other. The child who feels persistently unfairly treated and who feels defeated in efforts to modify the practice of inequity may become troublesome or emotionally disturbed. One pattern of inequity, scapegoating, has been described and analyzed by Vogel and Bell (1960).

Parents must deal with the problem of equity in a number of different contexts:

Unequal Performance. When two children perform differently in relation to some parental expectation, the parents must work out some strategy for dealing with the problem. They may reward good performance and punish unsatisfactory performance; they may reward only; they may punish only; or they may construct a more complex strategy. Mrs. GG wrestles with this problem in relation to the school performance of her two children. Grace, age 8, gets good grades; Gregory, age 7, does not. Asked, "Did you do anything about it?" Mrs. GG answers:

> No, we tried, that was one thing we tried to not do was, I mean, it was difficult because we wanted to praise Grace because she did, and yet we could see the reasons for Gregory's low grades, so what we made more of an issue of was the fact that he'd get checks for talking and not keeping profitably busy and things like that. We made more of that point than of his low grades. And then we tried to give him any incentive to do better.

Mrs. GG is here wrestling with the dilemma of how to be fair to one child without having a damaging impact on the other. As parents deal with problems of unequal performance they may have to struggle with the question of whether to adhere to a single standard for all their children or modify standards in accord with perceived differences among them. The consequences of different strategies for children's perceptions of parental equity can only be guessed at this point.

As parents wrestle with questions of expecting similar performance from different children and with consequences of responding to differential performances, the children are likely to be engaged in defining the parental behavior as fair or unfair. Each child is an audience for the interaction between parent and sibling.

The Application of Conduct Rules and Standards. A second context in which issues of equity arise is in the application of conduct rules and standards. A particularly candid recognition of this problem was provided by Mr. GG. When the interviewer asked, "Which of the children do you find it easiest to handle, would you say?" he responded:

Well, I think that in most cases I think that maybe the girl has a certain preference as far as my tenderness is concerned. She's the first born and the fact that she's a girl. I know I give her the benefit of a lot of doubts. I've been inclined at times to be more severe on the boy, only to look at him later that night or something and realize that he's only a little fellow and that maybe I shouldn't have been mean to him.

Grace clearly recognizes her father's disposition:

Interviewer: What kind of a person is your father?
Grace: Very nice and kind. . . . When I'm in trouble he takes care of the other person I'm in trouble with and that person is usually my dear little brother.

Gregory's interview does not yield a clear comment that bears on the issue of equity. It would be a mistake, however, to assume that the differential treatment is without impact. The school difficulties reported by his mother may be a response. The absence of comment directly from him is likely due to difficulty in eliciting it.

There is some evidence to suggest that a perception of being equitably treated contributes to a feeling of solidarity between siblings. Consider the R family with two sons, Ralph, 15, and Russell, 12. In the course of a series of questions relating to other members of the family, Ralph was asked: "Do your parents treat Russell any different from you?" He answered: "We both get a fair break." During an earlier interview, Ralph was asked, "What do you like to do best?" He answered:

There's three things, fishing, dating, and camping. I like to spend as much time outdoors as I can. And then Russell and I like to have a vision. He wants to be a naturalist of some kind and live in a small town. I'm going to be a lawyer, and as soon as I have my degree I'm going to the same town. And then when my dad retires they will come out there, too. We can do a lot of fishing and hunting together. . . .

Resolution of Disputes. A third context in which the issue of equity arises is in the resolution of disputes. These situations are of various kinds. In one type, a parent intervenes to break up a quarrel or fight. Both children receive the same treatment, but one may feel this is unfair because the other started it. To this child, the equal treatment (based on a parental presumption that both are culpable) is an expression of unfairness.

Another type of situation is one that siblings control themselves. In the P family, 12-year-old Paul says of his older sister, "If she wouldn't tease me, I wouldn't tease her." For him, fairness necessitates retaliation. He must make his sister uncomfortable if she makes him uncomfortable. Equity to him means "getting even." A related situation is one in which getting even is not handled by the siblings alone but draws the parents in as punishers. Thus, in the Z family, 14-year-old Zachary reports his 8-year-old sister's misdoings to their parents. He explains, "I tell on her because she has told on me." Equivalent victimization is Zachary's solution to the fairness problem presented by Zelda's initiatives.

Scarcity. A fourth context in which the issue of equity arises is that of access to scarce resources. An obvious type of instance is when two children, with one TV set, want to watch different programs at the same time. How can this scarce resource be apportioned so that both children feel fairly treated?

Different as their interests may be, children in the same family may nonetheless be attracted to or feel they have need or use for some possession of a sibling. They may not necessarily, however, accept the notion of equal access. Zelda complains that Zachary will not let her touch his possessions, particularly his model airplanes. She does not like this, because he touches her possessions. Equal access seems only fair to her.

In some families, equal access to parents' time and attention becomes an issue of potentially enduring significance. In the L family, an interview with 16-year-old Larry elicits his views of his father's treatment of him and his 12-year-old sister Lisa. Toward the end of a series of questions on ideal family members, he is asked what an ideal son is and how he feels he measures up. He answers:

> I don't suppose I measure up either, but that's because they aren't ideal parents. . . . (How about Lisa?) Depends on what you consider ideal. If it's someone who does everything you are told to do and never grunt, then she's ideal. Of course, I think they have been more ideal with her than with me. She's gotten more atten-

tion, usually what the younger child gets. (Have you ever felt jealous?) I don't any more. I used to feel jealous of the attention she'd get. I'm satisfied now.

Although he says he is no longer jealous, he also believes that the inequity in attention has made him a less ideal son than he might have been. . . .

Maturity

One of the factors which makes the attainment of equity difficult among siblings is the fact that they are of different ages. In Western society today as Ariés (1962) emphasized, fairly fine age differences in childhood constitute the basis for different expectations. As children grow and get older, they are expected to cast off behavior acceptable at earlier ages and to conduct themselves in ways that increasingly approximate adult ways. These expected changes are presented to children by their parents and others, and children take over these expectations as standards for judging themselves. Sibling relationships are to some extent shaped by these concerns, which we may designate generically as the issue of maturity in sibling relations.

Maturity arises as an issue among siblings in two principal forms.

Power. One common way in which differences in maturity enter into sibling relationships is the tendency of older siblings to attempt to exercise power over younger ones. For example, in the M family, one of the things that makes 12-year-old Morton angry is that when he and his 16-year-old brother Mark are watching television and the TV set requires adjusting, Mark always asks Morton to do it. Morton feels Mark could do it as easily. He resents his brother's use of his age status as a resource for exercising power.

Power is perhaps most commonly exercised by older over younger children, but not inevitably. In the V family, both 12-year-old Vance and 9-year-old Victor seem to agree that Victor has the upper hand in their relationship. When asked about differences between his parents on how the children should be treated, Vance says:

> My father thinks Victor should be punished when he's bad. Mother doesn't. I agree with father. Victor is always trying to make trouble, he's happy making trouble. Between any of us. . . . (What things do you do that make Victor mad?) Take all the blankets off him. He doesn't like that. He reaches over and takes all mine. I'd like to have a sister instead, a younger one who I could boss around . . . Victor tries to act too smart-alecky all the time.

In response to a question about fighting with his brother, Victor says, "I like to fight with him. I don't have to be mad at him, but he gets mad at me. I can handle him by putting a leg lock on him." He thwarts Vance's wish to dominate. . . .

Knowledge. The example of Xenia and Xavier suggests that in some families, at least, young siblings assign some responsibility to older ones, responsibility for helping them to grow up. Older siblings are seen as having knowledge which they can and ought to share freely.

An older sib's maturity can be alternately respected and denigrated by the younger. In the EE family, 12½-year-old Elizabeth says of her 15-year-old sister Eileen:

> She bosses me around too much at times. Other times we'll be awfully close. I used to be very neat and she wasn't and that would make me mad. When she's with older kids, she acts superior. But I go around with older kids, too. (What do you do that makes her mad?) I can't think. Maybe I pester her sometimes so she gets provoked. I ask her things over and over again. . . . (What characteristics about each person in the family do you like best?) Eileen, she's understanding compared to other sisters. She'll

have confidence in me and vice versa. . . . (Who do you usually go to with problems?) My sister. She usually gives me good advice. We talk over problems. I've helped her, too, like persuading Mother to let her stay out later.

The suggestion from this example, even more than from the preceding, is that older siblings may be perceived by younger as links to adulthood, people who know some of adulthood's secrets and should be willing to share them because they are also still "kids" themselves. The younger makes a claim upon the older as child to child, sib to sib, but does so because the older's greater maturity results in knowledge and understanding that the younger believes should be transferred. Even so, the older may be seen as sometimes taking her/his maturity too seriously, lording it over the younger with excessive self-importance.

Some of the secrets of maturity are sexual and sex-role-related, and so may have a particular fascination for a younger sibling of opposite sex. In the FF family, 9-year-old Florence is asked about her 16-year-old brother. In addition to some familiar themes, her response indicates her effort to gain knowledge of the world of older boys:

> (What things does Frank do that make you mad?) He wants his way, and he teases me and hits me. (And what do you do that makes him mad?) I'm under the bed and I listen to him and his friends. And once I put a pin on his chair and he sat on it. Sometimes I read his comics and forget to take them back, and I hang around when he's talking to his friends. That makes him real mad.

Younger children's efforts to learn from their older siblings seem to be quite easily defined by the latter as some form of pestering. Perhaps they are also defined as an effort to diminish the hard-won greater maturity of the older. If, after all, the secrets, the knowledge, the information, the know-how are freely passed over to the younger, then older and younger are less distinctive than they were. Under what circumstances do older sisters become willing teachers to younger sisters? To younger brothers? Older brothers to younger brothers or sisters? We do not know. We only know that it can happen, that an Eileen, despite being provoked by Elizabeth's pestering, can give advice that Elizabeth not only values but helps her define the relationship as one in which the sisters have confidence in each other. We do not know under what circumstances pestering remains the most salient feature of the sibling relationship and under what circumstances the relationship becomes characterized by teaching and learning in a context of mutual support.

Loyalty

Membership in a family imposes on its members multiple and conflicting loyalties. All are expected to be loyal to the family, and each is expected to be loyal to each other member. But these loyalties cannot remain fixed in place all the time. They are subject to stresses so that one loyalty may be temporarily weakened by another. A sibling may make a demand that conflicts with a parental demand. Family members have conflicting claims on each other; responsiveness to one claim strengthens the loyalty in that relationship. Disregarded claims loosen loyalty. The strengthening and loosening of loyalties are continuing processes. Fluctuations may take place within a narrow or wide range. Loyalty of one sibling to another is manifested and tested in a variety of contexts and has several dimensions. Four have emerged in this study.

Availability. Even as siblings pursue their individual interests and form individual associations with playmates or friends outside the family, they also often want the other(s) to be available on demand. Availability is desired for support in a particular situation, for advice, or for companionship in play. Availability for ad-

vice and support was exemplified in the discussion of Eileen and Elizabeth; the example suggested that the older attempts to understand and respond to the concerns of the younger, at the younger's behest most often, but perhaps also at the older's initiative.

A younger version of availability is provided in the GG family. In response to the opening question, "What are the important things about your family?" 8-year-old Grace answers:

> Like my mother, father and brother and my other relatives, our house and our car and all that stuff. We couldn't live without my mother. She sews and washes and changes our beds, and my father makes the money, and if we didn't have a car he couldn't make money. And my brother, well he's important to play with just to have someone around when I need him.

Later in the same interview, Grace illustrates the value of *her* availability to her brother:

> Sometimes on Sunday I like to watch TV instead of looking for new houses. I like to go but I like to watch TV. And one time when my brother was sick I was forced to stay home and they said they'd be home at 4:30 P.M. and they didn't come home until 6:30 P.M. He was crying but I finally made him some crackers and cheese and calmed him down.

In distress, or perplexity, or boredom, siblings turn to each other for or with appropriate manifestations of loyalty. . . .

Sharing. One child in a family may have possession of an item the other values. If it is shareable, there will often be an expectation by at least one of the siblings that it should be shared. A certain amount of interaction among siblings is devoted to constructing rules for sharing. The rules are often incomplete or ineffectual, and a fairly frequent complaint in these interviews is that one sibling takes or borrows something from another without asking. The taker or borrower is almost certainly acting on a presumption that the taking or borrowing is justified by shared family membership; it is unlikely that most of the borrowers would borrow equally freely from friends, without asking. In some fashion, children acquire the norm that shared family membership imposes on siblings an obligation to share possessions that is presumptively more compelling than obligations to share with outsiders.

When an expectation of sharing is not fulfilled, the disappointed sibling can become aggressive and evoke an aggressive response. A not untypical sequence is illustrated by the K family. As 13-year-old Karl describes his 11-year-old brother:

My little brother is fat and jolly. He's too jolly. Couple nights ago I had a piece of candy in my jacket and he kept nagging "give me some" and I told him "No" and he kept trying to get in my pocket and we were wrestling around and he got in and so I hit him.

Relatively little is known about family rules for sharing. To what extent are they promulgated by parents, to what extent constructed by the children themselves? What factors render them effective? Under what circumstances do they fail? To what extent to they foster sibling solidarity?

Handling Information Appropriately. At some early age—it is not clear just when—children begin to understand the importance of information as something that can be managed. They recognize that information management has some significant dimensions and that it has diverse consequences depending upon the nature of the information and the persons who have it.

One dimension is incrimination. Information can be incriminating. A child may feel that a sibling who has information of that kind should not share it with their parents. One's brother or sister should not tattle about something one has done. One's sibling ought to understand and respect the consequences of

information mismanagement. Violations of this expectation occur. In the C family, 12-year-old Caroline expresses her exasperation with her 6-year-old sister.

My mother is more often on Cynthia's side because both of us [Caroline and 10-year-old brother] are against Cynthia and Cynthia is such an innocent angel. If you ask her to promise not to tell my mother and father something, she promises and then she tells.

The problem is made difficult when the issue of maturity is confounded with the issue of loyalty. Thus, when 14-year-old Zachary, in pursuit of equity, "tells" on his sister because "she told on me," he knows what his way of managing information can lead to, but he seems unprepared to consider that his 8-year-old sister may not appreciate the consequences. He does not want to insist on a maturity gap here; he wants her to understand that loyalty requires that she not tell. Here is a type of situation in which the older child would like to see the younger grow up in a hurry because that would strengthen loyalty.

Another dimension of information is its status value. At some unknown age children become aware of secrets, and they come to recognize that those who share in a secret have more status than those who are excluded from it. The self is enhanced when one is deemed fit by others to be entrusted with a secret. In the B family, specifying what she likes best about each member of the family, 12-year-old Barbara says of her 10-year-old sister: "My sister, if anything happens, she always tells me about it. She doesn't keep anything from me." The transfer of information results in an exchange of esteem: Barbara feels valued by Bonnie and she values Bonnie for not keeping secrets.

Protection. Sibling loyalty is often put to a test outside the family, when one child is in conflict with peers. When neighborhood children give a child a hard time, that child is fortunate who has an older, tougher sib to back him up. Doreen, age 9, makes clear that she is the protector of her 8-year-old brother:

(Who do you usually go to when you feel worried or get into trouble?) Nobody. I worry about my own troubles, but if I did something. . . . I beat up my brother for fighting two little girls. I settled it. I did not tell my mother. I'll probably end up telling her if she is in a good mood. And if my little brother gets into trouble or if somebody is beating him up, he'd come to me. He said, 'Boy, my sister can beat you up.' I can beat him up so he thinks I can beat everybody. I can.

Doreen evidently sees herself as a protector of the underdog, which sometimes make her an enforcer against her brother, but when he is in the underdog role, she is his loyal protector.

Individuality

As much as siblings are involved with each other, expecting and seeking loyalty, they are endeavoring at the same time to become separate individuals capable of limiting the claims that others can make on them. They do not want the claims of loyalty to be limitless. One way of setting limits to loyalty claims is to establish a realm of privacy.

Privacy. Each child in a family wants jurisdiction over his or her own space and possessions, and wants siblings to accept rules for entering and operating within that jurisdiction. The widespread complaint of one sibling about another—"S/he borrows my things without asking"—is an effort to set limits to what may be claimed on the basis of family loyalty. The child seeks to maintain a realm of privacy, a realm of space and possessions that he or she has control of and from which siblings can be excluded at will. There is a dialectical opposition between privacy and loyalty, a constant tugging back and forth between the sibling who wants access on the basis of loyalty and the sibling who wants to deny access on the basis that "it's mine."

A related issue arises when one sibling is

with his own age-mates. Another may experience this as a temporary betrayal of loyalty and seek to be included, though sometimes in a way that expresses resentment for having been excluded. Something like this happens in the K family, where 13-year-old Karl says of his 11-year-old brother: "Oh, he's too nosey. Like today I was showing a friend some valuable stamps. He came in and said they were fakes and was teasing. He butts in."

The effort to maintain an arena and occasions of privacy is an effort by one sibling to limit the claims which other siblings, as well as parents, may make on the basis of the loyalties implied in shared family membership. It is a way of maintaining some control over those claims.

Self-Demarcation. In addition to its importance as a way of limiting the control of others over one's own circumstances, the insistence on privacy and personal ownership of possessions is one way of demarcating the self. Without at this point addressing the question of whether a clearly individuated self is a requisite for effective functioning in all societies, it indubitably is in Western societies. The formation of that individuated self begins in the family. Children in a family come to recognize that they share an identity as members. But each child enters into a family in his or her own way. Each is initially individuated on the basis of birth order; the fact of having a unique position in the birth order is sufficient basis for the initiation of an individuated self within the shared family identity. If of different sex, the children are additionally distinguished from each other on that basis. Beyond these categorical markers, which parents regard and act upon as individuating, each child discloses distinctive features of physiognomy and activity that parents and others interpret as individuating.

Proceeding from these initial distinctions, each child comes to regard himself or herself as marginally or significantly different from siblings. Self-demarcation can be done more or less matter-of-factly or insistently. A matter-of-fact version is 11-year-old Kenneth's, who talks about 13-year-old Karl and 9-year-old Kathy when asked, "How are you different from the other people in the family?"

I make so much noise. Nobody else hardly does. I think I like more fiction books. I like geography; only my Mom does. She likes Russian geography. (How are you different as a personality?) I ask silly questions all the time. (How are you different from Karl?) Smarter. When he was in my grade he got lower grades and everything. I'm a little better-tempered than he is. (And from Kathy?) I was just trying to think of that. I can't. She's just about like me. She likes dolls. Well, I'm a little dumber than she is. She got all A's and A pluses. I got B's. . . .

DISCUSSION

Sibling rivalry is a widespread, though reportedly not universal, occurrence. Although theories to explain its occurrence have been propounded, theories to explain non-occurrence have not (nor has non-occurrence been convincingly demonstrated.) Sibling supportiveness and friendship, also widespread, are not routinely expectable lifespan outcomes although they are normatively enjoined. This chapter is prompted by the question: Why do some siblings grow up to be friends while others remain rivalrous? The chapter addresses the question by conceptualizing the family as a problematic setting for siblings and their parents, who must construct some kind of relationship through interaction. By studying interviews with parents and children in 33 families, four central issues in sibling relationships were identified. I propose that studies of how these issues (and perhaps others yet to be identified) are resolved within families can contribute significantly to answering the questions posed. I therefore conceive of resolution as a process rather than a decision-point.

The four main issues delineated can usefully be regarded as standing in dialectical pairs. The issue of equity is concerned with treating siblings in such a way that they feel they have not been treated significantly differently. Significantly different treatment by parents tends to be regarded as inequitable. Similarly, privileges assumed by one sibling—such as uninhibited access to another's possessions—are construed as inequitable when reciprocal access is denied.

But the issue of maturity introduces contrary considerations. Greater age results in presumed greater competence and hence in greater status. Thus, solutions to the problems of sibling equity are made difficult by the issue of differential maturity. Solutions to problems of differential maturity are often likely to be regarded as dangerously close to approved inequity. The parent who is less stringent with a younger child on the ground of immaturity may arouse the older to a sense of injustice. A greater privilege to an older may seem unjust to a younger who cannot discern the grounds for judging a maturity difference. An older sib may feel justified in giving direction, a claim the younger may reject.

The issues of loyalty and individuality similarly are dialectical opposites in their implications. Loyalty provides the basis for making claims upon the other, while individuality provides the basis for rejecting such claims. Loyalty strains develop when one child wants to borrow something that a sibling does not want to lend. The would-be borrower loses some faith in the loyalty of the obdurate non-lender, while the latter, protecting self-interest, may lose some faith in the value of sibling loyalty itself. . . .

This study is based on intact families. Rising divorce and remarriage rates have led to a great increase in blended or post-divorce families. In 1978, 10 million children (one of every eight living in a two-parent family) lived in such families (Cherlin, 1981:30), where there might be children from two or three marriages—his, hers, and theirs. That type of family becomes problematic in a different way. Unshared parentage, or a combination of shared and unshared parentage, very probably recasts the issues that have been identified, but it is doubtful that their importance is diminished.

References

Aries, Philippe
1962 *Centuries of Childhood*. New York: Knopf.
Bank, Steven and Michael D. Kahn
1982a "Intense sibling loyalties." Pp 251–266 in Michael E. Lamb and Brian Sutton-Smith (eds.), *Sibling Relationships*. Hillsdale, New Jersey: Erlbaum.
1982b *The Sibling Bond*. New York: Basic Books.
Cherlin, Andrew J.
1981 *Marriage, Divorce, Remarriage*. Cambridge, Mass.: Harvard University Press.
Cicirelli, Victor
1982 "Sibling influence throughout the lifespan." Pp. 267–284 in Michael E. Lamb and Brian Sutton-Smith (eds.), *Sibling Relationships*. Hillsdale, New Jersey: Erlbaum.
Cumming, Elaine and David Schneider
1961 "Sibling solidarity: a property of American kinship." *American Anthropologist* 63:498–507.
Dunn, Judy and Carol Kendrick
1982 *Siblings*. Cambridge, Mass.: Harvard University Press.
Handel, Gerald
1967 *The Psychosocial Interior of the Family*. Chicago: Aldine.
Lofland, John
1976 *Doing Social Life*. New York: Wiley.
Ross, Helgola and Joel Milgram
1982 "Important variables in adult sibling relationships: a qualitative study." Pp. 225–249 in Michael E. Lamb and Brian Sutton-Smith (eds.), *Sibling Relationships*. Hillsdale, New Jersey: Erlbaum.
Straus, Murray A., Richard J. Gelles, and Suzanne K. Steinmetz
1980 *Behind Closed Doors: Violence in the American Family*. Garden City, New York: Doubleday Anchor.
Sussman, Marvin B.
1959 "The isolated nuclear family: fact or fiction?" *Social Problems* 6:333–39.
Vogel, Ezra F. and Norman W. Bell
1960 "The emotionally disturbed child as the family scapegoat." Pp. 382–397 in Norman W. Bell and Ezra F. Vogel (eds.), *A Modern Introduction to the Family*. Glencoe, Illinois: The Free Press.

DISCUSSION QUESTIONS

1. Based on Handel's article, under what circumstances is sibling rivalry least likely to occur?
2. Analyze your own family experiences in terms of Handel's argument.
3. What are the effects of no-fault divorce on the likelihood of sibling rivalries? Remarriages? Adoptions?

READING 9-3

Divorce in the USSR

William Moskoff

In a period of twenty years, the divorce rate in the USSR has quadrupled, rising from 0.9 per 1,000 population in 1958 to 3.6 per 1,000 population in 1979. The most recent figure stands second in the world only to the 5.1 per 1,000 population divorce rate of the United States (Mustafin, 1980; U.S. Bureau of the Census, 1979:81). This paper analyzes some of the causes for the sharp rise in divorce in the Soviet Union and explores some of the consequences of this important phenomenon. Specifically, it examines the quantitative data on divorce in the Soviet Union; traces the evolution of divorce law in the USSR, including legal changes in the access to divorce; explores the primary reasons for divorce in the USSR; and suggests some of the socioeconomic problems caused by divorce. The examinations should illuminate some emerging problems which are of deep concern to Soviet planners.

THE DATA BASE ON MARRIAGE AND DIVORCE

While the general divorce rate in the Soviet Union is high, there are substantial differences in divorce rates between urban and rural areas. For example, in 1972 86% of the divorces occurred in urban areas (Korolev, 1978:186), although only 59% of the population lived in urban areas during that year. In 1967 when the overall divorce rate was 2.7, it was 4.2 in urban areas (Perevedentsev, 1971). In the Ukraine in 1971, the number of divorces per 10,000 marriages was four times higher in urban areas than in rural areas (Chuiko, 1975:131); and the highest divorce rates in the country are found in the two largest cities, Moscow (5.1) and Leningrad (5.6) (Korolev, 1978: 136–137).

The higher divorce rate in urban areas apparently reflects the greater ease of obtaining a divorce in cities and the relative absence of social stigma attached to divorce among urbanites. In addition, the forces of migration from rural to urban areas have produced a younger population in the cities, which means more marriages and, therefore, a higher divorce rate since there is a disproportionately high rate of divorce among young marrieds.

Changes in divorce laws have made divorces easier to obtain in the Soviet Union, and the length of the typical Soviet marriage before divorce appears to be declining. In 1967 29% of the marriages lasted up to five years, and another 34% lasted 5-9 years. In urban areas in 1971, however, 35% of the divorces involved marriages lasting less than 5 years, while another 27% were in marriages 5-9 years long (Korolev, 1978:188). More recently, the noted Soviet demographer Perevedentsev said that one-third of all divorces occur in marriages that are less than a year old and another third in marriages 1-5 years long (Perevedentsev, 1978).

While it will take some time to determine whether these changes represent long-term trends, most indicators suggest that these tendencies will continue. The length of marriage at the time of divorce was probably greater in the mid-1960s because a great many couples who had been separated for a long time or were unable to divorce were suddenly able to take advantage of new laws. Given easier access to more liberal laws, Soviet couples seem likely to seek divorces earlier, now that the backlog of longer, more unhappy marriages has been depleted.

There are no national data on the average age of couples at the time of divorce, but the figures from some cities are helpful and revealing. In Kiev at the end of the 1960s, the average age of divorcing women was 34.0 years; for men it was 36.4 years (Chuiko, 1975:149). This should be seen in relation to the 1970 census data which showed that women typically marry between the ages of 18-24 years, men between the ages of 21-27 (Perevedentsev, 1977). While the average age at divorce is in the thirties, there is a disproportionate percentage of divorces involving young people. About one-third of the applicants for divorce (overwhelmingly women) in the Kiev study were under the age of 20 (Chuiko, 1975:149) even though the percentage of women marrying between the ages of 17 and 19 in the Soviet period has fallen steadily from a high of 29% in 1926 to 19% in 1970 (Vishnevskii, 1975). Ukrainian and Belorussian data both show that divorce is increasing most rapidly among the youngest age groups (under 25 years of age) and among people aged 40-49 (Chuiko, 1975:134; Korolev, 1978:140). . . .

THE CAUSES OF DIVORCE

Soviet research reveals that the three most commonly listed official reasons for divorce are: (a) alcoholism, (b) adultery, and (c) incompatibility of characters. While there is a significant amount of variation in the weight of each in the various studies, these three are consistently pre-eminent; moreover, alcoholism is particularly important in the petitions filed by women. In the early 1970s it was found to be the major cause of divorce in Belorussia (Chumakova, 1974:135), and six studies summarized by Kharchev and Matskhovskii (1978:142–145) showed that alcoholism was the identified cause of divorce in 10% to 44% of the cases studied. Perevedentsev reports that 47% of the women filing for divorce do so because of an alcoholic husband (Perevedentsev, 1978). In an interesting study, men were asked to identify both their frequency of alcohol usage and whether they were involved in a "happy,"

"satisfactory," or "unhappy" marriage. The results showed a clear inverse relationship between the frequency of usage and the percentage of men who say their marriage is "happy." Thus, 32% of the men who drink at least once a week identify their marriage as "happy," but 57% of those who usually drink only on holidays have a happy marriage (Iurkevich, 1970:151). Of course, unhappy marriages could have led to the heavy drinking, and the real cause of marital unhappiness may be found elsewhere.

With respect to adultery, the data summarized by Kharchev and Matskhovskii (1978) show it to be of lesser importance than alcoholism. In a Leningrad study, adultery was involved in 24% of all divorces (Korolev, 1978:143), and a Ukrainian study showed that the proportion of divorces due to adultery increases as the length of marriage increases. During the second year of married life, adultery is twice as likely to be a major cause of divorce as in the first year. In marriages ending after a duration of 5-20 years, two-thirds of the petitions filed by the husbands and three-fourths by the wives were because of adultery (Chuiko, 1975:165).

The concept of the "incompatibility of characters" escapes precise definition, and I have seen none attempted in Soviet literature. It appears to be a catchall term similar to what is called "irreconcilable differences" in the United States—an expression of the fact that the partners are no longer able to live with one another. The classification is convenient; it is not necessary then to assign fault to either party. It is not only a major reason offered in Soviet courts (64% of 1000 Latvian Supreme Court cases) (Korolev, 1978:145); it is also the most common reason offered by couples seeking divorce in the ZAGS. However, such a reason tells us almost nothing about the marriage. Often there is another reason such as alcoholism or adultery which the couple wishes to cover with a blander term (Korolev, 1978:141–142).

In a 1966 study of marriages that end in divorce during the first year and in which more than official grounds could be named, 75% of the people divorced because their marriages were without love, 47% because of the interference of parents and other relatives, and 34% because the respondent was to be imprisoned for at least three years. Adultery and alcoholism were mentioned in only 22% and 13% of the cases, respectively (Iurkevich, 1970:108).

While adultery, alcoholism, and incompatibility are universal problems, there are recent developments in the USSR that require a closer look as factors in the rising Soviet divorce rate, most notably urbanization and the change in the role of women. There is no way to quantify their impact, yet there is enough evidence to suggest that attention should be given to the role that these two variables play in causing divorce in the Soviet Union.

The process of modernization always creates pressures within a society, and the peculiar historical and institutional features of that society will determine how the dysfunctional dimensions of that pressure will be felt. Within the Soviet Union the problem of urbanization creates tensions in several ways, the most pressing of which is the chronic housing shortage. One study among divorced individuals revealed that only 5% of them had their own apartments when they were married (Kurganov, 1967:193). From the very beginning of their marriage, in other words, the young couple is faced with the pressure of accommodating to another set of vested emotional interests. When the couple lives with the wife's parents, it is typically the husband who files for divorce; the reverse is also true (Chuiko, 1975:166–167). This suggests that the extended-family concept within a high-pressure urban environment creates its own

dynamics of tensions. The benefits of grandparents who can assist in getting children to school and cooking meals are often neutralized by the apparent difficulties these living arrangements produce within Soviet marriages.

The housing problem affects marital relations most seriously at the new construction sites and in the new industrial towns where housing for couples is especially scarce (Korolev, 1978:136, 160). One example is the town of Naberezhnie Chelnie, where the giant Kama Truck Factory (KamAZ) is located. A characteristic of the town is that 70% of the young people, constituting 40% of the KamAZ labor force, live in sex-segregated hostels. This tension of living apart has led to an extremely high divorce rate in the town (Mustafin, 1975).

The severe housing shortage in the Soviet Union creates a separation period preceding divorce that is very different from that in the United States. While Soviet couples may no longer share the marriage bed, they must share the same apartment. A study showed that about two-thirds of all divorced Kiev couples live in the same apartment even after their marriage has ended (Chuiko, 1975:148). The average length of separation before application for divorce is 2.7 years (Chuiko, 1975:148). In the United States only 18.5% of those who divorce have a separation period of three years or longer (Weed, 1981). Thus, the true rate of marital dissolution in the Soviet Union is probably understated by the divorce rate because long separations precede divorce. In addition, there is the struggle with the everyday conditions of life—e.g., shopping, finding food, and traveling in a crowded mass transit system— all of which are more trying than in other industrialized nations (Perevedentsev, 1978).

The changed role of women as numerically equal participants in the labor force has created tensions in at least three ways. First, it has altered the traditional patriarchal family model and the power relationships and deference patterns embodied in that model. Soviet social scientists concede that tensions are created during this transition period between the rigid role model of the old order and the more modern ideal of equality (Perevedentsev, 1978; Korolev, 1978:160).

Second, the transition from old to new has imposed a double burden on women, who are often not only fulltime workers but also the primary caretakers of children and the home. One study stated that women work 80 hours a week while men work only 50 hours a week (Perevedentsev, 1978). There is tension in Soviet households because women are irritated with husbands who do not help with household responsibilities. According to a study conducted in the mid-1960s in Novosibirsk, 10.2% of unskilled women workers and 25.1% of skilled women divorced their husbands because of the husband's lack of participation in housework (Danilova, 1968:65). From the women's point of view, there is a contradiction between the official support of sexual equality, which raises expectations, and the paucity of daily help, which leaves those expectations unfulfilled. On the other hand, men reportedly miss the freedom of being single. The mutual dissatisfaction leads them to seek the company of other men and alcohol (Korolev, 1978:161).

Third, the independent work roles of men and women (including in some instances separate vacation schedules), in combination with the heavy reliance on institutional day care, reduces the role of the family as a unit of social action. All this may contribute to a sense that the enduring cohesion of the family is not very important.

THE SOCIOECONOMIC CONSEQUENCES OF DIVORCE

Soviet discussions of the implications of divorce consistently focus on four key themes:

(a) fatherless children, (b) the economic problems of women, (c) lonely women, and (d) remarriage. These problems are all interconnected, although they are treated separately here in order to see their individual dimensions.

Children affect the divorce rates in a number of significant ways. First, they are deterrents to divorce: divorce is most likely to occur among childless families. In families with children, the divorce rate is inversely correlated with the number of children (Korolev, 1978:137). Soviet writers are concerned that a growing number of children are living in homes without fathers (Perevedentsev, 1978; Urlanis, 1970:12), and this concern seems justified according to at least one study which shows that 69% of all fathers do not contact their children at all after divorce (Iurkevich and Burova, 1975).

Another adverse effect is on the academic performance of students. Two studies confirm that children in households without fathers because of divorce do more poorly in school than children in intact families. This is especially true where alcohol has been used (Danilova, 1968:66; Vasil'eva, 1973:20, 27). There is also a claimed link between teenage crime and divorce. In Novosibirsk 31% of the teenagers arrested for misdemeanors did not have fathers in their families (Danilova, 1968:66-67). Each of these studies has to be viewed with caution since neither indicates that they have controlled for such critical variables as income and level of educational attainment. United States studies are inconclusive on the impact of divorce on delinquency rates or the quality of school performance. They suggest the possibility that it is the family's socioeconomic group or the effect of an unstable marriage that leads to problems for children (Adam and Adam, 1979:10).

As in most countries, the financial consequences of divorce fall most heavily on children and women. For childless women it can be argued that their economic independence makes it easier for them to deal with divorce. This may account partially for the increase in the number of women who initiate divorce proceedings. On the other hand, women with children face severe financial constraints if they are divorced. In particular, the primary responsibility that women have for taking care of the home and children has not allowed women to reach the same social and economic level as men. As a consequence there is an incentive for women who are married to highly paid men to stay in their marriages (Chuiko, 1975:142).

If there is a divorce where children are involved, the economic outcome is somewhat problematic. A father is obliged to provide child support equal to one-fourth of his income. If the former husband and wife earned the same income or the husband earned more than the wife, income per person in the new single-parent household will fall; and the more children there are, the greater will be the decline. The situation is worse when Soviet fathers fail to pay child support on a regular basis. This is a common problem in the USSR, where the police are always looking for deserting fathers (Iurkevich and Burova, 1975:13). However, there is an interesting paradox embedded in a Minsk survey of divorced women: 88% of the sample said their financial situation was the same or better after divorce, and only 12% said it became worse. There are two explanations for this. First, in more than half the cases, alcoholism was the cause for divorce: thus, their situation has improved because the husband is no longer drinking away family income. The second reason is that women try to maintain the same standard of living after divorce by seeking other sources of income, such as overtime work (Iurkevich and Burova, 1975:13).

The aftermath of divorce brings loneliness to newly divorced individuals, both men and women. Yet, Soviet literature focuses on loneliness as a greater problem for women without discussing why this is so. It has been suggested that some childless women try to cope with their loneliness by having a child outside of marriage. These women are looked upon as pariahs by what one writer called the "Savonarolas of the communal apartments" (Zhukovitskii, 1977). Another writer contends that older women have children outside of marriage because they cannot find a husband and, therefore, seek consolation and companionship in a child (Kuznetsova, 1977).

A recent work asserts that less than half the divorced men remarry (Korolev, 1978:182) and an even smaller percentage of divorced women remarry in the Soviet Union (Iurkevich and Burova, 1975:13). In the United States by contrast, 83% of divorced men and 75% of divorced women remarry. Data from the Ukraine indicate that only 10%-15% of the women who remarry have children from their previous marriages (Chuiko, 1975:167). In other words a woman is much more likely to remarry if she does not have a child from her first marriage.

The large number of people who remain unmarried is of serious concern to Soviet economic planners because this contributes to a low birth rate which, in turn, adversely affects the potential size of the labor force and lowers Soviet economic growth and national security. However, even remarriage may not be the answer to this problem. In a Ukrainian study the average number of children in the first marriage is 1.2, while in the second marriage it drops to only 0.37 (Chuiko, 1975:192). There are probably four reasons for this: (a) the generally older age of remarried women, (b) a fear that their second marriage will also fail, (c) the presence of children from the first marriage; and (d) the possible reluctance of women to have more children because of the burdens involved in rearing them. In addition, of course, remarriage is probably constrained by the absence of suitable housing.

CONCLUSIONS

Divorce in the Soviet Union has increased dramatically, particularly in the urban areas of the country. The current legal framework is conducive to easy divorce, although it is obviously not responsible for the underlying pressures that lead to a high demand for divorce. Whatever the causes are, the outcomes have to be viewed as nothing short of dysfunctional from the perspective of planners. The most keenly felt impact is the negative effect this will have on the size of the future labor force.

The obvious policy options cannot be very attractive to planners. They could strengthen the divorce law and severely restrict the legal option for divorce. However, the Romanian experience with a repressive divorce law proved extremely unsuccessful, and they apparently have relaxed it in implementation (Moskoff, 1980). Another alternative would be to make much more residential housing available. This would require an amount and direction of investment thoroughly inconsistent with the current investment pattern. Nevertheless, even if there were a shift in Soviet priorities, the American experience of affluence and high divorce suggests that the good life would not necessarily decrease the Soviet divorce rate. Perhaps this problem in Soviet society escapes understanding and, therefore, remediation. If so, from the point of view of both economic and social planners, the present does not augur well for the future, given the likelihood that the existing patterns of Soviet life will persist in the foreseeable future.

References

Adam, J. H. and Adam, N. W.
  1979 *Divorce: How and When to Let Go.* Englewood Cliffs, NJ: Prentice-Hall.
Chuiko, L. V.
  1975 *Braki i Razvody.* Moscow.
Chumakova, T. E.
  1974 *Sem'ia, Moral', Pravo,* Minsk, USSR.
Danilova, E. Z.
  1968 *Sotsial'nye Problemy Truda Zhenshchiny-Rabotnitsy.* Moscow.
Iurkevich, G.
  1970 *Sovetskaia Sem'ia.* Minsk, USSR.
Iurkevich, N. and Burova, S.
  1975 "Etot legkii razvod." *Literaturnaia Gazeta* 46(October 1):13.
Kharchev, A. G. and Matskhovskii, M. A.
  1978 *Sovremennaia Sem'ia i ee Problemy.* Moscow.
Korolev, Iu. A.
  1978 *Brak i Razvod.* Moscow.
Kurganov, I. A.
  1967 *Sem'ia v SSSR: 1917–1967.* New York.
Kuznetsova, L.
  1977 "Dochki-materi." *Literaturnaia Gazeta* 48 (June 15):12.
Moskoff, W.
  1980 "Pronatalist policies in Romania." *Economic Development and Cultural Change* 28(April):597–614.
Mustafin, R.
  1975 "Slishkom mnogo svadaev?" *Literaturnaia Gazeta* 46(August 13):12.
  1980 *Narodnoe Khoziaistvo SSSR v 1979g.* Moscow.
Perevedentsev, V.
  1971 "Pora zhenit'sia, pora vykhodit zamuzh." *Literaturnaia Gazeta* 42(April 17):13.
  1977 "Zhenki i nevesty: dolgozhdannoe ravnovesie." *Literaturnaia Gazeta* 48(May 25):11.
  1978 "Ne soshlis; kharakterami." *Literaturnaia Gazeta* 49(February 15):13.
U.S. Bureau of the Census
  1979 *Statistical Abstract of the United States* (100th ed.). Washington, DC:U.S. Government Printing Office.
Urlanis, B.
  1970 "Bezotsovshchina." *Literaturnaia Gazeta* 41(January 7):12.
Vasil'eva, E. K.
  1973 *Sotsial'no Professional'nyi Uroven' Gorodskoi Molodezhi.* Leningrad.

Vishnevskii, A.
  1975 "Rannii brak?" *Literaturnaia Gazeta* 46 (March 26):12.
Weed, J.
  1981 U.S. Bureau of the Census (Interview, April 2).
Zhukovitskii, L.
  1977 "Liubov' i demografha." *Literaturnaia Gazeta* 48(May 4):12.

Discussion Questions

1. How is divorce in the U.S.S.R. different from that in the United States?

2. What effects do you see on Soviet family life as a result of Glasnost?

3. Using the information provided by O'Kelly and Carney on gender stratification in the Soviet Union (Reading 7-3), explain Moskoff's conclusions.

CHAPTER 10

Issues in Religion

INTRODUCTION

At first glance, religion may seem to be an inappropriate area of study for the sociologist. After all, is it not true that social science is, by definition, interested only in that which is empirically verifiable? The answer is yes, but this does not exclude religion as a field of study, because sociology is not concerned with proving religion to be true or false. Rather, its focus is on how people's belief or nonbelief influences their behavior and their thinking. In the larger sphere, sociologists want to understand how religious institutions fit in with the rest of society.

Among the major issues of interest to sociology are the cultural ideas that give birth to religious systems. *Polytheism* posits the idea of more than one God, while *monotheism* stresses a belief in one God. Both are *theistic* in that they accept the notion of a supreme being. Another category of religious beliefs, known as *animism*, sees the world as inhabited by a multitude of ghosts and spirits. Whatever the form of a religion, its believers are linked to one another both by a set of beliefs and by certain practices.

Religion has certain goals in the eyes of its members and leaders. One is to explain the world, to make sense of things. Another is to aid people in times of crisis, and a third is to provide structure for daily existence. Among the most important objectives is salvation, which means different things to different religious groups. In Taoism, salvation occurs when people achieve a state in which they have eliminated all earthly desires. For Christians, salvation means, quite simply, going to heaven when they die. The link between culture and religion is powerful, and a close examination of religious beliefs yields a clear understanding of just how powerful the link is. For example, Judaism's commandments emphasize human relationships, as in charity to the poor, marriage laws, and business ethics.

Religion is, however, far more than a set of cultural values and ideas. Generally highly structured, it exists within a complex web of institutional relationships that cut across entire societies. Membership and status in a religious group can be either achieved or ascribed, but most religious systems have a highly developed bureaucratic structure led by a hierarchy of leaders. Religious structures, unlike governments, are not bound by fixed time periods; they are timeless. Their timelessness, in fact, is for many people an important part of their appeal. They transcend human events and exist in a sphere that has a special status that is not easily challenged. Denominations are the most highly organized religious institutions, sects are somewhat less organized, and cults are the least organized. Perhaps the most important distinction between sects and cults is that charisma is the main form of authority in a cult, whereas in a sect, authority is vested in the formal structure of the institution.

Religious change, although it may happen slowly, does occur, and rather often at that. For example, the norms limiting participation of homosexuals in a variety of religions have been breaking down over the past twenty years. Similarly, women have achieved positions of power in Christianity and Judaism that were once not only denied to them but unthinkable.

One of the most important ideas to emerge within the field has been the concept of "civil religion." This concept, as posited by Robert Bellah (1973), is that, in modern society, the state has achieved a status similar to that of a religious institution. Bellah and others provide numerous examples to support their argument. Among them are the mentioning of God's name on currency; the tax-exempt status of property owned by churches, mosques, and synagogues; and the display of crèches and other religious symbols on government property. A civil religion is not a true religion, because it does not encompass a belief in the supernatural, and because it cannot answer questions about why we were put on this earth. It does, however, embody many characteristics of organized religious institutions.

In the first selection, Robert Bellah, one of the foremost sociologists in the United States,

evaluates religion as a social institution. Bellah examines religious pluralism in American society through the prism of the local congregation. Identifying Christianity as the center of religious life in this country, he demonstrates how it fits into and reflects the goals and values of our society in general. Within this center, there are elements of mysticism which, though they are connected to the religious mainstream, also stand apart from it. He concludes by observing that the civil rights movement, under the leadership of Dr. Martin Luther King, Jr., tried to unite all the different faiths by emphasizing a universal vision of tolerance and freedom.

The second article focuses on a quite different historical experience, that of Jonestown and its charismatic leader, Reverend Jim Jones. We see the horrifying results of fanaticism and megalomania—how one person can control the lives and fate of many others. John Hall, a sociologist, analyzes the movement and notes that Jones focused on "imminent apocalyptic disaster" rather than on any concept of salvation, such as the idea of Christ's millenial salvation. Hall explains how the resistance of Jones' followers was gradually broken down and how some came to believe that they owed everything to him. He also notes that the Jonestown community was racially integrated and protocommunist in its ideology. In the sense that it rejected the existence of God, it was not a classical religion. On the other hand, Jones did believe in reincarnation. Ultimately, as Hall observes, the mass suicide at Jonestown enabled people to achieve the twin goals of political revolution and religious salvation.

The third selection in this chapter takes us to an Italian village—a world unto itself, removed in both time and place from the United States. Feliks Gross, who teaches sociology in New York, makes the village come alive as he traces the daily lives of its people. We see what it means to begin the transition from traditional to industrial society. The change is not easily accomplished, and the villagers who live in Bonagente turn easily and often to Catholicism when in trouble. The role of sin, the importance of saints in the lives of the peasants, and the sociological functions of the great *festas* and processions are evaluated and described. Above all, Gross demonstrates how the removal of Catholicism from such communities amounts to destruction of an irreplaceable way of life. For better or for worse, the society that emerges, blinking in the new light of the modern era, can never be the same.

References

Bellah, Robert. *The Broken Covenant*. New York: Seabury Press, 1973.

Hall, John R. *The Ways Out: Utopian Communal Groups in an Age of Babylon*. Boston: Routledge & Kegan Paul, 1978.

Swanson, Guy E. *The Birth of the Gods: The Origin of Primitive Beliefs*. Ann Arbor, Mich.: University of Michigan Press, 1974.

Weber, Max. *The Protestant Ethic and the Spirit of Capitalism*. New York: Scribner, 1958 (first published in 1920).

Religion

Robert N. Bellah et al.

Religion is one of the most important of the many ways in which Americans "get involved" in the life of their community and society. Americans give more money and donate more time to religious bodies and religiously associated organizations than to all other voluntary associations put together. Some 40 percent of Americans attend religious services at least once a week (a much greater number than would be found in Western Europe or even Canada) and religious membership is around 60 percent of the total population.

In our research, we were interested in religion not in isolation but as part of the texture of private and public life in the United States. Although we seldom asked specifically about religion, time and again in our conversations, religion emerged as important to the people we were interviewing, as the national statistics just quoted would lead one to expect.

For some, religion is primarily a private matter having to do with family and local congregation. For others, it is private in one sense but also a primary vehicle for the expression of national and even global concerns. Though Americans overwhelmingly accept the doctrine of the separation of church and state, most of them believe, as they always have, that religion has an important role to play in the public realm. But as with every other major institution, the place of religion in our society has changed dramatically over time. . . .

RELIGIOUS PLURALISM

The American pattern of privatizing religion while at the same time allowing it some public functions has proven highly compatible with the religious pluralism that has characterized America from the colonial period and grown more and more pronounced. If the primary contribution of religion to society is through the character and conduct of citizens, any religion, large or small, familiar or strange, can be of equal value to any other. The fact that most American religions have been biblical and that most, though of course not all, Americans can agree on the term "God" has certainly been helpful in diminishing religious antagonism. But diversity of practice has been seen as legitimate because religion is perceived as a matter of individual choice, with the implicit qualification that the practices themselves accord with public decorum and the adherents abide by the moral standards of the community.

Under American conditions, religious pluralism has not produced a purely random assortment of religious bodies. Certain fairly determinate principles of differentiation—ethnic, regional, class—have operated to produce an intelligible pattern of social differentiation among religious groups, even though there remains much fluidity. Most American communities contain a variety of churches, and the larger the community the greater the variety. In smaller towns and older suburbs, church buildings draw significant public attention. They cluster around the town square or impressively punctuate the main streets. Local residents know very well who belongs where: the Irish and Italians go to the Catholic church and the small businessmen to the Methodist church, whereas the local elite belong to the Presbyterian and, even more likely, Episcopal churches.

Hervé Varenne has beautifully described the pattern in a small town in southern Wisconsin. Each congregation emphasized its own cultural style, often with implications about social class. Though the Protestant churches tended to be ranked in terms of the affluence and influence of their members,

Varenne discovered, it was a relatively small core group that gave them their identity and their actual membership was often diverse. Small fundamentalist sects appealed to the poorest and most marginal townspeople, and the Catholic church had the most diverse membership in terms of class background. Varenne gives an example of the social differentiation of religion in "Appleton" in the following paragraph:

> As perceived by many people in Appleton, the Presbyterian church, for example, was supposed to be "intellectual" and "sophisticated"; the Methodist was the church both of older, established small farmers and younger, "up-and-coming" businessmen in the town. Indeed, the Presbyterian church appealed mainly to professionals and high-level civil servants, the Methodist to merchants. The school board was dominated by Presbyterians, the town council by Methodists. There was clearly a feeling of competition between these two churches, the most important ones in Appleton. For the time being, the advantage appeared to lie with the Presbyterian church for the top spot in the ranking system. . . .

THE LOCAL CONGREGATION

We may begin a closer examination of how religion operates in the lives of those to whom we talked by looking at the local congregation, which traditionally has a certain priority. The local church is a community of worship that contains within itself, in small, so to speak, the features of the larger church, and in some Protestant traditions can exist autonomously. The church as a community of worship is an adaptation of the Jewish synagogue. Both Jews and Christians view their communities as existing in a covenant relationship with God, and the Sabbath worship around which religious life centers is a celebration of that covenant. Worship calls to mind the story of the relationship of the community with God: how God brought his chosen people out of Egypt or gave his only begotten son for the salvation of mankind. Worship also reiterates the obligations that the community has undertaken, including the biblical insistence on justice and righteousness, and on love of God and neighbor, as well as the promises God has made that make it possible for the community to hope for the future. Though worship has its special times and places, especially on the Sabbath in the house of the Lord, it functions as a model or pattern for the whole of life. Through reminding the people of their relationship to God, it establishes patterns of character and virtue that should operate in economic and political life as well as in the context of worship. The community maintains itself as a community of memory, and the various religious traditions have somewhat different memories.

The very freedom, openness, and pluralism of American religious life makes this traditional pattern hard for Americans to understand. For one thing, the traditional pattern assumes a certain priority of the religious community over the individual. The community exists before the individual is born and will continue after his or her death. The relationship of the individual to God is ultimately personal, but it is mediated by the whole pattern of community life. There is a givenness about the community and the tradition. They are not normally a matter of individual choice. . . .

THE RELIGIOUS CENTER

For a long time what have been called the "mainline" Protestant churches have tried to do more than this. They have offered a conception of God as neither wholly other nor a higher self, but rather as involved in time and history. These churches have tried to develop a larger picture of what it might mean to live a biblical life in America. They have sought to be communities of memory, to keep in touch with biblical sources and historical traditions not with literalist obedience but through an intelligent reappropriation illuminated by historical and theological reflection. They have tried to relate biblical faith and practice to the whole of contemporary life—cultural, social, political, economic—not just to personal and family morality. They have tried to steer a middle course between mystical fusion with the world and sectarian withdrawal from it.

Through the nineteenth century and well into the twentieth, the mainline churches were close to the center of American culture. The religious intellectuals who spoke for these churches often articulated issues in ways widely influential in the society as a whole. But for a generation or more, the religious intellectuals deriving from the mainline Protestant churches have become more isolated from the general culture. This is in part because they, like other scholars, have become specialists in fields where only specialists speak to one another. Their isolation also derives in part from the long pressure to segregate our knowledge of what is, gained through science, from our knowledge of what ought to be, gained through religion, morality and art. Finally, the religious intellectuals have themselves lost self-confidence and become vulnerable to short-lived fads. For some years now, they have failed to produce a Tillich or Niebuhr who might become the center of fruitful controversy and discussion. Without the leavening of a creative intellectual focus, the quasi-therapeutic blandness that has afflicted much of mainline Protestant religion at the parish level for over a century cannot effectively withstand the competition of the more vigorous forms of radical religious individualism, with their claims of dramatic self-realization, or the resurgent religious conservatism that spells out clear, if simple, answers in an increasingly bewildering world.

But just when the mainline Protestant hold on American culture seemed decisively weakened, the Roman Catholic church after Vatican II entered a much more active phase of national participation. Though never without influence in American society, the Catholic church had long been more concerned with the welfare of its own members, many of them immigrants, than with moulding the national society. The period 1930–60 was a kind of culmination of a long process of institution building and self-help. The church, still a minority, but long the largest single denomination, grew in confidence as the majority of its constituents attained middle-class respectability. An educated and thoughtful laity was thus ready to respond to the new challenges the Second Vatican Council opened up in the early 1960s. The unprecedented ecumenical cooperation that brought Catholics together with Protestants and Jews in a number of joint endeavors from the period of the Civil Rights movement to the present has created a new atmosphere in American religious life. With the American Catholic bishops' pastoral letter of May 3, 1983, on nuclear warfare, the promise of Vatican II began to be fulfilled. The Catholic church moved toward the center of American public life, invigorating the major Protestant denominations as it did so.

Recently Martin Marty, in the light of this new situation, has attempted to describe the religious center as what he calls "the public church." The public church, in Marty's sense, includes the old mainline Protestant churches, the Catholic church, and significant sectors of the evangelical churches. It is not a homogeneous entity but rather a "communion of communions" in which each church maintains the integrity of its own traditions and practices even while recognizing common ground with the others. Without dissolving its Christian particularity, the public church welcomes the opportunity for conversation, and on occasion joint action, with its Jewish, other non-Christian, and secular counterparts, particularly where matters of the common good are concerned. The public church is not triumphalist—indeed it emerges in a situation where Christians feel less in control of their culture than ever before—but it wishes to respond to the new situation with public responsibility rather than with individual or group withdrawal. The public church and its counterparts in the non-Christian religions offer the major alternative in our culture to radical religious individualism on the one hand and what Marty calls "religious tribalism" on the other.

It is possible to look at Art Townsend's liberal Presbyterian congregation, Larry Beckett's conservative evangelical church, and Ruth Levy's "community that's rooted in a synagogue" as examples of the public church or analogous to it. All reject the radical self-seeking of utilitarian individualism and none of them is content to be only a lifestyle enclave of warm mutual acceptance. For all of them, religion provides a conception, even if rudimentary, of how one should live. They all share the idea that one's obligations to God involve one's life at work as well as in the family, what one does as a citizen as well as how one treats one's friends. Yet, as we have seen, each of these communities has suffered to some degree from a therapeutic thinning out of belief and practice, a withdrawal into the narrow boundaries of the religious community itself, or both. As a result, continuity as a community of memory and engagement in the public world are problematic for each of them.

Let us turn, then, to another religious community, St. Stephen's Episcopal Church, which, while suffering from the same problems, seems to be able to combine a sense of continuity with the past and an engagement with the public world of the present. Like Art Townsend's and Larry Beckett's churches, St. Stephen's is in the San Francisco Bay area and has a largely middle-class membership. For a congregation of only a few hundred members, St. Stephen's is the center of a surprising amount of activity. There are prayer groups and bible study groups that meet weekly or more often. There is a pastoral care team to assist the rector, the only full-time cleric, at a variety of tasks such as visiting the sick, the shut-ins, those in convalescent hospitals, and so on. There are a number of people active in a local mission that consists mainly in feeding, clothing, and caring for the hungry and the homeless in the city where St. Stephen's is located. The church supports an Amnesty International group and a number of parishioners are involved in antinuclear activities. St. Stephen's has joined a local consortium of churches in a Sanctuary Covenant whereby they provide sanctuary for Salvadoran refugees.

But for all the parish's many activities, it is the life of worship that is its center. The Book of Common Prayer provides a pattern of liturgy that is continuous with the practices of worship from the early centuries of the church. Holy Communion is celebrated daily and three times on Sunday, with more than half the parish attending at least once a week. The liturgical year is taken seriously, with the Lenten and Easter seasons having a particular salience. Father Paul Morrison, rector of St. Stephen's, believes that for those who come regularly, worship "becomes a genuine source of life and focussing what they do during the week." The rector, a modest but articulate man of fifty, speaks with conviction balanced by self-searching. He attributes the effectiveness of worship not to the preaching but to the Eucharist, which "draws people in and somehow informs them of the source of life that is present at the heart of worship." In administering the sacraments, he finds he must keep some detachment in order not to be overwhelmed by the poignancy of all the individual lives he knows so well, of his people who "have brought their life, the heart of their life," to the communion rail and "they hold it up and find healing and comfort and walk away somehow renewed, restored, and fit for another week in a pretty tough world." In the Episcopal tradition, the sermon is less central than in most Protestant denominations, but Father Morrison's sermons are effective, sometimes moving, interpretations of the biblical readings and applications of them to contemporary personal or social problems. . . .

When asked whether the Episcopal church, which has traditionally stood close to the centers of power in our society and attempted to influence the power structure from within, should continue that policy or perhaps take a position closer to the margins of society, protesting against it, Father Morrison replied, "I wish I knew the answer to that." He often speaks in his sermons about people, not only in the United States but in Central America or southern Africa, who are on the margins and the edges and how the church must stand with them. He reminds his congregation that Christianity itself began among a peasant people at the margins of the Roman Empire. Yet he does not want to "abandon the world or undercut lay vocations." He sums up his view by saying, "If we recover to any extent our support of our people in their vocations and ministries in the world, then maybe one would have enough confidence to say 'yes, from the inside we certainly can take responsibility, because our best people are there and they are nourished and succored by the church and ready to do the job.' Right now it seems almost accidental if there is any relationships between Episcopalians in power and the Gospel."

CHURCH, SECT, AND MYSTICISM

In his comments on the relationship between the church and secular power, Father Morrison seems to be wavering between two conceptions of the religious community—what Ernst Troeltsch called "church" and "sect." Whereas the church enters into the world culturally and socially in order to influence it, the sect stands apart from the secular world, which it sees as too sinful to influence except from without. Troeltsch's third type, which he called "mysticism" or "religious individ-

ualism," is one in which the focus is on the spiritual discipline of the individual, however he or she relates to the world. Religious organization is important to both church and sect, but to mystics or religious individualists organization, being inessential, may be casual and transient. St. Stephen's, with its emphasis on individual spiritual discipline, seems to contain an element of mysticism as well as elements of church and sect. What this example suggests is that Troeltsch's types are dimensions of Christian (and often non-Christian) religious community. Individual congregations or denominations may emphasize one dimension more than another—St. Stephen's, for example, and the Episcopal church generally are predominantly of the church type— but examples of pure types will be rare. Nevertheless, by looking at American religion in terms of Troeltsch's types, we may gain a better understanding of how religion influences our society. . . .

The church type has been present in America from the beginning of European settlement, but it has never been dominant in pure form. Early New England Puritanism embodied much of the church type but with a strong admixture with the spirit of the sect. The more purely sectarian forms of Protestantism that were already present in the seventeenth century and grew markedly in the eighteenth century strongly colored all of subsequent American culture. The Roman Catholic church, even after massive immigration made it a significant force in the United States, remained a minority church. As it absorbed ever more of American culture, it too was affected by sect ideas. Indeed, in the United States, the church type has become harder and harder to understand. Our ontological individualism finds it hard to comprehend the social realism of the church—the idea that the church is prior to individuals and not just the product of them.

The sect type has been present in America virtually from the beginning, includes the

Protestant denominations with the largest numbers, and has in many ways been the dominant mode of American Christianity. The sect views a church as primarily a voluntary association of believers. The individual believer has a certain priority over the church in that the experience of grace is temporally prior to admission to membership, even though, once admitted, collective discipline in the sect can be quite strong. The sectarian church sees itself as the gathered elect and focusses on the purity of those within as opposed to the sinfulness of those without. Whereas the church type, with its ideal of communion, includes everybody in its hierarchical organic structure at some level or other, the sect with its ideal of purity draws a sharp line between the essentially equal saints within and the reprobates without. The strong sectarian emphasis on voluntarism and the equality of believers—the sect is anti-elitist and insists on the priesthood of all believers—is congenial to democratic forms of organization and congregational autonomy. There is a tendency for grace to be overshadowed by "the law of Christ" and for the sacraments to be less central than a moralism that verges on legalism. As Troeltsch pointed out, the sectarian group if often, especially in its beginnings, found primarily among lower income groups and the less educated. It is tempted toward a radical withdrawal from the environing society and a rejection of secular art, culture, and science. As Troeltsch also observed, the sect is especially close to the spirit of the synoptic gospels. Christianity began as a lower-class religion of people of no great education, although the urban churches founded by St. Paul in the Greco-Roman cities already had elements of the church type in New Testament times. . . .

Religious individualism is, in many ways, appropriate in our kind of society. It is no more going to go away than is secular individualism. Ours is a society that requires people to be strong and independent. As believers, we must often operate alone in uncongenial circumstances, and we must have the inner spiritual strength and discipline to do so. Objecting to its authoritarianism and paternalism, religious individualists have often left the church or sect they were raised in. Yet such people often derive more of their personal strength than they know from their communities of origin. They have difficulty transmitting their own sense of moral integrity to their children in the absence of such a community, and they have difficulty sustaining it themselves when their only support is from transient associations of the like-minded. It would seem that a vital and enduring religious individualism can only survive in a renewed relationship with established religious bodies. Such a renewed relationship would require changes on both sides. Churches and sects would have to learn that they can sustain more autonomy than they had thought, and religious individualists would have to learn that solitude without community is merely loneliness.

RELIGION AND WORLD

Throughout this chapter, we have seen a conflict between withdrawal into purely private spirituality and the biblical impetus to see religion as involved with the whole of life. Parker Palmer suggests that this apparent contradiction can be overcome:

> Perhaps the most important ministry the church can have in the renewal of public life is a "ministry of paradox": not to resist the inward turn of American spirituality on behalf of effective public action, *but to deepen and direct and discipline that inwardness in the light of faith* until God leads us back to a vision of the public and to faithful action on the public's behalf.

Palmer seems to be asserting with respect to religious individualism something similar to what we argued [earlier]—namely, that American individualism is not to be rejected but transformed by reconnecting it to the public realm.

Toward the end of the previous chapter, we discussed the social movement as a form of citizenship and pointed out how often in our history religion has played an important role in such movements. Time and again in our history, spiritually motivated individuals and groups have felt called to show forth in their lives the faith that was in them by taking a stand on the great ethical and political issues of the day. During the Revolution, the parish clergy gave ideological support and moral encouragement to the republican cause. Christian clergy and laity were among the most fervent supporters of the antislavery cause, just as Christians involved in the Social Gospel movement and its many ramifications did much to ameliorate the worst excesses of early industrial capitalism. Of course, the churches produced opponents of all these movements—the American religious community has never spoken with one voice. On occasion, a significant part of the religious community has mounted a successful crusade that the nation as a whole later came to feel was unwise—for example, the Temperance movement that led to a constitutional amendment prohibiting the sale of alcoholic beverages in the United States. But without the intervention of the churches, many significant issues would have been ignored and needed changes would have come about much more slowly.

To remind us of what is possible, we may call to mind one of the most significant social movements of recent times, a movement overwhelmingly religious in its leadership that changed the nature of American society. Under the leadership of Martin Luther King, Jr., the Civil Rights movement called upon Americans to transform their social and economic institutions with the goal of building a just national community that would respect both the differences and the interdependence of its members. It did this by combining biblical and republican themes in a way that included, but transformed, the culture of individualism.

Consider King's "I Have a Dream" speech. Juxtaposing the poetry of the scriptural prophets—"I have a dream that every valley shall be exalted, every hill and mountain shall be made low"—with the lyrics of patriotic anthems—"This will be the day when all of God's children will be able to sing with new meaning, 'My country 'tis of thee, sweet land of liberty, of thee I sing'"—King's oration reappropriated that classic strand of the American tradition that understands the true meaning of freedom to lie in the affirmation of responsibility for uniting all of the diverse members of society into a just social order. "When we let freedom ring, when we let freedom ring from every village and hamlet, from every state and every city, we will be able to speed up the day when all of God's children, black men and white men, Jews and Gentiles, Protestants and Catholics, will be able to join hands and sing the words of that old Negro spiritual. 'Free at last! Free at last! Thank God almighty, we are free at last!'" For King, the struggle for freedom became a practice of commitment within a vision of America as a community of memory. We now need to look at that national community, our changing conceptions of it, and what its prospects are.

DISCUSSION QUESTIONS

1. Explain the mystical elements in mainstream church life, according to Bellah.
2. How is it possible for religion to embody the seemingly contradictory values of private spirituality and acceptance of responsibility (as Martin Luther King did) for influencing society as a whole?
3. Do you find that Bellah's account of religion differs from your own experience? Explain differences, if any.

Apocalypse at Jonestown

John R. Hall

The events of November 1978 at Jonestown, Guyana have been well documented, indeed probably better documented than most incidents in the realm of the bizarre. Beyond the wealth of "facts" which have been drawn from interviews with survivors of all stripes, there remain piles of as yet unsifted documents and tapes; if they can ever be examined, these will perhaps add something in the way of detail. But it is unlikely they will change very much the broad lines of our understanding of Jonestown. The major dimensions of the events and the outlines of various intrigues are already before us. But so far as we have been caught in a flood of instant analysis; some of this has been insightful, but much of the accompanying moral outrage has clouded our ability to comprehend the events themselves. We need a more considered look at what sort of social phenomenon Jonestown was, and why (and how) Reverend Jim Jones and his staff led the 900 people of Jonestown to die in mass murder and suicide. On the face of it, the action is unparalleled and incredible.

"CRAZY LIKE A FOX"

The news media have sought to account for Jonestown largely by looking for parallels "in history"; yet we have not been terribly enlightened by the ones they have found, usually because they have searched for cases which bear the outer trappings of the event, but which have fundamentally different causes. Thus, at Masada, in 73 A.D., the Jews who committed suicide under siege by Roman soldiers knew their fate was death, and chose to die by their own hands rather than at those of the Romans. In World War II, Japanese kamikaze pilots acted with the knowledge that direct, tangible, strategic results would stem from their altruistic suicides, if they were properly executed. And in Hitler's concentration camps, though there was occasional cooperation by Jews in their own executions, the Nazi executioners had no intention of dying themselves.

Besides pointing to parallels which don't quite fit, the news media have targeted Jim Jones as irrational, a madman who had perverse tendencies from early in his youth. They have labelled the Peoples Temple as a "cult," perhaps in the hope that a label will suffice when an explanation is unavailable. And they have quite correctly plumbed the key issue of how Jones and his staff were able to bring the mass murder/suicide to completion, drawing largely on the explanations of psychiatrists who have prompted the concept of "brainwashing" as the answer.

But Jones was crazy like a fox. Though he may have been "possessed" or "crazed," both the organizational effectiveness of the Peoples Temple for more than 15 years, and the actual carrying out of the mass murder/suicide show that Jones and his immediate staff knew what they were doing.

Moreover, the Peoples Temple only became a "cult" when the media discovered the mass/suicide. As an Indiana women whose teenager died at Jonestown commented, "I can't understand why they call the Peoples Temple a cult. To the people, it was their church. . . ." It is questionable whether the term "cult" has any sociological utility. As Harold Fallding has observed, it is a value-laden term most often used by members of one religion to describe a heretical or competing religion, of which they disapprove. Of course, even if the use of the term "cult" in the press has been sloppy and inappropriate, some comparisons, for example to the Unification Church, the Krishna Society, and the Children of God, have been quite apt. But these comparisons have triggered a sort of guilt by association: in this view, Jonestown is a not so aberrant case among numerous exotic and weird religious "cults." The only thing stopping some people from "cleaning up" the "cult" situation is the constitutional guarantee of freedom of religion.

Finally, "brainwashing" is an important but incomplete basis for understanding the mass murder/suicide. There can be no way to determine how many people at Jonestown freely chose to drink the cyanide-laced Flav-r-ade distributed after Jonestown received word of the murders of U.S. Congressman Leo Ryan and four other visitors at the airstrip. Clearly over 200 children and an undetermined number of adults were murdered. Thought control and blind obedience to authority ("brainwashing") surely account for some additional number of suicides. But the obvious cannot be ignored: a substantial number of people—"brainwashed" or not—committed suicide. Insofar as "brainwashing" occurs in other social organizations besides the Peoples Temple, it can only be a necessary and not a sufficient cause of the mass murder/suicide. The coercive persuasion involved in a totalistic construction of reality may explain in part *how* large numbers of people came to accept the course proposed by their leader, but it leaves unanswered the question of *why* the true believers among the inhabitants of Jonestown came to consider "revolutionary suicide" a plausible course of action.

In all the instant analysis of Jones' perversity, the threats posed by "cults" and the victimization of people by "brainwashing," there has been little attempt to account for Jonestown sociologically, and as a religious phenomenon. The various facets of Jonestown remain as incongruous pieces of seemingly separate puzzles; we need a close examination of the case itself to try to comprehend it. In the following discussion based on ideal type analysis and *verstehende* sociology, I will suggest that the Peoples Temple Agricultural Project at Jonestown was an apocalyptic sect. Most apocalyptic sects gravitate toward one of three ideal typical possibilities: (1) preapocalyptic Adventism, (2) preapocalyptic war, or (3) postapocalyptic other-worldly grace. Insofar as the Adventist group takes on a communal form, it comes to approximate the postapocalyptic tableau of other-worldly grace. Jonestown was caught on the saddle of the apocalypse: it had its origins in the vaguely apocalyptic revivalist evangelism of the Peoples Temple in the United States, but the Guyanese communal settlement itself was an attempt to transcend the apocalypse by establishing a "heaven-on-earth." For various reasons, this attempt was frustrated. The Peoples Temple at Jonestown was drawn back into a preapocalyptic war with the forces of the established order. "Revolutionary suicide" then came to be seen as a way of surmounting the frustration, of moving beyond the apocalypse, to "heaven," albeit not "on earth."

In order to explore this account, let us first consider the origins of Jonestown and the ways in which it subsequently came to approximate the ideal typical other-worldly sect. Then we can consider certain tensions of the Jonestown group with respect to its other-worldly existence, so as to understand why similar groups did not (and are not likely to) encounter the same fate as Jonestown.

"A PROPHET CALLS THE SHOTS"

An other-worldly sect, as I have described it in *The Ways Out*, is a utopian communal group which subscribes to a set of beliefs based on an apocalyptic interpretation of current history. The world of society-at-large is seen as totally evil, and in its last days; at the end of history as we know it, it is to be replaced by a community of the elect—those who live according to the revelation of God's will. The convert who embraces such a sect must, perforce, abandon any previous understanding of life's meaning and embrace the new worldview, which itself is capable of subsuming and explaining the individual's previous life, the actions of opponents to the sect, and the demands which are placed on the convert by the leadership of the sect. The other-worldly sect typically establishes its existence on the "other" side of the apocalypse by withdrawing from "this" world into a timeless heaven-on-earth. In this millennial kingdom, those closest to God come to rule. Though democratic consensuality or the collegiality of elders may come into play, more typically, a preeminent prophet or messiah, legitimated by charisma or tradition, calls the shots in a theocratic organization of God's chosen people.

The Peoples Temple had its roots in amorphous revivalistic evangelical religion, but in the transition to the Jonestown Agricultural Mission, it came to resemble an other-worldly sect. The Temple grew out of the interracial congregation Jim Jones had founded in Indiana in 1953. By 1964, the Peoples Temple Full Gospel Church was federated with the Disciples of Christ. Later, in 1966, Jones moved with 100 of his most devout followers to Redwood Valley, California. From there they expanded in the 1970s to San Francisco and Los Angeles—more promising places for liberal, interracial evangelism than rural Redwood Valley. In these years before the move to Guyana, Jones engaged himself largely in the manifold craft of revivalism. Jones learned from others he observed—Father Divine in Philadelphia and David Martinus de Miranda in Brazil, and Jones himself became a purveyor of faked miracles and faith healings. By the California years, the Peoples Temple was prospering financially from its somewhat shady "tent meeting" style activities, and from a variety of other petty and grand money-making schemes; it was also gaining political clout

through the deployment of its members for the benefit of various politicians and causes.

"APOCALYPSE NOW"

Reverend Jones himself seems to have shared the pessimism of the Adventist sects about reforming social institutions in this world (for him, the capitalist world of the United States). True, he supported various progressive causes, but he did not put much stake in their success. Jones' prophecy was far more radical than those of contemporary Adventist groups: he focused on imminent apocalyptic disaster rather than on Christ's millennial salvation, and his eschatology therefore had to resolve a choice between preapocalyptic struggle with "the beast" or collective flight to establish a postapocalyptic kingdom of the elect. Up until the end, the Peoples Temple was directed toward the latter possibility. Even in the Indiana years, Jones had embraced an apocalyptic view. The move from Indiana to California was in part justified by Jones' claim that Redwood Valley would survive nuclear holocaust. In the California years, the apocalyptic vision shifted to Central Intelligence Agency persecution and Nazi-like extermination of blacks. In California too, the Peoples Temple gradually became communalistic in certain respects; it established a community of goods, pooled resources of elderly followers to provide communal housing for them, and drew on state funds to act as foster parents by establishing group homes for displaced youth. In its apocalyptic and communal aspects, the Peoples Temple more and more came to exist as an ark of survival. Jonestown, the Agricultural Project in Guyana, was built beginning in 1974 by an advance crew that by early 1977 still amounted to less than 60 people, most of them under 30 years old. The mass exodus of the Peoples Temple to Jonestown really began in

1977, when the Peoples Temple was coming under increasing scrutiny in California.

In the move to Guyana, the Peoples Temple began to concertedly exhibit many dynamics of other-worldly sects, though it differed in ways which were central to its fate. Until the end, Jonestown was similar in striking ways to contemporary sects like the Children of God and the Krishna Society (ISKCON, Inc.). Indeed, the Temple bears a more than casual (and somewhat uncomfortable) resemblance to the various Protestant sects which emigrated to the wilderness of North America beginning in the seventeenth century. The Puritans, Moravians, Rappites, Shakers, Lutherans, and many others like them sought to escape religious persecution in Europe in order to set up theocracies where they could live out their own visions of the earthly millennial community. So it was with Jonestown. In this light, neither disciplinary practices, the daily round of life, nor the community of goods at Jonestown seem so unusual.

"THE JUNGLE IS ONLY A FEW YARDS AWAY"

The disciplinary practices of the Peoples Temple—as bizarre and grotesque as they may sound, are not uncommon aspects of other-worldly sects: these practices have been played up in the press in an attempt to demonstrate the perverse nature of the group, so as to "explain" the terrible climax to their life. But as Erving Goffman has shown in *Asylums*, sexual intimidation and general psychological terror occur in all kinds of total institutions, including mental hospitals, prisons, armies, and even nunneries. Indeed, Congressman Leo Ryan, just prior to his fateful visit to Jonestown, accepted the need for social control: ". . . you can't put 1,200 people in the middle of a jungle without some damn tight

discipline." Practices at Jonestown may well seem restrained in comparison to practices of, say, seventeenth-century American Puritans who, among other things, were willing to execute "witches" on the testimony of respected churchgoers or even children. Meg Greenfield observed in *Newsweek* in reflecting on Jonestown, "the jungle is only a few yards away." It seems important to recall that some revered origins of the United States lie in a remarkably similar "jungle."

Communal groups of all types, not just other-worldly sects, face problems of social control and commitment. Rosabeth Kanter has convincingly shown that successful communal groups in the nineteenth-century U.S. often drew on mechanisms of mutual criticism, mortification, modification of conventional dyadic sexual mores, and other devices in order to decrease the individual's ties to the outside or personal relationships within the group, and increase the individual's commitment to the collectivity as a whole. . . .

What is unusual is the direction which coercive persuasion or "brainwashing" took. Jones worked to instill devotion in unusual ways—ways which fostered the acceptability of "revolutionary suicide" among his followers. During "white nights" of emergency mobilization, he conducted rituals of proclaimed mass suicide, giving "poison" to all members, saying they would die within the hour. According to one defector, Deborah Blakey, Jones "explained that the poison was not real and we had just been through a loyalty test. He warned us that the time was not far off when it would be necessary for us to die by our own hands." This event initially left Blakey "indifferent" to whether she "lived or died." A true believer in the Peoples Temple was more emphatic: disappointed by the string of false collective suicides, in a note to Jones he hoped for "the real thing" so that they could all pass beyond the suffering of this world. Some people yielded to Jim Jones only because their will to resist was beaten down; others, including many "seniors"—the elderly members of the Peoples Temple—felt they owed everything to Jim Jones, and provided him with a strong core of unequivocal support. Jones allowed open dissension at "town meetings" apparently because, with the support of the "seniors," he knew he could prevail. Thus, no matter what they wanted personally, people learned to leave their fates in the hands of Jim Jones, and accept what he demanded. The specific uses of coercive persuasion at Jonestown help explain how (but not why) the mass murder/suicide was implemented. But it is the special use, not the general nature of "brainwashing" which distinguishes Jonestown from most other-worldly sects.

MEAT EATERS AND BEAN EATERS

Aside from "brainwashing," a second major kind of accusation about Jonestown, put forward most forcefully by Deborah Blakey, concerns the work discipline and diet there. Blakey swore in an affidavit that the work load was excessive and the food served to the average residents of Jonestown, inadequate. She abhorred the contradiction between the conditions she reported and the privileged diet of Reverend Jones and his inner circle. Moreover, because she had dealt with the group's finances, she knew that money could have been directed to providing a more adequate diet.

Blakey's moral sensibilities notwithstanding, the disparity between the diet of the elite and of the average Jonestowner should come as no surprise: it parallels Erving Goffman's description of widespread hierarchies of privilege in total institutions. Her concern about the average diet is more the point. But here, other accounts differ from Blakey's report. Maria Katsaris, a consort of Reverent Jones, wrote her father a letter extolling the virtues of the Agricultural Project's "cutlass" beans used

as a meat substitute. And Paula Adams, who survived the Jonestown holocaust because she resided at the Peoples Temple house in Georgetown, expressed ambivalence about the Jonestown community in an interview after the mass murder/suicide. But she also remarked, "My daughter ate very well. She got eggs and milk everyday. How many black children in the ghetto eat that well?" The accounts of surviving members of Reverend Jones' personal staff and inner circle, like Katsaris and Adams, are suspect, of course, in exactly the opposite way as those of people like the "Concerned Relatives." But the inside accounts are corroborated by at least one outsider, *Washington Post* reporter Charles Krause. On his arrival at Jonestown in the company of U.S. Congressman Leo Ryan, Krause noted, "contrary to what the Concerned Relatives had told us, nobody seemed to be starving. Indeed, everyone seemed quite healthy." . . .

The "seniors" who provided social security checks, gardened, and produced handicraft articles for sale in Georgetown in lieu of heavy physical labor, as well as the fate of agricultural productivity—these both reinforce the assessment that Jim Jones' vision of the Peoples Temple approximates the "other-worldly sect" as an ideal type. In such sects, as a rule, proponents seek to survive *not* on the basis of productive labor (as in more "worldly" utopian" communal groups), but on the basis of patronage, petty financial schemes, and the building of a "community of goods" through proselytism. This was just the case with Jonestown: the community of goods which Jones built up is valued at more than $12 million. As a basis for satisfying collective wants, any agricultural production at Jonestown would have paled in comparison to this amassed wealth.

But even if the agricultural project itself became a charade, it is no easy task to create a plausible charade in the midst of relatively infertile soil reclaimed from dense jungle; this would have required the long hours of work which Peoples Temple defectors described. Such a charade could serve as yet another effective means of social control. In the first place, it gave a purposeful role to those who envisioned Jonestown as an experimental socialist agrarian community. Beyond this, it monopolized the waking hours of most of the populace in exhausting work, and gave them only a minimal (though probably adequate) diet on which to do it. It is easy to imagine that many city people, or those with bourgeois sensibilities in general, would not find this their cup of tea in any case. But the demanding daily regimen, however abhorrent to the uninitiated, is widespread in other-worldly sects. Various programs of fasting and work asceticism have long been regarded as signs of piety and routes to religious enlightenment or ecstacy. In the contemporary American Krishna groups, an alternation of nonsugar and high-sugar phases of the diet seems to create an almost addictive attachment to the food which is communally dispersed. And we need to look no later in history than to Saint Benedict's order to find a situation in which the personal time of participants is eliminated for all practical purposes, with procedures of mortification for offenders laid out by Saint Benedict in his *Rule*. The concerns of Blakey and others about diet, work, and discipline may have some basis, but they have probably been exaggerated, and in any case, they do not distinguish Jonestown from other-worldly sects in general.

COMMUNITY OF GOODS

One final public concern with the Peoples Temple deserves mention because it so closely parallels previous sectarian practice: the Reverend Jim Jones is accused of swindling people out of their livelihoods and life circumstances by tricking them into signing over their money and possessions to the Peoples Temple or its

inner circle of members. Of course, Jones considered this a "community of goods" and correctly pointed to a long tradition of such want satisfaction among other-worldly sects; in an interview just prior to the mass murder/suicide, Jones cited Jesus' call to hold all things in common. There are good grounds to think that Reverend Jones carried this philosophy into the realm of a con game. Still, it should be noted that in the suicidal end, Jones did not benefit from all the wealth the way a good number of other self-declared prophets and messiahs have done.

As with its disciplinary practices and its round of daily life, the community of goods in the Peoples Temple at Jonestown emphasizes its similarities to other-worldly sects—both the contemporary ones labelled "cults" by their detractors, and historical examples which are often revered in retrospect by contemporary religious culture. The elaboration of these affinities is in no way intended to suggest that we can or should vindicate the duplicity, the bizarre sexual and psychological intimidation, and the hardships of daily life at Jonestown. But it must be recognized that the Jonestown settlement was a good deal less unusual than some of us might like to think: the things which detractors find abhorrent in the life of the Peoples Temple at Jonestown prior to the final "white night" of murder and suicide are the core nature of other-worldly sects; it should come as no surprise that practices like those in Jonestown are widespread, both in historical and contemporary other-worldy sects. Granted that the character of such sects—the theocratic basis of authority, the devices of mortification and social control, and the demanding regimen of everyday life—predispose people in such groups to respond to the whims of their leaders, whatever fanatic and zealous directions they may take. But given the widespread occurrence of other-worldly sects, the other-worldly features of Jonestown are in themselves insufficient to explain the bizarre fate of its participants. If we are to understand the unique turn of events at Jonestown, we must look to certain distinctive features of the Peoples Temple—things which make it unusual among other-worldly sects, and we must try to comprehend the subjective meanings of these features for various of Jonestown's participants.

RACE AND IDEOLOGY

If the Peoples Temple was distinctive among other-worldly sects, it is for two reasons: first, the group was far and away more thoroughly racially integrated than any other such group today. Second, the Peoples Temple was distinctively proto-communist in ideology. Both of these conditions, together with certain personal fears of Jim Jones (mixed perhaps with organic disorders and assorted drugs), converged in the active mind of the reverend to give a special twist to the apocalyptic quest of his flock. Let us consider these matters in turn.

In the Peoples Temple, Jim Jones had consistently sought to transcend racism in peace rather than in struggle. The origins of this approach, like most of Jones' early life, are by now shrouded in myth. But it is clear that Jones was committed to racial harmony in his Indiana ministry. In the 1950s, his formation of an interracial congregation met with much resistance in Indianapolis, and this persecution was one impetus for the exodus to California. There is room for debate on how far Jones' operation actually went toward racial equality, or to what degree it simply perpetuated racism, albeit in a racially harmonious microcosm. But the Peoples Temple fostered greater racial equality and harmony than that of the society-at-large, and in this respect, it has few parallels in present-day communal groups, much less mainstream religious congregations. The significance of this cannot easily be assayed, but one view of it is captured in a letter from a 20-year-old Jonestown girl: she wrote to her mother in Evansville, Indiana that she could "walk down the street now without the fear of having little old white ladies call me nigger."

Coupled with the commitment to racial integration, and again in contrast with most other-worldly sects, the Peoples Temple moved strongly toward ideological communism. Most other-worldly sects practice religiously inspired communism—the "clerical" or "Christian" socialism which Marx and Engels railed against. But few, if any, to date have flirted with the likes of Marx, Lenin, and Stalin. By contrast, it has become clear that, whatever the contradictions other socialists point to between Jones' messianism and socialism, the Reverend Jim Jones and his staff considered themselves socialists. In his column "Perspectives from Guyana," Jim Jones maintained, "neither my colleagues nor I are any longer caught up in the opiate of religion . . . ." Though the practice of the group prior to the mass murder/suicide was not based on any doctrinaire Marxism, at least some of the recruits to the group were young radical intellectuals, and one of the groups' members, Richard Tropp, gave evening classes on radical political theory. In short, radical socialist currents were unmistakably present in the group.

PREACHING ATHEISM

It is perhaps more questionable whether the Peoples Temple was religious in any conventional sense of the term. Of course, all utopian communal groups are religious in that they draw together true believers who seek to live out a heretical or heterodox interpretation of the meaningfulness of social existence. In this sense, the Peoples Temple was a religious group, just as Frederick Engels once observed that socialist sects of the nineteenth century paralleled the character of primitive Christian and Reformation sects. Clearly, Jim Jones was more self-consciously religious than the socialist sects were. Though he "preached atheism," and did not believe in a God that answers prayer, he did embrace reincarnation, and a surviving resident of Jonestown remembers him saying, "Our religion is this: your highest service to God is service to your fellow man." On the other hand, it seems that the outward manifestations of conventional religious activity—revivals, sermons, faith healings—were, at least in Jim Jones' view, calculated devices to draw people into an organization which was something quite different. It is a telling point in this regard that Jones ceased the practice of faith healings and cut off other religious activities once he moved to Jonestown. Jones' wife Marceline once noted that Jim Jones considered himself a Marxist who "used religion to try to get some people out of the opiate of religion." In a remarkable off-the-cuff interview with Richard and Harriet Tropp—the two Jonestown residents who were writing a book about the Peoples Temple—Jones reflected on the early years of his ministry, claiming, "what a hell of a battle that (integration) was—I thought 'I'll never make a revolution, I can't even get those fuckers to integrate, much less get them to any communist philosophy.'" In the same interview, Jones intimated that he had been a member of the U.S. Communist party in the early 1950s. Of course, with Jones' Nixonesque concern for his place in history, it is possible that his hindsight, even in talking with sympathetic biographers, was not the same as his original motives. In the interview with the Tropps, Jones hinted that the entire development of the Peoples Temple down to the Jonestown Agricultural Project derived from his communist beliefs. This interview and Marceline Jones' comment give strong evidence of an early communist orientation in Jones. Wherever this orientation originated, the move to Jonestown was in part predicated on it. The socialist government of Guyana was generally committed to supporting socialists seeking refuge from capitalist societies, and they apparently thought Jones' flexible brand of Marxism fit well within the country's political matrix. By 1973, when negotiations with Guyana about an agricultural project were initiated, Jones and his aides were professing identification with the world-historical communist movement. . . .

In the struggle against evil, Jones and his true believers took on the character of what I have termed a "warring sect"—fighting a decisive Manichean struggle with the forces of evil. Such a struggle seems almost inevitable when political rather than religious themes of apocalypse are stressed, and it is clear that Jones and his staff at times acted within this militant frame of reference. For example, they maintained armed guards around the settlement, held "white night" emergency drills, and even staged mock CIA attacks on Jonestown. By doing so, they undermined the plausibility of an other-worldly existence. The struggle of a warring sect takes place in historical time, where one action builds on another, where decisive outcomes of previous events shape future possibilities. The contradiction between this earthly struggle and the heaven-on-earth Jones would have liked to proclaim (for example, in "Perspectives from Guyana") gave Jonestown many of its strange juxtapositions—of heaven and hell, of suffering and bliss, of love and coercion. Perhaps even Jones himself, for all his megalomaniacal ability to transcend the contradictions which others saw in him (and labelled him an "oppportunist" for), could not endure the struggle for his own immortality. If he were indeed a messianic incarnation of God, as he sometimes claimed, presumably Jones could have either won the struggle of the warring sect against its evil persecutors or delivered his people to the bliss of another world.

In effect, Jones had brought his flock to the point of straddling the two sides of the apocalypse. Had he established his colony beyond the unsympathetic purview of defectors, Concerned Relatives, investigative reporters, and governmental agencies, the other-worldly tableau perhaps could have been sustained with less-repressive methods of social control. As it was, Jones and the colony experienced the three interconnected limitations of group totalism which Robert Jay Lifton described with respect to the Chinese Communist revolution: (1) diminishing conversions, (2) inner antagonism (that is, of disillusioned participants) to the suffocation of individuality, and (3) increasing penetration of the "idea-tight milieu control" by outside forces. As Lifton noted, revolutionaries are engaged in a quest for immortality. Other-worldly sectarians in a way short-circuit this quest by the fiat of *asserting* their immortality—positing the timeless heavenly plateau which exists *beyond* history as the basis of their everyday life. But under the persistent eyes of external critics, and because Jones himself exploited such "persecution" to increase his social control, he could not sustain the illusion of other-worldly immortality.

On the other hand, the Peoples Temple could not achieve the sort of political victory which would have been the goal of a warring sect. Since revolutionary war involves a struggle with an established political order in unfolding historical time, revolutionaries can only attain immortality in the wide-scale victory of the revolution over the "forces of reaction." Ironically, as Lifton pointed out, even the initial political and military victory of the revolutionary forces does not end the search for immortality: even in victory, revolution can only be sustained through diffusion of its principles and goals. But as Max Weber observed, in the long run, it seems impossible to maintain the charismatic enthusiasm of revolution; more pragmatic concerns come to the fore, and as the ultimate ends of revolution are faced off against everyday life and its demands, the quest for immortality fades, and the immortality of the revolutionary moment is replaced by the myth of a grand revolutionary past.

The Peoples Temple could not begin to achieve revolutionary immortality in historical time, for it could not even pretend to achieve any victory against its enemies. If it had come to a pitched battle, the Jonestown defenders—like the Symbionese Liberation Army against the Los Angeles Police Department S.W.A.T. (strategic weapons and tactics) Team—would have been wiped out.

But the Peoples Temple could create a kind of "immortality" which is really not a possibility for political revolutionaries. They could abandon apocalyptic hell by the act of mass suicide. This would shut out the opponents of the Temple: they could not be the undoing of what was already undone, and there could be no recriminations against the dead. It could also achieve the other-worldly salvation Jones has promised his more religious followers. Mass suicide united the divergent public threads of meaningful existence at Jonestown—those of political revolution and religious salvation. It was an awesome vehicle for a powerful statement of collective solidarity by the true believers among the people of Jonestown—that they would rather die together than have the life that was created together subjected to gradual decimation and dishonor at the hands of authorities regarded as illegitimate.

Most warring sects reach a grisly end: occasionally, they achieve martyrdom, but if they lack a constituency, their extermination is used by the state as proof of its monopoly on the legitimate use of force. "Revolutionary" suicide is a victory by comparison. The event can be drawn upon for moral didactics, but this cannot erase the stigma that Jonestown implicitly places on the world that its members left behind. Nor can the state punish the dead who are guilty, among other things, of murdering a U.S. congressman, three newsmen, a Concerned Relative, and how ever many Jonestown residents did not willingly commit suicide. Though they paid the total price of death for their ultimate commitment, and though they achieved little except perhaps sustenance of their own collective sense of honor, still those who won this hollow victory cannot have it taken away from them. In the absence of retribution, the state search for living guilty, as well as the widespread outcry against "cults," take on the character of scapegoating. Those most responsible are beyond the reach of the law: unable to escape the hell of their own lives by creating an other-worldly existence on earth, they instead sought their "immortality" in death, and left it to others to ponder the apocalypse which they have unveiled.

DISCUSSION QUESTIONS

1. Describe the circumstances of the People's Temple in terms of Jim Jones' charismatic leadership.
2. How is it possible for Jones, as a Marxist, to be a religious leader?
3. From Hall's description of the People's Temple, how do you think this "cult" is different from more organized churches such as Roman Catholicism or branches of Protestantism?

READING 10-3

Il Paese

Feliks Gross

This is [an account of] an Italian village in a historical period of transition from a traditional to a technological society. It is a study of a society, of values, political views and social change in an Italian village community during the mid-twentieth century.

I was struck by the gentility, humanity and friendliness of the *contadini* and *cittadini of il Paese*. They knew how to love and how to hate; also how to gossip and to laugh; how to work hard under a scorching sun on a stony, steep mountain slope and later relax with a glass of wine, to the music of an old guitar and songs of an evening *suonata*. The people are politically minded, tough, and frequently ambivalent toward men and ideas. They are deeply religious, and their patron saints seem to accompany them when they walk the winding *mulattiere*, the ancient mule roads, and enter their houses to enjoy their company and share their sorrows.

Bonagente is very ancient. It perhaps was founded before the Roman era. The lore and knowledgeable scholars suggest that this was once the land of the Ernici (Hernici) who built the Acropolis of Alatri. The major towns of the province carry names which appear in early Roman history: Anagnia (today, Anagni) and Ferentinum (Ferentino), as well as Aletrium (Alatri) once belonged to the Hernican Confederation, defeated and conquered by Rome by the end of the fourth century, B.C. The Hernici later became Rome's allies.

The ancient castle-village on top of the mountain overlooks valleys and hills, neighbors with the Abruzzi. This village of scattered *contradas*—neighborhoods all over the valleys—is situated in the heart of once poverty-stricken but beautiful country called, for many generations, Ciociaria, the land of the sandal people. Bonagente may not be representative of all Italy, but it is very much so for the Ciociaria.

Italian villages and towns vary in this creative way which has contributed so much to the diverse and vigorous culture of this nation.

This diversity also harbors one of the secrets of the unusual, perhaps historically unprecedented creativity. Since antiquity, they have moved through their *fioriture*, flowerings of culture, and suffered sudden declines, only to recover and invigorate other nations of the world with their fresh outlook, with originality of thought and art, and with the genius of maintaining continuity, respecting the past and changing at the same time. The Italians are a nation of many nations, an historical result of the cultural fusion of defeated and victors, of allies and pilgrims, of races and nations. The traces of this integration which gives birth to genius are reflected in the speech and faces of the provinces, towns, and villages. This integration can be seen in the creations of man, such as the cathedral of Amalfi, which spans time and space, distant cultures, and nations, with its Roman or Greek columns built into a Gothic-Norman, thirteenth-century cathedral crowned with Moorish, Arab capstones on its towers, entered through a bronze porch brought from Constantinople. The cathedral still reflects a perfect harmony. The Italians did not develop or cherish theories of purity of race nor did they worship isolation. Makers of the Mediterranean culture, they fostered cultural exchange and communication and learned early to respect, not only to tolerate, cultural differences. . . .

Many still admire Garibaldi's values and views—what is popularly called "spirit." In fact, many educated Italians, somewhere between the democratic middle and democratic left are "garibaldini". And among the Communists one can find some pure "antipapalini." They are the radical ghibellini of today. There are not many, to be sure—and the few who exist are ready to make a compromise for political reasons if necessary. In spite of their views, many of the radical Italians, in a moment of personal crisis or great joy, fall back on their Catholicism and Catholic rituals.

DUAL LOYALTY—THE COMPLEX OF CANOSSA

The dual loyalty to Church and State persists today in the values and attitudes of many Italians. Those values and loyalties are often contradictory, and because they cannot easily be reconciled sometimes result in conflict. From the conflict comes a feeling of guilt. In a nation such as Italy, where the past is so often reflected in daily life, this ambivalence is quite common. It is not solely intellectual. In certain instances an Italian is at the same time a Catholic and an opponent of hierarchy. More often he is an Italian and a practicing Catholic, at least in terms of customs and rituals. The Italian looks for solutions in terms of political orientation. For the Catholic parties, primary loyalty is to the Church, but there are also various trends and factions within the Catholic parties.

The religious concept of sin is central to the guilt feelings. Values and norms of conduct are polarized; the positive are "good" and the negative "evil." A Catholic believes the evil deed is connected with extreme repression, pain and punishment (hell.) In the early training of the child, when the extreme negative norm of conduct (the "deadly sin") is associated with intense fear, the threat of hell is a moral sanction and sometimes affects his personality and especially affects the structure of his values. The absolute values of evil and good are associated with fear and release from anxieties. The guilt feeling appears here in association with the early concept of sin. . . .

The Church calls for a person's loyalty above all else, and it has its religious and moral sanctions to enforce this. The state and the nation in certain periods of Italian history also demanded complete and unconditional loyalty. Unlike other Catholic countries, Italy's capital is also the capital of the Church, and the conflict of loyalties is an Italian dilemma.

Philosophy and the conditions of everyday life have somewhat softened the extreme attitudes and humanized the conflicts, but the dilemma is still there. . . .

PATRON SAINTS

Every day is dedicated to a different saint, and important saints' days are celebrated not only in church but also at home. Saints are omnipresent in daily life here. They form the fulcrum of religious belief in Bonagente. They are close to the people. It is the Madonna and his patron saint to whom a Bonagentese refers and relates in an act of individual faith and loyalty. The holy pictures remind him of their presence and protection. . . .

LA FESTA

The great festas and processions have their social as well as religious function and meaning. Sociologically, the festas reintegrate the village community with the Church. But a festa is also an act of homage and respect to a local saint. This dual sociological and religious function is a source of continuity and collective appeal, even if the historical origin of the holy day or festa is forgotten.

During the festa for la Madonna del Soccorso Perpetuo, Professor Franco Cerase from the University of Rome attempted to find out the origin of the celebration.

> I recall that in other villages where there are similar holy days, they stem from some kind of a miracle, which is frequently related to the basic needs of the community, like water, or sometimes is connected with the defense from a danger. In consequence, a religious festa is ingrained in the community life. In this case we face an ignorance of the "origin." [Professor Cerase had asked the local teacher after the procession, and also the local medical doctor, and neither could explain the origin].

It is the ritual, the festa, which integrates this community around the Church and its teachings, for everyone participates in the procession and services. This is a communal festa, but it is also a family one. A child remembers the festa as a pleasant experience, a time of religious solemnity and of general joy when he received some minor gifts—perhaps candies, a bag of figs or a mandarin purchased for him by his godfather or parents. A festa is the sole celebration which combines the religious community, the village community, and the family. And on all such occasions, those three distinct social groupings merge into an integrated, even if only transient, unity. . . .

POLITICS AND RELIGION

Bonagentesi, like most Italians, change political parties easily but not their religion. For the Italian, core values and religion remain constant. The mystery of the Catholic religion, of its deeply rooted rituals, endures; they have changed very little throughout the centuries. Reale, a railroad worker in the United States, became a nationalist after he returned home; after a time he might become a monarchist and later perhaps a Social Democrat, but he remains a Catholic always.

The church hierarchy in Italy forms an extensive and powerful organization, a network which reaches every town and village of the nation. Thus, the hierarchy exercises its influence also in Bonagente through the bishop in the provincial capital, which is also a capital of the diocese, and through the local pastor. In addition to this formal hierarchical structure, every parish has its religious associations and fraternities of laymen. Women are organized in their own local religious organizations. All those activities are guided and controlled by the local pastor, who is the appointed chief religious executive of the entire community. Thus, the words from the pulpit and activities of the voluntary religious organizations reach directly or indirectly every single family. This complex organization in a devout, religious community exercises a powerful influence and the church does not remain neutral on major national issues or on significant local matters. On one hand political parties, but on the other also the church affects the views of the people. True, the latter not in all political matters, nor by direct decisions or advice.

But in an intelligent and subtle way, frequently indirectly the church has also its voice which is listened to and respected. It is listened to also in times of elections.

CATHOLICISM AND CULTURAL CONTINUITY IN BONAGENTE

Catholicism in Bonagente, at least in 1969, is an element of spiritual and psychological stability, of cultural continuity, and of a certain permanence. For how long? The drama of the Bersagliere of Porta Pia is not yet a drama of the *contadini* or the *contradas*. Perhaps the winds from Porta Pia blew here in 1957–58, but they have died down today. What will happen tomorrow?

Loyalties are changing in Bonagente. Admiration for the monarchy, which once commanded the loyalties of the *contadini*, is gone. The *contadino* asks now, "What have they done for us, *i conti, baroni e principi*?" Democracy, the belief in the equality of man (uguaglianza), has made inroads. In Bonagente, where a *carabiniere* was once a part of the landscape, one can hardly notice a uniform; perhaps during a festa, one will see a single *carabiniere* without arms, in a modest green costume. The pomp of the uniform and clothing by which man for centuries emphasized class distinction, is on the wane. Even military distinctions are discreet, as in democratic countries. Pomp remains for unusual festivities. Untouched by

the winds of the time, the Church still displays it, like an ancient relic.

Institutions have a general tendency to reach a *modus vivendi*. In an autocracy, the general pattern of command permeates the apparatus of state, and also in varying degrees, other institutions, such as school, church and family. A monarchy has its impact on other institutions. In Italy the monarchy and a monarchical church were compatible to a certain point. The Italian church hierarchy is a true and very ancient monarchy. Cardinals and bishops are princes, they live in princely residences, enjoy ancient, aristocratic status and personal comfort. This is one of the last feudal enclaves in a modern society. Can such a traditional, institution relate successfully to a welfare state in times of popular pressure for reform?

Should the Church remain unchanged, will the loyalty of the peasant-workers remain as strong as it is now? Should the Church grow very much weaker and the loyalty of the *contadini* decline, then what will remain? There is, at least at present, nothing to replace the powerful and profound sentiment of identification which it provides. This is one of Italy's major problems and it is also a problem of Bonagente. But the Church, although rooted in an ancient tradition, also has the experience of two thousand years of continuity and change. It is the oldest existing organization in the western world. And it has the wisdom and political skill to survive the shocks and changes of the present, and however erratically, to move forward in history.

For, the church, the *ecclesia*, in its social organization alone, is far more than a hierarchy. Monastic life in Italy still attracts a variety of personalities. Ascetism has survived in some orders in the form of daily modesty and relative poverty. Modern ideas have penetrated into others' and new approaches and interpretations are being explored. The monastic orders are still alive, still a part of the cultural landscape. The *frati* are visible everywhere and some of the orders are popular with the *contadini* of the Ciociaria. Neither their way of life nor their economic philosophy conflicts with modern social trends. The strength in times of change of religious forms may come from these orders in a country where religious traditions and needs are alive and real.

DISCUSSION QUESTIONS

1. What are the positive and negative aspects of life in Bonagente?
2. In general, what are the effects of modernization on traditional social life and religious values?
3. Explain Gross's findings in terms of the secularization of contemporary societies.

CHAPTER 11

Issues in Power and Politics

INTRODUCTION

Political sociology dates back to Plato and Aristotle, who were concerned with building more perfect societies and with the political means of achieving consensus. Contemporary sociologists have, to some degree, abandoned ideology in order to conduct empirical research. As any major textbook indicates, sociologists have extensively investigated such topics as: Why do people vote for certain parties in a democracy? Why do democratic processes break down, as they did in Nazi Germany? What causes revolution or counterrevolution? Why do political movements rise and fall? What is the relation between the growth of bureaucracy and the functioning of a democracy? What role does religion play in politics? What directions will the world political order and international relations take?

In an era characterized by nuclear weaponry, a grim division between industrialized and underdeveloped nations, and the rise of Asia, issues in power and politics have taken on even more import than before. To some degree, the gravity of the world political situation has engendered a reexamination of basic

philosophical issues by practicing politicians and civil servants who are responsible for policy decisions. The articles in this chapter provide an insight into the broader area of political sociology.

The first reading in this chapter, Seymour Martin Lipset's essay "The Sociology of Politics" analyzes seminal intellectual contributions to contemporary thought that were made by Max Weber (1864–1936), Robert Michels (1876–1936), Karl Marx (1818–1883), and Alexis de Tocqueville (1805–1859). Lipset, one of America's most distinguished social theorists and political researchers, argues that these four writers established the basic concepts of modern political sociology. His approach is distinctly macrosociological. This selection illustrates the profound influence of cultural and historical factors, as well as social unrest, on the development of political theories.

James Miller, a *Newsweek* editor, dissects the remarkable political spirit of the sixties in the second reading, "A Collective Dream." Writing in 1987, Miller looks back on the impact of a youth rebellion on the civil rights of blacks, on ending the carnage in Vietnam, or the demise of a President, and on development of new theories of "participatory democracy." In spite of frustrated revolutionaries who manufactured bombs and the collapse of "the movement" as a coherent whole, Miller suggests that "the ecstatic freedom" of the sixties left behind a major heritage in the ways it changed lives and institutions. Because Miller's analysis focuses on the lives of individuals who spearheaded the student movement of the 1960s, it is included here as an illustration of the individual level of analysis.

The dramatic political changes that have taken place in the world lately have given rise to much speculation on the fate of world politics. The cross-cultural reading by Daniel Bell offers some outlines of the twenty-first century from his perspective. Some observers see changes in eastern Europe as a victory for Western democracies. For example, Francis Fukuyama, deputy director of planning for the U.S. State Department, argues that Western liberalism, capitalism, and "consumerism" have won an "unabashed victory" throughout the world (Fukuyama, 1989). In a controversial article, Fukuyama foresees an end to major international conflicts and the death of Marxism as a believable doctrine. He contends that the "triumph of the West, of the Western *idea*,

is evident first of all in the total exhaustion of viable systematic alternatives to Western liberalism." Other observers are quick to disagree. Sociologist and U.S. Senator Daniel Patrick Moynihan, for one, has stressed that Fukuyama plays down the immense importance of ethnic conflict and nationalism in the contemporary world. You, the reader, must decide whether the views of Fukuyama (or Gorbachev) are merely "collective dreams" of reality.

Daniel Bell offers a brief summary of issues and forces in international politics that might put this question in perspective. He sees the collapse of communism, the reunification of Europe, the end of "The American Century" and the rise of the Pacific rim as the dominant issues at the close of this century. Bell discusses the reasons he sees for these trends and he speculates about future political axes. He also identifies the two major structural problems that loom on the horizon—aging populations in industrialized nations and the rising tensions between the pulls of a global economy and national politics.

Reference

Fukuyama, Francis. "The End of History?" *The National Interest.* Summer 1989.

The Sociology of Politics

Seymour Martin Lipset

THE SOCIOLOGY OF POLITICS[1]

One of political sociology's prime concerns is an analysis of the social conditions making for democracy. Surprising as it may sound, a stable democracy requires the manifestation of conflict or cleavage so that there will be struggle over ruling positions, challenges to parties in power, and shifts of parties in office; but without consensus—a political system allowing the peaceful "play" of power, the adherence by the "outs" to decisions made by the "ins," and the recognition by the "ins" of the rights of the "outs"—there can be no democracy. The study of the conditions encouraging democracy must therefore focus on the sources of both cleavage and consensus.

Cleavage—where it is legitimate—contributes to the integration of societies and organizations. Trade-unions, for example, help to integrate their members in the larger body politic and give them a basis for loyalty to the system. Marx's focus on unions and workers' parties as expediters of revolutionary tension was incorrect. . . . It is precisely in those countries where workers have been able to form strong unions and obtain representation in politics that the disintegrative forms of political cleavage are least likely to be found. And various studies have suggested that those trade-unions which allow legitimate internal opposition retain more loyalty from their members than do the more dictatorial and seemingly more unified organizations. Consensus on the norms of tolerance which a society or organization accepts has often developed only as a result of basic conflict, and requires the continuation of conflict to sustain it. . . .

THE INTELLECTUAL BACKGROUND

The crises of the Reformation and the industrial revolution which heralded modern society also brought the sociology of politics into being. The breakdown of a traditional society exposed to general view for the first time the difference between society and the state. It also raised the problem: How can a society face continuous conflict among its members and groups and still maintain social cohesion and the legitimacy of state authority?

The cleavage between the absolutist rulers of the seventeenth century and the emergent bourgeoisie made the distinctions between man and citizen, society and state, clear. These distinctions were both a cause and a consequence of the crisis over the legitimacy of the state, which some men were beginning to question and some to deny completely. Bodin, in the seventeenth century, formulated for the first time the principle of the sovereignty of the state over other institutions within the boundaries of the nation in order to justify the primacy of the state, particularly in an age of religious conflict. A number of philosophers—Hobbes, Locke, and Rousseau among them—tried, each in his own way, to solve the basic problem: the need for secular consensus which could substitute for the religious solution of the Middle Ages and bridge the gap between society and state.

The nineteenth-century fathers of political sociology took sides in the argument. Men like Saint-Simon, Proudhon, and Marx were on the side of society: for them it was the fabric which had to be strengthened and reinforced, while the state had to be limited, controlled by society, or abolished. On the other side were Hegel and his followers, Lorenz von Stein and others, who believed that the solution lay in the subordination of society's disparate elements to the sovereignty of the state.

The sociology of politics appears to have outgrown this controversy and solved the basic problem. The solution to the dilemma, like the solution to so many others, seemed to be that the question was asked in the wrong way. The error lay in dealing with state and society as two independent organisms, and asking which was the more important or preferable. Political sociologists now argue that the state is just one of many political institutions, and that political institutions are only one of many clusters of social institutions; that the relationships among these institutions and clusters of institutions is the subject of sociology in general; and that the relationship between political and other institutions is the special province of a sociology of politics. In debating with political scientists about the credentials of political sociology, sociologists have held that the independent study of the state and other political institutions does not make theoretical sense. Talcott Parsons, for example, perhaps the major contemporary sociological theorist, has suggested that the study of politics cannot be "treated in terms of a specifically specialized conceptual scheme . . . precisely for the reason that the political problem of the social system is a focus for the integration of all of its analytically distinguished components, not of a specially differentiated class of these components."[2]

From the standpoint of sociology, the debate between the "supporters" of the state and those of society is closed. But although the subjects of the controversy are no longer referred to as "state" and "society," the underlying dilemma—the proper balance between conflict and consensus—continues. It is the central problem with which this book deals.

Sociologists until fairly recently have been much more involved in studying the conditions producing cleavage than in determining the requisites of political consensus. The implications become clearer if we consider the four great Europeans whose ideas are, more or less, the basis of political sociology: Marx, Tocqueville, Weber, and Michels.

CLASS CONFLICT AND CONSENSUS: MARX AND TOCQUEVILLE

It was after the French Revolution that the problems of conflict versus consensus came into focus. The revolutionaries were naturally primarily concerned with furthering conflict, the conservatives with maintaining social stability. But for many years few men analyzed the conditions under which conflict and consensus were or could be kept in balance.

The most articulate spokesman for viewing conflict as the central interest in the study of politics was Karl Marx, and, as much of the later analysis in this book indicates, he had many fruitful insights into its causes. Alexis de Tocqueville, on the other hand, was the first major exponent of the idea that democracy involves a balance between the forces of conflict and consensus.

To Marx a complex society could be characterized either by constant conflict (even if suppressed) *or* by consensus, but not by a combination of the two. He saw conflict and consensus as alternatives rather than as divergent tendencies that could be balanced. On the one hand, he projected consensus, harmony, and integration into the communist future (and to some degree into the communist past); on the other hand, he saw conflict and absolutism as the great fact of history in the epoch between ancient primitive communism and the coming success of the proletarian revolution.

Marx's conception of the harmonious future society had significant bearing on his sociological outlook. The political system which he projected was not institutionalized democracy, but anarchy. This meant in particular the end of the division of labor, for elimination of the differentiation of roles in the economic spheres of life would, according to Marx, eliminate the major source of social conflict:

> In communist society, where nobody has one exclusive sphere of activity but each can become accomplished in any branch he wishes, society regulates the general production and thus makes it possible for me to do one thing today and another tomorrow, to hunt in the morning, fish in the afternoon, rear cattle in the evening, criticize after dinner, just as I have a mind, without ever becoming hunter, fisherman, shepherd, or critic.[3]

This statement is not simply Marx's daydream about a utopian future. It describes one of the basic conditions of communist society, for communism "is the true solution of the antagonism between man and nature, [and] man and man. . . ."[4] It is the elimination of all social sources of differences, even the distinction between town and country.[5]

Since consensus is impossible in a stratified society dominated by an exploiting class, Marx could not conceive of the sources of solidarity in precommunist society. His primary interest was an analysis of the factors making for the strength of the contending forces. He was, however, never really interested in understanding the psychological mechanisms through which the interests of individuals are disciplined, even for the purpose of increasing class strength. In an interesting passage, written when he was young, Marx did raise the problem in Hegelian terms:

> How does it come about that personal interests continually grow, despite the person, into class interests, into common interests which win an independent existence over against the individual persons, in this independence take on the shape of general interests, enter as such into opposition with the real individuals, and in this

opposition, according to which they are defined as general interests, can be conceived by the consciousness as ideal, even as religious, sacred interests.[6]

But he never tried to answer the question.[7] He was basically unconcerned with society's need to maintain institutions and values which facilitate stability and cohesion. To Marx, social constraints did not fulfill socially necessary functions but rather supported class rule.

Marx's theory has no place for democracy under communism. It has only two mutually exclusive social types: a society of conflict and a society of harmony. The first type, according to Marx, is inherently destructive of human dignity and must be destroyed. The second is freed of the sources of conflict and, therefore, has no need for democratic institutions, such as safeguards against state power, the division of powers, the protections of juridical guarantees, a constitution or "bill or rights."[8] The history of the Russian Revolution has already demonstrated some of the dire consequences of operating with a theory which deals only with nonexistent ideal types—that is to say, with societies of complete harmony and societies of constant conflict.

At first glance, Tocqueville's theory seems to be similar to Marx's, since both men emphasized the solidarity of social units and the necessity for conflict among these units. (For Marx the units were classes; for Tocqueville they were local communities and voluntary organizations.) However, Tocqueville, unlike Marx, deliberately chose to emphasize those aspects of social units which could maintain political cleavage and political consensus at the same time. He did not project his harmonious society into the future and did not separate in time the sources of social integration and the sources of cleavage. The same units—for example, federal and state governments, Congress and the President—which function independently of each other and therefore necessarily in a state of tension, are also dependent on each other and are linked by political parties. Private associations which are sources of restrictions on the government also serve as major channels for involving people in politics. In short, they are the mechanisms for creating and maintaining the consensus necessary for a democratic society.

Tocqueville's concern for a pluralistic political system resulted from his interpretation of the trends of modern society. Industrialization, bureaucratization, and nationalism, which were bringing the lower classes into politics, were also undermining the smaller local centers of authority and concentrating power in the state leviathan. Tocqueville feared that social conflict would disappear because there would be only one center of power—the state—which no other group would be strong enough to oppose.[9] There would be no more political competition because there would be no social bases to sustain it. He also feared that consensus as well would be undermined in the mass society. The atomized individual, left alone without membership in a politically significant social unit, would lack sufficient interest to participate in politics or even simply to accept the regime. Politics would be not only hopeless but meaningless. Apathy undermines consensus, and apathy was the attitude of the masses toward the state which Tocqueville saw as the outcome of an industrial bureaucratic society.

His study of America suggested to him two institutions which might combat the new leviathan: local self-government and voluntary associations. Involvement in such institutions seemed to him a condition for the stability of the democratic system. By disseminating ideas and creating consensus among their members, they become the basis for conflict between one organization and another. And, in the process of doing so, they also limit the central power, create new and autonomous centers of power to compete with it, and help to train potential opposition leaders in political skills.[10]

The approaches of Tocqueville and Marx did not result in contradictory analyses of the functions of various social institutions, although they did make for very different evaluations. Marx's statement that religion is the "opiate of the masses" is a recognition of its integrative function. Tocqueville also recognized the "opiative" quality of religion: "Religion, then, is simply another form of hope."[11] To Marx religion was a source of delusion for the lower strata, a mechanism to adjust them to their lot in life, and to prevent them from recognizing their true class interests. Tocqueville, conversely, saw that the need for religious belief grew in direct proportion to political liberty. The less coercive and dictatorial the political institutions of a society became, the more it needed a system of sacred belief to help restrict the actions of both the rulers and the ruled.

BUREAUCRACY AND DEMOCRACY: WEBER AND MICHELS

If one abiding interest of political sociology—cleavage and consensus—has been linked to the names of Marx and Tocqueville, another—the study of bureaucracy—is identified with the work of Max Weber and Robert Michels. The two problems are, of course, closely related, since bureaucracy is one of the chief means of creating and maintaining consensus and at the same time one of the major sources of the forces disrupting integration.

The difference between Marx and Tocqueville, with their emphasis on consensus and class conflict, and Weber and Michels, with their concern for the fulfillment or betrayal of values through bureaucracy, represents an accommodation of social thought to the subsequent stages of the industrial revolution. Many nineteenth-century social philosophers were worried about the disruptive effects of the industrial revolution on society, and about the possibility of achieving democratic political structures. Like Marx, some believed or hoped that political and social stability were inherently impossible in an urban industrial society characterized by economic competition and concern with profit, and they looked for a new, more stable, more moral system. In contrast, a number of twentieth-century thinkers, of whom Weber and Michels are the most significant, have moved away from the problem of the relationship between the economic system (as defined in terms of ownership and control of the means of production) and other social institutions. For them the problem is no longer the changes needed to modify or destroy the institutions of capitalism, but the social and political conditions of a bureaucratized society. Since few people now believe it feasible to return to small producers' communes, the question becomes: What institutional arrangements are possible *within* bureaucratic society?

Many opponents of Marxism said long ago that socialism would not end many of the evils it attacked. Weber and Michels were among the first, however, to engage in research on the postulate that the problem of modern politics is not capitalism or socialism but the relationship between bureaucracy and democracy. Weber saw bureaucratization as an institutional form inherent in all modern societies.[12] To Michels, oligarchy—government by a small group of persons who co-opt their successors—was a process common to all large organizations. Both men tried to demonstrate that socialist organizations and societies were or would necessarily be as bureaucratic and oligarchic as capitalist ones.

Weber's interest in bureaucracy was not primarily political. His belief that the growth of bureaucratic institutions was a prerequisite for a highly industrial society led him to view bu-

reaucratization as the single most important source of institutional change and hence a threat to existing forces of cohesion. As Parsons has pointed out, "Roughly, for Weber, bureaucracy plays the same part that the class struggle played for Marx and competition for Sombart."[13] However, Weber gave great importance to the integrative aspects of bureaucratization in a democratic society, such as the transfer to the entire society of the bureaucratic standards of equal treatment before the law and before authority, and the use of achievement criteria for selection and promotion.

In analyzing the actual operation of a democratic society, Weber considered control over the execution of the laws the greatest problem faced by politicians who held the confidence of the electorate: "the day-to-day exercise of authority was in the hands of the bureaucracy and even success in the struggle for votes and in parliamentary debate and decision-making would come to naught unless it was translated into effective control over administrative implementation."[14] And he was rather pessimistic about the ultimate effects of growing bureaucratization on democracy and freedom. Like Tocqueville, he feared that the growth of the superstate would eventually lead to the downfall of due process and the rule of law. Socialism meant for him the extension of bureaucratic authority to the entire society, resulting in a "dictatorship of the bureaucrats" rather than of the proletariat. It would be a world "filled with nothing but those little cogs, little men clinging to little jobs and striving towards bigger ones. The great question is therefore not how we can promote and hasten it [a situation of bureaucratic domination] but what can we oppose to this machinery in order to keep a portion of mankind free from this parcelling-out of the soul, from this supreme mastery of the bureaucratic way of life."[15]

Michels, too, was interested in the factors which maintain or undermine democracy. In analyzing political parties and trade-unions, he noted those elements inherent in large-scale organizations which make control by their mass membership technically almost impossible.[16] He pointed to the advantages of control over organizations for the incumbent leaders, to the political incapacity of rank-and-file members, to the causes of their apathy, and to the pressures on leaders to perpetuate themselves in office. And he saw the pattern of oligarchy within bureaucratic socialist parties extended to the society governed by such parties. . . .

The theories of Weber and Michels on bureaucracy and democracy, together with those of Marx and Tocqueville on conflict and consensus, established the basic concerns of modern political sociology. . . .

Notes

[1] A number of bibliographic reports dealing with political sociology and political behavior research may be of interest. A few recent bibliographic reports dealing with politics are: R. Bendix and S. M. Lipset, "Political Sociology—A Trend Report and Bibliography," *Current Sociology*, 6 (1957), pp. 79–169; Joseph R. Gusfield, "The Sociology of Politics," in Joseph B. Gittler, ed., *Review of Sociology* (New York: John Wiley & Sons, 1957), pp. 520–30. Compendia of important research are: Robert E. Lane, *Political Life* (Glencoe: The Free Press, 1959) and Heinz Eulau, Samuel J. Eldersveld, and Morris Janowitz, eds., *Political Behavior* (Glencoe: The Free Press, 1956).

[2] Talcott Parsons, *The Social System* (Glencoe: The Free Press, 1951), pp. 126–27.

[3] Karl Marx, *The German Ideology* (New York: International Publishers, 1939), p. 22.

[4] Quoted from the French edition of *The Holy Family*, in G. Gurvitch, "La Sociologie du jeune Marx," *Cahiers internationaux de sociologie*, 4 (1948), p. 25.

[5] Karl Marx, *op. cit.*, p. 44.

[6] K. Marx, "Ideology—'Saint Max,'" *Gesamtausgabe*, I, 5, p. 226, quoted in *The German Ideology*, p. 203.

[7] The best Marxist discussion of the problem of the development of class cohesion and the transcending of personal interests in favor of class interests may be found in Georg Lukacs, *Geschichte und Klassenbewusstsein* (Berlin: Malik, 1923).

[8] See his attack on the bill of rights of the Second French Republic as a sham in "The Eighteenth Brumaire of Louis Napoleon," in V. Adoratsky, ed., *Selected Works of Karl Marx* (Moscow: Cooperative Publishing Society of Foreign Workers in the USSR, 1935), pp. 328–29.

[9] Alexis de Tocqueville, *Democracy in America*, Vol. 1 (New York: Vintage Books, 1954), pp. 9–11. The drift toward a mass society through the elimination of local groups and intermediate centers of power between the individual and the national state has been analyzed by Robert Nisbet, *The Quest for Community* (New York: Oxford University Press, 1953).

[10] For an elaboration of these ideas see S. M. Lipset, M. Trow, and J. S. Coleman, *Union Democracy* (Glencoe: The Free Press, 1956).

[11] Tocqueville, *op. cit.*, p. 321.

[12] See Max Weber, "Zur Lage der bürgerlichen Demokratie in Russland," *Archiv für Sozialwissenschaft und Sozialpolitik*, 22 (1906), pp. 234–353; "Der Sozialismus," in *Gesammelte Aufsätze zur Soziologie und Sozialpolitik* (Tübingen: Mohr, 1924), pp. 492–518; Carlo Antoni, *From History to Sociology: The Transition in German Historical Thinking*, trans. by Hayden V. White (Detroit: Wayne State University Press, 1959), pp. 145–46.

[13] T. Parsons, *The Structure of Social Action* (New York: McGraw-Hill Book Co., 1937), p. 509. See also C. Wright Mills and Hans Gerth, "Introduction: The Man and His Work," in Max Weber, *Essays in Sociology* (New York: Oxford University Press, 1946), p. 49.

[14] Reinhard Bendix, *Max Weber: An Intellectual Portrait* (New York: Doubleday & Co., Inc., 1960), p. 433.

[15] Quoted in J. P. Mayer, *Max Weber and German Politics* (London: Faber & Faber, 1943), p. 128.

[16] Robert Michels, *Political Parties* (Glencoe: The Free Press, 1949). This book was first published in Germany in 1911 and in the United States in 1915.

DISCUSSION QUESTIONS

1. Compare the views of Marx and de Tocqueville on conflict in society.
2. According to Weber and Michels, can democratic political parties remain democratic?
3. In which respects do you think classical views of politics are inappropriate for contemporary societies?

A Collective Dream

James Miller

By the time the decade reached its end with episodes like the Weatherman rampage in Chicago, "The Sixties" represented not just a span of time but an impetuous, extreme spirit— youthful and reckless, searching and headstrong, foolhardy, romantic, willing to try almost anything. It was a spirit that *The Port Huron Statement* had helped to define. By exploring its vision of participatory democracy, a generation discovered (and eventually became addicted to) what one young radical called "breakaway experiences"—political and cultural moments when boundaries melted away and it seemed as if anything could happen. Such moments did in fact occur. They arose in the thick of passionate debate, during sit-ins, in marches, at violent confrontations—at times when people, discovering discontents and ideas and desires in common, sensed, often for the first time and sometimes in the teeth of danger, that together they could change the world. But the moments quickly passed. In the mounting enthusiasm for "breakaway experiences," the original vision of democracy was all but forgotten. The spirit of ecstatic freedom proved impossible to sustain. The Movement collapsed, leaving behind a congeries of smaller single-issue movements, demanding peace in Vietnam, dignity for blacks, liberation for women, respect for homosexuality, reverence for the balance of nature. Frustrated revolutionists built bombs, turning reveries of freedom into cruel, ineffectual outbursts of terrorism. And one by one, the political pilgrims who had created "the Sixties" fell back to earth.

For Tom Hayden, the end came in the early Seventies, through a dizzying series of events that left his sense of identity profoundly shaken. Called on the carpet in 1971 by his comrades in "The Red Family," the Berkeley commune he had joined, he was accused of manipulation, power-mongering and "male chauvinism." Humiliated, he packed his few belongings into an old Volkswagen and headed south. He moved into an apartment in Venice, by the Pacific, and changed his name to Emmett Garity, combining his middle name and his mother's maiden name. "I wanted to know what it was like not to be Tom Hayden," he says. Becoming preoccupied with his Irish roots, he flew to Dublin—only to be turned away at the airport as an undesirable alien. "I began to feel that I'd been stripped of my identity by the American assimilation process," he says. "My government wanted to put me in jail; there was a five-year sentence hanging over me. My father hadn't talked to me in ten years. And now the Irish didn't recognize that I was their son. I felt like I had nothing." He returned to California. In an effort to clarify America's national identity, he worked in solitude on a book, *The Love of Possession Is a Disease with Them*, a bitter critique of genocide in American history, from Wounded Knee to My Lai. Several months after he finished it, Rennie Davis, one of his oldest and steadiest friends, appeared on his doorstep. "Rennie told me the most fantastic story I'd ever heard," recalls Hayden. "Some woman had given him a ticket to go to India, to go meet the guru Maharaj-Ji," the adolescent "perfect master." Davis, who badly needed a vacation, had gone "thinking that this was just a great trip, that he was going to relax, and that he wasn't going to buy into this. Then, one day he was washing his clothes in a river. A giant black bird descended on him. He had a religious experience. He became convinced that the guru Maharaj-Ji was the son of God. He sat on my lawn telling me this. I thought I was in the presence of a character from *Invasion of the Body Snatchers*. It was one of the most shattering experiences of my life."

Slowly, Hayden backed away from the fantasies of apocalypse. Recovering his political nerve, he returned to public life. He helped start the Indochina Peace Campaign, an effort to lobby Congress and keep pressure on the Nixon administration to cut off American aid to the South Vietnamese. "In a strange way, I had to learn it from Vietnamese propaganda," he says, "but the American people were fundamentally good. They had a good Declaration of Independence, a bill of rights, they weren't evil—and I was one of them. I had to throw off all the ideology and guilt and self-hate and hostility that was burdening me and get back to my roots in the simplest sense." "The hope," he wrote in March, 1972, "should be that each act, . . . each organized protest, will have the effect of water dropping on stone, inevitably wearing the stone away. . . . No single drop will smash that stone. But in time, the weak become strong and the strong weak; the water continues and the stone is no more." In the fall of 1972, a federal appeals court, commenting that "the demeanor of the judge and prosecutors would require reversal if other errors did not," overturned Hayden's conviction in the Chicago conspiracy trial. By then, there was no Movement left to lead.

For Paul Booth, the decade had reached its symbolic end earlier, at the last SDS convention in Chicago in 1969. "Despite everything," he says, "SDS was still the main institution of the New Left." He attended one of the convention sessions, and watched silently as different factions spouted crude Marxist slogans from the podium, in an unwitting parody of a Communist Party plenum. It had been only three years since he had given up on his efforts to convince SDS of the need for structure and discipline.

After leaving Cleveland in 1967, Sharon Jeffrey had slowly drifted away from radical politics—she was alienated by the growing violence of the Movement. But her odyssey reached its true end only in 1973, when a two-week vacation in California turned into a three-month stay at the Esalen Institute in Big Sur. "It *uprooted* me entirely," she says. "It was the first time in my life that I had been in a situation where I had nothing to say." Her parents, who had supported her political activism, were distressed; old friends from Ann Arbor were bemused. "When I visited Dick and Mickey Flacks," recalls Jeffrey, "they said, 'Esalen? We know somebody who died there: committed suicide.'" Jeffrey, however, was undeterred. Studying different techniques of "self-actualization," she became convinced that authenticity was not simply a matter of creating the right kind of social structure.

For Dick Flacks, by contrast, the Sixties have in a way never really ended. In his intellectual work, he remains preoccupied with understanding an era that nearly cost him his life: in 1969, shortly after the *Chicago Tribune* had named him as a radical troublemaker, an unknown assailant burst into his office at the University of Chicago, beat him up and left him for dead. Fortunate to have survived, Flacks suffered a partially severed hand and multiple skull fractures. He had just finished serving as a staff consultant for the "Skolnik Report" to the President's Commission on the Causes and Prevention of Violence.

For what purpose, finally, had so many people made such sacrifices? What, in the end, had their search for a "democracy of individual participation" produced? These are hard questions to answer, in part because the sense of what democracy ideally meant underwent such a dizzying series of metamorphoses in the minds of young radicals during the Sixties, connoting at different times everything from registering black voters in the South, to rule-by-consensus in small communes, to street fighting in chaotic demonstrations. Convincing answers would require a more detailed study of the New Left as a whole, and of parallel trends in American society in the Sixties. But this much seems clear: the Movement that the young radicals had worked so hard to build fell apart in the wake of the killings at Kent State University in the spring of 1970. The war that they had tried to stop went on for several more years, although the United States withdrew its troops from Vietnam in 1973, in part in an effort to restore domestic tranquillity. Preoccupied with protesting the war and fatally handicapped by their inability to agree on what institutions (if any) were appropriate in a participatory democracy, they obviously did not succeed in reinventing "the neighborly community."

For all its failings, the New Left briefly affected the whole tone of political life in America, raising fundamental questions about the nature and limits of democracy in a modern industrial society. As the political scientist Samuel Huntington has pointed out in one of the most sharply critical evaluations of the era, "the 1960s witnessed a dramatic renewal of the democratic spirit in America"—a renewal that, in its sweep and intensity, Huntington ranks beside several other watershed periods in the development of American democracy: the revolution of 1776; the presidency of Andrew Jackson; the era of Progressive reforms. "The essence of the democratic surge of the 1960s," writes Huntington, "was a general challenge to existing systems of authority, public and private. In one form or another, this challenge manifested itself in the family, the university, business, public and private associations, politics, the governmental bureaucracy, and the military services. People no longer felt the same compulsion to obey those whom they had previously considered superior to themselves in age, rank, status, expertise, character, or talents. Within most organizations,

discipline eased and differences in status became blurred."

Writing in 1975, Huntington deplored these developments. American society, he felt, had come to suffer from "an excess of democracy." "The Welfare Shift" caused by the "internal democratic surge" on the part of "marginal social groups" in the Sixties had, he argued, badly strained the fiscal resources of the state, weakened its military power and created popular skepticism about such legitimate aspects of government as "hierarchy, coercion, discipline, secrecy, and deception." Huntington recommended a more balanced and tough-minded approach to government and a renewed respect for traditional institutions. Five years later, under the presidency of Ronald Reagan, such views became a commonplace of intellectual discourse and public policy. It is as if the strategy of the young radicals, as they had explained it in *America and the New Era*, had in some measure succeeded, only to create new—and unintended—opportunities for a kind of counterrevolution. Under the administration of President Reagan, it was neoconservatives who reaped the benefits of what the New Left, before its sudden collapse, had helped to sow—the delegitimation of liberal corporatism and the ideal of the welfare state.

Tom Hayden, speaking at the outset of Reagan's second term, doubted the long-term effectiveness of this counterrevolution. "Reagan," he said, "has tried through administrative methods to dismantle as much as possible of what the Sixties created. But he's accepted more of it than he recognizes, just as Eisenhower accepted more of the New Deal than was recognized at the time. I think democracy is the genie that's out of the bottle."

The spirit of Port Huron certainly left a lasting mark on those who experienced it firsthand. Al Haber, for one, remains an ardent activist. A cabinetmaker who lives in Berkeley, California, Haber in 1986 was involved with other Bay Area radicals in organizing everything from antiapartheid rallies to peace protests. He also has stayed in touch with most of his old friends from SDS. One of them is Bob Ross, an associate professor at Clark University in Worcester, Massachusetts. Ross in 1986 had recently finished a book, written in collaboration with Kent Trachte, presenting a new model of international capitalism. In addition, Ross was working as a policy analyst for Democrat Gerard D'Amico, an outspoken liberal—or "urban populist," in Ross's words—who was a Massachusetts state senator before becoming a candidate for lieutenant governor in 1986. Steve Max too maintains an active interest in stimulating what he calls a "resurgent populism." A full-time organizer who still lives in New York City, Max for years has been the curriculum director for the Midwest Academy, the training arm of Citizen Action, a national federation of grass-roots citizen organizations. As Max proudly points out, both Citizen Action and the Midwest Academy maintain cordial relations with the Democratic Socialists of America, which in 1986 was led by Michael Harrington—Max's old nemesis, now a firm friend and political ally. "Few things in my life have given me as much satisfaction as winning back the friendship of a good number of those whom I so wrongly attacked in 1962," says Harrington, who has played a major role in regrouping the socialist movement during the lean years of the late Seventies and Eighties. "I think I have proved that you can go home again."

"In the beginning, we were about discovering self-worth," says Sharon Jeffrey. "We were about breaking out of traditions, about breaking out of structures. I get angry with my friends who say that we accomplished very little. It's as if they won't take responsibility for what we did do—and for what we failed to do." Although she maintains an active interest in the psychological and spiritual traditions she discovered at Esalen, Jeffrey, like Max, remains an organizer. "My understanding of

what's entailed in participation," she says, "is so much greater now than it was then." In 1986, she was working in the San Francisco Bay Area as a free-lance consultant to small businesses and public agencies, as well as offering seminars on becoming a "visionary leader"—"somebody who creates desirable pictures of the future, inspires others to participate, mobilizes resources and designs organizational structures to produce the intended result." In her effort to fuse democratic ideals with therapeutic techniques of self-actualization—and in her continuing interest in the culture of modern feminism—Jeffrey embodies two important strands in the legacy of the New Left.

Paul Booth too has remained committed after his own lights to the project of democratic renewal defined at Port Huron. After nearly two decades of experience as a union organizer, he looks back on the politics of his youth with wry skepticism. "The direct-action model for political influence was about speaking truth to power," he says. "It was a theory that you could be influential because your thoughts were good and right, and you made the necessary sacrifices to get a podium to speak. We didn't start out with very good ideas about strategy, in part because the pacifist—direct-action people who influenced us weren't into strategy, they were into *witness*. And then there were the academic influences, and they weren't into strategy because they weren't into activity. Unfortunately, the Old Left *didn't* influence us: we viewed them as intellectually bankrupt. But they were the only people in the society who knew what mass action was, who knew what a mass organization was or how you worked in one." Still, as Booth hastens to add, "the willingness of Americans to take an activist approach to their society, which spread so dramatically in the Sixties, hasn't subsided very much; it is a major difference between our world in 1986 and the world we criticized in 1962." In 1986, Booth was working for

AFSCME, the American Federation of State, County and Municipal Employees, one of the most combative trade unions within the AFL-CIO.

Dick Flacks at the same time was putting the finishing touches on his second book, *Making History vs. Making Life*, a study of the tension between the vision of the left and mainstream American political beliefs. (His first book, *Youth and Social Change*, published in 1971, was a study of the student rebellions of the Sixties.) A professor of sociology at the University of California at Santa Barbara, Flacks, like Bob Ross and a host of other radicals from the Sixties, has found a home of sorts in the academy. "The New Left," he says, "helped open the political arena so that alternatives to capitalism can now be imagined, sought, debated and organized." One alternative—participatory democracy—still strikes Flacks as key. "I think we were on to something," he says. "I think people do have a basic impulse to have a voice in decisions about them. There certainly has been a tendency in this country for people to try to exercise that voice in more and more different areas. I mean, what is the environmental movement? It's an attempt to participate in decisions about land use and technology." The New Left fell apart at the end of the Sixties, he thinks, for a number of reasons: its inability to extend its middle-class base, its delusions of "revolutionary apocalypse," its failure to develop a durable organizational structure. "SDS," he says, "was trying to be too many things at once: a student group, an anti-war organization, and the party of the New Left. There's no way it could be all those things."

Like most of his old friends, Flacks has remained active in politics—he drafted the substance of "Make the Future Ours," the campaign platform that Tom Hayden used in his unsuccessful effort to defeat incumbent U.S. Senator John Tunney in the California Democratic primary election of 1976. But Flacks has grown increasingly skeptical about left-wing efforts to win power. "Basically," he says, "I think that the left in America is a cultural rather than a political force, defining 'political' as power-oriented. The claim that you are power-oriented is typically a sign that you are turning into a sect or that you are betraying the values that you once held. If that's true, the question for the left is what forms of organization are appropriate to being an intellectual, educative, moral force."

Although Tom Hayden was defeated in his bid to become the Democratic candidate for the Senate in 1976, he drew different lessons than Flacks did from his defeat. Shortly afterward, Hayden established the Campaign for Economic Democracy—in 1986, renamed Campaign California—a network of grass-roots citizen-action groups that has given him an independent base of power in California politics. Though the Campaign has concentrated on mobilizing voters and organizing "citizen lobbyists" to pepper elected officials with letters and phone calls, it also evokes the democratic ideals of the Sixties. "The process of trying to find a consensus rather than going ahead with a slim majority still strikes me as key," says Hayden of the Campaign's professed commitment to participatory democracy. "Simply counting votes doesn't encourage two people to find the best in each other and look for a deeper truth." However, he readily concedes that consensus has its limits. "Our meetings often drive people out because of their length," he says. "And if you want to participate on more than the most immediate, local level, for whatever reasons, something more than grass-roots organizing and neighborhood democracy is needed."

Although its effort to stimulate "participatory democracy" has had rather modest results so far, the Campaign has been successful in fielding candidates for more than fifty local and state offices in California. In the late Seventies, it developed an alliance with Governor Jerry Brown, which led to rent control and new energy-conservation measures, among other reforms that had been sought by its predominantly middle-class membership. At the same time, traditionally socialist goals that were part of the Campaign's original agenda—above all, the redistribution of wealth—have been sharply downplayed, in an apparent effort to broaden the group's appeal. In 1982, Hayden himself returned to the electoral arena. With support from CED members and financial help from the actress Jane Fonda, whom he married in 1973, he was able to win election to the California State Assembly, in a race that cost a staggering $1.7 million. Since then, Hayden has weathered several attempts by conservative opponents to impugn his loyalty and to have him thrown out of office. He has nevertheless succeeded in building a modest reputation as a tactician and iconoclast on the progressive wing of the Democratic Party, where his views—in 1986, he said that he still favored "economic democracy," but also described himself as an "armed dove"—linked him to such pioneering "new look" liberals as California Governor Jerry Brown and Colorado Senator Gary Hart. "I believe that the analysis of *America and the New Era* is still relevant," says Hayden. "Politicians of our generation, starting with Jerry Brown, are trying to understand the new era, which is one of limits—on our economic reach, on our military reach." At the same time, Hayden stresses the need to shore up "a very feeble center" within the Democratic Party—which may be one reason the political views he expresses often seem so ambiguous. "Is it co-optation to work with the corporate liberals?" he asked rhetorically shortly after being reelected to his State Assembly seat in 1984. "Or do you have virtually to define and defend what the corporate liberal agenda is? I think that it's important to defend

a centrist position that would allow a more progressive future to evolve."

Looking back on the Sixties, Hayden admits to "mistakes," but is reluctant to dwell on them. "You don't get to live your life over," he says. In a widely publicized speech delivered at Hofstra University in 1986, however, Hayden did express a number of "regrets"—that he was not more critical "of the cynical motives of the Soviet Union"; that he was "infected with a hostility" that alienated him from his own country; that "I compounded the pain of many Americans who lost sons and loved ones in Vietnam." It is also clear that Hayden has modified some of his basic convictions. "I used to reject Reinhold Niebuhr's philosophy that there was a flaw in the human condition, that perfectibility was unattainable," he says. "I now think that there's quite a bit of truth to that, for individuals, for revolutions, for nations." As a result, his old enthusiasm for a politics of "vision" has waned. "Ideology is an intellectual weapon you create to get your own way," he said in one of his more cynical moments.

But at other times, Hayden implies that he would do it all over again: "I don't think there's anything more satisfying politically than to be young in spirit, and to believe that the world is yours to change. And there's nothing better than to set a living example, if you can, by associating yourself with the victims of social injustice." Looking back, he also takes pride in many of the changes that the New Left triggered. "I don't know whether we caused the changes," he says, "or whether the changes were in the making and we just saw them coming. But obviously the system of segregation, which until 1960 was considered impregnable, collapsed. Students, who had never been considered a social force, became a political factor. The Vietnam War was brought to an end, partly because of the role of students. More than one President was thrown into crisis or out of office. And the Movement created an agenda. At the time, it was seen as anathema, as terrible—very unruly. But people have absorbed more of the agenda than they realize."

In the early Seventies, in the immediate aftermath of the collapse of the Movement, Hayden, like other young radicals, would have been incapable of delivering this sanguine verdict with such equanimity. Always more than an effort to win piecemeal reforms, the New Left—in this respect, as American as apple pie—had hoped for a new beginning, a new, more democratic order for the ages. Those who had committed their lives to the Movement experienced its violent, vertiginous crack-up as a personal calamity.

Although with more capable leaders, a more sharply defined theory of democracy, a sturdier sense of humility and skepticism, and a shrewder grasp of political reality, the Movement might have averted its disastrous collapse, the realization of its larger objectives—particularly in the chaotic circumstances of the late Sixties—was bound to be difficult, if not impossible. To search for a "democracy of individual participation," particularly if the goal is to restore the give-and-take of face-to-face relations in the "neighborly community," is to swim against the tide of history. The main drift in modern industrial life has been toward expanding scale and complexity, the centralization of power and the growth of hierarchical bureaucracies. Popular revolts against these overwhelming realities have been only sporadically successful, in part because the demand for individual autonomy and active participation in public life must sooner or later run up against the desire for stability, privacy and the material comforts promised by the modern industrial nation-state. Like virtually every other American mass movement for democratic renewal since the Civil War—socialist or populist, progressive or right-wing,

plebeian or middle-class—the New Left flourished in situations of relative moral simplicity and floundered when faced with the almost hopeless difficulties and immense strategic quandaries posed by the economic, social and political forces it wished to counteract. Its experiments in democracy perhaps most usefully demonstrated the incompatibility of rule-by-consensus with accountable, responsible government in a large organization—or even in a small group of people with divergent interests and a limited patience for endless meetings. But even this modest lesson proved difficult for many activists to assimilate. At the height of its influence in the late Sixties, the New Left had some of the virtues of a utopian and romantic revolt—passion, moral intensity, a shared joy in the sheer process of change—but also some of its most glaring vices: intransigence, impatience, an irrational and ultimately self-destructive sense of self-righteousness.

Nearly two decades later, the promise of democratic renewal leads a chastened existence in the thinking of intellectuals, the stubborn efforts of organizers and the disillusioned compromises of a handful of politicians. As the careers of Al Haber, Bob Ross, Steve Max, Sharon Jeffrey, Paul Booth, Richard Flacks and Tom Hayden all illustrate, many veterans of the Movement have continued to apply the precepts of Port Huron in the light of their mature experience, evincing modesty in their immediate goals, pragmatism in their tactics and a hard-earned realism in their evaluation of the prospects for social change. Numerous books, most of them aimed at an academic audience, have appeared in the wake of the New Left on the theory and practical problems of "economic democracy," "unitary democracy," "strong democracy," "empowered democracy." Left-wing legislators with power, cornered into fighting for the preservation of social reforms initiated in the Sixties, have desperately struggled to restore some luster to the liberal ideals of fairness, social justice and the welfare state. Some radical economists, no longer assuming America to be a society of potentially boundless prosperity, have argued that industrial productivity could be increased by the introduction of new forms of worker participation. At the same time, citizen-action groups and organizations like the Midwest Academy and Hayden's Campaign California have quietly continued to refine tactics honed in the Sixties, teaching techniques of grass-roots insurgency and small-scale self-govern-ment to disgruntled tenants, peace activists, environmentalists, feminists, small business-men, labor unionists. In bits and pieces and fragments that do not always fit together, the political vision of the New Left, and some of its original spirit, has survived, helping to keep open the possibilities for change.

"The American left is now powerless, dis-tracted, and confused," wrote C. Wright Mills in 1948, in a passage that rings true for the plight of American radicals throughout most of this century: "The program of the right can be presented as an implementation of what is now happening in and to the world, but no left program can honestly be asserted in such a compelling way. What is happening is destruc-tive of the values which the left would implant into modern society." That is why Mills, while clinging to the possibilities for democratic re-newal, conceded that "the ideas available on the left today are less a program than a collec-tive dream."

But for a time in the Sixties, for a generation that first found its political voice in *The Port Huron Statement*, the ideas of the left did not seem like a dream at all. In city streets and on college campuses, in thousands of small ex-periments in participatory democracy, my gen-eration tested for itself the limits of political freedom. Those limits proved sobering. In ret-rospect, our experience feels, almost literally, fantastic. Yet the spirit of Port Huron was real. A mass Movement to change America briefly flourished, touching countless lives and in-stitutions. And for anyone who joined in the search for a democracy of individual participa-tion—and certainly for anyone who remem-bers the happiness and holds to the hopes that the quest itself aroused—the sense of what politics can mean will never be quite the same again.

DISCUSSION QUESTIONS

1. Why was there an American "youth re-bellion" in the 1960s?
2. Miller discusses life-style changes among "rebels" of the 1960s. What institutional changes were wrought as a result of this period of rebellion?
3. What legacy will the 1980s leave for future Americans?

As We Go into the Nineties

Daniel Bell

As we enter the 1990s, the outline of the twenty-first century, with respect to the configuration of issues and forces, already seems clear. We can identify four:

1. The collapse of communism
2. The reunification of Europe
3. The end of "The American Century"
4. The rise of the Pacific rim

Beyond these are other, more inchoate and indistinct forms, whose outlines are not as clear, though this does not mean they are of lesser importance. In some instances, as the twenty-first century unfolds, they may, indeed, prove to be the most disruptive. These issues are the following: the problems of poverty in the Third World (exempting East Asia now from that configuration), the fratricidal rivalries in the Middle East, and the rising ethnic and nationalist rivalries in many different parts of the world, as the older issues of class and imperialism recede.

How can we understand these new forces in some systematic way? Is there some framework that allows us to order them in some explanatory fashion? More than fifteen years ago, in seeking to provide a coherent picture of the world at that time, I set forth four "axes" along which the alignments might be understood. These were, schematically put:

1. *East vs. West.* This rivalry was principally between the United States and the Soviet Union and the forces grouped behind them in the NATO and Warsaw Pact alliances.

The rivalries here were political and ideological, with the constant threat of military confrontation. This was the cold war.

2. *West vs. West.* This rivalry was principally between the United States on the one side and, on the other, Japan (putting her in this context within the West) and Germany. The rivalry here was economic.

3. *North vs. South.* Here were the OECD, or industrialized countries, versus the newly industrializing societies, the "Group of 77" within the United Nations, who were demanding a redistribution of world manufacturing capacity. The issues here were economic and ideological.

4. *East vs. East.* This rivalry was the Soviet Union against China, where the competitions were ideological and political with a thin threat of military conflict.

It was, and still is to some extent, a useful frame of reference.[1] The intention was to see which axis was salient, at what time. When this was first presented it was obvious that the East vs. West axis dominated all others. The West vs. West was only a dim cloud, and some writers thought it improbable. North vs. South was very strident. And East vs. East was very strained.

Today it is likely that the cold war is finished. West vs. West, in particular the rivalry between Japan and the United States on economic issues, has become highly salient. But there is also now the rise of the various East Asian "tigers," such as Korea, Taiwan, and Thailand, to add to that competition. North vs. South at the moment is somewhat muted. And East vs. East is, for the while, quiet.

That analytical framework may still have some limited use. But there is now a new intellectual challenge to provide a different, coherent framework to encompass the new alignments as they are emerging. Whether this can be done remains to be seen. But before we can do so, there is much detailed analysis to explore.

EVENTS OF THE PAST DECADE

For almost fifty years after the Russian Revolution of October 1917, it seemed as if Marxism would sweep the world. Nothing so blazing as revolutionary Marxism had been seen, as some historians compared it, since the rise of Islam more than a millennium before. Here was a new faith system that had inspired working-class movements in Europe, sparked a revolution in China, become a model for intellectuals in Latin America and new elites in Africa, and so on. And now it has collapsed, in less than a decade, like a house of cards. It would take many volumes to analyze the reasons why. For the moment, let us deal with two related groups, one the Soviet Union, the other Eastern Europe.

There are, I would say, three factors, now cojoined, that account for the crisis in the Soviet Union:

1. *The failure of the economic model.* Soviet planning was rigid and inflexible and, beyond an initial start, it could not manage a large and complex economy. In an early essay Lenin said that planning was a simple affair. If there were 200 million Russians and each one needed two pairs of shoes, one produced 400 million pairs. There is, paradoxically enough, a *surplus* of shoes today in Soviet warehouses. But nobody wants them. They are too ungainly, shoddily constructed, and of poor quality. What the Soviet Union had, in the early five-year plans, was not "planning" but a *mobilized* economy based on *physical* targets. But there was no price mechanism to judge whether resources were being used efficiently. In fact, for dogmatic reasons, Soviet planners did not use the mechanism of interest rates (since interest was usury and exploitative) as a measure of the relative efficiency of capital. At the same time there were heavy subsidies on such items as bread and housing rents. But no one knew the true costs; more resources were devoted to bread, and because it was relatively cheap, the product was misused. Lacking a true cost and accounting system (and using a double-ruble system to divert resources for military use) Soviet planners had no measures of the deficits they were running and the inflation that was hidden. Today the economy is in shambles.

2. *The failure of ideology.* Ideologies are worldviews (weltanschauungen) that mobilize their believers for a "cause" and provide a set of justifications on the basis of the "higher" goals. But the "revolutionary" goals of egalitarianism and of a classless society, and the ideas of socialized property, gave way, increasingly, to a "new class" of privileged, the *nomenklatura*; and the regime, particularly under Stalin, resorted to terror as a means of forcing compliance with its demands. The failure of ideology, when there are no other justifications, means a loss of legitimacy and the beliefs of the rulers and the ruled in their "right" to rule. For a period of time, the "patriotic war" against Nazi Germany provided a social cement. But the resumptions of terror and privilege eroded those commitments.

3. *The crumbling of "empire."* What was little known is that the Soviet Union was the *only* nation that came out of World War II with extensive territorial gains, at a time when almost all other imperial and colonial powers were surrendering their control over lands in Asia and Africa. Since 1940, starting with the Nazi-Soviet pact, the Soviet Union annexed Finnish Karelia, the Republics of Estonia, Latvia, and Lithuania, the Koenigsberg district of East Prussia, the eastern provinces of Poland, the sub-Carpathian district of Ruthenia from Czechoslovakia, Bukovina and Bessarabia from Romania, and the Sakhalin and Kurile islands from Japan.

In addition, badly drawn boundary lines within the older Soviet Union have left large pockets of ethnic rivalries, such as the Caucasus territory of Nagorno-Karabakh, which is heavily Armenian and Christian within the republic of Azerbaijan, which is Muslim. On the Black Sea, the small area of Abkazia wishes to secede from neighboring Georgia, while Georgia itself wants autonomy within the Soviet Union. And, more to the point, the most successful economic region of the Soviet Union, the Baltic republics of Estonia, Latvia, and Lithuania, are now demanding, if not freedom, then almost complete autonomy.

Almost twenty years ago, the Soviet dissident and writer Andrei Amalrik (who spent many years in the gulag and was killed tragically in an automobile accident) wrote a tract, *Will Russia Survive Until 1984?* It seemed odd and fanciful at the time. Now Russian politicians such as Boris Yeltsin (himself somewhat of an opportunist and demagogue) ask seriously whether the Soviet Union can last until 1994.

No one can provide an answer. It has been the genius of Mikhail Gorbachev that he has recognized all the problems and sought to provide reforms through *perestroika*. He has, at the same time, recognized that the party cannot rule alone and has begun to create political structures with a degree of independent power. Even if Gorbachev succeeds, it is evident that the Soviet Union cannot remain an effective superpower and that the military and ideological threat it once posed, especially to Europe, has now largely receded. If he fails? There was once an old Soviet joke that said that when Stalin died he left two envelopes. One said, "In case of trouble, open this." Trouble arose and the envelope was opened. In it was a message that said, "Blame me." The other envelope said, "In the event of more trouble, open this." More trouble came and the second envelope was opened. It said, "Do as I did."

That is now impossible. Deng Xiaoping could still have the authority among the veterans of the Chinese revolution to give an order to shoot. Gorbachev cannot. His destruction of Stalin and the legitimacy of that "revolution" makes it impossible. Yet if Gorbachev fails, the greater likelihood is that of a right-wing, nationalist reaction, using the symbols of old Russia and seeking to mobilize the Soviet people on the basis of traditional symbols. But such a move would alienate the intelligentsia and the modernizing elements in the Soviet Union, and even if a right-wing force came into power, its economic base would still be weak.

About Eastern Europe: the news has been electrifying. Within a few months the communist regimes of Poland, Hungary, Bulgaria, East Germany, and Czechoslovakia have crumbled. The reasons are fairly clear. In almost no country had there been strong, indigenous communist forces. The regimes were *imposed* almost entirely from the outside and reinforced by Soviet troops. More than that, in the first decade after World War II, Stalin purged the leadership of most of the native Communist parties in a sweeping set of trials. In Czechoslovakia, there was the Slansky trial. In Hungary, the Rajk trial. In Bulgaria, the Petkov trial, and so on. In 1956, an independent Hungarian regime led by *communists*, such as the premier Imre Nagy, was suppressed by Soviet tanks, and Nagy was executed and buried in an unmarked grave until the poignant moment last summer when his remains were given a public, ceremonial funeral. In 1968, the Prague Spring, the effort of Alexander Dubcek to put forth the new idea of "socialism with a human face," was smashed by Soviet tanks.

Once *glasnost* and political reforms had begun in the Soviet Union, how could the older regimes hold out against change? They could not. In Hungary, the Communist party has dissolved itself, and only *5 percent* of its former members have joined a new Communist party. In Poland, the Communist party, though nominally guaranteed a majority of seats in the lower house, could not even gain enough votes to ratify that agreement, and a non-Communist is the prime minister of Poland, received with amiable greeting by Gorbachev himself.

From all that political rubble, one thing is clear. Whatever the formal adherence to the Warsaw Pact may mean, Eastern Europe is no longer a reliable force for the Soviet Union. Nor is East Germany. So far as Europe is concerned, the cold war is over and new configurations are about to begin.

WHAT OF THE FUTURE?

Let me turn, now, to the new configurations:

1. *The reunification of Europe.* The framework with which we have all been operating has been the idea of the European Economic Community, the twelve-nation "commonwealth" scheduled to come to fruition in 1992 and that, already, has taken distinct shape.

Now three new factors have to be taken into account. One is the possible—and probable—reunification of the two Germanys into a single entity of eighty million persons, which will make it the most powerful economic unit of Europe. The second is the inclusion of Eastern Europe in a European trade bloc. And the third is the relation of the Soviet Union to Europe.

Historically, the Soviet Union has feared the emergence of a new, unified Germany. Historically, the two have been antagonists, even though a different set of dreamers, the German geopolitical strategists, such as Karl Haushofer, envisioned a new Eurasia, spanning the heartland of Europe and Asia and becoming the center of world power.

Although history has always been important in understanding the destinies of nations, it can also be misleading. England and France

were enemies at the beginning of the nineteenth century and allies at the beginning of the twentieth. History has been important when *land* and *territory* were the goals of national states. Today these are less important than *technology*. The overriding need of the Soviet Union is for technology. And here, Germany, even a reunified Germany, becomes a useful partner. Already a deal had been struck ten years ago for a new pipeline that would bring natural gas from Siberia to Germany.

Until now, the Soviet Union has depended upon Czechoslovakia and East Germany for much of its manufactured products and for steel and machine tools. But both economies have become increasingly outmoded and incapable of supplying the Soviet Union with the new modern technology that it needs, particularly computer technology and telecommunications. West Germany becomes the "natural" source of this technology.

In effect, the logic of the economic interdependencies and needs, the huge timber, oil and gas, and mineral resources of the Soviet Union and the technology of Western Europe, dovetail into a pattern. Eastern Europe itself, if its industries are modernized, can provide the light industry (shoes and textiles) as well as the older manufactured products, including steel, as well as cheaper labor, for Western Europe.

These closer bonds would mean the destruction of the older NATO and Warsaw Pact configurations. England and France are bound to be wary of such moves—unless the security issue is completely resolved. Here the key is the Soviet Union. If Gorbachev takes convincing steps to reduce the Soviet military posture, then the economic logic can begin to operate. From his point of view, there is a contradictory problem. Reducing the military sector means freeing resources for the consumer sector. At the same time, the military has been an important power base for him—especially as the Communist party itself has become weakened. The military remains the major organized base of power within the Soviet Union. How Gorbachev manages these tasks will be decisive for his own retention of power, as well as for the necessary economic moves he has to make vis-à-vis Europe.

2. *The end of "The American Century."* The American Century was a phrase fashioned by Henry Luce—proprietor of *Time, Life* and *Fortune,* the most influential periodicals of their day—during World War II to herald a new and majestic role for the United States. Like all such ambitions, it had a mixture of idealism and economic self-interest. Luce, the son of Christian missionaries, whose early years had been spent in China, saw the American Century as fulfilling the Christian obligations of the United States to be "the good Samaritan," the helper of the poor and the needy. At its best, this was expressed politically by the Marshall Plan, which led to the economic reconstruction of Europe, and by substantial aid to Japan. As the cold war developed, the United States—which had begun to disarm after World War II—became the military protector of both Europe and Japan against the Soviet Union. Its economic role became intertwined with its military role, creating what President Eisenhower called "the military-industrial complex." While military expenditure has never been the *necessary* basis for America's continuing economic growth, it has been an important one.

Four elements conjoin to reduce the centrality and power of the United States as the twenty-first century emerges: One is the reduction of the great power confrontations, and therefore the decisive political role of the United States as the "leader" of the world. Second is the rise of Japanese economic power, especially in the central high-technology sectors. Third are the low investment and productivity features of the American economy, which begin to sap its strength. And fourth comes the increasing difficulty of coping with domestic social problems such as crime and drugs, the aging infrastructures, and the declining quality of life in the central cities.

However, there has been a tendency, of late, to assume that the United States is almost "finished" as a major power. That would be misleading. The United States still maintains the general lead in technological *innovation*—if not always in development. (VCRs, facsimile, multivalve engines, and dozens of other products were created in the United States, though quickly developed elsewhere, as in Japan.) The United States maintains the foremost graduate education and scientific power of any country in the world. Japan, for example, has had strong universities but almost no graduate schools of any consequence. England and Europe, also with strong universities, do not have the scientific manpower and talent or the graduate schools of the United States. The United States remains the largest market for many export-led countries such as Korea to sell their products to. And in military and space technology, including aircraft, the United States maintains sizable leads.

The new free-trade pact with Canada and the growing integration of Mexican manufacture with U.S. industries provide a possible foundation for economic expansion. Nor should one ignore the political stability that provides a haven for jittery capital in other countries.

3. *The Pacific Rim.* What is evident here is the centrality of Japan as the major economic and financial power in the Pacific. And events in the last year have given Japan two "reprieves." One is the reduction of the Soviet military threat. In recent years, Japan has been under pressure from the United States to spend more on defense and military security. It has been yielding to that pressure. Now there is much less of that need. And the Soviet Union has even been making noises about returning some of the islands near Hokkaido to Japan, as a gesture of goodwill, and is seeking financial credits and technology from Japan. With the reduction of the Soviet threat, Japan is in a better position to resist American political and economic pressure on trade.

The second "reprieve" is China. The events in Tiananmen Square have, for the while, cut China off from the rest of the world. Historically, the United States, going back to the American Secretary of State John Hay, has always been *pro-China* in its policy. One of the "cards" open to the United States in recent years vis-à-vis Japan has been to develop political and economic relations with China. This was, particularly, the grand design of Henry Kissinger. And it would have led to a counterweight of U.S.- China relations to Japan and to the Soviet Union.

But as for Japan—and other East Asian countries—what is also evident is the recreation, with the cooperation of Australia and the Asian countries, of the old East Asia Co-Prosperity scheme. The industrialization of East Asia is proceeding rapidly, with Japan supplying most of the capital. A recent report of the Japan Center for Economic Research (October 1989) points out that in fiscal 1985 Japanese investments in manufacturing in Asian firms totaled $460 million. This increased 80 percent in the next year, and doubled the following one, and rose again by 40 percent in fiscal 1988. The total investments by electrical-machinery makers rose more than five times from 1985 to 1986 and have been increasing by 80 percent a year since then.

Given these emerging frameworks, what can one say, in summary, regarding the configuration of the twenty-first century as it is now appearing? I leave aside, as I said previously, the difficult questions of the increasing poverty and the widening gaps between the developed and the developing worlds, particularly in Africa. I leave aside the intractable passions of the Middle East. And there is the difficult question of the stability of the Soviet Union, given its economic and empire tensions.

North and South remain as an axis of division, which will likely become increasingly threatening after the first quarter of the twenty-first century. East vs. East is, for the while, in stasis, and much will depend upon the successors of Deng and even Gorbachev (who is likely to last, if he can surmount his difficulties, to the end of the century). And as for East vs. West, the United States and the Soviet Union may enter a period of détente.

The major new alignments that are coming into place are the regional blocs. These are economic-political units of a larger viability for nations to manage their problems of economic transition. A united Europe, a Continental North American economy, and a Japan-dominated Pacific region become the great landmass units for economic, and even political, power. It would mean, if economic logic also followed, the replacement of the dollar by a managed basket of the ECU (European currency unit), the dollar, and the yen as the mechanisms of exchange and trade balance.

One major caution: one cannot "predict" events and their outcomes, crucial as they may be; for example, the direction of China with the passing of Deng Xiaoping and his generation. One can only, as I have tried to do here, define "structural arrangements" to provide a grid for analysis.

If one looks ahead to the end of the century, there are two "structural" problems that loom quite large. One is demographic. In the United States, Western Europe, and Japan, we have aging populations. In most of the Third World countries—Algeria and Mexico are the prime examples—the youth cohort under seventeen years of age is between 40 and 50 percent of the population. Logically there are only three things one can do: take their people, buy their goods, or give them capital. All three pose difficulties that are not easy to resolve.

The second "structural" problem is the rising tension between the contrary pulls of the global economy and the national polities. Capital can flow easily; people cannot. No nation today controls its own currency and capital flows to take advantage of differential interest rates, cheaper labor, and better investment opportunities. But people, unless destitute or highly skilled, cannot move as readily; nor are many countries prepared to take them. More than that, as jobs slip away, the question before a regime is does it protect capital or people. In the United States we have seen this in the textile and automobile business and now in semiconductors. A large economy such as ours may be able to manage such transitions, but many cannot, and the fragmentation of many polities around the world because of economic difficulties, multiplied subsequently by ethnic clashes, increases the chances for what is called in the jargon of the Pentagon planner, "low-intensity conflicts."

These are the undertows and riptides in the world society. The interplay of demography, global economy, and national polity becomes the framework for trying to understand the problems of the twenty-first century.

Note

[1] Much of this scheme was elaborated in my essay "The Future World Disorder" (1977), reprinted in my book *The Winding Passage* (Basic Books, 1980).

DISCUSSION QUESTIONS

1. Briefly describe the four configurations of forces and issues that Bell believes will shape politics in the twenty-first century.
2. According to Bell, what does the future hold for East-West tensions?
3. Based on your knowledge of current events, will pressures for a global economy supersede nationalist interests?

CHAPTER 12

Issues in the Economy

INTRODUCTION

Momentous shifts are taking place in the United States economy which have far-reaching implications for all of society's institutions. The economic troubles that have become a harsh fact of life in the United States undergird many of the readings in this book, most particularly the selections on work, poverty, health, and the environment. The readings in this chapter specifically address contemporary issues in the economy. While the particular form economic changes take varies considerably, signs of fundamental shifts in the economy are unmistakable. The level of unemployment considered "normal" creeps higher every year. The automobile and steel industries, which traditionally symbolized American capitalism, have fallen on hard times. Inadequate government regulation and surveillance of economic activities permit unscrupulous profiteering. The status of the United States as the undisputed leader of world economies has been severely damaged by the success of our world competitors. Perhaps most pivotal of all, the shift from an economy based on the production of goods to a service economy signals deindustrialization and raises the possibility of a dual economy with a sharply segmented labor force and even greater income inequalities between the rich and poor.

The economy is concerned with the production, distribution, and consumption of goods and services for a given population. Although there are a variety of real-world economies, in the simplest terms two basic types of economic systems compete for people's allegiance. *Capitalist economies* rely heavily on free markets and privately held property to ensure that citizens' needs are met. *Socialist economies* rely primarily on state planning and publicaly held property to secure an equitable, or fair, distribution of goods and services in the population. Though this distinction between a capitalist, or "demand," economy and a socialist, or "command," economy seems clear, these economic systems share many features in common. Capitalist economies, like that of the United States, supplement the market with a variety of governmental supports such as grants and welfare benefits. They also regulate wages and many industries in a planned manner. Similarly, in socialist economies like that of the Soviet Union there are provisions for the private ownership of property, profit sharing does occur, and there are wide differences in income between workers and people in managerial and executive positions. Despite their differences, and in part because of their similarities, capitalist and socialist economies today are in a state of crisis. Recent changes in East Germany and other Soviet-bloc countries attest to the problems in command economies. In the United States and other market-driven economies, pressing issues portend change. The three readings in this chapter highlight contemporary issues in the U.S. economy.

The first reading tackles a critical issue in today's economy. George Benston and George Kaufman analyze the 1989 bailout of failed savings-and-loan associations by the federal government. Benston and Kaufman argue that because of peculiar accounting methods, rising interest rates during the period 1979 through 1981, mismanagement of funds by savings-and-loan officials, and a lack of effective government regulation, Congress was forced to authorize spending $155 billion to save the industry. The authors see several lessons in the history of the savings-and-loan debacle, and they offer recommendations on how to avoid similar catastrophes in the future.

We stated earlier that the most dramatic recent change in the U.S. economy may be the shift from an industrial economy to one in which the production of services is the driving force. This shift is influenced by the globalization of the economy and the internationalization of the division of labor. Not everyone views this structural change as sanguine. Generally, there are two different interpretations of current shifts in the U.S. economy. Some see the deep changes wrought by the shift to a service-dominated economy in optimistic terms, believing that more and better job opportunities will upgrade the workforce and improve access to desirable resources. Others take the pessimistic view that these structural shifts will result in a decline of middle-wage jobs, a contraction of the middle class, and the subsequent emergence of a two-tiered society due to growing income inequalities.

In their history of recent shifts in the U.S. occupational structure, Michael Harrington and Mark Levinson take a pessimistic view of the economic future. The evidence they present suggests that the trend toward a service economy has resulted in a decline in the number of middle-wage jobs and the subsequent rehiring of displaced workers in lower-paid, less-skilled positions. They express the fear that these shifts will lead to an entrenched dual economy with an occupational structure characterized by "polarization between highly paid professional and technical workers on the one hand and poorly paid, unorganized, lower-level workers on the other. . . ." Thus, their analysis of economic trends traces macrosociological changes in the U.S. economy down to the more microsociological level of individual job prospects.

The economic crisis in the United States may also be seen in the context of cross-cultural developments. The U.S. economy has failed to keep a competitive edge in an increasingly interdependent world economy. It was Ezra Vogel who, in 1979, first made this clear in his book *Japan as Number One*. From its position at the end of World War II as a devastated, A-bombed, and resourceless country, Japan has emerged into a paramount position in the world economy. In the third reading presented in this chapter, Vogel outlines some of the lessons that Americans should draw from this example.

Understanding the Savings-and-Loan Debacle

George J. Benston
George G. Kaufman

In August 1989 Congress made history when it earmarked about $115 billion to liquidate or to reorganize insolvent savings-and-loan associations (S&Ls). By far the largest single example of government financial assistance to any economic sector, the aid dwarfed the earlier "bailouts" of New York City in 1975 and of Chrysler in 1979 by factors of some fifty and eighty, respectively. How did we come to this pass? What lessons can we draw from our expensive mistake?

S&Ls were established as vehicles for home ownership. People who wanted to borrow funds for this purpose purchased shares in the S&Ls' predecessors, local building and loan societies (B&Ls). As funds accumulated, mortgage loans would be made to members who drew the winning lots or who offered the highest premiums. Savers and borrowers were often the same people. Borrowers pledged their shares to repay their loans, and periodic payments on the shares were required. The B&Ls emphasized borrowing more than saving; withdrawal of funds was subject to notification requirements and penalty fees and could be limited. As economists James Barth and Martin Regalia have written, "[I]t was not until the advent of federal deposit insurance for savings and loan associations in the 1930s that the taking of deposits as such became widespread."

B&Ls invested their assets almost entirely in home mortgages. In the 1920s the average contract length was about eleven years. Because their liabilities could not readily be withdrawn, the durations of the two sides of their balance sheets were probably not greatly mismatched, and the B&Ls ran little risk of being harmed by changes in interest rates. B&Ls' reserves for losses were low; state laws and regulators discouraged their accumulation, preferring that earnings be distributed to members.

Mutual savings banks (MSBs), which now are very similar to S&Ls, provide an interesting contrast. Unlike B&Ls, MSBs were established to serve generally low-income savers rather than potential home owners. MSBs originally provided conservative investment facilities for these groups; they tended to invest in "safe" marketable securities and moved gradually into mortgages. By 1930 they invested 55 percent of their assets in mortgages, 14 percent in government obligations, and 22 percent in other securities. Deposits in MSBs, like those in B&Ls, were not truly short-term investments; savings accounts could be subject to sixty-day notices of withdrawal.

The diversified and relatively conservative asset structure of MSBs, together with the limitations on withdrawals, appears responsible for the MSBs' superior survival during the Great Depression. Only eight of 598 (1.3 percent) MSBs failed; these banks had $28 million in deposits, or 0.3 percent of total MSB deposits. In contrast, of the 11,777 S&Ls operating in 1930, 526 failed (4.5 percent); the failed associations held about $400 million (4.5 percent) of the industry's $8.8 billion total assets. This disparity in performance was due to the S&Ls' investing almost entirely in a single type of asset—home mortgages—concentrated in a small geographic area. S&Ls, though, fared better than commercial banks, whose numbers dropped by 38.5 percent—from 24,970 in 1929 to 15,348 in 1934. The better experience of S&Ls appears to have resulted from the close relationship of shareholders and mortgagors, which provided strong incentives and opportunities for monitoring loans.

In the wake of the crash, the Federal Savings and Loan Insurance Corporation (FSLIC) was established in 1934, one year after the establishment of the Federal Deposit Insurance Corporation (FDIC). By guaranteeing the par value of shares up to $5,000 per shareholder, federal insurance effectively transformed the shares into deposits and shortened their durations. Although this change was not made as a matter of law until 1968, in practice insurance increased the mismatch between the durations of S&Ls' assets and those of their liabilities. It thereby increased the S&Ls' "interest-rate risk"; if one's assets are long-term and one's liabilities are short-term, rises in interest rates can be devastating.

Before 1950 FSLIC insurance was less liberal than FDIC insurance, as savers in S&Ls could be required to wait one to three years for cash repayment of claims. But in 1950 the two forms of federal deposit insurance were made identical, and deposit insurance was increased to $10,000 per account. Insurance coverage was increased to $15,000 in 1966, to $20,000 in 1969, to $40,000 in 1974, and to $100,000 in 1980. This near-blanket coverage virtually eliminated monitoring by depositors.

That the S&L industry's trouble was not apparent until the 1980s seems attributable to relatively high capital ratios and more stable interest rates. The capital cushion held by S&Ls gave owners and (for mutual associations) managers incentives to avoid risks that might result in failure. This cushion was built up over time, in part as a result of favorable tax laws. Until 1951 mutual associations were exempt from income taxation. The 1951 Revenue Act imposed a tax on net income, but only when surplus accounts exceeded 12 percent of liabilities were the excess retentions taxed; this exception gave S&Ls (and MSBs) considerable incentives and opportunities to increase their capital, at least up to the 12-percent level. The Revenue Act of 1962, however, limited these tax-free retentions and related them more closely to allowances for bad debts. For a thrift to qualify for income-tax benefits, it had to hold at least 60 percent of its assets in mortgages or mortgage-backed securities. Thus the tax laws helped thrifts increase their capital and kept them from diversifying out of mortgages.

The capital of S&Ls and MSBs also was supported by restrictions on the entry of competitors, which gave rise to an intangible asset—franchise values. Competition was restrained by the reluctance of the banking agencies to grant new charters, by the prohibition of interstate banking, and by restrictions on intrastate branching. Ceilings on bank-deposit interest rates also reduced competition, first from commercial banks and after 1966 from all depository institutions. These restrictions on competition, coupled with the growth of housing, raised the value of S&L charters and hence the amount of economic capital invested by their owners or managers.

Competition for deposits by nonchartered institutions increased in the 1970s as a result of an inflation-induced rise in nominal interest rates. Regulation Q, which put a ceiling on the interest rates that could be offered to depositors, increased the opportunity cost of keeping deposits in S&Ls and banks. Initially, Regulation Q ceilings benefited depository institutions. But the difference between the ceiling and market rates gave unregulated suppliers of similar types of savings accounts, such as money-market funds, greater incentives to develop and expand. Improvements in computer technology reduced these suppliers' transaction costs, which provided additional incentives for S&L depositors to withdraw their funds. The consequence was not only an outflow of funds from S&Ls but also a reduction in thrifts' charter values, and thus in their economic capital.

The Federal Home Loan Bank Board (FHLBB), however, assessed assets and liabilities in terms of historical cost, which does not require recognition of losses until a market transaction occurs (and sometimes not even then). Though the "economic" capital ratios of S&Ls were declining, their book-value capital ratios did not decline, and so the authorities did not react to the true picture.

RESPONSIBILITY FOR THE 1979-1981 DEBACLE

The problems caused by this accounting method greatly intensified when interest rates increased sharply in the late 1970s and early 1980s. While the thrifts' capital cushion was sufficient to enable them to survive the increase in interest rates in the late 1960s, it was not sufficient for them to survive the increase in the late 1970s. The very sharp increase in interest rates in 1979 to nearly 20 percent on short-term obligations and 15 percent on long-term obligations far exceeded previous increases, at least in modern times. Hence the reduction in the present values of thrifts' assets, which were primarily fixed-interest long-term mortgages, was much greater than it had ever been during previous interest-rate increases. Responsibility for this situation must be shared by three parties.

One is the Federal Reserve, which allowed the money supply to grow during the 1970s at rates that caused double-digit inflation. This inflation was reflected in higher nominal interest rates. Then in 1979 the Fed acted to reduce inflation quickly, causing interest rates to increase sharply and unexpectedly. As a result, holders of long-term fixed-interest-rate obligations, such as mortgages, suffered massive capital losses. Thousands of thrifts became "economically" insolvent—that is, the market value of their assets fell below that of their deposits.

Elected officials—members of Congress and the President—are also responsible. Both Congress and the executive ignored the fact that large unexpected increases in interest rates would cause severe economic damage to institutions offering long-term fixed-interest mortgages funded by short-term liabilities. They

also ignored the fact that this risk would be borne initially by a federally backed deposit-insurance agency. Instead, they led the public to believe that (or were led by the public to act as if) the means chosen to support housing—having specialized financial lenders and long-term fixed-rate mortgages—were not potentially costly. Indeed, Congress denied federally chartered thrifts the authority to make variable-rate mortgages, and it restrained them from diversifying their portfolios away from mortgages and savings deposits.

The third responsible party is the FHLBB, the independent agency that was charged with overseeing S&Ls. The FHLBB failed sufficiently to alert elected officials and the public to the fragility of an industry that funded long-term fixed-interest assets with short-term liabilities.

THE RESPONSE TO THE DEBACLE

By 1982 some two-thirds of the industry was economically insolvent, with aggregate negative net worth of about $100 billion; 85 percent of all thrift institutions were unprofitable in market-value accounting terms. At this time, a number of other forces came into play. Despite a prolonged fall in interest rates that greatly improved the solvency of the industry as a whole, the crisis worsened as many decapitalized institutions were permitted to substitute credit risk for interest-rate risk—in other words, to try to raise money by lending to people who were likely to default. The adoption of effective remedies was delayed until it was too late.

When Congress increased federal deposit insurance from $40,000 to $100,000 per account in 1980, the responsibility for monitoring S&Ls' risk taking was further shifted from depositors to the FSLIC. Deposit insurance not only prevented a depositor run on the insolvent and weak institutions, but also gave the institutions the opportunity to grow or to gamble their way out of their problems by attracting deposits and investing the proceeds in high-risk, high-yielding loans and other ventures.

Investors' monitoring of risks also was reduced by advances in telecommunications and computer technology, which allowed individual institutions to attract large amounts of money quickly from anywhere in the country. Where once deposit growth at individual institutions generally was restricted to funds available from local market areas and therefore depended more on the institution's risk profile, institutions could now expand their assets many-fold regardless of their financial strength.

Further regulatory changes exacerbated the crisis. The Garn-St Germain Act of 1982 and legislation in some states granted S&Ls the authority to make loans and investments other than long-term residential real-estate loans, such as consumer and commercial loans and equity investment in real-estate development. Like the liberalization in 1980 (and the eventual removal in 1986) of the ceilings on deposit rates, the deregulation of thrifts' activities was a response to market forces; it permitted thrifts to diversify more and to reduce their exposure to interest-rate risk. But this change also gave S&Ls the ability to take more credit risk faster than was previously possible.

As the industry's capital declined, the FHLBB also progressively reduced capital requirements in order to avoid having to reorganize deficient associations. In addition, the FHLBB adopted regulatory accounting principles that transformed many S&Ls—insolvent according to an established set of generally accepted accounting principles (GAAP)— into officially solvent institutions. Thus economically insolvent institutions were permitted to continue to operate, with costly consequences both for other associations and for the FSLIC. Indeed, 53 percent of all the S&Ls whose failures were resolved in 1988 had been insolvent under GAAP for three or more

years, and nearly 70 percent had been insolvent that long on a tangible capital basis. Economically insolvent institutions, with nothing to lose, had incentives to take more risks. Many, moreover, were generating insufficient revenues to pay the interest on deposits and to meet daily operating costs. To avoid regulatory insolvency, they offered high interest rates to outbid others for deposit funds. The deposit inflows were then used to pay deposit outflows, interest rates on deposits, and even operating expenses—a true "Ponzi scheme" of borrowing from Peter to pay Paul, made possible by federal deposit insurance. The higher deposit rates forced competing institutions also to pay higher rates in self-defense, increasing their costs and weakening them financially.

The Federal Home Loan Bank system and the FSLIC were not prepared for the increases in S&L risk taking and insolvencies. These agencies were geared to deal with the relatively calm environment of an earlier era. The sudden increases in allowable activities and risk taking found them greatly understaffed, undertrained, and underorganized; thrift supervision was grossly inadequate. Some associations were not examined for three or four years, and violations identified by field examiners frequently were not pursued by their supervisors. In addition, the FHLBB did not expand its examination staff to deal with the increasing scope and complexity of S&L operations, in part because of its own inadequacies and in part because it wanted to cooperate with Reagan administration efforts to restrain the growth of federal employment.

The problem was exacerbated in 1983 by the Little Rock Federal Home Loan Bank's move to Dallas. Only eleven of the forty-eight members of the supervisory staff were willing to make the move. As a result, the annual number of examinations in this district—which was in the heart of the problem area—declined from 261 in 1982–1983 to 183 in 1983–1984 and 173 in

1984–1985 before increasing again to 283 in 1985–1986.

With such inadequate supervision, it is not altogether surprising that massive fraud occurred at some institutions, particularly those purchased with minimal capital by promoters and real-estate developers when the S&Ls were already insolvent. Many of the S&Ls' owners and managers viewed the institutions as their own personal "piggy banks"; among other things, they falsified documentation to justify extending loans to themselves, their families, and their friends in amounts far in excess of the economic values of both the projects being financed and the associated collateral. They also made loans that provided for immediate interest prepayments, which were then reported as earnings to the association and used to pay dividends. A particularly outlandish case is that of the Vernon S&L in Vernon, Texas, which had $2 billion in outstanding loans when regulators finally took it over in 1987. Ninety-six percent of these loans were in default. The other 4 percent, moreover, were mostly deferred-interest loans on which the first interest payment had not yet come due—which means that the borrowers had not yet had the opportunity to default!

These abuses were exacerbated by sharp downturns in the economies of some local areas—particularly those dominated by energy or agriculture, such as Texas, Oklahoma, and Louisiana. These downturns lowered the values of residential and commercial real estate; as a result, mortgage defaults increased and the value of repossessed real estate decreased sharply. Risk-taking S&Ls had been attracted to these areas by economic booms, and they suffered greatly from the downturns.

RESPONSIBILITY FOR THE INEFFECTIVE REACTION

Some analysts blame deregulation for the debacle. The Depository Institutions Deregula-tion and Monetary Control Act of 1980 and the Garn-St Germain Act of 1982 accelerated the decontrol of the deposit interest-rate ceilings, and enabled thrifts and banks to bid—either directly or through brokers—for deposits from investors outside their market area. These laws, like the state legislation permitting thrifts to expand into commercial and consumer loans and to make direct investments, have been criticized as causing the great losses taken by the FSLIC. But the evidence does not support these charges. While some analysts have persuasively argued that the new powers increased the risks taken by institutions with inadequate capital, no evidence shows that they made failure itself significantly more likely. The removal of the Regulation Q ceilings, moreover, was inevitable. Their continuation would have caused investors to continue withdrawing their deposits and would have penalized savers who could not take advantage of such alternative investments as money-market mutual funds.

"Deregulation," we should note, does not mean no regulation at all. It simply means substituting market regulation for government regulation. For market regulation to work, however, market discipline must be permitted to function. One of the major reasons for the size of the S&L crisis is that authorities were reluctant to enforce some forms of market discipline—in particular, insistence on adequate capital reserves and the prompt liquidation or reorganization of economically insolvent S&Ls—that the market could not enforce itself under the deposit-insurance system.

Many groups share responsibility for the large losses that will be borne by U.S. taxpayers. Before the debacle, Congress prohibited S&Ls from offering variable-rate mortgages, which could have mitigated the damage from the 1979–1981 interest-rate increase. After the increase occurred, Congress failed to respond quickly by providing sufficient funds to enable the regulators to close, merge, or reorganize insolvent institutions under new management. In 1987, when the Administration asked for an adequate appropriation of $15 billion to recapitalize the FSLIC, Congress authorized only $11 billion. At the same time, to prevent the closure of S&Ls, it decreed mandatory forbearance for many economically insolvent associations in the Competitive Equality Banking Act of 1987.

As a result, the FSLIC was handicapped in resolving insolvencies and was forced to sell several bankrupt institutions to new investors at terms that sometimes were less advantageous to taxpayers than cash compensation for depreciated assets. These terms included issuing promissory notes on the FSLIC, granting tax breaks at below the cost to the U.S. Treasury, guaranteeing returns on assets, and waiving such regulatory requirements as minimum capital standards. Negotiations for the sales were complex and frequently carried out in secret, with few bidders and no public disclosure. Later announcements of these "deals" frequently gave the appearance of impropriety and caused sufficient public indignation to kill the program and to discredit the FSLIC and the FHLBB, further reducing the regulators' effectiveness.

The Reagan administration also contributed to the debacle. There is reason to believe that the Administration was unwilling to accept the very large increase in the federal deficit that recognition of S&L losses by 1982 would have required. While it was reasonable for the Administration to expect that interest rates would decline below the 1979 peak, it should have been clear by 1985 that much of the massive unbooked capital losses taken by S&Ls was attributable to credit risk and could not be reversed through monetary policy. The responsible position would have been to insist that the FHLBB recognize the S&L insolvencies and the unsolvency of the FSLIC, to request an appropriation from Congress to cover the losses, and to cover or to supervise very closely the insolvent institutions. Instead, the existence of the massive problem was denied until 1989. (In fact, neither political party made the S&L crisis an issue during the 1988 presidential campaign, which helped delay corrective actions.)

The FHLBB is also culpable. The Bank Board officially recognized only a few of the many insolvencies caused by the 1979–1981 interest-rate increase. It forebore from closing economically insolvent S&Ls, instead reducing its capital requirements and using accounting gimmickry. The FHLBB did not restrict practices that its chairman, Ed Gray, considered particularly risky, such as direct investments and brokered deposits; no credible evidence in support of Gray's views, however, was presented or discovered by independent studies. The FHLBB also exhorted S&Ls to make adjustable-rate mortgages the primary means of reducing interest-rate risk. After a costly delay the FHLBB increased its examination staff by transferring supervision responsibility to the Federal Home Loan Banks. But it did not require S&Ls to report capital on the basis of market values; hence it continued regulations that permitted economically insolvent institutions to remain open and to increase their risk exposure and losses. In fact, until restrictions on growth were instituted in the late 1980s, the FHLBB encouraged S&Ls to grow out of their problems by taking on new higher-yielding loans to offset their older lower-yielding fixed-rate mortgages.

Further blame can be attributed to the S&L industry itself. The industry made large political contributions to members of Congress in return for the postponement of legislative action that would have increased deposit-insurance premiums and other payments, reduced thrifts' independence, and resulted in the removal of managers and owners of insolvent or nearly insolvent institutions. Because the dollar amounts at stake were so massive, contributions were huge even by Washington standards. Many congressmen, who may not have been fully aware of either the technical roots of the problem or its severe consequences, delayed potentially corrective legislative and regulatory actions. Such congressional behavior was an important factor in the 1989 resignations of both Speaker of the House Jim Wright and Democratic House Whip Tony Coelho; it also tarnished the reputations of the "Keating Five" and other members of Congress.

What is more, some S&L owners and managers were simply thieves. When thrifts trying to raise new capital switched from being mutual organizations to being owned by stockholders, the regulators often did not carefully consider the backgrounds and characters of the new owners. As a result, more "high rollers" gained control of S&Ls. In particular, many real-estate developers used thrift associations to fund their own activities.

Even honest managers and owners of economically insolvent S&Ls increased their risk taking. Realizing that the amounts paid on their deposit liabilities would exceed the returns that they could ordinarily expect on their assets, they adopted high-return, high-risk strategies. If the ventures succeeded, the institutions kept all the gains. If the ventures failed, as was more likely, the losses were shifted to the FSLIC. Risk-seeking institutions did not need to use their new powers to increase their risks; many used the old powers to take more interest-rate or credit risk. But some of the new powers (particularly the power to make equity-participation commercial mortgage loans with large up-front fees and delayed interest payments) did give these institutions the ability to increase their income, and hence their capital, as calculated under regulatory accounting principles—which in turn let them take big risks faster.

The home-owning public must also accept some blame. Its demand for housing subsidies encouraged elected officials to support the ex-

pansion of specialized and inherently unstable depository-mortgage lenders, including S&Ls. The important role of S&Ls in financing housing created a close relationship—both direct and (through Congress) indirect—between the savings-and-loan industry and the Federal Home Loan Bank system. As a result, the regulators frequently bent over backward to avoid taking corrective actions that would have penalized or embarrassed the industry. The system frequently confused its role as regulator with that of cheerleader for the industry. This made it easier for both Congress and the FHLBB to conceal the true size of the crisis, its true causes, and the effective remedies.

THE CURE

Recognition of the enormous size of the crisis, coupled with horrifying reports of massive fraud and growing dissatisfaction with the regulators' handling of the problem, culminated in the Financial Institutions Reform, Recovery and Enforcement Act (FIRREA) of August 1989. In order to permit the closing or sale of the worst insolvent institutions, the bailout act raises some $115 billion over three years from general Treasury revenues and, to a lesser extent, from increased assessments on depository institutions. (Some $40 billion of the total was earmarked to support notes that the FSLIC had already issued for earlier failure resolutions.) Part of the $115 billion is recorded on the federal budget and part is off-budget—to be paid for by the government's new Resolution Financing Corporation. It should be noted that these funds represent a bailout of the depositors, not of the institutions, except to the extent that the managements responsible for the insolvencies are not replaced.

The act increases annual deposit-insurance premiums on S&Ls from .208 percent (.083 regular and 0.125 surcharge) to 0.23 percent in 1991, before lowering them to 0.18 percent in 1994 and to 0.15 percent in 1998. Commercial banks' premiums are raised from 0.083 percent to 0.12 percent in 1990 and to 0.15 percent in 1991. The FSLIC is separated from the FHLBB and reorganized as the Savings Association Insurance Fund (SAIF) within the FDIC, which will also administer a new Bank Insurance Fund (BIF); both funds are explicitly supported by the full faith and credit of the federal government up to $100,000 per deposit account. The chartering, regulatory, examination, and enforcement activities of the FHLBB are reorganized in the Treasury Department as the Office of Thrift Supervision (OTS), akin in structure to the Office of the Comptroller of the Currency.

The act also required S&Ls to maintain capital-to-asset ratios of at least 1.5 percent (excluding goodwill) and 3 percent (including goodwill) by the end of 1989; goodwill considerations will be phased out by the end of 1994. If these requirements are not met, deposit-growth constraints and other sanctions may be imposed until the association achieves the required minimum capital ratios. S&Ls are also required to increase their emphasis on residential mortgage lending. In general, the powers of state-chartered S&Ls are restricted to those permitted federally chartered associations, and S&Ls must have phased out their investments in real-estate equity and junk bonds by mid-1994. The act also allows S&Ls to be acquired by commercial bank-holding companies and to be operated as thrifts or converted into commercial banks, subject to SAIF premiums.

FIRREA transfers responsibility for managing and disposing of most insolvent associations to a new temporary Resolution Trust Corporation, which will exist until the end of 1996. During its existence, it is expected to manage many hundreds of insolvent associations pending their liquidation or sale.

The long-run effects of FIRREA are uncertain. The regulators now have the funds needed to resolve the worst of the insolvencies. But the new funds already appear to be insufficient to cover all the outstanding losses, and they provide little cushion either for potential problems at marginally capitalized institutions or for problems resulting from a rise in interest rates. Moreoover, the Resolution Trust Corporation has too little capital to resolve insolvencies quickly and efficiently.

Although FIRREA sets minimum capital standards, it does not do enough to reduce the incentives for insured depository institutions to take excessive risks. The capital standards are not as tough as advertised. They are considerably lower than they were in 1980, before the crisis was generally recognized, and they are still lower than they would be in the absence of deposit insurance. Indeed, because thrifts face lower capital requirements than banks, the Comptroller of the Currency has since proposed changes in the capital standards for national banks that may reduce their minimum requirements and may permit some banks to operate with near zero or even negative market-value net worth. FIRREA, moreover, does not specify that institutions breaching the minimum ratios must be recapitalized or reorganized immediately.

The act does call for the Treasury to make an eighteen-month study of deposit insurance. But this provision merely buys time; almost everything that anyone ever wanted to know about deposit insurance has already been studied and published. The delay may lead to inaction, because public pressure on Congress to make signifciant changes is likely to decline.

In addition, by restricting thrifts' product powers, the act reduces their ability to diversify both their interest-rate and credit risks. Thus it restores the conditions that initially resulted in the 1979–1981 debacle.

Although the act "punishes" the FHLB system and attempts to break up its cozy relationship with the industry, it does not significantly change the incentives that the regulators face. Discretionary forbearance is still permitted, and the OTS is not likely to be immune from congressional or industry influence simply because it is located in the Treasury Department. Indeed, political pressures on it may increase, since it may be viewed as an "administration" agency rather than an "independent" agency as before. In any event, the more discretion granted the regulators, the more vulnerable they are to political pressures.

LESSONS AND RECOMMENDATIONS

In light of the severity of both the S&L crisis and the embarrassment to the late but unlamented S&L regulators, one would expect the remaining bank regulators to move swiftly to minimize the probability of a recurrence. If there is a lesson to be learned from the debacle, it is that when the government provides deposit insurance, it must also use accurate accounting and monitoring systems and require individual institutions to maintain sufficient capital levels. Any set of recommendations for improving the safety and efficiency of the banking structure must include provisions for substantially higher capital requirements, mandatory early intervention by regulators, reorganization or recapitalization before capital is completely dissipated, and market-value accounting.

At best, the regulators have maintained current capital levels; in all likelihood they have actually reduced the levels. But higher capital should be required for two reasons. First, the greater an institution's capital, the better it can absorb losses. In the days before the FDIC, banks would display the amount of their capital and surplus on their windows, rather than "Member FDIC." More capital gives owners incentives to monitor the operations of their institution, because more of their money is at risk. This is especially important now that deposits are almost totally insured, in practice if not in law. Under the insurance system, depositors have little incentive to monitor the behavior of their institution; even if they

believe that they are at risk, they can generally remove their funds quickly when they believe that their institution may be in financial trouble.

Stockholders can benefit from risk taking when capital gets very low, because they enjoy the gains while most of the possible loss is borne by the FDIC. Debt holders, though, do not benefit from risk taking, as they receive only the promised coupon payments. Indeed, excessive risk taking jeopardizes these payments. It is useful, therefore, for capital to include debt subordinated to the claim of the FDIC. Such debt is truly uninsured. It is exactly the same as certificates of deposit that are not explicitly guaranteed by the FDIC. An institution's inability to find buyers for such debt indicates that the institution is not really healthy. Thus subordinated debt can give bank supervisors an early warning of trouble if interest rates on an institution's outstanding debt increase and the institution has trouble replacing debt as it matures. This debt should not be redeemable in less than one year, to prevent debtholders from "running" before the supervisory authorities can act.

It is sometimes argued that higher capital requirements could reduce profits and drive some healthy institutions out of business. It is true that one result of higher requirements would be to cut the subsidy provided by the present system of deposit insurance, where the premiums charged do not reflect risk. The subsidy, though, is paid by strong institutions, their customers, and taxpayers. An institution cannot be said to be healthy if it can survive only by receiving a subsidy.

Another objection to higher capital requirements is that capital is costly. Equity capital *can* be costly; but this objection does not apply to subordinated debt—primarily because interest payments on debt are deductible from income taxation, as are interest payments on deposits.

Mandatory early intervention by regulators before capital is completely dissipated can reduce the cost of bank failures to the taxpayers. The problem is that regulators are subject to considerable pressures—including "suggestions" from legislators and their own reluctance to admit that a bank has failed—to delay reorganizing or closing down banks. Instead, they prefer to delay action and to hope that conditions will improve or that the failure will occur on someone else's watch. That is why there should be a predetermined schedule for action as an institution's capital declines, as the Shadow Financial Regulatory Committee has recommended. If an institution has a capital-to-asset ratio of more than 10 percent, for example, it would need only general supervision. Should its ratio decline below 10 percent, the regulators could choose to suspend the institution's dividends and interest payments on subordinated debt, to prevent it from growing, and to require it to submit a plan to restore its capital. But when the ratio dipped below, say, 6 percent, the regulators would be *required* to suspend dividends and subordinated-debt payments and to restrain growth. At this point, bondholders and stockholders could be expected to step in to force recapitalization or to displace management. But if things deteriorated even further, the regulators would have to take over the institution when its capital fell below 3 percent, and to sell, merge, or—as a last resort—liquidate it.

Some might object that this plan amounts to the confiscation of solvent institutions. But the owners of a truly solvent bank would restore the capital before it hit the 3-percent point—even before dividends and interest on subordinated debt were suspended. Any capital remaining after the takeover, moreover, would be returned to the former owners.

Having capital measured in terms of market value rather than historical cost or regulatory accounting numbers is also important, because these latter numbers do not reflect an enterprise's actual economic condition. This fact was dramatically and disastrously illustrated by the savings-and-loan debacle.

Market-value accounting, however, is said to pose significant measurement problems. It is true that the market values of some important bank assets, particularly loans that are not marketed, are difficult to measure. But the alternative—of assuming that they have remained at their original levels—is worse.

Another objection is that market values emphasize the short run instead of the long run. Increases in interest rates, for example, are said not to affect the value of a fixed-rate mortgage that an institution plans to hold to maturity; the mortgage's value, moreover, will be restored when interest rates go down again. But while it holds the mortgage, the bank will be earning interest at a rate below the current market rate; if its deposits are short-term, it will be earning less than it is paying out. When the institution is likely to bleed to death over time, its owners will know that it is insolvent and will take excessively risky gambles. What is more, we usually have no more reason to expect interest rates to decrease than to expect them to increase further. Instead of being saved by future changes in interest rates, the institution could be plunged further into insolvency, to the detriment of other institutions and the taxpayers.

REGULATORS AND DISCRETION

No regulator has proposed or supported significant increases in capital requirements. Nor have the regulators supported mandatory reorganization, recapitalization when capital (however defined) is exhausted, or a change from book- to market-value accounting. Rather, they have responded that these proposals are unrealistic and unfeasible.

If these reforms are deemed worthy, it is important to identify the underlying motivations that cause the regulators to deny their value. It is relatively easy to rule out the possibility that regulators do not understand economics or accounting; regulators are generally quite intelligent and well-educated, and many senior-level regulators developed favorable reputations before being appointed to their current positions. It is somewhat more difficult to refute the hypothesis that regulators are knuckling under to adverse pressure from Congress or the S&L industry. But regulators have been known to stand up to Congress and the industry to preserve their independence.

Regulators seem to oppose proposals such as ours primarily because they want to maintain their discretionary powers. Discretion enables regulators to respond at any time and in any manner that they believe appropriate, with little need to define "appropriate" in an objective and reconstructible form. Under the discretionary system, regulators are supervised by "watchers" in the private sector, who frequently are former regulators and who tend to develop mutually supportive relationships with the regulators. Unfortunately, discretion makes it possible for regulators to refuse to recognize problems, or even to deny their existence.

Mandatory regulatory intervention and accurate market-value accounting are the antithesis of discretionary behavior; such rules put the regulators on "automatic pilot" and reduce their power and visiblity, as well as their sense of importance. Rules also reduce the regulators' ability to disguise or to cover up problems and to shift blame elsewhere; they force greater accountability.

Regulators favor discretion because they believe that they can acquire relevant information more quickly and more accurately than others. They believe, too, that they are more knowledgeable about the banking industry and its problems than others. Finally, they believe that the structure of the industry and the marketplace is unstable, so that rules designed for one period are not applicable to another; corrective actions, in their view, must be specially tailored to the unique aspects of each problem.

Yet the regulators' response to the thrift crisis was wholly ineffective. Because government failure is potentially far more costly than market failure, it is important to design incentives that force regulators to operate more responsibly. Until this is done, we are unlikely to avoid another crisis if and when the economic and technological forces that caused the current crisis reappear.

DISCUSSION QUESTIONS

1. What reasons do Benston and Kaufman provide for the failure of savings-and-loan associations in 1989?

2. Do you believe it is correct for Congress to authorize public funds to salvage bankrupt companies and associations like New York City in 1975, Chrysler in 1979, or the savings-and-loan associations in 1989? State your reasons.

3. Some might argue that the failure of savings-and-loans was a result of organizational failures (of various kinds) while others believe that it is a result of human errors and misdeeds. Which explanation do you find holds more weight in this case?

The Perils of a Dual Economy

Michael Harrington
Mark Levinson

In the wake of the economic recovery in 1983–84, a kind of euphoria spread through some, but by no means all, of the upper reaches of American society. John Naisbitt, author of the widely read book, *Megatrends*, wrote at the end of 1984 that "job creation is one of America's great untold stories." Indeed, he predicted that the United States was close to a time of labor shortages.

> With double-digit unemployment still fresh in our minds [Naisbitt conceded], the idea that labor shortages are imminent may be hard to swallow. How can it happen? Quite simply, the labor force is not growing at anywhere near the 2.2 percent annual growth experienced between 1965 and 1979, when most baby boomers entered the work force. Projections are that the labor force will grow by 21 million between 1982 and 1995, to 131 million from 110 million. New jobs are being created at a phenomenal rate—4 million in 1983, probably an equal number in 1984. . . . If job growth continues at the current rate, there still will be more jobs created than there are workers to fill them.[1]

In criticizing Naisbitt's analysis, we will focus not on the extremely optimistic assumptions about economic growth, which undergird it, but rather on the character of the jobs generated in the past, present, and future. We note, however, that the Department of Labor's projections, which yield a labor force of 131 million in 1995, assume even in the most moderate of three scenarios that GNP growth will outpace both the 1973–77 and 1977–82 rates in the low scenario. These projections envision a 2.8 percent growth rate in 1982–90 and a 2.7 percent pace in 1990–95, as against 2.2 percent in 1973–77 and 1.6 percent in 1977–82.[2]

We also will not dispute here Naisbitt's, and the Department of Labor's, hopeful economic premises. For we will argue *that, even if those growth rates are achieved, the changing American occupational structure is becoming bifurcated, and that this may create serious difficulties for many working people, as well as for American business.*

THE RECORD OF THE 1970S

Let us summarize some of the recent shifts in the American occupational structure. In the 11 years between 1970 and 1980, there was an enormous increase in the number of jobs, as the labor force added 23.655 million new participants. This was a 27 percent rise, almost 10 points higher than the rate of increase between 1960 and 1970.[3] In those years, it was not simply the number of people entering the labor force that signaled an important change; the very character of the occupational structure was in profound transition.

Women's labor-force participation was, of course, one of the most striking developments. It went from 36.5 percent in 1960 to 42.6 percent in 1970, to 51.9 percent in 1980. As *Business Week* pointed out in early 1985, fully two-thirds of the jobs created between 1974 and '84 had gone to women. *Business Week* noted that

> when women started flooding into the work force in the early 1970s, the gap [between male and female wages] actually widened. . . . Just as the shift from high-labor-cost manufacturing to low-labor-cost services was gaining momentum, the influx of women provided a cheap pool of labor for business.

This tendency, the article continued, is being somewhat counteracted. The female/male gap was 57 percent in 1973, 64 percent in the early

1980s, and is projected, in one study, to rise to 74 percent of the male wage by the year 2000.[4]

This analysis captures another aspect of the labor-market shift. Women are concentrated in clerical occupations (almost 80 percent of the total), the food and health sectors (60 percent), and sales (near 50 percent). The increase in female labor-force participation is an aspect of the trend toward a new occupational structure with educated and trained people at the top, a middle "sliding" down the wage scale, and a growing population of the marginalized. Most of those "women's jobs" were located in the sliding middle, a point to which we will return.

The blue-collar percentage of employed Americans dropped meanwhile from 35.3 percent in 1970 to 29.7 percent in 1980. The most significant gains in that decade were made at the top, where professional and technical workers increased by 4.8 million, and in the lower wage reaches of the middle, where service workers increased by 3.5 million, sales personnel by 2.84 million, and clericals by 4.7 million. These trends became even more pronounced during the economic recovery of 1982–84.

Granting that the quality of the new jobs generated in the 1970s did not correspond—in terms of either value-added or worker's pay— to that of the postwar boom period, doesn't this trend still stand in stark contrast to the European failure to create new work opportunities? And doesn't this explain why the American unemployment rate, which was normally higher than the European in the 1950s and '60s, is now lower than that of most European countries? (Sweden and Austria are obvious exceptions.)

These points are usually made by people who speak of the success of the American economy in recent years. An analysis by Lester Thurow emphasizes the complexities of these trends.[5]

In the '70s, Thurow points out, American research and development (R&D) fell while Europe's rose. And in the '80s, though U.S. R&D is on the increase, it has not reached European levels. Yet America has generated jobs and Europe has not. Thurow writes:

> The reason for this paradox can be found in the two continents' very different labor markets. Relative to the price of capital, American wages were 37 percent lower in 1983 than in 1972. After correcting for inflation, wages have fallen 6 percent in absolute terms. This has not happened in Europe.

In addition, Thurow continues, there are millions of Americans who work at levels well below the unenforced, legal minimum wage of $3.35, not to mention the average wage of $8.01. It is of some moment that the production workers in high-tech firms commonly labor for around $4 an hour.

"The worst-paid European workers," Thurow concludes, "make much more relative to the average European that the worst-paid American workers make relative to the average American." Under these conditions—the relative cheapness of workers in the United States and their high cost in Europe—the divergence between the two areas becomes quite explicable. Sweden has 13 times as many programmable robots in proportion to the size of its labor force as America, because it makes business sense in that economy to substitute machines for people. The United States had a boom in relatively low-paying jobs in the service sector because employing such workers was a profitable strategy.

There are Europeans who have interpreted these trends as proof of the superior flexibility of the American labor market. In 1983, for instance, the London *Economist* noted that between 1973 and 1982 real earnings for industrial workers in Britain rose by 10 percent while employment declined, and that real earnings dropped in America while employment went up by 16 percent. Part of the solution to the crisis, the *Economist* seemed to say, was that Europe should become more "American."[6]

Leaving aside the blithe disregard for the human and social cost of the American approach, there are economic reasons for being critical of it. In the United States, Thurow notes, management flexibility gives rise to a corresponding labor flexibility, and so the labor turnover rate in the States—4 percent a month—is vastly higher than in Europe. "Firms know employees are apt to leave before the costs of training can be recouped in higher productivity, and employees know that they may soon move to other jobs that require very different skills. The result is a much less well-trained labor force."

Thurow thinks that this is one of the reasons for the current crisis in the American machine-tool industry, which lost almost 50 percent of the market to the West Germans, Japanese, and South Koreans during the recovery.[7]

For now, however, we can make a preliminary generalization about the generation of jobs in the 1970s, which was obviously part of the transformation of the American economy from secondary to tertiary activity. Here the tertiary occupations are split into high- and low-wage sectors, with the latter being more numerous than the former. A few selective figures should reinforce this point. Between 1972 and 1982, the number of accountants grew by 473,000, computer specialists by 479,000, engineers by 463,000, engineering and scientific technicians by 279,000. That totals 1.694 million new, well-paid jobs. At the same time, if we look only at the service-sector proper, food, cleaning, health, and child-care services rose by 2.548 million jobs.

This analysis is not partisan. A New York Stock Exchange study of job trends in the United States came to empirical conclusions quite similar to ours. The difference is not primarily in the figures but in the interpretation. We are, the Stock Exchange agrees, generating more low-paying than high-paying jobs. But, it comments, "There has always been and probably will always be more people working in the lower-skill, lower-income jobs than in higher-skill, higher-income jobs."[8]

We disagree. In this case, the past is not a guide to the future. In an important study, Wassily Leontiev notes that, during the 19th century, "the 'productivity'—or should one say the 'indispensability'—of labor increased steadily and so did the demand and consequently the price paid for it." But, he says, this process is not taking place in today's technological revolution and, particularly as the service sector is more and more automated, it will occur less and less in the future.[9] All this anticipates a principal analytic proposition that will emerge at the end of this article. For now, we simply note that the New York Stock Exchange analysis coincides with our own regarding the basic trends. Let us now turn to the more recent developments during the recovery of 1983–84.

JOB GENERATION DURING THE 1983-84 RECOVERY

President Reagan's supporters argue that the principal reason for his landslide victory in the 1984 election was the extraordinary performance of the American economy in creating new jobs. Even critics of the president tend to be sanguine about the loss of jobs, confident that more and better jobs will be created. They argue that the trends described here are simply part of the process of economic development—a process that results in a shift of employment from agriculture to goods-producing industries and, finally, to services. In the past such growth was closely associated with economic progress and a rise in per capita GNP. Thus James Fallows:

> There are good reasons to believe that today's economic change is very much like past changes that the United States has undergone—and therefore to conclude that it will create many more opportunities than it destroys. . . . Why should we decide that the whole national history of migration, adjustment, and advancement must now come to an end?

There are good reasons to doubt Fallows' optimistic conclusion. In fact later in the same article Fallows seems to recognize this:

> [We] have to come to grips with certain uncomfortable human truths. One is that some—perhaps most—displaced workers will never again be as well off as they used to be. The [displaced worker] will not be filling the new professional slots that computerization will open up.[10]

What, one wonders, will they be doing? Fallows doesn't say. His claim that the current economic transformation will create more opportunities than it destroys requires careful examination. We will begin by looking at where the new jobs appeared and where old jobs disappeared (a point not much stressed by the Administration's supporters). There has been, it would seem, more than a little single-entry bookkeeping—with analyses of new jobs in gross terms that don't take into account the loss of existing jobs.

We first take the period from early 1983 to August 1984, utilizing Bureau of Labor Statistics figures for average employment in 1983 and preliminary estimates of employment from August 1984.[11] During that 20-month period, total employment went up by 4.9 million workers, and private-sector employment by 4.8 million. The goods-producing sector accounted for 26.3 percent of the job increase (1.299 million jobs), with a heavy concentration in the durable-goods sector (724,000 openings). But the "service-producing" sector

added 3.645 million jobs, or 73.7 percent of the total. The service sector proper (such as food and health) led the way with 1.6 million jobs; retail trade followed with 1.1 million.

What are the wage implications of these trends? The average weekly wage in manufacturing in 1983 was $478.98, in services it was $238.71, and in retail trade $171.05. The consequent yearly wage in retail trade is substantially under the poverty line for a family of four (which was just over $10,000 a year for an urban family of four in 1984), and it was just above that line in the service sector. The yearly manufacturing wage comes out to somewhat more than $24,000, or in the area of U.S. median income. But manufacturing occupations were down and retail and service up.

In short, the trends we have identified in the 1970s are at work in the recovery period of the 1980s—*only more so*. Blue-collar jobs are deteriorating at a rate that will lead to the further proportional decrease of that sector in our economy, and the importance of the low-wage strata, and their problems, is accelerating. The agony of restructuring suffered by these strata was the result of the 1981–82 recession, which had exacerbated the tendencies we have outlined in the previous section.

All the figures we have just cited compare the gross total of workers employed at the beginning and end of a time period. As a result, there is little sense of what happens to individuals during that period. A special study by the Bureau of Labor Statistics in late 1984 gets somewhat more concrete.[12]

The study looked at 5.1 million workers whose jobs were abolished or plants shut down between January 1979 and January 1984. These workers had been at their jobs for at least three years before they were discharged. Almost half of the jobs that were permanently ended were in manufacture, most of them in durable goods production. Retail trade accounted for less than 10 percent of the losses and services for about 10 percent. So the logic of job disappearance is the mirror image of job generation. In the former the losses are pimarily in manufacture; in the latter the gains are mainly in the service-producing sector.

Another familiar factor—economic geography—is also quite visible in the Bureau of Labor Statistics (BLS) analysis. The heaviest job losses were suffered in the Atlantic seaboard areas and parts of the industrial Midwest, which accounted for about half of the lost jobs. The Southeast and Southwest, the Mountain States, and the Pacific areas were much less affected.

What happened to these workers after their jobs disappeared? In January 1984, 60.1 percent of them had found other jobs, 25.5 percent were still unemployed, and 14.4 percent had left the labor force. But the men and women who had found new jobs had often been subjected to the "sliding" phenomenon—had been reemployed at a wage that was lower than the one they had earned before. For example, 27.4 percent of them were receiving 20 percent or even less of their previous pay; now 14 percent were below their old wage but not by more than 20 percent; 25 percent were above their old wage by 20 percent or less; and 23 percent had found a substantially better (by more than 20 percent) job. These percentages, however, are computed on the basis of those who had found full-time jobs. If one adds the 39.9 percent who are still unemployed or just left the work force, *the loss of income affected about 59 percent of the more than 5 million workers whose jobs had disappeared.*

A study by Michael Urquhart complements this analysis.[13] Urquhart found that new employees in the service sector are twice as likely not to have worked at all in the previous year than to have been employed in the goods-producing sector. So the employment shift to services *does not* essentially stem from an actual migration of workers from one sector to an-

other, but rather results from the expansion of the labor force and especially the increasing participation of women.

For a variety of technical reasons, the BLS study does not focus on office workers (the disappearance of manufacturing jobs is somewhat easier to define). In a *Business Week* analysis, the white-collar problem was put into focus. As a consequence of the decline in smokestack industries, it reported, a million white-collar (clerical and managerial) employees have lost their jobs. Since 1979, the numbers of steel-industry personnel of this type have declined by 40 percent, of auto personnel by 15 percent. Some of those let go find better jobs, but, as quoted in the BLS study, *Business Week* said that 34 percent of these people had to take pay cuts.[14]

These qualifications do not suggest that the recovery was a sham. We simply argue that the evolution of the American occupational structure is not as dynamic as some of President Reagan's more enthusiastic supporters suggest. But, more central to our analysis, the recent recovery has accelerated the shift to services that had become so visible in the '70s. What about the middle-range future?

THE FUTURE OF JOBS IN THE UNITED STATES

We shall rely primarily here on two analyses of the job future in the American economy, both of them previously cited (see Notes 2 and 8): *Employment Projections for 1995,* published in March 1984 by the Bureau of Labor Statistics (hereafter BLS), and *U.S. International Competitiveness: Perception and Reality,* published in 1984 by the New York Stock Exchange (hereafter NYSE).

Projections about 1995 are obviously very chancy, for one must make assumptions about the economic future—about such matters as growth and unemployment rates, and prices—

which are extremely difficult to establish in terms of next year, and even more so of the next decade. Thus the BLS "moderate" scenario assumes "stable economic growth through the mid-1990s" and expects productivity to do significantly better than in the 1973–79 period (when it declined compared to the '60s). Indeed, it is hypothesized that the '80s and the first half of the '90s will resemble the '60s in terms of productivity gains.

The Stock Exchange is, as one might expect, even more bullish. It anticipates 3.5 percent real growth in GNP per year between 1982 and 1995, with productivity rising by 2.2 percent. "These are fairly optimistic projections and some may be skeptical. . . ," the Exchange notes. In other contexts, we would strongly argue that these surprise-free and very optimistic projections are profoundly flawed. But for the analysis of our future occupational structure, *even if these excessively hopeful projections were to come true, our basic case would still stand*. We take the BLS and Stock Exchange scenarios, then, as the limit of the most optimistic expectations. And if, as we think likely, the American economy does much less well than those two studies assume, our somewhat pessimistic account of the shape of the labor force at century's end will be all the more compelling. . . .

The 10 top growth jobs on this list will account for 24.2 percent of the total employment increase projected for 1995. Three categories— noncollege teachers, registered nurses, and truck drivers—are in the "middle" of American society in terms of remuneration. There are very few classic blue-collar jobs on the list and most of the occupations predicted to grow are nonunion. Indeed, this projection puts the trends we have described here at the core of the 1995 reality: the growth of some well-paid professional and technical occupations (accountants, engineers, physicians, lawyers) and a large number of poorly paid service oc-

cupations (cashiers, salesclerks, kitchen helpers, and so on).

The Stock Exchange projections differ on a number of counts from those of the BLS, but the occupational universe described is essentially the same. The differences have to do, one suspects, with the job classifications used; for instance, machine-tool operators and metalworking craftsmen, which are 29 and 31 on the projected 1995 list in the Stock Exchange study, are not even found in the top 40 jobs of the BLS study. The Stock Exchange study also uses much more optimistic assumptions.

The conceptual problems can be seen in the Stock Exchange's valiant efforts to paint the economy as much less service-oriented than do the government's figures. This is accomplished primarily by including wholesale and retail trade in the "goods-producing sector," a stratagem that raises the job percentage of that sector in the economy to 45.7 percent. By the simple expedient of subtracting wholesale and retail trade from goods-producing—not the least because the pay in those sectors is significantly below that in manufacturing as well as for more obvious and traditional reasons—we find that goods-producing provided 28.8 percent of employment in 1982, which is more in line with the usual calculation.

The Stock Exchange engages in a related conceptual maneuver when it places sales workers and clerical workers (along with craft workers) in the "middle echelon" of occupations, and puts operatives in the "lower echelon." In that way—hardly realistic in terms of pay and status—the number of lower-echelon jobs declines in percentage terms between 1982 and 1995, from 37.3 percent to 35 percent.

The Exchange's account of the personal and business sector is somewhat more realistic. The main sources of new jobs in the American economy since 1962, the Exchange says, "have been personal and business services, government, and wholesale and retail trade." Wholesale trade pays, on the average, about 50 cents more than the average private-sector job ($8.02 was the average in 1983; wholesale trade paid $8.54); retail trade, at $5.74 an hour in 1983, is well under the national hourly average.[15]

Within the personal and business service sector, 27.6 percent of the employees are professionals, but 33 percent are service workers and another 17.3 percent are clericals. So if the growth sectors of the future are, as the Exchange maintains, dominantly wholesale and retail trade and personal and business services, that will even further accentuate the trends we have described here.

THE ROLE OF HIGH-TECH INDUSTRIES

But what about employment possibilities in the emerging high-tech industries?

First, it is important to define high-tech industries. Following Eileen Appelbaum, we define as high-tech those industries in which either the percentage of total investment devoted to Research and Development (R&D) expenditures or the number of scientists, engineers, and technical employees is at least twice the average of all U.S. industries. This definition encompasses 32 manufacturing industries as well as such service industries as computer programming, data processing, and research laboratories.[16]

Despite the widespread belief that high technology has been a major source of employment growth, high-tech industry growth rates did not differ much from employment growth in overall manufacturing, which measured 4.2 percent over the decade, and they compare unfavorably with the growth of total employment, which increased 27.6 percent. A subset of high-tech manufacturing industries, however, with both high R&D expenditures and high levels of scientific engineering and technical workers, did experience a 26.3 percent

growth rate. Yet these industries added only 444,000 new jobs, 2 percent of the 19 million jobs created during the 1969–79 decade.[17]

Employment in high-tech service-sector industries is growing rapidly, but the small size of the sector limits the total number of jobs created. Thus the computer and data-processing services industry, largest of the high-tech service industries, has added only about 300,000 jobs since 1969.[18]

Rapidly rising productivity in the high-tech industry, combined with the small size of the high-tech sector, constrains the ability of this sector to provide employment. Data Resources, Inc., estimates that the number of new high-tech jobs that will be created between 1983 and 1993 will be 730,000 to 1 million, less than half the jobs lost in manufacturing between 1979 and 1982.[19]

Moreover, assembly jobs in high-tech industries are subject to competition from low-wage labor, particularly in Third World countries such as Malaysia, Taiwan, the Philippines, and Mexico, where assembly workers earn as little as 50 cents an hour. Companies such as Intel, National Semiconductors, Atari, Apple Computers, and Wang Laboratories all have moved jobs to the Far East.

Furthermore, wages in the high-tech sector are two-tiered. Indeed, most of the jobs in high-tech industries are not high-tech jobs. The growth of high-tech employment has meant an increase in professional, technical, and managerial jobs at the top, but it has also meant an increase in clerical, sales, and nonprofessional service jobs at the bottom.

In 1977 the BLS surveyed the semiconductor industry, which then employed 242,600 workers. Of the workers employed in this industry, approximately 58 percent were production workers in the plant, 14 percent were office (nonplant) workers, and the remaining 28.9 percent were administrative, executive, professional, and technical employees. Only 28 percent of the jobs in this industry were good jobs (jobs in the top third of U.S. income distribution), 9.2 percent were in the middle, while 62.8 percent were low-paying jobs.[20] The low-wage production jobs in the industry are poor in other respects too: they are tedious, and many of them expose workers to substantial occupational health hazards. So even if high-tech industries employ more people than these studies indicate, the trend toward bifurcation of the labor market will continue.

All these data tend to support the theories developed by Barry Bluestone, Robert Kuttner, and others, that the "middle" of America's society is in deep trouble. There are, it should be noted, critics who seriously question this interpretation—Sar Levitan, Clifford Johnson, and Robert Samuelson are among them.[21] Part of the problems with these critics is that they rebut the thesis of a "cataclysmic" change in the American work force. But, as we emphasize throughout this article, there was no sudden, and surprising, discontinuity in the early 1980s—or, for that matter, in the 1970s.

Daniel Bell, for instance, was describing in 1960 trends toward the gradual transformation of work (and his data are from the 1950s). He extended that theme in an analysis he wrote in the early 1970s.[22] As we noted earlier, the trends we have outlined here have been visible for a decade and a half. . . .

Indeed, a chart cited by Samuelson to refute the notion of the sliding middle actually lends credence to it.

Samuelson emphasizes that there is very little shift in these percentages from 1982 to 1995. We believe that the categories used tend to conceal some of the changes that will take place, but this is not crucial here. Note, however, that between 1950 and 1982 (which are actual, not projected, figures) there was a 37 percent decrease in the jobs of machine operators, a 53 percent increase in clerical workers, and a 55 percent increase in service workers.

Samuelson insists that the 13 years between 1982 and 1995 will not see an equivalent transformation, which is right to some extent—but not as much as he thinks.[23]

The sociologist Steven Rose has published two editions of an intricate scholarly poster graphically representing the social structure of the United States. The first edition used 1978 statistics, the second was based on 1983 data.[24] In the second edition, Rose examined the dynamics of income distribution, using the poverty line of 1983 ($9,800 for an urban family of four), the BLS "Low Budget" ($17,000), Medium Budget ($27,500), and High Budget ($41,000). . . .

In fairness, it should be noted that the years compared—1978 and 1983—would tend to emphasize the worst aspects of these trends. The year 1978 was, in wage terms, the peak of the recovery from the 1974–75 slump. And 1983 was a time of partial recovery in which the effects of the worst recession in half a century were still being felt. Even so, the tendencies that are visible in Rose's chart reinforce the basic thesis developed here.

Finally, Robert Kuttner has written an excellent summary statement of the reality we are trying to define here:

> During the three decades after World War II, America not only generated lots of jobs, it generated plenty of good jobs. Between 1958 and 1968, for example, manufacturing added 4 million workers; state and local government added another 3.5 million. A working-class family's child with no education beyond a high-school diploma could nonetheless choose among a number of relatively well-paid jobs, and a wage sufficient to buy a house and support a family, usually on one income.
>
> These are precisely the jobs that are disappearing today. Manufacturing, which on average pays nearly three times the minimum wage, added only 1 million jobs between 1968 and 1978 and has lost nearly 3 million jobs between 1980 and 1982. Construction and production work,

taken together, accounted for one job in four in 1950; they account for just one job in eight in 1984. State and local government, a key source of good service jobs, peaked in 1981 and has reduced its labor force since then by several hundred thousand workers.[25]

The occupational shifts described here lead to an entrenched dual economy. This dual economy persists despite the current recovery. The old liberal wisdom—that in the long run the private economy will generate new and better paying jobs, and that this is the only real solution to poverty—becomes less and less relevant. An occupational structure characterized by a polarization between highly paid professional and technical workers on the one hand and poorly paid, unorganized, lower-level workers on the other will be threatened, not by revolution, but by social demoralization and/or constant outbreaks of individual, nihilistic violence. Only in the fairy-tale mind of Ronald Reagan is it possible to have "prosperity" *and* decreasing opportunity for the poor.

Notes

[1] John Naisbitt, "Reinventing the Corporation," *New York Times*, December 23, 1984.

[2] Arthur J. Andreassen, Norman C. Saunders, and Betty W. Su, "Economic Outlook for the 1990s: Three Scenarios for Economic Growth," *Employment Projections for 1995*, U.S. Department of Labor (Washington, D.C.: Government Printing Office—hereafter G.P.O.—March 1984).

[3] All statistics on the labor force in this section of our article, unless otherwise noted, are from *The Statistical Abstract of the United States, 1984*, U.S. Bureau of the Census (Washington, D.C.: G.P.O., 1984).

[4] "Women at Work," *Business Week*, January 28, 1985.

[5] Lester Thurow, "Jobs versus Productivity: The Euro-American Dilemma," *Technology Review*, October 1984.

[6] "How to Get Jobs," *Economist*, July 28, 1984.

[7] "The Bottom Could Drop Out of Capital Goods," *Business Week*, December 3, 1984.

[8] *International Competitiveness: Perception and Reality*, New York Stock Exchange (New York, 1984), p. 44.

[9] Wassily Leontiev, "Technological Advance, Economic Growth, and the Distribution of Income," *Population and Development Review*, September 1983, p. 403 and passim.

[10] James Fallows, "The Changing Economic Landscape," *Atlantic*, March 1985, pp. 47–68.

[11] "Current Statistics," *Monthly Labor Review*, October 1984, Table 11, p. 62.

[12] U.S. Department of Labor, Bureau of Labor Statistics, Publication no. 85–492, November 30, 1984.
A study of unemployed Michigan auto workers reaches similar conclusions. Over 100,000 Michigan auto workers experienced permanent or indefinite layoff between 1979 and 1982. By the summer of 1984, 30 percent of those surveyed had not been recalled. Of those who had not been recalled, 50 percent had found new jobs, 40 percent were still unemployed, and 10 percent had given up looking. Of those reemployed, 33 percent are in non-union jobs. The wages of those reemployed are on average 21 percent below their previous wage level. Only 50 percent of those reemployed are covered by health insurance. For a summary of this study, see *Research Bulletin*, April 1985 (Detroit: United Automobile Workers of America, Research Dept.).

[13] Michael Urquhart, "The Employment Shift to Services: Where Did It Come from?" *Monthly Labor Review*, April 1984.

[14] "Suddenly the World Doesn't Care," *Business Week*, February 4, 1985. See also, on long-term unemployment among blue-collar workers, *Chicago Steelworkers: The Cost of Unemployment* (Chicago: Hull House and Local 65, United Steelworkers of America, 1985).

[15] *Monthly Labor Review*, October 1984; Table 12, p. 63.

[16] Eileen Appelbaum, "High-Tech and the Structural Employment Problems of the 1980s," in *American Jobs and the Changing Industrial Base*, Eileen Collins and Lucretia Deway Tanner, eds. (Cambridge, Mass.: Ballinger, 1984), pp. 37–38.

[17] Donald Tomaskovic-Devey and S. M. Miller, "Can High-Tech Provide the Jobs?" *Challenge* (May-June, 1983), p. 60.

[18] Appelbaum, p. 38.

[19] *Business Week*, March 28, 1983, p. 85.

[20] Appelbaum, pp. 41–42.

[21] Sar Levitan and Clifford Johnson, "The Changing Work Place," *Annals of the American Academy of Political and Social Science*, May 1984; Robert Samuelson, "Middle-Class Media Myth," *National Journal*, December 31, 1983.

[22] Daniel Bell, *The End of Ideology*, (Glencoe, Ill.: Free Press, 1960), p. 268; *The Coming of Post-Industrial Society* (New York: Basic Books, 1973), p. 125ff.

[23] For a critical discussion of these issues, see David B. Bills, with the assistance of Virginia Lambert, "Changes in Social Stratification and Mobility in American Society," 1984 (Chicago: Illinois Institute of Technology, unpublished ms.).

[24] Steven Rose, *Social Stratification in the United States* (Baltimore: Social Graphics Co., 1983), p. 11.

[25] Robert Kuttner, *The Economic Illusion* (Boston: Houghton Mifflin, 1984), p. 170.

DISCUSSION QUESTIONS

1. According to Harrington and Levinson, how has the American occupational structure been affected by our shift to a service economy?

2. Compare the authors' conclusions to those of Zuboff in Chapter 4.

3. What suggestions would you offer to avoid the problems Harrington and Levinson see in a dual economy?

READING 12·3

Japan as Number One: Lessons for America

Ezra F. Vogel

After touring automobile assembly lines in both countries [America and Japan], a visitor observed, "The American factory seems almost like an armed camp. Foremen stand guard to make sure workers do not slack off. Workers grumble at foremen, and foremen are cross with workers. In the Japanese factory, employees seem to work even without the foreman watching. Workers do not appear angry at superiors and actually seem to hope their company succeeds."

Japanese workers' pride in their work and loyalty to their company are reflected in their capacity to produce goods that are not only competitive in price but reliable in quality. Some workers, especially younger workers in small plants, may be alienated from their company, but, compared to Americans, they are absent less, strike less, and are willing to work overtime and refrain from using all their allotted vacation time without any immediate monetary benefit. The average Japanese laborer may accomplish no more than a loyal hard-working American counterpart in a comparable factory, but loyalty to the company is typically higher and hard work more common.

Many an American businessman, after touring a Japanese company and inspecting figures on time lost from absenteeism and strikes, has expressed the wish that he had such a labor force.

It is tempting to account for the differences by historical tradition, but American workers have become less disciplined in recent decades, albeit with the same American tradition, and modern Japanese employees of large companies are far more loyal than, for example, Japanese textile workers at the turn of the century. It is common to assign American labor problems to our affluence, but discipline has remained strong in affluent Japan. Furthermore, Japanese companies establishing plants in America have achieved with a few years of modified Japanese-style management a level of employee devotion on the average higher than in comparable American plants. Before resorting to an explanation that centers on a semimystical "Oriental spirit," one might consider whether Japanese success bears any relationship to company management and treatment of workers.

THE EMERGENCE OF THE JAPANESE COMPANY SYSTEM

The Japanese company system as we know it today began to emerge only late in the nineteenth century. Craft shops, with paternalistic masters and their apprentices and journeymen, date back centuries, but these "feudalistic" shops are not totally different from the kind of paternalistic shops of Paul Revere's America or preindustrial Europe.

Modern Japanese corporate paternalism drew on the recent feudal past, but it emerged in industries that borrowed modern industrial technology and organization and required a high level of skill. In new industries with lower skill requirements like textiles, no long training was necessary. Here, young, dexterous employees were, if anything, more useful than older experienced ones with less dexterity, and young women were at least as agile as men. Late nineteenth- and early twentieth-century Japanese textile manufacturers, therefore, offered wages based on a piece rate system without significant salary increases for seniority. Wages were so low and factory conditions so unsatisfactory that most workers left before completing two or three years, and in some factories turnover was even more rapid.

Modern industries requiring a high level of skill faced different problems. As Ronald Dore has shown, the resulting late development pattern, unlike other industrialized countries' earlier indigenous development, relied on more concerted planning, training, and investment. In sizeable companies that manufactured steel, machine tools, electric equipment, and the like, companies needed to train both a group of highly skilled laborers and a group of white-collar managerial personnel. Because these skills were not based on experience with indigenous developments, it took considerable time and capital investment to train them. And since these new companies were in basic industries that were well-financed and ultimately backed by the government, the companies were in a position to guarantee long-term employment. They therefore developed a seniority system of wage increases such that the newly trained employees in whom the company invested so heavily would be motivated to remain. The system of seniority and permanent employment was by no means universal in Japanese industry, but it became the predominant pattern in the large-scale modern industrial sector and has since spread to the large commercial organizations as well. As the modern industrial sector expanded, a higher proportion of company employees has gradually been brought into this seniority and permanent employment pattern.

The modern form of the Japanese company has evolved considerably since the early 1900s. In the 1930s and during World War II Japanese companies were brought under increasingly tight government control. During the Allied Occupation, the large *zaibatsu* firms were split up into smaller independent firms, but they gradually recombined into the present-day loosely organized groups after the end of the Occupation. During the 1950s and 1960s under government guidance many smaller firms were consolidated in order to modernize, and new American technology and management were introduced. For a time companies even considered copying the American pattern whereby workers could be dismissed and laid off more easily and hired in midcareer: it might get rid of employees with low performance, reward bold, innovative employees held down by the system, increase flexibility, give employees stifled in one company more options elsewhere, and reduce costs in a declining sector. By the late 1960s, when Japanese businesses started outperforming companies in the West, Japanese management intellectuals were satisfied that their seniority system was preferable to the dominant Western pattern, and they began to articulate a new philosophy of management.

The new philosophy incorporates many concepts from modern Western management and has much in common with large companies of American origin such as IBM, Polaroid, and Kodak. There is attention to basic business strategy, the product life cycles, to market surveys and marketing strategy, to accounting, to econometric models, to modern advertising, to up-to-date information processing. But some basics of the pre-World War II Japanese system remain: long-term perspective, permanent employment, seniority, and company loyalty. In addition, certain features gradually developed have recently been articulated to a higher degree: separation of rank and task, low differentials in pay and status for workers of a given age, "bottom-up" management, and small-group responsibility.

The Japanese firm is less interested in short-term profits and more concerned with the long run. Executives may disparage their success in planning and forecasting, but they continue their best efforts and, when appropriate, boldly sacrifice profits for several years to build the groundwork for later success. They take care in cultivating good relations with institutions that might potentially be useful. They provide extensive training for personnel in skills that might be needed in the future. They invest in technology at seemingly high prices if it might later pay off. They invest heavily in plant modernization even when present plants meet immediate demands. As products become competitive, they conduct extensive preparatory work to lay a solid grounding for markets.

The companies' capacity to think in long-range terms is made possible in part by their relatively greater reliance on bank loans than on the sale of securities to meet their capital requirements. Since stock now accounts for less than one-sixth of a company's capital needs compared to one-half in the United States, stockholders lack power to pressure for showing a profit each year, and banks are as interested in a company's long-range growth as the company itself. When companies are able to pay interest, the banks want to continue to lend them money, for banks are as dependent on quality companies to lend to as companies are dependent on the banks for

borrowing. Indeed, when quality companies with their own capital want to cut costs by repaying loans, the banks try to make it attractive to continue borrowing.

Despite their interest in the future, most Japanese companies have not considered it profitable to invest heavily in basic research and development. It has made more sense to purchase foreign technology, for even if costs seemed high at the time of purchase, in retrospect the technology was obtained at bargain prices. The company concentrates research on adapting the technology for large-scale production, sometimes in such a way that it no longer needs to pay royalties on a particular patent. Japanese laws are such that processes, not functions, are patented. Thus, the company can buy technology, make new inventions that meet the same function as the original patent, and end its dependence on foreign technology. Until the 1970s many Western companies sold technology cheaply. Some did so because it was a perishable item likely to become obsolete or to be pirated, but often they were short-sighted in licensing patents—eager for a quick profit, ignorant of the long-term Japanese competitive threat, and unwilling to take the trouble to invest in developing the Japanese market. In recent years, as foreign companies are more clearly aware of the potential value of patents to Japanese mass producers, the prices and terms of technological transfer have become much higher, and the Japanese companies have therefore begun to move selectively into more research and development. Having caught up with much of Western technology, Japanese research is more concentrated in innovative rather than adaptive areas, and in areas with high potential economic payoff. Japan now has about as many people engaged in nonmilitary research as does the United States.

Just as MITI has tried to reorient industrial structure toward industrial sectors that can compete more effectively on world markets in the future, so each individual company tries to concentrate on product lines or segments that are likely to be more profitable in the future and to reduce its activity in declining sectors well before it is no longer profitable to continue.

It is not that Japanese are not interested in profitability, but that they are prepared to defer maximizing immediate profits in order to increase market share. Beginning in the late 1970s when the Japanese growth rate started leveling off, most Japanese companies have been trying even harder to find ways to cut costs to maintain profitability. But they tend to judge their company's success less by annual profit than by the annual changes in the market share their company has compared to other companies in the industrial sector. As the Boston Consulting Group has demonstrated, profitability is closely related to market share, for as firms expand they have more low-priced young labor and more modern plants. Therefore the companies' emphasis on market share has been well-placed.

The company's interest in the long term is also related to the system of permanent employment whereby an ordinary employee remains in the firm from the time he first enters after leaving school until he retires, which in most firms averages about fifty-seven or fifty-eight. The firm is committed to the employee and provides a sense of belonging, personal support, welfare and retirement benefits, and increased salary and rank with age. Barring serious long-term depression, the employee expects that he will never be laid off, and even if the company were to disband or be absorbed by another company, he expects that a new job elsewhere will be arranged. Companies are able to offer this kind of security despite economic fluctuations for several reasons. In times of temporary growth, additional temporary employees may be hired. For example, housewives may be added to the work force

with the clear understanding that they will remain only while business needs them. Employees retiring from the company may be offered special short-term assignments in the company, usually at a lower salary than before retirement. Work may be subcontracted to small companies with the understanding that these contracts imply no permanent relationship.

If a large, reliable company should encounter economic difficulty, it will not go out of business because it is backed by banks, and behind the banks are various government institutions. Japanese companies have large debts to banks, but virtually all major companies are considered important for the economy as a whole, and therefore the Bank of Japan, backed by the Finance Ministry, stands behind the city banks that lend to the companies. Every company borrows from a main bank and then from other banks. If the company should be badly in debt and need to be bailed out, the main bank arranges a new management team for the company, often from its own staff, thereby strengthening lines of control over the company, which had previously been essentially autonomous. To the company officials replaced, this is not only a loss of power for them and their followers but a disgrace, something to avoid at all costs. Similarly, even in a declining industry, management and unions consider consolidation and consequent loss of power a last resort, something to fight against as long as possible. Every large company that has collapsed in Japan has resorted to questionable practices and behaved improperly toward its main bank. There is virtually no danger of a reliable major firm collapsing, but this security does not lead companies to relax their determination to perform at a high level.

The Japanese company with a given amount of resources has much greater security than an American firm in making bold efforts to modernize and undertake new activities. In addition to financial backing through banks, the company can be sure that key government ministries are concerned with their success and will help out in unpredictable emergencies in finding land, getting resources, gaining crucial technology. They know the government will be unlikely to undertake antitrust or other legal action that will greatly upset the company's overall capacities. The Japanese company signs fewer contracts and works more with other firms with whom there is a high degree of mutual trust, especially within the same group. They can therefore make more flexible adjustments in case of unpredictable outside forces, greatly reducing legal risks which American companies would have to bear regardless of new circumstances.

A company that encounters economic difficulties has many ways of adjusting without sacrificing the permanent employment system. Usually in addition to monthly salary, the company pays sizeable semiannual bonuses amounting to several months' salary. The size of the bonus depends on company profits, and therefore in times of depression it may be reduced without affecting basic monthly salary. In the spring, when basic monthly salary is determined, salary increases can be reduced or eliminated. The company can request employees to take an immediate vacation with partial rather than full pay or to reduce working hours, or to take minor salary cuts while requesting high officials to take larger salary cuts. If the difficulty is more severe, a company will reduce its entering class or even take in no new employees, adjusting assignments within the company so that jobs that would have been done by new employees will be done by others. Since companies follow long-term trends very closely, in industries that are expected to level off or decline, as for example in family electronics products which are increasingly made in Taiwan and Korea, where labor costs are lower, companies will have anticipated the decline and admitted fewer em-

ployees in the years preceding the decline. Temporary employees will be released and permanent employees reassigned to their tasks. If the situation is very severe, the products formerly made by subcontractors are terminated. Some individual subcontracting firms may be in trouble, but until now there have been enough new opportunities that few workers still in their prime are unable to find new work. If the recession is so severe that this kind of remedy is not adequate, then the company may move into some product line where it can keep people busy, for it makes sense to the Japanese to employ steadily a devoted work force and to take a small loss in order to provide work opportunities for one's permanent staff. As a further remedy, a company may encourage its workers to retire somewhat earlier by providing special benefits. If all these strategies are insufficient, some employees may be transferred from a company in a declining sector to affiliated companies in growing sectors. In fact, however, the number of cases of permanent employees being transferred to other companies in hard times is small. The system has so many cushions that permanent employees in large companies have ample reason to feel secure. Japanese companies may trim around the edges but they are not about to abandon the system.

Because an employee has job security and knows his salary will rise with seniority, he is willing to accept moderately low wages during his first few years in the company. Also, since retirement age is normally in the late fifties, salary increments can go up fairly rapidly without a company's worrying about having very high-paid elderly employees for many years. Although the system is designed to provide incentives for the young person trained by the company to remain loyal throughout his career and to have a sense of advancement, one of the important side effects is that it creates great pressure on a company to hire young people. Companies are reluctant to hire a midcareer person not only because his sense of loyalty would be questionable but because it is to the company's advantage to employ him during his low-priced younger years. In boom years, school and university graduates usually have had several positions to choose from, and even in relatively depressed years unemployment among young people leaving school is virtually nonexistent, much lower than the general figure for unemployment which escalated to over two percent in the late 1970s.

The seniority system in the company works much as in the bureaucracy. Although there are pay differentials later in the career based on performance and responsibility, these are small compared to those accounted for by seniority pay. Responsible executives consciously try to keep pay distinctions among those with the same seniority no larger than, and if anything smaller than, what most employees consider appropriate. New employees ordinarily receive precisely the same pay for the first several years in the company; when differentials begin to appear later, they are minor, having more psychological than monetary significance. Equal pay tends to dampen competition and strengthen camaraderie among peers during their early years. If anything, the peer group recognizes that the ablest of their group are not being fully compensated in salary for their contribution, and this tends to dull any envy of peers toward the fastest rising in their group. Even those who rise more rapidly after differentials come into play can be promoted only if they enjoy the respect and approval of their associates; this prevents the growing distinctions from being overly disruptive. In a basic social sense, all those with the same seniority are considered as equals.

Those with higher positions continue to dress like others, often in company uniforms, and peers retain informal terms of address and joking relationships. Top officials receive less salary and fewer stock options than American top executives, and they live more modestly. It is easier to maintain lower pay for Japanese top executives because with loyalty so highly valued, they will not be lured to another company. This self-denial by top executives was designed to keep the devotion of the worker, and it undoubtedly succeeds.

It is understood that no one in a management track will be skipped over in advancement and no one will serve over another who entered the company at an earlier time. The same is true for technical track personnel and for laborers. Japanese executives at times considered increasing incentives for young people by allowing them to rise more rapidly and serve over their elders, but this caused undue strain in personal relations. The embarrassment for a person serving under a younger person is greater than in the United States. A person's official position can only rise until his retirement, and this eliminates any anxiety over the possibility that a worker will be relieved of his job or dropped to a lower position. After the first several years the able person begins to take on positions associated with the elite course inside the company and gradually rises to more important posts. But the differentials among age peers in title as well as pay are slight. A very able person might become section chief a year or two before his peers, or he might become section chief at the same time as his peers but be chief of a more important section.

As with elite bureaucrats, those who come up an elite course within the company have a broad range of experience in all parts of the company. The high official therefore has detailed understanding of issues in all sections as well as close friendships that ensure continuous frank communication. The highest officials just below the level of president have members of their peer group at all other important positions in the company, which makes for unusually effective communication and mutual understanding. It also makes it more difficult for younger men to break into the inner circles if they were to advance more rapidly than others of their age group and requires that they wait until their peer group holds the top positions. This also ensures classmate linkages with other companies and the government bureaucracy, where elite rise in pace, so that contacts with every important institution at every level can be conducted through long-term intimate channels. Managers of a large American corporation commonly have at least as broad a range of experience, and American companies can acquire some know-how by hiring workers with certain skills. However, with more turnover American employees lack the close personal connection within the company and with peers in other key organizations that contribute so much to Japanese company effectiveness.

As in the bureaucracy, only the top handful of officers work beyond normal retirement age, and when one man in an age cohort is chosen president, all his peers resign, usually to assume a high position with a subsidiary or subcontractor. One man therefore stands alone as the senior person concerned with daily affairs in the company, although the chairman of the board, usually the previous president, and board members or consultants, also former chief executives, may carry great weight on major issues or other issues in which they have special interest. It is conventional wisdom in Japan to concentrate the most experienced men at the top, in part because they have mature judgment but also because other senior people do not have to suffer the humiliation of serving under people younger than themselves and will wholeheartedly accept authority from those older who are also competent.

How is it possible for a unit to work effectively when a mediocre senior person is serving above an abler junior person? The answer lies not only in the senior person's lack of worry about being replaced by his junior but in the differentiation between task and title or position. The essential building block of a company is not a man with a particular role assignment and his secretary and assistants, as might

be the case in an American company. The essential building block of the organization is the section. A section might have eight or ten people, including the section chief. Within the section there is not as sharp a division of labor as in an American company. To some extent, each person in the same section shares the same overall responsibility and can substitute for another when necessary. The abler younger person knows that he cannot surpass his senior in rank and salary now, but that all concerned informally recognize that he is abler than his superior. He also knows that he will eventually rise higher than his present senior, but that he must cooperate with his present senior for his section to accomplish its tasks and for him to be considered promising. Similarly, the head of the section is held responsible for the successful work of the section. He knows that he needs to take advantage of the talents of the abler person under him, and he therefore eagerly gives him responsible work. He is in no fear of being upstaged by his underling, for they are lumped together when their accomplishments in the section are evaluated. Within the general work of a section, one's assignment to a task at a given time is affected by one's general abilities, skills, and aptitudes more than by one's title within the section. The section is, in a sense, an organic unit composed to match a variety of talents rather than a team with clearly distinct, independent role assignments. The section has a responsibility to perform, and each is expected to help out by dividing up what needs to be done, substituting for someone who is absent, or assisting another when necessary. The assignment is flexible, for the position and tasks are two different systems: the position rises with seniority, but the work depends on the tasks of the unit and the talents and complementarity of the individuals. Work is not determined by a specifically defined position.

When asked to describe a Japanese company, most Japanese managers list as one characteristic the practice of "bottom up" rather than "top down." The lowly section, within its sphere, does not await executive orders but takes the initiatives. It identifies problems, gathers information, consults with relevant parts of the company, calls issues to the attention of higher officials, and draws up documents. Of course the section acts within the context of the wishes of higher officials and is in constant communication with them. Proposals are not usually sent to higher levels until the section has consulted broadly with other sections and has formulated detailed plans. Nowhere in the process is there a fully organized presentation of several options to higher officials, and nowhere is there a neat package of conclusions flowing from higher levels. Good decisions emerge not from brilliant presentations of alternatives but from section people discussing all aspects of the questions over and over with all the most knowledgeable people. Some senior executives in companies play a central role in making decisions, but ordinarily they do so only after appropriate section leaders lay the groundwork through close consultation with other sections and only when lower levels cannot themselves resolve their differences. Section people take great pride in their work because of their initiatives and because they have a chance to develop their leadership and carry great weight within the company on matters relating to their sphere. Consequently, the morale of young workers in their thirties tends to be very high.

For this system to work effectively, leading section personnel need to know and to identify with company purposes to a higher degree than persons in an American firm. They achieve this through long experience and years of discussion with others at all levels. Company aims are not canonized into documents but continue to fluctuate with the changing environment, and therefore section leaders must avoid being locked into a specific list of aims but rather adapt to overall opportunities

for the company as a whole. Section leaders are sufficiently tuned to the overall thinking of the company for them to in fact achieve this, and they are given the leeway to act accordingly because higher officials know that section leaders are thoroughly committed to their company, where they will remain until retirement.

With so much authority concentrated at low levels and with so much discussion between levels, how can the company leaders make the bold decisions that have led to Japanese success? First, they operate in a climate of much greater security than the typical American firm. A company receives advice from well-informed bureaucrats, banks, affiliated trading companies, and other companies in its group. It is backed by banks and ultimately the government, which when necessary will assist it in obtaining special resources and facilities and will not pursue it in ways that create uncertainties and costly law suits. Second, because rivals are striving for market share and because the seniority system and bank lending require expansion, it becomes more dangerous to stand pat than to move ahead with bold modernization and innovation. Further, stockholders do not constrain executives with demands for short-term profits. As a result, Japanese companies have consistently been bolder than most of their Western counterparts in modernizing and expanding their capacity.

GROUP SPIRIT AND PERSONAL INCENTIVES

In addition to providing the employee with the economic incentives for long-term loyalty, company officials do their best to reinforce employee identification with the company. They provide elaborate annual ceremonies for inducting the new employees who enter as a group shortly after the end of the school year. The official training program may be anywhere from a few weeks to years, and includes not only useful background information but emotional accounts of company history and purposes. For spiritual and disciplinary training the employee may go on retreats, visit temples, or endure special hardships. To strengthen the bonds of solidarity, the new employee may be housed in company dorms while undergoing training, even if it means being separated from his spouse or parents. But even after the formal training program is over, the young employee continues to be treated as an apprentice for some time. He continues to receive training and supervision, and he is expected to behave with appropriate deference to his seniors. In American terms it is perhaps like a combination of the behavior of the fraternity pledge, without the hazing, and the young doctor in residency training.

Companies commonly have their own uniforms, badges, songs, and mottos. Each company has a special lore about the spirit of a ''Matsushita person'' or ''sumitomo person'' or ''Sanwa person,'' but to the outside observer the spirit sounds strikingly similar: enthusiastic, loyal, devoted. Company reception halls are available to employees' families for receptions and celebrations. Resort houses in the mountains and on the seacoast can be used by company employees who have put in the appropriate years of loyal service. Dormitories or apartment projects are available to employees of many companies. Unlike America, where mortgages are commonly obtained directly from banks, in Japan a high proportion of mortgages are obtained from the workers' company at subsidized interest rates. The company supplies gifts for many occasions in addition to the large semiannual bonuses. Special discounts of company products are available to employees and their families. Many companies have daily ceremonies—for opening the store, commencing work, or starting physical exercise. Parties large and small bid farewell to the old year, send off employees transferred to another city, welcome them

home, congratulate people on promotions or honors, greet visitors, and commemorate retirement. Weekend group trips celebrate the coming of cherry blossoms, fall foliage, or holidays. For family members there are parties, special-interest clubs, courses, lectures, and exhibitions.

In addition to providing gymnasiums and swimming pools, a large company usually has sports teams well-equipped with uniforms and often with showcase facilities. So they can do well in their leagues, many companies recruit talented athletes as company employees, much as American colleges do, and they are given only minor work responsibilities. Outstanding professional sports teams that in the United States would be privately owned and associated with a particular city are in Japan sponsored instead by companies. The very highest officials in the company commonly take off from work to attend important sports contests with their rival companies.

During Prime Minister Tanaka's time companies even tried sponsoring political candidates, but this was abandoned because they had limited appeal, even within the company, and it proved embarrassing for companies to have their candidate lose.

Executives generally want their employees to spend a certain amount of off-duty hours together, preferably under company sponsorship. One company, troubled that too many young employees had their own cars and sufficiently high salary to go off on their own rather than use company facilities, surveyed employee interests and, finding that bowling was then the current rage, provided very attractive uniforms, bowling balls, and other equipment. It also bought a regular block of time for workers at the most luxurious nearby bowling alley. By ensuring that more leisure time was under company auspices, the company reinforced group solidarity.

Loyalty in a large company is a many-layered overlapping labyrinth. Employees have layers of loyalty to the group with which the company is affiliated, to the particular factory or store, to the section, and to the immediate work group. Younger employees who are in a given specialty or career line may also enjoy a special link with senior sponsors in the same career line. Even with the immediate work group, one kind of group spirit thrives when the superior is absent, another when he is present. Part or all of the peer group assembles to commemorate earlier times and gossip about current events. Informal socializing, celebrations, and farewell or welcome-home parties occur at all of these levels.

At times a senior's concern about younger colleagues borders on what Westerners would consider "mothering," for Japanese of both sexes accept personal solicitousness that in the United States would ordinarily be considered unmasculine for men to give or receive. To avoid embarrassing an individual in public, criticism is commonly expressed in private in the spirit of a superior siding with a junior to help with a problem certain to cause him trouble.

With so much security and warmth, how does the system ensure high performance? In initially hiring employees, the company aims to be as merciless as entrance examinations in selecting people of quality. In preparation for selecting among employees of a peer group for more responsible positions, key line officers spend an enormous amount of time informally evaluating the performance of juniors, for decisions about personnel are considered too important to be left to personnel specialists. Employees are generally reassigned every two or three years, and each person knows that the quality of his overall performance is being evaluated to determine his next assignment. Those who rise to the top are chosen because in addition to high innate ability they have the capacity to see the big picture, to analyze problems clearly, to convey poise and confidence, to inspire support from fellow employees in all

parts of the company, and to form successful relationships with top-level people in other companies and in the government.

The Japanese company makes it clear that its substantial benefits to employees are not guaranteed. Benefits are not distributed automatically by contractual agreement to anyone simply because he is a company member or because he falls into a certain category of age, status, and length of service, for leaders believe flexibility of rewards is needed as a critical leverage to maintain discipline. Bonuses, sick leave, and use of company facilities are offered to the hard worker, but signs of disapproval to the dilatory cause doubts about how superiors will respond when they come with their next request.

For motivating the worker, superiors rarely need to talk directly about benefits. Since employees have such long-term personal relationships with each other, small systematic differentiations of treatment by superiors have great psychological significance. Those who receive subtle hints that they are likely to rise eventually to the top positions are tremendously motivated because there is sufficient continuity and predictability to ensure that the hints can be translated into reality. When peers become overly solicitous to see if they can be of help, the worker knows that others consider his performance below par, and he may be devastated. He will rise by seniority alone, but to be at the bottom of his age group is extremely embarrassing and to be at the bottom and disliked for not trying as well is something to be avoided at all costs. But unlike students at the Harvard Business School and members of the United States State Department, for example, those at the bottom of the Japanese peer group do not need to worry that they may become castoffs as long as they exert themselves; the threat of banishment is often implicit but rarely used.

The most important single criterion for assessing quality for regular term promotions is the capacity to work well with others. The person who rises more rapidly is not the one with the original ideas but the one who can cooperate with others in finding a conclusion satisfactory to everyone. Personal achievement cannot be separated from the capacity to work effectively in groups. Eventually the reward for performance and effort includes salary and position, but the proximate reward which foretells the eventual success in salary and position is the esteem of colleagues. In an American company without a strong group spirit and without expectations of permanent employment, an employee might come to feel that the only significant reward is salary and position, which in his view ought to be finely tuned to match performance. In the Japanese view, this custom, like tipping, which they still avoid, cheapens the sense of service and contributes to contentiousness. In a Japanese company with strong group spirit and a long time frame, the really significant reward, the thing an employee strives for, is the esteem of his colleagues.

THE COMPANY MAN: HARD WORK AND SELF-ESTEEM

Earlier generations of Western social scientists like Durkheim and Parsons thought that occupational specialty could provide the means for integrating the individual in modern society. However, the pace of modern technological and organizational change renders occupation specialty training too rapidly outdated to provide a stable source of life-long identification and basic social integration for the society. No structure in the West compares with the Japanese firm in its capacity to introduce rapid change and to provide identification for a substantial portion of the population. The young American employee hired as a specialist is not interested in learning as broad a range of things about the company as the young Japanese employee, who is more of a generalist. A Japanese employee who knows he will be kept and retrained in midcareer is less likely to worry about innovation and resist technological change. Featherbedding and the reluctance of American workers to be flexible in performing various jobs in a company are problems for American industry not only because workers are afraid of losing their jobs but because they want to protect their skill level. The Japanese worker concerned about the long-range future of his company eagerly seeks technological change and, because his status and future are less related to a special skill level, he is more willing to perform miscellaneous tasks and to assist fellow workers in different tasks as the need arises. The employer gets fuller and more flexible use of employees, and employees find the varied work less monotonous than their American counterparts who stick to the same work.

Like paternalistic craft structures in premodern America, Europe, and Japan, the large modern Japanese company is committed to the whole individual, not simply to the task-related part of the individual. Alfred Sloan once boasted that General Motors continued to pay dividends to stockholders right through the depression even though it had to lay off workers. A Japanese business leader would never say such a thing and, if he did anything remotely resembling it, he would try to hide it, for valuing profits above his employees would destroy his relationship with his workers. The primary commitment of a Japanese firm is not to its stockholders but to its employees.

Japanese workers reciprocate this commitment, for they prefer a company that is not simply "dry," cool, and calculated, but "wet" with human emotion. The American employee with specific assignments and responsibilities and strictly calculated pay per hour is not inclined to work beyond stated time or to do extra personal things for his colleagues, but a Japanese employee is. Every five years, beginning in 1953, there have been public opinion polls in Japan asking if people would prefer to work for someone who made specific assignments and provided help within the confines of the work or someone who expected extras beyond specific assignments but was prepared to offer personal help beyond the regular rules. The Japanese public, by a substantial majority, consistently prefers the supervisor who has personal relations going beyond the work requirements. Americans overwhelmingly prefer the opposite.

Even without company-sponsored activities, employees find time in the evenings or on weekends to have good times with one another without work in front of them. They often socialize on the way home from work. In many companies with a five- or five-and-a-half day week some employees at almost all levels come in on Saturday and stay later to play mahjong, go, *shoji*, or to go drinking. Even among more "modern" employees who, like Americans, want to spend weekend time with families, couples often spend their time with other couples connected with the same company. Socializing is partly for sheer fun, but many consciously try to have good times together to make it easier to work together during the week. Because employees know they have to have each other's goodwill until retirement, they are not as likely as Americans to become righteously indignant with each other. They look for ways to subdue tensions and rivalries and reinforce camaraderie. Inner feelings of competition, anxiety, and annoyance may be at least as strong as in American companies since relationships are so close and since escaping difficult problems by leaving the company is not ordinarily a realistic option. Informal sociability is not only an end in itself but a way to contain these potentially disruptive tendencies.

The success of Japanese companies in avoiding disruptive labor unrest must be understood in the context of long-run individual identification with the company, but it has been reinforced by company handling of labor unions. After World War II, when the Allied Occupation ordered a rapid expansion of labor unions, Japanese company executives moved quickly to make employees members of labor unions. Labor unions were thus born not from virulent struggles led by bitter union leaders but from the initiative of company leaders. Nonetheless, the labor movement, at first protected by the Allied Occupation, became a powerful and sometimes violent political force. Management moved to encourage faithful employees to take part in union activities with the hope of moderating the potentially devastating strikes. They encouraged white-collar employees to join the same company union as the blue-collar employees and provided rooms and other facilities for union activities. These same white-collar employees, after serving their stint in labor unions, then returned to their managerial career line without loss of seniority. When unions became too militant, companies sometimes used questionable tactics to break the union and sponsored a second union that was more sympathetic with company goals. Management realized that simply co-opting unions could not be successful, and they eagerly sought feedback from unions to find opportunities for meeting worker complaints in order to create better working relations and a more satisfied labor force. Japanese unions are organized by the enterprise, and national craft unions tend to be weak. Nonetheless, unions do energetically represent the interests of the workers in pushing for benefits. Otherwise, union leaders would lose the support of workers. Unions also play a role in aggregating worker opinion on issues directly affecting them as part of the root-binding process in the firm. Though very worried about the danger of unions in the late 1940s, management has come to regard their unions as friends in helping stabilize the company. To avoid an excessive adversary relationship and create a proper climate, management finds time to socialize with union leaders without waiting for disputes that engender an atmosphere of controversy.

Because Japan is a rapidly modernizing country, with a dual economy of a modern and less modern sector, workers in larger companies are elite, with better training, more security, and better working conditions than workers in small companies that are less modern. Employees in large companies therefore have felt privileged to be there. Furthermore, since companies were mostly formed by managers rather than independent owners, workers have no rich capitalist class above them but only a managerial class whose style of life is not so different from their own. Japanese executives feel that not only American company owners but managerial staff have given themselves too many emoluments compared to what they gave the workers. This modest differential between managers and workers of a given age tends to reinforce the worker's sense of identification with the firm.

In some areas unions have engaged in long disruptive strikes, but in all such cases workers were not afraid of company losses through strikes. Local government employees, public school teachers, national and private railway workers, workers in government monopolies like tobacco, and, in the early postwar period, mine workers have fought militantly, but they all share a common characteristic: they are convinced that disruptions will not endanger the future of their organization. Government employees know that taxes can be used to raise their wages and improve their conditions regardless of the effectiveness and efficiency of their government unit. Private railway workers know that company income is determined by the rate structure, which can be adjusted if wages are increased. And in the early postwar period, when coal was the main source of energy and the government provided necessary subsidies to private coal companies, workers were not afraid that militant struggle would

weaken the competitiveness of their company. In the late 1950s, when coal companies were going out of business because of the decline of available resources, miners struck because they knew they wanted the best possible settlement, backed by government support for a declining industry. In ordinary companies, where workers identify with the long-run interests of the company, strikes have been virtually unknown once the Occupation ended and the economy returned to normal in the early 1950s.

With growing affluence and full employment in the late 1960s, many young Japanese became confident of their ability to earn a living even if they should leave their present company, and this attitude threatened company discipline. Many worried managers therefore fought harder than ever to maintain company solidarity. At the height of rapid growth, when unemployment was less than one percent and many company employees could have found work elsewhere, they still remained in their company. Since the oil shock of 1973, with renewed fears of a depression and increased unemployment, workers have felt especially dependent on their company and discipline has improved further. Although the Japanese standard of living is now on a par with that of the most advanced countries in the world, affluence has not ended hard work.

Even in the public sector there have been few debilitating strikes in recent years. Strikes in the public sector are officially illegal, and when some unions tested this legality in 1976, the strike was stopped before the announced termination date by public opinion and not the law. Employees from private companies who worked hard and accepted what they considered reasonable salary raises would not tolerate the government providing more favorable conditions for striking workers in the public sector. Newspapers that initially had taken a somewhat favorable attitude toward strikers changed quickly with the vehemence of public reaction. They began reporting, for example, that children of striking workers were ridiculed by classmates for what their parents were doing to the general public. It would not be politically feasible for workers in the public sector to use their capacity to stop the operation of public facilities to raise salaries higher than their counterparts in the private sector. It is not simply that the majority of Japanese workers are basically satisfied because their interests are being served, but that the workers in the private sector who do not strike because of devotion to their company exert public pressure strong enough to contain strikers in the public sector.

Perhaps more important than the success of companies in mobilizing workers for production and avoiding disabling strikes is the impact the system has on the self-esteem of the individual. The American who is fired or laid off as soon as the company's financial statement is in the red and who must go on unemployment insurance finds it hard to maintain great self-respect for his capacity to work. The worker who knows he will then be out of work understandably might demand more salary now, but in so doing he begins to measure his contribution and even his own worth solely in monetary terms. Even a high American official who is dropped or demoted because his division is unprofitable or who is hastily removed when dissatisfaction rises about company performance cannot help but have doubts about himself as well as his company. Unless caught in a horrendous well-publicized scandal, no Japanese official would be comparably disgraced by his company, and even if an official were caught in such an extreme case, the other company officials find a way to cushion the blow if he has indeed performed well for the company. Officials who must be demoted to take responsibility for a public problem are often given substitute rewards and honor within the company so that they may not feel especially distraught. Success and failure come from group effort and are never laid on the shoulders of a single person. At worst, if an official performed badly, his term would be brought to a close slightly more rapidly or he might not be promoted to the next post quite as readily. Former officials do not need to be discredited by new officials and generally remain on good terms with their successors. Japanese workers who feel they do more than is required and feel they are appreciated by fellow workers enjoy a greater sense of individual worth than those who merely get by with the minimal effort, a more common American pattern.

In short, the large Japanese company, an institutional structure that originated not in traditional Japan but in the mid-twentieth century, has developed a very effective modern corporatism well adapted to the needs of the latter part of the twentieth century. It has not eliminated problems. There are bad managers as well as good ones, and workers feel unhappiness with boring assignments, anxiety over personal difficulties, disappointment at not being more appreciated. But by international standards the large modern Japanese corporation is a highly successful institution. It is successful not because of any mystical group loyalty embedded in the character of the Japanese race but because it provides a sense of belonging and a sense of pride to workers, who believe their future is best served by the success of their company. The pride and stability that so many Japanese have because a family member works in a large company helps stabilize the political process and set a tone for the society at large.

DISCUSSION QUESTIONS

1. Why has Japan outdistanced America in per capita production?
2. What unique problems did Japan face?
3. What new problems does a highly industrialized Japan face?

CHAPTER 13

Issues in Education

INTRODUCTION

In 1983 the National Commission on Excellence in Education made its report to President Reagan's Secretary of Education, and to the people of the United States. The report, entitled *A Nation at Risk*, caused renewed attention to be focused on the state of education in the United States. It also inspired a spate of critical books on American education, most notably Alan Bloom's *The Closing of the American Mind* (1987) and E. D. Hirsch's *Cultural Literacy* (1988), both of which became best-sellers.

Recognizing the achievements of the educational system of the United States, *A Nation at Risk* nevertheless states that the educational foundations of our society are presently being eroded by a rising tide of mediocrity that threatens U.S. preeminence in the world and has permitted other nations to challenge U.S. educational superiority. In locating fault within the nation's schools, which are buffeted by conflicting personal, social, and political demands, the report expressed concern not only about the areas in which the United States has fallen behind other nations in commerce and industry but also about the "intellectual, moral, and spiritual strengths of our people

which knit together the very fabric of our society." As indicators of this risk, the report points to the poor academic achievement of students in the United States, to the high rates of functional illiteracy, to falling SAT scores, and to the failure of students to match their talents to achievement. These deficiencies come at a time when the demand for highly educated and skilled workers is growing. The need for excellence in education has never been more pressing.

The Commission's report outlined a series of recommendations for educational reform, in an attempt to meet the crisis in U.S. education. The recommendations included strengthening high school graduation requirements, raising standards and expectations at all levels of the educational system, significantly increasing the amount of time devoted to learning, improving entrance requirements and performance of those in the teaching profession, and providing higher levels of support and leadership for the educational mission.

Each year some 5 million American children enroll in school for the first time, joining the 40 million returning students. Both the number and the proportion of young people attending school has increased, and there has been an accompanying increase in funds devoted to education. The educational institution is one of the most important institutions in the country, not only because of its size and cost but also because it has become the locus of a number of important societal issues. Education, a topic of central concern in U.S. society, is now often described as being in crisis. While the nature of the crisis is described in various terms, there is widespread agreement on its indicators, as described in *A Nation at Risk*.

The educational system has become a sort of laboratory in which various solutions are tested—solutions to the problems of declining quality in educational achievement and lack of equality in access to education—and in which attempts are made to determine what contributions teachers and schools make to these problems. Social science has become heavily involved in explaining the causes of these problems and formulating proposals for their resolution. Educational research has focused on such issues as tension between the goals of preparation for adult occupational roles and equality of educational opportunity, the relative effects of individual effort and schools on achievement, and the contribution of educational systems to structured social inequality. By some indicators, the American system of education is highly successful. Virtually all children receive some high school education, and a growing percentage of students go on to college. Young people today learn more than did their predecessors in earlier generations. And yet, the educational institution is buffeted by criticisms from many sides. The paradox of education in the United States is that, in a country where education is prized and universally provided, the educational system is often seen as a failure. The readings in this chapter address some of the more salient issues confronting contemporary educational institutions.

E. D. Hirsch, whose *Cultural Literacy* elicited an enraged response from the educational community following its publication in 1988, writes about the "primal scene of education," in the third reading presented in this chapter. The article, taken from *The New York Review of Books*, explores some of the individual consequences of skill-oriented education in America. Hirsch discusses the comparatively low science achievement scores of American students, their declining verbal SAT scores, the acute problems of variation in background knowledge which hampers learning in the elementary school classroom, and the existence of an academic caste system that puts poor and minority students at a distinct disadvantage. Hirsch attributes these deficiencies to the failure of American educators to emphasize factual knowledge. He concludes with some promising results from the New York State Regents exams and the success of the Swedish elementary school system.

Social scientists have long been interested in the relationship between educational opportunities and position in the stratification system of U.S. society. A college education, particularly, increases an individual's opportunities for greater access to the valued resources of income, prestige, and power. Educational organizations also contribute to structured inequalities through ascriptive processes. In the second reading of this chapter, Caroline Persell and Peter Cookson examine status ascription and the transmission of privilege in elite boarding schools. Their research on forty-two private boarding schools reveals the special status rights conferred upon graduates of these schools by virtue of the "charters" the schools have with Ivy League schools. Persell and Cookson also document the bartering about acceptances to elite colleges that goes on between boarding school advisers and college admission officers. These authors view the social networks between elite boarding schools and colleges as a critical element in the transmission of privilege across generations and the social reproduction of the elite class. We have selected their article in order to highlight the dramatic consequences revealed by an organizational level of analysis.

The cross-cultural reading on education, by Fred Strebeigh, examines some of the dilemmas created when foreign students study and do research in the United States. International study generates serious problems both for institutions of higher education and for the countries which send their brightest young people abroad for their educations. From the perspective of American universities, for example, the cost of training foreign students is not entirely covered by tuition fees. In addition, presence of large members of foreign students on American campuses, particularly in graduate programs, raises questions about the adequacy of our curriculums for their needs. Among the dilemmas faced by Third World nations that send their best students and researchers to the United States are (1) that the knowledge acquired by these students and researchers may not be relevant to their parent nations' problems and (2) that the educational exchange fosters cultural and informational dependencies which reinforce the economic dependency of less developed countries upon the United States and other Western industrialized nations. Equally serious is the so-called "brain drain" that results when foreign students opt to remain in the United States after their training, rather than returning to their native countries. Strebeigh explores the impact of a U.S. education on citizens of the People's Republic of China and concludes that while the adverse effects may be significant, they are often exaggerated.

References

Bloom, Allan. *The Closing of the American Mind.* New York: Simon & Schuster, 1987.

Hirsch, E. D. *Cultural Literacy.* New York: Vintage, 1988.

National Commission on Excellence in Education. *A Nation at Risk.* Washington, D.C.: Government Printing Office, 1983.

The Primal Scene of Education

E. D. Hirsch, Jr.

1

It is said that American prosperity is fading in a bleach of educational incompetence, and that a large proportion of our incoming work force can neither adjust to new technologies nor perform high-level communicative tasks. "In math and science," the education researcher John Chubb recently observed, "U.S. students rank dead last in any comparison with students from the nations that are our leading competitors."[1] Last October, an editorial in *The Washington Post* commented on

> the education-linked difficulty facing the large number of workers in this country who, not that long ago, could qualify for a wide range of entry-level, decently paying jobs without sophisticated technical skills or in many cases a high school diploma. As we constantly hear, these jobs are mostly gone, replaced by more technically demanding and autonomous jobs that need employees with higher-order skills. Many employers, especially urban employers in cities with troubled school systems, say they cannot fill these jobs with the available high school graduates.[2]

Current public concern over filling jobs and competing with other nations offers a historic opportunity to improve all dimensions of American education. Today, more than in any earlier time in our history, purely utilitarian aims happen to coincide with the highest humanistic and civic purposes of schooling, such as promoting a more just and harmonious society, creating an informed citizenry, and teaching our children to understand and appreciate the worlds of nature, culture, and history.

These aims coincide today with those of economic utility because the information age has made purely vocational training obsolete. Vocations change their character so rapidly that the most appropriate preparation for today's workplace is an ability to adapt to new kinds of jobs that may not have existed when one was in school. The best possible vocational training is to cultivate general abilities to communicate and learn—abilities that can only be gained through a broad humanistic and scientific education.

At a conference of college deans this fall, I heard a chorus of anecdotes about the declining knowledge and abilities of entering freshmen. To these administrators, the debate over Stanford University's required courses seemed interesting but less than momentous compared with the problem of preparing students to participate intelligently in any university-level curriculum. American colleges and universities at their best are still among the finest in the world. But in many of them the educational level of incoming students is so low that the first and second years of college must be largely devoted to remedial work. In the American school system, it is mainly those who start well who finish well. Elementary-school teachers have told me sadly that among their third and fourth graders they are able to identify future dropouts with great accuracy, because they know that the school system will not overcome the initial academic lag of poor minority children. Business leaders and the general public are coming to recognize that the gravest, most recalcitrant problems of American education can be traced back to secondary and, above all, elementary schooling.

The latest news of American school performance comes from the International Association for the Evaluation of Educational Achievement (IEA). Of the educational reports that have numbed our minds recently, none is more informative than the IEA's 1988 report on science achievement in seventeen countries.³ The schools of all nations teach the same basic knowledge about chemistry, physics, and biology. Hence, achievement in science is an excellent point of comparison for national systems of education. In the IEA comparisons, the rank order of the US was low for all three age groups tested: ages ten, fourteen, and sixteen to seventeen. But, as the report points out, the most significant results concern fourteen-year-olds. Age fourteen is pivotal, since children haven't yet started intensive training in specialized high schools, but they have, in effect, graduated from elementary school. Their test results are undistorted by variations in the sequence of instruction in different elementary systems. Moreover, international comparisons at that point in schooling are inherently fair, since at age fourteen, 90 percent of all children in the developed nations are still in school. We Americans cannot claim that our results are inferior because ours schools virtuously cast a broader demographic net than do other nations.

The performance of American fourteen-year-olds was singled out for special mention in the IEA executive summary, from which I quote:

> The U.S.A. was third to last out of seventeen countries, with Hong Kong and the Phillipines being in the sixteenth and seventeenth places. Thailand had a score equal to that of the U.S.A. . . . The IEA conducted its last survey of science achievement in 1970. . . . The United States has dropped from seventh out of seventeen countries to third from bottom.⁴

Why has there been so little discussion of such immensely significant news? Five years after the much publicized National Commission report *A Nation at Risk*, such reports perhaps no longer startle us or add to the picture we already have. Perhaps education reporters may assume that so much energy and thought are already going into school reform that it

serves no useful purpose to add to the literature of alarm. But my experiences with apologists for American education as well as with its critics and reformers during the months since the publication of my book *Cultural Literacy* have led me to think otherwise. Most reform efforts, including many that are highly promising, concentrate on the organization and administration of schooling. Recently, for example, there has been much emphasis on establishing cooperative relations with parents of poor children from minority groups, on merit pay for good teaching, and on the development of magnet schools. The IEA science report, with its emphasis on knowledge, has a special value because it encourages us to consider the specific curriculum of the elementary school.

Of course science is just one field of instruction in elementary school, and its significance can be exaggerated. More important than specific information, according to the most influential American education experts, is the possession of general academic skills. I shall not retrace the steps by which I argued in *Cultural Literacy* that a misguided emphasis on skills has been the single most disastrous mistake of American schooling during the past forty years. An emphasis on skills coupled with a derogation of "mere facts" is a cast of mind that distinguishes the thought-world of education professors from that of common sense. Ordinary people, as Aristotle observed, think facts are important, and take pleasure in knowing them. They assume that facts are essential to knowledge and education. This is not the case with most of the interlocking institutions that make up the educational establishment, including the people responsible for running most teachers' colleges and school districts, as well as professional curriculum organizations such as the ASCD (Association for Supervision and Curriculum Development) and the publishers and buyers of textbooks. Most of the experts who are in a position to affect the school curriculum think mere facts are deadening, unless they are instantly made meaningful by being "integrated" into the child's world.

This ambivalent attitude to specific information, so different from the attitude of most ordinary people, has a double importance to the educational establishment. American schools of education are conceived on the principle that pedagogy itself is a skill that can be applied to all subject matter. Many of the courses taken by prospective teachers emphasize techniques of teaching and ways of improving students' "inferencing skills" and other general abilities as they are defined by theories of educational psychology. Thus the principle that abstractly defined skills are more important than specific information cannot be relinquished without compromising the fundamental assumptions of education schools. If educationists did not assert that skill in pedagogy is more important than mere information (which can always be looked up) they would not be able to resist the common-sense view that the best teachers, in both the early grades and the later ones, would tend to be those who are well prepared in the subject that they teach. The derogation of mere facts, besides serving the institutional interests of education schools, is also politically useful to educational administrators in a contentious and diverse country where parents can often be depended upon to raise objections whenever the specifics of the school curriculum are openly discussed. An approach emphasizing "reading skills," for example, conveniently avoids argument about what is read.

The 1970 IEA report on science ranked the US seventh and the present IEA report ranks the US third from bottom. Our 1970 average scores on the verbal Scholastic Aptitude Test, soon after their high point around 1965, were also significantly higher than they are now. The historical parellel is significant, although the year 1970 was of no particular significance in educational history. Nineteen seventy happened to be the year that the previous IEA evaluation of science achievement was made and also a year when SAT scores had not yet reached bottom in their inexorable movement downward between 1965 and 1980. The causes of that decline had less to do with the turmoil of the 1960s than with the miseducation that had established itself on a vast scale in the preceding decades, when the high school graduates of the 1960s and 1970s were entering elementary school. During the 1940s and 1950s a new generation of educators, well indoctrinated in an antitraditional pedagogy emphasizing skills, finally gained control of the nation's schools and textbooks. Thus the 1940s and 1950s, not the 1960s, were the watershed decades in the recent history of American education.[5]

The verbal SAT has been much criticized for various kinds of bias, but studies correlating its results with school records have shown that it is a reliable indicator of the general level of education of the students who take it; so we would in any case expect the verbal SAT to show a close historical correlation with results on IEA achievement tests. By the same token, the latest IEA report on science knowledge has implications that are much broader than its immediate findings regarding science. In order to interpret those implications I shall try to explain why these two very different tests—the verbal SAT and the IEA test of science—show the same pattern of American decline between 1970 and the present. To understand that pattern is to begin to grasp one of the things that have gone wrong.

The Scholastic Aptitude Test is misnamed. As its critics have observed, it only measures aptitudes if we understand the term aptitude to mean *acquired* aptitude. It is really a vocabulary test, and the bookish vocabulary that it tests is inherently related to standard academic disciplines; it does not normally ask questions involving the vocabulary of popular culture. The test is divided into four question types: antonyms, analogies, sentence completion, and reading comprehension. All of these types of questions are ultimately grounded in vocabulary. The one exception might seem to be analogy questions, which are assumed to test thinking skill, but I doubt that they do so to any significant degree. For instance, most seventeen-year-olds will correctly answer the following question:

NAIL:HAND :: (A) talon:eagle (B) tooth:bite (C) toe:foot (D) claw:paw (E) hoof:horse

By contrast, fewer students can be expected correctly to answer this analogy question:

VINDICTIVE:REVENGE :: (A) belligerent:territory (B) repentant:guilt (C) ravenous:satiation (D) hostile:brutality (E) forgiving:clemency[6]

Yet the thinking skills required to answer both questions are the same. A student who can correctly answer the first ipso facto has the skill to answer the second—but only if he or she knows what the words mean. In short, the verbal SAT is essentially a vocabulary test in all of its components.

But calling the verbal SAT a vocabulary test is almost as misleading as calling it an aptitude test. Vocabulary is more than words; it is also knowledge. To know what a word means is to know the reality it refers to, and if you don't know the reality you don't know the word well enough to answer a question about it on the verbal SAT. Vindictiveness and revenge are realities as much as nails and hands. And since the verbal SAT is an extensive and diverse vocabulary test, it is implicitly at the same time a test of general knowledge. If you know a broad diversity of words you also most likely know a broad diversity of things. The verbal

SAT therefore correlates well with a broad range of tests that probe academic achievement. Knowledge builds upon knowledge. The best way to gain new knowledge is already to possess an informed mind that can assimilate various sorts of new information.

2

Because learning depends on prior knowledge, even at the earliest stages of schooling, young children ought ideally to arrive at first grade with a reasonably broad fund of information. But many children are not so fortunate as to come from families that provide them with a fairly extensive knowledge of words and ideas before they enter school. An excellent but enormously expensive way of making up deficiencies in elementary knowledge on the part of young children is to tutor them—the tutorial method being the fastest means for imparting new knowledge. A tutor becomes aware of the unique temperament of the child and will be able to arouse curiosity and make a child feel rewarded for learning. Also, since children learn new information by attaching it to already known information, a tutor's awareness of the child's own distinctive structure of conceptions will enable the tutor to impart further knowledge with great effectiveness.

For example, a tutor who wished to teach a pupil about atomic structure might use an analogy with the solar system—if the pupil already knew about the solar system. Analogies could then be drawn between planets revolving around the sun and electrons revolving around the nucleus, between the attractive force of gravity and the attractive force of opposed electrical charges, and so on. In short, a teacher's awareness of what a pupil already knows and consequent ability to form analogies based on that awareness is a characteristic advantage of tutorial instruction. The principle can be generalized. Since knowledge builds on knowledge, the technique of using analogies (including metaphors) is an indispensable device of all kinds of teaching, not just of tutorials.

Consider now the primal scene of education in the modern elementary school. Let us assume that a teacher wishes to inform a class of some twenty pupils about the structure of atoms, and that she plans to base the day's instruction on an analogy with the solar system. She knows that the instruction will be effective only to the extent that all the students in the class already know about the solar system. A good teacher would probably try to find out. "Now, class, how many of you know about the solar system?" Fifteen hands go up. Five stay down. What is a teacher to do in this typical circumstance in the contemporary American school?

If he or she pauses to explain the solar system, a class period is lost, and fifteen of the twenty students are bored and deprived of knowledge for that day. If the teacher plunges ahead with atomic structure, the hapless five—they are most likely to be poor or minority students—are bored, humiliated, and deprived, because they cannot comprehend the teacher's explanation. At the end of class they will not understand either the solar system or atomic structure. Under these circumstances, either one group of the other will be deprived of the knowledge the teacher had hoped to impart to all the pupils in the class.

The problem is more subtle and pervasive than the example suggests because a teacher's analogies are usually less elaborate and extended than the one between atomic structure and the solar system. Analogy forms part of the very texture of a teacher's discourse. Teachers refer constantly to concepts like Cinderella or the American Revolution in order to connect new pieces of information with things that are already familiar. But if the analogies are consistently unfamiliar to ill-prepared chil-

dren, they will fall ever further behind, or else the teacher will be compelled to make instruction very slow, repetitive, and inefficient, to the boredom of better prepared students.

No doubt the problem of imperfectly shared background knowledge is in some degree inherent in any classroom. But in American classrooms today, the problem has become pervasive and acute. I am told by those who teach mathematics and foreign languages, subjects which build upon careful sequences of knowledge, that new material cannot be introduced into the elementary-school classroom until the middle of November. And throughout the year, the chief shared experience that an American teacher can rely on in making analogies is often a topic or concept that has already been covered in the same class on a previous day. But what was "covered" was not necessarily understood and learned by all pupils, since in almost every class period some children will have been in the unfortunate position of the five students who did not know about the solar system.

The dilemma is almost inevitably resolved at the expense of poor and minority students. The pervasiveness of the academic caste system that is thus created was confirmed to me recently when a researcher who had visited elementary classrooms throughout the nation on behalf of the Carnegie Foundation for the Advancement of Teaching telephoned me saying that he needed to talk to somebody. He wanted to tell me about the observations he had made in dozens of schools. In a typical fifth-grade classroom, he said, all pupils are able to sound out the words from their books, and explain what the individual words mean. They apparently can "read," but when they are asked questions about a passage they have read, usually only middle-class pupils show an understanding of it. Many poor and minority pupils make little sense of the passage as a whole, and during class discussion of it they exhibit signs of boredom, discomfort, and hostility.

Educational specialists are of course aware of this situation, which they attribute to social forces beyond anyone's control. Like practically all people of good will, they favor Head Start, the training of parents, alliances between home and school, intensive remedial work, and other programs designed to improve the learning of minority pupils. These initiatives are in themselves of tremendous value. But unfortunately, given the cast of mind of educational specialists, the standard analysis of the bored and humiliated pupils described by the Carnegie researcher is that such children lack "inferencing skills," "organizing strategies," and other "higher-order thinking skills." These deficiencies should therefore be corrected through remedial training designed to develop the missing skills.

One wonders if the educational experts who make such analyses are aware that outside the school, these same minority children are street-smart and can deal quickly and effectively with a world of great complexity. Outside school, their language, as the sociolinguist William Labov has shown in detail, exhibits wit, narrative ability, syntactical sophistication, and complex inferencing skills that would tax the powers of any pedagogical expert who happened not to be familiar with the background knowledge and conventions the children take for granted.[7] A more likely explanation of the lack of "higher-order thinking skills" on the part of these children is therefore that they have been deprived of the background knowledge and conventions that they need in order to understand what is being said by teachers and books. Obviously children cannot learn from classroom discourse they do not understand; but the connection between the language of the classroom and learning goes deeper than that self-evident observation. In the solar-system analogy, it

would *not* have been sufficient to explain what the word "solar" means, or to substitute more familiar terms like "sun system." The children needed to have a concrete mental image of the solar system and how it works in order to learn from the teacher's analogy.

If we generalize from this example, we derive a principle that few experienced teachers would dispute, although many are not in a position to act upon it. Children who possess broad background knowledge will be able to learn new things more readily than those who lack it. This general principle of learning could be described, in an analogy with economics, as earning new wealth from old intellectual capital.[8] A diligent first grader who starts off with a dollar's worth of intellectual capital will be able to put it to work to gain, say, 15 percent a year. But a child who starts out with a dime's worth will not only gain less new intellectual wealth in absolute terms, but will earn even that pittance at a lower annual rate, say 7 percent. Why at a lower rate? Because, if we again imagine the classroom scene, we will notice that the use made of intellectual capital by deprived students is not only less extensive but also less efficient than the use made by well-informed students. Teachers I have talked to say that these deprived students, future dropouts, actively resist the enterprise that causes their boredom and humiliation; they develop an anti-school ethos; they are motivated not to use even that which they have.

3

Thus, inexorably, in the modern American classroom, the intellectual gap between the haves and have nots increases over time. The difficulty of overcoming this widening knowledge gap makes adult illiteracy an intractable problem. But adult illiteracy, as troubling and significant as it is, is not the chief symptom of American educational failure. About 80 percent of our population is neither illiterate nor poor. Yet today, even literate, middle-class students who have recently graduated from American high schools and colleges exhibit a significant knowledge gap when compared to students from other nations. On the international scene, American students are to their Swedish counterparts as, on the national scene, deprived students are to those of the middle class.

I believe that a chief cause of our poor showing in international educational comparisons is our failure to take a systematic approach to shared knowledge in elementary schools. American students participate in schooling under a tremendous disadvantage. Classroom transactions in which relevant knowledge is not widely shared are extremely ineffectual transactions. The impossibility of relying on common knowledge among the diverse pupils in American classrooms causes the children in our elementary schools to learn less for each day or hour in school than children in other countries. This low educational productivity may have mattered less when there was a smaller correlation between educational and economic productivity, but now it matters a lot.

The inherent ineffectualness of American elementary schooling not only handicaps our brightest pupils, it also creates, in the name of democratic diversity, one of the most unjust and inegalitarian school systems in the developed world. That is another implication of the IEA report on science achievement, which included findings about equality of education in various countries. One way of measuring equality of opportunity in a nation's school system is to compute the percentage of schools whose average scores fall below a minimal norm. It is reasonable to assume that the average score of other than the innate intellectual capacities of its students. Academic talent is randomly distributed throughout the population so far as innate capacities are concerned;

average scores tell us more about schools than about children. Moreover, we now know, from the extensive research published by the Brookings Institution, that the quality of schools, more than any other factor, determines the average level of academic achievement.[9]

One of the most disturbing features of the IEA report was its finding of severe inequality among American elementary schools. In nations with egalitarian school systems, only between 1 and 5 percent of elementary schools fall below a minimal standard. But in the US, 30 percent of our schools fall below the same standard— not a reassuring statistic for a nation that aspires to equality of opportunity for its children. The statistics supplied by the IEA do not tell us which of our schools perform poorly, but we can guess that among them are schools in our inner cities. Britain and Italy also performed badly by the same criterion of school equality, though their nationwide achievement scores are marginally higher than ours.

It happens that the most egalitarian elementary-school systems are also the best. With one exception (the Netherlands), the nations that score highest—Hungary, Japan, the Netherlands, English-speaking Canada, Finland, and Sweden—are also the nations that provide the greatest equality of opportunity to their young children. This finding contradicts the widespread belief that truly democratic education must sacrifice quality. The top-scoring nations do both a better and a more democratic job of early education than we do. By now, the reader will not be surprised to learn that the countries that achieve these results tend to teach a standardized curriculum in early grades. Hungarian, Japanese, and Swedish children have a systematic grounding in shared knowledge. Until third graders learn what third graders are supposed to know, they do not pass on to fourth grade. No pupil is allowed to escape the knowledge net.

Here is a general description of the curriculum for elementary schooling in Sweden:

All children in all schools have the same number of Swedish, mathematics, and English periods, etc., throughout their nine years of compulsory schooling. What is more, they cover the same main teaching items in every subject. The amount which pupils can assimilate varies, of course, depending on their individual aptitudes and interests. But the differentiation made in response to the personal aptitudes and interests of individual pupils is based on a common curriculum ensuring that everybody receives a basic grounding in every main teaching item specified for the compulsory or optional subjects. The curricula help to create a universal frame of reference on which to base co-operation and a sense of community.[10]

American educational specialists have told me that they believe the IEA comparisons are unfair. We are, they say, a pluralistic society, which has consciously decided against teaching our young children a standard curriculum. If our schooling is a little inefficient, so be it; we treasure our diversity. We don't want our children to know all the same things and think all the same thoughts. We don't want to be like other nations whose school systems produce automatons cut from the same cultural cookie cutters. Those who utter such clichés have not noticed how diverse, independent-minded, and eccentric Swedes and Hungarians and Canadians actually are, despite their having absorbed common knowledge during their elementary education. It is not obvious that a norm of commonly shared information in elementary school destroys diversity of thought any more than does a norm of commonly shared grammar and spelling.

But the basic importance of shared knowledge can be illustrated even if we ignore the un-American practices of other nations, and simply compare the educational performances of California and New York between 1965 and 1980. Both states exemplify American diversity; neither has the advantage of a homogenous culture. Yet in past decades, according to College Board statistics, students in New York have consistently outperformed students in California on the verbal SAT. Why? The basic conditions in the two states are very similar. Approximately the same number of students (100,000) take the test in each state each year. The test takers in each state are probably similar in their socioeconomic characteristics. Many poor and minority children drop out before the tests are given or do not take them. In both states, it is the better prepared students who tend to take the tests.

In the absence of another theory to explain the superior performance of the New York system, let me suggest the following. In the years between 1965 and 1980, before Bill Honig, the current head of public education in California, began applying his formidable energies to school reform, California's educational system was typically American in that it emphasized "skills" and neglected specific content. Its curriculum guide to language arts in the first six grades recommended no particular books or readings whatever. Its chief advice, much applauded in the introduction to the guide by the then head of public education, was that teachers should be solicitous of children's self-esteem. Under such "guidelines" it would have been a miracle if teachers in California found that the students had in common a wide range of knowledge.

New York had a different, rather special, tradition. With the threat of the Regents exams looming at graduation (at least for ambitious students), and with the politically protected Board of Regents setting standards of accomplishments for these exams, schools were provided with definite goals to aim for. The typical contents of the Regents exams were known. Throughout the New York system students and teachers expected that certain kinds of knowledge would be tested, and that schools' reputations and students' financial help in college depended on the outcomes of these exams. These expectations encouraged a concentration on specific kinds of knowledge in the New York system. We know that tests like the Regents exams encourage schools to include common elements in their curriculums. Indeed, the Dutch rely on such exams exclusively, instead of imposing specific curricular standards on the schools. Thus, while classroom instruction in New York was far from ideal between 1965 and 1980, teachers could depend somewhat more on shared knowledge than could teachers in California. This explanation has the advantage of coinciding with what we know about schooling in general and these two states in particular. It seems worth accepting until a better theory is proposed.

Some have hoped that television might provide children with a common basis for early learning. But television culture consists of multiple channels that randomly impart ephemeral information to random groups. Indeed, very little so-called "popular culture" is shared by a large proportion of American society, and that little is not diverse enough to provide an adequate basis for later schooling. In a modern nation, there is really just one effective vehicle for transmitting widely shared culture—the elementary school. It is the only channel that everyone must tune in. Although television is an immensely powerful medium that can supplement formal education, the elementary school is an even more powerful social-technological device. No cultural institution comes close in effectiveness to this now-rather-old modern invention. And, for reasons I have explained, the most effective elementary-school system uses a single channel—in the form of a standard curriculum.

No doubt American schools are unlikely to adopt a standard elementary-school curriculum on the Swedish model. The idea of such standardization would encounter vigorous resistance from curriculum experts in 15,000 school districts and fifty state departments of education. Even a suggestion of standardization in elementary textbooks would shake up the lucrative world of educational publishing and bring forth statements explaining why diversity of textbooks should be encouraged. American traditions of localism are so deeply established that the public would probably be sympathetic to arguments against standardization.

On the other hand, the evidence is clear that standardized elementary curriculums are inherently productive and egalitarian, and that they do not suppress diversity or dissent in other democratic nations, such as Sweden. Our extreme curricular localism, by contrast, has produced an unproductive and highly discriminatory system whose gravest victims are the poorest and most nomadic elements of our population. While children who stay in one school district sometimes stand a chance of receiving a coherent sequence of instruction, those who move from one district to another, often in the middle of the school year, have no such chance.

As more people come to understand that a fragmented curriculum in the early years causes problems in later ones, they may gradually come to favor some degree of standardization in elementary grades. But such a change will take a long time and, meanwhile, teachers and pupils are working under severe handicaps that should be alleviated as soon as possible. Although we cannot hope to institute a Scandinavian-style early curriculum, we might still hope to reach agreement among parents and teachers on some minimal goals of knowledge, grade by grade. Following these minimal guidelines would still leave local curriculum experts free to decide on emphases, introduce local subjects, choose textbooks, develop sequences, and, in short, determine most of the curriculum.

4

What should the minimal goals be, and who should decide them? The two questions are separate. The second question, who should decide, is easily and quickly answered. In the United States nobody has authority to decide upon the content of education for the nation as a whole, and no person or agency is ever likely to acquire such authority. If one set of goals were to be adopted in our 15,000 autonomous school districts, it would be because parents, administrators, principals, and teachers had concluded that a particular standard was useful for the moment and made sense. Among differing proposals for such goals, one of them might turn out to be more useful than others. Presumably that is how the IBM floppy-disk format became widely adopted. It wasn't necessarily the best format, but it served society much better than having no standard at all.

The second question, concerning what central core of knowledge should be taught to everyone, is not quite as difficult as it appears. About 50 percent of the basic knowledge taught in elementary education is common to all the developed nations. Math, science, world geography, economics, world history, world literature, and technology are similar in most countries. It would be very surprising if the contrary were true. Neither math, nor science, nor world geography much changes its character when it crosses a national or state border.

The other half of basic elementary-school work—that which is national rather than international in character—is, in my experience, at least 80 percent agreed upon right now. Ninety percent of the teachers and other edu-

cators I have talked to agree on about 90 percent of the basic items that should be taught in elementary school. I began to ask such questions about three years ago, before the publication of *Cultural Literacy*, when I formed a foundation to encourage the development of common goals of knowledge in schools.[11] The schools that make up the foundation's network currently number about eight hundred and are found in all fifty states and two protectorates.

The men and women who participate in the network represent black and Hispanic cultures as well as white, middle-class culture, and have been invited to suggest deletions and additions to the goals for knowledge that we have provisionally recommended, and that we constantly revise on the basis of members' suggestions. The members of the network have offered numerous recommendations for our twelfth-grade list, but have expressed virtually no dissent regarding the items that now appear on our cumulative sixth-grade list. The reason for this easy consensus may be that sixth grade is not the end of schooling, so that apparent omissions might reasonably be repaired in seventh grade or beyond.

Such a tolerant attitude to early minimal standards makes sense. What young pupils mainly need is a fairly broad range of knowledge that they share with their classmates, not absolute uniformity of information. They need to share enough information to make classroom communication effective. To that end, members of the network have been putting in a grade-by-grade sequence of information and ideas they believe should be taught during the first six grades. So far, we have had no dissent from members concerning our provisional sequence of items. At this early stage, the main frustration felt by members of the network is the lack of classroom materials and lesson plans designed to unify and teach the agreed-upon sequences, a crippling handicap. Nonetheless, our experiences so far offer hope that a consensus can be reached on a core of knowledge for the first six grades of schooling.

The reader may be curious to know what the network's sixth-grade list looks like. Here are just the first few items from some of the twenty categories conceived by the network. Each item merely stands for an event, episode, idea, or person that needs to be explained in depth and linked with others in sequences that will be clear and interesting.

American History to 1865

1492
1776
1861–1865
abolition
Alamo
all men are created equal
American Revolution
Apache Indians
Appleseed, Johnny
Appomattox Court House
Bill of Rights
Boone, Daniel
Booth, John Wilkes
Boston Tea Party
Brown, John
Battle of Bunker Hill
California Gold Rush
Cherokee Indians
Civil War
The Confederacy
The Constitution
Crockett, Davy
Davis, Jefferson
Declaration of Independence
Douglass, Frederick

Literature

Aesop's Fables
Aladdin's Lamp
Alice in Wonderland
Andersen, Hans Christian
Angelou, Maya
Arabian Nights
"Baa Baa Black Sheep"
"Beauty and the Beast"
The Big Bad Wolf
"The Boy Who Cried Wolf"
Brothers Grimm
Camelot
Carroll, Lewis
"Casey at the Bat"
Chicken Little
A Christmas Carol
"Cinderella"
Dickens, Charles
Dickinson, Emily
Doctor Jekyll and Mr. Hyde
Don Quixote
Dracula
"The Fox and the Grapes"

Life Sciences

amphibians
animals
balance of nature
biology
birds
carnivore
cell
chlorophyll
coldblooded
Darwin, Charles
deciduous

dinosaur

ecology

evergreen

evolution

fish

food chain

habitat

herbivore

heredity

hibernation

The reader who has followed my argument this far will understand why I think it is a good idea to make a list of what sixth graders should know, despite the fact that a list looks like a simple-minded gimmick. In the current American situation, in which lack of common knowledge impedes both teaching and learning, it has become an evasion *not* to make a list. The people who understand this best are teachers. After *Cultural Literacy* appeared, thousands of teachers wrote me to express their agreement with its thesis and their hope that schools would begin to emphasize shared knowledge. What they had been taught in pedagogy courses was being eroded by the realities of their daily experiences in the classroom. I received many moving letters, and teachers now send requests every day for teaching material incorporating the kinds of knowledge I have listed. Their response has been a genuine grass-roots movement, conducted mainly by word of mouth.

The modest efforts of the cultural literacy network are not by themselves going to change the results of the next IEA report. Imparting shared background knowledge is just one of several major reforms that are needed. James Comer, director of Yale's School Development Program, has explained in detail how, for poor black and other minority children, the "high degree of mutual distrust between home and school . . . makes it hard to maintain a link between child and teacher that can support development and learning." To create such a link, he writes, "requires fostering positive interaction between parents and school staff, a task for which most staff people are not trained." He argues convincingly that it also requires giving the school a new structure, involving teams of counselors and teachers, who would deal with the psychological and social problems of learning as well as the cognitive problems.[12] Significant improvement in academic performance cannot be achieved simply by offering children systematic knowledge when they are emotionally unprepared to believe that they can learn or use academic knowledge at all.

Moreover, compiling lists will not create teachers who are well-versed in history, science, and mathematics, and who are well-paid members of a respected profession. It will not convert poor textbooks into the coherent and well-written ones that have been called for by reformers such as Diane Ravitch, Paul Gagnon, and Harriet Tyson-Bernstein. Core knowledge will not convert pencil pushers into good principals and courageous administrators. That transformation is more likely to be encouraged by allowing parents the right to choose their children's schools. In the large view, the problems of American education are so vast as to make the creation of a few lists seem a trivial contribution, and indeed no single approach could quickly transform a system that has been wandering in the wilderness for forty years.

Despair is premature. The initiative for change in American education has to some extent been taken out of the monopolistic control of the bureaucratic establishment. Behind the elaborate state guidelines, the scope and sequence descriptions, the forms to be filled out, the competency measures to be met, the textbook adoption procedures to be followed, behind the commands emanating from state and local hierarchies, as set forth in documents of pseudoscientific jargon mixed with an officialese combined with pious slogans, behind the whole chaotic and fragmented scene, one feels the stirrings of change—not perhaps within the vast establishment itself, which is still engaged in defensive maneuvers, but among conscientious teachers, principals, and superintendents who are in the front lines.

Although the attempt to win adherence to a standard core of knowledge is but a small part of this larger effort, it is a necessary element. The effort to develop a standard sequence of core knowledge is, to put it bluntly, absolutely essential to effective educational reform in the United States. Amid the other improvements that may occur through better teacher training, better preschool education, stronger alliances between school and home, better remedial education, better textbooks, greater financial inducements, and more flexible school administration—amid all of these badly needed initiatives, the inherent logic of the primal scene of education itself still remains.

When I am feeling hopeful, I imagine to myself how things might change. A few schools scattered over the country will hold their pupils accountable for acquiring an agreed-upon minimum core of knowledge grade by grade. Because classroom work in such schools will be more effective and interesting for their pupils, children will feel more curious and eager. Their abilities to speak, write, and learn will improve noticeably. Students from such schools will make significantly higher scores on standardized tests of scholastic aptitude and achievement. Neighboring schools will observe the results, and, not wishing to be outshone, will follow the lead. District and state offices will find it convenient not to resist these successful undertakings. Even the education establishment itself may in time begin to say in its hundreds of conferences and dozens of journals, which are now vigorously resisting such changes, "We knew it all the time, That was what we were trying to tell you."

Notes

[1] Nathan Glazer, John Chubb, Seymour Fliegel, *Making Schools Better* (Manhattan Institute for Policy Research, 1988), p. 4.

[2] October 29, 1988.

[3] International Association for the Evaluation of Educational Achievement, *Science Achievement in Seventeen Countries: A Preliminary Report* (Pergamon, 1988).

[4] IEA report, p. 2.

[5] See Diane Ravitch, *The Troubled Crusade: American Education, 1945–1980* (Basic Books, 1983), especially pp. 43–80.

[6] The examples are taken from Karl Weber, *Complete Preparation for the SAT* (Harcourt Brace Jovanovich, 1986).

[7] See, for instance, William Labov, "The Logic of Nonstandard English," reprinted in *Language and Social Context*, P. P. Giglioli, ed. (Penguin, 1972), pp. 179–216.

[8] The term "intellectual capital" has been used in a different context by Pierre Bourdieu.

[9] See John Chubb and Terry Moe, *What Price Democracy? Politics, Markets and America's Schools* (Brookings Institution, 1988).

[10] Britta Stenholm, *The Swedish School System* (Stockholm: The Swedish Institute, 1984), p. 31.

[11] Activities of the Cultural Literacy Foundation include publishing a newsletter and offering provisional lists of what pupils should know at different grade levels. Its address is 2012-B Morton Drive, Charlottesville, VA 22901.

[12] See James Comer, "Educating Poor Minority Children," *Scientific American* (November 1988), pp. 42–48.

DISCUSSION QUESTIONS

1. What are the causes of educational incompetence in the United States according to Hirsch?

2. Do you think the Scholastic Aptitude Test (SAT) is a valuable tool in the college admissions process and in predicting academic success?

3. Do you think the Swedish model of a standard elementary school curriculum would work in a more heterogeneous society like the United States?

Chartering and Bartering: Elite Education and Social Reproduction

Caroline Hodges Persell
Peter W. Cookson, Jr.

The continuation of power and privilege has been the subject of intense sociological debate. One recurring question is whether the system of mobility is open or whether relationships of power and privilege are reproduced from one generation to the next. If reproduction occurs, is it the reproduction of certain powerful and privileged families or groups (cf. Robinson, 1984)? Or, does it involve the reproduction of a structure of power and privilege which allows for replacement of some members with new recruits while preserving the structure?

The role of education in these processes has been the subject of much dispute. Researchers in the status attainment tradition stress the importance for mobility of the knowledge and skills acquired through education thereby emphasizing the meritocratic and open basis for mobility (e.g., Alexander and Eckland, 1975; Alexander et al., 1975; Blau and Duncan, 1967; Haller and Portes, 1973; Otto and Haller, 1970; Kerckhoff, 1984; Sewell et al., 1969, 1970; Wilson and Portes, 1975). On the other hand, theorists such as Bowles and Gintis (1976) suggest education inculcates certain non-cognitive personality traits which serve to reproduce the social relations within a class structure; thus they put more emphasis on non-meritocratic features in the educational process.

Collins (1979) also deals with non-meritocratic aspects when he suggests that educational institutions develop and fortify status groups, and that differently valued educational credentials protect desired market posi-

tions such as those of the professions. In a related vein, Meyer (1977) notes that certain organizational "charters" serve as "selection criteria" in an educational or occupational marketplace. Meyer defines "charter" as "the social definition of the products of [an] organization" (Meyer 1970:577). Charters do not need to be recognized formally or legally to operate in social life. If they exist, they would create structural limitations within a presumably open market by making some people eligible for certain sets of rights that are denied to other people.

Social observers have long noted that one particular set of schools is central to the reproduction and solidarity of a national upper class, specifically elite secondary boarding schools (Baltzell, 1958, 1964; Domhoff, 1967, 1970, 1983; Mills, 1956). As well as preparing their students for socially desirable colleges and universities, traditionally such schools have been thought to build social networks among upper class scions from various regions, leading to adult business deals and marriages. Although less than one percent of the American population attends such schools, that one percent represents a strategic segment of American life that is seldom directly studied. Recently, Useem and Karabel (1984) reported that graduates of 14 elite boarding schools were much more likely than non-graduates to become part of the "inner circle" of Fortune 500 business leaders. This evidence suggests that elite schools may play a role in class reproduction.

Few researchers have gained direct access to these schools to study social processes bearing on social reproduction. The research reported here represents the first systematic study of elite secondary boarding schools and their social relations with another important institution, namely colleges and universities.

The results of this research illustrate Collins' view that stratification involves networks of "persons making bargains and threats . . . [and that] the key resource of powerful individuals is their ability to impress and manipulate a network of social contacts" (1979:26). If such were the case, we would expect to find that upper class institutions actively develop social networks for the purpose of advancing the interests of their constituencies.

By focusing on the processes of social reproduction rather than individual attributes or the results of intergenerational mobility, our research differs from the approaches taken in both the status attainment and status allocation literature. Status attainment models focus on individual attributes and achievements, and allocation models examine structural supports or barriers to social mobility; yet neither approach explores the underlying processes. Status attainment models assume the existence of a relatively open contest system, while reproduction and allocation models stress that selection criteria and structural barriers create inequalities, limiting opportunities for one group while favoring another (Kerckhoff, 1976, 1984). Neither attainment nor allocation models show how class reproduction, selection criteria, or structural opportunities and impediments operate in practice.

Considerable evidence supports the view that structural limitations operate in the labor market (e.g., Beck et al., 1978; Bibb and Form, 1977; Stolzenberg, 1975) but, with the exception of tracking, little evidence has been found that similar structural limitations exist in education. Tracking systems create structural impediments in an open model of educational attainment (Oakes, 1985; Persell, 1977; Rosenbaum, 1976, 1980), although not all research supports this conclusion (e.g., Alexander et al., 1978; Heyns, 1974).

In this paper we suggest that there is an additional structural limitation in the key transition from high school to college. We explore the possibility that special organizational "charters" exist for certain secondary schools

and that a process of "bartering" occurs between representatives of selected secondary schools and some college admissions officers. These processes have not been clearly identified by prior research on education and stratification, although there has been some previous research which leads in this direction.

EMPIRICAL LITERATURE

Researchers of various orientations concur that differences between schools seem to have little bearing on student attainment (Averch et al., 1972; Jencks et al., 1972; Meyer, 1970, 1977). Indeed, Meyer (1977) suggests the most puzzling paradox in the sociology of American education is that while schools differ in structure and resources, they vary little in their effects because all secondary schools are assumed to have similar "charters." Meyer believes that no American high school is specially chartered by selective colleges in the way, for instance, that certain British Public Schools have been chartered by Oxford and Cambridge Universities. Instead, he suggests that "all American high schools have similar status rights, (and therefore) variations in their effects should be small" (Meyer, 1977:60).

Kamens (1977:217–18), on the other hand, argues that "schools symbolically redefine people and make them eligible for membership in societal categories to which specific sets of rights are assigned." The work of Alexander and Eckland (1977) is consistent with this view. These researchers found that students who attended high schools where the social status of the student body was high also attended selective colleges at a greater rate than did students at other high schools, even when individual student academic ability and family background were held constant (Alexander and Eckland, 1977). Their research and other work finding a relationship between curricular track placement and college attendance (Alexander et al., 1978; Alexander and McDill,

1976; Jaffe and Adams, 1970; Rosenbaum, 1976, 1980) suggest that differences between schools may affect stratification outcomes.

Research has shown that graduation from a private school is related to attending a four-year (rather than a two-year) college (Falsey and Heyns, 1984), attending a highly selective college (Hammack and Cookson, 1980), and earning higher income in adult life (Lewis and Wanner, 1979). Moreover, Cookson (1981) found that graduates of private boarding schools attended more selective colleges than did their public school counterparts, even when family background and Scholastic Aptitude Test (SAT) scores were held constant. Furthermore, some private colleges acknowledge the distinctive nature of certain secondary schools. Klitgaard (1985: Table 2.2) reports that students from private secondary schools generally had an advantage for admission to Harvard over public school graduates, even when their academic ratings were comparable. Karen (1985) notes that applications to Harvard from certain private boarding schools were placed in special colored dockets, or folders, to set them apart from other applications. Thus, they were considered as a distinct group. Not only did Harvard acknowledge the special status of certain schools by color-coding their applicants' folders, attendance at one of those schools provided an advantage for acceptance, even when parental background, grades, SATs, and other characteristics were controlled (Karen, 1985).

NETWORKS AND THE TRANSMISSION OF PRIVILEGE

For these reasons we believe it is worth investigating whether certain secondary schools have special organizational charters, at least in relation to certain colleges. If they do, the question arises, how do organizational charters operate? Network analysts suggest that "the pattern of ties in a network provides significant

opportunities and constraints because it affects the relative access of people and institutions to such resources as information, wealth and power" (Wellman, 1981:3). Furthermore, "because of their structural location, members of a social system differ greatly in their access to these resources" (Wellman, 1981:30). Moreover, network analysts have suggested that class-structured networks work to preserve upper class ideology, consciousness, and life style (see for example Laumann, 1966:132–36).

We expect that colleges and secondary schools have much closer ties than has previously been documented. Close networks of personal relationships between officials at certain private schools and some elite colleges transform what is for many students a relatively standardized, bureaucratic procedure into a process of negotiation. As a result, they are able to communicate more vital information about their respective needs, giving selected secondary school students an inside track to gaining acceptance to desired colleges. We call this process "bartering."

SAMPLE AND DATA

Baltzell (1958, 1964) noted the importance of elite secondary boarding schools for upper class solidarity. However, he was careful to distinguish between those boarding schools that were truly socially elite and those that had historically served somewhat less affluent and less powerful families. He indicates that there is a core group of eastern Protestant schools that "set the pace and bore the brunt of criticism received by private schools for their so-called 'snobbish,' 'undemocratic' and even 'un-American' values" (Baltzell, 1958:307–08). These 16 schools are: Phillips (Andover) Academy (MA), Phillips Exeter Academy (NH), St. Paul's School (NH), St. Mark's School (MA), Groton School (MA), St. George's School (RI), Kent School (CT), The Taft School (CT), The Hotchkiss School (CT), Choate Rosemary Hall

(CT), Middlesex School (MA), Deerfield Academy (MA), The Lawrenceville School (NJ), The Hill School (PA), The Episcopal High School (VA), and Woodberry Forest School (VA). We refer to the schools on Baltzell's list as the "select 16."[1]

In 1982 and 1983, we visited a representative sample of 12 of the select 16 schools. These 12 schools reflect the geographic distribution of the select 16 schools. In this time period we also visited 30 other "leading" secondary boarding schools drawn from the 1981 *Handbook of Private Schools'* list of 289 "leading" secondary boarding schools. This sample is representative of leading secondary boarding schools nationally in location, religious affiliation, size, and the sex composition of the student body. These schools are organizationally similar to the select 16 schools in offering only a college preparatory curriculum, in being incorporated as non-profit organizations, in their faculty/student ratios, and in the percent of boarders who receive financial aid. They differ somewhat with respect to sex composition, average size, the sex of their heads, and

number of advanced placement courses (see Table 1). However, the key difference between the select 16 schools and the other "leading" schools is that the former are more socially elite than the latter. For instance, in one of the select 16 boarding schools in 1982, 40 percent of the current students' parents were listed in *Social Register*.[2]

All 42 schools were visited by one or both of the authors. Visits lasted between one and five days and included interviews with administrators, teachers and students. Most relevant to this study were the lengthy interviews with the schools' college advisors. These interviews explored all aspects of the college counseling process, including the nature and content of the advisors' relationships with admissions officers at various colleges. At a representative sample of six of the select 16 schools and a representative sample of 13 of the other "leading" schools a questionnaire was administered to seniors during our visits.[3] The questionnaire contained more than 50 items and included questions on parental education, occupation, income, number of books in the

TABLE 1			

COMPARISON OF POPULATION AND TWO SAMPLES OF BOARDING SCHOOLS[a]

	Total population (*N* = 289)	Other boarding school sample (*N* = 30)	Select 16 sample (*N* = 12)
Percent with college preparatory curriculum	100	100	100
Percent with no religious affiliation	65	70	67
Percent incorporated, not-for-profit	83	90	83
Average faculty/student ratio	0.17	0.15	0.15
Average percent of boarders aided	15	16	18
Percent of schools which are all-boys	28	17	33
Percent of schools which are all-girls	17	28	0
Percent coeducational schools	55	55	67
Percent with male heads	92	73	100
Average number of advanced courses	3.5	4.8	6.7
Average size	311	322	612

Note:
[a] Computed from data published in the *Handbook of Private Schools* (1981).

home, family travel, educational legacies as well as many questions on boarding school life and how students felt about their experiences in school. Overall, student survey and school record data were collected on 687 seniors from the six select 16 schools and 658 seniors from other leading schools. Although not every piece of data was available for every student, we did obtain 578 complete cases from six select 16 schools and 457 cases from ten leading schools.[4] School record data included student grade point averages, Scholastic Aptitude Test (SAT) scores, class rank, names of colleges to which students applied, names of colleges to which students were accepted, and names of colleges students will attend. This material was supplied by the schools after the seniors graduated, in the summer or fall of 1982 and 1983. With this population actual enrollment matches school reports with high reliability. The record data have been linked with questionnaire data from the seniors and with various characteristics of the college. The colleges students planned to attend, were coded as to academic selectivity, Ivy League, and other characteristics not analyzed here.[5]

CHARTERING

Historical evidence shows that the select 16 schools have had special charters in relation to Ivy League colleges in general, and Harvard, Yale, and Princeton in particular. In the 1930s and 1940s, two-thirds of all graduates of 12 of the select 16 boarding schools attended Harvard, Yale, or Princeton (Karabel, 1984). But, by 1973, this share had slipped noticeably to an average of 21 percent, although the rate of acceptance between schools ranged from 51 percent to 8 percent (Cookson and Persell, 1978: Table 4). In the last half century, then, the proportion of select 16 school graduates who attended Harvard, Yale or Princeton dropped substantially.

This decrease was paralleled by an increase in the competition for admission to Ivy League colleges. According to several college advisors at select 16 boarding schools, 90 percent of all applicants to Harvard in the 1940s were accepted as were about half of those in the early 1950s. In 1982, the national acceptance rate for the eight Ivy League schools was 26 percent, although it was 20 percent or less at Harvard, Yale and Princeton (*National College Data Bank*, 1984).

The pattern of Ivy League college admissions has changed during this time. Ivy League colleges have begun to admit more public school graduates. Before World War II at Princeton, for example, about 80 percent of the entering freshmen came from private secondary schools (Blumberg and Paul, 1975:70). In 1982, 34 percent of the freshman class at Harvard, 40 percent of Yale freshmen, and 40 percent of Princeton freshmen were from nonpublic high schools (*National College Data Bank*, 1984).

This shift in college admissions policy, combined with increased financial aid and an inflationary trend in higher education that puts increased emphasis on which college one attends, contributes to the large number of applications to certain colleges nationally. Thus, while in the past decade the number of college age students has declined, the number of students applying to Ivy League colleges has increased (Mackay-Smith, 1985; Maeroff, 1984; Winerip, 1984).

In view of these historical changes, is there any evidence that the select 16 schools still retain special charters in relation to college admissions? When four pools of applications to the Ivy League colleges are compared, the acceptance rate is highest at select 16 schools, followed by a highly selective public high school, other leading boarding schools, and finally the entire national pool of applications (Table 2).[6]

While we do not have comparable background data on all the applicants from these

TABLE 2

PERCENT OF APPLICATIONS THAT WERE ACCEPTED AT IVY LEAGUE COLLEGES FROM FOUR POOLS OF APPLICATIONS

College name	Select 16 boarding schools[a] (1982–83)	Other leading boarding schools[b] (1982–83)	Selective public high school[c] (1984)	National group of applicants[d] (1982)
Brown University				
Percent accepted	35	20	28	22
Number of Applications	95	45	114	11,854
Columbia University				
Percent accepted	66	29	32	41
Number of applications	35	7	170	3,650
Cornell University				
Percent accepted	57	36	55	31
Number of applications	65	25	112	17,927
Dartmouth				
Percent accepted	41	21	41	22
Number of applications	79	33	37	8,313
Harvard University				
Percent accepted	38	28	20	17
Number of applications	104	29	127	13,341
Princeton University				
Percent accepted	40	28	18	18
Number of applications	103	40	109	11,804
University of Pennsylvania				
Percent accepted	45	32	33	36
Number of applications	40	19	167	11,000
Yale University				
Percent accepted	40	32	15	20
Number of applications	92	25	124	11,023
Overall percent accepted	42	27	30	26
Total number of applications	613	223	960	88,912

Notes:
[a] Based on school record data on the applications of 578 seniors.
[b] Based on school record data on the applications of 457 seniors.
[c] Based on data published in the school newspaper.
[d] Based on data published in the *National College DataBank* (1984).

various pools, we do know that the students in the highly selective public high school have among the highest academic qualifications in the country.[7] Their combined SAT scores, for example, average at least 150 points higher than those of students at the leading boarding schools. On that basis they might be expected to do considerably better than applicants from boarding schools: which they do at some colleges but not at Harvard, Yale, or Princeton.

The most revealing insights into the operation of special charters, however, are provided by a comparison between select 16 boarding schools and other leading boarding schools—

the most similar schools and the ones on which we have the most detailed data.

Students from select 16 schools apply to somewhat different colleges than do students from other leading boarding schools. Select 16 school students were much more likely to apply to one or more of the eight Ivy League and at least one of the other highly selective colleges than were students from other leading boarding schools (Table 3). Among those who applied, select 16 students were more likely to be accepted then were students from other boarding schools, and, if accepted, they were slightly more likely to attend.

Before we can conclude that these differences are due to a school charter, we need to control for parental SES[8] and student SAT scores.[9] This analysis is shown in Table 4. One striking finding here is the high rate of success enjoyed by boarding school students in general. At least one-third and as many as 92

percent of the students in each cell of Table 4 are accepted. Given that the average freshman combined SAT score is more than 1175 at these colleges and universities, it is particularly notable that such a large proportion of those with combined SAT scores of 1050 or less are accepted.

In general, high SAT scores increase chances of acceptance, but the relationship is somewhat attenuated under certain conditions. Students with low SAT scores are more likely to be accepted at highly selective colleges if they have higher SES backgrounds, especially if they attend a select 16 school. These students seem to have relatively high "floors" placed under them, since two thirds of those from select 16 schools and more than half of those from other schools were accepted by one of the most selective colleges.[10]

The most successful ones of all are relatively low SES students with the highest SATs at-

TABLE 3

BOARDING SCHOOL STUDENTS' COLLEGE APPLICATION, CHANCES OF ACCEPTANCE, AND PLANS TO ATTEND

		Ivy league colleges	Highly selective colleges
A. Percent of boarding school samples who applied			
Select 16 boarding schools	%=	61	87
	N=	(353)	(502)
Other leading boarding schools	%=	28	61
	N=	(129)	(279)
B. Percent of applicants who were accepted			
Select 16 boarding schools	%=	54	84
	N=	(191)	(420)
Other leading boarding schools	%=	36	64
	N=	(47)	(178)
C. Percent of acceptees who plan to attend			
Select 16 boarding schools	%=	79	81
	N=	(151)	(340)
Other leading boarding schools	%=	53	77
	N=	(25)	(137)

TABLE 4

PERCENT OF STUDENTS WHO APPLIED TO THE MOST HIGHLY SELECTIVE COLLEGES WHO WERE ACCEPTED, WITH SAT SCORES, SES, AND SCHOOL TYPE HELD CONSTANTLY[a]

		Student combined SAT scores					
		High (1580–1220)		Medium (1216–1060)		Low (1050–540)	
		Select 16 schools	Other leading boarding schools	Select 16 schools	Other leading boarding schools	Select 16 schools	Other leading boarding schools
Student socio-economic status							
High	%=	87	70	80	64	65	53
	N=	(93)	(33)	(73)	(36)	(34)	(30)
Medium	%=	89	71	85	76	44	35
	N=	(100)	(28)	(66)	(46)	(18)	(51)
Low	%=	92	72	78	69	55	33
	N=	(72)	(25)	(51)	(32)	(33)	(49)

Note:
  [a] Based on student questionnaires and school record data on 1035 seniors for whom complete data were available.

---

tending select 16 schools—92 percent of whom were accepted. Students from relatively modest backgrounds appear to receive a "knighting effect" by attending a select 16 school. Thus, select 16 schools provide mobility for some individuals from relatively less privileged backgrounds. To a considerable degree all students with high SATs, regardless of their SES, appear to be "turbo-charged" by attending a select 16 school compared to their counterparts at other leading schools.

At every level of SATs and SES, students' chances of acceptance increase if they attend a select 16 school. Such a finding is consistent with the argument that a chartering effect continues to operate among elite educational institutions. The historical shifts toward admitting more public school students on the part of Ivy League colleges and the increased competition for entry, described above, have meant that more effort has been required on the part of select 16 schools to retain an advantage for their students. We believe that certain private boarding schools have buttressed their charters by an increasingly active bartering operation.

BARTERING

Normally, we do not think of the college admissions process as an arena for bartering. It is assumed that colleges simply choose students according to their own criteria and needs. Few students and no high schools are thought to have any special "leverage" in admissions decisions. Our research revealed, however, that select 16 boarding schools—perhaps because of their perennial supply of academically able and affluent students—can negotiate admissions cases with colleges. The colleges are aware that 16 schools attract excellent college prospects and devote considerable attention to maintaining close relationships with these schools, especially through the college admission officers. Secondary school college advisors actively "market" their students within a context of tremendous parental pressure and increasing competition for admission to elite colleges.

SELECT 16 COLLEGE ADVISORS AND IVY LEAGUE ADMISSIONS DIRECTORS: THE OLD SCHOOL TIE

Of the 11 select 16 school college advisors on whom data were available, 10 were graduates of Harvard, Yale, or Princeton. Of the 23 other leading boarding school college advisors on whom data were available, only three were Ivy League graduates, and none of them was from Harvard, Yale, or Princeton. College advisors are overwhelmingly white men. At the select 16 schools only one (an acting director) was a woman, and at other schools five were women. Some college advisors have previously worked as college admissions officers. Their educational and social similarity to college admissions officers may facilitate the creation of social ties and the sharing of useful information. Research shows that the exchange of ideas most frequently occurs between people who share certain social attributes (Rogers and Kincaid, 1981).

College advisors at select 16 schools tend to have long tenures—15 or more years is not unusual. On the other hand, college advisors at other schools are more likely to have assumed the job recently. A college advisor at one select 16 school stressed the "importance of continuity on both sides of the relationship." Thus, it is not surprising that select 16 schools hold on to their college advisors.

Select 16 college advisors have close social relationships with each other and with elite college admissions officers that are cemented through numerous face-to-face meetings each year. All of the select 16 schools are on the east coast, whereas only 70 percent of the other leading boarding schools are in that region. However, even those leading boarding schools

on the east coast lack the close relationships with colleges that characterize the select 16 schools. Thus, geography alone does not explain these relationships.

The college advisors at most of the boarding schools we studied have personally visited a number of colleges around the country. Boarding schools often provide college advisors with summer support for systematic visits, and a number of geographically removed colleges offer attractive incentives, or fully paid trips to their region (e.g., Southern California). These trips often take place during bitter New England winters, and include elegant food and lodging as well as a chance to see colleges and meet admissions officers.

However, the college advisors at select 16 schools are likely to have visited far more schools (several mentioned that they had personally visited 60 or 70 schools) than college advisors at other schools (some of whom had not visited any). They are also much more likely to visit regularly the most selective and prestigious colleges.[11]

Numerous college admissions officers also travel to these boarding schools to interview students and meet the college advisors. The select 16 schools have more college admissions officers visit than do other schools; more than 100 in any given academic year is not unusual. College advisors have drinks and dinner with selected admissions officers, who often stay overnight on campus. As one college advisor noted, "We get to establish a personal relationship with each other." Moreover, Ivy League colleges bring students from select 16 schools to their campus to visit for weekends.

By knowing each other personally, college advisors and admissions officers "develop a relationship of trust," so that they can evaluate the source as well as the content of phone calls and letters. We observed phone calls between college advisors and admissions officers when we were in their offices. Several college advisors mentioned, "It helps to know personally the individual you are speaking or writing to," and one college advisor at a select 16 school said, "I have built up a track record with the private colleges over the years."

Virtually all of the select 16 school college advisors indicated that in the spring—before colleges have finished making their admissions decisions—they take their application files and drive to elite colleges to discuss "their list." They often sit in on the admissions deliberations while they are there. In contrast, the other schools' college advisors generally did not make such trips. Such actions suggest the existence of strong social networks between select 16 school college advisors and elite college admissions officers.

HOW THE SYSTEM WORKS: "FINE TUNING" THE ADMISSIONS PROCESS

Bartering implies a reciprocal relationship, and select 16 schools and elite colleges have a well-developed system of information exchange. Both sides have learned to cooperate to their mutual benefit. College advisors try to provide admissions officers with as much information about their students as possible to help justify the acceptance of a particular applicant. Select 16 schools have institutionalized this process more than other schools. The most professional operation we found was in a select 16 school where about half the graduating class goes to Harvard, Yale or Princeton. There, the college advisor interviews the entire faculty on each member of the senior class. He tape records all their comments and has them transcribed. This produces a "huge confidential dossier which gives a very good sense of where each student is." In addition, housemasters and coaches write reports. Then the college advisor interviews each senior, dictating notes after each interview. After assimilating all of these comments on each student, the college advisor writes his letter of recommen-

dation, which he is able to pack with corroborative details illustrating a candidate's strengths. The thoroughness, thought, and care that goes into this process insures that anything and everything positive that could be said about a student is included, thereby maximizing his or her chances for a favorable reception at a college.[12]

Information also flows from colleges to the secondary schools. By sitting in on the admissions process at colleges like Harvard, Princeton, and Yale, select 16 school college advisors say they "see the wealth and breadth of the applicant pool." They get a first-hand view of the competition their students face. They also obtain a sense of how a college "puts its class together," which helps them to learn strategies for putting forward their own applicants.

By observing and participating in the admissions process, select 16 school college advisors gain an insider's view of a college's selection process. This insider's knowledge is reflected in the specific figures select 16 advisors mentioned in our conversations with them. One select 16 school college advisor said that a student has "two and one half times as good a chance for admission to Harvard if his father went there than if he did not." Another said, "while 22 percent in general are admitted to Ivy League colleges, 45 percent of legacies are admitted to Ivy League colleges." In both cases, they mentioned a specific, quantified statement about how being a legacy affected their students' admissions probabilities.[13] Similarly, several select 16 school college advisors mentioned the percentages of the freshman class at Harvard and Yale that were from public and private schools, and one even mentioned how those percentages have changed since 1957. College advisors at other schools do not lace their conversations with as many specific figures nor do they belong to the special organization that some of the select 16 schools have formed to share information and strategies.

The special interest group these schools have formed is able to negotiate with the colleges to their students' advantage. For instance, the college advisors explained that select 16 school students face greater competition than the average high school student and carry a more rigorous course load.[14] Therefore, this group persuaded the colleges that their students should not receive an absolute class rank, but simply an indication of where the students stand by decile or quintile. Colleges may then put such students in a "not ranked" category or report the decile or quintile rank. No entering student from such a secondary school is clearly labeled as the bottom person in the class. To our knowledge, only select 16 schools have made this arrangement.

Armed with an insider's knowledge of a college's desires, select 16 school college advisors seek to present colleges with the most appropriate candidates. As one select 16 school college advisor said, "I try to shape up different applicant pools for different colleges," a process that has several components. First, college advisors try to screen out hopeless prospects, or as one tactfully phrased it, "I try to discourage unproductive leads." This is not always easy because, as one said, "Certain dreams die hard." College advisors in other schools were more likely to say that they never told students where they should or should not apply.

One select 16 school requires students to write a "trial college essay" that helps the college advisor ascertain "what kind of a student this is." From the essay he can tell how well students write, determine whether they follow through and do what they need to do on time, and learn something about their personal and family background. With faculty and student comments in hand, college advisors can begin to assemble their applicant pools. One thing they always want to learn is which college is a student's first choice, and why. This is useful information when bartering with colleges.

Some college advisors are quite frank when bartering, for example, the select 16 college advisor who stressed, "I am candid about a student to the colleges, something that is not true at a lot of schools where they take an advocacy position in relation to their students. . . . We don't sell damaged goods to the colleges." College advisors at other schools did not define their role as one of weeding out candidates prior to presenting them to colleges, although they may do this as well. It would seem then that part of the gate-keeping process of admission to college is occurring in select 16 secondary schools. College advisors, particularly those with long tenures at select 16 schools, seem quite aware of the importance of maintaining long-term credibility with colleges, since credibility influences how effectively they can work for their school in the future.

While the children of certain big donors (so-called "development cases") may be counseled with special care, in general the college advisors have organizational concerns that are more important than the fate of a particular student. Several select 16 school college advisors spoke with scorn about parents who see a rejection as the "first step in the negotiation." Such parents threaten to disrupt a delicate network of social relationships that link elite institutions over a considerable time span.

At the same time, college advisors try to do everything they can to help their students jump the admissions hurdle. One select 16 school college advisor said,

> I don't see our students as having an advantage (in college admissions). We have to make the situation unequal. We do this by writing full summary reports on the students, by reviewing the applicants with the colleges several times during the year, and by traveling to the top six colleges in the spring. . . . [Those visits] are an advocacy proceeding on the side of the students. The colleges make their best decisions on our students and those from [another select 16

school] because they have the most information on these students.

Another select 16 college advisor said, "We want to be sure they are reading the applications of our students fairly, and we lobby for our students." A third select 16 college advisor made a similar statement, "When I drive to the [Ivy League] colleges, I give them a reading on our applicants. I let them know if I think they are making a mistake. There is a lobbying component here."

Select 16 college advisors do not stop with simply asking elite college admissions officers to reconsider a decision, however. They try to barter, and the colleges show they are open to this possibility when the college admissions officer says, "Let's talk about your group." One select 16 college advisor said he stresses to colleges that if his school recommends someone and he or she is accepted, that student will come. While not all colleges heed this warranty, some do.

One select 16 college advisor said, "It is getting harder than it used to be to say to an admissions officer, 'take a chance on this one,' especially at Harvard which now has so many more applications." But it is significant that he did not say that it was impossible. If all else fails in a negotiation, a select 16 college advisor said, "we lobby for the college to make him their absolute first choice on the waiting list." Such a compromise represents a chance for both parties to save face.

Most public high school counselors are at a distinct disadvantage in the bartering process because they are not part of the interpersonal network, do not have strategic information, and are thus unable to lobby effectively for their students. One select 16 advisor told us about a counselor from the Midwest who came to an Ivy League college to sit in on the admissions committee decision for his truly outstanding candidate—SATs in the 700s, top in his class, class president, and star athlete. The select 16 college advisor was also there, lobbying on behalf of his candidate—a nice undistinguished fellow (in the words of his advisor, "A good kid,") with SATs in the 500s, middle of his class, average athlete, and no strong signs of leadership. After hearing both the counselors, the Ivy League college chose the candidate from the select 16 school. The outraged public school counselor walked out in disgust. Afterwards, the Ivy League college admissions officer said to the select 16 college advisor, "We may not be able to have these open meetings anymore." Even in the unusual case where a public school counselor did everything that a select 16 boarding school college advisor did, it was not enough to secure the applicant's admission. Despite the competitive environment that currently surrounds admission to elite colleges, the admissions officers apparently listen more closely to advisors from select 16 boarding schools than to public school counselors.

CONCLUSIONS AND IMPLICATIONS

The graduates of certain private schools are at a distinct advantage when it comes to admission to highly selective colleges because of the special charters and highly developed social networks these schools possess. Of course, other factors are operating as well. Parental wealth (which is not fully tapped by a measure of SES based on education, occupation, and income), preference for the children of alumni, Advanced Placement (AP) coursework, sports ability especially in such scarce areas as ice hockey, crew or squash, and many other factors also influence the process of college admission. Elite boarding schools are part of a larger process whereby more privileged members of society transmit their advantages to their children. Attendance at a select 16 boarding school signals admissions committees that an applicant may have certain valuable educational and social characteristics.

Significantly, neither the families nor the secondary schools leave the college admissions process to chance or to formal bureaucratic procedures. Instead, they use personal connections to smooth the process, and there is reason to believe that those efforts affect the outcomes. The "knighting effect" of select 16 schools help a few low SES, high SAT students gain admission to highly selective colleges, evidence of sponsored mobility for a few worthy youngsters of relatively humble origins. Our findings are consistent with Kamens' (1974) suggestion that certain schools make their students eligible for special social rights. Furthermore, the interaction between social background, SATs, and select 16 school attendance suggests that both individual ability and socially structured advantages operate in the school-college transition.

These results illustrate Collins' (1979) view that stratified systems are maintained through the manipulation of social contacts. They show one way that networks and stratification processes are interconnected. College access is only one aspect of the larger phenomenon of elite maintenance and reproduction. Elite boarding schools no doubt contribute as well to the social contacts and marriage markets of their graduates. What this instance shows is that reproduction is not a simple process. It involves family and group reproduction as well as some structural replacement with carefully screened new members. There is active personal intervention in what is publicly presented as a meritocratic and open competition. The internal processes and external networks described here operate to construct class privileges as well as to transmit class advantages, thereby helping to reproduce structured stratification within society.

If this example is generalizable, we would expect that economically and culturally advantaged groups might regularly find or create specially chartered organizations and brokers with well-developed networks to help them successfully traverse critical junctures in their social histories. Such key switching points include the transition from secondary school to college, admission to an elite graduate or professional school, obtaining the right job, finding a mentor, gaining a medical residency at a choice hospital (Hall, 1947, 1948, 1949) getting a book manuscript published (Coser et al., 1982), having one's paintings exhibited at an art gallery or museum, obtaining a theatrical agent, having one's business considered for venture capital or bank support (Rogers and Larsen, 1984), being offered membership in an exclusive social club, or being asked to serve on a corporate or other board of directors (Useem, 1984).

In all of these instances, many qualified individuals seek desired, but scarce, social and/or economic opportunities. Truly open competition for highly desired outcomes leaves privileged groups vulnerable. Because the socially desired positions are finite at any given moment, processes that give an advantage to the members of certain groups work to limit the opportunities of individuals from other groups.[15] In these ways, dominant groups enhance their chances, at the same time that a few worthy newcomers are advanced, a process which serves to reproduce and legitimate a structure of social inequality.

Notes

[1] Others besides Baltzell have developed lists of elite private schools, including Baird (1977), Domhoff (1967, 1970, 1983), and McLachlan (1970).

[2] We were not able to compute the percent of students in *Social Register* for every school because most schools do not publish the names of their students. Hence, we were not able to look their families up in *Social Register*. We do know that less than .000265 percent of American families are listed in *Social Register*. See Levine (1980) for an historical discussion of the social backgrounds of students at several of the select 16 schools.

[3] We asked to give the student questionnaires at nine of the 12 select 16 schools and six of those nine schools agreed. At the other leading schools, we asked to give the questionnaires at 15 and 13 schools agreed.

[4] Three leading schools did not supply the college data.

[5] Following Astin et al. (1981:7), we measured selectivity with the average SAT scores of the entering freshmen.

[6] The entire national applicant pool includes the relatively more successful subgroups within it. If they were excluded, the national acceptance rate would be even lower.

[7] Students admitted to this selective public high school must be recommended by their junior high school to take a competitive entrance exam, where they must score very well. The school was among the top five in the nation with respect to the number of National Merit Scholarships won by its students, and each year a number of students in the school win Westinghouse science prizes. This school was selected for purposes of comparison here because academically it is considered to be among the very top public schools in the nation. However, it does not have the social prestige of the select 16 boarding schools.

[8] SES was measured by combining father's education, father's occupation, and family income into a composite SES score. These SES scores were then standardized for this population, and each student received a single standardized SES score.

[9] The combined verbal and mathematics scores were used.

[10] We performed separate analyses for boys and girls to see if sex was related to admission to a highly selective college when type of boarding school, SATs, and SES were held constant, and generally it was not. Girls who attend either select 16 or other leading boarding schools do as well or better in their admissions to college as do their male counterparts, with the single exception of girls at select 16 schools in the top third on their SATs and SES. In that particular group, 92 percent of the boys but only 77 percent of the girls were accepted at the most highly selective colleges. Since that is the only exception, boys and girls are discussed together in the text of the paper.

[11] Our field visits and interviews with college advisors at two highly selective public high schools and three open admission public high schools show that college advisors at even the most selective public high schools generally do not personally know the admissions officers at colleges, particularly at the most selective and Ivy League colleges, nor do they talk with them over the phone or in person prior to their admissions decisions.

[12] Such a procedure requires considerable financial and personnel resources. Select 16 schools have more capital-intensive and professional office services supporting their college admissions endeavor than other schools. Most of them have word processors, considerable professional staff, and ample secretarial and clerical help.

[13] We did not ask students what colleges their parents attended so we could not control for college legacy in our analysis. Further research on the admissions process should do so.

[14] One way select 16 schools establish their reputations as rigorous schools is through the numbers of their students who succeed on the Advanced Placement (AP) Exams given by the College Entrance Examination Board. Compared to other secondary schools, select 16 schools offer larger numbers of advanced courses (Table 1), encourage more students to take them, coach students very effectively on how to take the test, and maintain contacts with the people who design and read AP exams so that they know what is expected and can guide students accordingly. (See Cookson and Persell, 1985, for more discussion of these processes.) Other schools are much less likely than select 16 ones to have teachers who have graded AP exams or to know people who have helped write the tests.

[15] See Parkin (1979) for a discussion of social closure as exclusion and usurpation.

References

Alexander, Karl L., Martha Cook and Edward L. McDill
  1978 "Curriculum tracking and educational stratification: some further evidence." *American Sociological Review* 43:47–66.
Alexander, Karl L. and Bruce K. Eckland
  1975 "Contextual effects in the high school attainment process." *American Sociological Review* 40:402–16.
  1977 "High school context and college selectivity: institutional constraints in educational stratification." *Social Forces* 56:166–88.
Alexander, Karl L., Bruce K. Eckland and Larry J. Griffin
  1975 "The Wisconsin model of socioeconomic achievement: a replication." *American Journal of Sociology* 81:324–42.
Alexander, Karl L. and Edward L. McDill
  1976 "Selection and allocation within schools: some causes and consequences of curriculum placement." *American Sociological Review* 41:963–80.
Astin, Alexander W., Margo R. King, and Gerald T. Richardson
  1981 *The American Freshman: National Norms for Fall 1981.* Los Angeles: Laboratory for Research in Higher Education, University of California.
Averch, Harvey A., Steven J. Carroll, Theodore S. Donaldson, Herbert J. Kiesling, and John Pincus
  1972 *How Effective is Schooling? A Critical Review and Synthesis of Research Findings.* Santa Monica, CA: The Rand Corporation.

Baird, Leonard L.
1977 *The Elite Schools.* Lexington, MA: Lexington Books.

Baltzell, E. Digby
1958 *Philadelphia Gentlemen.* New York: Free Press.
1964 *The Protestant Establishment.* New York: Random House.

Beck, E. M., Patrick M. Horan, and Charles M. Tolbert II
1978 "Stratification in a dual economy." *American Sociological Review* 43:704–20.

Bibb, Robert C. and William Form
1977 The effects of industrial, occupational and sex stratification on wages in blue-collar markets." *Social Forces* 55:974–96.

Blau, Peter and Otis D. Duncan
1967 *The American Occupational Structure.* New York: Wiley.

Blumberg, Paul M.and P. W. Paul
1975 "Continuities and discontinuities in upper-class marriages." *Journal of Marriage and the Family* 37:63–77.

Bowles, Samuel and Herbert Gintis
1976 *Schooling in Capitalist America.* New York: Basic Books.

Collins, Randall
1979 *The Credential Society.* New York: Academic Press.

Cookson, Peter Willis, Jr.
1981 "Private secondary boarding school and public suburban high school graduation: an analysis for college attendance plans." Unpublished Ph.D. dissertation, New York University.

Cookson, Peter W., Jr. and Caroline Hodges Persell
1978 "Social structure and educational programs: a comparison of elite boarding schools and public education in the United States." Paper presented at the annual meeting of the American Sociological Association, San Francisco.
1985 *Preparing for Power: America's Elite Boarding Schools.* New York: Basic Books.

Coser, Lewis A., Charles Kadushin, and Walter W. Powell
1982 *Books: The Culture & Commerce of Publishing.* New York: Basic Books.

Domhoff, G. William
1967 *Who Rules America?* Englewood Cliffs: Prentice-Hall.
1970 *The Higher Circles.* New York: Vintage.
1983 *Who Rules America Now?* Englewood Cliffs: Prentice-Hall.

Falsey, Barbara and Barbara Heyns
1984 "The college channel: private and public schools reconsidered." *Sociology of Education* 57:111–22.

Hall, Oswald
1946 "The informal organization of the medical profession." *Canadian Journal of Economics and Political Science* 12:30–41.
1948 "The stages of a medical career." *American Journal of Sociology* 53:327–36.
1949 "Types of medical careers." *American Journal of Sociology* 55:243–53.

Haller, Archibald O. and Alejandro Portes
1973 "Status attainment processes." *Sociology of Education* 46:51–91.

Hammack, Floyd M. and Peter W. Cookson, Jr.
1980 "Colleges attended by graduates of elite secondary schools." *The Educational Forum* 44:483–90.

Handbook of Private Schools
1981 Boston: Porter Sargent Publishers, Inc.

Heyns, Barbara
1974 "Social selection and stratification within schools." *American Journal of Sociology* 79:1434–51.

Jaffe, Abraham and Walter Adams
1970 "Academic and socio-economic factors related to entrance and retention at two- and four-year colleges in the late 1960s." New York: Bureau of Applied Social Research, Columbia University.

Jencks, Christopher, Marshall Smith, Henry Acland, Mary Jo Bane, David Cohen, Herbert Gintis, Barbara Heyns, and Stephan Michelson
1972 *Inequality.* New York: Basic Books.

Kamens, David
1974 "Colleges and elite formation: the case of prestigious American colleges." *Sociology of Education* 47:354–78.
1977 "Legitimating myths and educational organization: the relationship between organizational ideology and formal structure." *American Sociological Review* 42:208–19.

Karabel, Jerome

1984 "Status-group struggle, organizational interests, and the limits of institutional autonomy: the transformation of Harvard, Yale, and Princeton 1918–1940." *Theory and Society* 13:1–40.

Karen, David
1985 Who Gets into Harvard? Selection and Exclusion. Unpublished Ph.D. Dissertation, Department of Sociology, Harvard University.

Kerckhoff, Alan C.
1976 "The status attainment process: socialization or allocation?" *Social Forces* 55:368–81.
1984 "The current state of social mobility research." *Sociological Quarterly* 25:139–53.

Klitgaard, Robert
1985 *Choosing Elites*. New York: Basic Books.

Laumann, Edward O.
1966 *Prestige and Association in an Urban Community: An Analysis of an Urban Stratification System*. Indianapolis: Bobbs-Merrill.

Levine, Steven B.
1980 "The rise of American boarding schools and the development of a national upper class." *Social Problems* 28:63–94.

Lewis, Lionel S. and Richard A. Wanner
1979 "Private schooling and the status attainment process." *Sociology of Education* 52:99–112.

Mackay-Smith, Anne
1985 "Admissions crunch: top colleges remain awash in applicants despite a smaller pool." *Wall Street Journal* (April 2):1,14.

Maeroff, Gene I.
1984 "Top Eastern colleges report unusual rise in applications." *New York Times* (February 21):A1,C10.

McLachlan, James
1970 *American Boarding Schools: A Historical Study*. New York: Charles Scribner's Sons.

Meyer, John
1970 "The charter: conditions of diffuse socialization in school." Pp. 564–78 in W. Richard Scott (ed.), *Social Processes and Social Structure*. New York: Holt, Rinehart.
1977 "Education as an institution." *American Journal of Sociology* 83:55–77.

Mills, C. Wright
1956 *The Power Elite*. London: Oxford University Press.

National College Data Bank
1984 Princeton: Peterson's Guides, Inc.

Oakes, Jeannie
1985 *Keeping Track: How Schools Structure Inequality*. New Haven: Yale University Press.

Otto, Luther B. and Archibald O. Haller
1979 "Evidence for a social psychological view of the status attainment process: four studies compared." *Social Forces* 57:887–914.

Parkin, Frank
1979 *Marxism and Class Theory: A Bourgeois Critique*. New York: Columbia University Press.

Persell, Caroline Hodges
1977 *Education and Inequality*. New York: Free Press.

Robinson, Robert V.
1984 "Reproducing class relations in industrial capitalism." *American Sociological Review* 49:182–96.

Rogers, Everett M. and D. Lawrence Kincaid
1981 *Communications Networks: Toward a New Paradigm for Research*. New York: Free Press.

Rogers, Everett M. and Judith K. Larsen
1984 *Silicon Valley Fever: The Growth of High-Tech Culture*. New York: Basic Books.

Rosenbaum, James E.
1976 *Making Inequality: The Hidden Curriculum of High School Tracking*. New York: Wiley.
1980 "Track misperceptions and frustrated college plans: an analysis of the effects of tracks and track perceptions in the national longitudinal survey." *Sociology of Education* 53:74–88.

Sewell, William H., Archibald O. Haller, and Alejandro Portes
1969 "The educational and early occupational attainment process." *American Sociological Review* 34:82–91.

Sewell, William H., Archibald O. Haller, and George W. Ohlendorf
1970 "The educational and early occupational status achievement process: replication

and revision." *American Sociological Review* 35:1014–27.

Social Register
1984 New York: Social Register Association.

Stolzenberg, Ross M.
1975 "Occupations, labor markets and the process of wage attainment." *American Sociological Review* 40:645–65.

Useem, Michael
1984 *The Inner Circle: Large Corporations and the Rise of Business Political Activity in the U.S. and U.K.* New York: Oxford University Press.

Wellman, Barry
1981 "Network analysis from method and metaphor to theory and substance." Working Paper Series 1B, Structural Analysis Programme, University of Toronto.

Wilson, Kenneth L. and Alejandro Portes
1975 "The educational attainment process: results from a national sample." *American Journal of Sociology* 81:343–63.

Winerip, Michael
1984 "Hot colleges and how they get that way." *New York Times Magazine* (November 18):68ff.

DISCUSSION QUESTIONS

1. In what respects is elite boarding school education different from mass education in public high schools?
2. Do you believe that admission to Ivy League colleges is based on merit alone?
3. Give a general description of the "chartering and bartering" process used by college and university educational institutions. What similarities and differences do you see between colleges and elite prep schools?

READING 13-3

Training China's New Elite

Fred Strebeigh

At *the New York Times*, in an oak-paneled and stained-glass seminar room that seems to have been lifted from Princeton or Yale, thirteen scholars from the People's Republic of China are meeting with Geneva Overholser, an editorial writer for the *Times*. These scholars have been brought to the *Times* by an American organization called the National Committee on U.S.-China Relations, but they are not short-term visitors getting a fast taste of America. They have been living in the United States for at least six months, some for as long as four years, in towns like Somerville, Massachusetts; Columbia, Missouri; and Riverside, California. Most are on leave from professorships, editorships, or chairmanships at prominent Chinese institutions. These visitors are a tiny sample of the tens of thousands of China's future leaders who are living in this country today—and who are engaged, in complex and unprecedented ways, in what could be called the modern Chinese discovery of America.

This morning Overholser (at the time of the visit a member of the *Times* editorial board, and now the editor of *The Des Moines Register*) is describing how *Times* editorials get written. Like her colleagues, Overholser says, she has developed a few specialties; hers are arms control and Russia and China. She has been fielding rapid questions from her Chinese audience. One scholar asks her if she does any research. "Oh, yes," Overholser responds, warming to a familiar question. She uses the fine *Times* library. She telephones overseas correspondents and American Sinologists. She requests clips of published *Times* articles.

Hearing this list of Overholser's resources, Yang Zidi, a pensive man in his late thirties, looks concerned. Do you, he asks her, read Xinhua publications?

Overholser's face shows surprise. Xinhua ("New China") is the official Chinese news agency, and Yang wants to know if Overholser reads the official story.

Yang's question is purposeful. He writes for Xinhua. He has spent most of his professional life explaining Chinese culture to overseas China-watchers. As he told me on another occasion, he has sensed during the past year, which he has spent earning a master's degree in journalism from the University of Missouri at Columbia, that many Americans disregard the work he does as a Chinese journalist. And now Overholser has just told him that her job includes watching China and formulating perhaps the most influential of American editorial opinions about it. Does she, too, disregard Xinhua? Will his work in China fail to reach Overholser and *The New York Times*?

Yang's question presents Overholser with a problem. She does not know if the fine *Times* library even receives Xinhua publications. She does not hedge about whether she reads China's official press. "I should," she replies. She tells him that she has begun reading reports from Tass, the Soviet news agency, and that they help her understand Russia. She announces a decision: that very afternoon she will find out whether her library gets materials from Xinhua; if not, she'll ask that they be ordered. Yang sits back, having scored a few points for Chinese journalism.

A few moments later different points will be scored. Another scholar asks Overholser,

When she writes editorials, to whom does she write?

Usually, to any well-read person, Overholser says—but not always. When, for example, the Senate must vote on an arms-control measure, Overholser will write the *Times* editorial on the subject. Hoping to influence American foreign policy, she will aim directly at Congress.

This comment brings a question from Zhu Shida. A man of playful and expansive intellect, who has spent the past year as a Fulbright scholar at Harvard studying John Dos Passos, Zhu teaches journalism in an elite graduate program at the Chinese Academy of Social Sciences.

Obviously fascinated by this editorialist, who regularly attempts to shape American diplomacy, Zhu stretches his lean frame across the table toward her. He asks, When *The New York Times* seeks to influence foreign policy, does Congress or the State Department impose guidelines?

Overholser misunderstands. Yes, she begins, you might say that an editorial writer tries to create "guidelines"—to direct the government toward proper policy. She begins to elaborate on the role of editorialist as guide. Someone in the audience gently cuts her off and restates Zhu's question. Overholser does a double take. "Guidelines from Congress or State?" she asks. "Well, they certainly wouldn't dare call them that." Overholser then proceeds, lest she seem naive about editorial freedom or Zhu feel embarrassed by his question, to talk about nongovernmental influences on editorial writing: possibly advertisers, perhaps social milieu, probably herd instinct.

As we walk away from the seminar room, Zhu Shida seems pleased to have heard the *Times* acknowledge the possibility that its editorials might, even in small ways, be affected by dubious influences. But he seems also to realize that his "guidelines" question departed so much from the reality of U.S. editorial-page procedure that Overholser could not even hear it.

ZERO TO THIRTY THOUSAND

Since 1982, when I first served as an adviser to a Chinese scholar who was visiting at Yale University, where I teach, I have witnessed many similar scenes. They usually contain just such a cast of well-informed people, displaying good intentions and betraying mutual ignorance. They reveal the intensity with which two nations separated through much of the last half of this century now struggle to understand each other.

For every scholar in that room at the *Times*, thousands are now scattered throughout the United States—living in hamlets and suburbs and slums, studying legal theory and laser physics and mass media, meditating on China and America and themselves.

These Chinese visitors range in age from their twenties to their sixties, and in status from undergraduate to full professor or fully accomplished professional. (The Chinese government in official documents tends to describe everyone whom it sends to the United States as a "student" and to make its most significant distinction between "officially sponsored" students, who receive some government or institutional funding and whom it attempts to control, and "self-sponsored" students, who pay their own way, usually with the help of friends or family abroad, and remain free of state control. American university administrators and individual Chinese visitors tend to distinguish between "students," who enroll in degree programs, and "scholars," who conduct research but do not enroll, a distinction I will observe.)

These visitors constitute the largest national group of foreign students and scholars now residing in the United States—they probably number more than 30,000. They also constitute the largest such group ever sent by a Communist nation to a Western one. In 1987–1988, the last year for which figures are available, the Soviet Union had fewer than a hundred students in the United States, and no other Communist nation had more than 1,900. The number of students and scholars from China who have studied in the United States in this decade—50,000—already exceeds the number who received training in the United States in the century prior to the creation of the People's Republic of China, in 1949, and greatly exceeds those trained in the Soviet Union since 1949.

But historical comparisons alone miss the impact of this cultural exchange on Chinese life. China today has approximately 120,000 graduate students within its borders, whereas it has some 20,000 enrolled here. Moreover, through national exams and institutional selection, China directs official support for overseas study to the cream of its intelligentsia—to an extent unprecedented among other nations. The selection process brings to America not just the Chinese scholarly elite but also the power elite. Douglas Murray, until recently the president of the China Institute in America, says, "Every Chinese leader seems to have a son or daughter in the United States."

These scholars and students, then, have importance beyond their numbers. For they likely represent a large segment of China's next generation of intellectual leadership, and perhaps much of the economic and political leadership as well. Their absence at times has so disrupted training in China that, in the words of Wang Ruizhong, the second secretary for education at the Chinese embassy in Washington, Chinese professors have worried that leading universities might become mere "prep schools for study abroad."

Most Americans who learn that tens of thousands of students from China are enrolled in this country seem astonished. They should be. None of the first American advocates for inviting Chinese students anticipated the current numbers of them. At the China Institute, Douglas Murray showed me an article he had published in 1976 in the *Annals of the American Academy of Political and Social Science*. It predicted that once China began to send students to the United States, "it would be overly optimistic to expect more than a few dozen per year."

Three years later, just before the reopening of formal Sino-American diplomatic relations, China made a surprising announcement: it wanted to send at least 500 students and scholars to American universities, beginning immediately, and it wanted its students to be free, like entrepreneurs, to wheel and deal among dozens of American universities.

Many American schools, lured, perhaps, by the exotic or by missionary impulses or by the prospect of additional tuition, opened their arms to China. By 1983 about a hundred American colleges and universities had set up exchanges with China. These connected such institutions as Harvard University and the Chinese Academy of Social Sciences, Oberlin College and Shanxi Agricultural University, the Thunderbird Graduate School of International Business and the Beijing Institute of Foreign Trade.

The welcome continued warm when Chinese students, particularly in the sciences, proved exemplary. In a survey of university officials, 44 percent reported that the grades of Chinese students were better than those of graduate students as a whole. The excellence of Chinese graduate students in physics, for example, has led American professors to rely on them as teaching and research assistants and American students to complain that they are distorting the grade curve. University departments such as physics, chemistry, computer science, and engineering now rely increasingly on Chinese talent, says Michael Holcomb, a graduate admissions officer at Rutgers University, which has approximately

350 Chinese students and scholars, and as a result "some programs have become hostages."

Because Chinese scientists contribute so much, they find American universities willing to support them financially. Although at first the Chinese government paid more than half the cost of sending students and scholars to the United States, by 1985 American universities paid 57 percent and the Chinese government only 17 percent of the $133 million spent for officially sponsored Chinese students and scholars in the United States, according to Leo A. Orleans, the author of a recent study titled *Chinese Students in America: Policies, Issues, and Numbers*, sponsored by the Committee on Scholarly Communication with the PRC.

If America's reasons for welcoming Chinese scholars seem complex and mutable, China's reasons for sending them seem straightforward and steady. At the national level officials proclaim that China needs well-trained intellectuals to assist its Four Modernizations (in agriculture, industry, science, and defense). At the institutional and individual levels students and scholars speak of enhancing their knowledge, technology, methods, and prestige.

Though straightforward, these reasons fail to explain why the number of Chinese studying in the United States has surged from zero to 30,000 in only ten years. This human outpouring implicitly acknowledges the squandering of intellectual resources during the decade of the Cultural Revolution, which began in 1966. When I asked Jay Henderson, of the Institute of International Education, why China had turned so decisively to Western education, he said, "They didn't have much other choice, because their domestic education system had been destroyed."

Henderson, who directs the institute's offices in Southeast Asia, explained, "China is a poor country. It's a country that from 1849 to

1949 ate the leaves off the trees and the grass off the ground, and was addicted to opium, and was the victim of every imaginable sort of exploitation. In 1949 the Chinese finally stood up. Then, from 1966 to 1976, they suffered the Cultural Revolution, and went almost totally out of control."

A large body of Chinese narrative, called "scar literature," describes that manic decade. Families saw their books burned before their eyes by revolutionary Red Guards. Universities closed and teachers departed for remote regions to learn from peasants and workers about labor and hardship. Old people and young were tortured to death. Famous intellectuals committed suicide rather than endure public criticism for purported crimes. To these horror stories most Chinese scholars in America today add tales of the milder scarring they suffered—as teenagers pulled from school and turned into melon-pickers or railroad-builders, as young professionals pulled from careers and made translators or clerks.

Finally, in the mid-1970s, China reopened its universities and began its Four Modernizations—which demanded trained intellectuals and modern technicians. These demands the Chinese could not meet. "They were in a desperate situation," says Glenn Shive, the Institute of International Education's representative to China. China had lost the "internal capacity to reproduce the next generation of scholars," he says. The old ones were dying or retiring, and few remained to teach.

"They had to do something fast," Shive says. "They had to do something dramatic. And they did, by investing in this study-abroad venture."

Although China's dramatic venture surprised every American who had studied the interaction of Chinese intellectuals with the West, the pattern is not a new one. When a Chinese government first sent students abroad, in 1872, it sent them to the United States, to live with families in New England.

Over the succeeding years Chinese students came in waves, flooding and receding. In all years prior to 1954 Chinese students earned more university degrees (13,797) from schools in the United States than from those in any other foreign country, and vastly more doctoral degrees (2,097). By 1964 three quarters of the board members and members of the departmental standing committees of the Chinese Academy of Sciences had Western training. On the basis of such evidence, Mary Bullock, the director of the Asia program at the Woodrow Wilson International Center for Scholars, argues that "the PRC's decision to send thousands of students to the West represents continuity, not a radical departure, in modern China's cultural policy."

Whatever its long-term continuity, China's policy suffers from frequent short-term discontinuities, as the fate of China's initial experiment reveals. In the early 1880s, a decade after it began to send them, China called back its first students from the United States. The Chinese government feared that its investment might yield inadequate returns, in part because some young scholars might stay overseas or become too Westernized.

In 1988, once again ten years after scholars had begun to study in the United States, the same fears seemed to strike the Chinese government. In March *The New York Times* reported that China planned "a drastic reduction in the number of its students abroad, especially in the United States." The Chinese government, the *Times* continued, feared that "too many young scholars may stay overseas or become too Westernized."

The *Times* went on to estimate that China might cut the number of new students arriving in the United States to 600 a year, noting that 8,000 had come in 1985 alone. That report alarmed many Chinese students in the United States. More than a thousand signed an open letter to the Chinese government expressing concern over the proposed reduction in numbers and objecting to new regulations that limited the number of years that government-sponsored students may study in the United States (two years for a master's degree, five for a doctorate).

The *Times* estimate that only 600 students would arrive in 1988 now seems misleading. Although China's State Education Commission did send the United States only 600 of the 3,000 students that it sent worldwide, an array of Chinese universities and academies sent another 4,000 students, out of 5,000 worldwide. In addition, according to the Institute of International Education, 2,000 to 3,000 Chinese students who paid their own way and thus were free of government control came to the United States. The United States, then, saw at least 6,600 new Chinese students arrive for the academic year 1988–1989.

SOURCES OF MISUNDERSTANDING

Because the number of Chinese scholars is so large, neither the Chinese nor the U.S. government can easily monitor their activities, much less assess how they are responding to American life. As a result, most information about their experiences is unavoidably anecdotal. The Chinese scholars with whom I have talked most tend to share my interest in the humanities and social sciences, in fields such as law, history, sociology, anthropology, English literature, and American studies, but I have also talked with scholars in, for example, radio engineering, atomic physics, and the history of science. Most are in their thirties and forties, but some are as young as twenty-five or as old as sixty-one. Their stories cannot reflect every experience possible for a Chinese scholar in the United States, but they do offer an illustrative sample of Chinese encounters with America.

Most scholars come here with professional goals foremost in mind. When discussing those goals Chinese scholars speak continually about access to research facilities and materials—facilities for learning American medical practices or experimenting in polymer chemistry, materials for analyzing American diplomacy or studying management techniques.

Access to materials often begins in libraries, and Chinese encounters with great American libraries can be revealing. The first scholar I helped at Yale asked for access to the "English-department library." Because he was studying American writing from the 1960s and 1970s and the English-department library contained only a few old books, I suggested that he try the *university* library. He resisted. I did not understand that valuable books at his university were kept in department libraries and made available primarily to faculty members, nor did I understand that some Chinese libraries give full access only to high-ranking officials. Finally he agreed to walk with me to Yale's great Sterling Library, the cathedral-like repository for the main university collection. As we entered its long nave, his worst fears were realized.

He saw vaulted arches, stained-glass windows, but no books at all. Within the nave's convoluted side chapels, students and teachers meandered—but not past bookshelves. They merely paused to make quick notes from cards in thousands of oak files. Turning to me, he insisted that the department library must hold more books.

I explained that the file cards represented millions of volumes on floors above our heads. I got him a library card, found him a study carrel at a window on an upper floor, and left him surrounded by unlimited books. Seldom have I seen an adult so happy.

As well as collecting new materials from America, students and scholars are discovering new scholarly methods and directions for their study of Chinese culture. A graduate student at the University of Wisconsin is working with types of sociological surveys and psychological experiments that are unknown in

China. A law student at Yale is doing a comparative study of freedom of speech—"a somewhat sensitive topic," he supposes. At the Center for Advanced Study, at Stanford University, Fu Zhengyuan, a professor from the Chinese Academy of Social Sciences, recently began a study of the determinants of political behavior in Britain, the United States, China, and the Soviet Union, including determinants that orthodox Marxist analysis overlooks.

All three studies reveal a desire to go beyond traditional materials and methods. Fu Zhengyuan, for example, speaks critically of the limitations imposed by Marxist analysis. In China, he says, "*Marxist* analysis is almost a dirty word among intellectuals. To use it means that your mind is sterile. It means that your work is annotational, not at all empirically oriented—that it stems from some hair-splitting scholastic analysis that has no basis in reality." Chinese scholars here seem to share the American desire to do fresh scholarship, in which, as one visiting scholar at Columbia University put it, you "don't have to eat what others have chewed."

The scholars seem attracted not just to openness in materials and methods but also to the open life of many American academics. American academic productivity (driven in part by the publish-or-perish system) and the related mobility of faculty members among universities has reshaped the professional ambitions of Chinese scholars. Glenn Shive, of the Institute of International Education, says that scholars returning to China have become critics of university "deadwood"—"all those professors reading from their aged, yellowing pages of notes." Returning scholars have also often become champions of mobility in the educational system and thus challengers of the *fenpei* system, which allocates workers through central planning. Scholars visiting America, Shive says, "realize that mobility in this culture is integral to the way sciences have

flourished in the West," and blame *fenpei* rigidity for one of China's deeply felt embarrassments: that no Chinese citizen has yet won a Nobel Prize for work done in China. "The whole personnel system in universities is unstable in China," Shive says, "partly as a result of their experience with the way American universities work. They're really impressed with the way we get our people to teach a lot, and publish a lot, and seek fame and fortune as scholars."

INHOSPITABLE AMERICANS

The enthusiasm shown by Chinese scholars for American professional life rarely extends to the social experiences they have in America. Many of China's most influential visiting scholars feel themselves snubbed or ignored. Some Chinese scholars I interviewed told me that I was the first American who had taken the time to talk with them.

During my first conversation with Ye Xiaoxin, sixty-one years old and a leading law professor at Fudan, one of China's major universities, I suggested we meet again. He seemed startled. "I would like very much to speak with an American," he said. Over tea a few days later, Ye described his efforts to get to know Americans. At Columbia he had approached a number of students whom he had selected carefully: each, he knew, was studying both law and Chinese. He has asked if they might like to talk. The students mentioned exams or other commitments. Politely, all refused him.

Such experiences force scholars to seek interaction in strange places. One visitor at Yale sought conversation in public parks with vagrants, because they would take time to talk. Liu Zongren, who studied at Northwestern University, once pretended he wished to get information from a local high school principal—just to speak English. In his memoir *Two Years in the Melting Pot*, Liu reported that one can sometimes make small talk with Americans but one can rarely make friends. Deprived of human conversation, some Chinese visitors settle for television. In five months Liu logged 750 hours of TV.

These Chinese experiences evoke American complaints about ostracism in China. What foreigners in Beijing experience "is remote from the life of this city," wrote Fred C. Shapiro in *The New Yorker*, in December of 1987, adding that even the persistent foreigner who becomes a "friend of China" learns that "the friendship will always be a formal and highly circumspect one." Similarly, a writer in *Conde Nast's Traveler* describes the Chinese instinct as "isolationist" and advises that "even an informal visit to a Chinese home remains a sometimes unobtainable prize for a foreigner."

Contrary to unflattering depictions of their instincts, many Chinese in the United States—perhaps thrilled by expatriation or plagued by loneliness—seem hungry to discuss not just America and China but also ideals and realities, lives and longings. They find, however, that few Americans will listen. One senior Chinese scholar caught the irony perfectly: "When I am at work in Beijing," the scholar said, "American visitors often wish to talk with me. Although I am very busy, I try to give them time. Now I am here and not so busy. No one wants to talk."

BETTER READ THAN FED

The social isolation felt by Chinese scholars derives in part from economics. The Chinese government provides the students and scholars whom it supports with stipends of $4,800 to $5,400 a year—$400 to $450 a month. This living allowance appalls American university administrators. Marvin Baron, the director of services for international students and scholars at the University of California at Berkeley, and a former president of the National Association for Foreign Student Affairs, has complained to the Chinese embassy in Washington, pointing

out that his university estimates that graduate students need at least $700 a month—$250 more than China gives its full-fledged scholars.

Although Americans disparage these stipends as miniscule, to Chinese they seem enormous. One month's check for $450 approaches a year's salary at home for most professors. Often the Chinese recipient of such wealth feels obligations like those of an American jackpot winner. He wants his family to benefit also, and the Chinese government accommodates his desire with special arrangements. In one version (details change often) the scholar pays the government $1,500 in American currency. The government waives its import duty (normally 300 to 400 percent) on certain purchases, often referred to as the "eight great items." A lifetime's cache of luxuries then awaits the scholar on his return to China—camera, refrigerator, computer, washer, color television, microwave oven, or whatever. The scholar returns to his family as if he were a winner on *Let's Make a Deal*.

The scholar's once-in-a-liftime chance to enrich family and self cuts into his small stipend. To survive, the scholar must live ingeniously. I know one scholar who, horrified by the high cost of American ginger, had a friend smuggle him a year's supply (he brought me a pungent bagful as a present, still moist with the red clay of his province).

Ingenuity, however, goes only so far. It will not buy books or bus fare or admission to cultural events. (The happiest recollections I hear from scholars often include the gift of a theater or intercity bus ticket). Nor will ingenuity allow scholars to escape their isolation. Chinese students who wish to share accommodations with Americans often cannot afford to, even in the crowded and run-down apartments surrounding major universities. Americans, they find, demand safer neighborhoods or more space than Chinese can afford. Thus many Chinese scholars crowd together, and some of them leave America speaking English little better than they did when they arrived. An administrator at the University of Iowa reports that returnees he has met in China all offer future students the same advice: Don't live with other Chinese.

Their ghettoization in urban neighborhoods give Chinese scholars not just a limited view but a tainted one. Some contend with slumlords and associated vermin. One scholar in New Haven told me, happily, that after he complained about the depletion of his apartment's food supply, his landlord gave him a mousetrap. The first night he used it, it caught seventeen mice.

The lives of scholars are also tainted by American crime. They speak frequently of wallets grabbed, bicycles stolen, friends attacked. A scholar in New Haven lent his apartment's communal bicycle to a neighborhood boy; the boy sold it. A scholar in Chicago, accosted by a young man demanding money, reached into his pocket to offer a few dollars; the man snatched the whole wallet.

Apart from the one major similarity—the difficulty of making friends in a culture that ignores foreigners—a Chinese scholar's social and economic perspective on America can be a near perfect reversal of the lofty vantage point from which most Americans see China. Chinese who are studying here live not in hotels but in ghettos, stay not days but months, encounter not the upbeat but the downcast, garner impressions that are not orchestrated but fragmented. This is a reversal of perspective that the Chinese government seems not to mind. Marvin Baron, of Berkeley, says that officials at the Chinese embassy in Washington told him "they don't want their people to become too indulgent and get more money than they actually need, because then it would become too difficult for them to readjust to life in China when they come back." As a result, while most American visitors to China gather images from an eagle's-eye view, Chinese scholars get what amounts to a worm's-eye view of America.

For Chinese studying in the United States, as for anyone anywhere, facts of professional, social, and economic life link ultimately to political concerns. These concerns surface frequently in conversation, but for me they were epitomized in the final seminar of a series moderated by Professor R. Randle Edwards at Columbia University's Center for Chinese Legal Studies. There the desire of Chinese scholars to understand how America works and thereby assess how China should or should not proceed politically became the dominant force.

For weeks Edwards and some American colleagues, along with five Chinese legal scholars, had discussed issues such as freedom of speech in China, China's growing private economy, and the applicability of Chinese law in capitalist Hong Kong—issues of shared concern, no doubt, but ones that interested the Americans primarily. For this final session the Chinese scholars had set their own agenda. They wished to talk only about how the American political system—the courts, the legal process, the selection of legislators, the making of foreign policy—was democratized, made "open to individuals."

For an hour the Chinese asked questions furiously. Edwards broke into a sweat as he dashed from seminar table to blackboard, scrawling "sunshine laws" and "urban affairs" and "conference committees." He cited Ralph Nader to explain interest groups and Pierre du Pont to explain the significance of campaign spending limits. No, he said, immigration law is not secret, and yes, Supreme Court decisions are public.

At the end of the seminar Edwards announced that he would like to celebrate with a banquet, a Chinese custom. One visitor countered that more talk was all they wanted. He said, "It's okay if we just eat bread."

When scholars discuss the political freedom they have encountered during their months or years in America, they speak most often about open exchange of information and ideas. Chinese students here freely create professional associations—the Chinese Young Economists, the Chinese Business Association, the Association of Life Sciences for Chinese Students and Scholars in the United States—some of which foster informal political discussion as readily as they sponsor technical seminars. They publish journals of opinion. They sign open letters questioning Chinese government policies. They spend many hours in library periodical rooms. They maintain a nationwide computer bulletin board, full of political debate, on the American interuniversity network called BITNET.

Easy access to information may be the single most radicalizing influence. A young graduate of Fudan University, Zhao Xinshu, recently conducted a survey of 112 Chinese students at the University of Wisconsin, where he is now a doctoral candidate in social and psychological research. He wished to discover what factors incline visiting students toward dissidence.

Zhao discovered that some presumed radicalizers—including many years of living in the United States or many hours of reading dissident publications—in fact have little effect. He found only two factors that seem to correlate with student opposition to official Chinese government ideology: youthfulness, and many hours spent reading *The New York Times*. The *Times* has influence, Zhao speculates, because students believe what it prints. Students who spend more than five hours a week with the *Times* prove particularly dissident.

FEARS OF A CHINESE BRAIN DRAIN

Chinese scholars immersed in these several aspects of American life—professional, social, economic, and political—often show signs of resistance to returning home. Some students and scholars say they are attracted to American ways. One will speak of testing his skills in a society that values competition; another,

more concretely, will compare his summer job as a New York lawyer at $1,300 a week with his permanent job as a Beijing lawyer at $10 a week. Some express criticism of Chinese political policy. One will endorse a letter challenging government directives; another will complain that China could never adopt a Freedom of Information Act. These and other signs suggest to some China-watchers that large numbers of Chinese students and scholars will not return home. Might China's ambitious experiment end in an enormous brain drain?

No one worries about this more than the Chinese government. Its State Education Commission, which reported that by 1987 slightly more than a quarter of the students and scholars it had sent to the United States had returned, has asked Americans to help enforce the new strict limits on duration of study abroad. It pressed the United States Information Agency, for example, to help ensure that Chinese students return to their homeland.

With questions of brain drain and non-return in mind, I sought out Hu Ping, a Chinese student who has become a symbol of political dissidence and an applicant for political asylum. Early in 1987 Hu enrolled as a doctoral candidate in political theory at Harvard, where he began a book on Chinese democracy. A year later he left Harvard to assume the editorship of the Chinese-language newspaper *China Spring*—itself a symbol of dissidence, and, according to a 1987 judgment by a Shanghai court, a "counterrevolutionary" publication. In the PRC one of *China Spring's* American-educated staff members had been sentenced to a two-year prison term when, during a visit home, he wrote posters encouraging student protest. Early last year, after Hu moved to *China Spring*, the Chinese government invalidated his passport. Students began to joke that the government had helped Hu in his application for American political asylum—which no Chinese student had yet received, but which the United States grants to "refugees" who demonstrate a "well-founded fear of persecution" if they return home. (Last August the United States made its first three grants of asylum to Chinese students or scholars—to three couples who had had second children in America and thus might, in the judgment of Edwin Meese, then the Attorney General, be subject to persecution for violating China's one-child limit.)

I found Hu in the railroad-car apartment in Queens, near the Brooklyn-Queens Expressway, that serves as the office for *China Spring*. Hu talked about his intellectual development as a student, reading Plato, Locke, and Hume at Beijing University. We discussed his essay "On Freedom of Speech"—notorious in China—which artfully quotes Milton, Hegel, and Mao, among others, to argue that the Chinese people deserve the freedom to "think, say, and write whatever they wish."

In answer to the charge that *China Spring* is counterrevolutionary, Hu insisted that it seeks not to oppose but to "correct" the Chinese Constitution. "We don't agree with the four basic principles," he continued, striking a moderate tone but making a radical argument. Those principles are the key Marxist elements of the Constitution's preamble: socialism, the dictatorship of the proletariat, the leadership role of the Chinese Communist Party, and Marxist-Leninist-Mao Zedong Thought. "We feel," he said, "that you have no right to force every citizen to be beneath Marxist-Leninist-Mao Zedong Thought—not in a government constitution. You can write it in a party constitution."

As Hu spoke, his colleages hauled down the corridor mailbags containing the latest issue of *China Spring*, which happened to carry the letter from students imploring the Chinese government not to limit their stays in the United States. I asked Hu if he thought most students and scholars would return to China. He believed that most would, he said, though in the "short term" he personally might find return

difficult. "Some [American] professor said to me, 'You are one of the most wanting-to-return-to-China-people.'" That's true, Hu told me: "Our cause is in China, not here."

Hu's words typify what I hear from Chinese students and scholars. Cong Dachang, an anthropologist at Yale whose family was one of the three that received political asylum last summer, told me that he finds it "hard to imagine growing old" in America. Liu Binyan, a controversial journalist whom China recently expelled from its Communist Party but who has been allowed to spend 1988–1989 as a Nieman fellow at Harvard, reportedly shrugs off questions about whether he will return. He says he would be useless anywhere but China.

Many knowledgeable Americans consider fears of a Chinese brain drain to be overblown. "Initially," says Marvin Baron, of Berkeley, "I expected a percentage to stay that would be nearly comparable to that from Taiwan"—a country that in most years during the past decade has had even more people studying in the United States than China has had, and that has suffered a non-return rate often estimated to be higher than 60 percent. "I very quickly realized," Baron says, "that that wouldn't be the case. The truth is, I still know of relatively few Chinese, five percent or so, who have tried to stay."

That most Chinese have been returning is confirmed in figures recently compiled by Leo A. Orleans, the author of *Chinese Students in America*. U.S. visa dates for 1979 to 1987 show that 34,000 Chinese students and scholars came here with J-1 visas—the visa category that roughly corresponds to what the Chinese government calls officially sponsored students. Of those students 12,500 have already returned to China. Another 21,000, most of whom have arrived too recently to finish degree programs, remain enrolled in American universities. Only 500 have changed their visa status—typically by marrying an American or getting an American employer to list them as essential personnel—to remain in the United States.

A different pattern is suggested by the statistics that Orleans compiled on students who came with F-1 visas—primarily "self-sponsored" students whose return China encourages but cannot control. Orleans estimates that 7,000 of these students have returned, 7,000 remained enrolled, and 8,000 have changed their visa status. This ratio represents a brain drain comparable to that suffered by other developing nations. For China it seems to represent a modest embarrassment but no great loss.

For those students abroad who do return, China has great expectations. "When you have finished your study and come home," it reassured scholars and students here a few years ago, "you should be fresh crack forces for China's cause of socialist modernization and pillars of the state by the first year of the 21st century."

But these pillars, some Chinese suggest, may not support the existing state—at least not without continued political reform. And as history shows, returning students have in the past shaken the Chinese state. Both the overthrow of China's last emperor and the arrival of Marxism in China drew strength from students educated overseas.

The ultimate impact of today's students and scholars remains open to question. Some analysts, including Glenn Shive, of the Institute of International Education, argue that an entire generation of leaders, many of them Soviet-trained, must retire before these American-trained students can come to power. "But eventually," Shive says, "they will get together, and they will move like a generation through the universities, legal system, and government." As they do, Shive predicts, "they are going to offend their colleagues. But they're going to persist, and eventually prevail. I think they're going to inherit the earth over there."

But just as history shows that foreign-trained students have helped transform China, it also shows that predictions about their effect have been exaggerated. In 1921, for example, *The Daily Mail* of London prophesied that the number of Chinese studying in America would lead to undue American—non-British, that is—influence on China's future. "Educated under the American system, constantly reminded of the happy associations of their school days through the influential alumni organization, aware that they owe their scholarships to American justice, and saturated with American sentiment by five to eight years' residence in the country," the *Mail* wrote, those students from Beijing would "look to the United States solely for cooperation in the troublous years to come." Not so, as it happened.

And not likely today. Chinese students and scholars seem as unsaturated with American sentiment as they seem unsatisfied in what could be called their lovers' quarrel with China. Whatever they eventually inherit in China—perhaps the earth, perhaps only the wind—the legacy of their American years will not be what the Chinese government derides as a "wholesale Westernization." It will be selective, cautious—in effect, retail Westernization.

Chinese students and scholars in America today speak in ways that recall Yen Fu, one of the first Chinese students sent to Britain, in 1876. Yen admired the West for its liberty and wealth and democracy. But ultimately he found the West inadequate, for he felt that it had made little progress toward the "three criteria of an ideal society—material sufficiently enjoyed by all, moral excellence attained by many, and crimes committed by none." Indeed, he suggested, "the West is heading toward the opposite direction."

DISCUSSION QUESTIONS

1. What are the advantages for the Chinese of an American education? What are the disadvantages for Chinese students and researchers?

2. If foreign students opt to remain in the United States to work about their educa-tion, it represents a so-called "brain drain." What problems does this create for their native countries?

3. Strebeigh identifies a number of misconceptions about foreign students studying in the United States. How serious are these misconceptions?

CHAPTER 14

Issues in Health and Medical Care

INTRODUCTION

Medical care has come to epitomize many of the critical dilemmas that confront contemporary societies, especially those pertaining to production and use of complex technology and use of scientific and professional knowledge. Issues in health and medical care are salient not only because they touch us individually in important respects but also because they expose many of the political, economic, social, and ethical dilemmas of our time. These issues are likely to continue to gain public attention and to consume increasing amounts of the nation's resources because of changing social attitudes and enormous social pressures to modify the organization, financing, and delivery of health and medical care services.

While matters such as birth technology and in vitro fertilization, organ transplantation, artificial life-sustaining measures, and the right to die are discussed daily in the popular media, issues concerning health and medicine are not limited to intractable ethical dilemmas. The social sciences have had a long-standing interest in medicine and have extended discussion of health issues beyond the exclusive purview of physicians and other medical care providers. In part, the effort of social scientists has been directed toward moving away from a strictly *medical* definition of health, in which disease is conceived of in purely physiological terms and health is the absence of disease, and toward a *sociocultural* view, in which health is defined positively in terms of physical, mental, *and* social well-being, rather than merely as the absence of disease. *Medical care*, according to this perspective, consists of services directed toward individuals who are sick or who think they are sick, while *health care* encompasses activities and services that promote or maintain health, including regular exercise, good nutrition, healthy life-style, and improved public health.

Both the significance of the distinction between health care and medical care and the significance of the underlying differences between the medical and sociocultural models have increased as the American people have come to expect much more from physicians and the medical care institution. These rising expectations are related to increased anxieties over the cost, quality, and accessibility of medical care. Many people believe that these mounting expectations and anxieties are a result of a definition of health that has become too broad and a medical profession that has become overly empowered. At a time when relations between health, illness, and medicine are being viewed in wholly different ways and are acquiring new meanings in U.S. culture, some critics believe that the United States has become "overmedicalized." These critics call for a measure of "demedicalization"—a return to a simpler set of health practices and less reliance on of complex, expensive medical intervention.

In the first selection, Renée C. Fox describes some of the dimensions of medicalization in American society and suggests that since there are indications that demedicalization is already taking place, concerns about overmedicalization may be exaggerated. However, there can be no doubt that the domain of medicine has enlarged considerably in this century. Child abuse, sexuality, death, obesity, alcoholism, addictions, and even homosexuality, among a number of other societal ills, have been defined and treated as medical problems. While the consequences of this "expansion and secularization" of medical problems are not entirely negative, the issue of medicalization has generated considerable discussion and reveals some of the cultural dimensions of health problems.

Medicalization suggests some ways in which physicians exercise power over who may legitimately act sick and over "appropriate" courses of action for dealing with disease and sickness. A most remarkable story about the rise of the medical profession to this position of authority is told by Paul Starr in his award-winning book, *The Social Transformation of American Medicine* (1982). Starr's historical analysis traces the rise of the medical profession to a sovereign position as its legitimacy and cultural authority expanded. Starr explores how the growth of medical authority allowed the profession to convert its cultural authority into high income, autonomy in fee setting, and other economic rewards as it gained control over both the market for its services and the various organizational hierarchies that govern medical practice, financing, and policy. Further, medicine's sovereignty thwarted challenges to its authority by large organizations and government until the 1970s when that very sovereignty resulted in a loss of public confidence in medicine, caused by the profession's insularity and social insensitivity. One consequence of the loss of confidence in medicine has been the rise in medical malpractice suits.

In the second selection, we turn to a different account of health problems—an individual physician's struggle with clinical uncertainty in the application of medical knowledge and the accompanying, ever-present danger of medical mistakes. David Hilfiker writes passionately about difficulties presented to practicing doctors. Medical mistakes, errors, and failings attract considerable media attention but are often couched in terms of the so-called "medical malpractice crisis" which is thought to be such a threat both to providers and to consumers of medical care services. Although what constitutes an instance of malpractice is not at all clear (Bosk, 1979; Danzon, 1985) and the extent of the crisis may have been overblown (Lieberman, 1981), there can be no doubt that medical mistakes injure, disfigure, and even kill patients. They can also have devastating emotional and, less frequently, financial consequences for physicians. Much of what has been written about malpractice from the individual level of analysis concerns injured patients. The problems of medical malpractice also affect doctors. Dr. Hilfiker's very human account of the causes and consequences of medical uncertainty examines the problem of malpractice from the perspective of the clinician and explores some unfortunate reactions of physicians to their errors.

The last reading in this chapter examines a major health problem in a cross-cultural context. Lori Heise describes the unfolding world epidemic, or pandemic, of acquired immuno-deficiency syndrome, AIDS.

Over 150,000 cases of AIDS have been diagnosed in the United States since 1981 when it was first identified, and world estimates of individuals infected with the virus that leads to full-blown AIDS exceed 10 million. While precise numbers on the extent of the AIDS pandemic are hard to come by, rapidly improving reporting methods suggest that Heise's data are out-of-date. However, her account of the impact of AIDS in the Third World and the alliances between developing and industrialized nations required to combat this deadly disease still ring true. In this selection, Heise argues that because of the realities of life in Third World nations, AIDS poses a greater threat there than in industrialized nations. It threatens to undermine decades of improved health and sustained economic development in Third World nations and has "multiplier"

effects on other health problems in already overburdened health budgets. Moreover, AIDS has become a "social crucible," bringing out the best and the worst of human nature. Heise discusses manifold responses to AIDS, including international cooperation on AIDS research and improved education programs as well as mean-spirited and irrational responses to AIDS victims. She concludes with the hope that there will be an international response to the global challenge that AIDS presents.

References

Bosk, Charles L. *Forgive and Remember: Managing Medical Failure*. Chicago: The University of Chicago Press, 1979.

Danzon, Patricia. *Medical Malpractice: Theory, Evidence and Public Policy*. Cambridge, Mass.: Harvard University Press, 1985.

Lieberman, Jethro K. *The Litigious Society*. New York: Basic Books, 1981.

Starr, Paul. *The Social Transformation of American Medicine: The Rise of a Sovereign Profession and the Making of a Vast Industry*. New York: Basic Books, 1982.

READING 14·1

The Medicalization and Demedicalization of American Society

Renée C. Fox

The statement that American society has become "medicalized" is increasingly heard these days. During the past decade or so, the allegation has been made by social scientists, jurists, politicians, social critics, medical scientists, and physicians. In many instances, it has been accompanied by the claim that the society is now "overmedicalized," and that some degree of "demedicalization" would be desirable. There are those who not only espouse "demedicalizing the society," but who also predict that, in fact, it will progressively come to pass.

One of the most extreme statements of this kind is Ivan Illich's monograph *Medical Nemesis*, which opens with the assertion that "the medical establishment has become a threat to health," and goes on to develop the many damaging ways in which the author considers modern medicine to be responsible for "social" as well as "clinical" and "structural iatrogenesis":

> The technical and non-technical consequences of institutional medicine coalesce and generate a new kind of suffering: anesthetized, impotent and solitary survival in a world turned into a hospital ward. . . . The need for specialized, professional health care beyond a certain point can be taken as an indication of the unhealthy goals pursued by society. . . . The level of public health corresponds to the degree to which the means and responsibility for coping with illness are distributed amongst the total population. This ability to cope can be enhanced but never replaced by medical intervention in the lives of people or by the hygienic characteristics of the environment. The society which can reduce professional intervention to the minimum will provide the best conditions for health. . . . Healthy people are those who live in healthy homes on a healthy diet; in an environment equally fit for birth, growth, work, healing and dying: sustained by a culture which enhances the conscious acceptance of limits to population, of aging, of incomplete recovery and ever imminent death. . . . Man's consciously lived fragility, individuality and relatedness make the experience of pain, of sickness and of death an integral part of his life. The ability to cope with this trio autonomously is fundamental to his health. As he becomes dependent on the management of his intimacy, he renounces his autonomy and his health *must* decline. The true miracle of modern medicine is diabolical. It consists not only of making individuals but whole populations survive on inhumanly low levels of personal health. That health should decline with increasing health service delivery is unforeseen only by the health managers, precisely because their strategies are the result of their blindness to the inalienability of life.[1]

There are numerous grounds on which Illich's thesis can be critized. He minimizes the advances in the prevention, diagnosis, and treatment of disease that have been made since the advent of the bacteriological era in medicine, and he attributes totally to nonmedical agencies all progress in health that has ensued. He implies that modern Western, urban, industrialized, capitalist societies, of which the United States is the prototype, are more preoccupied with pain, sickness, and death, and less able to come to terms with these integral parts of a human life, than other types of society. Although his volume appears to be well documented, a disturbing discrepancy exists between the data presented in many of the works that Illich cites in his copious footnotes and the interpretive liberties that he takes with them. Perhaps most insidious of all is the sophistry that Illich uses in presenting a traditional, orthodox, Christian Catholic point of view in the guise of a vulgar Marxist argument. For he repeatedly claims that, "when dependence on the professional management of pain, sickness and death grows beyond a certain point, the healing power in sickness, patience in suffering, and fortitude in the face of death must decline."[2] In Illich's view, this state is not ony morally dubious, but also spiritually dangerous. Because it entails the "hubris" of what he deems arrogant and excessive medical intervention, it invites "nemesis": the retribution of the gods.

But whatever its shortcomings, Illich's essay is a kind of lightning rod, picking up and conducting the twin themes of medicalization and demedicalization that have become prominent in the United States and a number of other modern Western societies. These themes will concern us here. We shall begin by identifying the constellation of factors involved in what has been termed "medicalization," offer an interpretation of these phenomena, and consider and evaluate certain signs of demedicalization. Finally, some speculative predictions about the probable evolution of the medicalization-demedicalization process in American society will be offered.

One indication of the scope that the "health-illness-medicine complex" has acquired in American society is the diffuse definition of health that has increasingly come to be advocated: "a state of complete physical, mental, and social well-being," to borrow the World Health Organization's phrase. This conception of health extends beyond biological and psychological phenomena relevant to the functioning, equilibrium, and fulfillment of individuals, to include social and cultural conditions of communal as well as personal import. Such an inclusive perspective on health is reflected in the range of difficulties that persons now bring to physicians for their consideration and help. As Leon Kass picturesquely

phrased it, "All kinds of problems now roll to the doctor's door, from sagging anatomies to suicides, from unwanted childlessness to unwanted pregnancy, from marital difficulties to learning difficulties, from genetic counseling to drug addiction, from laziness to crime. . . ."[3] A new term has even been coined by medical practitioners to refer to those clients who seem to have some legitimate need of their therapeutic services, but who technically cannot be considered to be ill. With discernible ambivalence, such people are often called "the worried well."

Accompanying the increasingly comprehensive idea of what constitutes health and what is appropriate for medical professionals to deal with is the growing conviction that health and health care are rights rather than privileges, signs of grace, or lucky, chance happenings. In turn, these developments are connected with higher expectations on the part of the public about what medicine ideally ought to be able to accomplish and to prevent. To some extent, for example, the rise in the number of malpractice suits in the United States seems not only to be a reaction to the errors and abuses that physicians can commit, but also a reflection of the degree to which the professional is being held personally responsible for the scientific and technical uncertainties and limitations of their discipline. The vision of an "iatrogenesis"-free furthering of health, which social critics such as Illich hold forth, is also an indicator of such rising expectations.

One significant form that the process of medicalization has taken is the increase in the numbers and kinds of attitudes and behaviors that have come to be defined as illnesses and treatment of which is regarded as belonging within the jurisdiction of medicine and its practitioners. In an earlier, more religiously oriented era of a modern Western society like our own, some of these same kinds of attitudes and behaviors were considered sinful rather than sick, and they fell under the aegis of religious authorities for a different kind of diagnosis, treatment, and control. In a more secular, but less scientifically and medically oriented, stage of the society than the current one, certain of these ways of thinking, feeling, and behaving were viewed and dealt with as criminal. Although sin, crime, and sickness are not related in a simple, invariant way, there has been a general tendency in the society to move from sin to crime to sickness in categorizing a number of aberrant or deviant states to the degree that the concept of the "medicalization of deviance" has taken root in social science writings. The sin-to-crime-to-sickness evolution has been most apparent with respect to the conditions that are now considered to be mental illnesses, or associated with serious psychological and/or social disturbances.[4] These include, for example, states of hallucination and delusion that once would have been interpreted as signs of possession by the Devil, certain forms of physical violence, such as the type of child abuse that results in what is termed the "battered child syndrome," the set of behaviors in children which are alternatively called hyperactivity, hyperkinesis, or minimal brain dysfunction, and so-called "addictive disorders," such as alcoholism, drug addiction, compulsive overeating, and compulsive gambling.

This "continuing process of divestment"[5] away from sin and crime as categories for abnormality, dysfunction, and deviance and toward illness as the explanatory concept has entailed what Peter Sedgwick calls "the progressive annexation of not-illness into illness." "The future belongs to illness," he proclaims, predicting that "we . . . are going to get more and more diseases, since our expectations of health are going to become more expansive and sophisticated."[6] If we include into what is considered to be sickness or, at least, non-health in the United States, disorders manifested by subjective symptoms that are not brought to the medical profession for diagnosis and treatment, but that do not differ significantly from those that are, then almost everyone in the society can be regarded as in some way "sick."

> At least two . . . studies have noted that as much as 90 percent of their apparently healthy sample had some physical aberration or clinical disorder. . . . It seems that the more intensive the investigation, the higher the prevalence of clinically serious but previously undiagnosed and untreated disorders. Such data as these give an unexpected statistical picture of illness. Instead of it being a relatively infrequent or abnormal phenomenon, the empirical reality may be that illness, defined as the presence of clinically serious symptoms, is the statistical *norm.*[7]

Such a global conception of illness sharply raises the question of the extent to which illness is an objective reality, a subjective state, or a societal construct that exists chiefly in the minds of its social "beholders," a question that will be considered in greater detail below.

The great "power" that the American medical profession, particularly the physician, is assumed to possess and jealously and effectively to guard is another component of the society's medicalization. In the many allusions to this medical "power" that are currently made, the organized "autonomy" and "dominance" of the profession are frequently cited, and, in some of the more critical statements about the physician, these attributes are described as constituting a virtual "monopoly" or "expropriation" of health and illness. The "mystique" that surrounds the medical profession is part of what is felt to be its power: a mystique that is not only spontaneously conferred on its practitioners by the public but, as some observers contend, is also cultivated by physicians themselves through their claim that they command knowledge and skills that are too esoteric to be freely and fully shared with lay persons.

However, it is to the biotechnological capacities of modern medicine that its greatest power is usually attributed: both its huge battery of established drugs and procedures and its new and continually increasing medical and surgical techniques. Among the actual or incipient developments that are most frequently mentioned are the implantation of cadaveric, live, or mechanical organs, genetic and other microcellular forms of "engineering," and *in vitro* fertilization, as well as various chemical, surgical, and psychophysiological methods of thought and behavior control. The potentials of medicine not only to prevent and to heal, but also to subjugate, modify, and harm are implicated in such references.

The high and rapidly growing cost of medical and health care is still another measure in increased medicalization. In 1975, Americans spent $547 per person for health care and related activities such as medical education and research. This represented 8.3 percent of the GNP. In 1950, 4.6 percent and in 1970, 7.2 percent of the GNP was spent. From 1963 to the present, health expenditures have risen at a rate exceeding 10 percent annually while the rest of the economy as reflected in the GNP has been growing at a rate between 6 and 7 percent.

In addition to allocating an ever-increasing proportion of society's economic resources for health care, greater amounts of political and legal energy are also being invested in health, illness, and medical concerns. The pros and cons of national health insurance, which continue to be vigorously debated in various arenas, are as much political, ideological, and legal issues, as they are economic ones. The volume of legislation relevant to health care has grown impressively. In 1974, for example, more than 1300 health-care bills were introduced in the Congress, and more than 900 such bills in the state legislature in New York alone. The health subcommittees of the Senate and the House of Representatives are particularly active, and they have become prestigious as well. Furthermore, partly as a consequence of various congressional investigations and hearings, the federal government is now significantly involved in bioethical questions (especially those bearing on human experimentation) in addition to their more traditional interests in medical economic and health-care-delivery problems.

During the past few years, a number of medico-legal decisions have been made that are of far-reaching cultural importance, affecting the society's fundamental conceptions of life, death, the body, individuality, and humanity. These include: the Supreme Court's decisions in favor of the legal right of women to decide upon and undergo abortion; the Court's ruling against the involuntary, purely custodial confinement of untreated mentally ill persons; the Uniform Anatomical Gift Act, adopted in fifty-one jurisdictions, which permits people to donate all or parts of their bodies to be used for medical purposes after their death; death statutes passed in various states that add the new, "irreversible coma" criterion of "brain death" to the traditional criteria for pronouncing death, based on the cessation of respiratory and cardiac function; and, in the case of Karen Ann Quinlan, the New Jersey Supreme Court's extension of "the individual's right of privacy" to encompass a patient's decision to decline or terminate life-saving treatment, under certain circumstances.

One other, quite different, way in which medical phenomena have acquired central importance in the legal system is through the dramatic escalation of malpractice suits against physicians. An estimated 20,000 or more malpractice claims are brought against doctors each year, and the number seems to be rising steadily. In New York, for example, the number of suits filed against physicians rose from 564 in 1970 to 1200 in 1974; in the past decade, the average award for a malpractice claim grew from $6000 to $23,400, with far more very large awards being made than in the past.[8]

Increasing preoccupation with bioethical issues seems also to be a concomitant of the medicalization process. Basic societal questions concerning values, beliefs, and meaning are being debated principally in terms of the dilemmas and dangers associated with biomedical advances. Consideration of particular medical developments such as genetic engineering, life-support systems, birth technology, organ implants, and population and behavior control have opened up far-reaching ethical and existential concerns. Problems of life, death, chance, "necessity," scarcity, equity, individuality, community, the "gift relationship," and the "heroic" world view are being widely discussed in medical, scientific, political, legal, journalistic, philosophical, and religious circles. A bioethics "subculture" with certain characteristics of a social movement has crystallized around such issues.

The unprecedented number of young people who are attempting to embark on medical careers is also contributing to the medicalization process. In this country, on the average, more than three persons apply for each medical-school place available to entering first-year students, and there is as yet no sign of leveling off. Paradoxically, this is happening during a period when medicine and the medical profession are being subjected to increased scrutiny and criticism.

Complex, and by no means consistent, the process of medicalization is not an easy one to analyze. Several preliminary *caveats* seem in order. In part, they are prompted by two sorts of assumptions made by critics of medicalization in America: one is that the central and pervasive position of health, illness, and medicine in present-day American society is histor-

ically and culturally unique, and the other, that it is primarily a result of the self-interested maneuvers of the medical profession. Neither of these assumptions is true without qualification.

To begin with, in all societies, health, illness, and medicine constitute a nexus of great symbolic as well as structural importance, involving and interconnecting biological, social, psychological, and cultural systems of action. In every society, health, illness, and medicine are related to the physical and psychic integrity of individuals, their ability to establish and maintain solidarity relations with others, their capacities to perform social roles, their births, survival, and death, and to the ultimate kinds of "human condition" questions that are associated with these concerns. As such, health, illness, and medicine also involve and affect every major institution of a society, and its basic cultural grounding. The family, for example, is profoundly involved in the health and illness of its members, and, especially in nonmodern societies, the kinship system is as responsible for health and illness as are specialized medical practitioners. The institutions of science, magic, and religion are the major media through which the "hows" and "whys" of health and illness, life and death are addressed in a society, and through which culturally appropriate action for dealing with them is taken. The economy is also involved in several ways: the allocation of resources that health, illness, and medicine entail; the occupational division of labor relevant to diagnosis and therapy; and the bearing of health and illness on the individual's capacity and motivation for work. The deviance and social-control aspects of illness have important implications for the policy, which, in turn, is responsible for the organized enforcement of health measures that pertains to the community or public welfare. And in all societies, the influence, power, and prestige that accrue to medical practitioners implicate the magico-religious and stratification systems as well as the polity.[9]

As the foregoing implies, there are certain respects in which health, illness, and medicine are imbued with a more diffuse and sacred kind of significance in nonmodern than in modern societies. For example, in traditional and neo-traditional Central African societies, the meaning of health and illness, the diagnosis and treatment of sickness, and the wisdom, efficacy, and power of medical practitioners are not only more closely linked with the institutions of kinship, religion, and magic than in American society; they are also more closely connected with the overarching cosmic view through which the whole society defines and orients itself. One indication of the larger matrix into which health, illness, and medicine fit in such a society is that in numerous Central African languages the same words can mean medicine, magico-religious charms, and metaphysically important qualities such as strength, fecundity, and invulnerability, which are believed to be supernaturally conferred.

In the light of the multi-institutional and the cultural significance of health, illness, and medicine in all societies, it is both illogical and unlikely to believe that the current process of medicalization in American society has been engineered and maintained primarily by one group, namely, the physicians. What the manifestations of medicalization that we have identified do suggest, however, is that the health-illness-medical sector has progressively acquired a more general cultural meaning in American society than it had in the past.[10]

Within this framework, the medicalization process entails the assertion of various individual and collective rights, to which members of the society feel entitled and which they express as "health," "quality of life," and "quality of death." The process also involves heightened awareness of a whole range of imperfections, injustices, dangers, and afflictions that are perceived to exist in the society, a protest against them, and a resolve to take action that is more therapeutic than punitive. Medicalization represents an exploration and affirmation of values and beliefs that not only pertain to the ultimate grounding of the society, but also to the human condition, more encompassingly and existentially conceived.

Thus, in American society, health and illness have come to symbolize many positively and negatively valued biological, physical, social, cultural, and metaphysical phenomena. Increasingly, health has become a coded way of referring to an individually, socially, or cosmically ideal state of affairs. Conversely, the concept of illness has increasingly been applied to modes of thinking, feeling, and behaving that are considered undesirably variant or deviant, as well as to more forms of suffering and disability. In turn, this medicalization of deviance and suffering has had a network of consequences.

Talcott Parsons's well-known formulation of the "sick role" provides important insights into what these effects have been. According to him,[11] the sick role consists of two interrelated sets of exemptions and obligations. A person who is defined as ill is exonerated from certain kinds of responsibility for his illness. He is not held morally accountable for the fact that he is sick (it is not considered to be his "fault"), and he is not expected to make himself better by "good motivation" or high resolve without the help of others. In addition, he is viewed as someone whose capacity to function normally is impaired, and who is therefore relieved of some of his usual familial, occupational, and civic activities and responsibilities. In exchange for these exemptions, which are conditionally granted, the sick individual is expected to define the state of being ill as aberrant and undesirable, and to do everything possible to facilitate his recovery from it. In the case of illness of any moment, the responsibility to try to get well also entails the obligation to seek professionally competent help. In a modern Western society, such as the United States, this obligation involves a willingness to confer with a medically trained person, usually a physician, and to undergo the modes of diagnosis and treatment that are recommended, including the ministrations of other medical professionals and hospitalization. Upon entering this relationship with institutionalized medicine and its professional practitioners, an individual with a health problem becomes a patient. By cooperating and collaborating with the medical professionals caring for him, the patient is expected to work toward recovery, or at least, toward the more effective management of his illness.

Because the exemptions and the obligations of sickness have been extended to people with a widening arc of attitudes, experiences, and behaviors in American society, what is regarded as "conditionally legitimate deviance" has increased. Although illness is defined as deviance from the desirable and the normal, it is not viewed as reprehensible in the way that either sin or crime is. The sick person is neither blamed nor punished as those considered sinful or criminal are. So long as he does not abandon himself to illness or eagerly embrace it, but works actively on his own and with medical professionals to improve his condition, he is considered to be responding appropriately, even admirably, to an unfortunate occurrence. Under these conditions, illness is accepted as legitimate deviance. But this also implies that medical professionals have acquired an increasingly important social-control function in the society. They are the principal agents responsible for certifying, diagnosing, treating, and preventing illness. Because a greater proportion of deviance in American society is now seen as illness, the medical profession plays a vastly more important role than it once did in defining and regulating deviance and in trying to forestall and remedy it.

The economic, political, and legal indicators of a progressive medicalization cited above also have complex origins and implications. For example, the fact that activities connected with health, illness, and medicine represent a rising percentage of the gross national product in the United States is a consequence of the fee-for-service system under which American health-care delivery is organized; the central importance of the modern hospital in medical care; the mounting personnel, equipment, and maintenance costs that the operation of the hospital entails; and the development of new medical and surgical procedures and of new drugs, most of which are expensive as they are efficacious. Some of this increase in costs results from the desire for profits that medical professionals, hospital administrators, and members of the pharmaceutical industry share to varying degrees. But how much is difficult to ascertain, though radical ideological criticisms and defensive conservative statements on the point are both rife at present.

In addition to such political and economic factors, the heightened commitment to health as a right and the medicalization of deviance have also contributed to the growth of health expenditures. Because health is both more coveted and more inclusively defined, and because a greater amount of medical therapeutic activity is applied to deviance-defined-as-illness, increasing economic resources are being invested in the health-illness-medicine sector of the society.

The political and legal prominence of questions of health care and medicine in American society at the present time reflects in part a widespread national discontent with the way medical care is organized, financed, and delivered, and with some of the attitudes and behaviors of physicians. The inequities that exist in access to care, and in its technical and interpersonal excellence, are among the primary foci of political and legal activities. Another major area of current political and legal action concerns the internal and external regulation of the medical profession better to insure that it uses its knowledge and skill in a socially as well as medically responsible way, and that it is adequately accountable both to patients and to the public at large. Various new measures, which represent a mixture of controls from within the medical profession and from outside it, have been set into motion. For example, in 1972, the Professional Standards Review Organization was established through the passage of amendments to the Social Security Act, which were designed to provide quality assessment and assurance, utilization review, and cost control, primarily for Medicare and Medicaid patients. Over the course of the years 1966 through 1971, a series of government regulations were passed which mandate peer review for all biomedical research involving human subjects, supported by the Department of Health, Education, and Welfare (and its subunits, the National Institutes of Health and the Public Health Service), as well as by the Food and Drug Administration. In 1975, the American College of Surgeons and the American Surgical Association set forth a plan for systematically decreasing the number of newly graduated doctors entering surgical training. In part, this plan represented an organized, intraprofessional attempt to deal with what appears to be an oversupply of surgeons in the United States, and thereby to reduce the possibility that federal health manpower legislation would have to be passed to remedy this maldistribution.

The extraordinary number of young people opting for careers in health, particularly as physicians, is the final concomitant of medicalization previously mentioned. Reliable and valid data are not available to explain the mounting wave of young persons who have been attracted to medicine since the 1960s. We do not know as much as we should about how they resemble their predecessors, or differ from them. We are aware that more women,

blacks, and members of other minority groups are being admitted to medical school than in the past, partly because of "affirmative action" legislation. But we do not have overall information about the characteristics of those who are accepted as compared with those who are not. Only sketchy materials are available on the impact of those changes in medical-school curricula during the past decade that were designed to make students more aware of the social and ethical dimensions of their commitment to medicine. We do not know whether their attitudes, their professional decisions, or their medical practice actually changed. More data are needed before we can interpret the short- and long-term implications of the rush of college youth toward medicine. As premedical and medical students themselves are first to testify, the prestige, authority, "power," autonomy, and financial rewards of medicine attract them and their peers to medicine, along with scientific interests, clinical impulses, and humanitarian concerns. But there is also evidence to suggest that even among those who readily contend that their reasons for choosing medicine are self-interested, a "new" medical-student orientation has been emerging. In fact, the very candor that medical students exhibit—and in some cases flaunt—when they insist that, regrettably, like their predecessors, their competitiveness, desire for achievement, and need for security have drawn them into medicine is part of this new orientation. Activist and meditative, as well as critical and self-critical, the "new medical student" not only wants to bring about change in the medical profession, but to do so in a way that affects other aspects of the society as well. The structural and symbolic meaning acquired by health, illness, and medicine has led such students to hope that their influence will be far-reaching as well as meliorative. How many students with this ostensibly "new" orientation will maintain it throughout their medical training and whether their entrance into the profession will significantly alter the future course of medicalization in American society remain to be seen.[12]

Along with progressive medicalization, a process of demedicalization seems also to be taking place in the society. To some extent the signs of demedicalization are reactions to what is felt by various individuals and groups to be a state of "*over*medicalization." One of the most significant manifestations of this countertrend is the mounting concern over implications that have arisen from the continuously expanding conception of "sickness" in the society. Commentators on this process would not necessarily agree with Peter Sedgwick that it will continue to "the point where everybody has become so luxuriantly ill" that perhaps sickness will no longer be "in" and a "backlash" will be set in motion;[13] they may not envision such an engulfing state of societally defined illness. But many observers from diverse professional backgrounds have published works in which they express concern about the "coercive" aspects of the "label" illness and the treatment of illness by medical professionals in medical institutions.[14] The admonitory perspectives on the enlarged domain of illness and medicine that these works of social science and social criticism represent appear to have gained the attention of young physicians- and nurses-in-training interested in change, and various consumer and civil-rights groups interested in health care.

This emerging view emphasizes the degree to which what is defined as health and illness, normality and abnormality, sanity and insanity varies from one society, culture, and historical period to another. Thus, it is contended, medical diagnostic categories such as "sick," "abnormal," and "insane" are not universal, objective, or necessarily reliable. Rather, they are culture, class, and time bound, often ethnocentric, and as much artifacts of the preconceptions of social biased observers as they are valid summaries of the characteristics of the observed. In this view, illness (especially mental illness) is largely a mythical construct, created and enforced by the society. The hospitals to which seriously ill persons are confined are portrayed as "total institutions": segregated, encompassing, depersonalizing organizations, "dominated" by physicians who are disinclined to convey information to patients about their conditions, or to encourage paramedical personnel to do so. These "oppressive" and "countertherapeutic" attributes of the hospital environment are seen as emanating from the professional ideology of physicians and the kind of hierarchical relationships that they establish with patients and other medical professionals partly as a consequence of this ideology, as well as from the bureaucratic and technological features of the hospital itself. Whatever their source, the argument continues, the characteristics of the hospital and of the doctor-patient relationship increase the "powerlessness" of the sick person, "maintain his uncertainty," and systematically "mortify" and "curtail" the "self" with which he enters the sick role and arrives at the hospital door.

This critical perspective links the labeling of illness, the "imperialist" outlook and capitalist behavior of physicians, the "stigmatizing" and "dehumanizing" experiences of patients, and the problems of the health-care system more generally to imperfections and injustices in the society as a whole. Thus, for example, the various forms of social inequality, prejudice, discrimination, and acquisitive self-interest that persist in capitalistic American society are held responsible for causing illness, as well as for contributing to the undesirable attitudes and actions of physicians and other medical professionals. Casting persons in the sick role is regarded as a powerful, latent way for the society to exact conformity and maintain the status quo. For it allows a semi-approved form of deviance to occur, which siphons off potential for insurgent protest and which can be controlled through the supervision or, in some cases, the "enforced therapy" of the medical profession. Thus, however permissive and merciful it may be to expand the category of illness, these observers point out, there is always the danger that the society will become a "therapeutic state" that excessively restricts the "right to be different" and the right to dissent. They feel that this danger may already have reached serious proportions in this society through its progressive medicalization.

The criticism of medicalization and the advocacy of demedicalization have not been confined to rhetoric. Concrete steps have been taken to declassify certain conditions as illness. Most notable among these is the American Psychiatric Association's decision to remove homosexuality from its official catalogue ("Nomenclature") of mental disorders. In addition, serious efforts have been made to heighten physicians' awareness that, because they share certain prejudiced, often unconscious assumptions about women, they tend to overattribute psychological difficulties to their female patients. Thus, for example, distinguished medical publications such as the *New England Journal of Medicine* have featured articles and editorials on the excessive readiness with which medical specialists and textbook authors accept the undocumented belief that dysmenorrhea, nausea of pregnancy, pain of labor, and infantile colic are psychogenic disorders, caused or aggravated by women's emotional problems. Another related development is feminist protest against what is felt to be a too great tendency to define pregnancy as an illness, and childbirth as a "technologized" medical-surgical event, prevailed over by the obstetrician-gynecologist. These sentiments have contributed to the preference that many middle-class couples have shown for natural childbirth in recent years, and to the revival of midwifery. The last example also illustrates an allied movement, namely a growing tendency

to shift some responsibility for medical care and authority over it from the physician, the medical team, and hospital to the patient, the family, and the home.

A number of attempts to "destratify" the doctor's relationships with patients and with other medical professionals and to make them more open and egalitarian have developed. "Patients' rights" are being asserted, codified and, in some states, drafted into law. Greater emphasis is being placed, for example, on the patient's "right to treatment," right to information (relevant to diagnosis, therapy, prognosis, or the giving of knowledgeable consent for any procedure), right to privacy and confidentiality, and right to be "allowed to die," rather than being "kept alive by artificial means or heroic measures . . . if the situation should arise in which there is no reasonable expectation of . . . recovery from physical or mental disability."[15]

In some medical milieux (for example, community health centers and health maintenance organizations), and in critical and self-consciously progressive writings about medicine, the term "client" or "consumer" is being substituted for "patient." This change in terminology is intended to underline the importance of preventing illness while stressing the desirability of a nonsupine, nonsubordinate relationship for those who seek to care to those who provide it. The emergence of nurse-practitioners and physician's assistants on the American scene is perhaps the most significant sign that some blurring of the physician's supremacy vis-à-vis other medical professionals may also be taking place. For some of the responsibilities for diagnosis, treatment, and patient management that were formerly prerogatives of physicians have been incorporated into these new, essentially marginal roles.[16]

Enjoinders to patients to care for themselves rather than to rely so heavily on the services of medical professionals and institutions are more frequently heard. Much attention is being given to studies, such as the one conducted by Lester Breslow and his colleagues at the University of California at Los Angeles, which suggest that good health and longevity are as much related to a self-enforced regimen of sufficient sleep, regular, well-balanced meals, moderate exercise and weight, no smoking, and little or no drinking, as they are to professionally administered medical care. Groups such as those involved in the Women's Liberation Movement are advocating the social and psychic as well as the medical value of knowing, examining, and caring for one's own body. Self-therapy techniques and programs have been developed for conditions as complicated and grave as terminal renal disease and hemophilia A and B. Proponents of such regimens affirm that many aspects of managing even serious chronic illnesses can be handled safely at home by the patient and his family, who will, in turn, benefit both financially and emotionally. In addition, they claim that in many cases the biomedical results obtained seem superior to those of the traditional physician-administered, health-care delivery system.

The underlying assumption in these instances is that, if self-care is collectivized and reinforced by mutual aid, not only will persons with a medical problem be freed from some of the exigencies of the sick role, but both personal and public health will thereby improve, all with considerable savings in cost. This point of view is based on the moral supposition that greater autonomy from the medical profession coupled with greater responsibility for self and others in the realm of health and illness is an ethically and societally superior state.

> We have the medicine we deserve. We freely choose to live the way we do. We choose to live recklessly, to abuse our bodies with what we consume, to expose ourselves to environmental insults, to rush frantically from place to place,

and to sit on our spreading bottoms and watch paid professionals exercise for us. . . . Today few patients have the confidence to care for themselves. The inexorable professionalization of medicine, together with reverence for the scientific method, have invested practitioners with sacrosanct powers, and correspondingly vitiated the responsibility of the rest of us for health. . . . What is tragic is not what has happened to the revered professions, but what has happened to us as a result of professional dominance. In times of inordinate complexity and stress we have been made a profoundly dependent people. Most of us have lost the ability to care for ourselves. . . . I have tried to demonstrate three propositions. First, medical care has less impact on health than is generally assumed. Second, medical care has less impact on health than have social and environmental factors. And third, given the way in which society is evolving and the evolutionary imperatives of the medical care system, medical care in the future will have even less impact on health than it has now. . . . We have not understood what health is. But in the next few decades our understanding will deepen. The pursuit of health and of well-being will then be possible, but only if our environment is made safe for us to live in and our social order is transformed to foster health, rather than suppress joy. If not, we shall remain a sick and dependent people. . . . The end of medicine is not the end of health but the beginning. . . .[17]

The foregoing passage (excerpted from Rick Carlson's book *The End of Medicine*) touches upon many of the demedicalization themes that have been discussed. It proclaims the desirability of demedicalizing American society, predicting that, if we do so, we can overcome the "harm" that excessive medicalization has brought in its wake and progress beyond the "limits" that it has set. Like most critics of medicalization on the American scene, Carlson inveighs against the way that medical care is currently organized and implemented, but he attaches exceptional importance to the health-illness-medical sector of the society. In common with other commentators, he views health, illness, and medicine as inextricably associated with values and beliefs of American tradition that are both critical and desirable. It is primarily for this reason that in spite of the numerous signs that certain *structural* changes in the delivery of care will have occurred by the time we reach the year 2000, American society is not likely to undergo a significant process of *cultural* demedicalization.

Dissatisfaction with the distribution of professional medical care in the United States, its costs, and its accessibility has become sufficiently acute and generalized to make the enactment of a national health insurance system in the foreseeable future likely. Exactly what form that system should take still evokes heated debate about free enterprise and socialism, public and private regulation, national and local government, tax rates, deductibles and co-insurance, the right to health care, the equality principle, and the principle of distributive justice. But the institutionalization of a national system that will provide more extensive and equitable health insurance protection now seems necessary as well as inevitable even to those who do not approve of it.

There is still another change in the health-illness-medicine area of the society that seems to be forthcoming and that, like national health insurance, would alter the structure within which care is delivered. This is the movement toward effecting greater equality, collegiality, and accountability in the relationship of physicians to patients and their families, to other medical professionals, and to the lay public. Attempts to reduce the hierarchical dimension in the physician's role, as well as the increased insistence on patients' rights, self-therapy, mutual medical aid, community medical services, and care by nonphysician health professionals, and the growth of legislative and judicial participation in health and medicine by both federal and local government, are all part of this movement. There is reason to believe that, as a consequence of pressure from both

outside and inside the medical profession, the doctor will become less "dominant" and "autonomous," and will be subject to more controls.

This evolution in the direction of greater egalitarianism and regulation notwithstanding, it seems unlikely that all elements of hierarchy and autonomy will, or even can, be eliminated from the physician's role. For that to occur, the medical knowledge, skill, experience, and responsibility of patients and paramedical professionals would have to equal, if not replicate, the physician's. In addition, the social and psychic meaning of health and illness would have to become trivial in order to remove all vestiges of institutionalized charisma from the physician's role. Health, illness, and medicine have never been viewed casually in any society and, as indicated, they seem to be gaining rather than losing importance in American society.

It is significant that often the discussion and developments relevant to the destratification and control of the physician's role and to the enactment of national health insurance are accompanied by reaffirmations of traditional American values: equality, independence, self-reliance, universalism, distributive justice, solidarity, reciprocity, and individual and community responsibility. What seems to be involved here is not so much a change in values as the initiation of action intended to modify certain structural features of American medicine, so that it will fully realize long-standing societal values.

In contrast, the new emphasis on health as a right, along with the emerging perspective on illness as medically and socially engendered, seems to entail major conceptual rather than structural shifts in the health-illness-medical matrix of the society. These shifts are indicative of a less fatalistic and individualistic attitude toward illness, increased personal and communal espousal of health, and a spreading conviction that health is as much a consequence of the good life and the good society as it is of professional medical care. The strongest impetus for demedicalization comes from this altered point of view. It will probably contribute to the decategorization of certain conditions as illness, greater appreciation and utilization of nonphysician medical professionals, the institutionalization of more preventive medicine and personal and public health measures, and, perhaps, to the undertaking of nonmedical reforms (such as full employment, improved transportation, or adequate recreation) in the name of the ultimate goal of health.

However, none of these trends implies that what we have called *cultural* demedicalization will take place. The shifts in emphasis from illness to health, from therapeutic to preventive medicine, and from the dominance and autonomy of the doctor to patients' rights and greater control of the medical profession do not alter the fact that health, illness, and medicine are central preoccupations in the society that have diffuse symbolic as well as practical meaning. All signs suggest that they will maintain the social, ethical, and existential significance they have acquired, even though by the year 2000 some structural aspects of the way that medicine and care are organized and delivered may have changed. In fact, if the issues now being considered under the rubric of bioethics are predictive of what lies ahead, we can expect that in the future, health, illness, and medicine will acquire even greater importance as one of the primary symbolic media through which American society will grapple with fundamental questions of value and belief. What social mechanisms we will develop to come to terms with these "collective conscience" issues, and exactly what role physicians, health professionals, biologists, jurists, politicians, philosophers, theologians, social scientists, and the public at large will play in their resolution remains to be seen. But it is a distinctive characteristic of an advanced modern society

like our own that scientific, technical, clinical, social, ethical, and religious concerns should be joined in this way.

Notes

[1] Ivan Illich, *Medical Nemesis: The Expropriation of Health* (London, 1975), 165–169.

[2] Illich, *Medical Nemesis*, passim.

[3] Leon R. Kass, "Regarding the End of Medicine and the Pursuit of Health," *The Public Interest*, 40 (Summer, 1975), p. 11.

[4] In his novel *Erewhon*, written in 1872, Samuel Butler satirized this evolution, and the degree to which what is defined as illness is contingent on social factors. In Erewhon (the fictitious country that Butler created by imagining late nineteenth- and early twentieth-century England stood on its head), persons afflicted with what physicians would call tuberculosis are found guilty in a court of law and sentenced to life imprisonment, whereas persons who forge checks, set houses on fire, steal, and commit acts of violence are diagnosed as suffering from a "severe fit of immorality" and are cared for at public expense in hospitals.

[5] Nicholas N. Kittrie, *The Right To Be Different: Deviance and Enforced Therapy* (Baltimore, 1971). See especially chapter 1, "The Divestment of Criminal Justice and the Coming of the Therapeutic State," 1–49.

[6] Peter Sedgwick, "Illness—Mental and Otherwise," *The Hastings Center Studies*, 1:3 (1973), p. 37.

[7] Irving Kenneth Zola, "Culture and Symptoms—An Analysis of Patients' Presenting Complaints," *American Sociological Review*, 31:5 (October, 1966), 615–616.

[8] These figures were cited in the June 9, 1976 issue of *Newsweek*, p. 59.

[9] These ideas are presented in more detail in the monograph I am currently writing on "Medical Sociology" which will appear as a volume in the Prentice-Hall *Foundations of Modern Sociology* series.

[10] See John H. Knowles, "The Responsibility of the Individual."

[11] Talcott Parsons's formulation of the sick role is the most important single concept in the field of the sociology of medicine. For his own elaboration of this concept, see, especially, Talcott Parsons, *The Social System* (Glencoe, Illinois), 428–79, and "The Sick Role and the Role of the Physician Reconsidered," *Milbank Memorial Fund Quarterly, Health and Society* (Summer, 1975), 257–77.

[12] See Renée C. Fox, "The Process of Professional Socialization: Is There a 'New' Medical Student? A Comparative View of Medical Socialization in the 1950's and the 1970's," in Laurence R. Tancredit, ed., *Ethics in Health Care* (Washington, D. C., 1974), 197–227.

[13] Sedgwick, "Illness—Mental and Otherwise," p. 37.

[14] In addition to Illich, *Medical Nemesis*, and Kittrie, *The Right To Be Different*, see, for example, Rick J. Carlson, *The End of Medicine* (New York, 1975); Michel Foucault, *Mad-*

ness and Civilization (New York, 1967); Eliot Freidson, *Professional Dominance* (Chicago, 1970); Erving Goffman, *Asylums* (New York, 1961); R. D. Laing, *The Politics of Experience* (New York, 1967); Thomas J. Scheff, *Being Mentally Ill* (Chicago, 1966); Thomas S. Szasz, *The Myth of Mental Illness* (New York, 1961); and Howard D. Waitzkin and Barbara Waterman, *The Exploitation of Illness in Capitalist Society* (Indianapolis, 1974).

[15] This particular way of requesting that one be allowed to die is excerpted from the "Living Will" (revised April, 1974, version), prepared and promoted by the Euthanasia Educational Council.

[16] See David Rogers, "The Challenge of Primary Care."

[17] Carlson, *The End of Medicine*, 44, 141, and 203–31.

DISCUSSION QUESTIONS

1. What are the indicators that Renée Fox believes have resulted in the overmedicalization of American society?
2. Select a behavior or attitude that has become medicalized and explain the advantages and disadvantages of its medicalization.
3. In this selection, written more than a decade ago, Fox predicts some demedicalization in the United States. Have her predictions come true?

READING 14-2

Uncertainty and Mistakes

David Hilfiker, M.D.

UNCERTAINTY

"I've been sick for the past six weeks, David. It started gradually with some sweats and chills and then got worse. I've felt weak and tired. I've got no appetite. I've lain in bed for a week now, but it hasn't seemed to help. What's going on?"

Carl Fitch is a close friend about my own age. I know him well enough to be sure that he wouldn't have come to the office unless he felt really sick. I can tell he's worried, but as I interview him and examine him I find nothing specific to explain his symptoms. I'm worried, too. Six weeks is a long time to be sick; his symptoms may represent a more serious underlying illness.

Fortunately, Carl has comprehensive medical insurance allowing us to investigate his illness without much regard to cost. I send him over to the hospital laboratory for an initial series of tests, but when he returns several days later for a consultation, none of the tests points definitively to an answer.

"Well, Carl, our initial lab tests look pretty normal. I'm not sure what's going on. The fact that your examination so far looks normal puts serious physical illness further down on the list of my concerns. You may have a persistent virus troubling you. Some of your white cells look a little reactive, suggesting a lingering infection, but I can't be sure. How about emotional stresses?"

Carl counsels people as part of his job, too, and he has observed how emotional tension can lead to physical symptoms. We discuss the pressures he is under, which, as for everybody else these days, are considerable. We talk about his family, his marriage, career satisfaction. There is stress, to be sure, but nothing has changed drastically in the last six months. There is no obvious diagnosis in this area, either. "Well, we're pretty much back where we started," I tell him. "It's very likely a persistent virus, but it also could be emotional exhaustion, and I can't completely rule out serious underlying illness, either."

"So . . . what do I do?" he asks. "I'm worried about the serious illness. How likely is it? I feel pretty sick."

"I'd like to be able to give you a percentage, Carl, but I can't. I'd guess that the chance of something serious is quite small, maybe one or two percent, but I don't know for sure. Why don't you take another week off from work and stay in bed? Let's see if that will help."

Carl remains quite concerned, and my doubts are not resolved either, so we decide to do some further tests while he is resting. When he returns a week later, he still feels the same and his tests still suggest an undetermined viral illness. Since I can't be sure, however, I think through the more exotic diseases: a smoldering infection of the heart valves, fungal infection of the lungs, hidden leukemia, Hodgkin's disease; the list goes on and on. Carl and I decide to search more thoroughly for evidence of serious underlying illness. Over the next week I order perhaps $1,000 worth of laboratory studies in addition to giving him another complete physical exam.

By the end of the third week since our initial interview, Carl is beginning to feel somewhat better. Most of his tests have returned with normal results, but there are still some virus studies which will not come back for several weeks. I do my best to reassure my friend. "I think it's a virus, Carl. You're getting better. Your tests are normal. Why don't we just wait and watch. Continue to rest and take care of yourself, let me know if anything new develops, and we'll let time give us the answer."

"Well, OK. I guess there isn't anything else to do. But are you sure there isn't anything serious going on? I've never felt this way for such a long time before . . ."

I almost consider lying, just to be reassuring, but decide to remain honest with him. "No, I can't be sure you don't have some bizarre illness just starting up. I don't think so, but I can't be sure."

After several more weeks, Carl does recover, and we do get some evidence suggestive of a viral infection. But we never make a firm diagnosis. Throughout Carl's illness both of us have lived with the discomfort of lingering doubt.

Medicine is a highly uncertain science. Not only is there far too much knowledge required for one person to grasp it all, but, even at its best, medicine usually cannot provide the definitive answers that patients and practitioners alike would want. Although there are obvious exceptions (lacerations, broken bones, earaches, bladder infections, to name a few), the majority of illnesses that patients bring their doctors are difficult or impossible to diagnose with any certainty, and their treatment is equally problematic. The everyday complaints of colds, viruses, skin rashes, bellyaches, fevers, childhood fussiness, sleeplessness, coughs, and indigestion are usually of uncertain etiology. The physician can often provide useful information and support to the patient ("It doesn't seem serious," "It will pass on its own," or "It's normal to experience this,"), but he usually cannot offer a precise diagnosis nor be sure he is helping in the cure. More serious problems of chronic disease (arthritis, heart disease, diabetes, cancer) usually are easier to diagnose (although the precise nature and cause of these conditions are often elusive), but even here the physician can rarely offer a cure or provide a certain prognosis.

Unfortunately, it is highly stressful for patient and physician alike to live with uncertainty. When I was a student and an intern, I would marvel at an often-repeated process. After a careful interview, meticulous examination, and thorough laboratory evaluation, no definitive diagnosis of a patient would seem apparent. At that point, the supervising physician often simply declared that, in his opinion, the patient suffered from the "X" problem. "X" usually would turn out to be a diagnosis such as "psychosomatic complaints," "such-and-such virus," or some obscure disease, all of which diagnoses were incapable of proof or disproof. We students and interns would murmur approvingly at the physician's wisdom (mostly because we couldn't think of anything else to offer), and we would all pass on to the next patient.

It was not until I had been in practice for several years that I realized the largely unconscious dynamic behind that familiar phenomenon. The doctor knew his students expected him to be able to make a secure diagnosis. When he could not do this, he needed something to protect his image of himself. So he had his own list of "wastebasket diagnoses" into which he threw all the problems that seemed to fit nowhere else. The stress of his own expectations and those of others in the face of endemic uncertainty tempts the physician to deny the complexities and limitations of medicine.

Not only is such uncertainty anxiety-producing for all concerned, it also subtly changes the nature of medical practice. Since neither definite diagnosis nor positive cure can be provided in most patient encounters, the physician must limit himself to doing as much as possible to rule out serious disease, prevent serious complications, provide information about the expected course of the problem, and offer, if possible, some alleviation of the patient's symptoms—an endeavor that combines science and art in a complex set of maneuvers through the murky waters of uncertainty. Unfortunately, this process may fulfill the expectations of neither patient nor physician.

Consider the following brief appointment: I enter the examining room to find Adele Johnson sitting uncomfortably on the table. I know her slightly since we have daughters in the same class in school. Thirty-one years old, the mother of three young children, a part-time employee at a small office downtown, Adele looks and sounds terrible—bloodshot eyes, runny nose, a hoarse voice.

"I've had this cold and sore throat for a week, Doc, and I can't seem to shake it. I'm weak and chilled, and I feel awful. I can hardly get through the morning at the office, much less the rest of the day. Terry is starting to come down with it, too, and I don't want the rest of the kids to get it. Can you give me something to knock it out?"

I avoid her questions and ask when the first symptoms started and what else has been bothering her. I ask briefly about other organ systems in the body. Although I expect from the moment I walk in that she has a cold, a "viral upper respiratory infection," my first concern is to make sure that there is nothing else going on. I examine her respiratory tract carefully, looking for other problems: no sign of ear infection, no evidence of an abscess near her tonsils, lungs clear without pneumonia. Adele seems impatient with all my fussing. "It's just a cold, Doc. All I want is a shot or something to get rid of it. We're supposed to go away this weekend and I have to get better."

When I've finished my questions and examination, I sit down on my stool. Adele is still perched on the examining table, wrapped in her sheet. "Well, I think you're right, Adele. It appears to be just a cold, but your throat looks pretty raw. I'd suggest doing a throat culture to make sure that you don't have strep throat."

She looks at me impatiently. "Is that going to help me get better? I heard they cost fifteen bucks."

"No, it won't help you get better at all, Adele." I think to myself that there must be some way to tape this conversation so I don't have to repeat it three times a day for the next twenty years. "But the only way to know for sure whether or not you have strep throat is to do a culture. I can't tell just by looking. If it is strep, you'll need penicillin to prevent the possibility of your getting rheumatic heart fever later on."

"Well, why don't you just give me the penicillin right now and know the thing out without a culture? That's all I really want, Doc, is to get rid of this thing." I can feel her frustration rising.

"Penicillin won't do a thing for you if this is a virus, and there are dangers in using antibiotics needlessly. Even if it is strep, the penicillin won't get you better any faster. The only reason I'd recommend it would be to prevent the small chance of getting rheumatic heart fever that can follow a strep throat."

Adele looks down on me in disbelief. "You mean you won't give me anything to make me feel better? Doc, we've got to go away this weekend. It's really important!"

In a small corner of my mind, I am amused at Adele's implication that if she can just convince me of the importance of her getting well, I will reach deep into my magic black bag and pull out a special medicine I reserve only for times when it is "really important."

"Well, I can suggest some things that will make you *feel* better. Aspirin, gargling, hot liquids, and throat lozenges will all help your throat feel better, but I think the most important thing to do is to go to bed. You can't push yourself with a job, kids, and a household and expect to get well. Take a few days off and just lie around."

"I can't do that, Doc. There's too much to do before the weekend. Why don't you just give me some of that penicillin, and we'll forget about the culture. Penicillin's always worked before."

We spar for a few minutes more. When it's all over, Adele gets her penicillin shot without the culture, a reasonable compromise medically. The compassionate part of me hopes that the placebo effect of the shot will help her feel better, but a more self-righteous part of me hopes her virus will linger a few more days to prove that I was right about the penicillin.

Adele's main concern, of course, was getting better. Although I too hoped she would get better soon, I knew that I couldn't do much to speed that process except encourage good health habits that Adele already knew about

but was ignoring. My main concerns were making a rough diagnosis, ruling out any serious illnesses, checking for strep in order to prevent the small chance of rheumatic fever, and then making some suggestions about how she could manage herself during the course of her illness. Thus, we were coming to our appointment with different priorities. It's little wonder that both of us felt frustrated.

The physician is a clinician who must make decisions on the basis of probabilities. Most patients, however, have little experience with this method of decision-making and are often unwilling to accept the uncertainty of medicine. If I express doubt that a particular diagnosis or treatment is completely reliable, this doubt may seem to my patient to be evidence that I am not competent, or haven't been thorough, or don't care. In Carl Fitch's case, for instance, I could tell him that the probability of serious disease was quite low, but I could not honestly tell him not to worry about it. Almost all decisions in medicine are made (whether consciously or not) on the basis of probabilities. When I am quite explicit about this process, it can become—even with sophisticated patients—a time-consuming matter (and the pressures of my schedule, if nothing else, often made me want to pull back from such explanations).

Terry Adolphson, for instance, was a thirty-six-year-old friend with a terrible family history of heart disease: all the male family members on his father's side had died with heart attacks before the age of forty. Terry has recently developed pain in the chest, or angina, suggesting that he too had a serious disease of the coronary arteries, the small blood vessels leading to the heart, a disease that could progress to a heart attack and quite possibly death. Recent articles in the medical literature had suggested that certain patients with angina not only had better pain relief but also lived longer if they underwent coronary-artery bypass surgery than if they were treated only with medicines. On the other hand, these patients had a definite chance of dying during surgery.

To complicate matters further, even the process of examining Terry to discover whether he had disease in the arteries which should be operated upon required a special examination of the coronary arteries (coronary arteriography). There was a small (usually less than 1 percent) change of heart attack and even death during such an examination.

As I discussed the situation with Terry, I realized that in order to recommend this single test, I had to review with him some very complicated medical studies. There were, at that time, differences of opinion among leading cardiologists about who should receive coronary bypass surgery, since the studies had not yet shown convincingly that such surgery was advantageous. Two studies of which I was aware had followed for five years patients who had symptomatic and arteriographically proven heart disease. In each study, the patients were randomly divided into two groups. One group had surgery, and the other was treated only with medicine. The studies showed that for blockages in certain coronary arteries there was no real difference in survival between the surgical and nonsurgical groups; in some cases the nonsurgical group even did better. However, for blockages in other coronary arteries—the left main artery, for example—a greater number of patients were alive five years later in the subgroup that chose surgery than in the subgroup that was treated with medicine alone.

Terry and I reviewed the reasons for his undergoing the coronary arteriography and the chances of his dying during the examination. Since there was no reason even to consider the arteriography test unless he was interested in surgery, we went over the studies that seemed to show advantage for the surgical treatment of some patients. We examined what the literature had to say about the statistical chances of dying during the surgery, as well as the chances of surviving with or without surgery. I realized that I was not merely informing Terry about a complex disease involving complex therapy but also about a method of decision-making which, though routine in medical circles, was quite alien to him. Medical science could only report what had happened to groups of other people; these statistical "certainties" could not be translated into an individual certainty—into a reliable prediction for Terry. The discussion was time-consuming and therefore expensive. It took him several days just to absorb the concepts. My only alternative (on the surface, the easier path) would have been to ignore this reasoning process and tell him: "I, as your physician and your friend, recommend that you have this operation. Trust me." But the situation was not at all black and white. It involved not only uncertainties but values. Did Terry wish to take a chance on death resulting from an "unnatural" surgical intervention or a "natural" death as a result of avoiding surgery? Did he wish to risk a smaller chance of dying sooner (with the surgery) or a larger chance of dying in the indefinite future? Although I could interpret the medical information for Terry so that he could understand it, ultimately he had to take responsibility for the decision.

Even so, I did not share with Terry certain more complex uncertainties. I decided not to complicate the discussion further by reminding Terry of the uncertain nature of any statistical analysis. Perhaps even the studies that showed improvement after surgery were the result of coincidence or of some unknown difference between the surgical and nonsurgical groups. A statistical analysis of the studies could tell me there was only a 5 percent chance that the results were due to coincidence, but we could not be 100 percent sure even that the studies were reliable. Nothing seems 100 percent certain in medicine! But Terry had enough uncertainty in his life. I chose to keep my "5 percent probabilities" to myself.

Terry decided, after much thought and consultation, to proceed with the coronary arteriography, and it indeed showed a blockage in those coronary arteries which, the statistics indicated, it would be advantageous to bypass. He underwent the surgery, but the first nine months after the operation were difficult. Symptoms continued, a repeat coronary arteriogram was required, and there was much uncertainty about the wisdom of surgery. Had I initially talked Terry into the surgery by insisting that he trust me, that trust would have been severely threatened by all the unforeseen complications he experienced. Instead, he was able to face his future with some equanimity because he had made a reasonable decision based on adequate, if sometimes frustrating, information.

This statistical basis for decision-making permeates day-to-day medical practice, although not usually as dramatically as in Terry's situation. Because of the time-consuming nature of the discussion, we physicians often are tempted to leave out the description of the process when talking with patients, thus leaving them with the impression that there is much more certainty than actually exists. The ensuing confusion when the outcome is poor frequently leaves the patient feeling angry and betrayed, sure that the physician was guilty of some gross negligence. For his part, the physician is impatient and angry with the patient's "unrealistic" expectations and, not infrequently, guilt-ridden for not fulfilling them.

Many patients acquire knowledge about illness through simplified information in newspapers and magazine articles, through their own friends' experiences, or even through overwrought hospital melodramas on television in which dramatic cures are regularly performed. Thus, they tend not to understand the necessity to work with probabilities. Patients and physicians, then, are poorly prepared to communicate with each other about the uncertainties of a patient's particular problem.

Mort Jesperson is a forty-seven-year-old plumber forced into early retirement by multiple sclerosis, a tragic neurological disease in which the nerves gradually deteriorate, leaving the patient with weakness, loss of sensation, severe tingling, and a multitude of other difficult problems. As an added frustration, multipe sclerosis is a disease of exacerbations and remissions: that is, it gets worse and then better and then worse again, all with no apparent reason. The usual course of the disease is a gradual decline, but the patient can frequently improve for months at a time, only to regress suddenly to a point even worse than before. This characteristic leads to hundreds of new-found "treatments": anything that happened to a patient just prior to the spontaneous improvement can be seen as a miraculous new cure. Since the disease also has no satisfactory medical treatment, the lay press is full of remedies—some crazy, some reasonable. Medical science itself has a very difficult time evaluating the treatments. Sophisticated studies are needed to be sure that a placebo effect is not responsible for the "cure," since it is well known that a patient's belief that she will improve frequently results in sustained remissions of the disease. Consequently, even the medical press is full of case reports of success in the treatment of multiple sclerosis.

Mort had increasingly severe disease over the years I was his physician. Every six months or so his wife would bring him into the office for evaluation, and he frequently showed me literature about a new treatment, which he would ask me to evaluate. At first, he wanted me to hospitalize him for intravenous doses of a powerful drug. This treatment had once been popular among physicians, but recent reports had been disappointing. I tried to explain this to Mort, but he was so sure the drug had helped him during previous treatments that I finally agreed to supervise its administration. At the next visit, he wanted to know about megavitamin therapy and then about some herbs he had read about in a magazine for multiple-sclerosis patients. During my first years working with Mort, I was impatient. Why couldn't he understand how difficult it was to evaluate these treatments properly? Why did he keep trying to talk me into giving him what I considered dangerous treatments with little hope of success? Why didn't he catch on as, year after year, each new treatment was ultimately discredited? As time went by and I continued to listen to Mort, I began to see his side of things. He had an incurable disease that was ravaging his life with little or no future to look forward to. He was not interested in how small the probabilities were or in the potential dangers. For him, any chance of even temporary improvement was important, a goal worth the risk. He saw me, I'm sure, as a stiff young know-it-all, continually squelching his hopes for a few days of relief. Mort and I were meeting each other from two different worlds. It took a great deal of patience on both our parts to continue our relationship.

Other patients were less understanding than Mort. Adele Johnson, for instance, did not really care about my opinion that penicillin would not help her viral upper respiratory infection. I could have quoted her chapter and verse of scientific studies demonstrating that "within 95 percent confidence limits," penicillin was no more effective than placebos. She "knew" that penicillin helped: "Everybody knows that. Two years ago I was sick for two months with some virus and I finally managed to talk the doctor into some penicillin. I was better in a week." The lengths to which the medical profession had to go to discredit Laetrile is recent evidence that physicians and patients simply perceive this aspect of health and disease differently.

The extremely unfortunate result of the inherent uncertainty of medicine and of the methods of coping with that uncertainty is that the patient has expectations of the physician which the physician cannot possibly fulfill—a discrepancy that leads easily to dissatisfaction and distrust. So stressful is the uncertainty itself and so difficult is it to communicate fully with the patient that the physician is tempted to avoid explanations altogether. It seems easier to retreat behind a mask of stony indifference, to appear certain, to reassure the patient that the doctor knows what is best. For her part, the patient cannot understand why the doctor seems so evasive, why he won't say what he is thinking, why so many questions are left unanswered. Because the fundamental issue of the uncertainty of medicine has not been addressed, both physician and patient are left feeling misunderstood.

In my own practice, I came to dread the simple complaints such as colds, viruses, and headaches, not so much because I was worried that I was missing something serious, but because people seemed so disappointed with the indefinite results of my examination and treatment. Often I would "know" (with a high degree of probability) before I stepped into the examining room that the next patient had a viral upper respiratory infection, and that I was not going to be able to offer her much except reassurance that her symptoms probably didn't represent a serious illness. Even as I walked into the room, I would catch myself trying out phrases in advance, variations upon my inevitably disappointing answers to her inevitable questions: "Are you *sure* this isn't something serious? Isn't there *anything* you can do?" I was always tempted (and more than once succumbed to the desire) to be definite, to be positive, to be the utterly authoritative healer of my patient's dreams: "Mrs. Smith, you *obviously* have a bad case of rhinopharyngitis. Take this magic elixir and come see me next Thursday. I'm *sure* you'll feel better!" Only my fear that somehow she would recognize "rhinopharyngitis" as doctor's lingo for a cold and my suspicion that she might not be better in a week kept me from making this a regular habit.

I am sure that if the time were all accumulated and tallied, I have literally spent days trying to explain the uncertainty of medicine to often understandably unwilling patients. Unless the patient already had significant faith in my competence, I usually left those consultations feeling that she was convinced only of *my* uncertainty and that she must be wishing she had gone to someone who would have given her more help. Occasionally I have described this process to my wife, expressing my frustration at the feelings of incompetence and mistrust that is so often brought out; and she has sometimes gently (and sometimes not so gently) suggested that perhaps it is my own fault, that people obviously want more assurance and more certainty from their doctor than I am willing to offer, that perhaps I should swallow my "less than five percent probability" and give these patients the reassurance they need to get well.

Laurel Tilson, a close friend, was seeing an obstetrician in Minneapolis prior to the delivery of her first child, and during the last weeks of her pregnancy she developed moderately severe "pregnancy-induced hypertension," or toxemia, a dangerous complication of pregnancy threatening both mother and baby. She described to us how concerned and anxious she was until she asked her doctor if the toxemia could possibly hurt her baby. "Not with *me* as your doctor," he replied and went on to the next question. "I was *so* relieved," Laurel said to us later. "I could relax for the rest of the pregnancy knowing that nothing was going to happen to the baby." Everything did turn out all right with her baby, and her obstetrician's self-confidence probably was therapeutic in allowing Laurel to relax and get her needed rest during the last weeks of pregnancy, but the obstetrician certainly was being less than honest about the dangers and uncertainties involved.

Perhaps my wife is right that my patients deserve that kind of reassurance to help them

muster their own personal resources in the struggle to get well. For me, however, there is something fundamentally dishonest in such a distortion of the truth. Life *is* uncertain. The physician who conceals that uncertainty with false reassurances ultimately is robbing the patient of her responsibility for her own life. Although my frustration sometimes leads me to compromise, the moral and emotional consequences of such misrepresentation seem to me too far-reaching to make it a regular part of my practice of medicine.

MISTAKES

On a warm July morning I finish my rounds at the hospital around nine o'clock and walk across the parking lot to the clinic. After greeting Jackie, I look through the list of my day's appointments and notice that Barb Daily will be in for her first prenatal examination. "Wonderful," I think, recalling the joy of helping her deliver her first child two years ago. Barb and her husband, Russ, had been friends of mine before Heather was born, but we grew much closer with the shared experience of her birth. In a rural family practice such as mine, much of every workday is taken up with disease; I look forward to the prenatal visit with Barb, to the continuing relationship with her over the next months, to the prospect of birth.

At her appointment that afternoon, Barb seems to be in good health, with all the signs and symptoms of pregnancy: slight nausea, some soreness in her breasts, a little weight gain. But when the nurse tests Barb's urine to determine if she is pregnant, the result is negative. The test measures the level of a hormone that is produced by a woman and shows up in her urine when she is pregnant. But occasionally it fails to detect the low levels of the hormone during early pregnancy. I reassure Barb that she is fine and schedule another test for the following week.

Barb leaves a urine sample at the clinic a

week later, but the test is negative again. I am troubled. Perhaps she isn't pregnant. Her missed menstrual period and her other symptoms could be a result of a minor hormonal imbalance. Maybe the embryo has died within the uterus and a miscarriage is soon to take place. I could find out by ordering an ultrasound examination. This procedure would give me a "picture" of the uterus and of the embryo. But Barb would have to go to Duluth for the examination. The procedure is also expensive. I know the Dailys well enough to know they have a modest income. Besides, by waiting a few weeks, I should be able to find out for sure without the ultrasound: either the urine test will be positive or Barb will have a miscarriage. I call her and tell her about the negative test result, about the possibility of a miscarriage, and about the necessity of seeing me again if she misses her next menstrual period.

It is, as usual, a hectic summer; I think no more about Barb's troubling state until a month later, when she returns to my office. Nothing has changed: still no menstrual period, still no miscarriage. She is confused and upset. "I feel so pregnant," she tells me. I am bothered, too. Her uterus, upon examination, is slightly enlarged, as it was on the previous visit. But it hasn't grown any larger. Her urine test remains negative. I can think of several possible explanations for her condition, including a hormonal imbalance or even a tumor. But the most likely explanation is that she is carrying a dead embryo. I decide it is time to break the bad news to her.

"I think you have what doctors call a 'missed abortion.'" I tell her. "You were probably pregnant, but the baby appears to have died some weeks ago, before your first examination. Unfortunately, you didn't have a miscarriage to get rid of the dead tissue from the baby and the placenta. If a miscarriage doesn't occur within a few weeks, I'd recommend a reexamination, another pregnancy test, and if nothing shows up, a dilation and curettage procedure to clean out the uterus."

Barb is disappointed; there are tears. She is college-educated, and she understands the scientific and technical aspects of her situation, but that doesn't alleviate the sorrow. We talk at some length and make an appointment for two weeks later.

When Barb returns, Russ is with her. Still no menstrual period; still no miscarriage; still another negative pregancy test, the fourth. I explain to them what has happened. The dead embryo should be removed or there could be serious complications. Infection could develop; Barb could even become sterile. The conversation is emotionally difficult for all three of us. We schedule the dilation and curretage for later in the week.

Friday morning, Barb is wheeled into the small operating room of the hospital. Barb, the nurses, and I all know one another—it's a small town. The atmosphere is warm and relaxed; we chat before the operation. After Barb is anesthetized, I examine her pelvis again. Her muscles are now completely relaxed, and it is possible to perform a more reliable examination. Her uterus feels bigger than it did two days ago; it is perhaps the size of a small grapefruit. But since all the pregnancy tests were negative and I'm so sure of the diagnosis, I ignore the information from my fingertips and begin the operation.

Dilation and curettage, or D & C, is a relatively simple surgical procedure performed thousands of times each day in this country. First, the cervix is stretched by pushing smooth metal rods of increasing diameter in and out of it. After about five minutes of this, the cervix has expanded enough so that a curette can be inserted through it into the uterus. The curette is another metal rod, at the end of which is an oval ring about an inch at its widest diameter. It is used to scrape the walls of the uterus. The operation is done completely by feel after the cervix has been stretched, since it is still too narrow to see through.

Things do not go easily this morning. There is considerably more blood than usual, and it is only with great difficulty that I am able to extract anything. What should take ten or fifteen minutes stretches into a half-hour. The body parts I remove are much larger than I expected, considering when the embryo died. They are not bits of decomposing tissue. These are parts of a body that was recently alive!

I do my best to suppress my rising panic and try to complete the procedure. Working blindly, I am unable to evacuate the uterus completely; I can feel more parts inside but cannot remove them. Finally I stop, telling myself that the uterus will expel the rest within a few days.

Russ is waiting outside the operating room. I tell him that Barb is fine but that there were some problems with the operation. Since I don't completely understand what happened, I can't be very helpful in answering his questions. I promise to return to the hospital later in the day after Barb has awakened from the anesthesia.

In between seeing other patients that morning, I place several almost frantic phone calls, trying to piece together what happened. Despite reassurances from a pathologist that it is "impossible" for a pregnant women to have four consecutive negative pregnancy tests, the realization is growing that I have aborted Barb's living child. I won't know for sure until the pathologist has examined the fetal parts and determined the baby's age and the cause of death. In a daze, I walk over to the hospital and tell Russ and Barb as much as I know for sure without letting them know all I suspect. I tell them that more tissue may be expelled. I can't face my own suspicions.

Two days later, on Sunday morning, I receive a tearful call from Barb. She has just passed some recognizable body parts; what is she to do? She tells me that the bleeding has stopped now and that she feels better. The abortion I began on Friday is apparently over. I set up an appointment to meet with her and Russ to review the entire situation.

The pathologist's report confirms my worst fears: I aborted a living fetus. It was about eleven weeks old. I can find no one who can explain why Barb had four negative pregnancy tests. My meeting with Barb and Russ later in the week is one of the hardest things I have ever been through. I described in some detail what I did and what my rationale had been. Nothing can obscure the hard reality: it killed their baby.

Politely, almost meekly, Russ asks whether the ultrasound examination would have shown that Barb was carrying a live baby. It almost seems that he is trying to protect my feelings, trying to absolve me of some of the responsibility. "Yes," I answer, "if I had ordered the ultrasound, we would have known the baby was alive." I cannot explain why I didn't recommend it.

Mistakes are an inevitable part of everyone's life. They happen; they hurt—ourselves and others. They demonstrate our fallibility. Shown our mistakes and forgiven them, we can grow, perhaps in some small way become better people. Mistakes, understood this way, are a process, a way we connect with one another and with our deepest selves.

But mistakes seem different for doctors. This has to do with the very nature of our work. A mistake in the intensive care unit, in the emergency room, in the surgery suite, or at the sickbed is different from a mistake on the dock or at the typewriter. A doctor's miscalculation or oversight can prolong an illness, or cause a permanent disability, or kill a patient. Few other mistakes are more costly.

Developments in modern medicine have provided doctors with more knowledge of the human body, more accurate methods of diagnosis, more sophisticated technology to help in examining and monitoring the sick. All of that means more power to intervene in the disease process. But modern medicine, with its invasive tests and potentially lethal drugs, has also given doctors the power to do more harm.

Yet precisely because of its technological wonders and near-miraculous drugs, modern medicine has created for the physician an expectation of perfection. The technology seems so exact that error becomes almost unthinkable. We are not prepared for our mistakes, and we don't know how to cope with them when they occur.

Doctors are not alone in harboring expectations of perfection. Patients, too, expect doctors to be perfect. Perhaps patients have to consider their doctors less prone to error than other people: how else can a sick or injured person, already afraid, come to trust the doctor? Further, modern medicine has taken much of the treatment of illness out of the realm of common sense; a patient must trust a physician to make decisions that he, the patient, only vaguely understands. But the degree of perfection expected by patients is no doubt also a result of what we doctors have come to believe about ourselves, or better, have tried to convince ourselves about ourselves.

This perfection is a grand illusion, of course, a game of mirrors that everyone plays. Doctors hide their mistakes from patients, from other doctors, even from themselves. Open discussion of mistakes is banished from the consultation room, from the operating room, from physicians' meetings. Mistakes become gossip, and are spoken of openly only in court. Unable to admit our mistakes, we physicians are cut off from healing. We cannot ask for forgiveness, and we get none. We are thwarted, stunted; we do not grow.

During the days, and weeks, and months after I aborted Barb's baby, my guilt and anger grew. I did discuss what had happened with my partners, with the pathologist, with obstetric specialists. Some of my mistakes

were obvious: I had relied too heavily on one test; I had not been skillful in determining the size of the uterus by pelvic examination; I should have ordered the ultrasound before proceeding to the D & C. There was no way I could justify what I had done. To make matters worse, there were complications following the D & C, and Barb was unable to become pregnant again for two years.

Although I was as honest with the Dailys as I could have been, and although I told them everything they wanted to know, I never shared with them my own agony. I felt they had enough sorrow without having to bear my burden as well. I decided it was my responsibility to deal with my guilt alone. I never asked for their forgiveness.

Doctors' mistakes, of course, come in a variety of packages and stem from a variety of causes. For primary care practitioners, who see every kind of problem from cold sores to cancer, the mistakes are often simply a result of not knowing enough. One evening during my years in Minnesota a local boy was brought into the emergency room after a drunken driver had knocked him off his bicycle. I examined him right away. Aside from swelling and bruising of the left leg and foot, he seemed fine. An x-ray showed what appeared to be a dislocation of the foot from the ankle. I consulted by telephone with an orthopedic specialist in Duluth, and we decided that I could operate on the boy. As was my usual practice, I offered the patient and his mother (who happened to be a nurse with whom I worked regularly) a choice: I could do the operation or they could travel to Duluth to see the specialist. My pride was hurt when she decided to take her son to Duluth.

My feelings changed considerably when the specialist called the next morning to thank me for the referral. He reported that the boy had actually suffered an unusual muscle injury, a posterior compartment syndrome, which had twisted his foot and caused it to appear to be dislocated. I had never even heard of such a syndrome, much less seen or treated it. The boy had required immediate surgery to save the muscles of his lower leg. Had his mother not decided to take him to Duluth, he would have been permanently disabled.

Sometimes a lack of technical skill leads to a mistake. After I had been in town a few years, the doctor who had done most of the surgery at the clinic left to teach at a medical school. Since the clinic was more than a hundred miles from the nearest surgical center, my partners and I decided that I should get some additional training in order to be able to perform emergency surgery. One of my first cases after training was a young man with appendicitis. The surgery proceeded smoothly enough, but the patient did not recover as quickly as he should have, and his hemoglobin level (a measure of the amount of blood in the system) dropped slowly. I referred him to a surgeon in Duluth, who, during a second operation, found a significant amount of old blood in his abdomen. Apparently I had left a small blood vessel leaking into the abdominal cavity. Perhaps I hadn't noticed the oozing blood during surgery; perhaps it had begun to leak only after I had finished. Although the young man was never in serious danger, although the blood vessel would probably have sealed itself without the second surgery, my mistake had caused considerable discomfort and added expense.

Often, I am sure, mistakes are a result of simple carelessness. There was the young girl I treated for what I thought was a minor ankle injury. After looking at her x-rays, I sent her home with what I diagnosed as a sprain. A radiologist did a routine follow-up review of the x-rays and sent me a report. I failed to read it carefully and did not notice that her ankle had been broken. I first learned about my mistake five years later when I was summoned to a court hearing. The fracture I had missed had not healed properly, and the patient had re-

quired extensive treatment and difficult surgery. By that time I couldn't even remember her original visit and had to piece together what had happened from my records.

Some mistakes are purely technical; most involve a failure of judgment. Perhaps the worst kind involve what another physician has described to me as "a failure of will." She was referring to those situations in which a doctor knows the right thing to do but doesn't do it because he is distracted, or pressured, or exhausted.

Several years ago, I was rushing down the hall of the hospital to the delivery room. A young woman stopped me. Her mother had been having chest pains all night. Should she be brought to the emergency room? I knew the mother well, had examined her the previous week, and knew of her recurring bouts of chest pains. She suffered from angina; I presumed she was having another attack.

Some part of me knew that anyone with all-night chest pains should be seen right away. But I was under pressure. The delivery would make me an hour late to the office, and I was frayed from a weekend on call, spent mostly in the emergency room. This new demand would mean additional presssure. "No," I said, "take her over to the office, and I'll see her as soon as I'm done here." About twenty minutes later, as I was finishing the delivery, the clinic nurse rushed into the room. Her face was pale. "Come quick! Mrs. Helgeson just collapsed." I sprinted the hundred yards to the office, where I found Mrs. Helgeson in cardiac arrest. Like many doctors' offices at the time, ours did not have the advanced life-support equipment that helps keep patients alive long enough to get them to a hospital. Despite everything we did, Mrs. Helgeson died.

Would she have survived if I had agreed to see her in the emergency room, where the requisite staff and equipment were available? No one will ever know for sure. But I have to live with the possibility that she might not have died if I had not had "a failure of will." There was no way to rationalize it: I had been irresponsible, and a patient had died.

Many situations do not lend themselves to a simple determination of whether a mistake has been made. Seriously ill, hospitalized patients, for instance, require of doctors almost continuous decision-making. Although in most cases no single mistake is obvious, there always seem to be things that could have been done differently or better: administering more of this medication, starting that treatment a little sooner . . . The fact is that when a patient dies, the physician is left wondering whether the care he provided was adequate. There is no way to be certain, for it is impossible to determine what would have happened if things had been done differently. Often it is difficult to get an honest opinion on this even from another physician, most doctors not wanting to be perceived by their colleagues as judgmental—or perhaps fearing similar judgments upon themselves. In the end, the physician has to suppress the guilt and move on to the next patient.

A few years after my mistake with Barb Daily, Maiya Martinen first came to see me halfway through her pregnancy. I did not know her or her husband well, but I knew that they were solid, hard-working people. This was to be their first child. When I examined Maiya, it seemed to me that the fetus was unusually small, and I was uncertain about her due date. I sent her to Duluth for an ultrasound examination—which was by now routine for almost any problem during pregnancy—and an evaluation by an obstetrician. The obstetrician thought the baby would be small, but he thought it could be safely delivered in the local hospital.

Maiya's labor was uneventful, except that it took her longer than usual to push the baby through to delivery. Her baby boy was born blue and floppy, but he responded well to routine newborn resuscitation measures. Fif-

teen minutes after birth, however, he had a short seizure. We checked his blood sugar level and found it to be low, a common cause of seizures in small babies who take longer than usual to emerge from the birth canal. Fortunately, we were able to put an IV easily into a scalp vein and administer glucose, and baby Marko seemed to improve. He and his mother were discharged from the hospital several days later.

At about two months of age, a few days after I had given him his first set of immunizations, Marko began having short spells. Not long after that he started to have full-blown seizures. Once again the Martinens made the trip to Duluth, and Marko was hospitalized for three days of tests. No cause for the seizures was found, but he was placed on medication. Marko continued to have seizures, however. When he returned for his second set of immunizations, it was clear to me that he was not doing well.

The remainder of Marko's short life was a tribute to the faith and courage of his parents. He proved severely retarded, and the seizures became harder and harder to control. Maiya eventually went East for a few months so Marko could be treated at the National Institutes of Health. But nothing seemed to help, and Maiya and her baby returned home. Marko had to be admitted frequently to the local hospital in order to control his seizures. At two o'clock one morning I was called to the hospital: the baby had had a respiratory arrest. Despite our efforts, Marko died, ending a year-and-a-half struggle with life.

No cause for Marko's condition was ever determined. Did something happen during the birth that briefly cut off oxygen to his brain? Should Maiya have delivered at the high-risk obstetric center in Duluth, where sophisticated fetal monitoring is available? Should I have sent Marko to the Newborn Intensive Care Unit in Duluth immediately after his first seizure in the delivery room? I subsequently learned that children who have seizures should not routinely be immunized. Would it have made any difference if I had never given Marko the shots? There were many such questions in my mind and, I am sure, in the minds of the Martinens. There was no way to know the answers, no way for me to handle the guilt feelings I experienced, perhaps irrationally, whenever I saw Maiya.

The emotional consequences of mistakes are difficult enough to handle. But soon after I started practicing I realized I had to face another anxiety as well: it is not only in the emergency room, the operating room, the intensive care unit, or the delivery room that a doctor can blunder into tragedy. Errors are always possible, even in the midst of the humdrum routine of daily care. Was that baby with diarrhea more dehydrated than he looked, and should I have hospitalized him? Will that nine-year-old with stomach cramps whose mother I just lectured about psychosomatic illness end up in the operating room tomorrow with a ruptured appendix? Did that Vietnamese refugee have a problem I didn't understand because of the language barrier? A doctor has to confront the possibility of a mistake with every patient visit.

My initial response to the mistakes I did make was to question my competence. Perhaps I just didn't have the necessary intelligence, judgment, and discipline to be a physician. But was I really incompetent? My University of Minnesota Medical School class had voted me one of the two most promising clinicians. My diploma from the National Board of Medical Examiners showed scores well above average. I knew that the townspeople considered me a good physician; I knew that my partners, with whom I worked daily, and the consultants to whom I referred patients considered me a good physician, too. When I looked at it objectively, my competence was not the issue. I would have to learn to live with my mistakes.

A physician is even less prepared to deal with his mistakes than is the average person. Nothing in our training prepares us to respond appropriately. As a student, I was simply not aware that the sort of mistakes I would eventually make in practice actually happened to competent physicians. As far as I can remember from my student experience on the hospital wards, the only doctors who ever made mistakes were the much maligned "LMDs"—local medical doctors. They would transfer their patients who weren't doing well to the University Hospital. At the "U," teams of specialist physicians with their residents, interns, and students would take their turns examining the patient thoroughly, each one delighted to discover (in retrospect, of course) an "obvious" error made by the referring LMD. As students we had the entire day to evaluate and care for our five to ten patients. After we examined them and wrote orders for their care, first the interns and then the residents would also examine them and correct our orders. Finally, the supervising physician would review everything. It was pretty unlikely that a major error would slip by; and if it did, it could always be blamed on someone else on the team. We had very little feeling for what it was like to be the LMD, working alone with perhaps the same number of hospital patients plus an office full of other patients; but we were quite sure we would not be guilty of such grievous errors as we saw coming into the U.

An atmosphere of precision pervaded the teaching hospital. The uncertainty that came to seem inescapable to me in northern Minnesota would shrivel away at the U as teams of specialists pronounced authoritatively upon any subject. And when a hospital physician did make a significant mistake, it was first whispered about the halls as if it were a sin. Much later a conference would be called in which experts who had had weeks to think about the case would discuss the way it should have been handled. The embarrassing mistake was frequently not even mentioned; it had evaporated. One could almost believe that the patient had been treated perfectly. More important, only the technical aspects of the case were considered relevant for discussion. It all seemed so simple, so clear. How could anyone do anything else? There was no mention of the mistake, or of the feelings of the patient or the doctor. It was hardly the sort of environment in which a doctor might feel free to talk about his mistakes or about his emotional responses to them.

Medical school was also a very competitive place, discouraging any sharing of feelings. The favorite pastime, even between classes or at a party, seemed to be sharing with the other medical students the story of the patient who had been presented to one's team, and then describing in detail how the diagnosis had been reached, how the disease worked, and what the treatment was. The storyteller, having spent the day researching every detail of the patient's disease, could, of course, dazzle everyone with the breadth and depth of his knowledge. Even though I knew what was going on, the game still left me feeling incompetent, as it must have many of my colleagues. I never knew for sure, though, since no one had the nerve to say so. It almost seemed that one's peers were the worst possible persons with whom to share those feelings.

Physicians in private practice are no more likely to find errors openly acknowledged or discussed, even though they occur regularly. My own mistakes represent only some of those of which I am aware. I know of one physician who administered a potent drug in a dose ten times that recommended; his patient almost died. Another doctor examined a child in an emergency room late one night and told the parents the problem was only a mild viral infection. Only because the parents did not believe the doctor, only because they consulted another doctor the following morning, did the

child survive a life-threatening infection. Still another physician killed a patient while administering a routine test: a needle slipped and lacerated a vital artery. Whether the physician is a rural general practitioner with years of experience but only basic training or a recently graduated, highly trained neurosurgeon working in a sophisticated technological environment, the basic problem is the same.

Because doctors do not discuss their mistakes, I do not know how other physicians come to terms with theirs. But I suspect that many cannot bear to face their mistakes directly. We either deny the misfortune altogether or blame the patient, the nurse, the laboratory, other physicians, the system, fate—anything to avoid our own guilt.

The medical profession seems to have no place for its mistakes. Indeed, one would almost think that mistakes were sins. And if the medical profession has no room for doctors' mistakes, neither does society. The number of malpractice suits filed each year is symptomatic of this. In what other profession are practitioners regularly sued for hundreds of thousands of dollars because of misjudgments? I am sure the Dailys could have successfully sued me for a large amount of money had they chosen to do so.

The drastic consequences of our mistakes, the repeated opportunities to make them, the uncertainty about our culpability, and the professional denial that mistakes happen all work together to create an intolerable dilemma for the physician. We see the horror or our mistakes, yet we cannot deal with their enormous emotional impact.

Perhaps the only way to face our guilt is through confession, restitution, and absolution. Yet within the structure of modern medicine there is no place for such spiritual healing. Although the emotionally mature physician may be able to give the patient or family a full description of what happened, the technical details are often so difficult for the layperson to understand that the nature of the mistake is hidden. If an error is clearly described, it is frequently presented as "natural," "understandable," or "unavoidable" (which, indeed, it often is). But there is seldom a real confession: "This is the mistake I made; I'm sorry." How can one say that to a grieving parent? to a woman who has lost her mother?

If confession is difficult, what are we to say about restitution? The very nature of a physician's work means that there are things that cannot be restored in any meaningful way. What could I do to make good the Dailys' loss?

I have not been successful in dealing with a paradox: I am a healer, yet I sometimes do more harm than good. Obviously, we physicians must do everything we can to keep mistakes to a minimum. But if we are unable to deal openly with those that do occur, we will find neurotic ways to protect ourselves from the pain we feel. Little wonder that physicians are accused of playing God. Little wonder that we are defensive about our judgments, that we blame the patient or the previous physician when things go wrong, that we yell at nurses

for their mistakes, that we have such high rates of alcoholism, drug addiction, and suicide.

At some point we must all bring medical mistakes out of the closet. This will be difficult as long as both the profession and society continue to project their desires for perfection onto the doctor. Physicians need permission to admit errors. They need permission to share them with their patients. The practice of medicine is difficult enough without having to bear the yoke of perfection.

DISCUSSION QUESTIONS

1. What are some of the problems for patients and doctors created by the uncertainty inherent in clinical treatment?
2. How differently do you think Barb, Dr. Hilfiker's patient, would describe her unwanted abortion?
3. Describe the different ways in which medical mistakes can occur and the typical responses of doctors and patients to these mistakes.

READING 14-3

Responding to AIDS

Lori Heise

Few tragedies in human history have captured the world's attention as has AIDS. No disease, past or present, has inspired an international response equal to the current AIDS mobilization of the World Health Organization (WHO). None in recent memory has provoked more anxiety, aroused such prejudice against the afflicted, or stimulated so many moral, ethical, and legal debates. And no disease has more

pointedly forced societies to confront issues otherwise conveniently ignored: drug abuse, sexuality, and the plight of the poor.

This global response is all the more remarkable given the relatively small number of people affected by acquired immunodeficiency syndrome so far. WHO estimates that by the end of 1988, at least 350,000 cases of the disease had occurred worldwide. The U.N. agency expects 1 million more cases by 1992, but even then, other killers will dwarf AIDS' toll. Each year, 2.5 million people die of smoking-related illnesses and 5 million children succumb to chronic diarrhea. Tuberculosis alone claims 3 million lives annually, 10 times the number of AIDS cases to date.[1]

This incongruity of numbers more likely reflects gross underattention to diarrhea and tuberculosis than overreaction to AIDS. The world is rightly alarmed at AIDS' potential to surpass other killers if it continues to spread unchecked. Moreover, body counts alone do not reflect what sets AIDS apart. Unlike most diseases, AIDS is almost always fatal; there is no cure and no vaccine. Carriers may go for years without symptoms, evoking the paranoia and fear that accompany uncertainty. And AIDS deals with the most intimate of human activities, the most powerful of human emotions.

Together these factors give AIDS a psychological charge unmatched by any other illness. Significantly, though, AIDS is one of the few diseases that poses a substantial threat to both industrial and developing nations. This convergence of interests provides opportunities to forge new alliances and new models for international cooperation. As Jonathan Mann, Director of WHO's Global Programme on AIDS, observes: "AIDS has the potential to bring us together, if we can thwart those who would use it to drive us apart."[2]

THE PANDEMIC UNFOLDS

In 1981, astute physicians in California and New York began to recognize a strange clustering of symptoms among some of their male homosexual patients. Something was destroying the immune systems of these individuals, rendering them susceptible to an odd assortment of opportunistic infections and cancers. Almost simultaneously, doctors in Central Africa, Europe, and Haiti began to note patients with similar conditions. By 1982, the new disease had a name: AIDS. And one year later, it had a cause: the human immunodeficiency virus, or HIV.[3]

HIV exhibits a unique combination of characteristics that makes it intrinsically hard to control. Like genital herpes, once caught, the virus stays with its carrier for life. Once disease develops, AIDS is almost always fatal—usually within two years. But instead of manifesting within a few days or weeks, like most viral diseases, AIDS on average takes eight or nine years to develop. During this interval, carriers look and feel healthy but can pass the virus to others. Researchers now believe that most if not all individuals infected with HIV will eventually develop AIDS.[4]

The good news, however, is that compared with other viruses—such as polio and the common cold—HIV is fragile and relatively difficult to transmit. AIDS is overwhelmingly a sexually transmitted disease, communicated through body fluids and blood during vaginal or anal intercourse. To a significant but lesser extent, the virus is also transmitted through blood transfusions, through the sharing or re-using of contaminated needles, and from mother to child during pregnancy or birth. Contrary to widespread fears, AIDS cannot be caught through casual contact, sneezes, kissing, toilet seats, or insects.

Although the virus is transmitted the same way everywhere—through blood, through sexual intercourse, or from mother to child—the pattern of transmission and infection varies among regions. Indeed, the international AIDS picture can best be understood in terms of three broadly defined subepidemics, each with its own dynamic.

In North America, Western Europe, and certain Latin American countries, AIDS is mainly transmitted through homosexual intercourse and the sharing of needles among drug addicts. As a result, those infected are overwhelmingly male, and transmission from mother to child is limited. Less than 1 percent of the population is thought to be infected, but the infection rate among intravenous (IV) drug users and homosexual men exceeds 50 percent in some cities. Heterosexual sex is responsible for a small but increasing proportion of cases. Interestingly, despite its potential, sex with prostitutes is not a major mode of transmission.[5]

By contrast, in sub-Saharan Africa and parts of the Caribbean, AIDS is primarily a heterosexually transmitted disease, with women infected as often as men. Because so many women are infected, transmission from mother to child is disturbingly common. Blood transfusions—a route largely eliminated in the industrial world—remain a source of infection in many countries where blood supplies still are not screened. Since intravenous drug use and homosexuality are rare, these modes of transmission are not significant, although reuse of contaminated needles by health workers remains a likely source of infection. In some countries, infection in the total population exceeds 1 percent, with 5–33 percent of sexually active adults in select urban areas infected. Male contact with prostitutes is thought to play a major role in the epidemic's spread.[6]

In the third set of countries, HIV has been introduced only recently. Infection rates remain extremely low even among people with multiple sex partners, such as prostitutes. Most cases have originated outside of the country either through sex with a foreigner or through imported blood products contaminated with HIV. Although there is increasing evidence of in-country spread, no strong pattern of heterosexual or homosexual transmission has emerged. Asia, Eastern Europe, northern Africa, the Middle East, and most of the Pacific all fall in this category.[7]

These variations evolve from a combination of factors, including when and where the virus first entered the population and the different social practices and behaviors that exist among cultures. In Africa, for example, the epidemic involved the heterosexually active population first, whereas in the United States the epidemic was initially introduced and amplified in predominantly male populations: homosexuals, people with hemophilia, and IV drug users. Researchers also believe that the greater

prevalence of untreated sexually transmitted diseases (STDs) in Africa has facilitated the spread of AIDS there and may largely explain the greater efficiency of heterosexual sex in transmitting the virus among Africans.[8]

It is becoming increasingly clear, for example, that chlamydia and STDs that cause genital sores (such as syphilis, herpes, and chancroid) make it easier for HIV to pass between sexual partners. Sadly, in developing countries where treatment is less accessible, STDs are far more endemic than in the industrial world. Laboratory evidence also suggests that an individual whose immune system has been activated by chronic infections might be more susceptible to HIV infection. This factor may operate to increase heterosexual transmission in the Third World, where viral and parasitic diseases are endemic. There is no convincing evidence that genetic differences or variations in viral strains account for the African pattern of transmission.[9]

Although scientists have mapped the virus's surface chemistry in minute detail, the world has only the vaguest notion of where HIV is and where it is going. As of December 1, 1988, 142 countries had reported a total of 129,385 AIDS cases to the World Health Organization. (See Table 7–1.) Due to gross underreporting and underrecognition, however, WHO suspects that the true global caseload is more than twice that figure. Moreover, AIDS cases represent only the tip of the iceberg: for every AIDS case, anywhere from 20 to 100 people may carry the virus but not yet show symptoms. All told, WHO estimates that 5 million to 10 million people worldwide may be infected with HIV.[10]

Lacking any better measure, many people have used WHO data on reported AIDS cases to compare the severity of the epidemic in different parts of the world. Such comparisons can be misleading, however, because countries vary greatly in the accuracy and completeness of their reporting. Also, because of the virus's

TABLE 1

OFFICIALLY REPORTED AIDS CASES, SELECTED COUNTRIES, DECEMBER 1, 1988

Country	Prevalence (cases)	Rate (cases per million population)
United States	78,985	321
Uganda	5,508	336
Brazil	4,436	31
France	4,211	75
Tanzania	3,055	126
Kenya	2,732	117
Malawi	2,586	336
West Germany	2,580	42
Italy	2,556	45
Canada	2,156	83
Mexico	1,502	18
Haiti	1,453	231
Burundi	1,408	271
Congo	1,250	568
Zambia	1,056	141
Rwanda	987	139
Switzerland	605	92
French Guiana	113	1,228
Japan	90	0.7
Bermuda	81	1,396
China	3	0.003

Sources: World Health Organization data base; Population Reference Bureau, *1988 World Population Data Sheet* (Washington, D.C.: 1988).

long latency period, a country's current number of AIDS cases is actually a snapshot of the epidemic five to eight years ago, when those who now have AIDS first got infected. The severity of today's epidemic is best represented by studies that measure how many people are currently infected with HIV by testing individuals' blood for antibodies to the virus.

Because antibody testing is expensive and difficult to conduct on a large scale, only a handful of countries—including Uganda and Rwanda—have attempted to design and im-plement surveys that would yield national estimates of HIV prevalence. Even in these small countries, the logistical and design problems of testing "representative" cross sections of society have proved immense, making it un-likely that many countries will undertake sim-ilar ventures. Without systematic testing, epidemiologists will have to rely on small-scale blood surveys of select groups for estimating the scope of infection.[11]

By testing enough people with different backgrounds and risk factors—factory workers, prostitutes in cities, rural blood donors—epidemiologists can piece together a fairly accurate picture of the epidemic's extent. Researchers at WHO are now using such surveys to derive country-specific estimates of infection within different age-groups. Although estimates of infection by country are not yet available, the sum total of data lead WHO to believe that Africa is the most affected continent and Asia the least. (See Table 7–2.) Infection in Africa appears largely concentrated in the center, extending west from Tanzania to the Congo, and dipping south to include Zambia and Malawi. The United States is also severely affected, with an estimated 1–1.5 million infected individuals.[12]

TABLE 2

Estimated HIV Prevalence, Selected Regions, 1987/88

Region	Prevalence (number infected)
Africa	2–3 million
United States	1–1.5 million
Latin America	500,000–750,000
Europe	280,000–800,000
Asia	fewer than 100,000
World	5–10 million (probably closer to 5 million)

Source: Worldwatch Institute, compiled from various World Health Organizations sources.

Antibody surveys likewise reveal that throughout the world AIDS is primarily an urban disease, although it is gradually spreading from major urban centers to smaller cities and towns. In parts of Zambia, northwestern Tanzania, and southwestern Uganda, however, there are major rural outbreaks, emanating from the movement of people and disease along the Trans-African Highway and in areas of military conflict.[13]

Even more difficult than determining the world's current AIDS picture is predicting how the epidemic will evolve. Already there have been important shifts in the persons most at risk in various countries and in the relative significance of different transmission routes. Such shifts are meaningful because they indicate where new prevention activities should be focused and have important implications for the spread of infection beyond those presently affected.

The United States and Western Europe, for example, are now experiencing a second wave of epidemic among intravenous drug users. Whereas most AIDS cases used to involve homosexual men, evidence indicates that rates of new infection are declining among gay men but accelerating among drug addicts. In fact, in certain parts of Europe—including Italy, Spain, and Scotland—IV drug users now account for the majority of all cases. Overall, the proportion of total European AIDS cases involving drug injection rose from 2 percent in September 1984 to 24 percent in mid-1988.[14]

This new pattern is important because of both its impact on the drug-using community and its potential to facilitate the spread of AIDS into the general population. Although it is too early to predict whether AIDS will move into the heterosexual mainstream in these areas, addicts could facilitate this process by communicating the virus to their sexual partners who in turn could infect people outside the drug community. Seventy percent of heterosexually transmitted cases in native-born U.S. citizens currently occur in partners of IV drug users.[15]

Indeed, it is difficult to overemphasize the role that drug abuse could play in the future of the American and European AIDS epidemic. Already, more than 70 percent of cases in American children are due to IV drug use by their mother or her sexual partner. Half of all AIDS cases in American women are related to drug use, with even higher proportions among black and Hispanic women (70 and 83 percent, respectively). Even among female prostitutes, the likelihood of infection is more closely linked to IV drug use than to prostitution itself.[16]

Certain Central American and Caribbean nations have also experienced shifts in AIDS epidemiology, with heterosexual sex gradually replacing homosexual activity as the dominant route of transmission. This change is best exemplified in Haiti, where the percentage of cases involving men who contracted AIDS through homosexual activity declined from 50 percent in 1983 to 1 percent in 1987, while the share transmitted heterosexually increased from 26 to over 80 percent. As a result, the proportion of cases among women has doubled since 1979, and the number of babies born with AIDS has increased greatly.[17]

Latin American health officials suspect that the high prevalence of bisexuality among some Latin men has contributed to this shifting epidemiology. Because homosexuality is less acceptable in Latin culture and the pressure to have children is acute, many men who engage in homosexual activity marry or have steady female lovers. This sets the stage for increasing AIDS incidence among women and children, a pattern already documented in Trinidad and Tobago, the Dominican Republic, and Honduras, among others. Health officials fear that other Latin American countries could follow Haiti's lead. In Brazil and Mexico, for example, bisexuals account for 23 percent of reported AIDS cases; in Ecuador, for 40 percent.[18]

THE IMPACT IN THE THIRD WORLD

Estimating the social and economic impact of AIDS in the Third World is an endeavor fraught with uncertainty. Scientists have too few data on the prevalence of HIV infection or on the conditions—both behavioral and social—that determine its spread to project with any confidence the future course of the epidemic. Even less information is available for translating rising death rates into potential impacts on overtaxed health care systems, economic output, or future population growth. Yet one thing is certain: AIDS will have a profound impact in the Third World, and one that exceeds the impact in the West, where resources are plentiful and basic infrastructure better developed.

A look at existing health care systems in the Third World provides a glimpse of the disadvantage that developing countries face in responding to AIDS. In 1984, Haiti had $3.25 to spend on health care per citizen; Mexico had $11.50. Rwanda's pitiful annual budget of $1.60 per person would not even buy a bottle of aspirin in the industrial world. By contrast, Sweden annually spends over $1,100 on health care per person and the United States invests more than $760. Yet meager Third World health budgets must contend with existing epidemics of frightening proportion. Three million Third World children die each year from preventable diseases such as measles, tetanus, and whooping cough. In Africa alone, malaria annually claims 1 million lives.[19]

Data from countries already responding to AIDS confirm that the costs of prevention will be high. In 1988, for example, Brazil's prevention program was estimated to cost $28 million, $8 million of which went to screen blood at state-run blood banks. Health officials in Peru put the start-up costs of screening their national blood supply at $20 million in 1987, a sum that could otherwise cover the total annual health care bill for 1.5 million Peruvians.

If borne alone by developing countries, these costs could derail already fragile and inadequate health care systems.[20]

Developing countries also have fewer options for treating AIDS patients than countries in the West do. Physicians in industrial countries largely respond by treating the secondary diseases, such as *Pneumocystis carinii* pneumonia, that accompany AIDS. It is an expensive ordeal that often involves frequent hospital stays. The only drug currently known to attack HIV directly—zidovudine, commonly known as AZT—costs roughly $8,000 per patient annually, and causes anemia so severe that over a quarter of recipients require blood transfusions. In the Third World, where per capita incomes are measured in hundreds of dollars and blood is in short supply, a life-prolonging drug like AZT might as well not exist.[21]

Indeed, preliminary cost data from around the world suggest that the amount spent per AIDS patient roughly correlates with a country's gross national product (GNP). As with health care in general, poor countries are forced to spend less on each patient. If Zaire spent at a level comparable to the United States, the cost of treating 10 AIDS patients would exceed the entire budget of Mama Yemo, the nation's largest public hospital. Although costs in industrial countries are inflated by higher salaries, more expensive equipment, and added malpractice insurance, AIDS treatment undoubtedly suffers in countries where even antibiotics and syringes are in short supply.[22]

Given such constraints, AIDS naturally raises the question of triage. Where hospital space and medical supplies are scarce and where people regularly die of treatable illnesses, diverting resources to AIDS treatment may actually cost lives by crowding out patients who can be cured. From a quarter to half of precious hospital beds in some central African hospitals are occupied by patients who are infected with HIV; Costa Rican officials predict a similar situation by the mid-1990s. Already, AIDS patients are being discharged from some health facilities in Africa, Haiti, and Brazil to give preference to patients with curable illnesses.[23]

In terms of overall health investment, however, AIDS prevention activities may actually deserve high priority, even in countries heavily burdened by other diseases. A World Bank/ WHO research team of western and African researchers has estimated that preventing one case of HIV infection in Africa would save more years of life than would preventing a case of malaria, measles, tuberculosis (TB), or pneumonia. To determine the relative merits of investing in AIDS prevention versus other disease control programs, decision makers need to consider how many people are affected by each disease and the comparative costs of each prevention program. Significantly, preventing a case of AIDS stops secondary and tertiary transmission of the virus, whereas preventing a case of measles or malaria would affect transmission little if at all, because such diseases are already so pervasive in Africa.[24]

Not only does AIDS compete with other diseases for limited health budgets, HIV actually magnifies existing epidemics. By weakening the immune system of its host, the virus makes carriers more susceptible to renewed attack from other microbes lying dormant. For example, some 30–60 percent of adults in many developing countries are carriers of the tuberculosis bacteria, even though their bodies have conquered outward signs of the disease. By suppressing the immune system, HIV allows dormant TB bacteria to become active, leading to the contagious form of tuberculosis.[25]

Although it is too early to measure worldwide increases in TB prevalence, some evidence suggests that HIV may already be having a multiplier effect on this deadly disease. New York City—home to almost half of all U.S. AIDS patients—reported a 35-percent jump in TB cases between 1984 and 1986. Studies also document a close association between TB and HIV: in Kinshasa, Zaire, 38 percent of TB patients tested were HIV-positive, compared with only 2.5–8 percent of healthy adults. An HIV-TB link is especially worrisome in the Third World, where poverty, overcrowding, and lack of access to treatment make tuberculosis more lethal than in the West.[26]

It is in the area of child health, however, that AIDS has the greatest potential to erode hard-won health gains in the Third World. Over the last three decades, developing regions have inaugurated a "child survival revolution" through encouraging oral rehydration therapy for diarrhea, immunization, breastfeeding, and birth spacing. Together with economic growth and increased female literacy, these simple interventions have cut Third World child deaths by slightly more than half since 1955, with Southeast Asia making the greatest progress and Africa the least.[27]

Left unchecked, AIDS will undermine these gains as more and more pregnant women become infected and transmit the virus to their children *in utero*. Already 9–24 percent of pregnant women in some African cities—such as Kinshasa and Kampala—are infected. Up to half the children born to these women will contract the virus and die. Preliminary models of the most affected regions in Africa suggest that infant mortality could increase by more than 25 percent, eroding three decades of progress in infant and child health.[28]

These models also show that although adult death rates in Africa could rise dramatically, AIDS will likely have only modest impacts on population growth. The notion—advanced by some—that parts of Africa are already "lost" to AIDS or that the disease eliminates the need for family planning funds is not supported by the evidence. A model by John Bongaarts of the Population Council in New York, for example, predicts that a typical African growth rate of 3 percent could fall to 2 percent over 25 years if 20 percent of the total population became infected. Even if death rates were to double—with AIDS adding as many deaths as all other causes combined—population growth would not cease.[29]

The demographic effects of AIDS may be small, but the economic impact of a fatal epidemic focused on sexually active adults could be immense. Unlike other diseases that cull the weakest members of society—the sick, the old, and the very young—AIDS eliminates the most productive segment of a population. In Africa, HIV infection in women peaks during their third decade—the prime childbearing years—and for males during their fourth decade, the most productive years at work and in the community. Where the ranks of people with certain specialized skills and training may be small, the loss of even a handful of engineers, health planners, or agronomists can be debilitating.[30]

Although predicting AIDS' impact on specific economic sectors will require detailed country-by-country analysis, hints of what may be in store have started to emerge. Zambian researchers fear that labor losses due to AIDS could cripple their nation's copper mining industry, which accounts for one fifth of Zambia's GNP. One study in the nation's Copper Belt found that 68 percent of men testing positive were the skilled professionals upon whom the mining industry depends. Since the companies provide both retirement and benefits and comprehensive medical and social services for miners and their families, Zambian researchers fear that the financial drain of AIDS could jeopardize the entire mining sector.[31]

These economic disruptions come at a time when developing nations—especially in Africa—are already laboring under severe economic hardship. Per capita income is declining

and foreign debt is mounting. Against this backdrop, AIDS threatens to further complicate balance-of-payment problems. Foreign exchange will be lost as governments seek to import items necessary to combat the epidemic, tourist dollars may decline in response to travelers' fears, and economic growth will slow as people and governments divert savings from investment to treatment. Indeed, in industrial and developing countries alike, the indirect economic costs of AIDS will far exceed any direct costs related to prevention or treatment.[32]

Researchers at the Harvard Institute of International Development are attempting to quantify these indirect costs by modeling the impact of AIDS on certain central African economies. According to their projections, by 1995 the annual loss to Zaire's economy due to premature deaths and reduced savings will be between $350 million and $670 million—equal to 8 to 16 percent of the nation's GNP in 1984. Even without including direct treatment costs or losses due to illness, these figures exceed the $314 million that Zaire received from all sources of development assistance in 1984.[33]

In human terms, this economic slowing will mean that by 1995, the average Zairian will have roughly $18 less income per year than he or she would have had in an economy without AIDS (measured in constant 1984 dollars). A mere pittance in industrial societies, $18 represents a 10-percent loss in income for Zairians, who average only $170 per year. Tragically, this decline comes on top of an already seriously eroded income base: per capita income in Zaire declined roughly 42 percent between 1965 and 1985. AIDS is an added burden these people cannot afford.[34]

Even more devastating are the costs of caring for family members stricken with AIDS. Although employers or the state pay health care costs in many developing countries, not all citizens have access to such assistance, either because they are unemployed or because they live in remote areas. In one study of children with AIDS in Kinshasa, over half the parents were either unemployed or dead, meaning that treatment costs fell to family and friends. Children's hospital expenses typically were three times their parents' average monthly wages, and funerals and burial cost almost a year's salary.[35]

Yet the true costs of AIDS are both economic and personal. Economists can count up the direct costs and calculate the indirect cost of lost wages from disability and death. But what of the psychological toll on those left behind? Economic tally sheets cannot capture the pain of a child left without parents or of a generation whose future is short-changed by AIDS.

PROGRESS TOWARD PREVENTION IN INDUSTRIAL COUNTRIES

For a world used to solving problems with a technical fix, AIDS is frustrating. Today, prospects for a vaccine or cure seem even more distant than they did two years ago, when scientists were reeling from the thrill of rapid discovery. The AIDS virus has proved a wily opponent: It hides within the very immune cells that the body normally uses to ward off invaders, making vaccines and treatments exceedingly difficult to devise. And it mutates at a furious pace—perhaps even faster than the influenza virus that requires researchers to alter the flu vaccine every year. Prevention will likely remain the world's primary weapon against AIDS for at least the next decade.[36]

In the industrial world, where transmission through blood transfusions has essentially ceased, stopping AIDS means getting people to change high-risk behavior. Risky behavior includes unprotected sex, especially with multiple partners, and the sharing of contaminated needles among drug addicts. The best way to avoid AIDS is to have a mutually monogamous sexual relationship with a partner

known to be uninfected. Short of that, condoms provide good, although not foolproof protection against HIV transmission. The spermicide nonoxyl-9 has also been shown to kill the virus in laboratory tests, but its ability to prevent HIV transmission between sexual partners has yet to be proved.[37]

It is important to recognize that it is what people do, not who they are, that puts them at risk. As the Panos Institute has pointed out in its groundbreaking work *Blaming Others*, talk of "high-risk groups," such as Haitians, gay men, or prostitutes, tends to invite finger-pointing and erroneously suggests that anyone not in these groups is safe. Moreover, categorization fails to acknowledge that not all group members practice high-risk behavior. AIDS is not a "gay disease" or an "African disease" or a "disease of drug addicts." Anyone who engages in high-risk behavior can contract HIV.[38]

Given these risks, industrial countries have responded in a variety of ways, some constructive, others less so. In general, European governments were quicker than the United States to launch broad-based AIDS education programs, even though their epidemics were not yet as severe. Seven European countries sent information booklets to their citizens more than a year before the United States did so in June 1988. Across the board, these public information campaigns have achieved roughly the same result: people now know that sex, blood, and needles can transmit AIDS, but they still cling to many misperceptions. In 1987, 40 percent of Canadians polled, for instance, believed that AIDS could be transmitted through insects, as did 38 percent of Americans.[39]

Regrettably, some nations have also espoused superficially attractive but ineffective responses, such as screening and deportation of infected foreigners, premarital testing, and mandatory testing of those perceived to be at risk. For example, 29 countries—including various developing ones—now impose some form of travel restriction or mandatory screening of foreigners even though WHO has determined that such measures are costly, repressive, and will not stem the epidemic's tide. Entry restrictions are born of a desire to erect a barrier between the virus and the uninfected, to label the afflicted as "foreign," "different," "not me." In reality, by providing a false sense of security, they allow the disease to spread unchecked.[40]

In the United States, bills for premarital screening for HIV have been introduced in 35 states and become law in Illinois, Louisiana, and Texas. (The law in Texas will not go into effect unless HIV prevalence exceeds a certain threshold.) Like travel restrictions, such bills are politically attractive because they are highly visible; yet they are dangerous because they deflect attention and resources from those truly at risk. Even premarital syphilis testing has never efficiently identified new syphilis cases: in 1978, premarital screening accounted for only 1.27 percent of all tests found positive, but the program cost $80 million annually. Not surprisingly, Louisiana has already repealed its AIDS law after realizing that it uncovered few cases and pushed couples to neighboring states to get married. Illinois likewise is having second thoughts.[41]

Other countries and constituencies have responded with calls for mandatory testing, compulsory reporting of HIV-positive individuals, or required partner tracing. The Soviet Union, Hungary, and Bavaria in West Germany, for example, all require testing of high-risk individuals, including prostitutes, drug addicts, and—with the exception of Bavaria—homosexuals. Yet health officials are unanimous in the view that mandatory measures merely drive underground those most in need of testing. In Charleston, South Carolina, the number of homosexual men seeking testing dropped by 51 percent after the state began requiring all those who tested positive to be reported to the public health department. When anonymous and voluntary, however, testing counseling, and partner tracing have proved to be useful and effective tools for AIDS prevention.[42]

Despite these false starts, many countries now have innovative prevention programs in place, including school-based education, information campaigns aimed at the general public, condom promotion, and specialized outreach programs designed to reach those at highest risk. Many of the most impressive initiatives come from outside the government and draw on the skills and energy of the homosexual community, which rallied early to protect its members. The Gay Men's Health Crisis in New York (founded in 1982) and the Terrence Higgins Trust in London (founded in 1983) probably still have more experience in AIDS education than any other groups in the world.[43]

So far it appears that among heterosexuals, prevention campaigns have increased knowledge but have changed sexual behavior only marginally. Change among gay men, however, has been dramatic and may well constitute the most rapid and profound behavioral response ever documented in public health. Studies throughout the United States and Western Europe have found that gay men have reduced their number of sexual partners, increased their use of condoms, and decreased their participation in unprotected anal intercourse. One review of 24 American and European studies concluded that, on average, gay men have 63 percent fewer sexual partners since AIDS. The incidence of receptive anal intercourse has similarly declined, by 59 percent.[44]

Because of HIV's long latency period, these behavior changes have not yet translated into fewer new AIDS cases, but in parts of the United States rates of new HIV infection among gay men have declined. Less than 1 percent of noninfected homosexual men in San

Francisco, for example, were being infected annually by 1988, down from 18 percent in 1983. AIDS-induced behavior change is also probably responsible for recent declines in the number of new gonorrhea and syphilis cases among gay men in Denmark, Finland, the Netherlands, Sweden, and the United Kingdom. Because these STDs have shorter incubation periods than HIV, reductions in high-risk behavior register more quickly with syphilis and gonorrhea than with AIDS.[45]

Unfortunately, studies on both continents confirm that a minority of gay men still engage in dangerous behavior despite understanding the risks involved. Risky behavior is most often associated with the use of uninhibiting drugs during sex, suggesting that programs aimed at alcohol and recreational drugs may be important for AIDS control. Moreover, gays living in lower risk areas do not seem to have modified their behavior as much, perhaps because they do not feel as personally at risk. It is unsafe to assume, therefore, that the entire gay male population in the United States and Europe has been educated and that attention is better placed elsewhere. Promising progress has been made, but much remains to be done.[46]

Intravenous drug users have also proved capable of change, although curbing HIV infection among drug addicts has received far too little attention, especially in the United States. Response has been hampered by debate over the moral and legal appropriateness of certain interventions, such as needle exchange programs, and the pervasive view that addicts somehow "deserve" AIDS. Inaction, however, is both inhumane to drug users and shortsighted, given that IV drug users are the most likely bridge between HIV and the general population.

Without a doubt, helping addicts kick their habit is the favored approach to stopping AIDS transmission among drug users, but in many countries treatment capacity is sorely lacking.

The United States, for example, can treat only 15–20 percent of its more than 1.2 million needle addicts, and waiting lists of up to six months for treatment are not uncommon. During this time, addicts continue to shoot drugs, increasing their chances of contracting and spreading HIV and diminishing their resolve to fight their addiction. When treatment is affordable and accessible, IV drug users have shown that they will seek it out to reduce their risk of AIDS. In New Jersey, addicts redeemed 84 percent of 970 coupons for free treatment that AIDS outreach workers distributed. More than half said they were largely motivated by fear of AIDS.[47]

For those unable or unwilling to break their addiction, programs aimed at safer injection are important for AIDS control. Needle-sharing is deeply ingrained in the drug culture, both as a form of social bonding and because new syringes are expensive, hard to obtain, and illegal to possess in many areas. But studies confirm that addicts will reduce their use of contaminated needles, especially if given the means to do so, either through needle-syringe exchange programs or through the provision of bleach for cleaning syringes between uses. Indeed, several studies suggest that supplying the means to change behavior is critical; programs that provide information alone have tended to fail.[48]

Despite the importance of providing the hardware of behavior change, needle exchange programs have been extremely controversial, especially in the United States, where only two small pilot programs have been approved. On both sides of the Atlantic, people argue that to supply syringes is to condone drug use. To refuse addicts access to clean needles in the age of AIDS, however, is to deny them the opportunity to protect themselves—and eventually others—from a deadly infection.[49]

While still controversial, other countries have been more willing than the United States to experiment with needle exchange programs. So far, Switzerland, Denmark, the Netherlands, the United Kingdom, and Australia have initiated programs and all report significantly less needle-sharing among addicts. France has also liberalized its policy by making needles available for sale at pharmacies without prescription or identification. Despite widespread concern that increased availability of needles would encourage drug use, there is no evidence that this is occurring. Indeed, in the Netherlands the number of addicts actually decreased from roughly 8,500 in 1984 to 6,800 in 1988 after the government implemented a comprehensive AIDS prevention campaign aimed at addicts, including needle exchange, methadone treatment, and outreach.[50]

Disturbing evidence indicates, however, that changes in sexual behavior among American and European drug addicts lag considerably behind changes in drug-use behavior. Even more distressing, the least amount of change has occurred within committed, heterosexual relationships, where HIV transmission is most likely to occur (because of frequency of intercourse) and where children are most likely to be conceived. Given that three fourths of American IV drug users are male and have a primary partner who does not use drugs, there is clearly need for more education on safer sex among addicts as part of an effort to prevent the spread of HIV.[51]

AIDS prevention programs to date have also been singularly ineffective at reaching U.S. minority communities. Studies show that blacks and Hispanics are less well informed than whites about AIDS and that they have not modified their behavior as much. This is particularly worrisome because blacks and Hispanics are at extremely high risk. Already they account for 41 percent of AIDS cases, even though they constitute only 19 percent of the U.S. population. Eighty-five percent of children who acquired AIDS from their mother

and 71 percent of all women with AIDS are black or Hispanic.[52]

This pattern of infection is partly due to the fact that a disproportionate number of IV drug users are black or Hispanic. But even among drug addicts, minorities are more likely to be infected than whites. The reasons for this are unclear, although for cultural and economic reasons, blacks and Hispanics may have less access to clean needles, drug treatment, and AIDS information. Particularly disturbing is evidence that blacks also account for a disproportionate share of new HIV infection occurring outside of big cities, where IV drug use would be less common.[53]

These trends emphasize the need for more culturally relevant AIDS information aimed at minorities. Recently, the Centers for Disease Control of the U.S. Public Health Service has attempted to fill this gap by earmarking almost $45 million for minority outreach projects in 1989, up from only $14 million in 1987. Experience suggests that initiatives arising from the minority communities themselves have the greatest chance of success.[54]

ALLIANCE FOR PREVENTION IN DEVELOPING COUNTRIES

Stopping AIDS in developing countries will take a worldwide alliance of professional skills, resources, and experience. Left unaided, the Third World would have to divert scarce resources from other essential development initiatives or be forced to accept ever-rising death tolls. Even industrial countries cannot fight this scourge alone. Barring a vaccine or a cure, no country can independently protect itself from HIV, for the disease respects no national boundaries. Like several of today's most pressing problems—global warming, ozone depletion, Third World debt—unless all nations work together against AIDS, there is little hope in acting separately.

Although nations have collaborated before

on action aimed at disease control, there is no precedent for the level of cooperation that will be required to battle AIDS. Even WHO's successful effort to eradicate smallpox during the seventies is not fully analogous: Smallpox could be prevented with a single vaccine that was already available and relatively easy to deliver. Industrial nations had already conquered the disease, and carriers were easily identified by a characteristic rash. By contrast, HIV infection is invisible and insidious. And there is no vaccine. Stopping AIDS means getting people to change their behavior, a task that governments and international agencies are ill prepared to do.

With a threat this great and requiring so much coordination, central leadership is essential. WHO accepted this role in February 1987 when it formed the Special Programme on AIDS, later renamed the Global Programme on AIDS (GPA). Since then, the program has grown rapidly, largely due to the determined leadership of its director, Dr. Jonathan Mann. Starting with one secretary and a $580,000 budget, Mann has built the AIDS program into one of the agency's largest and most active, with a proposed budget of $95 million for 1989 and a year-end staffing target of 222 professionals.[55]

GPA acts primarily as a coordinating body for AIDS surveillance, prevention, and research and as a resource to governments trying to develop national AIDS control plans. With WHO's encouragement and assistance, more than 150 nations now have national AIDS committees, and 119 have developed short-term plans for combatting the disease (including every country in sub-Saharan Africa). Forty-eight countries, mostly in the Third World, have gone on to develop three- to five-year plans. WHO also serves as an intermediary between donors and developing countries hoping to arrange funding for their national AIDS programs. As of December 1988, $99 million had been raised to support 30 medium-term plans, mostly in Africa and the Caribbean.[56]

That so many nations have mobilized is a testament to WHO's effectiveness, given that two years ago most governments still denied the presence or extent of AIDS. The challenge now is to translate these paper plans into functioning programs, a task that will be particularly hard in developing countries. Most experts agree that it is preferable to integrate AIDS prevention activities into existing health and educational systems rather than develop "vertical" AIDS programs that would compete for resources and attention. But it is impossible to graft AIDS control programs onto nonexistent or rudimentary rural health care systems or to introduce blood screening in countries without adequate labs, trained technicians, or functioning blood banks. Indeed, to be successful in some poorer countries, the whole health infrastructure will have to be expanded and fortified.

WHO's leadership has clearly inspired some countries to act, but many nations had nascent education campaigns even before WHO entered the scene. As in industrial countries, many of the earliest efforts were implemented by nongovernmental groups, the vanguard of AIDS education. In Kenya, for example, the Red Cross distributed over a million leaflets counseling "Help Crush AIDS" and "Spread facts . . . not fear." The Rwandan Red Cross launched an impressive campaign using radio announcements, posters, and leaflets. And in the Dominican Republic, the government distributed free condoms, printed hundreds of thousands of brochures, posters, and bumper stickers, and passed legislation requiring all motels to provide complimentary condoms.[57]

Indeed, the picture that emerges from the Third World is one of many small acts that combine to form a growing tide of prevention activities. In Guatemala, the Association for Sexual Education has produced two pamphlets and a series of wallet-sized cards that describe how to protect oneself from AIDS. In Mexico, a dynamic woman named Gloria Ornelas Hall runs an AIDS hotline that handles over 70 calls a day. And in Uganda, a physiotherapist and a doctor whose lives were personally touched by AIDS have formed a counseling service for sufferers and their families. With few resources but much foresight, these individuals are reaching out into their communities to educate others about AIDS.[58]

As WHO has helped mobilize outside funds, Third World governments have become more involved in prevention. Often one of their first priorities has been to secure the nation's blood supply, primarily because it is one route that can be eliminated with a technical fix. In 1985, when a blood test for HIV first became available, from 8 to 18 percent of blood donors in the capitals of Uganda, Rwanda, and Zaire were infected. With screening units costing up to $10,000 apiece and each test costing on average $1–4, developing countries could not afford screening and hospitals became part of the chain of infection. In Central Africa, transfusions probably account for 5–10 percent of HIV transmission among adults and up to a quarter of all AIDS cases in children.[59]

The majority of developing countries now have at least some screening capacity, mostly in major urban areas. By the end of 1988, limited testing equipment was available in most capital cities in Africa and Latin America and some countries—such as Zimbabwe, Zambia, and Mexico—had nearly universal screening. Blood screening should become considerably more common in the near future as a new generation of simple, rapid blood tests for HIV become available. Field tests are nearing completion on several that yield results in 2–4 minutes, and that use only a slide and medicine dropper instead of expensive equipment and reagents. The ability to screen quickly is especially important in developing countries where blood is often not banked but donated as needed when an emergency arises.[60]

Although worth doing, screening blood will have a relatively small impact on the spread of AIDS because at least 80 percent of transmission in the Third World is through heterosexual sex. Thus the bulk of prevention must come from encouraging fidelity and greater use of condoms. Also important is expanding access to treatment for other sexually transmitted diseases that may be facilitating the spread of HIV.

The best strategy for curtailing sexual transmission depends in part on whether HIV has infiltrated the general population or not. In countries where the virus is already widely dispersed, prevention activities must be broad in scope. But where HIV prevalence is still low, as in West Africa and Asia, countries have an opportunity to target interventions and thereby save vital resources. Experience has shown that HIV generally spreads outward from pockets of infection among individuals whose behavior increases their risk of contracting and transmitting the virus, such as prostitutes, men in the military, and IV drug users. By helping such groups to protect themselves, governments can prevent HIV from gaining a foothold in their country.[61]

The speed at which the virus can infiltrate unsuspecting populations argues persuasively for acting before HIV is an obvious problem. Studies in Bangkok, Thailand, for example, show that among the city's estimated 60,000 IV drug users, HIV prevalence rose from 1 percent in 1987 to over 30 percent by mid-1988. Had prevention programs been in place, this precipitous rise might have been avoided. These individuals now represent a large pool for spread of HIV both within the drug community and, through sexual contact, outside of it.[62]

Even where HIV is already widespread, there is urgent need for more community-based programs designed to reach populations at highest risk: clients of STD clinics, long-distance truck drivers, and bisexual men in Latin America, among others. The message must be delivered in their own language and by a source they can trust. So far, programs that use peers as AIDS educators seem the most promising. In Accra, Ghana, for example, prostitutes trained as AIDS educators increased condom use significantly within their community: 67 percent of prostitutes now use condoms all the time and another 24 percent report frequent or occasional use. (Only 13 percent used condoms before the program.) Similar gains have been achieved by peer educators working with prostitutes in Nairobi, Kenya, and in Santo Domingo, Dominican Republic.[63]

Encouraging though this may be, these results are but small victories in what is destined to be a protracted and expensive war. Consider the challenge of expanding condom use alone. Programs to supply condoms vary greatly in cost depending on how the condoms will be distributed and how actively they will be promoted. Even the least expensive option—subsidizing their sale through existing commercial outlets—costs roughly $12 per couple annually, half of which is the cost of the condoms themselves. Just to ensure that commercial channels supply enough condoms for one third of all couples in the nine hardest-hit countries of Africa would cost $110 million annually, more than WHO's total AIDS budget for 1989.[64]

Yet the bigger challenge—both in terms of difficulty and expense—is getting couples to use condoms in cultures where birth control itself is not readily accepted and where condoms are especially disdained. In most African countries, less than 5 percent of married women practice any form of modern contraception and only 0.3 percent use condoms. Efforts to promote condoms throughout the

Third World will have to overcome strong cultural and religious prohibitions as well as daunting logistical problems.[65]

Such observations capture the magnitude of the prevention task at hand and raise the question, Are we doing enough? The answer is most certainly no if the number of lives at risk is considered. Yet world priorities have seldom bowed to the exigencies of body counts. In 1988, industrial countries probably spent in the neighborhood of $100–150 million on AIDS control in the Third World, a reasonable amount when compared with other health, nutrition, and population assistance. But the world spent more than $100 million *each hour* on the global military apparatus. It is not that AIDS deserves a bigger share of the health and development pie, but that health and development themselves have been vastly underattended.[66]

Admittedly, money alone will not solve the AIDS dilemma. But money is an important catalyst for action. The challenge ahead is to find new international funds for AIDS control with an eye toward helping the Third World develop the infrastructure and indigenous human talent necessary to sustain the effort over the long haul. So far donors have been forthcoming with development assistance to fight AIDS, but this money appears largely to have been subtracted from other development accounts. If AIDS control comes at the expense of other life-promoting initiatives, we will have won the battle, but lost the war.

AIDS AS SOCIAL CRUCIBLE

AIDS is both a product of social change and its instrument. Rapid urbanization in Africa, the rise of gay liberation in the West, and the advent of modern air travel have all fueled this pandemic. In turn, AIDS has already triggered profound changes in every aspect of human endeavor, from how we care for the dying to how we relate to the living. Perhaps most significant, AIDS compels societies to confront issues and aspects of the human condition that are otherwise easily ignored. While heightening awareness, the disease does not dictate our response. How societies choose to act on the issues raised by AIDS may stand as a key measure of our time.[67]

Like all crises, AIDS has brought out the best and the worst of human nature. The pulling together of the American gay community to respond to a crisis within its ranks, the generous and often courageous actions of thousands of professional and voluntary caregivers, and the outpouring of global resources and talent to fight the disease are all expressions of human compassion at its best. But if compassion has been at work, so too have fear and denial.[68]

AIDS has aroused mean-spirited and irrational responses, often provoked by gross misconceptions about how the disease can be transmitted. American children with AIDS have been barred from school, despite repeated assurances by health professionals that they pose no risk to other students. In Colombia, one man with AIDS was forced to guard his house with a shotgun to keep villagers from burning it down to avoid "contamination." And in the United States, gay rights groups note that physical attacks against homosexuals have risen sharply since the epidemic began.[69]

These panic responses have been made worse by the fact that AIDS first struck already stigmatized populations—gay men, IV drug users, and foreigners in the West; prostitutes and those with multiple sex partners in developing countries. This has reinforced thinly veiled prejudices and encouraged scapegoating. Regrettably, the global mobilization against AIDS has been hampered by the human tendency to blame others for a problem rather than tackle the problem itself. AIDS has

been blamed on everything from Western decadence to sexual promiscuity among Africans. Such accusations have merely bred resentment, encouraged denial, and thwarted the global cooperation so desperately needed to fight this disease.[70]

The potential for discrimination and persecution is so great, in fact, that Jonathan Mann recently made an unprecedented call for an international human rights network to monitor discrimination and abuse against HIV-infected individuals. Without a supportive and tolerent social environment, fear and retribution will undermine communication, reinforce prejudice, and make infected people unwilling to come forward. Indeed, health officials consider tolerance so important to AIDS control that the London World Summit of Health Ministers and the U.S. Presidential Commission on the Human Immunodeficiency Virus Epidemic both endorsed antidiscrimination policies as a top AIDS priority.[71]

In addition to exposing human vulnerabilities, AIDS has thrown into sharp relief certain inadequacies and inequities in the existing social order. The crisis has underscored the dismal state of health infrastructure in the developing world, where even syringes are in short supply. It has highlighted the structural flaws in economic systems that fail to provide gainful alternatives to prostitution and drug dealing. And in the United States, it has made painfully obvious shortcomings in the nation's health care system: the underfunding of preventive health measures, the lack of care options for the chronically ill, and the plight of the poor and uninsured.

By highlighting these flaws and adding a sense of urgency, AIDS may galvanize societies to tackle the underlying problems that allow HIV to flourish. Stopping AIDS among drug users, for example, may have more to do in the long term with fighting unemployment, poverty, and welfare dependence than with needle exchange or more treatment. As Harvey Fineberg, Dean of Harvard's School of Public Health, observes: "Jobs, schools and housing . . . would go a long way toward creating the individual self-respect, dignity and hope for the future that can forestall the turning to drugs in the first place." Similarly, societies may come to realize that prostitution is seldom a profession of choice, but one of economic necessity. Already, a family planning association in Ghana is fighting AIDS by retraining prostitutes in other types of work.[72]

AIDS has also forced societies to look again and with new eyes at issues such as sex education in schools, drug addiction, and the standards of public discourse. The urgency of AIDS has encouraged reappraisal of the appropriateness of certain interventions and has tabled debates over offending "public sensibilities." Formerly taboo subjects such as condoms are now topics of conversation in settings as diverse as western dinner parties and village tea stalls. In the Soviet Union, Vadim Pokrovskiy, director of the Moscow AIDS Clinic, appeared on television in August 1987, strongly urging the use of condoms. Suck frankness in Soviet broadcasting would have been unthinkable in a world without AIDS.[73]

Indeed, AIDS has forged its own special form of *glasnost* in the Eastern bloc. For the first time, governments are responding with candor about the existence of drug abuse, prostitution, and homosexuality within their societies. Bulgaria, for example, now acknowledges some 600 addicts in a population of 9 million. The Soviet Union has gone from denying that drug addiction exists to implementing a program to register addicts. And the Policy weekly *Polityka* now reports that Poland has approximately 270,000 homosexual men—about 1.5 percent of the male population—and twice as many bisexuals.[74]

It is in the area of health care, however, that AIDS will likely catalyze the greatest changes. In both industrial and developing countries, for example, AIDS is already encouraging a shift from hospital to community- or home-based care to limit cost and preserve vital hospital beds. Interestingly, AIDS' influence to date appears to be operating through its ability to overwhelm local health care services rather than through its impact on national health care expenditures. In the United States, the cost of AIDS treatment and prevention accounted for only 0.4 percent of total medical spending in 1986. Even by 1991, AIDS will likely account for only 1.5 percent of U.S. health expenditures, largely because deaths from other diseases will still overwhelm those from AIDS.[75]

In the world's hardest-hit cities, however, the financial and health impacts of AIDS are already substantial. By 1991, AIDS patients will occupy one out of every four hospital beds in New York City, a proportion already exceeded in some central African cities. In fiscal year 1988, San Francisco spent $17 million of city funds on AIDS; New York plans to spend $170 million in 1989. Medical care alone for San Francisco's AIDS patients in 1991 is expected to cost some $350 per city resident. Of course, city taxpayers will share these costs with private insurers, the federal government, and the patients themselves, but the local burden will still be great.[76]

Faced with such burdens, cities around the world are experimenting with new models of community-based care that may forever change how societies cope with chronic illness. San Francisco, which pioneered this approach, now has expanded hospice care, improved home nursing, residential facilities for patients who are homeless, and outpatient clinics for AIDS treatment. Cost per patient has declined, as has the percentage of patients requiring hospitalization and the average hospital stay. Likewise, in southern Zambia, Chikankata Hospital has cooperated with the Salvation

Army to establish roving health teams that care for and counsel AIDS patients in their homes. In 1987, the program avoided an estimated 35 hospital admissions, more than paying for itself.[77]

Ultimately, the power of AIDS lies in its ability to reveal ourselves to ourselves. AIDS raises the questions, and the quality of our response may define our humanity. What if scientists develop a solution to AIDS that works in industrial nations but is either impractical or too costly for the developing world? Will western nations consider further AIDS research a priority? Or will AIDS become like schistosomiasis and other Third World diseases that can be ignored because Americans and Europeans are not dying? What if AIDS becomes largely a disease of minorities and drug users? Will money for treatment and prevention still be forthcoming? As Jonathan Mann observes, "AIDS will . . . put our global conscience to the test." Let us hope that compassion and tolerance prevail.

Notes

[1] Smoking-related deaths from William U. Chandler, *Banishing Tobacco*, Worldwatch Paper 68 (Washington, D.C.: Worldwatch Institute, January 1986); diarrhea figure from Katrina Galway et al., *Child Survival: Risks and The Road to Health* (Columbia, Md.: Institute for Resource Development/Westinghouse, 1987); tuberculosis figure from G. Slutkin et al., "Effect of AIDS on the Tuberculosis Problem and Programmes and Priorities for Control and Research," abstract of paper presented at the IV International Conference on AIDS, Stockholm, Sweden, June 12–16, 1988 (hereinafter cited as Stockholm Conference).

[2] Quote from "Interview: Jonathan Mann," *AIDS Patient Care* (New York), June 1988.

[3] Renée Sabatier, *Blaming Others: Prejudice, Race and Worldwide AIDS* (Philadelphia: New Society Publishers, for Panos Institute in association with Norwegian Red Cross, 1988).

[4] Observations about control from Dr. Malcolm Potts, "Preparing for the Battle," *People* (London), Vol. 14, No. 4, 1987; incubation period from Roy M. Anderson and Robert M. May, "Epidemiological Parameters of HIV Transmission," *Nature*, June 9, 1988; observation about progression to AIDS from Institute of Medicine, National Academy of Sciences, *Confronting AIDS, Update 1988* (Washington, D.C.: National Academy Press, 1988).

[5] World Health Organization (WHO), "Global Programme On Aids: Progress Report Number 3," Geneva, May 1988; role of prostitutes from Don C. Des Jarlais et al., "HIV Infection and Intravenous Drug Use: Critical Issues in Transmission Dynamics, Infection Outcomes, and Prevention," *Reviews of Infectious Diseases*, Vol. 10, No. 1, 1988, and from Bruce Lambert, "AIDS Among Prostitutes Not as Prevalent as Believed, Studies Show," *New York Times*, September 20, 1988.

[6] Until recently, researchers commonly cited 5–20 percent of sexually active adults infected in major urban areas of East and Central Africa; see Jonathan M. Mann et al., "The International Epidemiology of AIDS," *Scientific American*, October 1988. New data from urban centers in the Kagera region of Tanzania reveal 32.8 percent of adults (aged 15–54) infected; see J. Killewo et al., "The Epidemiology of HIV-1 Infection in the Kagera Region of Tanzani," abstract of paper presented at the Third International Conference on AIDS and Associated Cancers in Africa, Arusha, Tanzania, September 14-16, 1988 (hereinafter cited as Arusha Conference). Prostitute observation from Peter Piot and Michel Caraël, "Epidemiological and Sociological Aspects of HIV-infection in Developing Countries," *British Medical Bulletin*, Vol. 44, No. 1, 1988.

[7] Dr. Jonathan Mann, "Global AIDS: A Status Report," Testimony before the Presidential Commission on the Human Immunodeficiency Virus Epidemic (hereinafter cited as Presidential Commission), April 18, 1988.

[8] Nancy S. Padian, "Heterosexual Transmission of Acquired Immunodeficiency Syndrome: International Perspectives and National Projections," *Review of Infectious Diseases*, September/October 1987; Sabatier, *Blaming Others*.

[9] J. O. Ndinya-Achola et al., "Co-Factors in Male-Female Transmission of HIV," abstract of paper presented at Arusha Conference; Mann et al., "International Epidemiology of AIDS"; Michael Specter, "Herpes Found to Increase Susceptibility to AIDS Virus Infection," *Washington Post*, June 16, 1988; D. Zagury et al., "Long Term Cultures of HTLV-III-infected T-cells: A Model of Cytopathology of T-cell Depletion in AIDS," *Science*, February 21, 1986.

[10] WHO computer printout and Mann et al., "International Epidemiology of AIDS."

[11] Dr. James Chin, Chief, AIDS Surveillance Unit, WHO, Geneva, private communications, September 27 and October 21, 1988.

[12] U.S. estimate from William L. Heyward and James W. Curran, "The Epidemiology of AIDS in the U.S.," *Scientific American*, October 1988; European estimate from J. B. Brunet, "Aids and HIV Infection in Europe," abstract of paper presented at Stockholm Conference; Latin American estimate from Pan American Health Organization (PAHO), "The Epidemiology of AIDS in the Americas," Testimony before Presidential Commission, April 18, 1988; Asian estimate from Chin, private communication.

[13] Rural outbreaks from Dr. Samuel Ikwaras Okware, "Towards a National AIDS-Control Program in Uganda," *The Western Journal of Medicine*, December 1987, and from William Lyerly, Jr., AIDS Coordinator, Bureau for Africa,

U.S. Agency for International Development (AID), Washington, D.C., private communication, October 10, 1988.

[14] The percentage of European cases involving drug injection has leveled off in 1988 and includes cases where there are risk behaviors in addition to IV drug use; see Don C. Des Jarlais, "HIV Infection Among Persons Who Inject Illicit Drugs: Problems and Prospects," paper presented at Stockholm Conference.

[15] *Report of the Presidential Commission on the Human Immunodeficiency Virus Epidemic* (Washington, D.C.: U.S. Government Printing Office, 1988).

[16] Cases in American children from James W. Curran et al., "Epidemiology of HIV Infection and AIDS in the United States" *Science*, February 5, 1988; IV drug link to cases in American women from Donald R. Hopkins, "AIDs in Minority Populations in the United States," *Public Health Reports*, November/December 1987; prostitutes' IV drug link from Dr. June E. Osborn, "AIDS: Politics and Science," *New England Journal of Medicine*, February 18, 1988.

[17] J. W. Pape et al., "Epidemiology of AIDS in Haiti (1979–1987)," Testimony before Presidential Commission, April 18, 1988.

[18] PAHO, "Epidemiology of AIDS in the Americas"; C. Bartholomew et al., "Transition From Homosexual to Heterosexual AIDS in Trinidad and Tobago," abstract of paper presented at Arusha Conference; observations about Dominican Republic, Honduras, Ecuador, Brazil, and Mexico from Renée Sabatier, *AIDS and the Third World*, Panos Dossier 1 (Philadelphia: New Society Publishers, for Panos Institute, 1988).

[19] Figures on Haiti, Mexico, and Rwanda from Ruth Leger Sivard, *World Ministry and Social Expenditures 1987–88* (Washington, D.C.: World Priorities, 1987); Swedish figure refers to per capita health spending in 1984, as cited in ibid.; U.S. number refers to 1986 spending, from National Center for Health Statistics, U.S. Department of Health and Human Services, *Health, United States 1987* (Washington, D.C.: U.S. Government Printing Office, 1988); United Nations Children's Fund (UNICEF), *State of the World's Children 1988* (New York: Oxford University Press for UNICEF, 1988).

[20] Hesio Cordeiro et al., "Medical Costs of HIV and AIDS in Brazil," paper presented at the First International Conference on the Global Impact of AIDS, London, March 8–10, 1988 (hereinafter cited as London Conference); Renée Sabatier, "The Global Costs of AIDS," *The Futurist*, November/December 1987.

[21] AZT costs from Fred J. Hellinger, "Forecasting the Personal Medical Care Costs of AIDS from 1988 Through 1991," *Public Health Reports*, May/June 1988; anemia observation from Sabatier, *AIDS and the Third World*.

[22] Relationship between GNP and cost of treatment from Mead Over et al., "The Direct and Indirect Cost of HIV Infection in Developing Countries: The Cases of Zaire and Tanzania," paper presented at Stockholm Conference; Mama Yemo hospital example from Thomas C. Quinn, "AIDS in Africa: An Epidemiologic Paradigm," *Science*, November 21, 1986; observation about quality of care from Sabatier, *AIDS and the Third World*.

[23] Hospital bed rates from Mann et al., "International Epidemiology of AIDS," and from Sabatier, *AIDS and the Third World:* patient discharge from J. Wilson Carswell, "Impact of AIDS in the Developing World," *British Medical Bulletin*, Vol. 44, No. 1, 1988, and from Raisa Scriabine-Smith, unpublished manuscript prepared for the Hudson Institute, Indianapolis, Ind., 1988.

[24] Over et al., "Direct and Indirect Cost of HIV Infection."

[25] Slutkin et al., "Effect of AIDS on the Tuberculosis Problem and Programmes."

[26] Sabatier, *AIDS and the Third World*; R. Colebunders et al., "HIV Infection in Patients with Tuberculosis in Kinshasa, Zaire," abstract of paper presented at Arusha Conference.

[27] United Nations, *Mortality of Children Under Age 5: World Estimates and Projections, 1950–2025* (New York: 1988).

[28] Figures on pregnant women from Carswell, "Impact of AIDS in the Developing World"; mother-to-child infection rate from T. Manzila et al., "Perinatal HIV Transmission in Two African Hospitals: One Year Follow-Up," abstract of paper presented at Arusha Conference; impact on child survival from Mann et al., "International Epidemiology of AIDS," and from Rodolfo A. Bulatao, "Initial Investigation of the Demographic Impact of AIDS in One African Country" (draft), World Bank, Washington, D.C., unpublished, June 15, 1987.

[29] John Bongaarts, "Modeling the Demographic Impact of AIDS in Africa," paper presented at the Annual Meeting of the American Association for the Advancement of Science, Boston, February 11–15, 1988; Philip J. Hilts, "Aids Impact on Population," *Washington Post*, May 24, 1988.

[30] Carswell, "Impact of AIDS in the Developing World."

[31] "Mining Companies Face Increasing Burden," *New Scientist*, March 17, 1988; Copper Belt study from Renée Sabatier, *AIDS and the Third World*, 2nd ed. (London: Panos Institute, 1987).

[32] Indirect costs from Over, "Direct and Indirect Cost of HIV Infection," and from David E. Bloom and Geoffrey Carliner, "The Economic Impact of AIDS in the United States," *Science*, February 5, 1988.

[33] Over, "Direct and Indirect Cost of HIV Infection."

[34] Ibid.

[35] F. Davachi et al., "Economic Impact of Families of Children with AIDS in Kinshasa, Zaire," paper presented at London Conference.

[36] Sharon Kingman and Steve Conner, "The Answer is Still a Condom," *New Scientist*, June 23, 1988; Marilyn Chase, "AIDS Virus in Infected People Mutates At a Dizzying Rate, Two Studies Show," *Wall Street Journal*, August 4, 1988.

[37] Dr. Jeffrey Harris, AIDS Coordinator, AID, Washington, D.C., private communication, October 8, 1988.

[38] Sabatier, *AIDS and the Third World* (1988).

[39] European booklet mailings from Scriabine-Smith, unpublished manuscript; Canadian poll from a study conducted by the Alberta provincial government, as cited in

Sabatier, *AIDS and the Third World* (1988); American data from the National Health Interview Survey of August 1987, as cited in Institute of Medicine, *Confronting AIDS, Update 1988*.

40 Steve Conner and Sharon Kingman, "The Trouble with Testing," *New Scientist*, January 28, 1988; number of countries with travel restrictions from the Panos Institute, as cited in "AIDS Said to Claim a Victim a Minute," *Washington Post*, September 28, 1988.

41 Alan M. Brandt, "AIDS in Historical Perspective: Four Lessons from the History of STDs," *American Journal of Public Health*, April 1988; Sandra G. Boodman, "Premarital AIDS Testing Annoying Many in Illinois," *Washington Post*, July 30, 1988.

42 Hungarian testing information from Radio Free Europe, February 23, 1987, as cited in Scriabine-Smith, unpublished manuscript; Bill Keller, "New Soviet Law Makes AIDS Testing Mandatory," *New York Times*, August 27, 1987; "Mandatory AIDS Test on Basis 'of Slight Suspicion' in Bavaria," *Nature*, June 10, 1988; Wayne D. Johnson, "The Impact of Mandatory Reporting of HIV Seropositive Persons in South Carolina," abstract of paper presented at the Stockholm Conference; for evidence that voluntary and anonymous testing and partner tracing are successful, see Nancy Padian et al., "Partner Notification as a Means to Prevent Further HIV Transmission," M. L. Rekart, "A Modified System of Contact Tracing for HIV Seropositives—A Year's Results," and J. E. Kristoffersen, "Case Contact Tracing and Testing in HIV Infection," all abstracts of papers presented at Stockholm Conference; see also Institute of Medicine, *Confronting AIDS, Update 1988*.

43 Sabatier, *AIDS and the Third World* (1988).

44 Marshall H. Becker and Jill G. Joseph, "Aids and Behavioral Change to Reduce Risk: A Review," *American Journal of Public Health*, April 1988; Office of Technology Assessment (OTA), U.S. Congress, *How Effective is AIDS Education?* Staff Paper, Washington, D.C., May 1988; Robert R. Stempel and Andrew R. Moss, "Changes in Sexual Behavior By Gay Men in Response to AIDS," abstract of paper presented at Stockholm Conference.

45 Rates in San Francisco from Dr. Warren Winklestein, School of Public Health, University of California, Berkeley, private communication, September 13, 1988; M. Paalman et al., "Condom Promotion in the Netherlands: Evaluation," abstract of paper presented at Stockholm Conference; Finland information from S. Valle, "The Occurrence of STD's in a Cohort of Homosexual Men Prior To and After Repeated Personal Counseling," abstract of paper presented at Stockholm Conference: C. A. Carne et al., "Prevalence of Antibodies to Human Immunodeficiency Virus, Gonorrhea Rates, and Changed Sexual Behavior in Homosexual Men in London," *The Lancet*, March 21, 1987; G. von Krogh et al., "Declining Incidence of Syphilis Among Homosexual Men in Stockholm," *The Lancet*, October 18, 1986, as cited in the Scriabine-Smith, unpublished manuscript; Asmus Poulsen and Susanne Ullman, "AIDS-Induced Decline of Incidence of Syphilis in Denmark," *Acta Dermata Vernereologica*, Vol. 65, No. 6, 1985, as cited in ibid.

46 R. R. Stempel et al., "Changes in Sexual Behavior by Gay Men in Response to AIDS," R. Stall et al., "Intravenous Drug Use, the Combination of Drugs and Sexual Activity and HIV Infection Among Gay and Bisexual Men: The San Francisco Men's Health Study," and M. Miller et al., "Relationships Between Knowledge About AIDS Risk and Actual Risk Behaviour in a Sample of Homosexual Men," all abstracts of papers presented at Stockholm Conference; Valle, "The Occurrence of STD's in a Cohort of Homosexual Men Prior To and After Repeated Personal Counseling." See also OTA, *How Effective is AIDS Education?* and C. Beeker et al., "Gay Male Sexual Behavior Change in a Low-Incidence Area for AIDS," abstract of paper presented at Stockholm Conference.

47 Treatment capacity for addicts from Dr. Roy Pickens, Associate Director for AIDS, National Institute on Drug Abuse, Rockville, Md., private communication, August 23, 1988; coupon data from Joyce F. Jackson, AIDS Community Support Unit, New Jersey Department of Health, Testimony before Presidential Commission, December 18, 1987.

48 OTA, *How Effective is AIDS Education?*

49 Pilot programs have been approved in New York City and Portland, Oregon, according to Don C. Des Jarlais, New York State Division of Substance Abuse Services, private communication, August 18, 1988.

50 Doug Lefton, "Nations Report on Needle Distribution," *American Medical News*, March 4, 1988; "European Countries Develop Programs to Fight AIDS," *AIDS Patient Care* (New York) June 1988; E. C. Buning, "The Evaluation of the Needle/Syringe Exchange in Amsterdam," abstract of paper presented at Stockholm Conference; decline in Dutch drug users from Lefton, "Nations Report."

51 *OTA, How Effective is AIDS Education?* three fourths figure from Des Jarlais et al., "HIV Infection and Intravenous Drug Use."

52 Centers for Disease Control (CDC), "Weekly Surveillance Report," Atlanta, Ga., August 1, 1988; 19 percent figure from Martha F. Rogers and Walter W. Williams, "Aids in Blacks and Hispanics: Implications for Prevention," *Issues in Science and Technology*, Spring 1987; rates for children and women from Dr. James Mason, Opening Address of the National Conference on the Prevention of HIV Infection and AIDS Among Racial and Ethnic Minorities in the United States, Washington, D.C., August 15, 1988.

53 "Needle Sharing and AIDS in Minorities," *Journal of the American Medical Association*, September 18, 1987; Rogers and Williams, "Aids in Blacks and Hispanics"; black HIV infection outside cities from Lytt I. Gardner et al., "Race Specific Trend Analysis of HIV Antibody Prevalence in the United States," abstract of paper presented at Stockholm Conference.

54 "CDC Spends Over $30 Million to Prevent HIV Infection Among Minorities at Risk," press release from CDC, Atlanta, Ga., September 6, 1988; fiscal year 1989 funding information from Debbie Mathis, Budget Office, CDC, Atlanta, Ga., private communication, October 21, 1988.

55 WHO, "Global Programme on AIDS: Proposed Pro-

gramme & Budget for 1989," Geneva, September 1988.

56 Tom Natter, Public Information Officer, WHO, Geneva, December 12, 1988; sub-Saharan countries from William Lyerly, Jr. et al., "Impact of Epidemiology and Demographic Patterns on Regional HIV/AIDS Control Strategies in Africa," abstract of paper presented at Arusha Conference.

57 "Kenyans Respond to Red Cross Alert," *People* (London), Vol. 14, No. 4, 1987; Susan Allen et al., "AIDS Education in Urban Rwanda: Change In Knowledge and Attitudes From 1986 to 1987," abstract of paper presented at Stockholm Conference; Edward C. Green, "AIDS and Condoms in the Dominican Republic: Evaluation of an AIDS Education Program," paper presented at the Annual Meeting of the American Association for the Advancement of Science, Boston, February 11, 1988.

58 Guatemala and Mexico examples from Kathryn Carovano, AIDSCOM project, Washington, D.C., private communication, August 30, 1988; Uganda example from Robin Le Mare, Ugandan desk officer, Action AID, London, U.K., private communication, September 16, 1988.

59 Infection rates from Quinn, "AIDS in Africa"; percentage of cases attributable to AIDS from Piot and Caraël, "Epidemiological and Sociological Aspects of HIV-infection."

60 "HIV Screening in the Americas," PAHO, Washington, D.C., unpublished mimeograph, January 19, 1988; "Strategy for Countrywide Screening of Blood Donors in Zambia," abstract of paper presented at Stockholm Conference; Zimbabwe from "A Specially Prepared Update of the Panos Dossier 'AIDS in the Third World'," London, unpublished mimeograph, October 1987; Mexico from Dr. Gonzales Pacheco, PAHO, Washington, D.C., private communication, August 15, 1988; new blood tests from T. C. Quinn et al., "A Rapid Enzyme Immunoassay for the Detection of Antibodies to HIV-1 and HIV-2," and from J. P. Galvin et al., "HIV-CHEK—A Sensitive, Rapid, Manual Test for the Detection of HIV Antibodies," abstracts of papers presented at Arusha Conference.

61 Malcolm Potts, "The Imperative Intervention: Targeting AIDS Control Activities Toward High-Risk Populations," unpublished discussion paper from Family Health International (FHI), Research Triangle Park, N.C., undated; B. Auvert et al., "Characteristics of the HIV Infection in Kinshasa as Determined By Computer Simulation," abstract of paper presented at London Conference.

62 Chin, private communication.

63 Ghana data from Sharon Weir, Program Coordinator of AIDSTECH, FHI, Research Triangle Park, N.C., private communication, August 29, 1988 (based on a pilot project conducted by FHI among 72 prostitutes between June 1987 and January 1988); Francis Plummer et al., "Durability of Changed Sexual Behavior in Nairobi Prostitutes: Increasing Use of Condoms," and E. Antonio De Moya and Ernesto Guerrero, "The Breaking of the Condom Use Taboo in the Dominican Republic," abstracts of papers presented at Stockholm Conference.

64 In mid-1988 the total population in Burundi, Central African Republic, Congo, Kenya, Rwanda, Tanzania, Uganda, Zaire, and Zambia was an estimated 122.1 million, according to the Population Reference Bureau, Washington, D.C. In these nine countries, women of childbearing age (15–49) constitute on average 22.5 percent of the total population, according to age distributions available in United Nations, *World Demographic Estimates and Projections, 1950–2025* (New York: 1988). Thus the total number of people needing condoms is 27.5 million. Condoms cost about 4.4¢ apiece and an average couple uses 100–144 per year, according to Carl Hemmer, Chief of Commodity and Program Support Division, AID, Washington, D.C., private communication, October 12, 1988. Shipping adds 20 percent to cost and subsidizing their sale through commercial channels adds another 70 percent, making total costs roughly $12 per couple, according to Jerald Bailey, Deputy Division Chief of Research, Office of Population, AID, Washington, D.C., private communication, October 12, 1988. Community-based distribution of programs that actively promoted condom use through education, advertising, and so on would cost considerably more.

65 W. Parker Mauldin and Sheldon J. Segal, *Prevalence of Contraceptive Use in Developing Countries: A Chart Book* (New York: Rockefeller Foundation, 1986); condom use in Africa applies to married women of reproductive age, from John W. Townsend and Luis Varela, The Population Council, Testimony before Presidential Commission, April 18, 1988.

66 Estimate of funding available for AIDS control in developing countries from Harris, private communication. No one has yet compiled data on funds available for AIDS control in the Third World so this number is necessarily a ballpark estimate. WHO's budget for AIDS control in 1988 was $66 million and AID gave an additional $15 million in bilateral aid. World military expenditure in 1987 from Sivard, *World Military and Social Expenditures, 1987–88.*

67 Harvey V. Fineberg, "The Social Dimensions of AIDS," *Scientific American*, October 1988.

68 Kenneth Presitt, "AIDS in Africa: The Triple Disaster," in Norman Miller and Richard C. Rockwell, eds., *AIDS in Africa: The Social and Policy Impact* (Lewiston, N.Y.: The Edwin Mellen Press, 1988).

69 Clare Ansberry, "AIDS, Stirring Panic and Prejudice, Tests the Nation's Character," *Wall Street Journal,* November 13, 1987; Colombian example from Sarita Kendall, "Latin American Conference Increases AIDS Awareness," AIDS Watch No. 1, 1988, supplement to *People* (London).

70 For an excellent discussion of these issues, see Sabatier, *Blaming Others.*

71 Dr. Jonathan Mann, "Worldwide Epidemiology of AIDS," Address to London Conference; "London Declaration on AIDS Prevention," World Summit of Ministers of Health on Programmes for AIDS Prevention, January 28, 1988; *Report of Presidential Commission.*

72 Fineberg, "Social Dimensions of AIDS"; Ghana example from "Family Planners Define Their Role in Preventing Viral Spread," *New Scientist*, July 21, 1988.

73 Bill Keller, "New Soviet Law Makes AIDS Testing Mandatory," *New York Times*, August 27, 1987.

[74] Bulgaria from Sophia Miskiewicz, "AIDS in Eastern Europe and the Soviet Union," Radio Free Europe Research Report No. 24, February 23, 1987; registration of addicts from United Press International, B Wire, Moscow Bureau, "Soviet Scientist Says 'Positive Results' in AIDS Research," February 11, 1987; Poland from Radio Free Europe Research Report, Poland No. 3, February 19, 1986; all broadcasts cited in Scriabine-Smith, unpublished manuscript.

[75] Bloom and Carliner, "Economic Impact of AIDS in the United States."

[76] New York hospital bed data from Paul S. Jellinek, "Case-Managing AIDS," *Issues in Science and Technology*, Summer 1988; San Francisco funds for AIDS form Mona J. Rowe and Caitlin C. Ryan, "Comparing State-Only Expenditure for AIDS," *American Journal of Public Health*, April 1988; New York data from Robert Blake, Budget Officer, New York City Budget Office, private communication, September 13, 1988; cost per resident from Bloom and Carliner, "Economic Impact of AIDS in the United States."

[77] Bloom and Carliner, "Economic Impact of AIDS in the United States"; P. S. Arno and R. G. Hughes, "Local Policy Response to the AIDS Epidemic: New York and San Francisco," *New York State Journal of Medicine*, May 1987; Robert T. Chen et al. "Hospital Utilization by Persons with AIDS in San Francisco, January 1984–June 1987," abstract of paper presented at Stockholm Conference; Ian Douglas Campbell, "AIDS Care and Prevention in a Zambian Rural Community," paper presented at London Conference.

DISCUSSION QUESTIONS

1. What is the extent of the AIDS epidemic in the world and why do you think some nations are harder hit by this epidemic than others?

2. Why is it that cases of AIDS are likely to be underreported in Third World nations? What would be the political and economic implications if all cases were reported to authorities?

3. Heise describes AIDS as a "social crucible." What does she mean by this expression?

PART 5

Social Environments

CHAPTER 15

Issues in City and Community

INTRODUCTION

Nothing better exemplifies modern society than the city itself. Before 1850, only about 2 percent of the world's people lived in cities with populations of over 100,000. Today, most people in the United States live in metropolitan areas. There is even a new term, *megalopolis*, which describes areas in which two or more cities have merged, simply because they have grown so large. The result has often been battles between suburbs and cities, and between adjoining metropolises, for control of resources.

Such changes are, of course, not limited to the United States. Throughout the world there has been a massive shift to urban life. There are many reasons for this shift, including population growth, economic changes, and the expansion of jobs and opportunities in urban areas. Because of the accelerated pace of growth, many cities cannot handle the populations residing within their boundaries. Calcutta, Port-Au-Prince, and Cairo are examples of cities that have great difficulty in caring for their residents.

Sociologists have developed models of what cities look like in order to better understand them. One model, called the *concentric zone*, looks at the city as a series of rings with the business district at its center. Another scheme, the *sector zone*, analyzes the city in terms of transportation routes. A third model, the *multiple nuclei model*, divides the city into different nuclei. All these models are useful, depending on which city is under consideration, but perhaps the most useful is *social area analysis*, which looks at changes taking place in society at large and how they influence the use of land in urban areas.

A major issue in urban sociology has been whether urbanization is good or bad. When we hear the word "city," what often comes to mind first is an impression of slums, crowding, crime, and alienation—and yet, there are also clear-cut advantages to living in a large metropolis. Some of the advantages are anonymity, variety, economic and social opportunities, and the freedom to do what one pleases without having others constantly looking over one's shoulder. Moreover, many urban dwellers find a sense of community in their own neighborhoods. They may form clubs and associations based on ethnic groups or simply on the fact that they live on a particular block. Herbert Gans has beautifully portrayed the richness of such life in his writing on Italians living in Boston (1982). Nevertheless, the problems faced by decaying urban areas are of great significance. The crime, drugs, and general poverty associated with such areas threaten to affect not only their residents but also those who live in more affluent suburbs and rural areas. Thus, the city's problems are, quite literally, everyone's problems.

Perhaps the most important question is: what will be the future of our cities? In other words, can they be saved and revitalized, or are they doomed to deterioration and decay? In the case of the United States, some people believe that eventually the migration of businesses and factories to the South and West will slow down as the costs of operating industries equalize. The expectation is that the same companies that have been leaving will someday return to the now-depressed Midwest and Northeast. Adherents of this position cite the renovation that has gone on in cities such as New York; Washington, D.C.; and San Francisco in recent years.

Other people disagree, citing gentrification of neighborhoods and displacement of their former residents as evidence that the city can serve only the yuppie community. Emphasis upon how young urban professionals benefit from city life obscures the fact that many city people are compelled to live in substandard housing, because they would have to have public housing to satisfy their needs and such housing is often not readily available.

Changing the tax system so that it will assess people in an entire region of suburbs and inner cities has been proposed as a way of increasing the cities' piece of the pie. Such proposals have been met with considerable resistance from people who left the city and no longer identify with, or even need it. Another idea has been greater involvement on the part of the private sector, but these programs, while they result in improvements in the city as a whole, have not always benefited the poor. These and other approaches offer hope for the future, but that future is, at this point, still uncertain.

In the first essay, one of the most prominent sociologists in the United States, William Julius Wilson, challenges what is often taken as a given. He argues that problems in the inner city cannot be explained simply in terms of whites' prejudice and discrimination against blacks. Nor is there, in his view, a "culture of poverty" thesis that could account for most problems related to urban life. Rather, inner-city problems stem from complex sociological dilemmas and are often related to demographic and economic factors. Since Wilson stresses the problems of social dislocation in the inner city in terms of cultural and structural changes in the economy and migration patterns, his approach illustrates the first level of analysis. Central to his argument is an analysis of migration patterns within this country and how they have affected the cities themselves.

The second selection focuses on the individual level. It is a moving account of the life of Carolina Maria De Jesus, who lived in a shack in Sao Paulo, Brazil. After a background explanation by the translator of her diary, we turn to an excerpt from de Jesus' diary. She talks about hunger in a way that makes us appreciate our own good fortune. We see that the residents of the *favela*, or slum, still hope and dream of a better life, even as they despair of ever reaching it. Her message is both eloquent and sad.

The last contribution in this chapter is by Hoda Sobhi, an Egyptian scholar who specializes in problems of urbanization. His subject is Cairo. The discussion focuses on the twin problems of surplus labor in the city and the ever-growing demand for services in large cities. Sobhi makes an argument for a national urban strategy, because urban concerns are directly related to the welfare of the country, in this case Egypt, as a whole. This is especially true in developing countries like Egypt, which is highly urbanized and has a high degree of geographical centralism. Since Cairo is the epitome of the large city in the Middle East and Africa, an urban-biased approach is absolutely necessary for Egypt.

References

Gans, Herbert J. *The Urban Villagers: Group and Class in the Life of Italian Americans.* New York: The Free Press, 1982, augmented edition.

Lieberson, Stanley. *A Piece of the Pie: Black and White Immigrants Since 1880.* Berkeley: University of California Press, 1981.

Suttles, Gerald D. *The Social Order of the Slum.* Chicago: University of Chicago Press, 1968.

Weber, Max. *The City.* New York: The Free Press, 1958.

Inner-City Dislocations

William Julius Wilson

The social problems of urban life in advanced industrial America are, in large measure, viewed as problems of race. Joblessness, urban crime, addiction, out-of-wedlock births, female-headed families, and welfare dependency have risen dramatically in the past several decades. Moreover, . . . these rates reflect an amazingly uneven distribution by race. These problems are heavily concentrated in urban areas, but it would be a mistake to assume that they afflict all segments of the urban minority community. Rather, . . . they disproportionately plague the urban underclass—a heterogeneous grouping of families and individuals in the inner city that are outside the mainstream of the American occupational system and that consequently represent the very bottom of the economic hierarchy. It is my view that the increasing rates of social dislocation in the inner city cannot be explained simply in terms of racial discrimination or in terms of a "culture of poverty," but should be viewed as having complex and interrelated sociological antecedents, ranging from demographic changes to the problems of societal organization.

Racial discrimination is the most frequently invoked explanation of racial variation in certain forms or urban social dislocation. Proponents of the discrimination thesis, however, often fail to make a distinction between the effects of historical discrimination and the effects of contemporary discrimination.

There is no doubt that contemporary discrimination has contributed to or aggravated the social and economic problems of the black poor. But is discrimination greater today than it was in 1948, when black unemployment (5.9%) was less than half the rate in 1980 (12.3%), and when the black/white unemployment ratio (1.7) was almost a quarter less than the ratio in 1980 (2.1)? There are obviously many reasons for the higher levels of black joblessness since the mid-1950s, but to suggest contemporary discrimination as the main factor is, as I shall soon show, to obscure the impact of major demographic and economic changes and to leave unanswered the question of why black unemployment was lower not after, but prior to, the mid-1950s.

It should also be pointed out that, contrary to prevailing opinion, the black family showed signs of deterioration not before, but after, the mid-twentieth century. Until the publication of Herbert Gutman's impressive historical study of the black family, it had been widely assumed that the contemporary problems of the black family could be traced back to slavery. Gutman, however, produced data demonstrating that the black family was not particularly disorganized either during slavery or during the early years of their first migration to the urban North, thereby suggesting that the present problems of black family disorganization are a product of more recent forces. But are these problems mainly a consequence of contemporary discrimination, or are they related to other factors that ostensibly have little to do with race? If contemporary discrimination is the main culprit, why have its nefarious effects produced the most severe problems of inner-city social dislocation—including joblessness—during the *1970s*, a decade that followed an unprecedented period of antidiscrimination legislation and that ushered in the proliferation of affirmative-action programs.

To repeat, the problem is to unravel the effects of contemporary discrimination, on the one hand, and historical discrimination, on the other. Even if all contemporary discrimination were eliminated, the problems of social dislocation in the inner city would persist for many years, until the effects of historical discrimination disappeared. However, a full appreciation of the legacy of historical discrimination is impossible without taking into account other historical and contemporary forces that have helped shape the experiences and behavior of impoverished urban minorities.

One of the major consequences of historical discrimination is the presence of a large black underclass in our central cities, plagued by problems of joblessness and other forms of social dislocation. Whereas blacks made up 23 percent of the population of central cities in 1977, they constituted 46 percent of the poor in those cities. In accounting for the historical developments that contributed to this concentration of urban black poverty, I will draw briefly upon Stanley Lieberson's recent and original study *A Piece of the Pie: Black and White Immigrants since 1880*. On the basis of a systematic analysis of early U.S. censuses and various other data sources, Lieberson showed that in many areas of life, including the labor market, blacks in the early twentieth century were discriminated against far more severely than the new immigrants from Southern, Central, and Eastern Europe. However, be cautious against attributing this solely to racial bias. The disadvantage of skin color—the fact that the dominant white population preferred whites over nonwhites—is one that blacks have certainly shared with the Chinese, Japanese, American Indians, and other nonwhite groups. Nonetheless, even though blacks have experienced greater discrimination, the contrast with the Asians does reveal that skin color per se was "not an insurmountable obstacle." Indeed, Lieberson argues that the greater success enjoyed by Asians may well be explained largely by the different context of their contact with whites. Because changes in immigration policy cut off Asian migration to America in the late-nineteenth and earlier-twentieth century, the Japanese and Chinese populations—in sharp

contrast to blacks—did not reach large numbers and therefore did not pose as great a threat to the white population. Lieberson concedes that the "response of whites to Chinese and Japanese was of the same violent and savage character in areas where they were concentrated," but he also notes that "the threat was quickly stopped through changes in immigration policy."

Furthermore, the discontinuation of large-scale immigration from Japan and China enabled these groups to solidify networks of ethnic contact and to occupy particular occupational niches. The 1970 census records 22,580,000 blacks and only 435,000 Chinese and 591,000 Japanese. "Imagine," Lieberson exclaims, "22 million Japanese Americans trying to carve out initial niches through truck farming!"

THE IMPORTANCE OF MIGRANT FLOWS

If different population sizes accounted for a good deal of the difference in the economic success of blacks versus Asians, they also helped determine the dissimilar rates of progress of urban blacks and the new Europeans. The dynamic factor behind these differences, and perhaps the most important single contributor to the varying rates of urban ethnic progress in the twentieth century, is the flow of migrants. Changes in U.S. policy first halted Asian immigration to America and then curtailed the new European immigration. However, black migration to the urban North continued in substantial numbers several decades after the new European immigration had ceased. Accordingly, the percentage of northern blacks who are recent migrants substantially exceeds the dwindling percentage of Europeans who are recent migrants.

In this connection, Lieberson theorizes that the changes in race relations that accompany shifts in racial composition are not caused by any radical alteration in white dispositions but, rather, that shifts in composition activate dispositions that were present all along. "In other words," writes Lieberson, "there is a latent structure to the race relations pattern in a given setting, with only certain parts of this structure observed at a given time." The sizable and continuous migration of blacks from the South to the North, coupled with the cessation of immigration from Eastern, Central, and Southern Europe, created a situation in which other whites muffled their negative disposition toward the new Europeans and focused antagonism toward blacks. In the words of Lieberson, "the presence of blacks made it harder to discriminate against the new Europeans because the alternative was viewed less favorably."

The flow of migrants made it much more difficult for blacks to follow the path of the Asians and new Europeans, who had overcome the negative effects of discrimination by finding special occupational niches. Only a small percentage of a group's total work force can be absorbed in such specialties when the group's population increases rapidly or is a sizable proportion of the total population. Furthermore, the flow of migrants had a harmful effect on the earlier-arriving or longer-standing black residents of the North. Lieberson insightfully points out that

> sizable numbers of newcomers raise the level of ethnic and/or racial consciousness on the part of others in the city; moreover, if these newcomers are less able to compete for more desirable positions than are the longer-standing residents, they will tend to undercut the position of other members of the group. This is because the older residents and those of higher socioeconomic status cannot totally avoid the newcomers, although they work at it through subgroup residential isolation. Hence, there is some deterioration in the quality of residential areas, schools, and the like for those earlier residents who might otherwise enjoy more fully the re-

wards of their mobility. Beyond this, from the point of view of the dominant outsiders, the newcomers may reinforce stereotypes and negative dispositions that affect all members of the group.

In sum, because substantial black migration to the North continued several decades after the new European and Asian migration ceased, urban blacks, having their ranks constantly replenished with poor migrants, found it much more difficult to follow the path of the new Europeans and the Asian immigrants in overcoming the effects of discrimination. The net result is that as the nation entered the last quarter century, its large urban areas continued to have a disproportionate concentration of poor blacks who, as I shall show, have been especially vulnerable to recent structural changes in the economy.

It should also be emphasized, however, that black migration to urban areas has been minimal in recent years. Indeed, between 1970 and 1977, blacks actually experienced a net out-migration of 653,000 from the central cities. In most large cities, the number of blacks increased only moderately; in some, in fact, the number declined. As the demographer Philip Hauser pointed out, increases in the urban black population during the 1970s were "mainly due to births." This would indicate that, for the first time in the twentieth century, the ranks of blacks in our central cities are no longer being replenished by poor migrants. This strongly suggests, other things being equal, that urban blacks will experience a steady decrease in joblessness, crime, out-of-wedlock births, single-parent homes, and welfare dependency. In other words, just as the Asian and new European immigrants benefited from a cessation of migration, there is now reason to expect that the cessation of black migration will help to upgrade urban black communities. In making this observation, however, I am in no way overlooking other factors that affect the differential rate of ethnic progress at different periods of time, such as structural changes in the economy, population size, and discrimination. Nonetheless, one of the many obstacles to urban black advancement—the constant flow of migrants—has been removed.

Hispanics, on the other hand, appear to be migrating to urban centers in increasing numbers. The status of Hispanics vis-à-vis other ethnic groups is not entirely clear because there are no useful figures for 1970 on their type of residence. But data collected since 1974 indicate that their numbers are increasing rapidly in central cities, as a consequence of immigration as well as births. Indeed, in several large cities (including New York, Los Angeles, San Francisco, San Diego, Phoenix, and Denver) Hispanics apparently outnumber black Americans. Accordingly, the rapid growth of the Hispanic population in urban areas, accompanied by the opposite trend for black Americans, could contribute significantly to different outcomes for these two groups in the last two decades of the twentieth century. Specifically, whereas blacks could very well experience a decrease in their rates of joblessness, crime, out-of-wedlock births, single-parent homes, and welfare dependency, Hispanics could show a steady increase in each of these problems. Moreover, whereas blacks could experience a decrease in the ethnic hostility directed toward them, Hispanics, with their increasing visibility, could become victims of increasing ethnic antagonism. . . .

In short, recent increases in crime, out-of-wedlock births, female-headed homes, and welfare dependency are related to the explosion in numbers of young people, especially among minorities. However, as James Q. Wilson pointed out in his analysis of the proliferation of social problems in the 1960s, a decade of general economic prosperity, changes in the age structure of the population cannot alone account for the social dislocations

in those years. Wilson argues, for instance, that from 1960 to 1970 the rate of serious crime in the District of Columbia increased by more than 400 percent, heroin addiction by more than 1,000 percent, welfare rates by 100 percent, and unemployment rates by 100 percent, yet the number of young persons between 16 and 21 years of age increased by only 32 percent. Also, the number of murders in Detroit increased from 100 in 1960 to 500 in 1971, "yet the number of young persons did not quintuple."

Wilson, drawing from published research, notes that the "increase in the murder rate during the 1960s was more than ten times greater than what one would have expected from the changing age structure of the population alone," and that "only 13.4 percent of the increase in arrests for robbery between 1950 and 1965 could be accounted for by the increase in the numbers of persons between the ages of ten and twenty-four." Speculating on this problem, Wilson advances the hypothesis that the abrupt increase in the number of young persons had an "exponential effect on the rate of certain social problems." In other words, there may be a "critical mass" of young persons such that when that mass is reached or is increased suddenly and substantially, "a self-sustaining chain reaction is set off that creates an explosive increase in the amount of crime, addiction, and welfare dependency."

This hypothesis seems to be especially relevant to densely populated inner-city neighborhoods, especially those with large public housing projects. The 1937 United States Housing Act provided federal money for the construction of housing for the poor. But, as Roncek and colleagues pointed out in a recent article in *Social Problems*, opposition from organized community groups trying to prevent public housing contruction in their neighborhoods "led to massive, segregated housing projects, which become ghettos for minorities and the economically disadvantaged." As large poor families were placed in high-density housing projects in the inner city, both family and neighborhood life suffered. Family deterioration, high crime rates, and vandalism flourished in these projects. In St. Louis, for example, the Pruitt-Igoe project, which housed about 10,000 children and adults developed serious problems only five years after it opened and became so unlivable that it was closed in 1976, less than a quarter-century after it was built. . . .

ECONOMIC CHANGES AND ETHNIC CULTURE

Problems of social dislocation in the inner city have also been profoundly exacerbated by recent structural changes in the economy. Indeed, the population explosion among young minorities in recent years occurred at a time when changes in the economy are posing serious problems for unskilled workers, both in and out of the labor force.

Urban minorities are particularly vulnerable to structural economic changes: the shift from goods-producing to service-producing industries, the increasing segmentation of the labor market, the growing use of industrial technology, and the relocation of manufacturing industries out of the central cities. Such economic changes serve to remind us, as John Kasarda notes in this issue, that for several decades America's urban areas have been undergoing what appears to be an irreversible structural transformation—from centers of production and distribution of material goods to centers of administration, information exchange, finance, trade, and government services. This process has effectively eliminated millions of manufacturing, wholesale, and retail jobs since 1948, a process that has accelerated since 1967. At the same time, there has been an increase in "postindustrial society" occupational positions that usually require levels of training and education beyond the reach of disadvantaged inner-city residents. These

changing employment patterns have accompanied shifts in the demographic composition of our central cities—from predominantly European white to predominantly black, Hispanic, and other minorities—leading to a decrease both in the total population size of the central cities and in aggregate personal-income levels.

The cumulative effect of these technological-employment and population changes, as Kasarda points out, has been a growing mismatch between the level of skill or training of city residents and the formal prerequisites for urban jobs. Thus we have deeper "ghettoization," solidification of high levels of urban poverty, increased institutional problems in the inner city (e.g., the declining quality of public schools, poorer municipal services), and a rise in such social dislocations as joblessness, crime, single-parent homes, and welfare dependency.

The changes brought about by the cessation of migration to the central cities and by the sharp drop in the number of black children under age 13 seem to make it more likely that the economic situation of urban blacks as a group will noticeably improve in the near future. However, the present problems of black joblessness are so overwhelming (less than 30 percent of all black-male teenagers and only 62 percent of all black young-adult males [ages 20 to 24] were employed in 1978) that perhaps only an extraordinary program of economic reform can possibly prevent a significant segment of the urban underclass from being permanently locked out of the mainstream of the American occupational system.

In focusing on different explanations of the social dislocation in the inner city, I have yet to say anything about the role of ethnic culture. Even after considering racial discrimination, migrant flows, changes in ethnic demography, and structural changes in the economy, a number of readers will still maintain that ethnic cultural differences account in large measure for the disproportionate and rising rates of social dislocation in the inner city. But any cultural explanation of group behavioral differences must deal with, among other things, the often considerable variation within groups on several aspects of behavior. For example, whereas only 7 percent of urban black families having incomes of $25,000 or more in 1978 were headed by women, 85 percent of those having incomes below $4,000 were headed by women. The higher the economic position of black families, the greater the percentage of two-parent households. Moreover, the proportion of black children born out of wedlock (See Diana Pearce's article in this issue) is partly a function of the sharp decrease in fertility among married blacks (i.e., two-parent families) who have a higher economic status in the black community. By treating blacks and other ethnics as monolithic groups, we lose sight of the fact that *high-income* blacks, Hispanics, and Indians have *even fewer* children than their counterparts in the general population.

Nonetheless, in the face of some puzzling facts concerning rates of welfare and crime in the 1960s, the cultural explanation seems to hold validity for some observers. From the Great Depression to 1960, for example, unemployment accounted in large measure for welfare dependency. During this period, the correlation between the nonwhite-male unemployment and the rate of new AFDC cases was very nearly perfect. As the nonwhite-male unemployment rate increased, the rate of new AFDC cases increased; as the former decreased, the latter correspondingly decreased. Commenting on this relationship in his book *The Politics of a Guaranteed Income*, Daniel P. Moynihan stated that "the correlation was among the strongest known to social science. It could not be established that the men who lost their jobs were the ones who left their families, but the mathematical relationship of the two statistical series—unemployment rates and new AFDC cases—was astonishingly close." However, the relationship suddenly

began to weaken at the beginning of the 1960s, had vanished by 1963, and had completely reversed itself by the end of the decade—a steady decline in the rate of nonwhite-male unemployment and a steady increase in the number of new AFDC cases.

Some observers quickly seized on these figures. Welfare dependency, they argued, had become a cultural trait; even during an economic upswing, welfare rates among minorities were increasing. Upon closer inspection, though, one sees that even though nonwhite-male unemployment did drop during the 1960s, the percentage of nonwhite males who dropped out of the labor force increased steadily throughout the decade, thereby maintaining the association between economic dislocation and welfare dependency. The importance of labor-force participation in explaining certain types of social problems was also demonstrated in a recent empirical study relating labor-market opportunities to the increasing rate of crime among youths, reported in the *Journal of Political Economy*:

> The labor force/not-in-the-labor-force formulation has greater explanatory power than the non-working formulation, demonstrating the importance of participation rates relative to unemployment rates in explaining crime rates. This point is reinforced when one observes that during the middle and latter sixties, crime rates rose while unemployment rates declined. It is the decline in the participation rate which provides an explanation of the rise in crime during this period. . . .

Adaptive responses to recurrent situations take the form of behavior patterns, norms, and aspirations. As economic and social opportunities change, new behavioral solutions originate, form patterns, and are later upheld and complemented by norms. If new conditions emerge, both the behavior patterns and the norms eventually undergo change. As Herbert Gans has put it: "some behavioral norms are more persistent than others, but over the long run, all of the norms and aspirations by which people live are nonpersistent: they rise and fall with changes in situations."

ALLIES NEEDED

To suggest that changes in social and economic situations will bring about changes in behavior patterns and norms raises the issue of public policy: how to deal effectively with the social dislocations that have plagued the urban underclass over the past several decades. Space does not permit a detailed discussion of public policy and social dislocations in the inner city, but it must be emphasized that any significant reduction of inner-city joblessness, and of the related problems of crime, out-of-wedlock births, single-parent homes, and welfare dependency, will call for a program of socioeconomic reform far more comprehensive than what Americans have usually regarded as appropriate or desirable.

A shift away from the convenient focus on "racism" would probably result in a greater appreciation and understanding of the complex factors that account for recent increases in the social dislocations of the inner city. Although discrimination undoubtedly still contributes to these problems, in the past twenty years they have been more profoundly affected by shifts in the American economy that have both produced massive joblessness among low-income urban minorities and exacerbated conditions stemming from historical discrimination, the continuous flow of migrants to the large metropolises, changes in the urban-minority age structure, and population changes in the central city. For all these reasons, the urban underclass has not significantly benefited from race-specific policy programs (e.g., affirmative action) that are designed only to combat discrimination. Indeed, the economic and social plight of the underclass calls for public policies that benefit all the poor, not just poor minorities. I have in

mind policies that address the broader, and more difficult to confront, problems of societal organization, including the problems of generating full employment, achieving effective welfare reform, and developing a comprehensive economic policy to promote sustained and balanced urban economic growth. Unless these problems are seriously addressed, we have little hope that public policy can significantly reduce social dislocation in the inner city.

I am reminded, in this connection, of Bayard Rustin's plea in the early 1960s—that blacks ought recognize the importance of *fundamental* economic reform and the need for an effective and broad-based interracial coalition to achieve it. It is evident—more now than at any time in the last half of the twentieth century—that blacks and other minorities will need allies to effect a program of reform that can improve the conditions of the underclass. And since an effective political coalition will partly depend upon how the issues are defined, the political message must underscore the need for socioeconomic reform that benefits *all* groups in society. Civil rights organizations, as one important example, will have to change or expand their definition of racial problems in America and broaden the scope of their policy recommendations. They would, of course, continue to stress the immediate goal of eliminating racial discrimination; but they will have to recognize that low-income minorities are also profoundly affected by problems in social organization that go beyond race (such as structural changes in the economy) and that the dislocations which follow often include increased joblessness, rising crime, family deterioration, and welfare dependency.

Readings Suggested by the Author:

Gans, Herbert. "Culture and Class in the Study of Poverty." In Daniel P. Moynihan, ed., *On Understanding Poverty: Perspectives for the Social Sciences*. New York: Basic Books, 1968.

Lieberson, Stanley. *A Piece of the Pie: Black and White Immigrants since 1880.* Berkeley: University of California Press, 1981.

Steinberg, Stephen. *The Ethnic Myth: Race, Ethnicity, and Class in America.* New York: Atheneum, 1981.

Wilson, James Q. *Thinking about Crime.* New York: Basic Books, 1971.

DISCUSSION QUESTIONS

1. Do you agree with Wilson's thesis? Why or why not?

2. If migration into large urban centers can have destructive effects on the city and its social services, do you think large cities should control migration, as the United States controls immigration into the country?

3. Compare the problems of U.S. inner cities with those of Cairo.

READING 15-2

Child of the Dark

Carolina Maria de Jesus
David St. Clair, Translator

TRANSLATOR'S PREFACE

July 15, 1955. The birthday of my daughter Vera Eunice. I wanted to buy a pair of shoes for her, but the price of food keeps us from realizing our desires. Actually we are slaves to the cost of living. I found a pair of shoes in the garbage, washed them, and patched them for her to wear.

Thus begins this book, the diary of a simple uneducated slum Negress that has been called by critics "possibly one of the best books to come from a Brazilian in this century."

Carolina is a product of her time and is acutely aware of the time and the way her life is moving. She writes of contemporary society and its impact around her. She has not tried to be artistic—just sincere.

Brazil is a modern paradox. Discovered by the Portuguese sea captain Pedro Álvares Cabral in 1500 (just eight years after Columbus), the land was turned into a colony of the King, who promptly started taking things out of it rather than putting things in. Not as ruthless as the Spanish in Peru (possibly because there were no golden Inca-like cities), the Portuguese merely put the Indians to work on their huge sugar and cocoa plantations. Spices and rich woods had to be exported to luxury-loving Lisbon, and when the Indians died off because of the heavy work, Portugal raided the coast of Africa and brought in thousands of Negro slaves.

The colony prospered and the shoreline sprang up with cities rich with gilt churches and baroque slave blocks. When the emperor Dom João VI decided to move the capital from easily sacked Bahia to Rio de Janeiro in 1763, the wealth and the culture moved with him.

But it was always along the coast. The interior remained virgin and unexploited. There were those that looked for rubber along the banks of the Amazon, or those that dug diamonds and amethysts in Minas Gerais, but Brazil was too big (actually larger than the continental United States) and what little industry was available settled into easy living along the pleasant tropical coast.

Slaves were freed in 1888 and Brazil became a republic with equal rights for all. Equal rights and freedom meant the Negro had to work for his daily ration of beans and rice, and the work was in the cities.

But the work wasn't there. Not for all of them anyway, and those who couldn't find work settled on low unwanted swamplands in São Paulo or on high hills in Rio and built their shacks. Thus the *favelas*, the slums, began.

The north of Brazil is dry. When the great droughts hit every two years or so, hundreds die of thirst. Cattle wander in circles looking for water and their rotting carcasses are picked apart by the vultures. The northern farmer (*nordestino*) sees his family decimated. He remembers tales of famine and abject poverty from his father and grandfather. So when the droughts hit he bundles his family and his few possessions into an open truck and takes the long hot dusty journey to Rio or São Paulo. There, there should be work. There, there should be abundant food and water. There, there should be opportunity.

There is. But not for the uneducated and unskilled. Shops and offices will not hire a man who cannot write his own name or speak correct Portuguese. Factories can't be bothered with illiterate men who have only agricultural experience, and it takes too long to train them. So the distraught father looks around for a place to put his family until things get better. He has no money. He has no friends. He finds a place in a favela. In Rio there are 200 favelas with a population of 337,500 souls, a 99 per cent increase over the 1950 census. In São Paulo (where work has been more plentiful these past few years) there are only seven favelas, with 50,000 living there. They grow and grow and grow until they are small cities of filth, perversion, and prostitution.

The local governments do nothing about them. Some churches and charities try to help but the problem is staggering and heartbreaking. Each year more and more people are forced to the favelas as they search for work in the cities. Erasing the cancerous growths is not the answer. It would be like trying to kill a tree by pulling off its leaves. The real solution is industrialization of the underdeveloped areas, so the distraught fathers would not have to come to the cities in the first place.

Politicians make big promises to the *favelados*. They're going to do all sorts of things if elected. But once elected they forget about their problem children and spend their time thinking of pleasanter things.

This breeds discontent among the people. And discontent breeds Communism. Middle- and upper-class Brazilians look with growing fear upon this powerful mass of the hungry in the heart of their two richest cities. If there should appear a Brazilian Fidel Castro, and if he should give these hungry illiterates guns. . . .

Carolina Maria de Jesus came to the favela of Canindé in 1947. She was unemployed and pregnant. No one wanted her. Her lover had abandoned her and the white family where she worked as a maid refused to let her in the house. She was desperate and turned to the favela. Carrying boards on her head from the construction site of a church five miles away, she built a shack, roofed it with flattened tin cans and cardboard. Three months later her son João was born. Then began the fight for survival that only ceased with the publication of her diary.

Carolina was born in 1913 in the little town of Sacramento in the state of Minas Gerais, in the interior of Brazil. Her mother, an unmarried farm hand, was worried about her daughter having the same kind of life and insisted that Carolina attend school. The little girl hated it, and every morning her mother practically had to spank her all the way to the one-room building. It was only when she learned to read, three months after opening day, that she enjoyed her education.

It was a Wednesday, and when I left school I saw a paper with some writing on it. It was an announcement of the local movie house. "Today. Pure Blood. Tom Mix." I shouted happily—"I can read! I can read!"

She wandered through the streets reading aloud the labels in the drugstore window and the names of the stores.

For the next two years Carolina was first in her class. Then her mother got a better job on a farm far away from Sacramento and Carolina had to give up her beloved school. She never went back. Her education stopped at the second grade.

Her first days in the country were spent crying, but with time she began to appreciate the beauties of nature: trees, birds, creeks, silence. The miracle of seeds especially intrigued the girl. But when she was completely at home in the country her mother moved again, this time to the city of Franca near São Paulo. Carolina was sixteen years old. She got a job in a hospital, ran away to sing in a circus, sold beer and cleaned hotel rooms. Then she wandered to the big city of São Paulo. She slept under bridges and in doorways, until she got a job as maid in a white family. "But I was too independent and didn't like to clean up their messes. Besides I used to slip out of the house at night and make love. After four months they fired me." Six more jobs and six more dismissals ended with the discovery that she was pregnant. "He was a Portuguese sailor, and he got on his ship fast when I told him I was going to have a baby."

Carolina built her shack like the others there. When it rained the water came in the roof, rotting her one mattress and rusting the few pots and pans. There was a sack over the window that she'd pull for privacy and late at night she would light a small kerosene lamp "and cover my nose with a rag to take away some of the favela stench."

With a baby she couldn't get work. He had to be looked after constantly. She heard that junk yards paid for scrap paper and so, strapping her tiny son to her back, she walked the streets of rich São Paulo looking for trash. She filled a burlap bag with everything she could find, and foraged in rich houses' garbage cans for bits of food and old clothes. Usually by noon she would have enough paper to sell. She got one cruzeiro (about one-fourth of a U.S. cent) per pound. "On good days I would make twenty-five or thirty cents. Some days I made nothing."

Carolina was attractive and liked men and so two years later a Spaniard "who was white and gave me love and money" went back to Europe and her second son José Carlos was born. Life continued as it was, collecting paper, ransacking garbage cans, but now with two children clinging to her. In 1943 "I met a rich white man who thought I was pretty. I would visit him and he would give me food and money to buy clothes for my sons. He didn't know for a long time that I bore his daughter. He has many servants and I guess that's where Vera Eunice gets her fancy ways."

With three children to raise life became torture. "How horrible it is to see your children eat and then ask: 'Is there more?' This word 'more' bounces inside a mother's head as she searches the cooking pot knowing there isn't any more."

In order to keep from thinking about her troubles she started to write. Poems, novels, plays, "anything and everything, for when I was writing I was in a golden palace, with crystal windows and silver chandeliers. My dress was finest satin and diamonds sat shining in my black hair. Then, I put away my book and the smells came in through the rotting walls and rats ran over my feet. My satin turned to rags and the only things shining in my hair were lice."

After a day of carrying paper her arms and back would ache so that she couldn't sleep. "I would lie on the bed and start to worry about the next day. I knew there was no bread in the house and that Vera needed a pair of shoes. I was so nervous about my children that many times I'd vomit, but there was nothing there but bile. Then I'd get up, light the lamp, and write." Her notebooks were those she found in the trash, writing on the clean side of the page with a treasured fountain pen, making slow even letters.

Her neighbors knew of her writings and made fun of them. Most of them couldn't even read, but thought she should be doing other things with her spare time than writing and saving old notebooks. They called her "Dona" (Madame) Carolina. Because of her standoffish ways she was accused of causing trouble, sleeping with everyone's husband, and calling the police each time there was a fight. Her children were stoned and charged with stealing by the neighbors. Once in a jealous rage, because Carolina wouldn't attend a drunken party-orgy, a woman filed a complaint against her son João, who was then eleven, claiming he had raped her two-year-old daughter. Carolina's life was miserable but she refused to lower the standards she had set for herself and her children and mingle with those she couldn't stand.

She had as little as possible to do with her neighbors. She hated standing at the city-installed water spigot waiting to fill her can and hated haggling with the *favelado* who had the only electric line in the section and made a living running wires from his box to neighbors' shacks and illegally charging for the electricity.

In April of 1958, Audalio Dantas, a young reporter, was covering the inauguration of a playground near Canindé for his newspaper. When the politicians had made their speeches and gone away, the grown men of the favela began fighting with the children for a place on the teetertotters and swings. Carolina, standing in the crowd, shouted furiously: "If you continue mistreating these children, I'm going to put all your names in my book!"

Interested, the reporter asked the tall black woman about her book. At first she didn't want to talk to him, but slowly he won her confidence and she took him to her shack. There in the bottom drawer of a dilapidated dresser she pulled out her cherished notebooks. The first ones she showed him were fiction—tales of kings and princesses, plays about the fancy rich, and poems about the forest and open countryside. They were crude, childlike works, much like a primitive painting done in words. After more prodding, Dantas got her to admit that she was writing a diary. He sat on the floor reading avidly the daily notations until Carolina had to light the lamp. Enthused, he told her he wanted to show her diary to a publisher, but she told him: "I didn't write it for anyone to see. It is filled with ugly things and ugly people. Maybe after I die it will be published, but not now."

Dantas persuaded her to let him take one of the notebooks—there were twenty-six of them covering a three-year span—to his newspaper. And the next day while the story on the playground got small notice, a two-column full-length excerpt from Carolina's diary appeared.

The story electrified the town. People telephoned and stopped by the newspaper office asking if there was going to be more. "Even my cynical newspaper cronies were interested," says Dantas, "and felt it should be published. Some thought it should be cleaned up a bit, as there were some rough remarks and unkind political comments, but others thought all it needed was editing." Then, as with all newspaper stories, the furor died down.

Shortly after this Dantas was offered the important position of chief of the São Paulo bureau of *O Cruzeiro* magazine, Brazil's biggest weekly. Here, he saw an even better opportunity to bring the story of Carolina's life to the attention of all Brazilians. For one full year he worked on her notebooks, ignoring the childlike novels, and concentrating on her diary, extracting the best of each day. It took a great deal of convincing on his part to get her to agree to publish excerpts from her account of her daily life. She wanted her short stories and poems published first. Dantas, with his sharp reporter's mind, saw the value and the urgency of her diary, and soon she was working on it and nothing else.

After almost a lifetime in the favela she was not used to kindness from anyone and there were times when she distrusted what he was doing for her, and refused to talk to him or give up the precious manuscripts. Then sometimes he would visit and she'd put a fresh ribbon in her hair and write "Viva Audalio" on the walls of the shack.

As Carolina is a perfectionist she started every entry telling what time she got up, what she did before she went out to gather paper, and what she saw in the streets. Most of this was repetitive and Dantas cut savagely until he got the diary down to its present size. "But I did not rewrite," he insists. "The words and ideas are Carolina's. All I did was edit."

Published, her diary became the literary sensation of Brazil. Over a thousand people swamped the bookshop on the first day of sales. (In Brazil book publishers have their own retail shops; the publisher of *Quarto de Despejo* had a publication day autographing party at his shop, and did not release the book to other booksellers for one week.) Carolina signed 600 copies that afternoon, and would have done more if she hadn't stopped to talk to each of the buyers. She asked what their names were, where they lived, and if they were happy. When a state senator appeared with flash bulbs popping, Carolina wrote in his book: "I hope that you give the poor people what they need and stop putting all the tax money into your own pocket. Sincerely, Carolina Maria de Jesus."

Never had a book such an impact on Brazil. In three days the first printing of 10,000 copies was sold out in São Paulo alone. In less than six months 90,000 copies were sold in Brazil and today it is still on the best-seller list, having sold more than any other Brazilian book in history.

Carolina was invited to speak about the favela problem on radio and television, and she gave lectures on the problem in Brazilian universities. Her book has become required reading in sociology classes and the São Paulo Law University has given her the title of "Honorary Member," the first such person so honored who has not a university education. The title was originally slated for Jean Paul Sartre, but the students decided that Carolina was "far worthier in the fight for freedom" than the French philosopher.

Two months after the publication of the diary Carolina loaded her table, two small beds and a mattress, a closet, a bookshelf, six pots, herself and her children into the back of an open truck and prepared to leave the favela that she had lived in for twelve years. She had used the first proceeds from the book for the down payment on a brick house in the suburbs. But the neighbors had other ideas. They swarmed around the truck and wouldn't let her leave. "You think you are high class now, don't you, you black whore," shouted one man. "You write about us and make lots of money and then leave without sharing it."

Carolina refused to reply.

"You wrote bad things about me," shouted a drunken skinny woman named Leila. "You did worse things than I did." And with this she hurled a rock that hit young José Carlos on the cheek, making a deep gash and causing blood to flow. Others started to scream and throw stones. Vera was struck in the back and on the arm, while Carolina tried to shield her with her body. She beat on the hood of the truck and the driver roared through the crowd, who came surging behind with sticks and rotten vegetables. They chased the truck as far as the police station, then fell away.

Carolina is not really the main personage in her diary. It is a bigger character—Hunger. From the first to the last page he appears with an unnerving consistency. The other characters are consequences of this Hunger: alcoholism, prostitution, violence, and murder.

The human beings who walk through these pages are real, with their real names, but with slight variations they could be other men who live with Hunger in New York, Buenos Aires, Rome, Calcutta, and elsewhere.

Carolina's words are the words of the street. Her Portuguese is not the flowing classical language spoken by the upper classes, but the short choppy urgent speech of the poor. She wasn't taught in school to make paragraphs or to be consistent with her tenses. None of this has been altered in the translation, for to do it would be to alter the woman herself. She writes directly, roughly, and without artifice. She recorded what she saw in such a way that she makes the reader feel it too. No small feat.

Recently on a television program a well-dressed, well-fed Carolina said:

> If I wasn't so happy I would cry. When I first gave my manuscript to Brazilian editors they laughed at this poor Negro woman with calloused hands who wore rags and only had two years of schooling. They told me I should write on toilet paper. Now these same editors are asking for my works, actually fighting for them.

Today I had lunch in a wonderful restaurant and a photographer took my picture. I told him: "Write under the photo that Carolina who used to eat from trash cans now eats in restaurants. That she has come back into the human race and out of the Garbage Dump."

THE DIARY OF CAROLINA MARIA DE JESUS: 1958

May 2, 1958   I'm not lazy. There are times when I try to keep up my diary. But then I think it's not worth it and figure I'm wasting my time.

I've made a promise to myself. I want to treat people that I know with more consideration. I want to have a pleasant smile for children and the employed.

I received a summons to appear at 8 p.m. at police station number 12. I spent the day looking for paper. At night my feet pained me so I couldn't walk. It started to rain. I went to the station and took José Carlos with me. The summons was for him. José Carlos is nine years old.

May 3   I went to the market at Carlos de Campos Street looking for any old thing. I got a lot of greens. But it didn't help much, for I've got no cooking fat. The children are upset because there's nothing to eat.

May 6   In the morning I went for water. I made João carry it. I was happy, then I received another summons. I was inspired yesterday and my verses were so pretty, I forgot to go to the station. It was 11:00 when I remembered the invitation from the illustrious lieutenant of the 12th precinct.

My advice to would-be politicians is that people do not tolerate hunger. It's necessary to know hunger to know how to describe it.

They are putting up a circus here at Araguaia Street. The Nilo Circus Theater.

May 9   I looked for paper but I didn't like it. Then I thought: I'll pretend that I'm dreaming.

May 10   I went to the police station and talked to the lieutenant. What a pleasant man! If I had known he was going to be so pleasant, I'd have gone on the first summons. The lieutenant was interested in my boys' education. He said the favelas have an unhealthy atmosphere where the people have more chance to go wrong than to become useful to state and country. I thought: if he knows this why doesn't he make a report and send it to the politicians? To Janio Quadros, Kubitschek,[1] and Dr. Adhemar de Barros? Now he tells me this, I a poor garbage collector. I can't even solve my own problems.

Brazil needs to be led by a person who has known hunger. Hunger is also a teacher.

Who has gone hungry learns to think of the future and of the children.

May 11   Today is Mother's Day. The sky is blue and white. It seems that even nature wants to pay homage to the mothers who feel unhappy because they can't realize the desires of their children.

The sun keeps climbing. Today it's not going to rain. Today is our day.

Dona Teresinha came to visit me. She gave me 15 cruzeiros and said it was for Vera to go to the circus. But I'm going to use the money to buy bread tomorrow because I only have four cruzeiros.

Yesterday I got half a pig's head at the slaughterhouse. We ate the meat and saved the bones. Today I put the bones on to boil and into the broth I put some potatoes. My children are always hungry. When they are starving they aren't so fussy about what they eat.

Night came. The stars are hidden. The shack is filled with mosquitoes. I lit a page from a newspaper and ran it over the walls. This is the way the favela dwellers kill mosquitoes.

May 13   At dawn it was raining. Today is a nice day for me, it's the anniversary of the Abolition. The day we celebrate the freeing of the slaves. In the jails the Negroes were the scapegoats. But now the whites are more educated and don't treat us any more with contempt. May God enlighten the whites so that the Negroes may have a happier life.

It continued to rain and I only have beans and salt. The rain is strong but even so I sent the boys to school. I'm writing until the rain goes away so I can go to Senhor Manuel and sell scrap. With that money I'm going to buy rice and sausage. The rain has stopped for a while. I'm going out.

I feel so sorry for my children. When they see the things to eat that I come home with they shout:

"*Viva Mama!*"

Their outbursts please me. But I've lost the habit of smiling. Ten minutes later they want more food. I sent João to ask Dona Ida for a little pork fat. She didn't have any. I sent her a note:

"Dona Ida, I beg you to help me get a little pork fat, so I can make soup for the children. Today it's raining and I can't go looking for paper. Thank you, Carolina."

It rained and got colder. Winter had arrived and in winter people eat more. Vera asked for food, and I didn't have any. It was the same old show. I had two cruzeiros and wanted to buy a little flour to make a *virado*.[2] I went to ask Dona Alice for a little pork. She gave me pork and rice. It was 9 at night when we ate.

And that is the way on May 13, 1958 I fought against the real slavery—hunger!

May 15   On the nights they have a party they don't let anybody sleep. The neighbors in the brick houses near by have signed a petition to get rid of the *favelados*. But they won't get their way. The neighbors in the brick houses say:

"The politicians protect the *favelados*."

Who protects us are the public and the Order of St. Vincent Church. The politicians only show up here during election campaigns. Senhor Candido Sampaio, when he was city councilman in 1953, spent his Sundays here in the favela. He was so nice. He drank our coffee, drinking right out of our cups. He made us laugh with his jokes. He played with our children. He left a good impression here and when he was candidate for state deputy, he won. But the Chamber of Deputies didn't do one thing for the *favelados*. He doesn't visit us any more.

I classify São Paulo this way: The Governor's Palace is the living room. The mayor's office is the dining room and the city is the garden. And the favela is the back yard where they throw the garbage.

The night is warm. The sky is peppered with stars. I have the crazy desire to cut a piece of the sky to make a dress. I hear some yelling and go into the street. It is Ramiro who wants to give it to Senhor Binidito. A misunderstanding. A tile fell on the electric line and turned off the lights in Ramiro's house. For this Ramiro wants to beat Senhor Binidito. Because Ramiro is strong and Binidito is weak.

Ramiro got angry because I was on Binidito's side. I tried to fix the wires. While I was trying to repair them Ramiro wanted to hit Binidito but was so drunk he couldn't even stand up. I can't describe the effects of alcohol because I don't drink. I drank once, just to try it, but the alcohol made me silly.

While I was working to repair the light, Ramiro said: "Turn on the light! Turn on the light or I'll smash your face."

The wire wasn't long enough to connect. It needed to be mended. I'm not an expert in electrical matters. I sent for Senhor Alfredo, who is professionally an electrician. He was nervous and kept glancing at Binidito. Juana, who is the wife of Binidito, gave 50 cruzeiros to Senhor Alfredo. He took the money, didn't smile, but was pleased. I could tell by his face. In the end money always dissipates nervousness.

May 16   I awoke upset. I wanted to stay at home but didn't have anything to eat.

I'm not going to eat because there is very little bread. I wonder if I'm the only one who leads this kind of life. What can I hope for the future? I wonder if the poor of other countries suffer like the poor of Brazil. I was so unhappy that I started to fight without reason with my boy José Carlos.

A truck came to the favela. The driver and his helper threw away some cans. It was canned sausage. I thought: this is what these hardhearted businessmen do. They stay waiting for the prices to go up so they can earn more. And when it rots they throw it to the buzzards and the unhappy *favelados*.

There wasn't any fighting. Even I found it dull. I watched the children open the cans of sausages and exclaim:

"Ummm! Delicious!"

Dona Alice gave me one to try, but the can was bulging. It was rotten.

May 18   In the favela everything spreads in a minute. The news has gone around that Dona Maria José is dead. Various persons came to see her. The St. Vincent brother who took care of her showed up. He had come to visit her every Sunday. He is not disgusted by the *favelados* and treats their miseries with tenderness. There's no comparison with that so-called State Social Service.

The coffin arrived. It was purple. The color of the bitterness that encloses the hearts of the *favelados*.

Dona Maria was a Believer and said that the Believers before dying were already in Heaven. The burial is at 3 this afternoon. The Believers are singing a hymn. Their voices are sweet. I have the feeling that it's the angels who are singing. I don't see one drunk. Maybe out of respect for the dead, but I doubt it. I think it's because they don't have the money.

The coach arrived to deliver the lifeless body of Dona Maria José to her true home— the tomb. Dona Maria José was very good. They say that the living must forgive the dead, and that all of us have our moments of weakness. The funeral car arrived and is waiting for the hour to leave for the burial.

I'm going to stop writing. I'm going to wring the clothes I left soaking yesterday. I don't like to see burials.

May 19   I left the bed at 5 a.m. The sparrows have just begun their morning symphony. The birds must be happier than we are. Perhaps happiness and equality reigns among them. The world of the birds must be better than that of the *favelados*, who lie down but don't sleep because they go to bed hungry.

What our President Senhor Juscelino has in his favor is his voice. He sings like a bird and his voice is pleasant to the ears. And now the bird is living in a golden cage called Catete Palace. Be careful, little bird, that you don't lose this cage, because cats when they are hungry think of birds in cages. The *favelados* are the cats, and they are hungry.

I broke my train of thought when I heard the voice of the baker:

"Here you go! Fresh bread, and right on time for breakfast!"

How little he knows that in the favela there are only a few who have breakfast. The *favelados* eat only when they have something to eat. All the families who live in the favela have children. A Spanish woman lives here named Dona Maria Puerta. She bought some land and started to economize so she could build a house. When she finished construction her children were weak with pneumonia. And there are eight children.

There have been people who visited us and said:

"Only pigs could live in a place like this. This is the pigsty of São Paulo."

I'm starting to lose my interest in life. It's beginning to revolt me and my revulsion is just.

I washed the floor because I'm expecting a visit from a future deputy and he wants me to make some speeches for him. He says he wants to know the favelas and if he is elected he's going to abolish them.

The sky was the color of indigo, and I understood that I adore my Brazil. My glance went over to the trees that are planted at the beginning of Pedro Vicente Street. The leaves moved by themselves. I thought: they are applauding my gesture of love to my country. I went on looking for paper. Vera was smiling and I thought of Casemiro de Abreu, the Brazilian poet who said: "Laugh, child. Life is beautiful." Life was good in that era. Because now in this era it's necessary to say: "Cry, child, Life is bitter."

I went on so preoccupied that I didn't even notice the gardens of the city. It's the season for white flowers, the predominating color. And in the month of May the altars must be adorned with white flowers. We must thank God or Nature, who gave us the stars that adorn the sky, for the flowers that adorn the parks and the fields and the forests.

When I was going up Southern Cross Avenue I saw a woman with blue shoes and a blue handbag. Vera told me:

"Look, Mama, what a beautiful woman. She is going in my car."

My daughter Vera Eunice says she is going to buy a car and will only drive beautiful people in it. The woman smiled and Vera went on:

"You smell so good!"

I saw that my daugher knew how to flatter. The woman opened her bag and gave me 20 cruzeiros.

Here in the favela almost everyone has a difficult fight to live. But I am the only one who writes of what suffering is. I do this for the good of the others. Many look in the garbage for shoes to wear. But the shoes are weak and only last six days. In the old days, that is from 1950–1958, the *favelados* sang. They had parties. 1957, 1958 life was getting tougher and tougher. Now there isn't even money for them to buy *pinga*. The parties were shortened until they snuffed themselves out. The other day I met a policeman. He asked me:

"You still live in the favela?"

"Why?"

"Because your family has left the Radio Patrol in peace."

"There's no money left over to buy booze!" I snapped.

I put João and Vera to bed and went looking for José Carlos. I telephoned the Central Police

Station. The phone doesn't always resolve things. I took a street car and went there. I didn't feel cold. I felt as if my blood was 40 degrees. I spoke with the Female Police who told me that José Carlos was at Asdrubal Nascimento Street (juvenile court). What a relief! Only a mother could appreciate it.

I went toward Asdrubal Nascimento. I don't know how to walk at night. The glare of the lights turns me around. I have to keep asking. I like the night only to contemplate the shining stars, to read and to write. During the night it is quieter.

I arrived at Asdrubal Nascimento and the guard told me to wait. I looked at the children. Some were crying but others were furious with the interference of a law that didn't permit them to do as they pleased. José Carlos was crying. When he heard my voice he became happy. I could feel his contentment. He looked at me and it was the tenderest look I have ever received in my life.

At 8:30 that night I was in the favela breathing the smell of excrement mixed with the rotten earth. When I am in the city I have the impression that I am in a living room with crystal chandeliers, rugs of velvet, and satin cushions. And when I'm in the favela I have the impression that I'm a useless object, destined to be forever in a garbage dump.

May 20 Day was breaking when I got out of bed. Vera woke up and sang and asked me to sing with her. We sang. Then José Carlos and João joined in.

The morning was damp and foggy. The sun was rising but its heat didn't chase away the cold. I stayed thinking: there are seasons when the sun dominates. There's a season for the rain. There's a season for the wind. Now is the time for the cold. Among them there are no rivalries. Each one has a time.

I opened the window and watched the women passing by with their coats discolored and worn by time. It won't be long until these coats which they got from others, and which should be in a museum, will be replaced by others. The politicians must give us things. That includes me too, because I'm also a *favelado*. I'm one of the discarded. I'm in the garbage dump and those in the garbage dump either burn themselves or throw themselves into ruin.

The women that I see passing are going to church begging for bread for their children. Brother Luiz gives it to them while their husbands remain home under the blankets. Some because they can't find jobs. Others because they are sick. Others because they are drunk.

I don't bother myself about their men. If they give a ball and I don't show up, it's because I don't like to dance. I only get involved in fights when I think I can prevent a crime. I don't know what started this unfriendliness of mine. I have a hard cold look for both men and women. My smile and my soft smooth words I save for children.

There is a teen-ager named Julião who beats his father at times. When he hits his father it is with such sadism and pleasure. He thinks he is unconquerable. He beats the old man as if he were beating a drum. The father wants him to study law. When Julião was arrested the father went with him with his eyes filled with tears. As if he was accompanying a saint in a procession. Julião is a rebel, but without a cause. They don't need to live in a favela; they have a home on Villa Maria hill.

Sometimes families move into the favela with children. In the beginning they are educated, friendly. Days later they use foul language, are mean and quarrelsome. They are diamonds turned to lead. They are transformed from objects that were in the living room to objects banished to the garbage dump.

For me the world instead of evolving is turning primitive. Those who don't know hunger will say: "Whoever wrote this is crazy."

But who has gone hungry can say:

"Well, Dona Carolina. The basic necessities must be within reach of everyone."

How horrible it is to see a child eat and ask: "Is there more?" This word "more" keeps ringing in the mother's head as she looks in the pot and doesn't have any more.

When a politician tells us in his speeches that he is on the side of the people, that he is only in politics in order to improve our living conditions, asking for our votes, promising to freeze prices, he is well aware that by touching on these grave problems he will win at the polls. Afterward he divorces himself from the people. He looks at them with half-closed eyes, and with a pride that hurts us.

When I arrived from the Palace that is the city, my children ran to tell me that they had found some macaroni in the garbage. As the food supply was low I cooked some of the macaroni with beans. And my son João said to me:

"Uh, huh. You told me we weren't going to eat any more things from the garbage."

It was the first time I had failed to keep my word. I said

"I had faith in President Kubitschek."

"You had faith, and now you don't have it any more?"

"No, my son, democracy is losing its followers. In our country everything is weakening. The money is weak. Democracy is weak and the politicians are very weak. Everything that is weak dies one day."

The politicians know that I am a poetess. And that a poet will even face death when he sees his people oppressed.

May 21 I spent a horrible night. I dreamt I lived in a decent house that had a bathroom, kitchen, pantry, and even a maid's room. I was going to celebrate the birthday of my daughter Vera Eunice. I went and bought some small pots that I had wanted for a long time. Because

I was able to buy. I sat at the table to eat. The tablecloth was white as a lily. I ate a steak, bread and butter, fried potatoes, and a salad. When I reached for another steak I woke up. What bitter reality! I don't live in the city. I live in the favela. In the mud on the banks of the Tietê River. And with only nine cruzeiros. I don't even have sugar, because yesterday after I went out the children ate what little I had.

Who must be a leader is he who has the ability. He who has pity and friendship for the people. Those who govern our country are those who have money, who don't know what hunger is, or pain or poverty. If the majority revolt, what can the minority do? I am on the side of the poor, who are an arm. An undernourished arm. We must free the country of the profiteering politicians.

Yesterday I ate that macaroni from the garbage with fear of death, because in 1953 I sold scrap over there in Zinho. There was a pretty little black boy. He also went to sell scrap in Zinho. He was young and said that those who should look for paper were the old. One day I was collecting scrap when I stopped at Bom Jardim Avenue. Someone had thrown meat into the garbage, and he was picking out the pieces. He told me:

"Take some, Carolina. It's still fit to eat."

He gave me some, and so as not to hurt his feelings, I accepted. I tried to convince him not to eat that meat, or the hard bread gnawed by the rats. He told me no, because it was two days since he had eaten. He made a fire and roasted the meat. His hunger was so great that he couldn't wait for the meat to cook. He heated it and ate. So as not to remember that scene, I left thinking: I'm going to pretend I wasn't there. This can't be real in a rich country like mine. I was disgusted with that Social Service that had been created to readjust the maladjusted, but took no notice of we marginal people. I sold the scrap at Zinho and returned to São Paulo's back yard, the favela.

The next day I found that little black boy dead. His toes were spread apart. The space must have been eight inches between them. He had blown up as if made out of rubber. His toes looked like a fan. He had no documents. He was buried like any other "Joe." Nobody tried to find out his name. The marginal people don't have names.

Once every four years the politicians change without solving the problem of hunger that has its headquarters in the favela and its branch offices in the workers' homes.

When I went to get water I saw a poor woman collapse near the pump because last night she slept without dinner. She was undernourished. The doctors that we have in politics know this.

Now I'm going to Dona Julita's house to work for her. I went looking for paper. Senhor Samuel weighed it. I got 12 cruzeiros. I went up Tiradentes Avenue looking for paper. I came to Brother Antonio Santana de Galvão Street, number 17, to work for Dona Julita. She told me not to fool with men because I might have another baby and that afterward men won't give anything to take care of the child. I smiled and thought: In relations with men, I've had some bitter experiences. Now I'm mature, reached a stage of life where my judgment has grown roots.

I found a sweet potato and a carrot in the garbage. When I got back to the favela my boys were gnawing on a piece of hard bread. I thought: for them to eat this bread, they need electric teeth.

I don't have any lard. I put meat on the fire with some tomatoes that I found at the Peixe canning factory. I put in the carrot and the sweet potato and water. As soon as it was boiling, I put in the macaroni that the boys found in the garbage. The *favelados* are the few who are convinced that in order to live, they must imitate the vultures. I don't see any help from the Social Service regarding the *favelados*.

Tomorrow I'm not going to have bread. I'm going to cook a sweet potato.

May 22   Today I'm sad. I'm nervous. I don't know if I should start crying or start running until I fall unconscious. At dawn it was raining. I couldn't go out to get any money. I spent the day writing. I cooked the macaroni and I'll warm it up again for the children. I cooked the potatoes and they ate them. I have a few tin cans and a little scrap that I'm going to sell to Senhor Manuel. When João came home from school I sent him to sell the scrap. He got 13 cruzeiros. I was furious with him. Where had he seen a *favelado* with such highborn tastes?

The children eat a lot of bread. They like soft bread but when they don't have it, they eat hard bread.

Hard is the bread that we eat. Hard is the bed on which we sleep. Hard is the life of the *favelado*.

Oh, São Paulo! A queen that vainly shows her skyscrapers that are her crown of gold. All dressed up in velvet and silk but with cheap stockings underneath—the favela.

The money didn't stretch far enough to buy meat, so I cooked macaroni with a carrot. I didn't have any grease, it was horrible. Vera was the only one who complained yet asked for more.

"Mama, sell me to Dona Julita because she has delicious food."

I know that there exist Brazilians here inside São Paulo who suffer more than I do. In June of '57 I felt rich and passed through the offices of the Social Service. I had carried a lot of scrap iron and got pains in my kidneys. So as not to see my children hungry I asked for help from the famous Social Service. It was there that I saw the tears slipping from the eyes of the poor. How painful it is to see the dramas that are played out there. The coldness in which they treat the poor. The only things they want to know about them is their name and address.

I went to the Governor's Palace.[3] The Palace sent me to an office at Brigadeiro Luis Antonio Avenue. They in turn sent me to the Social Service at the Santa Casa charity hospital. There I talked with Dona Maria Aparecida, who listened to me, said many things yet said nothing. I decided to go back to the Palace. I talked with Senhor Alcides. He is not Japanese yet is as yellow as rotten butter. I said to Senhor Alcides:

"I came here to ask for help because I'm ill. You sent me to Brigadeiro Luis Antonio Avenue, and I went. There they sent me to the Santa Casa. And I spent all the money I have on transportation."

"Take her!"

They wouldn't let me leave. A soldier put his bayonet at my chest. I looked the soldier in the eyes and saw that he had pity on me. I told him:

"I am poor. That's why I came here."

Dr. Osvaldo de Barros entered, a false philanthropist in São Paulo who is masquerading as St. Vincent de Paul. He said:

"Call a squad car!"

The policeman took me back to the favela and warned me that the next time I made a scene at the welfare agency I would be locked up.

Welfare agency! Welfare for whom?

May 23 I got up feeling sad this morning because it was raining. The shack is in terrible disorder. And I don't have soap to wash the dishes. I say "dishes" from force of habit. But they are really tin cans. If I had soap I would wash the clothes. I'm really not negligent. If I walk around dirty it's because I'm trapped in the life of a *favelado*. I've come to the conclusion that for those who aren't going to Heaven, it doesn't help to look up. It's the same with us who don't like the favela, but are obliged to live in one. . . . It doesn't help to look up.

I made a meal. The grease frying in the pan was beautiful. What a dazzling display! The children smile watching the food cooking in the pans. Still more when it is rice and beans— it's a holiday for them.

In the old days macaroni was the most expensive dish. Now it's rice and beans that have replaced the macaroni. They've crossed over to the side of the nobility. Even you, rice and beans, have deserted us! You who were the friends of the marginal ones, the *favelados*, the needy. Just look. They are not within reach of the unhappy ones of the Garbage Dump. Who has not flown off is senhor cornmeal. But the children don't like cornmeal.

When I put the food on the table João smiled. He ate and didn't mention the black color of the beans.[4] Because black is our life. Everything is black around us.

In the streets and shops I see the posters with the names of candidates for deputy. Some names are already known. They are the repeaters who have already failed once at the ballot boxes. But the people are not interested in elections. Our elections are just a Trojan Horse that appears once every four years.

The sky is beautiful, worthy of contemplation because the drifting clouds are forming dazzling landscapes. Soft breezes pass by carrying the perfume of flowers. And the sun is always punctual at rising and setting. The birds travel in space, showing off in their happiness. The night brings up the sparkling stars to adorn the blue sky. There are so many beautiful things in the world that are impossible to describe. Only one thing saddens us: the prices when we go shopping. They overshadow all the beauty that exists.

Theresa, Meryi's sister, drank poison. And for no reason. They say she found a note from a woman in her lover's pocket. It ate away her mouth, her throat, and her stomach. She lost a lot of blood. The doctors say that even if she does get well she will be helpless. She has two sons, one four years old and the other nine months.

May 26   At dawn it was raining. I only have four cruzeiros, a little food left over from yesterday, and some bones. I went to look for water to boil the bones. There is still a little macaroni and I made a soup for the children. I saw a neighbor washing beans.[5] How envious I became. It's been two weeks that I haven't washed clothes because I haven't any soap. I sold some boards for 40 cruzeiros. The woman told me she'd pay today. If she pays I'll buy soap.

For days there hasn't been a policeman in the favela, but today one came because Julião beat his father. He gave him such a violent blow that the old man cried and went to call the police.

May 27   It seems that the slaughterhouse threw kerosene on their garbage dump so the *favelados* would not look for meat to eat. I didn't have any breakfast and walked around half dizzy. The daze of hunger is worse than that of alcohol. The daze of alcohol makes us sing, but the one of hunger makes us shake. I know how horrible it is to only have air in the stomach.

I began to have a bitter taste in my mouth. I thought: is there no end to the bitterness of life? I think that when I was born I was marked by fate to go hungry. I filled one sack of paper. When I entered Paulo Guimarães Street, a woman gave me some newspapers. They were clean and I went to the junk yard picking up everything that I found. Steel, tin, coal, everything serves the *favelado*. Leon weighed the paper and I got six cruzeiros.

I wanted to save the money to buy beans but I couldn't because my stomach was creaming and torturing me.

I decided to do something about it and bought a bread roll. What a surprising effect food has on our organisms. Before I ate, I saw the sky, the trees, and the birds all yellow, but after I ate, everything was normal to my eyes.

Food in the stomach is like fuel in machines. I was able to work better. My body stopped weighing me down. I started to walk faster. I had the feeling that I was gliding in space. I started to smile as if I was witnessing a beautiful play. And will there ever be a drama more beautiful than that of eating? I felt that I was eating for the first time in my life.

The Radio Patrol arrived. They came to take the two Negro boys who had broken into the power station. Four and six years old. It's easy to see that they are of the favela. Favela children are the most ragged children in the city. What they can find in the streets they eat. Banana peels, melon rind, and even pineapple husks. Anything that is too tough to chew, they grind. These boys had their pockets filled with aluminum coins, that new money in circulation.

May 28   It dawned raining. I only have three cruzeiros because I loaned Leila five so she could go get her daughter in the hospital. I'm confused and don't know where to begin. I want to write, I want to work, I want to wash clothes. I'm cold and I don't have any shoes to wear. The children's shoes are worn out.

The worst thing in the favela is that there are children here. All the children of the favela know what a woman's body looks like. Because when the couples that are drunk fight, the woman, so as not to get a beating, runs naked into the street. When the fights start the *favelados* leave whatever they are doing to be present at the battle. So that when the woman goes running naked it's a real show for Joe Citizen. Afterward the comments begin among the children:

"Fernanda ran out nude when Armin was hitting her."

"Oh, I didn't see it. Damn!"

"What does a naked woman look like?"

And then the other, in order to tell him,

puts his mouth near his ear. And the loud laughter echoes. Everything that is obscene or pornographic the *favelado* learns quickly.

There are some shacks where prostitutes play their love scenes right in front of the children.

The rich neighbors in the brick houses say we are protected by the politicians. They're wrong. The politicians only show up here in the Garbage Dump at election time. This year we had a visit from a candidate for deputy, Dr. Paulo de Campos Moura, who gave us beans and some wonderful blankets. He came at an opportune moment, before it got cold.

What I want to clear up about the people who live in the favela is the following: the only ones who really survive here are the *nordestinos*.[6] They work and don't squander. They buy a house or go back up north.

Here in the favela there are those who build shacks to live in and those who build them to rent. And the rents are from 500 to 700 cruzeiros. Those who make shacks to sell spend 4,000 cruzeiros and sell them for 11,000. Who made a lot of shacks to sell was Tiburcio.

May 29   It finally stopped raining. The clouds glided toward the horizon. Only the cold attacked us. Many people in the favela don't have warm clothing. When one has shoes he won't have a coat. I choke up watching the children walk in the mud. It seems that some new people have arrived in the favela. They are ragged with undernourished faces. They improvised a shack. It hurts me to see so much pain, reserved for the working class. I stared at my new companion in misfortune. She looked at the favela with its mud and sickly children. It was the saddest look I'd ever seen. Perhaps

she has no more illusions. She had given her life over to misery.

There will be those who reading what I write will say—this is untrue. But misery is real.

What I revolt against is the greed of men who squeeze other men as if they were squeezing oranges. . . .

Notes

[1] Juscelino Kubitschek: President of Brazil from 1956 to 1961.

[2] *Virado*: a dish of black beans, manioc flour, pork, and eggs.

[3] Like most Brazilians, Carolina believes in going straight to the top to make her complaints.

[4] Black beans in almost every part of Brazil, except Rio, are looked down upon as the lowest thing that can be eaten. In the northeast poor families shut their windows out of shame that neighbors will see them eating black beans rather than brown ones.

[5] Beans, like rice, must be picked over to get rid of the rotten kernels, and then washed to take away dust and pieces of dirt and other foreign matter. The *favelados* buy these staples at street fairs from huge wooden bins that are never covered over.

[6] *Nordestinos*: forced by land-parching droughts and almost no industry, the poor of the north swarm into cities like São Paulo and Rio looking for work. Needing a place to live, they choose the favelas and end up worse off than they were before.

DISCUSSION QUESTIONS

1. Do you feel that Carolina Maria de Jesus could have done more to escape her situation? Why or why not?
2. In which respects are urban centers in developing countries different from those in postindustrialized societies?
3. What are some of the structural and contextual forces which effect urban life?

The Big Urban Bias

Hoda M. Sobhi

INTRODUCTION

The pace of urban growth in the developing countries poses great challenges for national, regional and city policy-makers. To show how big these challenges are in the field of socio-economic development in such countries we should note that:[1]

- It is expected that 95% of the increase in world population up to the end of this century would take place in developing countries. 50% of this increase is expected to be urban population.
- The increase in the number of big cities has been quite tremendous in the last decade. The number of cities with more than four million inhabitants has increased from 28 to 41. In the developing countries this figure almost doubled; it increased from 15 to 27 big cities.

In cities of developing countries the problems faced by urban authorities are serious, yet the resources to deal with them are quite scarce. In addition, fundamental improvements in the institutional framework are considered an important prerequisite for more efficient and equitable urban growth. This is true since spatial development and the growth of any particular urban area are interrelated aspects of the same process of transformation experienced in all developing countries.

A diagnosis of the problems of urban policy in developing countries can be summarized as consisting of two interrelated phenomena. First, urban labor supply tends to expand more rapidly than urban labor demand; this limits the growth of urban wages and incomes, especially for unskilled workers. Second, the demand for urban services expands more rapidly than their supply; this leads to rising prices for urban land and housing, overcrowded housing, and shortages of essential services, all of which affect the urban poor especially. Since these imbalances are largely the result of inefficient management of labor demand and service supply by governments, the efficiency and equity of urban development can be increased by improving the policies that create the imbalance.[2]

The rising concern with the need for decentralization, the problems of rural-to-urban balance, regional inequalities, the growing squatter settlements and slums, and the rising backlog in urban services—these and other factors forced planners to realize that the spatial distribution of socio-economic activities cannot be treated independently from issues of national economic, social and political development. Development involves much more than just the expansion of output. . . .

For several essential reasons the need for a national urbanization strategy is much stronger among developing countries than it ever was in the developed countries. In practically all developing countries the role of the state is dominant. The government has an inevitable influence through its policies, the location of infrastructure investment, and the public enterprises it controls. In many developing countries national spatial development is marked by a higher degree of economic dualism and inequality among regions and urban areas. The rapid rate of growth of the population has led to the concentration of large groups of low-income households in a few large cities. This, in turn, complicated the task of development. Effective settlement strategies may alleviate this problem.[3]

THE URBAN BIAS OF NATIONAL ECONOMIC POLICIES

A good understanding of the spatial effects of national economic policies is essential to developing countries. These policies have a definite effect on where people live and where they work. In countries that have begun to tackle their spatial problems seriously, the effect of the incentives on business location decisions is very strong.[4]

One major reason for the failure of national urbanization policies in developing countries is the exclusive concentration on problems of urban decentralization while ignoring the fact that national economic policies provide strong implicit incentives to locate in the dominant urban centers. Therefore, many of the objectives selected by policy-makers address the symptoms and not the causes of resource misallocation and severe regional disparities. The social and political objectives behind many announced spatial strategies are in clear conflict with the forces set in motion by national economic policy. Therefore, urban policies must make sure that national economic and social policies do not accentuate the concentration of population and economic activities in large urban centers.

The proper formulation of a national urbanization policy strategy requires the systematic discussion of three major aspects of population distribution and national settlement.[5]

1. The implicit spatial effects and biases of national policies
2. The appropriate policies to deal with problems of large cities such as congestion and pollution
3. The problems of regional inequality and the direct explicit policy instruments for the redistribution of economic activities

REGIONAL INEQUALITIES, PRIMACY AND CONGESTION

The great economic and social difference between regions sharply distinguishes the problems of a large number of developing countries from those of advanced economies. In the most advanced economies, the ratio between the poorest and the richest regions is in the order of two to one; in many middle-income countries this ratio can go up to ten to one. This contrast between the richer, more advanced regions and the poorer regions had led to differentiating the core region of a country from its periphery and to the notion of polarized development.[6]

In the developing countries there is a basic contradiction between the desire to reduce disparities among regions and the need to improve the overall efficiency of the national economy. In order to enhance future development in all the regions, growth in modern urban regions must be intensified, since they are the ones with high growth potential and high saving rates. They also generate investment surplus in the future which could be allocated to the less-developed and poorer regions. This is more or less the "trickle-down" theory in economic development. Of course, in the short run this is in direct contradiction with the goal of equity.[7] Therefore, there is little doubt that these pronounced spatial inequalities are associated with the biases of the above national economic policies. Inter-regional inequality is greater during the transition stage or intermediate level than at the low or high levels of development. The concentration of industrial development in growth centers is the result of attempts to derive the full benefits of external economies. This leads to a dual structured economy: a center of rapid intense growth and a periphery whose economy is either stagnant or declining. Later on, as the process of concentration of economic activities accentuates, the influx from the periphery to the center leads to congestion and over-urbanization.[8]

Here it is very important to distinguish between the concentration of a large percentage of total urban population in the largest city (primacy), and the existence of a large urban center in a country. These two conditions are not synonymous. Also, congestion is not synonymous with concentration of economic activities in space but refers only to situations where, at the margin, increases in concentration add more to total diseconomies than to total economies.

What matters here is economic efficiency and city size. Economic efficiency of a city is the net result of the benefits or urban agglomeration and the losses created by congestion and environmental deterioration. At the lower end of the size range, economies of scale increase rapidly as a city expands, but beyond a certain size the additional gains diminish rapidly.[9]

URBANIZATION TRENDS IN EGYPT

Egypt is highly urbanized for a country with its economic structure and per capita income. This phenomenon is not of recent origin, but has characterized the country from the beginning of the century. The over-urbanization is real and has increased with time.[10]

Many observers have noted that Egypt's over-urbanization is out-distancing its economic development in general and its industrialization in particular. Compared to Western societies which launched industrialization in the nineteenth century, Egypt is said to have twice as many urban dwellers as these societies had during their economic take-off.[11]

However, an opposite point of view exists. Gamal Hamdan, a distinguished Egyptian writer, does not think that Egypt is over-urbanized. He argues that modern civilization has reached a stage which is quite different from the post-industrial revolution stage. Urbanization is no longer a function of the degree of industrial growth; therefore, it is possible, and even natural, to have big cities without big industries. Or, at least it has become possible for the growth of big cities to precede industrial development as long as industrialization comes later and corrects the imbalance. In short, he considers the high rate of urbanization without industrialization a new pattern in

modern societies and a natural outcome of modern advanced technology.[12]

Of course, there is no doubt that urbanization, provided it takes place within the right limits and necessary prerequisites, is a healthy and natural phenomenon. On the contrary, it is a sign of progress on the national level since it conforms with the long-term global trends. However, inasmuch as a great portion of our scarce capital is diverted away from industrial development in order to relieve the strains on urban infrastructure and services, there exists a problem of over-urbanization in Egypt.

Table 1 shows the dramatic rise in the share of urban population. The real jump to urban life came during World War II when the percentage of urban population suddenly jumped to 30%. For a whole decade after that the urbanization process continued rapidly, then it began to slow down. This trend is expected to continue, and by the year 2000, Egypt's urban population is expected to be 50%. This will give Egypt the same urbanization rate as the rest of the world by the beginning of the twenty-first century.

However, the situation is complicated since Egypt's pattern of urbanization has been dominated by the growth of the country's primary city, Cairo. The largest city in the Middle East and Africa, Cairo ranked the sixth largest among the capitals of the world in 1980. Moreover, as Issawi notes, Egyptian regimes have

TABLE 1		
URBANIZATION IN EGYPT RURAL-URBAN (%)		
Date	Rural	Urban
1907	81.0	19.0
1917	77.4	22.7
1927	77.1	22.9
1947	70.4	29.6
1960	62.6	37.4
1966	59.5	40.5
1976	56.1	43.9
2000	50.0	50.0

Source: G. Hamdan, p. 315.

been strongly urban biased for centuries, long before important substitution industrialization strategies were known. This urban bias has always been and continues to mean a bias to the capital, Cairo.[13] . . .

Cairo is at the top of the Egyptian urban life and urban hierarchy. This contradiction explains many of Cairo's features and problems.

ELEMENTS OF THE BIAS

One of the most important characteristics of Egypt has always been the very high degree of geographical centralism. Cairo seemed always to be the destination of the whole country. All roads lead to Cairo; it is the center of the valley as well as the center of the desert. This is true although, distance-wise, Cairo is not exactly at the center of the country, however, it is precisely at the center of the densely inhabited part.

The pattern of population distribution and densities make Cairo a natural demographic peak. In fact, one-third of the total population lives within a 45-mile radius of Cairo (according to 1976 census data).[14]

The administrative factor has always been a very important factor leading to more centralization. This is because Egypt is a hydraulic society and therefore the central government has always played a very important role in the economic life and prosperity of the whole country. Moreover, there has always been a strong relationship between the bureaucracy and the urban bourgeoisie, and based on this relationship it is said that the main Egyptian cities are cities of bureaucrats.[15] The administrative apparatus was always located mainly in Cairo, leaving the whole countryside totally deprived from the minimum level of its services.

Unfortunately, Egypt has always been divided into a big city, the capital, and a big village, the countryside. This has been the great contradiction and the peak of dualism in Egypt's history. There was always the glorious capital as contrasted with the poor country-side. This means Egypt was never a pyramid-shaped hierarchy of cities. In this sense, Cairo has conquered all other Egyptian cities, and this is the reason Egypt has a very imbalanced and skewed hierarchy of cities.

Feudalism, before the 1952 revolution, divided the country not only socially and functionally, but also geographically and spatially. Absentee ownership created two geographical classes: rich absentee landlords living in the capital, and poor landless peasants living in the countryside. Even after the end of feudalism, the same center-periphery relationship still existed in a much stronger form because of the growing bureaucracy, commercial bourgeoisie and later the industrial capitalists. Finally came the "infitah" (open-door) economic policy to give Cairo its highest stage of growth and to make it look like a giant on the Egyptian landscape.

THE STAGE OF DISECONOMIES: THE CONSEQUENCES OF THE BIAS

Cairo today is a city of great and acute contradictions. Cairo is the city of the rich and most fortunate. Over 200,000 millionaires live in Cairo. Only 5% of the Cairene population has all the power and wealth, while the rest suffers from Cairo's diseconomies of agglomeration.[16]

Cairo therefore has the severest class differentials in the country. It is estimated that 50% of Cairo's income goes to only 5% of its inhabitants. Therefore, Cairo's poor are the victims of its rich.[17]

Cairo today has become a real national issue because the congestion represents a frightening and vicious problem. All the positive externalities and the economics of scale Cairo had provided for a long time have now been exceeded by negative externalities and diseconomies of scale.

The rapid and sustained growth of urban population and the low level of resources available for housing and municipal services have all contributed to poor conditions in the cities, particularly in Cairo. Urban housing in particular seems to have steadily deteriorated since the early 1960s.[18]

On the one hand, there are the high modern and luxurious buildings in Zamalek, Maadi, Mohandesin and Heliopolis and on the other hand, the tomb cities are getting more and more crowded every day. The population of the "Dead City" was estimated at 900,000 inhabitants in 1984, and the illegal low-standard houses represent 80% of the annual increase in housing units in Cairo, in spite of the fact that Cairo's share of public expenditure in subsidy to low-income housing is more than 50%. Cairo has an estimated shortage of 200,000 housing units today. Housing conditions in Cairo, probably the best served in Egypt, are very poor.

In 1970 only 44% of the buildings in Greater Cairo were connected to public or private systems of sewerage. Over 50% of the buildings did not have tap water supply. More than one-third of the buildings did not have electric connections.[19]

In 1984, room densities in Cairo reached a very high level [Table 2]. Some housing units, in districts like Babas-Sh'arriya, have 10 persons per room. The average of the old and poor districts of Cairo today is seven persons per room. In such residential units, it is quite usual for generations to live together in a single housing unit.[20]

Babas-Sh'arriya, the first destination for many bewildered new peasant migrants, now has a density of about 60,000 per square mile, three times the average of the slums of Calcutta or Djakarta.[21]

Looking at the problem from a different angle, we find that 400,000 of Cairo's dwellings are structurally unsound, and about 40% of Cairo's dwellings are on the verge of total collapse. The crisis is more aggravated by illegal urban squatters. We may distinguish between two basic types of clandestine squatters in Cairo: one form is roof-dwellers who build huts, shacks and the like on roofs of buildings in old districts of Cairo, which house about half a million Cairenes; the other is people living in the "dead city."[22]

The transport problem is even worse than the housing problem. Transportation reaches a standstill in the center of the city during rush hours, and the lines of cars are getting longer and longer. Today the cruelest problem facing anyone living in Cairo is the daily trip to work and the trip back home. This goes for those who drive their own cars, and in a much more dramatic way, for those who use public transportation. This is because there has never been any real coordination between working locations, especially industry, and dwelling loca-

---

TABLE 2

ROOM DENSITIES FOR THE CITY OF CAIRO 1947–1972

Year	City population	No. of housing units	Number of rooms	Persons per room
1947	2,090,064	448,333	1,039,742	2.0
1960	3,348,779	687,858	1,439,158	2.3
1966	4,232,663	779,789	1,559,578	2.7
1972	5,200,000 (Est.)	860,039 (Est.)	1,720,078 (Est.)	3.1

Source: Mahmoud A. Fadil: *Political Economy of Nasserism*, Cambridge Univ. Press, Cambridge, U.K. 1980, p. 128.

tions. Therefore, a high percentage of the Cairene population works where others live, and lives where others work. The zoning system simply does not work. Moreover, there are more people than the vehicles could support, and there are more vehicles than the capacity of roads can handle.[23] This means that increasing the numbers of vehicles does not solve the problem, on the contrary, it complicates the problem.

An answer to Cairo's public transport system has been sought for about 30 years. The possibility of an underground system was first explored in 1954, and the cost was estimated at slightly below 770,000 U.S. dollars per mile (1985 rate of exchange). As the transportation crisis worsened, cost estimates have grown proportionately. In 1968 the cost of 12 miles running along the north-south axis of the city was estimated to be over five million U.S. dollars per mile (1985 rate of exchange). The five miles of track proposed to join the southern railway system with the northern metro, thus bypassing the highly congested central area, would cost approximately 12 million U.S. dollars per mile (1985 rate of exchange). In any case, the underground train system is presently being executed.

Of course, an underground system is the most expensive solution to the problem, and at the same time it may not be the perfect one. It is expected to relieve about 30% to 40% of the problem. There is also the fear that, in the future, this huge project would cause more growth and more concentration in the capital.

Finally, the pollution problem of Cairo, i.e., noise, air, odors and sewerage, comes on top of all the other problems. The rate of pollution in Cairo has far exceeded the international safety levels. The physical density of the population, the huge numbers of vehicles, the absence of parks and green areas, the industrial siege around Cairo, and the sands and dusts of the surrounding hills and desert all add up to the problem. Therefore, the capital has developed a very unhealthy environment.

CONCLUSION

Cairo is a typical case of strong urban bias due to national economic policies. It is also a good example of many of the problems facing cities in the developing countries where resources to deal with such problems are quite scarce. Allocation of investments among governorates in Egypt illustrates the bias in favor of Cairo quite clearly. The results of the infitah policies show how the laissez-faire approach can only strengthen the trends of concentration of different economic activities, especially high income-generating activities in the primate region. The price the Egyptian economy has to pay today for this bias, which has long historical roots, is unfortunately a heavy burden. The social consequences of the resulting problems from this bias are quite serious.

Notes

[1] *Al-Ahram*, November 11, 1984.

[2] Johannes F. Linn, *Cities in The Developing World.* New York: Oxford University Press, 1983, p. XIV.

[3] Bertrand Renand, *National Urbanization Policy in Developing Countries.* New York: Oxford University Press, 1981, pp. 5–6.

[4] *Ibid.*, p. 101.

[5] *Ibid.*, p. 98.

[6] *Ibid.*, p. 117.

[7] Hoda M. Sobhi, "Regional Disparities and The Problem of Regional Allocation of Investments" (in Arabic). A paper presented to the 4th Egyptian Economists Conference, 1979.

[8] Frank Stillwell, *Regional Economic Policy.* London: MacMillan Press, 1972, pp. 9–15.

[9] Renand, *op. cit.*, pp. 107–108.

[10] Kingsley Davis and Hilda Golden, "Urbanization and the Development of Pre-industrial Areas," in *Economic and Cultural Change.* 3, no. 1, 1954, pp. 6–24.

[11] Saad Eddin Ibrahim, "Over-urbanization and Under-urbanism: The Case of the Arab World," in *International Journal of Middle East Studies.* Vol. 1, 1975, pp. 1–23.

[12] Gamal Hamdan, *The Identity of Egypt.* Part 4 (in Arabic), Alam El-Kotob, Cairo, 1984, pp. 320–321.

[13] Alan Richards, "Ten Years of Infitah: Class, Rend (sic) and Policy Stasis in Egypt," in *The Journal of Development Studies*, 1983. p. 324.

[14] Hamdan, *op. cit.*, p. 262.

[15] *Ibid.*, pp. 271–273.

[16] Hamdan, *op. cit.*, p. 340.

[17] Khalid Ikram, *Economic Management in a Period of Transition.* U.S.: Johns Hopkins University Press, 1980, p. 147.

18 *Al-Ahali, op. cit.*

19 *Al-Mussaware*, no. 3138, Nov. 30, 1984.

20 Mahmoud A. Fadil: *Political Economy of Nasserism*, Cambridge University Press, Cambridge, UK, 1980, p. 128.

21 *Ibid.*, p. 129.

22 Ikram, *op. cit.*, p. 161.

23 Hamdan, *op. cit.*, p. 358.

DISCUSSION QUESTIONS

1. Based on your reading of Sobhi's essay, do you think that Egypt should decentralize Cairo and adopt a policy of forcing people to live elsewhere?

2. Describe some of the unique geographic, historical, social, and economic factors that make Cairo's problems unique.

3. Does the United States have a "big urban bias"?

CHAPTER 16

Issues in the Environment

INTRODUCTION

The "oil shocks" of the 1970s, unbearable urban pollution, the world's exploding population, the "greenhouse" effect, sub-Saharan famines, and the ever-present threat of nuclear obliteration have made sociologists aware, as never before, of the fragility of the earth's environment. Far more than in past history, humanity itself, rather than nature, poses a profound threat to mankind's survival.

Since the time of the ancient Greeks, Western thought has emphasized the concept of mankind conquering nature. With the advent of the scientific and industrial revolutions, it seemed that humans had actually overcome— or would overcome—the obstacles to evolution that nature created. Early sociologists such as Claude-Henry de Rourroy Saint-Simon (1760–1825), Auguste Comte (1798–1857), Herbert Spencer (1820–1903), and even Karl Marx (1818–1883) embraced the idea of eternal progress, giving little or no thought to its impact on the physical environment. The eradication of smallpox and malaria, humanity's leap into space, the advent of the computer age—all signaled human mastery of the environment.

Ironically, the very process of scientific evolution produced a series of contradictions. The progress of industrialization, for example, created greater wealth than ever before but brought with it pollution of the seas and cities, a scarcity in mineral and energy resources, and a hole in the ozone layer—a vital atmospheric layer that protects people and other denizens of earth from the potentially lethal rays of the sun.

Contemporary medicine has dramatically decreased infant mortality, freed humans from many debilities, conquered plagues, and increased longevity. In so doing, it has also produced dramatic increases in the world's population. The resultant threat is that the planet's food supply may not be adequate to feed the ever-expanding numbers of human beings.

Modern physics has broadened our understanding of the universe, made advanced technology possible, and allowed the first explorations of outer space, but it has also manufactured atomic weapons, the ultimate instruments of death that may yet destroy the earth.

Most sociologists, natural scientists, and

489

economists, as well as some statesmen, now realize that an imperative challenge is to re-establish a balance between mankind and nature. Failure to do so will result in not only ecological disasters but the possible disappearance of the human species. The selections in this chapter address this vastly important topic.

In the first selection, Albert Gore, Senator from Tennessee, argues, "Humankind has suddenly entered into a new relationship with the planet Earth." He examines the population crisis, the spread of carbon dioxide, greenhouse gas emissions, and the exhaustion of fossil energy supplies. Gore points out,

> We are destroying forest land at the rate of one acre per second; we are poisoning our rivers, lakes, groundwater, and oceans; we are causing living species to be destroyed at a rate 1,000 times greater than at any time in the last 65 million years; we are filling the atmosphere with gaseous wastes that threaten changes in the climactic system in the next 75 years as large as those that accompanied the ice age.

Senator Gore calls for a "globalistic" approach that would stop man's destruction of his environment and save the planet for future generations.

The last two readings on the environment offer diametrically opposite views on the future of planet earth. Julian Simon, an economist, is optimistic about the future. In his book *The Ultimate Resource*, he argues that natural resources and energy are getting less scarce, that pollution is decreasing, that the world's food supply is improving, and that population growth has long-term benefits. He suggests, "The ultimate resource is people-skilled, spirited, and hopeful people who will exert their wills and imaginations for their own benefit, and so, inevitably, for the benefit of us all." In this excerpt from his book, Simon gives a summary based on his review of the evidence, of his conclusions about the population problem and associated environmental ills. While he acknowledges shortages of natural resources in the short run, Simon fervently believes that there are no physical or economic reasons why human resourcefulness and enterprise cannot expand resource limits and ensure continued human progress. Central to Simon's optimism is his belief that long-run economic indicators do *not* indicate that we have entered an age of scarcity.

A very different conclusion is reached in the Worldwatch Institute Report on Progress toward a Sustainable Society, *State of the World 1990*. Lester R. Brown sees an "illusion of progress" in economic indicators. He argues that while economic trends have traditionally shaped environmental trends, the situation is now reversed. Environmental trends are beginning to shape economic trends. Moreover, as they are typically used to document progress, economic indicators such as the gross national product (GNP) are fundamentally flawed: They do not distinguish between resource uses that sustain progress and those that undermine progress. If all the environmental consequences of economic activity were included in economic indicators, Brown believes, it would be apparent that real progress would be much less. He locates the key to our future, not in gross economic indicators, but rather in the declining productivity of the earth's "biological product." The three biological systems that sustain the world economy—croplands, forests, and grasslands—are the keys to shaping civilization. They share the common feature of photosynthesis, which is being undermined by environmental degradation. Brown argues that it is the size of this photosynthesis product that affects the problem of population growth (How many people can be supported?) and stabilizing the climate (At what level can they be supported?), the two major fronts in our race to save the planet.

Though Brown offers a different, and far more pessimistic, reading of the measures of progress than we have seen thus far in this chapter, he does see evidence of a political awakening to environmental issues. The question that remains is whether the world's governments, and people, have sufficient wisdom and can muster the will to save the globe in a new age of environmental diplomacy.

The Ecology of Survival

Albert Gore

Theories about history are built on sand. Yet millions have died believing in their ultimate truth. It's because we have paid such a high price for historical theorizing that we can ill afford to lose our perspective now, or to stop thinking about where we've been and what it tells us about where we're going. To paraphrase Santayana, those who cannot remember the past ought to be condemned to reread it.

Seventy-five years, the measure of one magazine, is now the measure of one human lifetime—the number of years an American child born today can expect to live. Looking back 75 years, we can accept or ignore any number of political, cultural, or strategic lessons. Looking ahead into the life of that child, however, we see two indisputable patterns. With the invention of nuclear weapons we changed the character of warfare in ways that must preclude any conflict on the scale of the one that began in 1914. That lesson is widely understood, and we have some basis for hoping that it will guide our future affairs. The second dramatic change has not yet been so widely accepted. Humankind has suddenly entered into a new relationship with the planet Earth. Our survival depends upon our capacity to grasp, and quickly, the extent to which the current pattern or world civilization threatens the ecological system that sustains life as we know it.

From this side of the Atlantic, at least, the future looked better in 1914. Back then America didn't need a coup in Panama; that year we opened the Canal. Productivity growth in the United States was almost too fast to measure.

In the fall of 1913 a Model T came off the assembly line at Henry Ford's new Highland Park plant every 12 hours. By the spring of 1914 that plant was producing one car every hour. The world environment was as untrampled as the poppies in Flanders Fields. The biggest threat to the rain forest was Tarzan, created that year by Edgar Rice Burroughs.

From politics to art, the world was breaking loose from the old order. The acceleration of history was already well under way. Einstein's theory of relativity had jolted science. Cubism was fracturing the way artists interpreted the world. Ancient dynasties and immense empires began to die with the Archduke Ferdinand. The World War hardly made the world safe for democracy, but it did put the foes of democracy on notice. The period since then represents a succession of struggles between democratic powers and tyranny in all its guises. In 1914, as Europe descended into carnage, by far the greater number of the world's peoples lived under tyrannies. But of the major nations that went to war in Europe, only the established democracies survived with their political systems intact. The interwar years were marked by philosophical as well as geopolitical struggles on a global scale, with the ideologies of fascism, communism, and democracy in contention. In World War II, not only was fascism defeated; its exemplars underwent apparently permanent societal conversions, from which they emerged as democracies themselves. Now we appear to be experiencing the rapid dissolution of Communist tyranny. The process is advancing in Europe and perhaps gathering strength in Asia, the result of irresistible internal forces that can be set back but not permanently stopped.

In the developing worlds of Latin America, Africa, and Asia, the battle between democratic and tyrannical forms of government has been less decisive. Nevertheless, over the last decade the trend has been toward democratic forms, from Argentina and Brazil to the Philippines. Looking at this pattern, some conclude that humankind is maturing out of tutelage, throwing off submission to the arbitrary rule of those who claim legitimacy by divine right or historical "law" and embracing instead the self-rule that derives its legitimacy from the will of the electorate. Perhaps so. But experience ought to make us wary of premature declarations of victory, and we should certainly reject the ideas that we have arrived at the end of political history. The human imagination is much too fertile for that, and the human capacity for inventing systems of political belief has not exhausted itself. We can expect that "isms" will continue to appear, displacing others in the hearts and minds of millions, over cycles of time that may run from decades to centuries and even to millennia.

Yet because of the events and accomplishments of the last 75 years, there are indeed critical, and permanent, new factors in the life of humanity. These relate to the physical world, whose constants are beyond the power of ideological manipulation. We have, in the course of a single life span, managed to grasp the levers of our own destruction: first, in the form of nuclear weapons; and second, in the form of the industrial destruction of the biosphere, which has begun to move ahead of geometric rates of increase. When you consider the relationship of the human species to the planet Earth, not much change is visible in a single year, in a single nation. Yet if you look at the entire pattern of that relationship from the beginning of the modern era in 1914 until today, the contrast is starkly clear.

In 422 years, from the time of Christopher Columbus until 1914, world population tripled, to 1.6 billion. In the last 75 years it has tripled again, to 5.2 billion. We are told that in the next 75 years it will double and perhaps even triple once more. Nearly every index of the impact of modern industrial society follows the same pattern of sudden, unprecedented

acceleration. Americans consumed around 40 billion kilowatt-hours of electricity in 1914. Last year we used 60 times that much. U.S. production of synthetic organic chemicals (from PCBs to pesticides to plastics) has gone from almost nothing to 225 billion pounds per year—half a ton for every American. The world's fossil fuel use has increased ten times over, and with it, carbon dioxide has flooded the Earth's atmosphere. Other greenhouse gases have soared upward at similar rates: U.S. nitrogen oxide emissions are up 800 percent since 1914; methane concentrations have nearly doubled; and the world's emissions of chlorofluorocarbons, which had not yet been invented in 1914, have increased by 80 times since World War II, and are still doubling every decade, posing a deadly threat to the Earth's protective ozone shield.

The hole in the ozone layer is only the most widely accepted manifestation of a much broader challenge to the Earth's environment. We are destroying forest land at the rate of one acre per second; we are poisoning our rivers, lakes, groundwater, and oceans; we are causing living species to be destroyed at a rate 1,000 times greater than at any time in the last 65 million years; we are filling the atmosphere with gaseous wastes that threaten changes to the climatic system in the next 75 years as large as those that accompanied the ice ages over hundreds of thousands of years. These dramatic changes are taking place not only because the human population is surging and our standard of living has increased, but because we tolerate environmental vandalism on a global scale.

For 75 years the price we would have to pay for our actions has seemed impossibly remote. Only now are we beginning to see, in Ivan Illich's phrase, "the shadow our future throws." Whether we look forward in hopes of glimpsing what the future holds or gaze backward at the events that have dominated the world since 1914, we see something that resembles one of those artist's depictions of relativity theory, with time and space curved like a checkerboard grid painted by Salvador Dali. Our political awareness of the world is shaped and bent by events. Vast calamities such as the world wars exert a powerful gravitational pull on every idea we have around the world around us. And, just as in Einstein's theory, future events can exert the same gravitational pull on our thinking as events in the past. The political will to slow down the nuclear arms race came from the feeling that we were being pulled toward a future we had never seen but didn't want. Now, as we are being drawn toward the brink of ecological collapse, we must be willing to consider drastic ecological action.

There is no way for humanity to forget its skills for self-destruction, by war upon each other or by war upon the environment. In an exchange of Promethean proportions, we have acquired deadly knowledge that we can never lose but must learn to keep under control forever. That is the new and permanent point of departure for political wisdom. And if we are to succeed in keeping civilization intact, it is clear that one ism must be revived and renewed: globalism—by which I mean not some kind of world order prescribed and imposed from above, but rather a sense of responsibility for the good order of the world, rising upward from all of its peoples, and ultimately manifesting itself in the behavior of their governments, both domestically and in international relations.

A new globalism cannot be based on some transformation of human nature, by which people will be endowed with new virtues of foresight and restraint. In the last 75 years we have had enough of efforts to create the New Man in one image or another. Jefferson's educated citizenry will have to suffice. The globalism we need can develop out of roots already universally present. It will be an enlightened, informed extension of our desire to survive, and of our often even more intense desire to provide for the survival and well-being of our children and grandchildren. Globalism will be marked by the sense that if our affairs are conducted on the basis of an unlimited struggle for supremacy—whether among nations or over nature—the result will be an increasingly high risk of almost immeasurable loss for all. It will be marked also by a sense that at some level, cooperation secures for all of us what strife cannot.

Mikhail Gorbachev now speaks as an advocate of a globalist approach based on mutual consent, rather than hegemony. It is certainly a revolution of sorts to hear such things from a Soviet leader. But it is well to remember that Gorbachev has at best caught up with the doctrine of collective security as propounded by Woodrow Wilson in 1918 and again by Franklin Roosevelt in 1945.

The essence of the doctrine of collective security is that security is indivisible and mutual: it must be provided for all, by actions to which all must contribute, or it exists for no one. That is certainly the lesson we must apply as we struggle to redefine our security relationship in military terms. Reductions of strategic and conventional weapons are desirable, but not in the abstract. They must seek a result in which the residual forces are perceived by all concerned parties to be stable, in the sense of lacking the capacity for decisive surprise. And reductions must be carried out in a political context that buttresses the expectation of peace and justifies diminished preparation for war.

But the notion of mutual security must now move from an exclusive concern with security as an issue of peace or war to a definition of security that includes the global environment. With that in mind, I have proposed a Strategic Environment Initiative (SEI). Let's face it: the Strategic Defense Initiative can't assure our survival for the next 75 years. A Strategic Environment Initiative might. I am no admirer of SDI, but one doesn't have to be an admirer to recognize that it drew together previously scattered facilities and resources and that it attracted a generous share of the government's budget for research and development. We need to approach the technological challenge of environmental protection and economic growth with at least the same intensity—and with comparable or greater levels of funding.

If we continue our current pattern of technology and production, we will be able to achieve economic growth in the near term only at the cost of massive environmental disorder in the not so distant future. For the developing world, the problems of reconciling economic growth and environmental protection are compounded by high rates of population growth and a massive debt burden. Yet the cooperation of Third World nations is crucial to controlling problems as vast as global warming. Their share of greenhouse gas emissions from fossil fuels could grow from about 20 percent today to as much as 60 percent by 2050. A Strategic Environment Initiative would promote environmentally sustainable development by identifying and spreading new technologies to developing countries, where 95 percent of world population growth will take place during the next century. Here in the United States, the Strategic Environment Initiative must modernize technologies and practices in every economic sector, from more fuel-efficient cars and energy-efficient appliances to manufacturing that relies on recycled material, to a second green revolution requiring fewer fertilizers and pesticides. The emerging consensus for environmental protection is opening the door to solutions once considered politically impossible.

It will not be enough, however, to change our laws, policies, and programs. We must also change the way we think about ourselves, our children, and our future. For a very long time, we have seen ourselves as separate from the world around us. At least since the beginning of the scientific method, and probably since Aristotle, we have seen nature as the object of our experiments, exploitation, and dominion. As scientists reflected on Einstein's revolution, they discovered that the act of observing alters what is observed. Heisenberg established that "uncertainty principle" in 1923. But its philosophical application is not limited to the subatomic world he described. In a kind of Heisenberg Principle writ large, we have altered—without realizing it—our relationship to nature itself. We must now create a new pattern of thinking in which we once again see ourselves as a part of the ecological system in which we live. We have lost, so to speak, our eco-librium.

How can we gain sufficient distance from ourselves to see a pattern that contains us in a larger context? My own religious faith teaches me that while we are given dominion over the Earth, we also are required to be good stewards of the Earth. If our actions cause the destruction of half the living species God put on this Earth during our lifetimes, we will have failed in the responsibility of stewardship. Are those actions, because of their result, "evil"? The answer depends not upon the everyday nature of the actions, but upon our knowledge of their consequences. For the individual actions that collectively produce the world's environmental evil are indeed banal when they are looked at one by one: the cutting of a tree, the flicking on of an air conditioner, the dumping of some inconvenient waste.

"Evil" and "good" are terms not used frequently by politicians. Yet I do not see how this problem can be solved without reference to spiritual values found in every faith. For many scientists on the edge of new discoveries in cosmology and quantum physics, the reconciliation of science and religion sometimes now seems near at hand. It is a reconciliation not unlike the one we seek between humankind and nature. But even without defining the problem in religious terms, it is possible to conclude that the solutions we seek will be found in a new faith in the future of life on

Earth after our own, a faith in the future that justifies sacrifices in the present, a new moral courage to choose higher values in the conduct of human affairs, and a new reverence for absolute principles that can serve as stars by which to map the future course of our species and our place within creation.

DISCUSSION QUESTIONS

1. What explanations would you offer for the destruction of planet earth?

2. In what ways, if any, can Gore's hope for a "globalistic" approach be implemented in a practical way.

3. How has the development of a global economy contributed to the destruction of the environment and how can it be used to "save the planet"?

The Ultimate Resource

Julian Simon

WHAT ARE THE *REAL* POPULATION AND RESOURCE PROBLEMS?

Is there a natural-resource problem now? Certainly there is—just as there has always been. The problem is that natural resources are scarce, in the sense that it costs us labor and capital to get them, though we would prefer to get them for free.

Are we now "entering an age of scarcity"? You can see anything you like in a crystal ball. But almost without exception, the best data—the long-run economic indicators—suggest precisely the opposite. The relevant measures of scarcity—the costs of natural resources in human labor, and their prices relative to wages and to other goods—all suggest that natural resources have been becoming *less* scarce over the long run, right up to the present.

How about pollution? Is this not a problem? Of course pollution is a problem—people have always had to dispose of their waste products so as to enjoy a pleasant and healthy living space. But on the average we now live in a less dirty and more healthy environment than in earlier centuries.

About population now: Is there a population "problem"? Again, of course there is a population problem, just as there has always been. When a couple is about to have a baby, they must prepare a place for the child to sleep safely. Then, after the birth of the child, the parents must feed, clothe, guard, and teach it. All of this requires effort and resources, and not from the parents alone. When a baby is born or a migrant arrives, a community must increase its municipal services—schooling, fire and police protection, and garbage collection. None of these are free.

Beyond any doubt, an additional child is a burden on people other than its parents—and in some ways even on them—for the first fifteen or twenty-five years of its life. Brothers and sisters must do with less of everything except companionship. Taxpayers must cough up additional funds for schooling and other public services. Neighbors have more noise. During these early years the child produces nothing, and the income of the family and the community is spread around more thinly than if the baby were not born. And when the child grows up and first goes to work, jobs are squeezed a bit, and the output and pay per working person go down. All this clearly is an economic loss for other people.

Almost equally beyond any doubt, however, an additional person is also a boon. The child or immigrant will pay taxes later on, contribute energy and resources to the community, produce goods and services for the consumption of others, and make efforts to beautify and purify the environment. Perhaps most significant of all for the more-developed countries is the contribution that the average person makes to increasing the efficiency of production through new ideas and improved methods.

The real population problem, then, is *not* that there are too many people or that too many babies are being born. It is that others must support each additional person before that person contributes in turn to the well-being of others.

Which is more weighty, the burden or the boon? That depends on the economic conditions, about which we shall speak at some length. But also, to a startling degree, the decision about whether the overall effect of a child or migrant is positive or negative depends on the values of whoever is making the judgment—your preference to spend a dollar now rather than to wait for a dollar-plus-something in twenty or thirty years, your preferences for having more or fewer wild animals alive as opposed to more or fewer human beings alive, and so on. Population growth is a problem, but not *just* a problem; it is a boon, but not just a boon. So your values are all-important in judging the net effect of population growth, and whether there is "overpopulation" or "underpopulation."

An additional child is, from the economic point of view, like a laying chicken, a cacao tree, a new factory, or a new house. A baby is a durable good in which someone must invest heavily long before the grown adult begins to provide returns on the investment. But whereas "Travel now, pay later" is inherently attractive because the pleasure is immediate and the piper will wait, "Pay now, benefit from the child later" is inherently problematic because the sacrifice comes first.

You might respond that additional children will *never* yield net benefits, because they will use up irreplaceable resources. Much of this book is devoted to showing that additional persons do, in fact, produce more than they consume, and that natural resources are not an exception. But let us agree that there is still a population problem, just as there is a problem with all good investments. Long before their are benefits, we must tie up capital that could otherwise be used for immediate consumption.

Please notice that I have restricted the discussion to the *economic* aspect of investing in children—that is, to a child's effect on the material standard of living. If we also consider the non-economic aspects of children—what they mean to parents and to others who enjoy a flourishing of humanity—then the case for adding children to our world becomes even stronger. And if we also keep in mind that most of the costs of children are borne by their parents rather than by the community, whereas the community gets the lion's share of the benefits later on, especially in developed countries, the essential differences between children and other investments tend to strengthen rather than weaken the case for having more children. . . .

Food Contrary to popular impression, the per capita food situation has been improving for the three decades since World War II, the only decades for which we have acceptable data. We also know that famine has progressively diminished for at least the past century. And there is strong reason to believe that human nutrition will continue to improve into the indefinite future, even with continued population growth.

Land Agricultural land is not a fixed resource, as Malthus and many since Malthus have thought. Rather, the amount of agricultural land has been, and still is, increasing substantially, and it is likely to continue to increase where needed. Paradoxically, in the countries that are best supplied with food, such as the U.S., the quantity of land under cultivation has been decreasing because it is more economical to raise larger yields on less land than to increase the total amount of farmland. For this reason, among others, land for recreation and for wildlife has been increasing rapidly in the U.S. All this may be hard to believe, but solid data substantiate these statements beyond a doubt.

Natural Resources Hold your hat—our supplies of natural resources are not finite in any economic sense. Nor does past experience give reason to expect natural resources to become more scarce. Rather, if the past is any guide, natural resources will progressively become less scarce, and less costly, and will constitute a smaller proportion of our expenses in future years. And population growth is likely to have a long-run *beneficial* impact on the natural-resource situation.

Energy Grab your hat again—the long-run future of our energy supply is at least as bright as that of other natural resources, though political maneuvering can temporarily boost prices from time to time. Finiteness is no problem here either. And the long-run impact of additional people is likely to speed the development of a cheap energy supply that is almost inexhaustible.

Pollution This set of issues is as complicated as you wish to make it. But even many ecologists, as well as the bulk of economists, agree that population growth is not the villain in the creation and reduction of pollution. And the key trend is that life expectancy, which is the best overall index of the pollution level, has improved markedly as the world's population has grown.

Pathological Effects of Population Density This putative drawback of population growth is sheer myth. Its apparent source is faulty biological and psychological analogies with animal populations.

The Standard of Living In the short run, additional children imply additional costs, though the costs to persons other than the children's parents are relatively small. In the longer run, however, per capita income is likely to be higher with a growing population than with a stationary one, both in more-developed and less-developed countries. Whether you wish to pay the present costs for the future benefits depends on how you weigh the future relative to the present; this is a value judgment.

Immigration Immigration usually has a positive effect on most citizens. The few persons whom the immigrants might displace from their jobs may be hurt, of course, but many of them only temporarily. On balance, immigrants contribute more to the economy than they take, in the U.S. and most other places.

Human fertility The contention that poor and uneducated people breed like animals is demonstrably wrong, even for the poorest and most "primitive" societies. Well-off people who believe that the poor do not weigh the consequences of having more children are simply arrogant or ignorant, or both.

Future Population Growth Population forecasts are publicized with confidence and fanfare, but the record of even the official forecasts made by U.S. government agencies and by the UN is little (if any) better than that of the most naive predictions. For example, experts in the 1930s foresaw the U.S. population as declining, perhaps to as little as 100 million people, long before the turn of the century. And official UN forecasts made in 1970 for the year 2000, a mere thirty years in advance, were five years later revised downward by almost 2 billion people, from 7.5 billion to 5.6 billion. Nor is the record better with more modern statistical methods. Perhaps most astonishing is a forecast made by the recent President's Commission on Population Growth and the American Future. In 1972 the commission published its prediction that "there will be no year in the next two decades in which the absolute number of births will be less than in 1970." But in the year *before* this prediction was made—1971—the number of births has *already* fallen lower than in 1970. The science of demographic forecasting clearly had not yet reached perfection.

World Population Policy Tens of millions of U.S. taxpayers' money is being used to tell the governments and people of other countries that they ought to take strong measures to control their fertility. The head of the Population Branch of the U.S. State Department Agency for International Development (AID)—the single most important U.S. population official for many years—has publicly said that the U.S. should act to reduce fertility worldwide for its own economic self-interest. But no solid economic data or analyses underlie this assertion. Furthermore, might not such acts be an unwarranted interference in the internal affairs of other countries?

Domestic Population Activities Other millions of U.S. taxpayers' funds go to private organizations making up the population lobby, whose directors believe that, for environmental and related reasons, fewer Americans should be born. These funds are used to propagandize the rest of us that we should believe—and act—in ways consistent with the views of such organizations as the Population Crisis Committee, the Population Reference Bureau, the Worldwatch Institute, the Environmental Fund, and the Association for Voluntary Sterilization.

Still more tens of millions of U.S. taxpayers' funds are being spent to reduce the fertility of the poor in the U.S. The explicit justification for this policy (given by the head of Planned Parenthood's Alan Guttmacher Institute) is that it will keep additional poor people off the welfare rolls. Even were this to be proven—and as far as I know it has not been proven—is this in the spirit or tradition of America? Furthermore, there is statistical proof that the public birth-control clinics, which were first opened in large numbers in the southern states, were positioned to reduce fertility among blacks.

Involuntary Sterilization Tax moneys are being used to involuntarily sterilize poor people (often black) without medical justification. As a result of the eugenics movement, which has been intertwined with the population-control movement for decades, there are now laws in thirty states providing for the involuntary sterilization of the mentally defective, and many thousands have been so sterilized. And these laws have led to perfectly normal women being sterilized, without their knowledge, after being told that their operations were other sorts of minor surgery.

In the chapters to come, you will find evidence documenting these statements and many others about resources, population, environment, and their interconnections. You will also find a foundation of economic theory that makes sense of the surprising facts. And you will find my offer to back with my own hard cash my forecasts about the things we can bet about—natural resources and energy. If you believe that scarcities are coming, you can take advantage of my offer and make some money at my expense. . . .

ABOUT THIS AUTHOR AND HIS VALUES

This book originated in my interest in the economics of population. In order to show that population growth is not a straightforward evil, I had to show that more people need not cause scarcities or environmental decay in the long run. That's how this book came to be written.

Ironically, when I began to work on population studies, I assumed that the accepted view was sound. I aimed to help the world contain its "exploding" population, which I believed to be one of the two main threats to mankind (war being the other). But my reading and research led me into confusion. Though the standard economic theory of population (which has hardly changed since Malthus) asserts that a higher population growth implies a lower standard of living, the available empirical data do not support that theory. My technical book, which is the predecessor of this volume, is an attempt to reconcile that contradiction. It leads to a theory that suggests population growth has positive economic effects in the long run, though there are costs in the short run.

When I began my population studies, I was in the midst of a depression of unusual duration (whose origins had nothing to do with population growth or the world's predicament). As I studied the economics of population and worked my way to the views I now hold—that population growth, along with the lengthening of human life, is a moral and material triumph—my outlook for myself, for my family, and for the future of humanity became increasingly more optimistic. Eventually I was able to pull myself out of my depression. This is only part of the story, but there is at least some connection between the two sets of men-

tal events—my population studies and my increasing optimism.

One spring day about 1969 I visited the AID office in Washington to discuss a project intended to lower fertility in less-developed countries. I arrived early for my appointment, so I strolled outside in the warm sunshine. Below the building's plaza I noticed a sign that said "Iwo Jima Highway." I remembered reading about a eulogy delivered by a Jewish chaplain over the dead on the battlefield at Iwo Jima, saying something like, "How many who would have been a Mozart or a Michelangelo or an Einstein have we buried here?" And then I thought, Have I gone crazy? What business do I have trying to help arrange it that fewer human beings will be born, each one of whom might be a Mozart or a Michelangelo or an Einstein—or simply a joy to his or her family and community, and a person who will enjoy life?

I still believe that helping people fulfill their desires for the number of children they want is a wonderful service. But to persuade them or coerce them to have fewer children than they would individually like to have—that is something entirely different.

The longer I read the literature about population, the more baffled and distressed I become that one idea is omitted. Enabling a potential human being to come into life and to enjoy life is a good thing, just as enabling a living person's life not to be ended is a good thing. Of course a death is not the same as an averted life, in part because others feel differently about the two. Yet I find no logic implicit in the thinking of those who are horrified at the starvation of a comparatively few people in a faraway country (and apparently more horrified than at the deaths by political murder in that same faraway country, or at the deaths by accidents in their own country) but who are positively gleeful with the thought that 1 million or 10 million times that many lives will never be lived that might be lived.

Economics alone cannot explain this attitude, for though the economic consequences of death differ from those of non-life, they are not so different as to explain this difference in attitude. So what is it? Why does Kingsley Davis (one of the world's great demographers) respond to the U.S. population growth during the 1960s with, "I have never been able to get anyone to tell me why we needed those 23 million"? And Paul Ehrlich: "I can't think of any reason for having more than one hundred fifty million people [in the U.S.], and no one has ever raised one to me."

I can suggest to Davis and Ehrlich more than one reason for having more children and taking in more immigrants. Least interesting is that the larger population will probably mean a higher standard of living for our grandchildren and great-grandchildren. (My technical book and a good many chapters in this book substantiate that assertion.) A more interesting reason is that we need another person for exactly the same reason we need Davis and Ehrlich. That is, just as the Davises and Ehrlichs of this world are of value to the rest of us, so will the average additional person be of value.

The most interesting reason for having additional people, however, is this: If the Davises and Ehrlichs say that their lives are of value to themselves, and if the rest of us honor that claim and say that our lives are of value to us, then in the same manner the lives of additional people are of value to those people themselves. Why should we not honor their claims, too?

If Davis or Ehrlich were to ask those 23 million additional Americans born between 1960 and 1970 whether it was a good thing that they were born, many of them would be able to think of a good reason or two. Some of them might also be so unkind as to add, "Yes, it's true that you gentlemen do not *personally* need any of us for your own welfare. But then, do you think that *we* have greater need of you?"

What is most astonishing is that these simple ideas, which would immediately spring to the minds of many who cannot read or write, have never even come into the heads of famous scientists such as Davis and Ehrlich—by their own admission.

The same absence of this basic respect for human life is at the bottom of Ehrlich's well-known restatement of Pascal's wager. "If I'm right, we will save the world [by curbing population growth]. If I'm wrong, people will still be better fed, better housed, and happier, thanks to our efforts. [He probably *is* wrong.] Will anything be lost if it turns out later that we can support a much larger population than seems possible today?"

Please note how different is Pascal's wager: Live as if there is God, because even if there is no God you have lost nothing. Pascal's wager applies entirely to one person. No one else loses if he is wrong. But Ehrlich bets what he thinks will be the economic gains that we and our descendants might enjoy against the unborn's very lives. Would he make the same sort of wager if his *own* life rather than others' lives were the stake? . . .

DISCUSSION QUESTIONS

1. According to Simon, what is the ultimate resource?
2. What indications does Simon provide for an improved environment?
3. How do Gore and Simon differ on the state of the environment?

The Illusion of Progress

Lester R. Brown

For most of the nearly four fifths of humanity born since World War II, life has seemed to be a period of virtually uninterrupted economic progress. Since mid-century, the global economic product has nearly quintupled. On average, the additional economic output in each of the last four decades has matched that added from the beginning of civilization until 1950.

World food output during this period also grew at a record pace. Soaring demand fueled by population growth and rising affluence provided the incentive, and modern technology the means, to multiply the world's grain harvest 2.6 times since mid-century. No other generation has witnessed gains even remotely approaching this.

Such gains would seem to be a cause for celebration, but instead there is a sense of illusion, a feeling that they overstate progress. The system of national accounting used to measure economic progress incorporates the depreciation of plant and equipment, but not the depletion of natural capital. Since mid-century, the world has lost nearly one fifth of the topsoil from its cropland, a fifth of its tropical rain forests, and tens of thousands of its plant and animal species.

During this same period, atmospheric carbon dioxide (CO_2) levels have increased by 13 percent, setting the stage for hotter summers. The protective ozone layer in the stratosphere has been depleted by 2 percent worldwide and far more over Antarctica. Dead lakes and dying forests have become a natural accompaniment of industrialization. Historians in the twenty-first century may marvel at this economic performance—and sorrow over its environmental consequences.

Throughout our lifetimes, economic trends have shaped environmental trends, often alerting the earth's natural resources and systems in ways not obvious at the time. Now, as we enter the nineties, the reverse is also beginning to happen: environmental trends are beginning to shape economic trends.

The environmental degradation of the planet is starting to show up at harvest time. The cumulative effects of losing 24 billion tons of topsoil each year are being felt in some of the world's major food-producing regions. Recent evidence indicates that air pollution is damaging crops in both auto-centered economies of the West and coal-burning economies of the East. Meteorologists cannot yet be certain, but the hotter summers and drought-reduced harvests of the eighties may be early indications of the greenhouse effect.

Environmental degradation undoubtedly contributed to the slower growth in world grain output during the eighties. The 2.6-fold gain in world grain output just mentioned occurred between 1950 and 1984; since then, there has been no appreciable increase. The 1989 estimated harvest (1.67 billion tons) was up only 1 percent from that of 1984, which means that grain output per person is down nearly 7 percent. Some two thirds of this fall in production has been offset by drawing down stocks, reducing them to a precariously low level; the remainder, by reducing consumption. Although five years is obviously not enough time to signify a long-term trend, it does show that the world's farmers are finding it more difficult to keep up with growth in population.

Nowhere is this more clear than in Africa, where the combination of record population growth and widespread land degradation is reducing grain production per person. A drop of 20 percent from the peak in 1967 has converted the continent into a grain importer, fueled the region's mounting external debt, and left millions of Africans hungry and physically weakened, drained of their vitality and productivity. In a 1989 report sketching out several scenarios for this beleaguered continent, World Bank analysts termed the simple extrapolation of recent trends the "nightmare scenario."

In both Africa and Latin America, food consumption per person is lower today than it was when the decade began. Infant mortality rates—a sensitive indicator of nutritional stress—appear to have turned upward in many countries in Africa and Latin America, reversing a long-term historical trend. Nations in which there are enough data to document this rise include Brazil, the Dominican Republic, El Salvador, Ghana, Madagascar, Mexico, Peru, Uruguay, and Zambia.

Environmental degradation is affecting more than economic and social trends: 1989 was the year environmental issues moved into the political mainstream. In Western Europe, environmentalists won resounding gains in legislative races. And environmental issues moved to the forefront of political debate in Poland, the Soviet Union, Japan, and Australia. Unfortunately, rising political awareness has not yet translated into policies that will reverse the deteriorating situation.

On the two most important fronts in the race to save the planet—stopping population growth and stabilizing climate—the world is losing ground. Some progress has been made in slowing the rate of population growth since 1970, but the decline has been so gradual that the annual increment grows larger each year. During the eighties, world population increased by 842 million, an average of 84 million a year. (See Table 1.) During the next 10 years it is projected to grow by 959 million, the largest increment ever for a single decade. As the annual excess of births over deaths continues to widen, the date of population stability is pushed ever further into the future.

TABLE 1			
WORLD POPULATION GROWTH BY DECADE, 1950–90, WITH PROJECTION TO 2000			
Year	Population (billion)	Increase by decade (million)	Average annual increase (million)
1950	2.515		
1960	3.019	504	50
1970	3.698	679	68
1980	4.450	752	75
1990	5.292	842	84
2000	6.251	959	96

Source: United Nations, Department of International Economic and Social Affairs, *World Population Prospects 1988* (New York: 1989).

Progress in stabilizing climate is equally disappointing. (See Chapter 2.) Carbon emissions from fossil fuel use declined for several years as countries invested heavily in energy efficiency measures. But in the last few years they have started to rise again. Leading industrial economies, such as the United States and Japan, are the primary contributors to this unfortunate global upturn. In 1987, global carbon emissions from fossil fuels rose 1.5 percent and in 1988, 3.7 percent, reaching a record total of 5.7 billion tons.

Reading the daily newspapers gives the impression that changes in economic indicators such as the gross national product (GNP), interest rates, or stock prices are the keys to the future. But it is changes in the biological product that are shaping civilization. It is changes in the size of the photosynthetic product that determine ultimately how many of us the earth can support and at what level of consumption.

THE EARTH'S DECLINING PRODUCTIVITY

Three biological systems—croplands, forests, and grasslands—support the world economy. Except for fossil fuels and minerals, they supply all the raw materials for industry; except for seafood, they provide all our food. Forests are the source of fuel, lumber, paper, and numerous other products. Grasslands provide meat, milk, leather, and wool. Croplands supply food, feed, and an endless array of raw materials for industry such as fiber and vegetable oils.

Common to all these biological systems is the process of photosynthesis, the ability of plants to use solar energy to combine water and carbon dioxide to produce carbohydrates. Although an estimated 41 percent of photosynthetic activity takes place in the oceans, it is the 59 percent occurring on land that underpins the world economy. And it is the loss of terrestrial photosynthesis as a result of environmental degradation that is undermining many national economies.

The biological activity that supplies the bulk of our food and raw materials takes place on the nearly one third of the earth's surface that is land, some 13 billion hectares. According to a U.N. Food and Agriculture Organization tabulation for 1986, 11 percent of this—nearly 1.5 billion hectares—is used to produce crops. Roughly 25 percent is pasture or rangeland, providing grass or other forage for domesticated livestock and wild herbivores. A somewhat larger area (31 percent) is in forests, including open forests or savannahs only partly covered with trees. The remaining 33 percent of the world's land supports little biological activity. It is either wasteland, essentially desert, or has been paved over or built on.

The share of land planted to crops increased from the time agriculture began until 1981, but since then the area of newly reclaimed land has been offset by that lost to degradation and converted to nonfarm uses. The grassland area has shrunk since the mid-seventies, as overgrazing slowly converts it to desert. The forested area has been shrinking for centuries, but the losses accelerated at mid-century and

even more from 1980 onward. The combined area of these three biologically productive categories is shrinking while the remaining categories—wasteland and that covered by human settlements—are expanding.

Not only is the biologically productive land area shrinking, but on part of it productivity is falling. In forests, for example, output is being lowered on some remaining stands, apparently by air pollution and acid rain. Evidence of this damage in industrial countries is now widespread. In the United States, it can be found throughout much of the country, and in Europe it stretches from the Atlantic coast in the west to the remote reaches of Siberia in the east.

Even an experienced forester often cannot see any changes in the trees that would indicate slower growth; only careful measurements over time show how much pollutants are stressing trees. A Forest Inventory Analysis conducted regularly by the U.S. Forest Service reports that the annual growth of yellow pines, a major species covering some 42 million hectares in the Southeast, declined by 30–50 percent between 1955 and 1985. From 1975 to 1985, the dead pines increased from 9 percent of all trees to 15 percent. Soviet foresters report a decline in tree growth rates in central Siberia over the last few decades that is remarkably similar.

While forest productivity is being diminished by chemical stress, that of grasslands is being reduced by the physical stress of overgrazing. Widespread grassland degradation can now be seen on every continent. Although the data for grassland degradation are even more sketchy than for forest clearing, the trends are no less real. This problem is highly visible throughout Africa, where livestock numbers have expanded nearly as fast as the human population. In 1950, 238 million Africans relied on 272 million livestock. By 1987, the human population had increased to 604 million, and the livestock to 543 million.

In a continent where grain is scarce, 183 million cattle, 197 million sheep, and 163 million goats are supported almost entirely by grazing and browsing. Everywhere outside the tsetse-fly belt, livestock are vital to the economy, but in many countries their numbers exceed grassland carrying capacity by half or more. A study charting the mounting pressures on grasslands in nine southern African countries found that the capacity to sustain livestock is diminishing. As grasslands deteriorate, soil erosion accelerates, further reducing the carrying capacity and setting in motion a self-reinforcing cycle of ecological degradation and deepening human poverty.

Fodder needs of livestock in nearly all developing countries now exceed the sustainable yield of grasslands and other forage resources. In India, the demand by the end of the decade is expected to reach 700 million tons, while the supply will total just 540 million. The National Land Use and Wastelands Development Council there reports that in states with the most serious land degradation, such as Rajasthan and Karnataka, fodder supplies satisfy only 50–80 percent of needs, leaving large numbers of emaciated cattle. When drought occurs, hundreds of thousands of these animals die. In recent years, local governments in India have established fodder relief camps for cattle threatened with starvation, much as food relief camps are set up for people similarly threatened.

Overgrazing is not limited to the Third World. In the United States, where the Bureau of Land Management (BLM) is responsible for 66 million hectares of government-owned grazing land, overgrazing is commonplace. A 1987 survey found that only 33 percent of the BLM's rangeland was in good to excellent condition; 58 percent was fair to poor. (See Table 2.)

As the deterioration of grazing lands continues, some of it eventually becomes wasteland, converted to desert by the excessive

TABLE 2	
CONDITION OF BUREAU OF LAND MANAGEMENT GRAZED LAND, 1987	
Condition	**Percent[1]**
Excellent	3
Good	30
Fair	39
Poor	19

[1] Column totals 91 because the condition of 9 percent of land was not reported.
Source: U.S. Department of the Interior, Bureau of Land Management, *Public Land Statistics, 1987* (Washington, D.C.: 1988).

demands of growing livestock populations. And as the forage available to support animals diminishes, pressure shifts to croplands to produce more grain to feed livestock, thus intensifying the competition between humans and animals for scarce food supplies.

The loss of productive woodland, grassland, and cropland to nonfarm uses is also progressing on every continent, though at varying rates. Each year, millions of hectares of biologically productive land are paved over or built upon. Growth in the world's automobile fleet, though it has slowed dramatically over the last decade, is nonetheless leading to the paving of more and more of the earth's surface with streets, roads, and parking spaces. Each car added to the world fleet competes with farmers.

Stanford University biologist Peter M. Vitousek and his colleagues estimate that humans now appropriate close to 40 percent of the land's net primary biological product. In other words, nearly 40 percent of the earth's land-based photosynthetic activity is devoted to the satisfaction of human needs or has been lost as a result of human degradation of natural systems. As our own share continues to increase, it becomes more difficult for other species to survive. Eventually, life-supporting systems could begin to unravel.

To summarize, at a time when demand for

various biological products is rising rapidly, the earth's biological production is shrinking. The even greater annual additions to world population in prospect for the nineties will further reduce the earth's ability to supply our food and raw materials. These two trends cannot continue indefinitely. At some point, the continuing decline in the photosynthetic product will translate into a decline in the economic product.

RECALCULATING ECONOMIC PROGRESS

Looking at the basic biological systems just discussed, the world is not doing very well. Yet key economic indicators show the world is prospering. Despite a slow start at the beginning of the eighties, global economic output expanded by more than a fifth during the decade. The economy grew, trade increased, and millions of new jobs were created. How can basic biological indicators be so bearish and economic indicators so bullish at the same time?

The answer is that the economic indicators are flawed in a fundamental way: they do not distinguish between resource uses that sustain progress and those that undermine it. The principal measure of economic progress is the gross national product. In simple terms, this totals the value of all goods and services produced and subtracts depreciation of capital assets. Developed a half-century ago, GNP accounts helped establish a common means among countries of measuring changes in economic output over time. For some time, this seemed to work reasonably well, but serious weaknesses are now surfacing. As noted earlier, GNP includes depreciation of plant and equipment, but it does not take into account the depreciation of natural capital, including nonrenewable resources such as oil or renewable resources such as forests.

This shortcoming can produce a misleading sense of national economic health. According to the conventional approach, for example, countries that overcut forests actually do better in the short run than those that manage forests on a sustained-yield basis: the trees cut down are counted as income but no subtraction is made to account for depletion of the forest, a natural asset. The advantage is short-lived, however, as overcutting eventually destroys the resource base entirely, leading to a collapse of the forest products industry.

To illustrate the flaws in current GNP accounting, economist Robert Repetto and his colleagues at the World Resources Institute recalculated the GNP of Indonesia, incorporating the depletion of natural capital. Considering only oil depletion, soil erosion, and deforestation, he showed that Indonesia's economic growth rate from 1971 to 1984, originally reported at 7 percent, was in reality only 4 percent. The conventional system not only sometimes overstates progress, it may indicate progress when there is actually decline. In Repetto's revised system of national economic accounting, natural capital depletion gets a line entry just as depreciation of plant and equipment does.

Including changes in the stock of natural capital represents a major advance in national economic accounting, but if this system is to be a basis for policymaking in an era when environmental issues loom large, it will have to go one step further and incorporate the environmental effects of economic activity. For instance, the deforestation that led to a net loss in Indonesia's natural capital also contributed to the buildup of CO_2 around the world, thus hastening global warming. How much will it cost to cope with the share of climate change due to deforestation in Indonesia?

Or consider the oil produced in Indonesia, which Repetto incorporated as a net reduction in the country's natural capital. To what extent is it contributing to the serious air pollution problem in Jakarta and to respiratory illnesses among the residents? How much is the Indonesian oil burned in the Netherlands contributing to the air pollution and acid rain destroying lakes in Scandinavia and forests in West Germany? It is certainly true that data on the costs of lost forest productivity in Europe or of global warming are not very good. But is that a good reason to ignore them entirely rather than try to make some estimates, however crude they are, and incorporate them into the national economic accounts? The consequences are so profoundly important that it would be better to include even the roughest of estimates.

Another way to grasp the importance of natural capital depreciation would be to look at a particular sector of the world economy, such as food, and subtract from national accounts the value of output that is produced unsustainably. This would also help determine how much of our consumption is at the expense of future generations. Grain is currently produced, for example, by cultivating highly erodible land that will eventually become wasteland or by intensifying farming in ways that lead to excessive soil erosion and cropland loss.

In the United States, an estimated 13 million hectares of cropland was losing topsoil so rapidly that Congress has provided for its conversion to grassland or woodland before it becomes wasteland. If this were all Great Plains wheatland, it would produce roughly 2.5 tons of grain per hectare, for a total of 33 million tons. Since a minor share is higher yielding midwestern cornland, this is a lower bound estimate for unsustainable grain output.

In addition, one fifth of the 20 million hectares of U.S. irrigated land is being watered by drawing down water tables by 15-152 centimeters (6 inches to 5 feet) per year. If, for purposes of calculation, it is assumed that water tables are eventually stabilized under 2 million hectares of this 4 million hectare total by increasing water use efficiency and that the

other 2 million hectares reverts to dryland farming, grain output on the latter would be reduced by perhaps 4 tons per hectare or 8 million tons. Thus the 41 million tons of grain produced with the unsustainable use of land and water in the United States alone would offset most of the excess production capacity in world agriculture.

If adjustment were made for all grain produced with the unsustainable use of land and water worldwide, it would show a grain output well below consumption and provide a much bleaker sense of global food security. When the unsustainable use of land and water is eventually abandoned, it will dramatically tighten world food supplies, pushing prices upward.

With the existing economic accounting system, those who overplow and overpump appear to be doing very well in the short run, even while facing a disastrous collapse over the long run. Although the loss of topsoil does not show up in the national economic accounts or resource inventories of most countries, it is nonetheless serious. And it is largely unrecognized, since the intensification of cropping patterns and the plowing of marginal lands that lead to excessive erosion over the long run can lead to production gains in the short run, thus creating the illusion of progress and a false sense of food security.

If all the environmental consequences of economic activity—from resource depletion to the numerous forms of environmental damage—were included, real economic progress would be much less than conventional economic measures indicate. The challenge to governments is to revise national accounting systems so as to reflect more precisely real changes in output. Just as we deflate reported economic growth with a price deflator, we must also apply an ecological deflator if we are to measure real progress. Without this, we will continue to delude ourselves into thinking we are making progress when we are not.

A few governments and international organizations are starting to move in this direction. Laws enacted by the U.S. Congress in 1989 require the federal government to calculate a "gross sustainable productivity" for the United States each year in conjunction with the annual GNP figures, and to work with international organizations and agencies to revise national accounting systems. Further, the United Nations is considering a revision of its own system.

THE BOTTOM LINE

We know that we cannot continue to damage our life-support systems without eventually paying a price, but how will we be affected? What will the price be? Is it likely to be a buildup of carcinogens in the environment so severe it increases the incidence of cancer, dramatically raising death rates? Or will the rising concentration of greenhouse gases make some regions of the planet so hot that they become uninhabitable, forcing massive human migrations? Or will it be something we cannot even anticipate yet?

We also know we cannot keep adding ever more people to the planet each 12 months. Adding 88 million people a year—the equivalent of the population of the United Kingdom combined with those of Belgium, Denmark, Ireland, Norway, and Sweden—will eventually get us into trouble. What form will that trouble take? And is it imminent or in the distant future?

Amidst the uncertainty, food scarcity in developing countries is emerging as the most profound and immediate consequence of global environmental degradation, one already affecting the welfare of hundreds of millions. All the principal changes in the earth's physical condition—eroding soils, shrinking forests, deteriorating rangelands, expanding deserts, acid rain, stratospheric ozone depletion, the buildup of greenhouse gases, air pollution, and the loss of biological diversity—are

affecting food production negatively. Deterioration diets in both Africa and Latin America during the eighties, a worldwide fall in per capita grain production since 1984, and the rise in world wheat and rice prices over the last two years may be early signs of the trouble that lies ahead.

After a generation of record growth in world food output, it sometimes seemed that the rapid ascent in production of this essential commodity could continue indefinitely. The 2.6-fold increase in the world grain harvest between 1950 and 1984 (nearly 3 percent a year) raised per capita production by more than one third. But between 1984 and 1989, overall output rose by only 1 percent. (See Figure 1.) This five-year period is too short to show a trend because weather fluctuations could be partly responsible for the slowdown, but it is an unsettling interruption in food output growth.

The downturn in grain production per capita that became firmly established in Africa during the seventies and spread to Latin America during the early eighties thus engulfed the entire world in the late eighties. In 1989, higher grain prices to farmers, the return

FIGURE 1.
World grain production per capita, 1950–89.

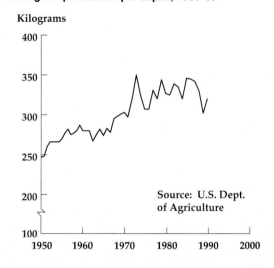

Source: U.S. Dept. of Agriculture

to production of idled U.S. cropland, and near-normal weather were expected to restore production and permit a rebuilding of depleted grain stocks. But this did not happen. With carryover stocks now amounting to little more than pipeline supplies, there is little cushion for short harvests in the future. Falls in production will translate directly into falls in consumption.

Why has production not increased during this five-year period, a time in which the world's farmers invested billions of dollars to expand output, and in which fertilizer use increased by 18 million tons, a gain of 14 percent? There is no single explanation. Three historical trends are converging to make it more difficult to expand world food output. One is the growing scarcity of new cropland and fresh water that affects most of the world. The second is the lack of any new technologies, such as hybrid corn or chemical fertilizer, that can dramatically boost output. And the third is the negative effects of planetary environmental degradation on food production. Any one of these trends could slow the growth in food output. But the convergence of all three could alter the food prospect for the nineties in a way the world is not prepared for.

The sad reality is that the contributions to increased output of greater fertilizer use, continuing modest expansion in irrigated areas, and other technological advances are being partly offset by soil erosion, the waterlogging and salinity of irrigated cropland, air pollution, and several other forms of environmental degradation. . . .

The first concrete economic indication of broad-based environmental deterioration now seems likely to be rising grain prices. After reaching an all-time low of $224 per ton in 1986 (in 1988 dollars), rice prices rose to an estimated $309 for 1989, an increase of 38 percent. Wheat prices, which bottomed in 1987 at $117 per ton, rose 48 percent, to an estimated $173 per ton in 1989 (See Figure 2.) If world grain production should surge upward in the nine-

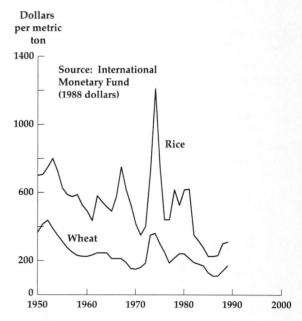

FIGURE 2.
World wheat and rice prices, 1950–89.

ties, this price rise will be checked. If, on the other hand, the world's farmers still have difficulty expanding production at the 28 million tons a year required merely to maintain current per capita consumption levels, prices could rise dramatically—as they did in the mid-seventies.

The combination of falling incomes in most of Africa and Latin America and the grain price rises of the last few years has forced consumption below the level of survival for millions. An estimated 40,000 infants die each day in the Third World as a result of severe nutritional stress and infectious disease. Tragically, higher grain prices also mean that food assistance, which is determined by budgetary allocations, is actually falling just as chronic food scarcity becomes a part of the landscape in much of the Third World.

The world enters the nineties not only with a low level of grain in reserve, but with little confidence that the "carryover" stocks can be rebuilt quickly. Sketching out the consequences of a poor harvest while stocks are this low sounds like the outline of a science fiction catastrophe novel. If before stocks are rebuilt the United States experiences a drought-reduced harvest similar to that of 1988, which dropped grain production below domestic consumption, U.S. grain exports will slow to a trickle. Nearly everything produced would be needed to satisfy domestic consumption. By early fall, the more than 100 countries that import U.S. grain would be competing for meager exportable supplies from Argentina, Australia, and France. Fierce competition could double or triple grain prices, driving them far above any level previously experienced.

By early winter, the extent of starvation, food riots, and political instability in the Third World would force governments in affluent industrial societies to consider tapping the only remaining food reserve of any size—the 600 million tons of grain fed to livestock. If they decided to restrict livestock feeding and use the grain saved for food relief, governments would have to devise a mechanism for doing so. Would they impose a meat tax to discourage consumption and free up grain? Would they ration livestock products, much as was done in many countries during World War II?

Forcing millions of the world's poor to the brink of starvation would be the most immediate and tragic consequence of such a food emergency, but the international monetary system would also be in jeopardy. Third World governments desperately trying to import enough high-priced grain to avoid widespread starvation would have little foreign exchange for debt payments. Whether all the major international banks could withstand such a wholesale forfeiture of income is problematic. At this point, the effects of food scarcity would spread beyond the Third World hungry, driving interest rates upward and threatening the integrity of leading international financial institutions. The linkage between the environ-

mental degradation of the planet and the economic prospect would have become all too apparent.

The number of hungry people in the world has increased dramatically during the eighties. Reversing the spread of hunger will depend on a massive effort to cut the world rate of population growth and restore the health of the planet. We can no longer separate our health from that of our home. If the health of the planet continues to deteriorate, so will that of its inhabitants.

In many ways, changes in the amount of grain that can be sustainably produced per person may be the best single indicator of success in the battle to save the planet. If an upward trend can be restored in the years immediately ahead—one that reduces hunger and malnutrition—it will be a clear sign of victory. If, on the other hand, per capita grain supplies continue to decline, leading the world into an era of food scarcity, rising food prices, and political instability, it will be a sure sign that the battle is being lost.

A POLITICAL AWAKENING

Scenes of people and nations competing for scarce grain supplies after another drought thankfully did not make the front pages last year. But the news of the planet's health was dire enough to keep the environment on magazine covers and in television broadcasts day after day. And it finally brought the issue into the political mainstream. Concern over the future of the planet pushed the environment toward center stage in political structures at all levels, from town councils to the U.N. General Assembly. International diplomacy, national political campaigns, and grassroots political activity are increasingly being shaped by environmental issues. In every corner of the world, environmentalism is on the rise.

Initially, international environmental issues were confined to local transboundary concerns, such as discussions on acid rain between the United States and Canada or the pollution of internationally shared rivers like the Rhine in Europe. More recently, genuinely global issues such as ozone depletion, climate change, and the preservation of biological diversity have attracted the attention of national political leaders and the international community. Environmental security issues now share the stage with more traditional economic and military concerns, inaugurating a new age of environmental diplomacy.

Political leaders organized several important meetings in 1989. In early March, Prime Minister Thatcher—impressed by new scientific evidence on depletion of the ozone layer—hosted a three-day international conference on the subject. Specifically, her aim was to convince more countries to support the Montreal Protocol goal of halving the use of chlorofluorocarbons (CFCs), the family of chemicals responsible for the damage, by the end of the nineties. By the close of the London conference, 20 more countries had agreed to sign the protocol, bringing the total to 66. And 11 more indicated they were seriously considering doing the same.

A meeting in the Hague the following week, organized by the governments of France, the Netherlands, and Norway, considered the challenges to international governance posed by the twin problems of global warming and ozone depletion. Political representatives of 24 countries, including 17 heads of government, attended the conference. The three-page Hague Declaration they agreed to began: "The right to live is the right from which all other rights stem. Guaranteeing this right is the paramount duty of those in charge of all States throughout the world. Today, the very conditions of life on our planet are threatened by the severe attacks to which the earth's atmosphere is subjected."

This tone set the stage for a statement in which the international community went the furthest ever in recommending that the United Nations be given enforcement powers. It ar-

gued for a new or newly strengthened U.N. institutional authority to deal with global warming and ozone depletion that would "involve such decision-making procedures as may be effective even if, on occasion, unanimous agreement has not been achieved." And it discussed the need to "develop instruments and define standards to enhance or guarantee the protection of the atmosphere and monitor compliance," questions on which would be referred to the International Court of Justice.

Though it remains unclear when—if ever—the Hague Declaration's call will be heeded, it is becoming increasingly clear that some reform of the current international environmental machinery is on the horizon. It is widely expected that institutional reform will figure prominently on the agenda of the 1992 World conference on Environment and Development, on the twentieth anniversary of the Stockholm meeting. The various proposals on the table at the moment include a British one to give the existing U.N. Security Council an environmental role, a Soviet suggestion to establish an ecological council separate from but equal in stature to the present Security Council, a private proposal to transform the moribund Trusteeship Council into an environmental body, and near-universal support for a strengthened U.N. Environment Programme.

In late March 1989, 116 countries met in Basel to negotiate a treaty on the international transport and disposal of hazardous waste. The result was a compromise between industrial countries, which wanted to retain the right to export toxic materials under controlled conditions, and some developing countries that wanted to ban international movements of such materials altogether. Following by 18 months of adoption of the Montreal Protocol to reduce CFC use, this treaty also underlined the growing importance of environmental issues in international affairs.

The Basel treaty was signed on the spot by 34 countries, and 71 more nations tentatively agreed to it, exceeding by a wide margin the 20 required for the accord to take effect. Mostafa Tolba, Executive Director of the U.N. Environment Programme, recognized that the treaty was a step in the right direction, albeit a small one, when he said, "Our agreement has not halted the commerce in poison, but it has signaled the international resolve to eliminate the menace that hazardous wastes pose to the welfare of our shared environment and to the health of the world's peoples."

The single event of 1989 that best symbolized the new age of environmental diplomacy was the agenda at the Group of Seven's annual summit meeting hosted by President Mitterand in Paris during July. These meetings were initiated in 1976 as an economic summit when the world was in a turmoil following the doubling of grain prices and the fourfold rise in oil prices; by 1989, much of the meeting was devoted to environmental issues. Discussions on climate change, deforestation, and ozone depletion consumed a good part of the weekend conference and dominated the communiqué released at its end.

In Europe, the results of elections for the European Parliament provided unmistakable evidence that the electorate cares about the environment. The Greens gained 19 seats in the European Community's governing body, for a total of 39 of the 518-seat assembly. Although still small compared with the Socialist Party, which led the multiparty assembly with 180 seats, they became nonetheless a force to be reckoned with. The results in local terms were even more impressive. In France's elections for the European Parliament, the Greens won 11 percent of the vote, up from 3 percent in the 1984 elections. And in the United Kingdom, the Green share of the vote increased from less than 1 percent in 1984 to 15 percent.

In national parliaments, the Greens are also now represented. For example, they hold 20 seats of a 349-seat total in the Swedish Riksdag and 13 of 630 seats in the Italian House of Deputies. In the Australian state of Tasmania,

Greens hold the balance of power, with 5 out of 35 seats in the parliament. They captured 1,800 city council seats in France last year, establishing a foothold in local governments there as well. In West Germany, where they have been represented for many years, gains in 1989 were less impressive, partly because the federal government has already adopted many of the Greens' issues, such as disarmament.

Similar opportunities to deal with global issues developed in other key areas. In Poland, environmental issues figured prominently in the Round Table discussion between the Communist Party and Solidarity that paved the way for the power-sharing arrangement. Elections to the Supreme Soviet and the Congress of People's Deputies also recognized the need to broaden the base of participation if the Soviet Union's economic and environmental issues were to be resolved. And the success of Japan's Socialist Party in wresting control of the Upper House from the long-entrenched Liberal Democratic Party reflected a growing concern in the electorate over both social and environmental issues.

Three governments—the Netherlands, Norway, and Australia—announced longterm environmental plans in 1989. In varying degrees, each recognized both domestic and global environmental issues.

The Dutch National Environmental Policy Plan developed by the federal government was presented to the Parliament for debate following the September 1989 election. Given the combination of high population density and uncontrolled use of automobiles, pollution problems in this small nation are severe. The government proposes to adopt various incentives, disincentives, and regulations to encourage greater use of bicycles for trips of 5–10 kilometers. For longer trips, it will encourage people to use trains, not cars or planes. It plans to install emission controls in power plants to reduce sulfur dioxide and nitrogen oxide discharges sharply. The plan also calls for building 2,500 megawatts of cogeneration capacity this decade to increase energy efficiency. The goal is to halt the growth in CO_2 emissions by the end of the nineties.

The Norwegian plan, which like the Dutch one is designed as a national response to the report of the World Commission on Environment and Development, also sets the goal of stabilizing carbon dioxide emissions by the year 2000 at the latest. Combined with efforts to reduce CFCs and nitrous oxide, this is intended to reduce total greenhouse gas emissions by Norway from the end of the decade on.

The Australian plan is much less comprehensive than the other two. The major specific action it calls for is the planting of 1 billion trees during the nineties. If successful, this would replace roughly half the tree cover removed since European settlement began two centuries ago. Recognizing that Australia has lost 18 species of mammals and 100 of flowering plants since European settlement, the plan also launched an endangered species program; this is designed to save the 40 species of mammals at risk of extinction and the 3,300 rare or endangered plants. Although the plan recognizes the near-desperate need to conserve Australia's topsoil, it includes no detailed program for doing so. Likewise, it talks about the need to reduce CO_2 emissions, but has no specific steps to lower fossil fuel use.

A number of national governments responded to specific environmental threats in 1989. Thailand, for example, concerned about increasingly destructive floods and landslides associated with deforestation, announced a ban on logging. Brazil, responding in part to international criticism of the burning of the Amazon rain forest, withdrew tax incentives from ranchers doing much of the burning.

Many local governments throughout the world have taken their own specific steps on particular environmental issues, without waiting for a national strategy to materialize. In the United States, for instance, some states and numerous municipal governments have adopted mandatory recycling laws. Vermont has banned several major applications of CFCs, including their use in car air conditioners by 1993. Even more ambitious, Governor Madeleine Kunin is developing a state-level program to combat global warming.

Grassroots groups are also joining the battle. Their efforts range from those of the rubber tappers in the Amazon to protect the rain forest to those of Soviet groups organizing to block construction of nuclear plants in their communities. No one knows how many grassroots environmental groups now exist, but it must surely be in the tens of thousands. Issues they commonly organize around include the cleanup of toxic waste sites, recycling, and the protection of forests. Increasingly, people are realizing that protecting the environment requires organizing at the local level.

Public opinion polls show rising concern with environmental degradation throughout the world. A U.N.-commissioned poll conducted in 14 disparate countries—rich and poor, East and West, North and South—found "in every major area of the world nothing less than alarm about the state of the environment."

Is the recent political awakening too little and too late? Overall, the effort to protect the earth's life-support systems is lagging badly. Despite growing public concern, government expenditures to defend against military threats still dwarf those to protect us from environmental ones. For example, the United States plans to spend $303 billion in 1990 to protect the country from military threats but only $14 billion to protect it from environmental threats, a ratio of 22 to 1. Unfortunately, this national distribution of resources in response to these two threats is not atypical.

All in all, 1989 was a year of much activity, a

year of many conferences and declarations, but with little concrete action. Few major new laws were passed or new programs adopted. Some progress was made on reducing the threat to the ozone layer: as noted earlier, 66 countries have signed or agreed to sign the Montreal Protocol. A few countries, such as Sweden, have decided to phase out CFC use entirely. So, too, have some of the major manufacturers, such as U.S.-based Du Pont and Allied Chemical.

With the major threats to food security, such as population growth, climate change, and soil erosion, little or no progress was made last year. The annual addition to world population, which reached a record high in 1989 of 88 million people, is likely to average 96 million during the nineties. As noted earlier, the buildup of carbon dioxide, the principal heat-trapping gas in the atmosphere, is accelerating; not a single national government has adopted a plan to reduce CO_2 emissions. And as far as soil goes, only the United States, which has reduced losses by one fifth since 1985, has succeeded in slowing the depletion of this essential resource.

This past year brought the promise of change, but little real change. Proclamations and statements of concern were many, but actual steps to restore the planet's health were few. If the world does not seize the opportunities offered by the promise of change, the continuing environmental degradation of the planet will eventually lead to economic decline.

DISCUSSION QUESTIONS

1. According to Lester Brown, how is it that economic indicators provide us with only the "illusion" of progress with respect to environmental issues?

2. How do Julian Simon and Lester Brown differ in their readings of progress in the economy and on the environmental front?

3. What measures do you think must be taken to increase the political awareness of nation-states about the future of planet earth?

PART SIX

Epilogue

CHAPTER 17

Emerging Issues

INTRODUCTION

In an era in which crime has reached an all-time high in the United States, the traditional family is crumbling, and the world is facing nuclear obliteration, we are sometimes numbed by the multiplicity and magnitude of issues confronting our society. This book is an attempt to treat these issues with understanding and to offer reasonable solutions—as perceived by a variety of observers—for our current dilemmas. Such solutions, however, should be regarded as only a first step.

Looming on the horizon of future history, new and alarming problems have emerged. How will we deal with dramatic changes in technology? Will America be displaced as the dominating power in world affairs? How will the emergence of new societies and "miracle" economies in Asia alter the pattern of world relationships? How we will grapple with the projected overheating of the planet? These are among the gravest issues which the next generation must understand and resolve. The readings in this chapter will help to illuminate some of these new concerns.

In the first reading, Paul Kennedy, a historian, argues first that Spain, Great Britain, and Germany fell from preeminent world positions when the cost of empire and of projecting their military power exceeded the strength of their economies. He argues that the relative decline of the American economy—linked with an expensive effort to maintain a world-girdling military presence—may well doom the United States to a similar decline.

Sociologist William McCord examines the development of East Asia over the last thirty years, in the second selection. He notes that Japan alone has become the world's largest creditor and donor of aid—while America has become the world's largest debtor. He analyzes the ramifications of this "miracle" for other developing countries.

The final reading is taken from *The Human Prospect* by Robert Heilbroner, a distinguished economist. In this book Heilbroner examines two global trends: the race between an expanding world population and the food supply, and warfare generated by the competition for resources. In the developing world, Heilbroner points out, population doubles about every twenty-five years. He prophesies that the most probable solution to this problem is the rise of "iron" governments—dictatorships capable of suppressing population growth. Such ruthless governments might also resort to "nuclear blackmail"—a threat to obliterate the world unless food and other resources are more liberally shared. Heilbroner argues that there is no escape from this vicious situation. He writes,

> The outlook for man is painful, difficult, perhaps desperate, and the hope that can be held out for his future prospect seems to be very slim indeed. . . . The answer to whether we can conceive of the future other than as a continuation of the darkness, cruelty, and disorder of the past seems to me to be no; and to the question of whether worse impends, yes.

This excerpt from Heilbroner's work includes his statement about the "ultimate certitude" of environmental deterioration. He contends that "industrial growth must surely slacken and likely come to a halt." If that occurred what would happen to the dreams of progress in currently industrialized lands and the expectations of people in the developing world? Heilbroner offers little hope for the future, because mankind's "command over natural processes and forces far exceeds the reach of our present mechanisms of social control."

READING 17-1

The Rise and Fall of Great Powers

Paul Kennedy

. . . The United States today has roughly the same massive array of military obligations across the globe as it had a quarter-century ago, when its shares of world GNP, manufacturing production, military spending, and armed forces personnel were so much larger than they are now. Even in 1985, forty years after its triumphs of the Second World War and over a decade after its pull-out from Vietnam, the United States had 520,000 members of its armed forces abroad (including 65,000 afloat). That total is, incidentally, substantially more than the overseas deployments in peacetime of the military and naval forces of the British Empire at the height of its power. Nevertheless, in the strongly expressed opinion of the Joint Chiefs of Staff, and of many civilian experts, it is simply not enough. Despite a near-trebling of the American defense budget since the late 1970s, there has occurred a "mere 5 percent increase in the numerical size of the armed forces on active duty." As the British and French military found in their time, a nation with extensive overseas obligations will always have a more difficult "manpower problem" than a state which keeps its armed forces solely for home defense; and a politically liberal and economically laissez-faire society—aware of the unpopularity of conscription—will have a greater problem than most.

Possibly this concern about the gap between American interests and capabilities in the world would be less acute had there not been so much doubt expressed—since at least the time of the Vietnam War—about the *efficiency* of the system itself. Since those doubts have been repeatedly aired in other studies, they will only be summarized here; this is not a further essay on the hot topic of "defense reform." One major area of contention, for example has been the degree of interservice rivalry, which is of course common to most armed forces but seems more deeply entrenched in the American system—possibly because of the relatively modest powers of the chairman of the Joint Chiefs of Staff, possibly because so much more energy appears to be devoted to procurement as opposed to strategical and operational issues. In peacetime, this might merely be dismissed as an extreme example of "bureaucratic politics"; but in actual wartime operations—say, in the emergency dispatch of the Rapid Deployment Joint Task Force, which contains elements from all four services—a lack of proper coordination could be fatal.

In the area of military procurement itself, allegations of "waste, fraud and abuse" have been commonplace. The various scandals over horrendously expensive, *under*performing weapons which have caught the public's attention in recent years have plausible explanations: the lack of proper competitive bidding and of market forces in the "military-industrial complex," and the tendency toward "gold-plated" weapon systems, not to mention the striving for large profits. It is difficult, however, to separate those deficiencies in the procurement process from what is clearly a more fundamental happening: the intensification of the impacts which new technological advances make upon the art of war. Given that it is in the high-technology field that the USSR usually appears most vulnerable—which suggests that American *quality* in weaponry can be employed to counter the superior Russian *quantity* of, say, tanks and aircraft—there is an obvious attraction in what Caspar Weinberger termed "competitive strategies" when ordering new armaments. Nevertheless, the fact that the Reagan administration in its first term spent over 75 percent more on new aircraft than the Carter regime but acquired only 9 percent more planes points to *the* appalling military-procurement problem of the late twentieth century: given the technologically driven tendency toward spending more and more money upon fewer and fewer weapon systems, would the United States and its allies really have enough sophisticated and highly expensive aircraft and tanks in reserve after the early stages of a ferociously fought conventional war? Does the U.S. Navy possess enough attack submarines, or frigates, if heavy losses were incurred in the early stages of a *third* Battle of the Atlantic? If not, the results would be grim; for it is clear that today's complex weaponry simply cannot be replaced in the short times which were achieved during the Second World War.

This dilemma is accentuated by two other elements in the complicated calculus of evolving an effective American defense policy. The first is the issue of budgetary constraints. Unless external circumstances became much more threatening, it would be a remarkable act of political persuasion to get national defense expenditures raised much above, say, 7.5 percent of GNP—the more especially since the size of the federal deficit . . . points to the need to balance governmental spending as the first priority of state. But if there is a slowing-down or even a halt in the increase in defense spending, coinciding with the continuous upward spiral in weapons costs, then the problem facing the Pentagon will become much more acute.

The second factor is the sheer variety of military contingencies that a global superpower like the United States has to plan for—all of which, in their way, place differing demands upon the armed forces and the weaponry they are likely to employ. This again is not without precedent in the history of the Great Powers; the British army was frequently placed under strain by having to plan to fight on the Northwest Frontier of India *or* in Belgium. But even that challenge pales beside the task facing today's "number one." If the critical issue for the United States is preserving a nuclear deterrent against the Soviet Union, at *all* levels of escalation, then money will inevitably be poured into such weapons as the MX missile, the B-1 and "Stealth" bombers, Pershing IIs, cruise missiles, and Trident-bearing submarines. If a large-scale conventional war against the Warsaw Pact is the most probable scenario, then the funds presumably need to go in quite different directions: tactical aircraft, main battle tanks, large carriers, frigates, attack submarines, and logistical services. If it is likely that the United States and the USSR will avoid a direct clash, but that both will become more active in the Third World, then the weapons mix changes again: small arms, helicopters, light carriers, an enhanced role for the U.S. Marine Corps become the chief items on the list. Already it is clear that a large part of the controversy over "defense reform" stems from differing assumptions about the *type* of war the United States might be called upon to fight. But what if those in authority make the wrong assumption?

A further major concern about the efficiency of the system, and one voiced even by strong supporters of the campaign to "restore" American power, is whether the present decision-making structure permits a proper grand strategy to be carried out. This would not merely imply achieving a greater coherence in military policies, so that there is less argument about "maritime strategy" versus "coalition warfare," but would also involve effecting a synthesis of the United States' long-term political, economic, and strategical interests, in place of the bureaucratic infighting which seems to have characterized so much of Washington's policymaking. A much-quoted example of this is the all-too-frequent *public* dispute about how and where the United States should employ its armed forces abroad to enhance or defend its national interests—with the State Department wanting clear and firm responses made to those who threaten such interests, but the Defense Department being unwilling (especially after the Lebanon debacle) to get involved overseas except under special conditions. But there also have been, and by contrast, examples of the Pentagon's preference for taking unilateral decisions in the arms race with Russia (e.g., SDI program, abandoning SALT II) without consulting major allies, which leaves problems for the State Department. There have been uncertainties attending the role played by the National Security Council, and more especially individual national security advisers. There have been incoherencies of policy in the Middle East, partly because of the intractibility of, say, the Palestine issue, but also because the United States' strategical interest in supporting the conservative, pro-Western Arab states against Russian penetration in that area has often foundered upon the well-organized opposition of its own pro-Israel lobby. There have been interdepartmental disputes about the use of economic tools—from boycotts on trade and embargoes on technology transfer to foreign-aid grants and weapons sales and grain sales—in support of American diplomatic interests, which affect policies toward the Third World, South Africa, Russia, Poland, the EEC, and so on, and which have sometimes been uncoordinated and contradictory. No sensible person would maintain that the many foreign-policy problems afflicting the globe each possess an obvious and ready "solution"; on the other hand, the preservation of long-term American interests is certainly not helped when the decision-making system is attended by frequent disagreements within.

All this has led to questions by gloomier critics about the overall political culture in which Washington decision-makers have to operate. This is far too large and complex a matter to be explored in depth here. But it has been increasingly suggested that a country needing to reformulate its grand strategy in the light of the larger, uncontrollable changes taking place in world affairs may not be well served by an electoral system which seems to paralyze foreign-policy decision-making every two years. It may not be helped by the extraordinary pressures applied by lobbyists, political action committees, and other interest groups, all of which, by definition, are prejudiced in respect to this or that policy change; nor by an inherent "simplification" of vital but complex international and strategical issues through a mass media whose time and space for such things are limited, and whose *raison d'être* is chiefly to make money and secure audiences, and only secondarily to inform. It may also not be helped by the still-powerful "escapist" urges in the American social culture, which may be understandable in terms of the nation's "frontier" past but is a hindrance to coming to terms with today's more complex, integrated world and with *other* cultures and ideologies. Finally, the country may not always be assisted by its division of constitutional and decision-making powers, deliberately created when it was geographically and strategically isolated from the rest of the world two centuries ago, and possessed a decent degree of time to come to an agreement on the few issues which actually concerned "foreign" policy, but which may be harder to operate when it has become a global superpower, often called upon to make swift decisions vis-à-vis countries which enjoy far fewer constraints. No single one of these presents an insuperable obstacle to the execution of a coherent, long-term American grand strategy; their cumulative and interacting effect is, however, to make it much more difficult than otherwise to carry out needed changes of policy if that seems to hurt special interests and occurs in an election year. It may therefore be here, in the cultural and domestic-political realms, that the evolution of an effective overall American policy to meet the twenty-first century will be subjected to the greatest test.

The final question about the proper relationship of "means and ends" in the defense of American global interests relates to the economic challenges bearing down upon the country, which, because they are so various, threaten to place immense strains upon decision-making in national policy. The extraordinary breadth and complexity of the American economy makes it difficult to summarize what is happening to all parts of it—especially in a period when it is sending out such contradictory signals. Nonetheless, the features which were described in the preceding chapter still prevail.

The first of these is the country's relative industrial decline, as measured against world production, not only in older manufactures such as textiles, iron and steel, shipbuilding, and basic chemicals, but also—although it is far less easy to judge the final outcome of this level of industrial-technological combat—in global shares of robotics, aerospace, automobiles, machine tools, and computers. Both of these pose immense problems: in traditional and basic manufacturing, the gap in wage scales between the United States and newly industrializing countries is probably such that no "efficiency measures" will close it; but to lose out in the competition in future technologies, if that indeed should occur, would be even more disastrous. In late 1986, for example, a congressional study reported that the U.S. trade surplus in high-technology goods had plunged from $27 billion in 1980 to a mere $4 billion in 1985, and was swiftly heading into a deficit.

The second, and in many ways less expected, sector of decline is agriculture. Only a decade ago, experts in that subject were predicting a frightening global imbalance between feeding requirements and farming output. But such a scenario of famine and disaster stimulated two powerful responses. The first was a massive investment into American farming from the 1970s onward, fueled by the prospect of ever-larger overseas food sales; the second was the enormous (western-world-funded) investigation into scientific means of increasing Third World crop outputs, which has been so successful as to turn growing numbers of such countries into food *exporters*, and thus competitors of the United States. These two trends are separate from, but have coincided with, the transformation of the EEC into a major producer of agricultural surpluses, because of its price-support system. In consequence, experts now refer to a "world awash in food," which in turn leads to sharp declines in agricultural prices and in American food exports— and drives many farmers out of business.

It is not surprising, therefore, that these economic problems have led to a surge in protectionist sentiment throughout many sectors of the American economy, and among businessmen, unions, farmers, and their congressmen. As with the "tariff reform" agitation in Edwardian Britain, the advocates of increased protection complain of unfair foreign practices, of "dumping" below-cost manufactures on the American market, and of enormous subsidies to foreign farmers—which, they maintain, can only be answered by U.S. administrations abandoning their laissez-faire policy on trade and instituting tough countermeasures. Many of those individual complaints (e.g., of Japan shipping below-cost silicon chips to the American market) have been valid. More broadly, however, the surge in protectionist sentiment is also a reflection of the erosion of the previously unchallenged U.S. manufacturing supremacy. Like mid-Victorian Britons, Americans after 1945 favored free trade and open competition, not just because they held that global commerce and prosperity would be boosted in the process, but also because they knew that they were most likely to benefit from the abandonment of protectionism. Forty years later, with that confidence ebbing, there is a predictable shift of opinion in favor of protecting the domestic market and the domestic producer. And, just as in that earlier British case, defenders of the existing system points out that enhanced tariffs might not only make domestic products *less* competitive internationally, but that there also could be various external repercussions—a global tariff war, blows against American exports, the undermining of the currencies of certain newly industrializing countries, and a return to the economic crisis of the 1930s.

Along with these difficulties affecting American manufacturing and agriculture there are unprecedented turbulences in the nation's finances. The uncompetitiveness of U.S. industrial products abroad and the declining sales of agricultural exports have together produced staggering deficits in visible trade—$160 billion in the twelve months to May 1986—but what is more alarming is that such a gap can no longer be covered by American earnings on "invisibles," which is the traditional recourse of a mature economy (e.g., Great Britain before 1914). On the contrary, the only way the United States can pay its way in the world is by importing ever-larger sums of capital, which has transformed it from being the world's largest creditor to the world's largest debtor nation *in the space of a few years*.

Compounding this problem—in the view of many critics, *causing* this problem—have been the budgetary policies of the U.S. government itself. Even in the 1960s, there was a tendency for Washington to rely upon deficit finance, rather than additional taxes, to pay for the increasing cost of defense and social programs. But the decisions taken by the Reagan administration in the early 1980s—i.e., large-scale increases in defense expenditures, plus considerable decreases in taxation, but *without* significant reductions in federal spending elsewhere—have produced extraordinary rises in the deficit, and consequently in the national debt, as shown in Table 1.

TABLE 1		

U.S. FEDERAL DEFICIT, DEBT, AND INTEREST, 1980–1985

(Billions of Dollars)

	Deficit	Debt	Interest on debt
1980	59.6	914.3	52.5
1983	195.4	1,381.9	87.8
1985	202.8	1,823.1	129.0

The continuation of such trends, alarmed voices have pointed out, would push the U.S. national debt to around $13 *trillion* by the year 2000 (fourteen times that of 1980), and the interest payments on such debt to $1.5 *trillion* (twenty-nine times that of 1980). In fact, a lowering of interest rates could bring down those estimates, but the overall trend is still very unhealthy. Even if federal deficits could be reduced to a "mere" $100 billion annually, the compounding of national debt and interest payments by the early twenty-first century will still cause quite unprecedented totals of money to be diverted in that direction. Historically, the only other example which comes to mind of a Great Power so increasing its indebtedness in *peacetime* is France in the 1780s, where the fiscal crisis contributed to the domestic political crisis.

These American trade and federal deficits are now interacting with a new phenomenon in the world economy—what is perhaps best described as the "dislocation" of international capital movements from the trade in goods and services. Because of the growing integration of the world economy, the volume of trade both in manufactures and in financial services is much larger than ever before, and together may amount to some $3 trillion a year; but that is now eclipsed by the stupendous level of capital flows pouring through the world's money markets, with the London-based Eurodollar market alone having a volume "at least 25 times that of world trade."

While this trend was fueled by events in the 1970s (the move from fixed to floating exchange rates, the surplus funds flowing from OPEC countries), it has also been stimulated by the U.S. deficits, since the only way the federal government has been able to cover the yawning gap between its expenditures and its receipts has been to suck into the country tremendous amounts of liquid funds from Europe and (especially) Japan—turning the United States, as mentioned above, into the world's largest debtor country by far. It is, in fact, difficult to imagine how the American economy could have got by *without* the inflow of foreign funds in the early 1980s, even if that had the awkward consequence of sending up the exchange value of the dollar, and further hurting U.S. agricultural and manufacturing exports. But that in turn raises the troubling question about what might happen if those massive and volatile funds were pulled out of the dollar, causing its value to drop precipitously.

The trends have, in turn, produced explanations which suggest that alarmist voices are exaggerating the gravity of what is happening to the U.S. economy and failing to note the "naturalness" of most of these developments. For example, the midwestern farm belt would be much less badly off had not so many individuals bought land at inflated prices and excessive interest rates in the late 1970s. Again, the move from manufacturing into services is an understandable one, which is occurring in all advanced countries; and it is also worth recalling that U.S. manufacturing *output* has been rising in absolute terms, even if employment (especially blue-collar employment) in manufacturing industry has been falling—but that again is a "natural" trend, as the world increasingly moves from material-based to knowledge-based production. Similarly, there is nothing wrong in the metamorphosis of American financial institutions into *world* financial institutions, with a triple base in Tokyo, London, and New York, to handle (and profit from) the great volume of capital flows; that can only boost the nation's earnings from services. Even the large annual federal deficits and the mounting national debt are sometimes described as being not too serious, after allowance is made for inflation; and there exists in some quarters a belief that the economy will "grow its way out" of these deficits, or that measures will be taken by the politicians to close the gap, whether by increasing taxes or cutting spending or a combination of both. A too-hasty attempt to slash the deficit, it is pointed out, could well trigger off a major recession.

Even more reassuring are said to be the positive signs of growth in the American economy. Because of the boom in the services sector, the United States has been creating jobs over the past decade faster than at any time in its peacetime history—and certainly a lot faster than in western Europe. As a related point, its far greater degree of labor mobility eases such transformations in the job market. Furthermore, the enormous American commitment in high technology—not just in California, but in New England, Virginia, Arizona, and many other parts of the land—promises ever greater outputs of production, and thus of national wealth (as well as ensuring a strategical edge over the USSR). Indeed, it is precisely because of the opportunities that exist in the American economy that it continues to attract millions of immigrants, and to stimulate thousands of new entrepreneurs; while the floods of capital which pour into the country can be tapped for further investment, especially into R&D. Finally, if the shifts in the global terms of trade are indeed leading to lower prices for foodstuffs and raw materials, that ought to benefit an economy which still imports enormous amounts of oil, metal ores, and so on (even if it hurts particular American producers, like farmers and oilmen).

Many of these individual points may be

valid. Since the American economy is so large and variegated, some sectors and regions are likely to be growing at the same time as others are in decline—and to characterize the whole with sweeping generalizations about "crisis" or "boom" is therefore inappropriate. Given the decline in raw-materials prices, the ebbing of the dollar's unsustainably high exchange value of early 1985, the general fall in interest rates—and the impact of all three trends upon inflation and upon business confidence—it is not surprising to find some professional economists being optimistic about the future.

Nevertheless, from the viewpoint of American grand strategy, and of the economic foundation upon which an effective, long-term strategy needs to rest, the picture is much less rosy. In the first place, given the worldwide array of military liabilities which the United States has assumed since 1945, its capacity to carry those burdens is obviously less than it was several decades ago, when its share of global manufacturing and GNP was much larger, its agriculture was not in crisis, its balance of payments was far healthier, the government budget was also in balance, and it was not so heavily in debt to the rest of the world. In that larger sense, there is something in the analogy which is made by certain political scientists between the United States' position today and that of previous "declining hegemons."

Here again, it is instructive to note the uncanny similarities between the growing mood of anxiety among thoughtful circles in the United States today and that which pervaded all political parties in Edwardian Britain and led to what has been termed the "national efficiency" movement: that is, a broad-based debate within the nation's decision-making, business, and educational elites over the various measures which could reverse what was seen to be a growing uncompetitiveness as compared with other advanced societies. In terms of commercial expertise, levels of training and education, efficiency of production, standards of income and (among the less well-off) of living, health, and housing, the "number-one" power of 1900 seemed to be losing its position, with dire implications for the country's long-term *strategic* position; hence the fact that the calls for "renewal" and "reorganization" came at least as much from the Right as from the Left. Such campaigns usually do lead to reforms, here and there; but their very existence is, ironically, a confirmation of decline, in that such an agitation simply would not have been necessary a few decades earlier, when the nation's lead was unquestioned. A strong man, the writer G. K. Chesterton sardonically observed, does not worry about his bodily efficiency; only when he weakens does he begin to talk about health. In the same way, when a Great Power is strong and unchallenged, it will be much less likely to debate its capacity to meet its obligations than when it is relatively weaker.

More narrowly, there could be serious implications for American grand strategy if its industrial base continued to shrink. Were there ever to be a large-scale future war which remained conventional (because of the belligerents' mutual fear of triggering a nuclear holocaust), then one is bound to wonder what the impact upon U.S. productive capacities would be after years of decline in certain key industries, the erosion of blue-collar employment, and so on. In this connection, one is reminded of Hewins's alarmed cry in 1904 about the impact of British industrial decay upon *that* country's power:

> Suppose an industry which is threatened [by foreign competition] is one which lies at the very root of your system of National defence, where are you then? You could not get on without an iron industry, a great Engineering trade, because in modern warfare you would not have the means of producing, and maintaining in a state of efficiency, your fleets and armies.

It is hard to imagine that the decline in

American industrial capacity could be so severe: its manufacturing base is simply that much broader than Edwardian Britain's was; and—an important point—the "defense-related industries" have not only been sustained by repeated Pentagon orders, but have paralleled the shift from materials-intensive into knowledge-intensive (high-technology) manufacturing, which over the longer term will also reduce the West's reliance upon critical raw materials. Even so, the very high proportion of, say, semiconductors which are assembled in foreign countries and then shipped to the United States, or—to think of a product as far removed from semiconductors as possible—the erosion of the American shipping and shipbuilding industry, or the closing down of so many American mines and oilfields—such trends cannot but be damaging in the event of another long-lasting, Great Power, coalition war. If, moreover, historical precedents are of any validity at all, the most critical constraint upon any "surge" in wartime production has usually been in the area of skilled craftsmen—which, once again, causes one to wonder about the massive long-term decline in American blue-collar (i.e., usually skilled-craftsmen) employment.

A quite different problem, but one equally important for the sustaining of a proper grand strategy, concerns the impact of slow economic growth upon the American social/political consensus. To a degree which amazes most Europeans, the United States in the twentieth century has managed to avoid ostensible "class" politics. This is due, one imagines, to the facts that so many of its immigrants were fleeing from socially rigid circumstances elsewhere; that the sheer size of the country allowed those who were disillusioned with their economic position to "escape" to the West, and simultaneously made the organization of labor much more difficult than in, say, France or Britain; and that those same geographical dimensions, and the entrepreneurial opportunities within them, encouraged the development of a largely unreconstructed form of laissez-faire capitalism which has dominated the political culture of the nation (despite occasional counterattacks from the left). In consequence, the "earnings gap" between rich and poor in the United States is significantly larger than in any other advanced industrial society; and, by the same token, state expenditures upon social services form a lower share of GNP than in comparable countries (except Japan, which appears to have a much stronger family-based form of support for the poor and the aged).

This lack of "class" politics despite the obvious socioeconomic disparities has obviously been helped by the fact that the United States' overall growth since the 1930s offered the prospect of individual betterment to a majority of the population; and by the more disturbing fact that the poorest *one-third* of American society has not been "mobilized" to become regular voters. But given the differentiated birthrate between the white ethnic groups on the one hand and the black and Hispanic groups on the other—not to mention the changing flow of immigrants into the United States, and given also the economic metamorphosis which is leading to the loss of millions of relatively high-earning jobs in manufacturing, and the creation of millions of poorly paid jobs in services, it may be unwise to assume that the prevailing norms of the American political economy (low government expenditures, low taxes on the rich) would be maintained if the nation entered a period of sustained economic difficulty caused by a plunging dollar and slow growth. What this also suggests is that an American polity which responds to external challenges by increasing defense expenditures, and reacts to the budgetary crisis by slashing the existing social expenditures, may run the risk of provoking an eventual political backlash. As with all of the other Powers surveyed in this chapter, there are no easy answers in dealing with the constant three-way tension between defense, consumption, and investment in settling national priorities.

This brings us, inevitably, to the delicate relationship between slow economic growth and high defense spending. The debate upon "the economics of defense spending" is a highly controversial one, and—bearing in mind the size and variety of the American economy, the stimulus which can come from large government contracts, and the technical spin-offs from weapons research—the evidence does not point simply in one direction. But what is significant for our purposes is the comparative dimension. Even if (as is often pointed out) defense expenditures formed 10 percent of GNP under Eisenhower and 9 percent under Kennedy, the United States' relative share of global production and wealth was at that time around *twice* what it is today; and, more particularly, the American economy was not then facing the challenges to either its traditional or its high-technology manufactures. Moreover, if the United States at present continues to devote 7 percent or more of its GNP to defense spending while its major economic rivals, especially Japan, allocate a far smaller proportion, then *ipso facto* the latter have potentially more funds "free" for civilian investment; if the United States continues to invest a massive amount of its R&D activities into military-related production while the Japanese and West Germans concentrate upon commercial R&D; and if the Pentagon's spending drains off the majority of the country's scientists and engineers from the design and production of goods for the world market while similar personnel in other countries are primarily engaged in bringing out better products for the civilian consumer, then it seems inevitable that the American share of world manufacturing will steadily decline, and also likely that its economic growth rates will be slower than in those countries dedicated to the marketplace

and less eager to channel resources into defense.

It is almost superfluous to say that these tendencies place the United States on the horns of a most acute dilemma over the longer term. Simply because it is *the* global superpower, with far more extensive military commitments than a regional Power like Japan or West Germany, it requires much larger defense forces—in just the same way as imperial Spain felt it needed a far larger army than its contemporaries and Victorian Britain insisted upon a much bigger navy than any other country. Furthermore, since the USSR is seen to be the major military threat to American interests across the globe and is clearly devoting a far greater proportion of *its* GNP to defense, American decision-makers are inevitably worried about "losing" the arms race with Russia. Yet the more sensible among these decision-makers can also perceive that the burden of armaments is debilitating the Soviet economy; and that if the two superpowers continue to allocate ever-larger shares of their national wealth into the unproductive field of armaments, the critical question might soon be: "Whose economy will decline *fastest*, relative to such expanding states as Japan, China, etc.?" A low investment in armaments may, for a globally overstretched Power like the United States, leave it feeling vulnerable everywhere; but a very heavy investment in armaments, while bringing greater security in the short term, may so erode the commercial competitiveness of the Americn economy that the nation will be *less* secure in the long term.

Here, too, the historical precedents are not encouraging. For it has been a common dilemma facing previous "number-one" countries that even as their relative economic strength is ebbing, the growing foreign challenges to their position have compelled them to allocate more and more of their resources into the military sector, which in turn squeezes out productive investment and, over time, leads to the downward spiral of slower growth, heavier taxes, deepening domestic splits over spending priorities, and a weakening capacity to bear the burdens of defense. If this, indeed, is the pattern of history, one is tempted to paraphrase Shaw's deadly serious quip and say: "Rome fell; Babylon fell; Scarsdale's turn will come."

In the largest sense of all, therefore, the only answer to the question increasingly debated by the public of whether the United States can preserve its existing position is "no"—for it simply has not been given to any one society to remain *permanently* ahead of all the others, because that would imply a freezing of the differentiated pattern of growth rates, technological advance, and military developments which has existed since time immemorial. On the other hand, this reference to historical precedents does *not* imply that the United States is destined to shrink to the relative obscurity of former leading Powers such as Spain or the Netherlands, or to disintegrate like the Roman and Austro-Hungarian empires; it is simply too large to do the former, and presumably too homogeneous to do the latter. Even the British analogy, much favored in the current political-science literature, is not a good one if it ignores the differences in *scale*. This can be put another way: the geographical size, population, and natural resources of the British Isles would suggest that it ought to possess roughly 3 or 4 percent of the world's wealth and power, *all other things being equal*; but it is precisely because all other things are *never* equal that a peculiar set of historical and technological circumstances permitted the British Isles to expand to possess, say, 25 percent of the world's wealth and power and its prime; and since those favorable circumstances have disappeared, all that it has been doing is returning down to its more "natural" size. In the same way, it may be argued that the geographical extent, population, and natural resources of the United States suggest that it ought to possess perhaps 16 or 18 percent of the

world's wealth and power, but because of historical and technical circumstances favorable to it, that share rose to 40 percent or more by 1945; and what we are witnessing at the moment is the early decades of the ebbing away from that extraordinarily high figure to a more "natural" share. That decline is being masked by the country's enormous military capabilities at present, and also by its success in "internationalizing" American capitalism and culture. Yet even when it declines to occupy its "natural" share of the world's wealth and power, a long time into the future, the United States will still be a very significant Power in a multipolar world, simply because of its size.

The task facing American statesmen over the next decades, therefore, is to recognize that broad trends are under way, and that there is a need to "manage" affairs so that the *relative* erosion of the United States' position takes place slowly and smoothly, and is not accelerated by policies which bring merely short-term advantage but longer-term disadvantage. This involves, from the president's office downward, an appreciation that technological and therefore socioeconomic change is occurring in the world faster than ever before; that the international community is much more politically and culturally diverse than has been assumed, and is defiant of simplistic remedies offered either by Washington or Moscow to its problems; that the economic and productive power balances are no longer as favorably tilted in the United States' direction as in 1945; and that, even in the military realm, there are signs of a certain redistribution of the balances, away from a bipolar to more of a multipolar system, in which the conglomeration of American economic-cum-military strength is likely to remain larger than that possessed by any one of the others individually, but will not be as disproportionate as in the decades which immediately followed the Second World War. This, in itself, is not a bad thing if one recalls Kissinger's observations about the disadvantages of carrying out policies in what is always seen to be a bipolar world; and it may seem still less of a bad thing when it is recognized how much more Russia may be affected by the changing dynamics of world power. In all of the discussions about the erosion of American leadership, it needs to be repeated again and again that the decline referred to is relative not absolute, and is therefore perfectly natural; and that the only serious threat to the real interests of the United States can come from a failure to adjust sensibly to the newer world order.

Given the considerable array of strengths still possessed by the United States, it ought not *in theory* to be beyond the talents of successive administrations to arrange the diplomacy and strategy of this readjustment so that it can, in Walter Lippmann's classic phrase, bring "into balance . . . the nation's commitments and the nation's power." Although there is no obvious, single "successor state" which can take over America's global burdens in the way that the United States assumed Britain's role in the 1940s, it is nonetheless also true that the country has fewer problems than an imperial Spain besieged by enemies on all fronts, or a Netherlands being squeezed between France and England, or a British Empire facing a bevy of challengers. The tests before the United States as it heads toward the twenty-first century are certainly daunting, perhaps especially in the economic sphere; but the nation's resources remain considerable, if

they can be properly organized, and *if* there is a judicious recognition of both the limitations and the opportunities of American power.

Viewed from one perspective, it can hardly be said that the dilemmas facing the United States are unique: Which country in the world, one is tempted to ask, is *not* encountering problems in evolving a viable military policy, or in choosing between guns and butter and investment? From another perspective, however, the American position is a very special one. For all its economic and perhaps military decline, it remains, in Pierre Hassner's words, "the decisive actor in every type of balance and issue." Because it has so much power for good or evil, because it is the linchpin of the western alliance system and the center of the existing global economy, what it does, *or does not do*, is so much more important than what any of the other Powers decides to do.

DISCUSSION QUESTIONS

1. According to Kennedy, which countries have fallen from preeminent world positions and why?
2. Is Kennedy correct that America is in "relative" decline? What are the likely consequences of its decline?
3. From the readings in other chapters of this book, what evidence do you find to support Kennedy's position that the United States is in decline?

Explaining the East Asian "Miracle"

William McCord

The most striking economic development in the past thirty years has been the rise of the

Asian societies. Not much more than a generation ago, Japan, Korea, Taiwan, Hong Kong, and Singapore lay nearly prostrate, devastated by war and political unrest. All but Japan lacked any industrial base. Since then they have grown at such rapid rates that Staffan Linder predicts that East and Southeast Asia—not including China—will by the year 2000 produce more than Europe and the United States combined. East Asia's astounding success stands in startling contrast to most of the Third World, which remains mired in seemingly intractable poverty and economic stagnation.

While such a drastic shift in the world's distribution of income and power has considerable strategic consequences for Europe, the United States, and the Soviet Union, for the poor of the world it raises questions of a different order. Simply put:

Is there a distinct East Asian "model" of development?

Can the East Asian path be emulated by nations in Latin America, Africa, South Asia, and the Middle East?

Theorists have attributed the economic success of the East Asian nations to their ethnic cultures, their Confucian ethic, their sheer luck in timing an entry into the world market, their political structures, or to unfair trade practices; rarely have they been traced to a common set of social and economic policies. If these explanations were sufficient, it would be futile for non-Asian countries to try to emulate them. But while each of them has some plausibility, all of them, under scrutiny, prove less than an adequate guide to Asia's striking success.

Culture. The more successful regions have in common a largely Oriental population and a strong Chinese cultural influence. Even in those Asian nations that have not yet quite lived up to their potential, such as Malaysia and Indonesia, a minority of Chinese entrepreneurs has taken the lead in economic activity.

Clearly, the folk cultures—as opposed to the classic traditions—of Japan, China, and Korea stress pragmatism, hard work, discipline, and an active rather than contemplative way of life. A pronounced tendency to save— an obvious prerequisite for capital investment—has also been described as a facet of Oriental culture. In many ways, these traits

reflect worldly asceticism. They contrast vividly with other cultural traditions such as the fatalism of Hinduism, the "mañana" mentality of Latin America, and the other-worldliness of Buddhism.

There is, however, a major problem with this explanation: for many centuries, these same traditions that are now allegedly producing dynamic growth were associated with economic stagnation. The Chinese, for example, have always worked hard and saved for the future but their efforts brought few material rewards.

Further, Pacific countries that have a meager Chinese or Japanese heritage (but are now following similar economic policies) are making strides comparable to what Japan and the other newly industrialized countries achieved earlier. In 1988, for example, Thailand's economy grew at a rate of 9 percent annually. Exports of industrial goods surged by 40 percent. But Thailand's dominant culture is Buddhism, a tradition not previously considered a spiritual source for economic innovation.

Most importantly, growth in the successful countries improved only after their governments adopted new economic strategies: land reform (in Japan, Korea, and Taiwan), financial measures to encourage investment, mechanisms to hold down inflation, incentives for labor-intensive, outward-looking industries, government intervention to correct distortions in free market operations, and heavy investment in education. Their ancient cultures remained essentially unchanged through stagnation and growth.

It would seem reasonable, then, to conclude that certain socio-economic policies—combined with political stability—have played a more decisive role than culture in promoting modernization. At most, pre-existing cultural tendencies stressing activism and self-discipline may have been "mobilized in a new economic environment."

In some cases, it would be plausible to consider these traits as part of an "immigrant ethic." Chinese migrants have played a major role in the development of Singapore and Malaysia, Indonesia and even Thailand. But so have other migrants from different backgrounds in other environments—Lebanese in the Ivory Coast, Indians in East Africa, Basques in Venezuela. The common element among these groups is that they chose to take risks in an alien culture, sought out new economic opportunities, and applied their energies in a diligent fashion. No culture commands a monopoly of the entrepreneurial talents that seem to blossom so freely among those adventurous people who dare to leave their original homes.

The Confucian Ethic. One specific variant of the culturalists' argument is to credit East Asian success to the "Confucian Ethic."

For many years scholars such as Max Weber regarded the "Confucian Ethic"—with its demands for filial piety, its emphasis on hierarchy and deference, its glorification of stability, and its disdain for mere merchants— as a major obstacle to economic modernization.

With the rise of the Asian countries, however, some scholars now cite elements of Confucianism, such as its reverence for education, as a prime reason for East Asia's growth. Michio Morishima, for example, argues that Confucianism played a key role in Japan's development, while Peter Berger has contended that a "vulgar Confucianism" provided a "dynamic trigger" for East Asian growth.

In making such comparisons, it is wise to remember that regions untouched by the Confucian ethic, such as the Ivory Coast, have achieved similar advances. On the other hand, "Confucian" countries, such as Taiwan and Korea, initially followed economic policies that inhibited rapid economic growth. After specific reforms, they moved forward dramatically. Again, these facts point to the importance of social, economic, and political policies as the true initiators of change.

Timing. Avoiding the ambiguities of the culturalists' positions, some scholars explain the success of the East Asian countries by the timing and circumstances of their entry into the world market.

The Asia Pacific region moved into the world economy in the 1950s and 1960s, when there was an abundance of capital and fewer trade barriers. Consequently, the argument goes, well-made labor-intensive goods could find a niche in foreign markets. Certainly, too, countries such as Japan, Korea, and Taiwan temporarily benefited from American aid (although in much smaller amounts than Europe) and were able to build new industries from scratch. Since such conditions do not apply today, one might conclude that newly developing nations have fewer opportunities.

Nonetheless, Japan, the newly industrializing countries (NICS), and post-1977 China have prospered in spite of the twists and turns of the world economy, the "oil shocks," the debt crisis, the cessation of American aid, and the partial closing of European and American markets. They have done so by exploiting flexibly their comparative advantages, opening new markets, moving quickly into high-tech industries, investing in other countries to avoid trade barriers, and, in some cases, inviting foreign capital investments on attractive terms. Thus it may be that Japan in 1953, Singapore in 1968, and China in 1977 benefited from certain advantages, but their achievements since then have demonstrated that they do not depend on the vagaries of the world economy.

Although Korea, Taiwan, and Japan could be considered "success stories" of American aid, economic assistance ended long before the real expansion of these countries. Singapore and Hong Kong never received such aid. Japan, Taiwan, Korea (and implicitly Deng's

China) do benefit from the American military umbrella, but the importance of that umbrella to their economies may well be exaggerated. Taiwan and Korea, for instance, spend as large a slice of their GNP on military activities as the United States and Europe; while Japan and post-Mao China spend much less, all four have grown dramatically in economic terms.

In another version of the "timing" theory, Lucian Pye has proposed that the East Asian nations have prospered precisely because they faced severe military and economic threats that made it a necessity to learn from and adapt to the outside world. He notes the impact of Perry's invasion and the defeat in World War II of Japan, the Kuomintang's retreat to Taiwan, the Korean War—perhaps even China's disastrous "Cultural Revolution"—as events that forced the various elites to ensure their legitimacy and indeed their survival by stimulating outstanding economic advances.

Certainly, the elites of East Asia once had to face the possibility that their regimes would collapse. Clearly, too, the existence of an internal or external enemy can serve to mobilize people around national goals.

Nonetheless, two facts stand out. First, the East Asian economies have continued to grow although most of their peoples no longer perceive any real threat to their survival or stability. Second, other developing countries throughout the world have experienced terrible "shocks"—repeated defeats by Arab countries at the hands of Israel, civil war in Nigeria, bloody revolutions in Zaire—without any improvement in their government's policies or the pace of their economies. If the "shock theory" has validity, it is not universal.

"Unfair" Trade Practices. It is a common American and European belief that East Asian countries have competed unfairly. Supposedly, their governments protect them from foreign competition, their companies are encouraged

to "dump" goods on the world market, and they underpay their exploited workers.

Japan and some other East Asian countries do protect some of their industries (particularly the "infant industries") and agriculture from European or American competition. Protectionism most often takes the form of applying worrisome inspection procedures, taxes, and bureaucratic delays to the entrance of new products into the market, rather than direct tariffs. The Japanese government also helps ease the transition of new companies into the world economy and aids certain uncompetitive industries out of the domestic and world markets. Mechanisms such as the devaluation of the yen aid the process.

The East Asian societies cannot, however, be accused of direct protectionism. The Japanese have, after all, imposed voluntary quotas on some of their exports and opened their markets to competition from the NICS. Products that have a certain "cachet" in Japan—Mercedes, BMWs, French perfume, and wine—enjoy a good market. Only the American products, with their reputation for "shoddiness," do not sell well.

In Japan and the smaller Asian economies, such as Singapore and Taiwan, government officials fully realize that a protectionist policy would merely provoke more intense retaliation from Europe and America. Rather than blaming protectionist policies, it is more disquieting but more realistic to admit that the thriving Asian economies have beaten the West because of their superior planning and effort.

Dumping. Dumping, the practice of selling below cost abroad in order to ensure a greater market share in the long run, has undoubtedly been practiced, particularly in new high-tech industries such as semiconductors. Such a policy cannot work indefinitely, since Asian businessmen, like any others in a capitalist society, cannot forever sell their goods below actual price.

Clearly, all of the high growth economies began their expansion on the basis of labor intensive industry and generally undercut the wages paid in the industrialized world. Yet, unlike the initial stages of industrialization in the West, the strategy benefited the poor, narrowed the gap between the rich and the impoverished, and very quickly raised wages to a decent level. Today, the average Japanese worker earns wages comparable to the typical European or American, and Singaporean workers are not far behind. Thus, the continued expansion of these economies cannot currently be attributed principally to low pay. In fact, some of the East Asian economies have been forced to abandon low-wage industries such as textiles and thus have opened a door for less developed countries to take over the market. Meanwhile, nations like Japan are adjusting their economies to meet unfulfilled needs for domestic consumption, housing, and social investments.

Political Structures. Some observers have emphasized government-business cooperation and even despotism as the fundamental reasons for the economic dynamism in East Asia. Admittedly, it is hard to picture how fundamental reforms in many parts of Asia—such as the enfranchisement of women in Japan under MacArthur's rule or land reforms in Taiwan under the Kuomintang—could have been brought about under pre-existing or purely democratic regimes.

Nonetheless, commentators who emphasize the authoritarian nature of some East Asian regimes ignore several central facts. Many despotic regimes in Asia and elsewhere have actually ruined their economies. Some purely democratic regimes (such as Japan after MacArthur) and partially democratic regimes (such as Singapore before 1987) achieved marked economic gains. The trend in countries such as Taiwan, Korea, and Thailand seems to lie in the direction of increasing liberalization,

and yet their economies continue to thrust ahead.

In fact, the high growth economies do share some rather prosaic similarities in public policy; significantly, these are not policies which could only be carried out under Asian conditions, but could well be reproduced elsewhere.

Since the 1960s, all of the East Asian nations (including China after 1977) have been politically stable. In some areas, such as Korea and Taiwan until the 1980s, governments achieved political tranquility only at the price of heavy repression of the opposition. Korea also experienced the assassination of Park Chung Lee, but a military government remained. In other places, such as Japan, a free press and vociferous dissenters have operated within a fully democratic system but the same political party has remained in power. Such political stability allows for foreign investment, repayment of debts, and an adherence to international trade laws and customs. The East Asian governments have generally run balanced budgets since the late 1950s, thus aiding in the control of inflation. (Korea experienced inflation briefly in the 1970s and amassed a large foreign debt but the economy's growth has allowed the nation to meet its bills promptly.) Political stability may be regarded as one prerequisite, but hardly the source of economic growth.

Unlike the usual pattern traced by the "Kuznets curve," the income gap between classes decreased while the economies grew. Careful fiscal and income policies, an accretion of foreign debt (in some cases), and encouragement of foreign investment (in other cases) allowed Asian economies to expand while the income of the masses grew. Since their people received an increasingly "fair share" in the economy, political stability was reinforced.

The East Asian governments have engaged in planning of a very special type: removing distortions in the market economy, particularly the export sector. Thus, in Japan, government taxes have been heaviest on domestic consumer industries, and the Ministry of International Trade and Investment (MITI) has targeted certain export industries for special aid to meet foreign competition. The same pattern has been repeated in post-Mao China, South Korea, Taiwan, and even in supposedly "laissez-faire," but finely managed, Hong Kong.

All of the East Asian governments have invested heavily in education, particularly of the vocational variety, and have often adjusted admissions to higher education in accord with the future needs of the economy. The education of females has received particular attention, and virtually 90 percent of East Asian girls finish primary school.

Many of the elements of the Asian success could be emulated by other developing countries. One common element was land reform and the invigoration of agriculture, a crucial first step in Japan, Taiwan, and Korea. Dengist China has also offered peasants the incentives to produce abundantly for their home markets. These governments provided technical assistance, credit, and improved seeds to promote agricultural expansion. As their incomes grew, peasants acquired the capital to fund labor-intensive industries and the money to buy new products. The city states, Singapore and Hong Kong, did not need major agricultural reforms while other areas, such as Indonesia's outer islands and Thailand, originally possessed large amounts of untilled or peasant-owned land. Where necessary, the reforms increased the land ownership and material incentives for peasants without (except in the case of Japan) major subsidies.

Labor-intensive industrialization allowed most of these originally impoverished countries to use their most abundant resource, unskilled labor, as the next stage in economic growth. For varying but very short periods of time, the NICs all depended on labor-intensive activities which required little capital, skills, or technology. This approach did not represent exploitation of the poor since, without the new industries, there would have been no jobs at all. Moreover, because of an equitable income policy, economic inequalities were reduced. Thus, the wages of Korean textile workers surged from $32 a month in the 1950s to $242 a month in the 1980s; wages of construction workers in Japan jumped from $41 a month to $1,200; and the earnings of manufacturing labor in Hong Kong went from $0.64 a day in the 1950s to $11.50 a day in the 1980s.

All of the fast growing economies controlled but did not dismantle trade unions, which served to keep inflation low. Most of the labor associations were "enterprise unions" located in a particular company or industry, which were supposed to share the same goals as managers in the company. In any case, widespread strikes were kept to a minimum. In Singapore, as one example, a tri-partite arbitration board of unions, management, and government set basic wages while most union officers were also officials in the ruling PAP government.

Government intervention to promote export industries helped the free enterprise system in the more affluent Asian nations. Among other measures, the governments manipulated their foreign exchange and bank credit rates to encourage exports and discourage imports. At the same time, the government or (in Korea and Japan) large banks associated with particular industrial groups offered relatively "hidden" subsidies, particularly in the form of guarantees for the liquidity of new enterprises, in order to aid export industries. Singapore followed a deliberate policy of encouraging foreign investments while China is now widely engaged in joint ventures with foreign companies. Such efforts relieved entrepreneurs and enterprises of the initial risks of entering the world market.

Government planning did not necessarily

require corporations to follow a specific blue-print, as in the Soviet bloc. Fortunately, the advice of various planning agencies has not always been followed. In the early 1950s, for example, the supposedly omniscient MITI of Japan recommended against any attempt by the country to expand its export of auto-mobiles. Private companies—most riskily, Honda—ignored the government and forged ahead in spite of the mistaken counsel.

Since the 1950s, the successful regions have had consistently high rates of investment and high returns on investments. East Asian coun-tries exhibited a very good rate of either com-pulsory or voluntary savings (at least 24 percent more than other developing countries) during their early stages of industrialization. Investment of these savings, particularly in la-bor-intensive industries, brought large returns to investors who were virtually guaranteed against nationalization of their enterprises. In the 1950s and 1960s, Japan (through its postal savings system) and Hong Kong depended upon internal savings for investment and the willingness of their peoples to give up quick profits for long-term growth. Taiwan and Korea drew on foreign aid, capital from rural areas, or foreign debts. Singapore relied on private foreign capital, as well as its Central Provident Fund. As a beneficent cycle began, high investment led to rapid growth which, in turn, encouraged further expansion. (By the 1980s, savings declined in countries such as Japan as the government allowed expenditure on consumer goods, a market which had long been bottled up.)

The successful Asian regions also encour-aged a meritocracy in both business and gov-ernment. In contrast to many developing countries—and, indeed, some of their own traditions—the successful Asian countries have generally turned away from person-alistic, family-based, ethnic or political criteria as their standard for appointment and ad-vancement. Instead, they have emphasized educational attainment, examination results, and actual performance on the job for moving people into the elite civil service and first-ranked corporations.

The high growth regions have, with more or less success, followed conscious policies of population control, thus lessening the pres-sure of their people upon limited food sup-plies. Japan and Singapore have reached a point of zero population growth; Taiwan and Thailand have drastically reduced their birth rates. Urban Chinese have also cut their popu-lation growth, although newly "rich" rural Chinese show signs of once again creating large families.

The East Asian nations have been notably successful in absorbing alien economic and cultural intrusions. Under the Meiji regime, of course, Japan deliberately copied the policies and technologies of the West. More recently, Singapore opened its doors to multinationals, post-Mao China has welcomed joint ventures, and Korea has imported Japanese technology. Other Pacific countries, such as Malaysia, have begun "to look East" (to Japan and Korea) for capital, technology, and ideas. While political rhetoricians still demand a defense of "authen-tic culture," the fact is that "Eastern" culture has absorbed "Western" culture. The mix is understandably confusing: Singaporean chil-dren are, for example, taught a required course on Confucius but they must learn his teachings in English.

Taken together, these common policies—political stability, investment in education, land reform, government—guided free enter-prise with an original emphasis on labor-inten-sive and export-oriented industries, a high rate of savings and private profit with a decrease in real poverty, an emphasis on meritocracy, population control, an acceptance of alien in-fluences—have been strikingly successful.

Upon first examination, it would seem that other developing countries might find it diffi-cult to follow the examples from the Pacific.

One reason is historical: the Pacific Rim nations have already co-opted the export market, leaving no room for newly developing countries.

Further, unlike East Asian nations at the beginning of their expansion, many developing countries suffer from a heavy burden of debt. What would motivate richer nations to invest in such crippled economies as Argentina's or Nigeria's?

The social systems of the "Third World"— rampant with factionalism and corruption, governed by feudal elites or minor dictators— would hardly seem receptive to the policies followed in East Asia.

In addition, most developing nations suffer from cultural burdens that history did not impose on East Asian nations. Caste, linguistic, and religious divisions threaten to rip apart South Asia. A heavy Islamic tradition, hardly noted for innovation in recent centuries, hangs over the Middle East, as well as much of Asia and Africa. Tribal hatreds create bloody divisiveness in Africa.

Military governments in Africa and tenuous democracies in Latin America hardly offer a stable rule of law, exemption from the threat of nationalization, or a solid promise against defaulting on loans. Many have not conquered inflation, built a reliable infrastructure, or created educational systems geared to merit. In lands ruled by a traditional elite, some of the first steps in Asian development, such as land reform and education of women, seem virtually impossible.

Despite all this, and while it would require a Pangloss to argue that many developing nations could copy wholesale the Asian example, a closer look suggests reasons for believing that policies adopted from the East Asian model could succeed elsewhere.

First, in the 1950s and 1960s, it was frequently asserted that an expansion of manufactured exports from developing countries was impossible. Many theorists advocated an import substitution strategy. Nonetheless, the East Asian countries followed another path and expanded their exports at the rate of 20 to 40 percent a year, while the import substitution countries went into huge debt. It would be difficult to replicate such an outstanding export record in today's protectionist climate but, as the economist Gustav Papenek has argued in *In Search of An East Asian Development Model*, efficient export producers in developing countries could "gradually replace the middle-income East Asian countries in such industries as textiles and garments, just as the four 'little tigers' . . . earlier replaced Japan."

Second, the debt burden, while awesome, has perhaps been over-emphasized. The truth is that foreign capital still flows to developing countries that show signs of stability and progress. Korea is in the front rank of debtor countries and yet no one questions the nation's ability to repay its debts. Moreover, the emergence of the Pacific countries has opened new avenues of investment and aid that did not exist in the 1950s. The fact that Japan is now the major donor and creditor in the world means that a fresh source of capital and technology exists for newly developing nations.

Third, social systems in developing countries differ substantially from the East Asian "model" but they do not present any more difficult obstacles to development than East Asia once faced and overcame. After all, the Asian social system was itself once regarded as an intractable barrier to economic progress. And, in the 1940s and 1950s, all of the now prospering countries suffered from terrible social dislocations. Military defeat devastated Japan's assumption of superiority. Civil war tore apart China. A corrupt and discredited Kuomintang ruled Taiwan. Singapore fell victim to ethnic riots. War ruined the former "Hermit Kingdom" of Korea. Hong Kong absorbed millions of refugees. These burdens were as severe as those experienced by developing countries today, and did not prevent East Asia's eventual triumph.

Outstanding political leadership, such as Lee Kuan Yew's in Singapore, often made the difference. More usually, politicians followed the sound advice of economic technocrats, often Western trained, who introduced the strategies outlined above, which are the common features of the East Asian example. Indeed, in spite of vast differences in culture, politics, and resources, some other regions of the world have consciously or by coincidence followed the East Asian pattern. In recent years, these societies have begun to prosper, a hopeful indication that East Asian policies can be adapted in completely different environments.

In Africa, the economy of the Ivory Coast, a mildly authoritarian society governed by octogenarian Felix Houphouet-Boigny has grown at an annual rate of 6 percent in the 1980s. Per capita income leapt from $70 annually in 1960 to $2,150 now. Four factors, reminiscent of the East Asian example, stand out in explaining the Ivory Coast's success: the country has stressed export-oriented agricultural production; opened its doors to foreign (primarily French) investment and personnel; stressed education by investing 20 percent of its national budget in schooling; and encouraged capitalism. Although burdened by tribal divisions, corruption, and some two million refugees from poorer parts of Africa, the Ivory Coast has demonstrated that economic "miracles" can occur in Africa.

In India, two quite different economic strategies have been followed with strikingly contrasting results. The Punjab, although wracked by religious discontent and virtual civil war, has become India's shining example of economic advance. Punjabis grow two-thirds more wheat per acre than the agro-business-men in America. They "export" large amounts of rice to India's central reserves and now account for about 45 percent of the national reservoir. Farm income has doubled over the last decades, literacy has soared, and most of the untouchables have risen from their despised position in society. The ingredients in this success story are familiar: middle-income landowners took the lead in "export" trade with India; the government contributed the seeds, credit facilities, and irrigation necessary for a "green revolution"; and Sikh entrepreneurs built small-scale, labor intensive industries.

In contrast, the state of Bihar—potentially the richest region of India with two-fifths of the nation's mineral resources—followed a different path. The Indian government nationalized the state's industries, allowed the education system to deteriorate (students struck for the right to cheat, and won), neglected agricultural reform, and sought the elusive goal of self-sufficiency. The results were disastrous. Thirty-eight of Bihar's forty public-owned enterprises failed to make a profit in the 1980s while landlords treated farmers as serfs. "Bihar has become a symbol of waywardness and dashed hopes," Trevor Fishlock observes. "Corruption, gangsterism, intimidation and the rusting of standards in public life had combined to give it a nightmarish quality."

In Latin America, those nations that have the most direct investment from Pacific countries and the greatest cultural contact are even more likely to benefit from the East Asian example. Chile's newest trading partner, for example, is now the Asian Pacific region. Japan exchanges automobiles for fruit, timber, flowers, and even wine grapes. China imports Chile's copper and timber. In 1988, Australians purchased a gold mine in Chile's Northern desert and bought 60 percent of the largest unexploited copper deposits in the world. Hong Kong secured 45 percent of the Chilean telephone system. Due to exports, however, Chile maintains a favorable balance of trade with the Asian Pacific region.

In sum, while the barriers to adapting the East Asian example are great, they are not insurmountable. In fact, developing countries today have advantages—huge new markets in Asia, sources of investment from the Pacific, a new supply of foreign aid, and the successful "demonstration effect" of the region—that were not available thirty years ago. Some nations, from Thailand to Chile, are taking advantage of these new options. The challenge for the less developed countries is to grasp the new opportunities, learn the lessons of the Asian success, and respond with political courage to the new realities.

DISCUSSION QUESTIONS

1. What are the reasons for the success of East Asian nations in the world economy?
2. How can the rise of Asia have an impact on developing countries? On developed countries?
3. Will social obstacles block the adoption of an "Asian model"?

READING 17-3

The External Challenges

Robert Heilbroner

. . . Here we come to a crucial stage of our inquiry. For unlike the threats posed by population growth or war, there is an ultimate certitude about the problem of environmental deterioration that places it in a different category from the dangers we have previously examined. Nuclear attacks may be indefinitely avoided; population growth may be stabilized; but ultimately there is an absolute limit to the ability of the earth to support or tolerate the process of industrial activity, and there is reason to believe that we are now moving toward that limit very rapidly.

When we examine the actual timetable of environmental disruption, however, we soon encounter a baffling set of considerations. Despite the certainty of our knowledge that a limit to growth impends, we have only a very imprecise capability of predicting the time span within which we will have to adjust to that impassable barrier. As we shall see, this makes it difficult to formulate appropriate policies, or to forecast the rate of social change that will be required to bring about the necessary environmental safeguards.

Take, as our initial problem, the availability of the resources necessary to sustain industrial output. In the developed world, industrial production has been growing at a rate of about 7 percent a year, thereby doubling every ten years. If we project this growth rate for another fifty years, it would follow that the demand for resources would have doubled five times, requiring a volume of resource extraction thirty-two times larger than today's; and if we look ahead over the ten doublings of a century, the amount of annual resource requirements would have increased by over a thousand times.

Do we have the resources to permit us to attain—or sustain—such gargantuan increases in output? Here the problem begins to reveal its complexity. A considerable proportion of the resources we extract today does not become industrial output but ends up as waste. To the extent that we can reduce waste, or use old outputs as new inputs—for example, recycling junked cars as new steel—we will be able to reduce the need for new resources, although by how much no one knows. Further, the problem is complicated because we are largely ignorant of the extent of most of the world's resources, petroleum being perhaps an exception. Indeed, not only is the world still largely "unexplored," so far as its potential mineral and other riches are concerned, but the very definition of a resource changes as our ability to extract minerals or other substances improves. For example, today we utilize enormous reservoirs of iron ore that were not even considered to be reserves when we were still mining the rich iron deposits of the Mesabi Range, now long exhausted. In point of fact, reserves of all known elements exist in "limitless" quantities as trace elements in granite or sea water, so that, given the appropriate technology and the availability of sufficient energy, no insurmountable barrier to growth need arise from resource exhaustion for millennia to come.

This conclusion depends, however, on several assumptions. It assumes that we will develop the necessary technology to refine granite or sea water before we run out of, say, "copper"—meaning copper in its present degree of availability.[1] More important yet, it assumes that the ecological side effects of extracting and processing the necessary vast quantities of rock or sea water would not be so deleterious as to rule out the new extraction technologies because of their environmental impact. Most important of all, as we shall see, the gigantic energy requirements for mining ordinary rocks or refining sea water bring us to the consideration of whether a continuously increasing application of energy is compatible with environmental safety.

To many of these questions no clear-cut answers exist. We do not know how rapidly new technologies of extraction or refining can be developed, or the degree to which anti-pollution technologies can suppress their ecological disturbance. Today, for example, the practical

limit to open-pit mining, which appears to be the most economical way to extract common rock, is about 1,500 feet. It seems unlikely that this depth can be doubled, and it is a certainty that the rock extracted from such a vast pit will diminish exponentially unless ways can be found to dig pits with vertical walls.[2] In addition, as T. S. Lovering has written, "The enormous quantities of unusable waste produced for each ton of metal are more easily disposed of on a blueprint than in the field."[3]

But even if we make the heroic assumption that all these difficulties will be overcome, so that another century of uninterrupted industrial growth, with its thousandfold increase in required inputs, will face no constraints from resource shortages, there remains one barrier that confronts us with all the force of an ultimatum from nature. It is that all industrial production, including, of course, the extraction of resources, requires the use of energy, and that all energy, including that generated from natural processes such as wind power or solar radiation, is inextricably involved with the emission of heat.

The limit on industrial growth therefore depends in the end on the tolerance of the ecosphere for the absorption of heat. Here we must distinguish between the amount of heat that enters the atmosphere from the sun or from the earth, and the amount of heat we *add* to that natural and unalterable flow of energy by man-made heat-producing activities, such as industrial combustion or nuclear power. Today the amount of heat added to the natural flow of solar and planetary heat is estimated at about 1/15,000 of the latter—an insignificant amount.[4] The emission of man-made heat is, however, growing exponentially, as both cause and consequence of industrial growth. This leads us to face the incompatibility of a fixed "receptacle," however large, and an exponentially growing body, however initially small. According to the calculations of Robert Ayres and Allen Kneese, of Resources for the

Future, we therefore confront the following danger:

> Present emission of energy is about 1/15,000 of the absorbed solar flux. But if the present rate of growth continued for 250 years emissions would reach 100% of the absorbed solar flux. The resulting increase in the earth's temperature would be about 50° C.—a condition totally unsuitable for human habitation.[5]

Two hundred and fifty years seems to give us ample time to find "solutions" to this danger. But the seemingly extended timetable conceals the gravity of the problem. Let us suppose that the rate of increase in energy use is about 4 percent per annum, the worldwide average since World War II. At a 4 percent rate of growth, energy use will double roughly every eighteen years. This would allow us to proceed along our present course for about 150 years before the atmosphere would begin to warm up appreciably—let us say by about three degrees. At this point, however, the enormous multiplicative effects of further exponential growth would suddenly descend upon us. For beyond that threshold, extinction beckons if exponential growth continues for only another generation or two. Growth would therefore have to come to an immediate halt. Indeed, once we approached the threshold of a "noticeable" change in climate, even the *maintenance* of a given industrial level of activity might pour dangerous amounts of man-made heat into the atmosphere, necessitating a deliberate cutting back in energy use.

In point of fact, serious climatic problems may be encountered well before that dangerous threshold. Noticeable perturbations are anticipated by climatologists when global man-made heat emissions reach only 1 percent of the solar flux, little more than a century from now.[6] This timetable assumes, however, that the rate of energy dissipation will not rise from its present rate of annual increase of 4 percent to, say, 5 percent or even higher. These esti-

mates therefore make no allowance for *increases* in the rate of global heat dissipation if massive industrialization is undertaken in the underdeveloped regions. Per capita energy consumption in these areas is now only about one-tenth of that of the more advanced portions of the globe, although populations in the backward regions outnumber populations of the industrialized areas by two or three times. To raise per capita energy consumption in the poor regions of the world to Western levels would therefore require a twenty- to thirty-fold increase in energy use in these areas—a calculation that, however staggering, still fails to take into account the potential demands for energy from populations, within these areas, that will certainly double and possibly quadruple over the next hundred years.

It is important, in considering this last element of the human prospect, to avoid a prediction of imminent disaster. The timetable for global climatic disturbance is not only fairly distant, as we are accustomed to judge the time scale of events, but it can be pushed still farther into the future. Increases in the efficiency of power generation or utilization may considerably augment the amount of industrial production obtainable per unit of energy. New technologies, above all the use of solar energy, which adds nothing to the heat of the atmosphere since it utilizes energy that would in any case impinge on the earth, may greatly reduce the need to rely on man-made energy. From yet a different perspective, the technologies required to supplant the present fossil fuels— safe and efficient fission reactors, economical solar or wind machines, large-scale geothermal plants—may not arrive "on time," thereby enforcing a slowdown in the rate of energy use and postponing the advent of an ecological Armageddon. More important, the vast energy sources required to "melt the rocks and mine the seas," notably fusion power, may also remain beyond our capability for a very long period, thereby curbing our fatal growth curve by depriving us of the needed resources. Finally, a wholesale shift away from material production to the production of "services" that demand far less energy would also greatly extend the period of safety—a possibility that we will look into in our next chapter.

Thus imminent disaster is not the problem here. It is the inescapable need to limit industrial growth that emerges as the central challenge. Indeed, the main lesson of the heat problem is simply to drive home with the greatest possible force the conclusion that such a limitation must sooner or later impose a straitjacket on the never-ending growth of industrial production, even under the most optimistic or unrealistic assumptions with regard to resource availability or technology.[7]

The problem of global thermal pollution, for all its awesome finality, therefore stands as a warning rather than as an immediate challenge. Difficulties of a much more matter-of-fact kind—resource availability, energy shortages, the pollution resulting from noxious by-products of industrial production—are likely to exert their throttling effect long before a fatal, impassable barrier of irreversible climatic damage is reached. Every sign, however, points in the same direction: industrial growth must surely slacken and likely come to a halt, in all probability long before the climatic danger zone is reached.

Once again, however, we must stress an aspect of the environmental problem that is largely overlooked in the mounting literature on the ecological threat. Most of this literature focuses on the technical aspects of the problem, whose dimensions we have generally described. Of far greater importance for the human prospect are its socio-economic and political consequences. It is these aspects which will therefore mainly occupy us in the chapters to come.

There remains one concluding comment, before we proceed. At the outset I said that three elements of the current human predicament would be unanimously selected if we were to seek the source of the pervasive unease of our contemporary mood. Now, without going beyond the specific dangers of population growth, war, and environmental deterioration, I must identify a fundamental element in the external situation—not so much a fourth independent threat as an unmentioned challenge that lies behind and within all of the particular dangers we have singled out for examination. This is the presence of science and technology as the driving forces of our age.

It is hardly necessary, I think, to spend much time defending the cogency of this unifying proposition. The population explosion that looms with such horrifying possibilities is directly traceable to the consequences of new techniques of science and technology in the area of medicine and public health: it is not a rise in fertility rates but a science-induced fall in death rates that has set off the unstable demographic situation that now threatens to overwhelm the underdeveloped areas. The responsibility of science and technology for nuclear armaments is self-evident, as is also their joint effect in bringing about both the rate of industrial expansion and the peculiarly dangerous nature of modern industrial processes. That science and technology may also be indispensable agents for the mitigation of these external dangers, through birth-control techniques, sophisticated means of arms detection or defense, or greatly improved methods of energy production and pollution suppression, does not vitiate the contention that these external dangers arise in the first instance because of the development of science and technology in that era we call "modern history."

The very possibility of using science and technology to mitigate our present problems indicates, however, that it is not the extraordinary development of these forces, as such, that underlies our predicament. It is, rather, their fusion in a civilization that has developed scientific technology in a lopsided manner, giving vent to its disequilibrating or perilous aspects without matching these ill effects with compensating "benign" technologies or adequate control mechanisms. In turn, this raises the question of whether scientific research and technological application follow their "own" courses of development, or whether these forces are imperfectly constrained and directed because of inadequacies of the economic and social milieu within which they have arisen. . . .

Here it is enough to claim that the external challenge of the human prospect, with its threats of runaway populations, obliterative war, and potential environmental collapse, can be seen as an extended and growing crisis induced by the advent of a command over natural processes and forces that far exceeds the reach of our present mechanisms of social control. It goes without saying that this unequal balance between power and control enters into, or provides the underlying basis for, that "civilization malaise" of which I spoke earlier. . . .

Notes

[1] See T. S. Lovering, "Non-Fuel Mineral Resources in the Next Century," in *Global Ecology*, eds. John P. Holdren and Paul Ehrlich (Harcourt, Brace, Jovanovich, 1971); and Preston Cloud, "Mineral Resources in Fact and Fancy," in *Toward a Steady-State Economy*, ed. Herman Daly (W. H. Freeman, 1971).

[2] Cloud, *op. cit.*, p. 61.

[3] Lovering, *op. cit.*, p. 45.

[4] W. R. Frisken, "Extended Industrial Revolution and Climate Change," *E⊕S, American Geophysical Union*, vol. 52 (July 1971), p. 505.

[5] Robert U. Ayres and Allen V. Kneese, *Economic and Ecological Effects of a Stationary State*, Resources for the Future, Reprint No. 99, December 1972, p. 16. See also Frisken, *op. cit.*, and John P. Holdren, "Global Thermal Pollution," in *Global Ecology*.

[6] Frisken, *op. cit.*, p. 505.

[7] I must add a footnote here, lest it be thought that the availability of safe solar energy obviates the problem of an energy constraint. Ayres and Kneese (page 51) point out that 250 years of growth, with its present associated emission of heat, would reach 100 percent of the total solar flux. It follows therefore that even the fantasy of a complete capture of all sunlight falling on the earth would yield no more energy than 250 years of growth of conventional (including nuclear) sources. Beyond that lies the exotic possibility of capturing additional solar energy in space and safely relaying it to earth by microwaves, or using microwaves to radiate manmade energy into space. The substantial application of such technologies seems far beyond any realistic capabilities of the next century or so.

DISCUSSION QUESTIONS

1. Does Heilbroner believe that human disaster is imminent?
2. What evidence could you offer that Heilbroner's vision is too pessimistic?
3. What do you see as the future of institutions in contemporary societies?

Author Index

Subject Index